Multinationals and Economic Growth in East Asia

This is a comprehensive examination of the role of foreign direct investment in East Asia before and after the financial crisis of mid-1997. Developing countries in East Asia recorded remarkable economic growth until the Asian financial crisis erupted in mid-1997. Although several countries experienced devastating setbacks, most of them recovered to achieve reasonable rates of economic growth over the next few years. Sound macroeconomic management, export-oriented policies, and the availability of skilled and low-wage labor are among the factors that contributed to the rapid economic growth before the crisis and the recovery thereafter. Especially noteworthy in this regard is the role played by foreign direct investment (FDI) by multinational companies. This book identifies the factors that contributed to the expansion of FDI inflows in East Asia and the factors that enabled recipient countries to utilize FDI effectively. It discusses the strategies of the multinational companies making the investments, and also the impact on the countries affected. It includes case studies on China, South Korea, Taiwan, Indonesia, Malaysia, the Philippines, Singapore, Thailand, and Vietnam. Also included is a comparative study of investing firms headquartered in the United States, Japan, and Hong Kong.

Shujiro Urata is Professor of Economics at Waseda University, Japan.

Chia Siow Yue is Senior Research Fellow at the Singapore Institute of International Affairs.

Fukunari Kimura is a Professor in the Faculty of Economics at Keio University, Japan.

Routledge International Business in Asia Series

Series editor: Hafiz Mirza,
Bradford University School of Management

The primary aim of this series is to publish original, high-quality, research-level work, by both new and established scholars in the West and East, on all aspects of international business in Asia. Works of synthesis, reference books and edited collections will also be considered. Submissions from prospective authors are welcomed, and should in the first instance be sent to the series editor: Professor Hafiz Mirza, Bradford University School of Management, Emm Lane, Bradford BD9 4JL. Email: h.r.mirza@bradford.ac.uk.

1. The Future of Foreign Investment in Southeast Asia
Edited by Nick J. Freeman and Frank L. Bartels

2. Multinationals and Asia
Organizational and institutional relationships
Edited by Axèle Giroud, Alexander T. Mohr and Deli Yang

3. Multinationals and Economic Growth in East Asia
Foreign direct investment, corporate strategies and national economic development
Edited by Shujiro Urata, Chia Siow Yue and Fukunari Kimura

Multinationals and Economic Growth in East Asia

Foreign direct investment, corporate strategies and national economic development

Edited by
Shujiro Urata, Chia Siow Yue and Fukunari Kimura

LONDON AND NEW YORK

First published 2006
by Routledge
2 Park Square, Milton Park, Abingdon, Oxon OX14 4RN

Simultaneously published in the USA and Canada
by Routledge
711 Third Avenue, New York, NY 10017

Routledge is an imprint of the Taylor & Francis Group, an informa business

First issued in paperback 2012

Typeset in Palatino by
Carol Levie, Grammarians, Inc.

British Library Cataloguing in Publication Data
A catalogue record for this book is available from the British Library

Library of Congress Cataloging in Publication Data
Multinationals and economic growth in East Asia : foreign direct investment, corporate strategies and national economic development / edited by Shujiro Urata, Chia Siow Yue, and Fukunari Kimura.
p. cm. — (Routledge international business in asia series 3)
Includes bibliographical references and index.
ISBN 0-415-38271-8 (hardback : alk. paper) 1. Investments, Foreign—East Asia. 2. East Asia—Economic conditions. I. Urata, Shujiro, 1950– II. Chia, Siow Yue. III. Kimura, Fukunari. IV. Series.

HG5770.5.A3M85 2006
332.67'3095—dc22 2006014389

ISBN13: 978-0-415-51238-1 (pbk)
ISBN13: 978-0-415-38271-7 (hbk)
ISBN13: 978-0-203-96669-3 (ebk)

Contents

Boxes

Tables

Figures

Foreword

This book is the result of a research project managed by the World Bank Institute as part of a program for the Study of the Japanese Development Management Experience (often referred to as the Brain Trust Program) that is financed by the government of Japan through the World Bank's Policy and Human Resources Development Trust Fund. We are most grateful for the Japanese government's generous support.

The Brain Trust Program conducts studies primarily on the Japanese and East Asian development management experience and shares the lessons learned with developing economies. The program often covers the experiences of regions and countries other than Japan and East Asia. Several important books have resulted from these research projects.

The main objective of this study of foreign direct investment in East Asia is to identify and analyze the factors that contributed to the expansion of FDI inflows in East Asia as well as the factors that enabled the recipient countries to use FDI effectively. The study contrasts FDI activity before and after the 1997–98 financial crisis that had significant effects on FDI inflows to East Asian developing countries. The countries covered by the research project—China, the Republic of Korea, Taiwan (China), Indonesia, Malaysia, the Philippines, Singapore, Thailand, and Vietnam—provide examples of both large and small economies with different degrees of openness in their FDI regimes and different levels of economic success. A country study of India is included for comparison with China, since both countries are very large and both have been liberalizing their FDI regimes. This research project provides useful insights on formulating FDI policies not only for the East Asian developing countries but also for other developing regions and countries interested in FDI as an instrument of economic growth and development.

Identifying the factors influencing FDI flows and the effects of FDI on recipients required an examination of the strategies of FDI suppliers, particularly multinational corporations (MNCs). Therefore, the research project also examines FDI flows from the United States, Japan, and Hong Kong (China) and the FDI strategies of their MNCs. A key question is whether behavioral differences exist between investing firms from these economies. The study of MNC strategies will help decisionmakers in the FDI recipient countries formulate appropriate policies to attract and maximize the benefits of FDI.

Tsutomu Shibata
Senior Adviser and Task Manager of the Brain Trust Program
World Bank Institute

Contributors

Titik Anas
Centre for Strategic and International Studies
Jakarta, Indonesia

Mitsuyo Ando
Assistant Professor
Hitotsubashi University, Japan

Myrna S. Austria
Associate Professor
De La Salle University, Philippines

Bee-Yan Aw
Professor
Pennsylvania State University

Taeho Bark
Professor
Seoul National University
Republic of Korea

Peter Brimble
President
Asia Policy Research Company Ltd., Thailand

Edward K. Y. Chen
President
Lingnan University
Hong Kong (China)

Chia Siow Yue
Singapore Institute of International Affairs

Fukunari Kimura
Professor
Keio University, Japan

Nagesh Kumar
Director-General
Research and Information System for Developing Countries (RIS)
India

Robert E. Lipsey
Professor
City University of New York and
National Bureau of Economic Research

Hwy-Chang Moon
Professor
Seoul National University
Republic of Korea

Mari Pangestu
Centre for Strategic and International Studies
Jakarta, Indonesia

Sieh Lee Mei Ling
Director
Southern Bank Berhad, Malaysia

Tran Van Tho
Professor
Waseda University, Japan

Shujiro Urata
Professor
Waseda University, Japan

Yu Yongding
Director
Institute of World Economics and Politics
Chinese Academy of Social Sciences, China

Introduction

Shujiro Urata, Chia Siow Yue, and Fukunari Kimura

Developing countries in East Asia recorded remarkable economic growth until the Asian financial crisis erupted in mid-1997. Several of these countries experienced devastating setbacks, but most of them recovered to achieve reasonable rates of economic growth over the next few years. The soaring growth of the economic miracle years of the 1990s, however, appears not to be repeatable in the short run. Sound macroeconomic management, export-oriented policies, and the availability of skilled and low-wage labor are among the factors that contributed to the rapid economic growth before the crisis and the recovery thereafter. Especially noteworthy in this regard is the role played by foreign direct investment (FDI).

FDI before and after the Asian Crisis of 1997

East Asian developing countries were very successful in attracting FDI in the pre-crisis period. FDI contributed significantly to their rapid economic growth from the mid-1980s until the crisis. The positive contribution of FDI inflows to economic growth in East Asia has been well documented.[1] The benefits to FDI recipient countries include financial resources for fixed investment as well as technological and managerial know-how. These factors play a crucial role in upgrading industrial competitiveness and

1. See Urata (2001). In their statistical analyses of the experiences of other developing countries, Borensztein et al. (1998) and United Nations (1999) found FDI's impact on economic growth to be positive.

accelerating economic growth. FDI has enabled recipient economies to utilize sales, procurement, and information networks developed by foreign multinational corporations (MNCs). Through these networks, the recipient countries realize more efficient production and marketing and participate in global supply chains. Indeed, FDI has fundamentally changed the industrial structure and international trade patterns of host countries.

FDI played an important role in keeping East Asian developing countries from further collapse during the financial crisis and in fostering their recovery. Unlike the massive withdrawal of bank loans and portfolio investments that triggered the financial crisis, there was no massive outflow of FDI from East Asia, and most of the affiliates of MNCs remained in the region. FDI proved to be a much more resilient and stable source of financial capital. Some MNCs were able to inject additional funds into struggling joint ventures. Multinational corporations operating in these countries also were able to expand exports to take advantage of the improved competitiveness following the sharp devaluations in currency. Trends in FDI inflows into the region after the crisis, however, have varied by country. China has maintained its appeal as an FDI host, but some countries, such as Indonesia, have lost their attractiveness.

Mergers and acquisitions (M&As) increased markedly after the crisis, whereas before the crisis greenfield investments dominated. Several governments relaxed their restrictions on foreign investors to facilitate cross-border M&As in the hopes of aiding distressed corporations. Thus MNC investments and exports contributed to the East Asian economic recovery. It is interesting to note that the substantial changes in industrial structure and trade, as well as the formation of international production networking, caused partly by FDI inflows, continued even during the recovery.

Objectives of the Research Project

The main objectives of the research project that culminated in this book were to identify the factors that contributed to the expansion of FDI inflows in East Asia and to discern and analyze the factors that enabled the recipient countries to utilize FDI effectively. Developments before and after the financial crisis were contrasted, since the crisis appeared to affect East Asian developing countries and FDI inflows significantly. The following recipient economies were selected for study: China, the Republic of Korea, Taiwan (China), Indonesia, Malaysia, the Philippines, Singapore, Thailand, and Vietnam. They represent economies big and small, with different degrees of openness in FDI regimes, and with successful and less successful records. A country study of India, although not an East Asian developing economy, is included to provide a comparison with China, since both are very large countries, and both have been liberalizing their FDI regimes. The research project has provided insights on FDI policies that are useful not only for developing countries in East Asia but also for other developing countries that are interested in FDI as an instrument of economic growth and development.

Previous studies have examined the factors influencing investment locations. For example, Urata and Kawai (2000a) examined the determinants of the location of Japanese FDI. Low economic risks (small variations in the exchange rate and a low inflation rate), low wages, a well-developed infrastructure, agglomeration of industrial activities, and good governance were identified as important factors for attracting Japanese FDI. Other studies have examined the impact of FDI on economic growth. Urata (2001) noted the importance of FDI for promoting trade, and Kawai and Urata (2003) showed how FDI upgraded the technological capability of the recipient economies. OECD (2002) and Yusuf, Altaf, and Nabeshima (2004) identified the role of FDI in fostering recipients' participation in global production networks. Many of these studies are either cross-country comparisons or industry case studies. Although the studies' observations and conclusions are useful, important factors intrinsic to particular countries are not discussed.

To shed light on these factors, this project conducted detailed case studies of individual recipient countries, including studies of specific industries and specific firms. It also examined the strategies of FDI suppliers, particularly the multinational corporations, in order to identify the factors influencing FDI flows and impacts on recipients. By including analyses of FDI flows from the source countries of Japan, the United States, and Hong Kong (China), and by describing the FDI strategies of their MNCs, this project complements studies of FDI recipients. Japan, the United States, and Hong Kong were chosen mainly for two reasons. One is their active FDI in East Asia, and the other is the availability of the information needed for carrying out the research. MNCs from economies in Europe and East Asia—including the Republic of Korea, Taiwan (China), and Singapore—are actively undertaking FDI in East Asia, but information on MNCs from these countries is quite limited. As for European MNCs, an analysis of their behavior is made more difficult because the MNCs are from different European countries.

A key question is whether there are behavioral differences between investing firms from the United States, Japan, and Hong Kong. Also of interest are the common economic and political factors determining corporate strategies and performance. The study of MNC strategies will help policy makers in the FDI recipient countries formulate appropriate policies to attract FDI and to maximize the benefits from those investments.

Major Findings

The major findings of the research project are presented in this chapter. These findings cover four primary subject areas: FDI flows in East Asia; the FDI strategies of multinational corporations from Japan, the United States, and Hong Kong (China); factors influencing FDI in the host economies; and the impact of FDI in East Asia on recipient economies.

FDI Flows in East Asia

To provide a comparative perspective, Shujiro Urata (Chapter 1) examines the changing patterns of FDI flows in East Asia with reference to world FDI flows. World FDI increased substantially in the 1990s before experiencing a decline in 2001–2. The rapid increase in FDI in the 1990s is attributable to several factors. Technological progress and deregulation in communication services reduced the cost of international communication, enabling multinational corporations to conduct international business through FDI. Liberalization in FDI policies by many countries also contributed to the expansion of foreign direct investment.

As a whole, developing countries in East Asia have been quite successful in attracting FDI. From the early 1990s to the early 2000s, when world FDI inflows increased substantially, the region maintained its share of world FDI inflows at around 10 to 20 percent. Fukunari Kimura and Mitsuyo Ando (Chapter 2) and Robert E. Lipsey (Chapter 3), in their studies of Japanese and U.S. outward FDI, respectively, also note the increasing importance of East Asia as a host region for FDI.

FDI inflows among East Asian developing economies vary widely. China experienced a steady increase in its FDI inflows from the early 1990s to 2002. In contrast, ASEAN5 (Indonesia, Malaysia, the Philippines, Thailand, and Vietnam) saw a steady increase in FDI inflows until 1997 and the outbreak of the financial crisis; thereafter FDI inflows declined dramatically. As a result of these contrasting patterns, China surpassed ASEAN5 in the early 1990s as an FDI recipient, and since then the gap has notably widened. By 2001, FDI inflows to China were more than ten times as large as FDI inflows for ASEAN5.

In Chapter 4, Edward K. Y. Chen explains the importance of Hong Kong's FDI in China, especially in the Guangdong Province and the Pearl

River Delta. FDI in four newly industrializing economies (NIEs)—namely, Hong Kong, Korea, Singapore, and Taiwan—increased steadily from the early 1990s until 1998, and FDI increased dramatically in 1999 and 2000. A precipitous decline in 2001 and 2002 followed.

With respect to FDI outflows worldwide, the industrial economies have a dominant share (90 percent from 1990 to 2002). This can be attributed to the fact that they are well endowed with the capital, technology, and management know-how required for undertaking FDI. Among industrial countries, the United States accounted for 15 to 30 percent of world FDI outflows from the early 1990s to the early 2000s. It should be noted, however, that the United States is also one of the largest FDI recipients in the world. Japan invested actively, especially in the early 1990s, but since the middle of the decade it has not been investing actively, mainly because of the poor financial performance of Japanese firms. As a result, the share of Japan in world FDI declined from around 15 percent in the early 1990s to around 5 percent in the early 2000s.

Unlike Japanese firms, firms in developing countries in East Asia, especially firms in the newly industrializing economies, increased their foreign direct investments in the 1990s. During that decade, the share of East Asian developing countries in world FDI outflows increased slightly (from 4 percent to 5 percent). The increasing importance of East Asian developing countries as foreign investors reflects their success in economic development and the growing global and regional reach of their corporations. Looking at East Asia, one can identify a sequential pattern of successful economic development and outward FDI. At the lead is Japan, followed by the NIEs, then ASEAN, and then China. This sequential development has been frequently described as the "flying geese" pattern.

In recent years the characteristics of FDI in East Asia have changed. For example, intraregional FDI has become more important than in the past. This is attributable to East Asian countries' greater attractiveness as FDI recipients on the one hand and their increased capability as FDI suppliers on the other. Another interesting development is the rapid expansion of FDI in machinery sectors, especially electronics machinery. The factors behind Japan's active FDI in machinery sectors are examined by Kimura and Ando in Chapter 2. They found that Japanese machinery firms are actively setting up regional production and distribution networks in East Asia through FDI. The country studies also found the growing importance of FDI in services, reflecting the liberalization and deregulation of service sectors in many host countries.

Mergers and acquisitions (M&As) became the dominant form of FDI in East Asia after the 1997 financial crisis, in contrast to the overwhelming dominance of greenfield investments in the pre-crisis period. The crisis created severe financial problems for many corporations, and consequently many governments relaxed the restrictions governing cross-border M&As. It remains to be seen whether mergers and acquisitions will remain a major activity once the recapitalization need of corporations diminishes. M&As have different implications for measuring host-country benefits. Unlike greenfield investments, M&As do not expand facilities physically, and therefore host countries eagerly expect the positive contribution from the transfer of technology and management know-how. As the Hong Kong study by Chen makes clear, equity investment is not the only way for firms to internationalize their production systems. In addition to traditional forms of FDI in China, Hong Kong firms are engaged in nonequity forms such as outward processing and subcontracting activities.

The changing characteristics of FDI in East Asia in recent years largely reflect changes in FDI strategies by MNCs and other foreign investors as well as changes in the FDI environment in recipient countries. Our findings on these two issues are explored in the next two sections.

FDI Strategies of MNCs from Japan, the United States, and Hong Kong

Multinational corporations have several motives for undertaking FDI. First, MNCs undertake FDI to expand sales in the host-country market. Such market-seeking FDI takes place in countries where serving the market through exports is difficult because of import protection or because proximity to consumers is important. Second, MNCs undertake FDI in host countries to produce for export to either the home market or to third markets. Such efficiency-seeking FDI is carried out in countries where production costs are low. The availability of abundant low-wage labor and well-developed infrastructure attracts efficiency-seeking FDI. Both market-seeking and efficiency-seeking FDI are commonly found in East Asia in recent years. The third motive is to acquire natural resources such as minerals. This resource-seeking FDI helps secure crucial natural resources for resource-poor countries.

By examining the characteristics of host countries, Urata (Chapter 1) and Lipsey (Chapter 3) shed light on the motives of MNCs in undertaking FDI. They found that FDI is directed to countries with a sizable market and substantial openness to trade. Global FDI flows to Asia are strongly related to trade openness, while those to Latin America are more related to market size and rate of economic growth. The FDI undertaken in East Asia is largely efficiency seeking, while FDI in Latin America is largely market seeking. However, there is an emerging trend of FDI in China that is market seeking as well.

FDI in East Asia by Japanese manufacturing firms, specifically machinery firms, can be characterized as the efficiency-seeking type. In Chapter 2 Kimura and Ando describe the formation by Japanese firms of international production and distribution networks involving vertical division of labor across a number of countries in East Asia. Active FDI by Japanese small and medium-size enterprises (SMEs), which supply parts and components to assemblers, has contributed to the formation of these networks. Kimura and Ando examine the patterns of sales and procurements by Japanese firms and their affiliates in East Asia. The transactions, they note, are open to both Japanese and non-Japanese firms. The Japanese government helped Japanese firms, especially SMEs, invest abroad in three ways: by providing modest financial assistance, by providing information on East Asia, and by providing official development assistance (ODA) to host countries for fostering local supporting industries and building infrastructure. This facilitated FDI by Japanese firms. In explaining the FDI strategies of Japanese machinery firms in East Asia, Kimura and Ando point to the importance of the following three factors: fragmentation of the production system, agglomeration of industrial activities, and internalization of production and distribution activities.

In Chapter 4 Chen identifies efficiency-seeking or cost-minimization as an important motive for Hong Kong firms undertaking outward FDI, regardless of whether the firms' sales serve export markets or local markets. Like Japanese firms, Hong Kong firms set up international production and distribution networks to increase efficiency and minimize costs. Chen observes, however, that international production and distribution networks developed by Hong Kong firms are less sophisticated than those developed by MNCs from developed countries such as Japan. As Chen explains, the sophistication of the international production and distribution networks is related to the country's level of economic development. More specifically, FDI is influenced by ownership-specific advantages.

The chapters on the United States, Japan, and Hong Kong as investing countries suggest a number of important differences in the competitive strengths of their multinational corporations. Japanese MNCs concentrate on manufacturing activities; U.S. MNCs have a competitive edge in service industries as well. Hong Kong firms particularly utilize proximity, both geographical and ethnic/cultural, to Mainland China. Regardless of their nationality, MNCs in East Asia tend to conduct efficiency-seeking operations and to explore the benefits of participating in international production and distribution networks. These findings indicate that factors of host economies or regions may be more influential than those of nationalities of MNCs in determining the characteristics of MNCs' activities.

Factors Influencing FDI in the Host Economies

Ten host-country studies, including one on India, confirm the findings from studies of investing countries. Political and social stability is the most important factor influencing FDI inflows. Without stability, foreign investments are deterred, since investors face a risk of losing their invested assets, not only financial funds but also sunk resources such as human resources and various networks. Political and social instability is often associated with policy instability. Shifts and changes in policies, and labor market unrest, may negatively affect the presence and performance of foreign firms.

In Chapter 6 Chia Siow Yue shows how political, social, and policy stability has helped Singapore garner and sustain high levels of FDI inflows. Chapter 8 by Mari Pangestu and Titik Anas highlights the problem of political and social instability that has deterred investments in Indonesia since the 1997 financial crisis. Indeed, this problem deterred investments in the Philippines for much of the 1990s (see Chapter 10 by Myrna Austria).

Macroeconomic stability is important for foreign investors. During much of the 1990s, stability in the exchange rate of the East Asian currencies vis-à-vis the U.S. dollar led to a substantial expansion of FDI inflows in the region. Then, with the onset of the financial crisis in 1997, investors became wary. In a highly unstable macroeconomic environment with high inflation, firms are discouraged from investing because of the uncertainty of economic prospects and difficulties in predicting cost levels and profit margins. As a result of expansionary fiscal policies adopted to deal with the crisis, future macroeconomic stability is emerging as a concern in some East Asian countries including the Philippines and Vietnam.

Directly affecting FDI inflows is a country's FDI policy regime. The most influential policy concerns the right of establishment. Host countries commonly bar or restrict foreign investors from certain sectors, activities, or locations to protect domestic natural resources, strategic industries and services, and domestic small enterprises and retail distributors. Many countries also have restrictions on foreign ownership of land. Singapore has adopted and maintained open FDI policies for many decades, providing national treatment and imposing minimal sectoral restrictions (see Chapter 6). Early in their economic development, Taiwan (Chapter 7 by Bee-Yan Aw) and Malaysia (Chapter 9 by Sieh Lee Mei Ling) also opened up to foreign firms. Recognizing the important contribution that FDI could make toward their economic growth, other East Asian countries also liberalized FDI policies in the 1980s and 1990s. This promoted the expansion of FDI inflows. Many East Asian countries further liberalized their FDI policy regimes in the wake of the financial crisis in an effort to revive investments. Despite the liberalization in recent decades, restrictions remain in sectors that host countries consider to be of strategic national importance. For example, in the manufacturing sector, the automobile industry is restricted in many countries, including Malaysia and China. Likewise, many countries have yet to open up their service sectors, particularly in finance and distribution, to foreign investors.

Many East Asian countries have imposed various types of performance requirements (including local content requirements, export requirements, and local employment requirements) to obtain desired effects from FDI. Although performance requirements sometimes serve their purposes, as will be discussed in the next section on the effects of FDI, in many countries these requirements are counterproductive. It is important to note that under the agreement on trade-related investment measures (TRIMs), the World Trade Organization (WTO) prohibits performance requirements affecting trade flows; included in this prohibition are the use of local content requirements, trade balancing requirements, restrictions on foreign exchange transactions, and local sales requirements.

FDI policy regimes in East Asia, as in other regions of the world, often contain a mix of restrictions and incentives. Sectoral exclusions and performance requirements restrict FDI, and investment incentives encourage FDI inflows and attempt to attract them into particular sectors and activities. Income tax holidays and tariff exemptions on imported inputs are common fiscal incentives. Other investment incentives include the provision of infrastructure and industrial facilities in special export processing zones and industrial estates, and permission for foreign firms to employ foreign nationals in certain senior positions. Investment incentives giving preferential treatment to foreign firms over local firms would theoretically be justified if market failure, such as external economies due to technology spillover, existed.

Incentives are expected to increase FDI inflows, but their effectiveness in attracting FDI is not easily evaluated. The results of country case studies are mixed. The Singapore study found that incentives played an important role in attracting FDI inflows into desired sectors as well as into activities such as regional headquarter functions and research and development. In the Philippines, incentives had positive but rather marginal effects on FDI. The China study by Yu Yongding (Chapter 13) argues that incentives caused serious distortions in the market. For example, to attract FDI, the Chinese government set rental prices for land excessively low, and this resulted in wasteful use of this natural resource. It is important to note that even if incentives serve the objective of attracting FDI, they can impose a fiscal burden, either because of tax revenue forgone or because of government expenditures to provide FDI-specific services. Governments' intent on achieving sound fiscal discipline should carefully evaluate the use of incentives.

In East Asia the liberalization of FDI policies certainly promoted FDI inflows. Country studies affirm the importance of consistency, transparency, and effective implementation of FDI policies in attracting investment. It is also true that frequent and unpredictable changes in policy affecting FDI, lack of transparency regarding rules and regulations, and inconsistencies in the regulations and administrative practices of government agencies create a policy and administrative environment that deters FDI. Administrative implementation can be impeded by bureaucratic red tape, inefficiency, and corruption. In some countries the processing of applications for FDI takes far too long. The reasons vary: lack of capability on the part of government officials; the complexity of the process requiring examination by several government offices; corruption. The Singapore study highlighted the importance of policy consistency/transparency and administrative efficiency in processing and approval of FDI applications. The satisfactory experience of foreign investors in the country is reflected in the high level of reinvestment.

A number of country studies emphasize the need for a comprehensive policy environment conducive to economic development; FDI policy is one important component in such an environment. Singapore and Malaysia have pursued such an approach; Thailand, as Peter Brimble points out in Chapter 11, has not. The policy environment in Indonesia also has made FDI policy there rather ineffective (see Chapter 8). Several chapters evaluate the role of trade liberalization in attracting export-oriented FDI. Policy coordination also is essential. Domestic deregulation in various areas, such as infrastructure, can promote FDI as well as increase the benefits from FDI. Deregulation not only broadens the scope of private economic activities, allowing foreign firms to enter; it also can improve the quality of infrastructure (energy supply as well as communication and transportation services, for example).

Many country studies emphasize the importance of well-developed "hard" and "soft" infrastructure. Indeed, many East Asian countries have been successful in improving the quality of both hard and soft infrastructure. For example, Singapore, with the active support of the government, has been very effective in this regard. Yet there remains in other countries (such as the Philippines and Indonesia) much room for improvement.

A reliable supply of electricity is crucial for plants manufacturing high-quality electronic products such as semi-conductors. Efficient and low-cost transportation and communication services are crucial for supply-chain management and regional and global production networks. These are examples of the hard infrastructure that is needed. Combined with trade and FDI facilitation, lowering the service link cost is the key for cross-border production sharing. Soft infrastructure is a fundamental requirement for well-functioning market mechanisms and supporting economic activities, and for formulating and implementing FDI policies. Without soft infrastructure, foreign investors cannot be assured of security and smooth operation of their businesses. Taeho Bark and Hwy-Chang Moon in their study of the Republic of Korea (Chapter 5) address the issue of soft infrastructure and point out the importance of protecting intellectual property rights, adhering to global accounting standards, and controlling hostile labor unions.

Despite their importance for attracting FDI, many East Asian countries lack competitive local supporting industries. Recognizing that supporting industries not only attract FDI but also increase the host-country benefits from FDI, many countries in East Asia have actively tried to develop supporting industries, although with limited success. Several countries have developed supporting industries, but the suppliers are frequently foreign. When they venture abroad, many foreign firms ask their parts and components suppliers back in their home countries to follow them and continue supplying parts and components because of the absence of local suppliers.

Tran Van Tho in Chapter 12 on Vietnam and Nagesh Kumar in Chapter 14 on India emphasize the importance of supporting industries, suppliers of parts and components, for attracting FDI in machinery sectors. Although assembly firms can procure parts and components from foreign countries, they would rather procure them locally because of savings in transportation costs and because of shorter delivery times. It is also important to emphasize that competitive supporting industries promote technology spillover, one of the positive effects of FDI for host economies.

The Impact of FDI in East Asia

Foreign direct investment can make a positive contribution to the prospects for economic growth. As Urata observes in Chapter 1, multinational corporations have helped generate employment, output, and investment for many East Asian countries, although the importance of MNCs varies widely among them. For example, in Malaysia and Singapore, foreign MNCs are very prominent, and they employ 40 to 50 percent of all workers in manufacturing. The benefits of FDI also vary by country. In Malaysia, Singapore, and Thailand, FDI has generated jobs for both skilled and unskilled labor. MNCs provide opportunities for skilled workers to use and upgrade their skills. However, the supply of skilled workers for MNCs is limited. The shortage of the kinds of workers MNCs want to recruit is reflected in significant wage differentials between MNCs and local firms (see Chapter 11). This points up the need to develop capable workers for the benefit not only of foreign firms but also local firms. The Thai study emphasizes the contribution of FDI to poverty reduction. In addition to generating jobs, FDI triggers indirect interindustry job creation. In other words, the jobs and income created by FDI in one sector increase the output of other sectors, which in turn leads to employment generation in those sectors.

FDI has contributed to capital formation in the host East Asian countries. Urata notes that the ratio of FDI inflows to domestic capital formation exceeded 10 percent for seven out of fifteen East Asian countries in 2001. Because FDI inflows do not reflect all investment activities by MNCs, this ratio is only a rough indicator of the contribution of MNCs to capital formation in the host economies. Opinions differ on the net impact of FDI on domestic investment. Some argue that FDI inflows crowd out investment by local firms, resulting in the overvaluation of FDI's contribution to domestic capital formation. We did not analyze this issue statistically in this project, but the India study pointed out the possibility of a crowding-in effect, that is, that FDI inflows promoted domestic investment. Positive effects of FDI on domestic investment seem to hold more strongly when the policy regime is favorable for efficiency-seeking FDI.

One common observation in the country studies is the very important role of FDI in exports in East Asia. MNC exports contribute to economic growth by providing the foreign exchange to import technologies, intermediate and capital goods, and other items from foreign countries. Chapters 6 and 10 note the importance of the importance of MNCs in the exports of Singapore and the Philippines. The huge FDI outflow, first from Japan and then from the NIEs in the second half of the 1980s, was export oriented and precipitated by the great appreciation of the various countries' currencies. The trade-FDI nexus was strong in the machinery sectors, particularly in electronics machinery.

Although many East Asian countries are integrated into the global and regional production and distribution networks, which were created via the trade-FDI nexus, the extent of integration differs from country to country. Singapore, Malaysia, Thailand, the Philippines, Taiwan (China), and China are deeply integrated into the networks, but Indonesia, the Republic of Korea, and Vietnam are much less so. These differences are largely attributable to the differences in trade and FDI policies. Countries with open trade and FDI policies tend to be deeply integrated into the networks. For those countries integrated into the global and regional networks of MNCs, FDI has played significant roles in upgrading production and trade structures from resource-intensive products, such as food and textiles, to machinery products. Although many East Asian countries are increasingly specializing in machinery production and export, they are still engaged in production processes that rely on unskilled labor, such as assembly, and not in high-skill intensive processes, such as research and development.

Host countries are eager to acquire technology and management know-how through FDI. Indeed, many developing countries consider technology transfer to be one of the most important FDI benefits, and consequently they encourage joint ventures between foreign MNCs and local firms. Technology transfer can refer to the transfer of core production technology or the transfer of management and marketing know-how and practices. Technology transfer takes two forms. One is the transfer from parent firms of MNCs to their overseas affiliates, and the other is the transfer from overseas affiliates of MNCs to local firms. The former is described as intrafirm technology transfer, while the latter is described as technology spillover. Intrafirm technology transfer is carried out by various means, including provision of production blueprints to affiliates and training programs for local employees. Technology spillover may also be realized in various ways. Technology may be transmitted from foreign firms to joint ventures and to local firms when local workers at MNC firms become employed by local firms or start new businesses after having acquired know-how from their MNC employers. Local firms also acquire technology from foreign firms by imitating the latter's production methods and management and marketing practices. Technology spillover is accelerated once local firms can successfully participate in MNCs' production networks. Close geographical proximity between foreign firms and local firms facilitates these types of spillover.

Previous empirical studies of technology transfer have found that intrafirm technology transfer has been successfully undertaken in many cases, but evidence on technology spillover is mixed.[2] On intrafirm technology transfer, several studies have found that the affiliates with a large share of equity held by parent firms tend to successfully acquire technology.[3] The

2. For a survey of technology transfer, see Kawai and Urata (2003) and Nabeshima (2004).

3. See, for example, Urata and Kawai (2000b).

reason behind this relation is that the threat of misuse of technologies declines with the increase in the equity holding by parent firms, since the monitoring capability of parent firms on the use of technologies by affiliates increases with the level of equity holding by parent firms. The findings on intrafirm technology transfer and technology spillover from the country studies in this project are more or less consistent with these previous findings. The studies of Indonesia, Korea, the Philippines, and Singapore report some evidence of intrafirm technology transfer. A detailed study of foreign and local firms in Taiwan (China) by Aw revealed that total factor productivity (TFP) of foreign firms is higher than that of local firms, indicating the presence of intrafirm technology transfer. However, Aw also found that high TFP of foreign firms is mainly attributable to export activities rather than their foreign ownership, indicating the importance of exposure to foreign competition for improving technical efficiency.

The findings on the presence of technology spillover are mixed for the country studies. Studies of China, Indonesia, and the Philippines showed weak evidence of technology spillover. Studies of the Republic of Korea and Vietnam report technology spillover in a broad sense to encompass managerial and marketing know-how. In Korea, a foreign firm is reported to have introduced new and high-quality after-sales services in the electronics industry, while in Vietnam, which is going through a transition from a centrally planned economy to market economy, foreign firms have introduced "new" management systems. The Taiwan study found evidence of technology spillover from foreign firms to small local firms in close geographical proximity. The India study found that the chance of technology spillover was greater when the technology gap between foreign and local firms was small. The Thailand study reported that MNCs sponsored a number of projects (for example, scholarships to technical institutes) to promote technology transfer, but the effectiveness of these programs was not examined.

Country studies on India, Indonesia, the Philippines, Singapore, and Vietnam stress the importance of supporting industries and strong linkages between foreign and local firms to successfully promote technology spillover. Limited success in technology spillover is largely attributable to underdevelopment of supporting industries and a lack of linkage between foreign and local firms. It should be noted that underdevelopment of supporting industries and a lack of linkage are closely related. Foreign firms form a link with local firms, if competitive supporting industries consisting of local firms exist in the host country. Underdevelopment of supporting industries limits the extent of technology spillover. The Singapore study shows the importance of government support in promoting technology spillover between foreign MNCs and local suppliers of parts and components through the Local Industry Upgrading Program.

Underdevelopment of supporting industries also has an important implication for foreign exchange earnings. Earlier we observed that foreign firms contributed significantly to export expansion for East Asian countries. However, it is often argued that export expansion does not contribute much to foreign exchange earnings because of the high import content of export production, since foreign firms procure parts and components from foreign countries and not locally. Underdevelopment of supporting industries keeps foreign firms from procuring parts and components locally.

Finally, it should be noted that technology transfer cannot be achieved without local workers who are capable in terms of technical ability or managerial ability. Without that, neither intrafirm technology transfer nor technology spillover can be achieved.

Conclusions

East Asia as a whole was quite successful in attracting FDI inflows until the outbreak of the financial crisis in 1997. Since then, there have been two divergent trends. FDI inflows to China have continued to rise; FDI inflows to the developing economies of Southeast Asia have fallen. The studies in this research project examined the factors influencing the FDI flows.

The impacts of FDI on the recipient countries in East Asia vary. The recipients have benefited substantially from FDI mainly in terms of employment generation and export expansion; the evidence on technology transfer is mixed. Many East Asian countries have experienced difficulties in acquiring production technology and management know-how from foreign firms, although acquisition of these intangible assets is one of the most desired benefits for FDI recipients.

This book offers important lessons and policy implications for developing countries that are eager to promote economic growth by utilizing FDI. One important finding is that multiple factors, rather than a single factor, influence the volume and pattern of FDI flows and their effects on recipient economies. These factors include political and social stability, sound macroeconomic environment, well-developed soft and hard infrastructure, competitive supporting industries, the availability of skilled labor, and open trade and FDI regimes. Indeed, these factors are considered "fundamentals"; they create an environment that enables foreign firms to enter an economy and contribute to its growth and development.

We offer here four major conclusions based on this research project. First, changes in a country's FDI policy regime are not enough to ensure the desired inflow of FDI. As the Asian financial crisis clearly demonstrated, deteriorating political and social stability, a deteriorating macroeconomic environment, and poor prospects for economic growth deter foreign investors. Although some countries afflicted by the crisis improved their FDI policy regimes, relaxing restrictions and performance requirements and increasing investment incentives, the result was disappointing until the political, social, and macroeconomic environment improved and prospects for economic growth brightened.

Unfortunately, the political and social environment cannot be easily corrected by government policy. It is the responsibility of governments, however, to make decisions that create a sound economic environment. It is hoped that governments in East Asia have learned their lessons from the financial crisis and will take public governance seriously. As the East Asian economies become increasingly integrated, the failures and successes of one country are sure to spill over into the neighborhood. Indeed, this "neighborhood" effect should not be overlooked. Since the financial crisis, East Asian economies have put in place a "peer review" process under the ASEAN Plus Three (China, Japan, and the Republic of Korea) framework.

A second major conclusion of the research study is that FDI policies do matter. Restrictions on right of establishment and performance requirements imposed on foreign investors have positive effects, when certain conditions are met, as discussed below. These policies protect local ownership of land and natural resources, promote national strategic industries and small and medium-size enterprises (SMEs), create jobs, upgrade technology and workers' skills, improve research and development capability, and develop linkages through joint ventures and the use of local inputs. These policies and measures, however, also have negative effects on FDI inflows and FDI performance as well as on overall economic performance.

Protection of domestic industries and activities can be economically justified only on "infant industry" grounds. Such protection should not be permanent, and it should encourage the protected to pick up know-how and efficiency quickly and develop economies of scale. Performance requirements (such as local content, employment of local managerial and professional staff, technology transfer, and research and development) will work only if there exists a competitive local supporting industry and a ready and competitive supply of managers, professionals, and R&D scientists and engineers and other skilled workers. The export requirement works only if the host country has competitive production and transportation and logistics costs. China has been able to attract large volumes of FDI despite some performance requirements because it has political and social stability, a huge market, an abundant supply of skills, and an even more abundant supply of low-wage labor. No other country in East Asia can replicate China's advantages.

FDI recipient countries in East Asia need to re-examine their plethora of restrictions and performance requirements. What are the economic and political rationales for their use? Where the objectives are clearly political, what are the economic costs and benefits? Two policy areas are positive-sum games and should be the highest priorities: human resource development and the development of local supporting industries.

Human resource development not only ensures an adequate supply of skill for foreign investors. It helps a country achieve overall economic efficiency and move up the economic development ladder. Aspirations for high-tech industries cannot be realized without human resource development. Perhaps because of pressing competing claims for financial resources, several East Asian governments have neglected human resource development. Such neglect is sure to have dire consequences for a country's long-term development potential.

The development of local supporting industries, which are critical in machinery industries, also is essential. An increasing number of MNCs are constructing global production and distribution networks to produce and distribute their products and services more efficiently. MNCs are attracted to locations where competitive supporting industries exist.

Host countries benefit not only from FDI but also from the technology spillover from foreign MNCs to local firms. Limited success in acquisition of technology in many East Asian developing countries is largely attributable to a lack of linkage between MNCs and local firms. The incentive for foreign MNCs to source parts and components through imports diminishes when there is a well-developed and competitive local supporting industry. Governments can encourage the emergence and development of local supporting industries through technical and financial assistance to local small and medium-size enterprises. Dissemination of information and know-how through seminars and consulting services is beneficial. It is important that governments formulate and implement these measures in collaboration with the private sector to ensure their effectiveness.

Evidence is mixed on the efficacy and impact of the use of investment incentives. Provision of infrastructure, skills, and supporting industries do contribute to economic efficiency. However, if such provision requires government subsidies, as in the case of export processing zones, then foreign MNCs should not be favored over domestic enterprises. The use of tax holidays remains controversial. Governments must ensure that the tax holiday does not become a convenient investment promotion tool; all aspects of the investment environment should be improved. Governments also need to examine carefully whether the tax holiday is effective in encouraging FDI inflows. The type of inflows that are encouraged and the fiscal burdens that may result from the tax holiday are issues meriting governments' close attention.

A third major conclusion of the research project is that policy coherence, consistency, transparency, and effective implementation matter. For example, performance requirements and investment incentives can work at cross-purposes and cancel out efforts to promote investment. FDI policy liberalization and trade liberalization should work hand in hand to maximize the positive effects of FDI. Liberalization of regulations on goods imports is necessary to ensure ready import supplies at world prices and to make export production competitive. For countries lacking the domestic market size and potential of China or India, the formation of free trade areas with neighboring countries could attract FDI to produce for a large integrated regional market.

While it is positive to have flexible policies that respond to a changing business environment, unpredictable policy changes and inconsistency in implementation across government agencies create confusion and increase investment risks and transaction costs for foreign investors. Governments can reduce investors' concerns by providing a developed legal framework, dispute settlement mechanisms, and protection of intellectual property rights. By signing onto existing international agreements or entering into bilateral investment treaties, governments can lessen investors' concerns. The transparency of policies, rules, and administrative practices also lowers the transaction costs facing foreign investors, including reducing the incidence of corruption. In the forefront of effective implementation of FDI policies is the speedy processing and approval of FDI applications.

Finally, to support public governance on the part of host-country governments there must also be corporate governance on the part of MNCs. In industrial countries the public increasingly expects corporations, whether operating domestically or abroad, to be socially responsible. Likewise they expect the MNCs in their midst to give due regard to workers' safety and working conditions, to protect the environment, and to help in poverty reduction programs and efforts. The foreign MNCs could be role models for local private enterprise.

References

Borensztein, Edward, Jose de Gregorio, and Jong-Wha Lee. 1998. "How Does Foreign Direct Investment Affect Economic Growth?" *Journal of International Economics* 45, 115–35.

Chia, Siow Yue. 2000. *FDI Policy Regimes and Practices in ASEAN and their Applicability to Africa.* Report commissioned by the United Nations Conference on Trade and Development.

Dobson, Wendy, and Chia Siow Yue, eds. 1997. *Multinationals and East Asian Integration.* Canada and Singapore: International Development Research Council and Institute of Southeast Asian Studies.

Kawai, Hiroki, and Shujiro Urata. 2003. "Competitiveness and Technology: An International Comparison." In Sanjaya Lall and Shujiro Urata, eds., *Competitiveness, FDI and Technological Activity in East Asia,* 55–82. Cheltenham, UK: Edward Elgar.

Nabeshima, Kaoru. 2004. "Technology Transfer in East Asia: A Survey." In Shahid Yusuf, M. Anjum Altaf, and Kaoru Nabeshima, eds., *Global Production Networking and Technological Change in East Asia,* 394–434. New York: Oxford University Press for the World Bank.

OECD (Organization for Economic Cooperation and Development). 2002. *Foreign Direct Investment for Development: Maximising Benefits, Minimising Costs.* Paris.

United Nations. 1999. *World Investment Report 1999.* New York.

Urata, Shujiro. 2001. "Emergence of an FDI-Trade Nexus and Economic Growth in East Asia." In Joseph E. Stiglitz and Shahid Yusuf, eds., *Rethinking the East Asian Miracle,* 409–60. New York: Oxford University Press.

Urata, Shujiro, and Hiroki Kawai. 2000a. "The Determinants of the Location of Foreign Direct Investment by Japanese Small and Medium-sized Enterprises." *Small Business Economics* 15, 79–103.

———. 2000b. "Intrafirm Technology Transfer by Japanese Manufacturing Firms in Asia." In Takatoshi Ito and Anne O. Krueger, eds., *The Role of Foreign Direct Investment in East Asian Economic Development*, 49–74. Chicago and London: The University of Chicago Press.

Yusuf, Shahid, M. Anjum Altaf, and Kaoru Nabeshima, eds. 2004. *Global Production Networking and Technological Change in East Asia.* New York: Oxford University Press for the World Bank.

1

FDI Flows, their Determinants, and Economic Impacts in East Asia

Shujiro Urata

Foreign direct investment (FDI) has contributed to the economic growth of the recipient (or host) economies in important and varied ways. Not only has FDI brought financial resources for fixed investment. It also has brought new technology and managerial know-how to the recipient economies, thus further promoting economic growth. In addition, FDI has enabled the recipient economies to utilize sales, procurement, and information networks developed by foreign firms. This has greatly improved efficiency in production and marketing.

Several studies confirmed the positive contribution of FDI to economic growth. Borensztein, de Gregorio, and Lee (1998) examined the economic growth of sixty-nine developing countries from 1970 to 1989. Their regression analysis showed that FDI had a marginally positive impact on economic growth, but it had a significantly positive impact when the FDI was undertaken in the countries with high educational attainment. Their findings suggest that education plays an important role in the effective use of FDI. United Nations (1999) examined the economic growth of more than sixty countries from 1971 to 1995 and obtained results similar to those of Borensztein, de Gregorio, and Lee (1998). Kawai and Urata (2003) found that FDI had significantly positive impacts on economic growth by analyzing the data for 133

The author thanks the participants of the "Foreign Direct Investment and Economic Development: Lessons from East Asian Experience" project for their helpful comments. He is particularly indebted to Chia Siow Yue for detailed and helpful suggestions on an earlier version of this chapter.

countries from 1970 to 1997. Among the countries in various groups, East Asian countries experienced particularly strong positive effects on economic growth from FDI.

Various factors help explain East Asian economies' rapid economic growth in recent decades. Among them are high savings and investments, export expansion, and the availability of educated and hard-working labor. In addition, FDI has made an important contribution to remarkable economic growth in East Asia since the mid-1980s. Indeed, the formation of the FDI-trade nexus has played a crucial role in achieving high economic growth (Urata 2001). Although FDI inflows to many East Asian economies declined as a result of the outbreak of the crisis in the late 1990s, some economies (such as the Republic of Korea and Thailand) saw an increase in FDI inflows, and this aided in their economic recovery. Even in East Asian economies that experienced a decline in FDI inflows, the magnitude of the decline was much smaller than the decline in other types of financial flows, such as bank lending and portfolio investments. Based on this observation, one could argue that FDI lessened the negative effects of the crisis in many East Asian economies.

Aware of the important connection between FDI inflows and economic growth, many East Asian governments are keenly interested in attracting foreign direct investment. This chapter examines the recent patterns of FDI flows in East Asian economies and attempts to identify the factors that have influenced these flows. Such analysis may prove useful for other economies seeking to attract FDI. In addition, the notable impact of FDI on trade and production systems in East Asia is examined.

The chapter begins with a discussion of FDI inflows and outflows in East Asia. The policy environment affecting foreign direct investment is then examined at the global, regional, and bilateral levels. Topics addressed include the following: trade-related investment measures (TRIMs) in the World Trade Organization (WTO); Non-Binding Investment Principles affirmed by Asia-Pacific Economic Cooperation (APEC) members; bilateral investment treaties and free trade agreements; and FDI regimes in East Asia. Next the chapter evaluates the extent of FDI liberalization by East Asian economies and the determinants of FDI inflows. The effects of FDI on intraregional trade and emerging regional production systems in East Asia are also explored. The chapter concludes with a review of the findings.

FDI Inflows and Outflows of East Asian Developing Economies

FDI inflows worldwide increased substantially in the 1990s before beginning to decline in 2001 (Figure 1.1). This rapid increase is attributable to several factors. Technological progress and deregulation in communication services reduced the cost of international communication, helping multinational corporations (MNCs) to conduct international business through FDI. Liberalization in FDI policies by many countries also contributed to the expansion of FDI. The decline in the annual flow of world FDI in 2001 was largely attributable to a slowdown in economic growth in the United States and in members of the European Union. The main cause of this slowdown was the bursting of the information technology bubble and the terrorists' attacks in the States.

Similar to the pattern observed for world FDI, FDI inflows in East Asian developing economies experienced an increase in the 1990s and a decline in the early 2000s. The rate of change, however, was significantly smaller than that experienced by the economies in other regions. Specifically, annual FDI inflows to East Asian developing economies increased sharply from approximately $20 to $30 billion in the early 1990s to $136 billion in 2000. From this peak they declined to $93 billion in 2001 and to $84 billion in 2002 (Appendix Table A1.1). According to United Nations (2003), major causes of the

Figure 1.1. *FDI Inflows to the World, Developing Countries, and Developing Countries in East Asia, 1990–2002*

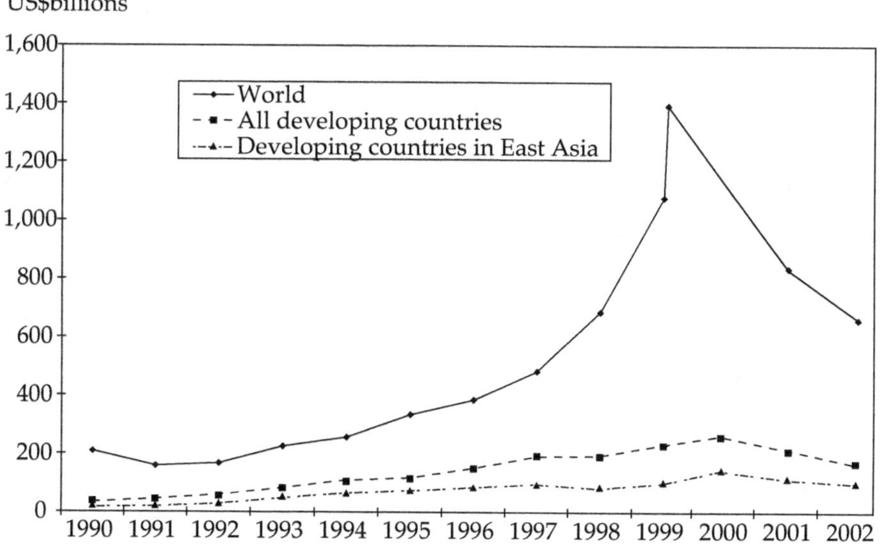

Source: United Nations Conference on Trade and Development (UNCTAD), Foreign Direct Investment database on line.

decline include weak economic growth, low corporate profits, and the winding down of privatization.

FDI inflows in East Asian developing economies varied widely (Figure 1.2). China experienced a steady increase in its FDI inflows from the early 1990s to 2002. Unlike China, ASEAN5 saw a steady increase in FDI inflows until the outbreak of the currency and financial crisis in 1997; FDI in those five countries dramatically declined in the following years.[1] China surpassed ASEAN5 in the early 1990s and has widened the gap notably since then. In 2001 FDI inflows to China were more than ten times larger than for ASEAN5. The newly industrializing economies (NIEs4)—Hong Kong, China; the Republic of Korea, Singapore, and Taiwan, China—experienced a steady increase in FDI inflows from the early 1990s to 1998 and a dramatic

Figure 1.2. *FDI Inflows to Developing Countries in Asia, 1990–2002*

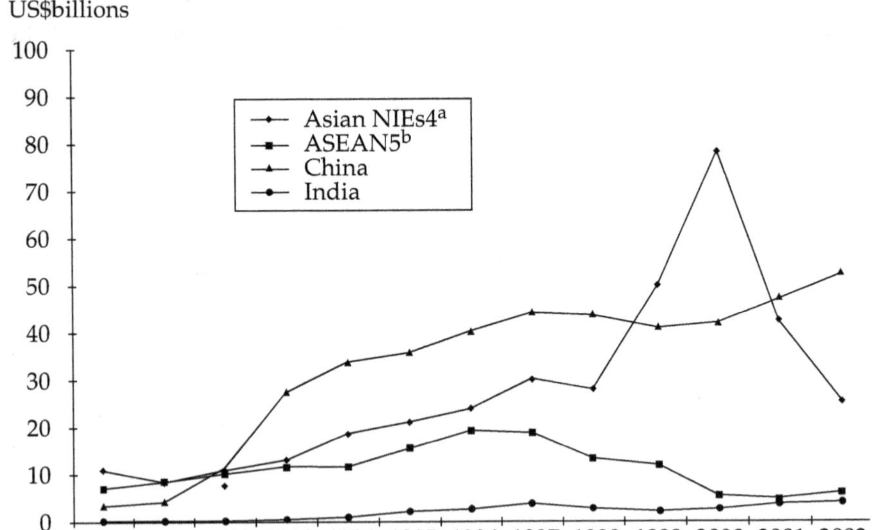

a. The Asian newly industrializing economies are Hong Kong, China; Taiwan, China; Republic of Korea; and Singapore.

b. Indonesia, Malaysia, the Philippines, Thailand, and Vietnam are the ASEAN (Association of Southeast Asian Nations) 5.

Source: United Nations Conference on Trade and Development (UNCTAD), Foreign Direct Investment database on line.

1. This reference to the Association of Southeast Asian Nations (ASEAN) is a reference to Indonesia, Malaysia, the Philippines, Thailand, and Vietnam.

increase in 1999 and 2000. In the following two years, however, NIEs4 saw a precipitous decline in FDI.

As noted earlier, among East Asian developing economies, China has attracted FDI successfully since the early 1990s. Indeed, China has been the largest recipient of FDI among developing economies since the early 1990s, and it became the world's largest recipient of FDI in 2002. Some of the factors that make China an attractive host country for foreign direct investment include its large market and low-wage workers, trade and FDI liberalization, and accession to the World Trade Organization.

Among ASEAN5 countries, Thailand, Malaysia, and Indonesia recorded notable increases in FDI inflows before the 1997 crisis (Figure 1.3). Thereafter, FDI inflows to Malaysia and Indonesia dropped significantly. In Indonesia they turned negative in 1998, and this disinvestment continued through 2002. Political instability appears to be an important factor behind the decline in FDI in Indonesia.[2] In Thailand, unlike Indonesia, FDI inflows

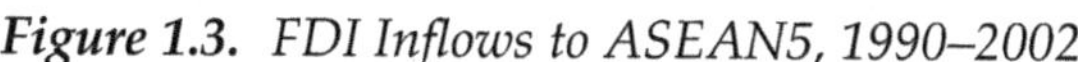
Figure 1.3. *FDI Inflows to ASEAN5, 1990–2002*

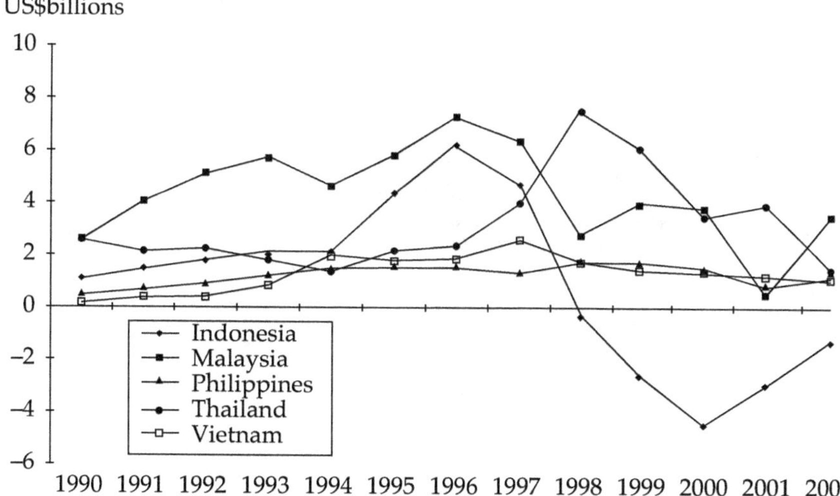

Note: ASEAN refers to the Association of Southeast Asian Nations.

Source: United Nations Conference on Trade and Development (UNCTAD), Foreign Direct Investment database on line.

2. The Business Risk Service lowered Indonesia's political risk rating from 46 in 1997 to 39 in 1998 (the year Suharto's presidency ended). Reflecting continued political instability, the rating for Indonesia declined to 36 in 2000.

increased after the crisis and remained at relatively high levels through 2001. The Thai government promoted FDI inflows by liberalizing FDI policies. From 1990 to 2002 FDI inflows to the Philippines and Vietnam remained relatively constant.

Among the Asian NIEs4, Hong Kong exhibited substantial growth in FDI inflows in 2000 (Figure 1.4). Although they declined sharply in 2001, the level of FDI inflows to Hong Kong was still substantially larger than the levels achieved by other NIEs. It is important to note, however, that FDI inflows to Hong Kong may be overestimated. This is because a substantial portion of them were reinvested in China. A large increase in 2000 was due to a single large investment in the telecommunication sector worth $23 billion (United Nations 2001, 25). Singapore, which kept pace with Hong Kong until the outbreak of the financial crisis, experienced a decline in FDI inflows after 1997, although it regained its attractiveness quickly. Korea recorded a substantial increase in FDI inflows in 1998 that can be largely attributable to the Korean government's drastic liberalization of FDI policies to deal with the negative impacts of the crisis. Similar to the pattern observed for Korea, FDI inflows in Taiwan increased after the crisis, although the magnitude of the increase was much smaller.

Figure 1.4. *FDI Inflows to Asian NIEs4, 1990–2002*

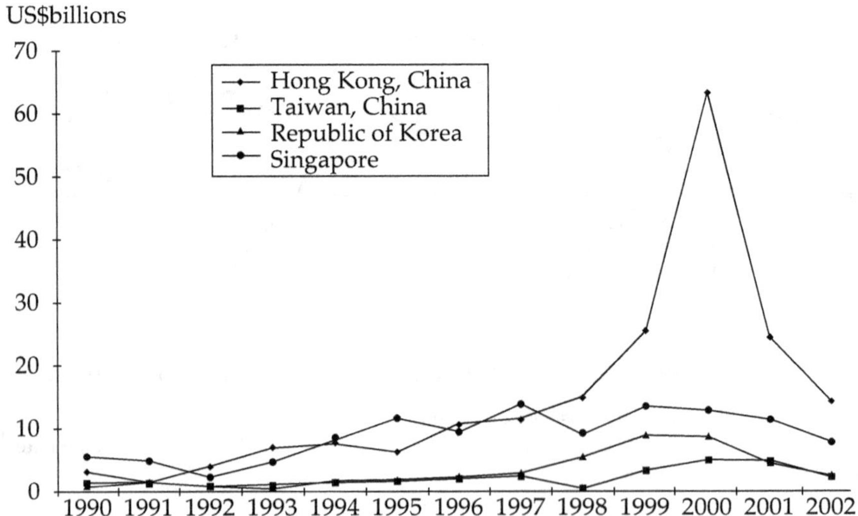

Note: NIEs refers to newly industrializing economies.

Source: United Nations Conference on Trade and Development (UNCTAD), Foreign Direct Investment database on line.

FDI inflows to India remained small until the mid-1990s when they began to grow (Figure 1.2).[3] The pace of the increase accelerated in the 2000s, largely reflecting liberalization of FDI policies.

A substantial part of FDI inflows in East Asia appears to have taken the form of reinvestment financed by earnings from the overseas affiliates of multinational corporations. According to the International Monetary Fund (2002), the shares of reinvested earnings in FDI inflows for China, Hong Kong, and the Philippines in recent years were approximately 30 to 50 percent. High shares of reinvested earnings reflect multinational corporations' favorable performance in these countries and mature investments that yield profits for reinvestment. In addition, FDI policies of the recipient countries that restricted or discouraged the repatriation of profits resulted in high shares of reinvested earnings.

One notable development concerning FDI in East Asia in recent years is the rapid expansion in crossborder mergers and acquisitions (M&As), a development observed in developed economies as well. M&A transactions in East Asia increased sharply after the crisis in 1997, their value growing from $8.4 billion in 1996, to $16.7 billion in 1997, to $31.7 billion in 2001 (Figure 1.5).[4] Among developing economies in East Asia, the crisis countries (Korea, Indonesia, Malaysia, the Philippines, and Thailand) recorded substantial increases in M&A transactions. The percent of FDI inflows for East Asian economies represented by mergers and acquisitions increased from 10 percent in 1996, to 18 percent in 1997, to 34 percent in 2001.

At least two factors contributed to the expansion of M&A transactions. First, a sharp decline in the value of equity in terms of foreign currency (currency depreciation) increased the attractiveness of M&A purchases for foreign investors. Second, liberalization of restrictions on M&A transactions facilitated crossborder mergers and acquisitions. The host economies' capability to assimilate technology and management know-how, in order to reap benefits from FDI inflows, became more important. Because mergers and acquisitions do not expand physical capacity, an improvement in technological capability through successful technology transfer is a major source of benefits. After the 1997 crisis, mergers and acquisitions played a crucial role in the survival of firms by injecting capital and introducing a new management style.

---

3. India is not in East Asia, but it is included in the analysis because of its importance for East Asian developing economies, not only as their competitor in attracting FDI but also as a business partner.

4. Appendix Tables A1.2 and A1.3 contain information on M&A sales for East Asian economies.

Figure 1.5. *Mergers and Acquisitions in East Asia, 1990–2001*

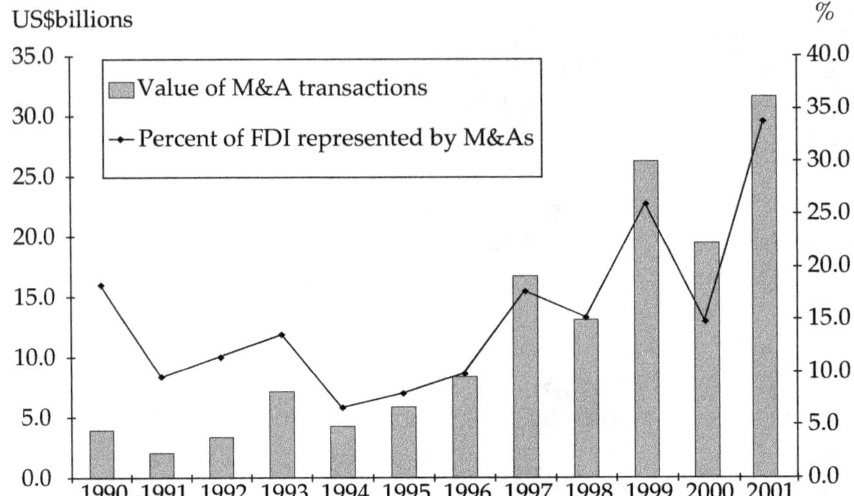

Source: United Nations Conference on Trade and Development (UNCTAD), Foreign Direct Investment database on line.

As FDI inflows to East Asian developing economies expanded, MNCs became more important (Table 1.1). This table shows two types of information for selected East Asian economies: the importance of MNCs in employment, sales, and value added, and the ratio of FDI inflows to domestic capital formation. The importance of multinational corporations to the East Asian economies varies widely. MNCs have a sizable presence in Singapore, Malaysia, and Hong Kong; in terms of employment and/or sales for the manufacturing sector in these economies, MNCs contribute as much as 40 to 80 percent. Although significant, the presence of MNCs in Taiwan, China, and Vietnam is smaller than in Singapore, Malaysia, and Hong Kong. Multinational corporations' presence in Indonesia and India is very limited.

For many countries, the ratio of FDI inflows to domestic capital formation increased in the mid-1990s, reflecting the increase in these investments (Table 1.1).[5] The economies with a high ratio—around 30 to 50 percent—include Sin-

5. The ratio of FDI inflows to domestic capital formation does not accurately reflect the importance of multinational corporations' activities in the host economies. MNCs procure investment funds not only from foreign countries in the form of FDI but also from local sources. Therefore, FDI represents only one part of the investment activities of MNCs. Despite its deficiency, this measure is used as a proxy because of its availability for many East Asian developing economies.

gapore and Hong Kong. Those economies registering around 10 to 20 percent include China, Malaysia, Thailand, and Vietnam. Very low ratios (less than 10 percent) are observed in Taiwan, Indonesia, Korea, and India.

FDI inflows and their importance in the economic activities of East Asian economies differ as a result of various factors, including current economic conditions, the FDI policy environment, and the country's future economic outlook. Before examining the FDI policy environment in the next section of this chapter, we briefly consider the patterns of FDI outflows from East Asian economies and the United States, a major investor in East Asia.

Most foreign direct investment for the period 1990 to 2002 was provided by developed countries. Indeed, FDI outflows from developed countries represented 90 percent of the world total (Appendix Table A1.4). This dominance of developed countries in FDI outflows is particularly notable once one realizes that for FDI inflows developed countries had 73 percent of the world total for the 1990–2002 period; the corresponding value for developing countries was 27 percent. The high share of developed countries in FDI outflows when compared to FDI inflows can be explained by developed countries' abundance in capital, technology, and management know-how, so necessary for making foreign direct investments. The United States saw large and growing FDI outflows in the 1990s, reaching $175 billion in 1999 before starting to decline in 2000. Unlike U.S. FDI outflows, Japanese FDI outflows stayed at a low level (around $25 billion) in the 1990s before starting to increase in 2000 and 2001. The sharp contrast between the United States and Japan in terms of FDI outflows largely reflects the two countries' contrasting economic performance. The U.S. economy was performing extremely well, and therefore U.S. firms actively invested overseas. Japanese firms did not invest actively abroad because of their poor performance at home.

Among East Asian developing economies, Hong Kong has been a very large supplier of FDI flows (Appendix Table A1.4). As noted earlier, however, the data presented in the table include not only FDI from local Hong Kong firms but also FDI from foreign firms, because Hong Kong was an intermediary for foreign firms from other countries. In addition to Hong Kong, Singapore, Taiwan, and Korea have been actively investing abroad. These findings indicate very interesting developments in East Asia. An increasing number of developing economies that once were only recipients of FDI have become FDI suppliers after achieving economic growth. Through such developments, FDI has become very active in East Asia.

This chapter has examined FDI inflows and outflows in East Asia separately. It would be of interest to examine the pattern of intraregional FDI in East Asia. Because of a lack of consistent and comparable information on FDI

Table 1.1. *Foreign Multinational Corporations' Role in East Asian Economies, 1990–2002*
(Percent)

Item	*1990*	*1991*	*1992*	*1993*	*1994*	*1995*	*1996*	*1997*	*1998*	*1999*	*2000*	*2001*	*2002*
Employment (manufacturing)[a]													
Hong Kong, China	12.9	13.4	13.2	14.2	16.9	19.3	20.3	22.5	—	—	—	—	—
Indonesia	—	—	3.3	—	—	—	4.7	—	—	—	—	—	—
Malaysia	—	—	43.2	45.6	45.9	43.2	43.7	38.5	—	—	—	—	—
Singapore	—	—	59.7	58.1	56.8	55.1	55.1	54.8	53.4	52.3	49.9	48.5	—
Taiwan, China	—	—	12.8	11.9	9.9	10.6	—	—	—	—	—	—	—
Vietnam	—	—	—	—	—	—	22.6	—	—	—	—	—	—
Sales (manufacturing)[a]													
China	2.3	5.3	7.1	9.1	11.3	14.3	15.1	18.6	24.3	27.7	31.3	—	—
Hong Kong, China	22.6	26.0	27.0	30.8	35.7	43.5	44.6	44.8	—	—	—	—	—
India	5.4	5.5	—	6.1	5.5	3.1	—	—	—	—	—	—	—
Malaysia	44.1	45.4	47.6	48.6	52.6	50.1	—	—	—	—	—	—	—
Singapore	76.9	75.4	74.7	74.8	75.1	75.6	75.9	75.8	76.0	81.1	—	—	—
Taiwan, China	17.8	19.2	20.9	18.7	21.5	—	—	—	—	—	—	—	—
Value added (whole economy)[a]													
China	—	—	—	—	—	4.4	4.2	4.8	—	—	—	—	—
Malaysia	17.5	18.6	20.1	20.6	23.1	23.8	—	—	—	—	—	—	—
Vietnam	—	—	—	—	—	11.3	11.6	12.5	—	—	—	—	—

Capital formation (whole economy)[b]													
Cambodia	—	—	17.0	18.8	15.5	23.5	36.1	28.7	56.4	48.2	31.1	32.1	—
China	3.5	3.9	7.4	12.2	17.3	14.8	14.3	14.6	13.1	11.3	10.4	10.5	—
Hong Kong, China	16.3	4.4	13.8	21.5	19.8	14.4	21.4	19.5	29.4	58.6	138.9	54.2	35.2
Macao	0.1	1.0	–1.2	–0.2	0.2	0.1	0.4	0.2	–1.5	0.9	–0.1	20.8	21.5
Taiwan, China	3.7	3.2	1.8	1.6	2.3	2.4	3.0	3.4	0.4	4.4	6.8	7.8	2.9
India	0.3	0.1	0.4	0.9	1.4	2.4	2.9	4.0	2.9	2.2	2.3	3.2	—
Indonesia	3.4	4.1	4.7	4.8	4.3	7.6	9.2	7.7	–1.5	–9.7	–14.3	-10.8	—
Korea, Rep. of	0.8	1.0	0.6	0.5	0.6	1.0	1.2	1.7	5.7	8.3	7.1	3.1	1.6
Lao PDR	—	—	—	—	—	19.3	23.6	18.2	14.4	15.7	9.8	7.2	—
Malaysia	18.0	22.6	23.7	22.1	15.3	15.0	17.0	14.7	14.0	22.2	16.5	2.5	—
Myanmar	4.6	5.4	3.4	1.7	1.4	2.2	2.9	3.7	2.1	0.8	0.7	0.6	—
Philippines	5.4	6.1	7.0	9.6	10.5	9.6	8.3	6.3	12.5	11.9	9.7	8.0	8.7
Singapore	46.8	33.6	12.5	23.1	36.1	40.8	26.6	37.0	24.7	47.6	45.6	43.8	—
Thailand	7.5	5.0	4.9	3.7	2.4	3.0	3.1	7.6	29.9	23.8	12.4	14.4	3.7
Vietnam	21.2	35.9	28.0	32.2	49.3	34.7	29.5	37.3	23.9	20.1	15.0	13.7	—

— Not available.

a. The share of indicated domestic economic activity contributed by overseas subsidiaries of foreign multinational corporation.

b. FDI inflows as a percentage of gross fixed capital formation.

Source: For employment, sales, and value added, United Nations (2002); for capital formation, United Nations Conference on Trade and Development (UNCTAD), Foreign Direct Investment database on line.

flows by destinations and sources, only a rough picture of intraregional FDI flows can be drawn (Table 1.2).[6] Several interesting observations, however, may be made based on the available data. First, the magnitude of FDI inflows in East Asia from other East Asian economies, or groups of economies, increased in the 1990s, with the exception of China-ASEAN bilateral FDI flows. Second, the importance of East Asia as a source of FDI increased for China and ASEAN4 and declined for the NIEs. Third, intraregional dependence on FDI in East Asia increased in the 1990s. Intraregional FDI as a share of FDI inflows to East Asia increased from 28 percent in the first half of the 1990s to 32 percent in the second half of the decade. This finding is similar to the case for international trade, which will be discussed in a later section.[7]

Table 1.2. *Intraregional Foreign Direct Investment in East Asia*
(Average annual value in US$millions)

	Recipients of FDI							
	China		*NIEs4*		*ASEAN4*		*Developing economies in East Asia*	
Investors	*1990–95*	*1996–2000*	*1990–95*	*1996–2000*	*1990–95*	*1996–2000*	*1990–95*	*1996–2000*
East Asia	12,854	14,239	1,603	4,876	12,507	15,477	26,964	34,592
Japan	3,072	3,511	1,336	2,766	6,042	7,306	10,450	13,583
China			4	25	131	89	135	114
NIEs4	8,364	9,671	145	987	5,561	6,517	14,070	17,175
ASEAN4	1,418	1,057	118	1,098	773	1,565	2,309	3,720
Total	60,349	55,997	5,209	18,338	30,995	33,836	96,553	108,171
EastAsia as percentage of total	21.3	25.4	30.8	26.6	40.4	45.7	27.9	32.0

Note: NIEs4 are Hong Kong, China; Rep. of Korea; Singapore; and Taiwan, China. ASEAN4 are Indonesia, Malaysia, Philippines, and Thailand. The figures are either committed or approved values. Strictly speaking, FDI based on different definitions cannot be compared. Thus, these figures should be interpreted as approximations.

Source: Ministry of Economy, Trade and Industry (2003).

6. The data in Table 1.2 are not strictly comparable to those shown in Figures 1.1 to 1.4 or in Appendix Table A1.1. The data in Table 1.2 are either committed or approved values, while the other data are on the balance of payments basis. Because of these differences, the data in Table 1.2 are used only to examine the directional patterns of FDI.

7. United Nations (2001, Figure II.10, 57) found a similar pattern of increasing intraregional dependence on FDI in South, East, and Southeast Asia.

FDI Policy Environment in East Asia

A number of economic, political, and institutional factors in recipient and investing countries influence FDI flows. Statistical analysis will be used later in the chapter to analyze the importance of these factors. Here we focus on the FDI policy environment in East Asian developing economies.[8] Many of them have recognized the importance of FDI inflows as a means of promoting economic growth and have responded to requests or pressure from multinational corporations for a freer FDI environment. A variety of institutional frameworks regarding FDI—including multilateral, regional, and bilateral approaches—have been established.

GATT/WTO Trade-Related Investment Measures

The Uruguay Round of the General Agreement on Tariffs and Trade (GATT) reached an agreement on investment rules in 1994. This was the first time in the history of GATT multilateral negotiations that the members took up the issue of foreign direct investment. After intense debate, an agreement was reached to prohibit trade-related investment measures (TRIMs) that violate the GATT rules. The agreement was a compromise between developed and developing countries; neither side was entirely happy with the outcome. The United States argued strongly to prohibit export requirements, fearing that they might lead to the expansion of exports bound for the U.S. market. However, this provision was not included in the agreement. Developing countries argued for a clause to restrict the monopolistic behavior of MNCs, but it was not included either.

In the end the agreement prohibited TRIMs that violate the following two GATT rules: national treatment applied to imported products (Article III) and general elimination of quantitative restrictions on imports (Article XI). TRIMs that violate the national treatment rule include the local content requirement and trade balancing requirements (requirements that imports of foreign firms do not exceed their exports). TRIMs that violate the general elimination of quantitative restrictions are trade balancing requirements, restrictions on foreign exchange transactions, and local sales requirements. Local sales requirements force foreign firms to limit their exports.

TRIMs practiced by governments, not TRIMs practiced voluntarily by the private sector, violate GATT rules. Trade-restricting measures that are sanctioned under the GATT for security reasons, among others, are recognized in

8. This section draws on Urata (1998).

the agreement on TRIMs. Special provisions are accorded to developing countries under Article XVIII. Specifically, section B permits developing countries to restrict their imports in order to deal with balance-of-payments difficulties, and section C permits developing countries to apply the same restrictions to promote a particular industry.

The contracting parties of the World Trade Organization (WTO), a successor to the GATT, must abolish trade-related investment measures that are reported to the Council for Trade in Goods within the agreed period: within two years for developed countries, within five years for developing countries, and within seven years for the least developed countries. To increase the transparency of TRIMs, WTO member countries are required to notify all TRIMs that they adopt. They are also required to furnish information on TRIMs to any member country that requests it. Several East Asian developing economies have notified the list of existing TRIMs (Ministry of Economy, Trade, and Industry 2003, 288-90). Specifically, Indonesia, Malaysia, and Thailand notified the application of local content requirement, while the Philippines notified the application of local content requirement and foreign exchange balancing. The transition period for the elimination of notified TRIMs expired at the end of 1999. However, the TRIMs Agreement provides for an extension of the transition period, if the WTO members can demonstrate particular difficulties. The Philippines, Malaysia, and Thailand requested extensions, and after intense discussions they were granted extensions until the end of June 2003 for the Philippines, and until December 2003 for Malaysia and Thailand.

The rules regarding FDI that were established in the WTO are limited to issues of FDI that are related to foreign trade. Agreements were not reached on other restrictive measures related to FDI, such as restrictions on the extent of equity participation and requirements for technology transfer and exports. Many government interventions still must be removed before a truly free FDI environment can be established. It is worth noting that in the General Agreement on Trade in Services (GATS), an agreement was reached to protect the right of establishment in service trade, a significant step toward ensuring the right of establishment for firms undertaking FDI.

At the first ministerial meeting of the WTO, held in Singapore in December 1996, it was agreed that a working group should be established to examine the relationship between trade and FDI. This was a compromise between developed countries, which were interested in setting up stronger regulation of FDI, and developing countries, such as Malaysia and India, which were against such rules. At the third ministerial meeting of the WTO in Doha in November 2001, an agreement was reached to initiate a new round of trade negotiations under the WTO; negotiations started in January 2002 and a target of finishing negotiations in three years was set. A working group on investment has been set up, and it has been discussing the issues related to possible investment rules. Although several developed countries, including Japan and the European Union (EU) members, are eager to establish investment rules under the WTO, strong opposition from developing countries has precluded an agreement so far. Indeed, disagreement on investment rules contributed to the failure of the ministerial meeting in Cancun in October 2003.

APEC's Non-Binding Investment Principles

Achieving free trade and investment in the Asia-Pacific region has been one of the central objectives of members of the Asia-Pacific Economic Cooperation (APEC) forum. The members have liberalized their trade and FDI policies unilaterally in recent years, but in a number of APEC member economies, many areas still have not been liberalized. Recognition of these issues led to the agreement on Non-Binding Investment Principles (NBIP) in November 1994. An increasing number of developing countries belonging to APEC have been recipients of foreign direct investment. They are now becoming active investors, contributing to the establishment of the NBIP.

Since the creation of APEC in 1989, expansion of FDI has been recognized as an important means of promoting economic growth in the Asia-Pacific region. The framework for the liberalization of FDI has been shaped gradually since then.

At the Bangkok meeting in 1992, ministers proposed that senior officials prepare a guidebook on APEC members' rules and procedures regarding FDI. This proposal led to the APEC *Guidebook on Investment Regimes*. The Seattle meeting in 1993 reaffirmed the importance of trade and FDI liberalization for economic growth in the APEC region by creating the Committee on Trade and Investment (CTI). The committee's objectives are twofold: to formulate opinions on trade and FDI issues by APEC members and to devise ways to reduce or remove obstacles to the free flow of trade and FDI. The newly formed committee was given the task of developing a set of non-binding investment principles.

In Indonesia in 1994, APEC leaders issued the Bogor Declaration, which expressed their intention to achieve free and open trade and investment in the APEC region. The declaration established a target date for reaching that goal: no later than 2010 for the industrial members and no later than 2020 for the developing-country members. Prior to the Bogor Declaration at the APEC meeting in Jakarta, the ministers endorsed the Non-Binding Investment Principles prepared by the Committee on Trade and Investment.

These principles are divided into four sections: principles that govern international relations, codes of conduct for government, codes of conduct for investors, and a system for dispute settlement. The three general principles of international relations are transparency, national treatment, and nondiscrimination. The codes of conduct for government stipulate the use of specific policies related to FDI: investment incentives, performance requirement, expropriation and compensation, transfer of funds, settlement of investment disputes, entry and stay of expatriates, tax measures, and capital movements. The codes of conduct are meant to discourage the use of investment-distorting policies, but the diversity of APEC members has made it difficult to implement these codes uniformly.

Despite the divergent views of APEC members, codes of conduct for investors were included in the Non-Binding Investment Principles because they were considered to balance the set of principles. These codes of conduct state that foreign investors should abide by the host country's laws, regulations, administrative guidelines, and policies, just as domestic investors do. A dispute settlement provision is included in the NBIP, but it lacks a detailed mechanism or procedure. The provision suggests only that disputes will be settled promptly through consultations and negotiations between parties under arbitration procedures acceptable to all. Finally, the NBIP states that it must not violate existing bilateral or multilateral treaties, including the agreement on TRIMs under the WTO.

After agreeing on the Non-Binding Investment Principles in order to establish an open investment regime in the region, APEC members have not achieved much progress toward FDI liberalization. The NBIP has not been effective. Some fault its nonbinding nature. Others favor making the principles binding, but the opposition has argued that this would conflict with the fundamental APEC principle of voluntarism. Today APEC is at a critical juncture as an organization with the mission of promoting FDI and trade liberalization in the Asia-Pacific region.

Bilateral Investment Treaties and Free Trade Agreements

Multilateral and regional frameworks to liberalize FDI policies have been established. They contribute to the promotion of FDI flows in East Asia and other regions. Despite the presence of these frameworks, bilateral and plurilateral investment treaties, some of which are included in free trade agreements, have been increasing in number.

Bilateral investment treaties (BITs) have been recognized as instruments for the promotion and legal protection of foreign direct investment. They determine the scope of application of the treaty (that is, the investments and investors covered by it). In addition, virtually all BITs cover four substantive areas: admission, treatment, expropriation, and the settlement of disputes. Recent BITs stipulate the rules on the right of establishment, national treatment, prohibition of certain performance requirements, and other matters. In some cases BITs may put local firms at a competitive disadvantage vis-à-vis their foreign counterparts (United Nations 1999, 118).

Bilateral investment treaties have been increasing rapidly since the early 1990s, as multinational corporations have become active in making foreign direct investments. Indeed, the cumulative number of BITs worldwide increased fivefold in twelve years from 446 in 1990 to 2,181 in 2002 (Table 1.3). In the past BITs were concluded between developed countries, or between developed and developing countries. In recent years BITs have been concluded between developing countries, reflecting their recognition of the importance of a stable and transparent FDI environment. Similar to the pattern observed in the rest of the world, developing economies in East Asia have been active in concluding BITs since the 1990s. Among East Asian developing economies, China has been the most active, with 107 bilateral investment treaties concluded as of 2002. Malaysia, Korea, and Indonesia also have been active, with 67, 62, and 56 BITs, respectively, as of 2002.

Free trade agreements (FTAs) are a traditional framework for promoting free trade among member countries. However, recent FTAs go beyond free trade, and some have arrangements for free FDI. For example, the North American Free Trade Agreement (NAFTA) has agreements on MFN (most-favored-nations) and national treatment for foreign firms, and a mechanism for dispute settlement. The newly enacted FTA between Japan and Singapore has various components that promote free FDI including national treatment of foreign companies, protection of investors, and abolition of performance requirements.

Plurilateral investment arrangements also have been established. The Association of Southeast Asian Nations (ASEAN) Investment Area is one of the few such arrangements in East Asia. The framework agreement for the ASEAN Investment Area (AIA) was concluded in 1998. AIA, with its more liberal and transparent investment environment, was created to attract FDI to ASEAN member countries from both ASEAN and non-ASEAN sources. Initially, the deadline for the opening up and adoption of national treatment of all industries was set for 2010 for ASEAN investors and 2020 for non-ASEAN investors.[9] However, ASEAN leaders brought forward the target

9. See Chia (2000) on the ASEAN Investment Area.

Table 1.3. *Bilateral Investment Treaties, 1990–2002*
(Cumulative numbers)

Area	*1990*	*1991*	*1992*	*1993*	*1994*	*1995*	*1996*	*1997*	*1998*	*1999*	*2000*	*2001*	*2002*
World	446	527	651	780	971	1,173	1,384	1,556	1,727	1,856	1,940	2,099	2,181
Developing countries	364	425	511	603	743	904	1,068	1,211	1,355	1,465	1,538	1,675	1,745
East Asia	97	118	166	198	248	291	343	383	417	440	462	482	495
NIEs4	31	35	46	54	61	74	89	98	106	111	115	117	117
Hong Kong, China	0	0	1	2	5	8	11	13	14	14	14	14	14
Korea, Rep. of	20	24	28	32	35	41	49	52	57	60	60	62	62
Singapore	10	10	11	12	12	15	16	19	20	21	24	24	24
Taiwan, China	1	1	6	8	9	10	13	14	15	16	17	17	17
ASEAN5	37	50	71	83	113	136	155	176	193	207	220	224	234
Indonesia	8	12	17	17	24	28	34	41	46	52	53	55	56
Malaysia	16	17	22	25	36	43	49	53	61	63	65	65	67
Philippines	4	4	7	8	12	18	18	23	26	30	32	33	34
Thailand	8	12	13	14	16	18	20	22	23	23	31	31	37
Vietnam	1	5	12	19	25	29	34	37	37	39	39	40	40
Other ASEAN countries	2	2	3	4	8	10	19	22	26	28	31	37	37
Brunei Darussalam	0	0	0	0	0	0	0	0	2	2	2	2	2
Cambodia	0	0	0	0	1	2	5	6	6	8	10	13	13
Lao PDR	2	2	3	4	7	8	14	16	17	17	18	19	19
Myanmar	0	0	0	0	0	0	0	0	1	1	1	3	3
China	27	31	46	57	66	71	80	87	92	94	96	104	107
South Asia													
India	0	0	0	0	2	9	14	24	27	35	39	43	46

Source: United Nations Conference on Trade and Development (UNCTAD), Foreign Direct Investment database on line.

date to 2003 for the original ASEAN-6 and Myanmar; Vietnam and Laos will try to achieve early realization of AIA by no later than 2010.

The boom in bilateral and plurilateral investment treaties stems from many countries' dissatisfaction with multilateral and regional frameworks. Several reasons can be found for such sentiment. First, many members of the World Trade Organization, especially those from developed countries, are not satisfied with the rules in the trade-related investment measures mainly because of their limited coverage. As noted earlier, TRIMs regulate restrictions on FDI that are related to trade only. Fundamental restrictions on FDI, such as those on the right of establishment and national treatment, are not included. Second, APEC's Non-Binding Investment Principles cannot be enforced since FDI liberalization under APEC is carried out voluntarily in response to peer pressure. Third, negotiations on multilateral and regional frameworks take enormous time and effort because of the numerous participants. Because of the problems with multilateral and regional frameworks, many countries have chosen bilateral and plurilateral investment agreements.

Benefits of bilateral and plurilateral investment treaties include "high-level" contents and a short negotiating time. These treaties certainly have helped expand foreign direct investment.[10] However, problems exist with these treaties. Their varied and inconsistent contents make the FDI environment complex and confusing. Bilateral and plurilateral investment treaties cannot be concluded without many negotiations, thus incurring enormous costs. It may be possible to liberalize FDI regimes with less difficulty if the liberalization is carried out regionally or multilaterally. This is because the negative effects of FDI liberalization on some groups in the economy are likely to be offset by favorable effects in other areas.

Foreign Direct Investment Regimes of East Asian Developing Economies

Many developing economies in East Asia liberalized their FDI policies in recent years because they recognized the importance of FDI in promoting economic growth. Figure 1.6 presents our assessment of FDI regimes in ten East Asian developing economies for which the data are available. The assessment is based on the information given in the Individual Action Plans (IAPs) submitted to APEC. Figure 1.7 evaluates the investment regimes for these ten economies in terms of the following eleven categories: right of

10. World Bank (2002) provides empirical evidence on the effectiveness of bilateral investment treaties in attracting foreign direct investment.

Figure 1.6. *FDI Regimes in Selected East Asian Economies, 1996, 1999, and 2000*

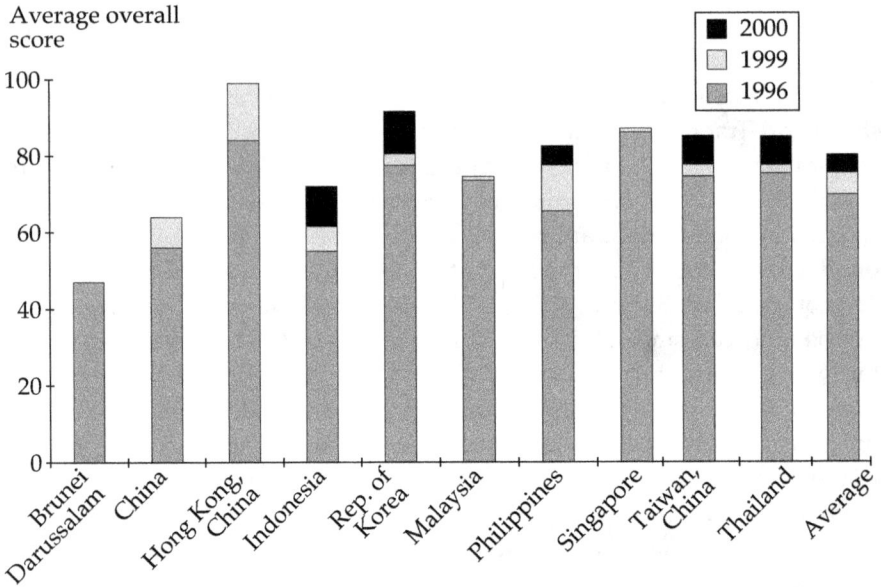

Source: Japan National Committee for Pacific Economic Cooperation Council (2002).

Figure 1.7. *FDI Regimes in East Asian Economies by Category, 1996, 1999, and 2000*

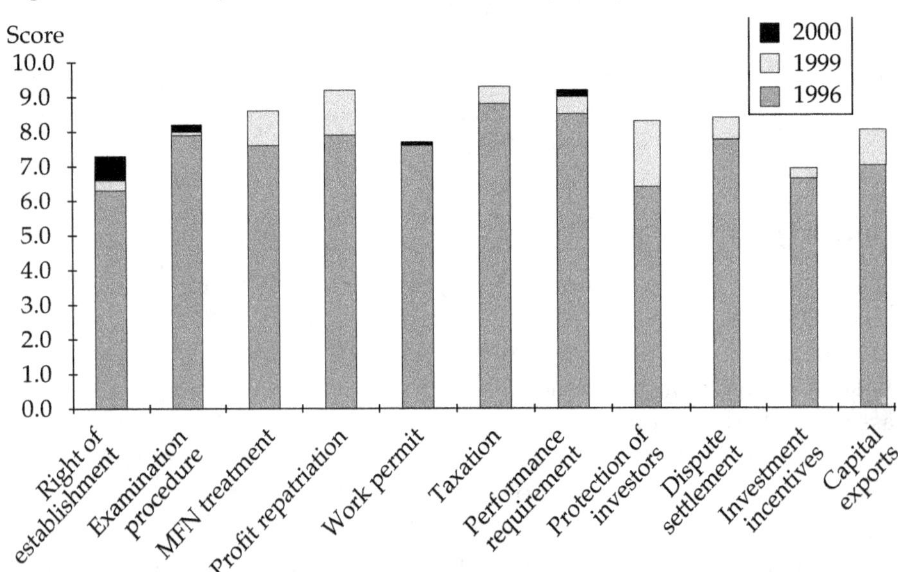

Source: Japan National Committee for Pacific Economic Cooperation Council (2002).

establishment, examination procedure, MFN treatment, profit repatriation, work permit, taxation, performance requirement, protection of investors, dispute settlement, investment incentives, and capital exports.

Shortcomings in certain categories can restrict FDI inflows. For example, problems with regard to right of establishment (market access), work permit, taxation, performance requirement, protection of investors, and dispute settlement can restrict foreign firms' activities and create an unstable business environment. Investment incentives, which have a favorable impact on FDI inflows, can negatively affect resource allocation because they do distort investment flows. In addition, it should be emphasized that investment incentives result in "beggar-thy-neighbor" policy making since all the economies offering investment incentives would end up wasting resources by trying to attract investments. Restrictions on capital exports discourage FDI outflows. The economies with these restrictions are viewed as restrictive FDI regimes.

For each of the eleven categories, scoring is conducted on a scale of 1 to 10. A score of 10 reflects no restrictions; a score of zero is given when no information is provided in the IAP; this score is justifiable because a lack of disclosure of the rules is a serious obstacle to FDI. To obtain the average overall score for all the categories, the scores for individual categories are summed with the following weights. The right of establishment (market access) is given a weight of 10; other categories are given a weight of 1. This treatment reflects the fact that the right of establishment is the most important regulation on inward FDI.

East Asian developing economies liberalized their FDI regimes during the 1996–2000 period; the average overall scores increased from 73 in 1996 to 81 in 2000 (see Figure 1.6). In 2000 Hong Kong had the highest score, 99; Korea, Singapore, Taiwan, Thailand, and the Philippines also scored high (above 80). In contrast, Brunei Darussalam and China received low scores, although China's score improved between 1996 and 1999. Indonesia and Malaysia are placed in between the high-scoring and low-scoring groups. As one would expect, more developed economies exhibit high scores, reflecting open FDI regimes, while less developed economies show relatively low scores, indicating restrictive FDI regimes. Of the eleven FDI categories, taxation, profit repatriation, and performance requirement register high scores in 2000, and investment incentives, right of establishment, and work permit register low scores (Figure 1.7). Scores for the right of establishment improved substantially, while scores for work permit and investment incentives remained low despite some improvement.

The scores for the right of establishment and investment incentives vary widely among the selected East Asian economies listed in Appendix Table

A1.5. Brunei and China register very low scores at 4 and 5, respectively; entry by foreign firms is restricted. By contrast, Hong Kong, and Korea have high scores; their markets are very open to foreign firms. As to investment incentives, both Korea and Malaysia register low scores of 6, while the score of 10 was given to Hong Kong.

For the work permit category, unlike the right of establishment and investment incentives categories, scores vary little among the sample economies. This reflects the difficulties associated with opening up labor markets; increased foreign personnel can negatively affect domestic unemployment. Comparing the scores for 1996, 1999, and 2000, one finds that profit repatriation and protection of investors improved markedly. Hong Kong, Indonesia, Korea, and the Philippines increased their respective scores by more than 10 points.

Scores are based on the information given in Individual Action Plans. IAPs describe the regulations concerning foreign direct investment and thus they provide very useful information for the assessment of the FDI regimes. However, IAPs do not capture the complete picture because regulations on FDI are not always practiced in the ways that are documented. To obtain a more accurate picture of FDI regimes, we use information obtained from the survey conducted by the Japan Machinery Center for Trade and Investment (Table 1.4). It collected information on impediments to trade and investment from its member companies. Of the eleven economies listed in the table, China received the highest number (65). Behind China are Malaysia (38), Thailand (24), and Indonesia (21). Economies with few impediments include Brunei (0), Singapore (0), and Hong Kong (1).

Although Brunei had the lowest score based on IAPs (Figure 1.6), no incidents were reported for Brunei concerning FDI impediments (Table 1.4). One reason for this inconsistency is the limited importance of Brunei for Japanese firms' FDI activities. Another reason is our treatment of "not mentioned" in the evaluation of IAPs. Brunei has by far the largest number of such cases. In our evaluation, a score of zero is given if the policies are "not mentioned," probably reflecting the restricted nature of the FDI regime (Appendix Table A1.5). However, this score may overstate the degree of restrictiveness, a possibility that should be kept in mind when evaluating the results in Figure 1.6.

Evaluations of Singapore and Korea also differ. Korea ranked higher than Singapore in the IAP evaluation, but the number of incidents of FDI impediments is higher for Korea than for Singapore. These "inconsistencies" may be due to ineffective application and enforcement of FDI regulations in Korea, resulting in the high score shown in Table 1.4. Singapore, on the other hand, has a very effective application and enforcement mechanism.

Table 1.4. *Impediments to FDI Reported by Japanese Companies, 2000*

Economy	*Right of establishment*	*Real estate acquisition*	*Equity restriction*	*Examination procedure*	*MFN treatment*	*Profit repatriation*	*Work permit*	*Taxation*	*Performance requirement*					*Investor protection*	*FDI regime*	*Total no. of incidents*	*FDI cases*	*Rate of incidence*
									Total	*Export*	*Local content*	*Technology transfer*	*Other*					
Brunei Darussalam																0	33	0.00
China	13		2	5		5	2	7	18	6	3	1	8	5	8	65	4,512	14.41
Hong Kong, China	1															1	4,820	0.21
Indonesia	4	1	3	1			4	3	4	1			3		1	21	2,991	7.02
Korea, Rep. of	4					3			1	1						8	2,204	3.63
Malaysia	2	1	7			3	4	1	11		1		10	2	7	38	2,183	17.41
Philippines	1	2	5	1		1	3	1	5	1	3		1			19	1,383	13.74
Singapore																0	3,327	0.00
Taiwan, China	1	1		1			5	1	5	2	2		1			14	2,826	4.95
Thailand	1	1	6	6	1		1	1	5	2	3		2			24	3,747	6.41
Vietnam	1	1	1	1		3	1	1	6	2	2		2			15	274	54.74
Total	28	7	24	15	1	15	20	15	55	15	14	1	27	7	16	205	28,300	7.24

Note: FDI regime means a changeable, inefficient, nontransparent regime. The numbers in the table are the cumulative number of reported FDI cases by Japanese firms from 1951 to 1999. The rate of incidence is measured in terms of 1,000 FDI cases.

Source: Author's compilation based on the data collected by Japan Machinery Center for Trade and Investment.

The findings above on the rate of incidence are biased in such a way that gives countries with a large number of FDI cases (projects) a large number of reported incidents of FDI impediments. To deal with this bias, we computed the rate of incidence by dividing the number of reported cases of FDI impediments by the number of FDI cases by Japanese firms. The results of this adjustment show that Vietnam registers a very high incidence rate at 55 per 1,000 FDI cases. Vietnam is followed by Malaysia (17), China (14), and the Philippines (13).

An examination of impediments by category (Table 1.4) reveals the largest number of impediments for performance requirements (55). Scores for China and Malaysia in this category were particularly high. Among the different types of performance requirements, the export requirement and local content requirement are the two most commonly applied (scores of 15 and 14, respectively). The technology transfer requirement is allegedly used by the host economy government to absorb technology. Only one case was reported. As to the local content requirement, China, the Philippines, and Thailand had a score of 3; Taiwan and Vietnam had a score of 2. China is reported to have many incidents (6) of export requirement.

The next most frequently reported FDI impediments include restricted right of establishment (market access), restriction on the level of equity participation, difficulty obtaining a work permit, lack of transparency in FDI regime, and taxation. As to the right of establishment, China received the largest number of reported cases at 13; Indonesia and Korea each registered 4 cases. Restriction on equity participation is reported to be a prevalent impediment to FDI in Malaysia, Thailand, and the Philippines.

Difficulty in obtaining a work permit, an FDI impediment in many East Asian developing economies, was a problem frequently reported in Taiwan, Indonesia, Malaysia, and the Philippines. From the analysis of IAPs, Indonesia and the Philippines were found to have restrictive policies toward issuing work permits, while Taiwan and Malaysia were assessed to have relatively open policies on work permits. Again, the inconsistencies between the findings in Figure 1.7 and in Table 1.4 appear to result from the differences between actual practices and reported practices.

Lack of transparency regarding FDI rules is reported to be a problem in China, Malaysia, and Indonesia. Taxation is reported to be an impediment in many East Asian developing economies, with China at the top of the list (7 cases) and Indonesia with the next largest number (3 cases).

An examination of FDI regimes for East Asian economies found that FDI regimes have been liberalized in recent years, but there is ample room for improvement, especially in the areas of right of establishment, work permit, and performance requirement.

The Determinants of FDI Inflows

Several studies have examined the determinants of FDI inflows. United Nations (1998) provides a good survey of the past studies and evaluates host countries in terms of their policy framework for FDI, economic determinants, and business facilitation. The policy framework includes economic, political, and social stability, FDI policy, trade policy, and other factors. Economic determinants are categorized based on motives for foreign direct investment. For FDI with market-seeking motives, market size, market growth, access to regional and global markets, and country-specific consumer preferences are important factors. For FDI with resource/asset-seeking motives, the important factors are the availability of raw materials, low-cost unskilled labor, skilled labor, technological assets, and physical infrastructure. Finally, for FDI with efficiency-seeking motives, the availability of low-cost unskilled labor, intermediate inputs, and participation in a regional integration agreement conducive to the establishment of regional corporate networks are the factors considered to be important determinants of FDI inflows. The measure "business facilitation" includes investment incentives, administrative efficiency, and social amenities (such as bilingual schools).

In the previous analyses, variables representing some of the determinants of FDI inflows were tested to explain FDI inflow values. Typical studies include nominal gross domestic product (GDP), growth in real GDP, GDP per capita, and political stability as explanatory variables. The first three variables capture the elements related to market size and market growth; political stability is used as a proxy for stability in political as well as institutional environments. The studies generally find positive and statistically significant coefficients on market size, real GDP growth, and political stability, while the estimated coefficients on GDP per capita are mixed, reflecting two different meanings of this variable. GDP per capita is a proxy for the purchasing power of the host-country population, yet it can be a proxy for the wage rate. One would expect a positive impact of GDP per capita on FDI inflow if the objective of FDI is to expand sales in the host economy. One would expect the impact to be negative if FDI is of the efficiency-seeking type.

In this section we examine the determinants of FDI inflows by extending the previous analyses in terms of country and period coverage, and in terms of explanatory variables. In addition to GDP (ln GDP), real GDP growth (GROWTH), per capita GDP (GDPCAP), and political stability measured by political risk (RISK), we include these five variables: inflation (INF), exchange rate (EX), the share of trade (exports and imports) to GDP

(TRADE), secondary school enrollment ratio (EDU), and electricity generation per capita (ELEC).[11] Inflation and exchange rate are included to examine the impact of macroeconomic stability on FDI inflows. Foreign investors tend to avoid risk and thus we expect INF to be negative; EX is expected to be positive because depreciation of the host currency is likely to increase the host country's attractiveness.[12] Open trade and investment regimes would attract FDI inflows. To test this hypothesis, we include the share of trade (exports + imports) to GDP (TRADE) as an explanatory variable. One would expect the estimated coefficient of TRADE to be positive. The availability of educated labor attracts FDI since these workers can contribute to achieving high productivity for multinational corporations. Good infrastructure also is a benefit since it can reduce multinational corporations' transaction costs. To test these hypotheses, we included the following variables—secondary school enrollment ratio and electricity generation per capita—to reflect the availability of educated labor and infrastructure. We expect both of these variables to have positive impacts on FDI inflows.[13]

We conducted regression analysis to identify the determinants of FDI inflows. Our panel data set has 120 countries (95 of them are developing countries), and the data cover the period from 1980 to 2001. The data set is not a full panel, since many observations are missing. After testing the validity of the type of estimation (random-effect model or fixed-effect model), we applied the fixed-effect model for the estimation. We conducted the analysis by using all countries and developing countries only since the objectives of FDI in devel-

---

11. Urata and Kawai (2000), in their study of the locational determinants of Japanese FDI, examined the importance of the following variables: exchange rate, exchange rate volatility, wage rate, market size, macroeconomic stability, labor quality, infrastructure, agglomeration (cumulative FDI cases by Japanese firms), and governance of the host-country government. They found that exchange rate volatility and wage rate have negative impacts, while market size, macroeconomic stability, infrastructure, agglomeration, and governance of the host-country government have positive impacts. These results are consistent with expectations. The exchange rate and labor quality variables did not show expected effects, but they are not statistically significant.

12. Exchange rate is defined as the number of host currency units per US$. Therefore, depreciation of the host currency is expressed by the increase in the value.

13. The sources of data for the analysis are as follows. FDI inflows are taken from UNCTAD's Foreign Direct Investment Database. Information on RISK is taken from Business Risk Service, and the data for the remaining variables are obtained from the *World Bank's World Development Indicators 2003* CD-ROM. The information on Taiwan is taken from the Taiwan Statistical Yearbook (the Republic of China).

oped and developing countries may differ. Because of limited availability of information on RISK, we conducted the analysis with and without RISK.

The results of the estimation are shown in Table 1.5. They are generally consistent with our expectations. Specifically, the estimated coefficients on GDP, GROWTH, TRADE, EDU, ELEC are positive and statistically significant, while those on GDPCAP and INF are negative and statistically significant. The results on EX are negative and insignificant, while the coefficients on RISK are mixed. These findings indicate that large market size and the presence of a growing market attract foreign direct investment. Open trade regimes and a stable macroeconomic environment are important factors for multinational corporations in determining the location of FDI. Moreover, good infrastructure and the availability of well-educated and low-wage workers contribute to attracting FDI. Unexpectedly, political risk did not show any discernible impacts on the decision of MNCs on where to invest. The unexpected result may be due to a lack of appropriate measure of political risk for a large number of countries.

To examine how East Asian economies performed in attracting FDI, we compare the actual FDI inflow to the expected or predicted value, which is computed from the estimated results. Table 1.6 shows the ratio of actual to predicted values for eleven East Asian economies from 1990 to 2000.[14] For most of this period, Singapore and China are overachievers, while Taiwan and Malaysia are underachievers. The performance for the other economies is mixed. Korea and India improved their performance in the latter half of the 1990s; the performance of Indonesia, Malaysia, the Philippines, and Vietnam deteriorated.

The explanatory variables do not capture the quality of institutions, such as government agencies and corporations, in these economies or their FDI policies—factors that are very important in determining FDI inflows. Indeed, the countries with a favorable FDI performance, such as China, Korea, India, and Singapore, improved their investment environment by liberalizing FDI policies or by improving the quality of institutions. By contrast, Indonesia, Malaysia, the Philippines, and Vietnam, whose FDI performance worsened in the 1990s, continued to have various problems including political instability and a restrictive environment for foreign direct investment, as later chapters will explain in detail.

---

14. The values for some explanatory variables are not available for some countries. In these cases interpolation or extrapolation is used to obtain the values.

Table 1.5. *The Determinants of FDI Inflows*

	All sample economies				*Developing economies*			
	(1)		(2)		(3)		(4)	
Variable	*coefficients*	*t-statistic*	*coefficients*	*t-statistic*	*coefficients*	*t-statistic*	*coefficients*	*t-statistic*
ln GDP	1.85 ***	9.91	1.83 ***	12.81	1.93 ***	7.53	1.91 ***	10.28
GROWTH	0.007	0.49	0.03 ***	3.18	0.02 *	1.70	0.03 ***	3.30
GDPCAP	–0.00004 **	–2.04	–0.00003 **	–2.00	–0.0001 *	–1.93	–0.0001 **	–2.18
INF	–0.0004 ***	–3.22	–0.0003 ***	–4.29	–0.0003 ***	3.09	–0.0003 ***	–3.92
EX	–8.5E-07	–0.38	–5.2E-07	–0.19	–1.2E-6	–0.54	–6.8E-7	–0.24
TRADE	0.01 **	2.43	0.02 ***	6.02	–0.002	–0.49	0.01 ***	5.00
EDU	0.01 **	2.17	0.01 ***	2.77	0.02 ***	2.98	0.02 ***	3.09
ELEC	0.0002 ***	3.15	0.0001 ***	3.38	0.0004 ***	2.75	0.0001 **	2.00
RISK	–0.0003	–0.02			0.004	0.30		
c	–28.55 ***	–6.31	–26.91 ***	–8.15	–29.77 ***	–4.93	–28.28 ***	–6.75
R-sq	0.641		0.717		0.454		0.600	
F[a]	45.35 ***		71.55 ***		31.84 ***		48.60 ***	
rho[b]	0.865		0.818		0.863		0.759	
chi2[c]	45.04 ***		110.08 ***		2507.34 ***		83.98 ***	
No. of observations	518		1157		294		881	

* Level of statistical significance at 10 percent.
** Level of statistical significance at 5 percent.
*** Level of statistical significance at 1 percent.
a. F: H_0: all beta are zero.
b. fraction of variance due to u_i.
c. Hausman specification test.
Source: Author's estimation.

Table 1.6. *The Ratio of Actual to Expected Values of FDI Inflows for Selected East Asian Economies, 1990–2000*

Year	*Hong Kong, China*	*Rep. of Korea*	*Singapore*	*Taiwan, China*	*Indonesia*	*Malaysia*	*Philippines*	*Thailand*	*Vietnam*	*China*	*India*
1990	0.97	1.20	1.11	1.44	1.10	2.03	1.81	3.08	1.64	0.85	0.47
1991	0.20	1.65	1.14	1.12	1.27	2.14	1.62	1.74	1.86	0.73	0.18
1992	0.59	0.89	0.44	0.68	1.25	2.14	1.54	1.34	2.03	1.43	0.64
1993	1.10	0.54	0.86	0.63	1.11	1.72	1.90	0.79	2.32	3.36	0.97
1994	1.49	0.50	1.30	0.84	0.85	0.82	1.67	0.40	2.47	2.19	1.28
1995	0.85	0.79	1.39	0.76	1.29	0.60	1.12	0.41	1.33	1.41	2.29
1996	1.74	0.92	1.15	0.85	1.54	0.73	0.84	0.52	0.71	1.25	2.50
1997	1.05	1.50	1.12	0.95	1.33	0.49	0.96	1.45	0.60	1.37	3.09
1998	1.33	2.38	1.03	0.09	–1.28	0.25	1.08	1.09	0.48	1.24	2.44
1999	1.23	3.27	1.20	1.05	–1.22	0.26	0.88	0.72	0.32	0.96	1.62
2000	1.12	2.94	1.22	1.70	–1.12	0.21	0.68	0.47	0.19	1.04	1.55

Source: The actual values are from United Nations Conference on Trade and Development (UNCTAD), Foreign Direct Investment database on line. The expected values are obtained from the estimated coefficients from column (4) in Table 1.5.

The Effects of FDI on Trade and Production Patterns in East Asia

The changing patterns of trade and production in East Asia appear to have been greatly influenced by foreign direct investment. Although the role of FDI cannot be easily proved empirically because of the absence of necessary information, evidence showing trade by multinational corporations as a large share of global foreign trade indicates the significant impact of FDI.[15] The positive, strong effects of FDI on foreign trade are emphasized by several studies, including Kawai and Urata (1998). Therefore, this section examines the effects of FDI on the patterns of international trade and production in East Asia, with a focus on its impacts on intraregional trade and production networks.

To analyze the changing patterns of regional trade in East Asia, we computed two measures: absolute and relative. The absolute measure compares the scale of a particular bilateral trading relationship to world trade; the relative measure compares it to trade of one or the other of the two partners participating in the relationship.

The absolute measure can be expressed

$$A = Xij \ / \ X..$$

The relative measure can be expressed

$$B = A \ / \ (Xi. \ / \ X..) = Xij \ / \ Xi.$$

where *Xij* represents exports from region *i* to region *j*, and "." indicates the summation across all *i* or *j*. Therefore, *Xi.* represents total exports of region *i*, *X.j* represents total imports (or inward FDI flows) of region *j*, and X.. represents world trade.

Table 1.7 shows the estimated values of these two measures of foreign trade for East Asia, the North American Free Trade Agreement (NAFTA) members, and the European Union (EU) members. Intraregional trade in East Asia became more important not only in terms of world trade but also in terms of regional trade.

The importance of intra–East Asian trade in world trade, shown by the absolute measure, increased notably from 8 percent in 1990 to 12 percent in

15. According to United Nations (1999), two-thirds to three-quarters of world exports are conducted by MNCs, and a third of world exports is between affiliated firms belonging to MNCs.

Table 1.7. Regionalization in Foreign Trade in East Asia, NAFTA, and EU Countries, 1990 and 2001
(Percent)

	1990	2001
Absolute measure		
East Asia[a]	8.3	11.9
NAFTA[b]	6.7	10.0
EU[c]	29.1	22.3
Relative measure		
Exports & imports		
East Asia	43.2	51.8
NAFTA	37.9	47.5
EU	66.3	61.4
Exports		
East Asia	39.8	47.5
NAFTA	41.4	54.6
EU	66.0	60.8
Imports		
East Asia	47.2	56.9
NAFTA	35.0	42.0
EU	66.5	62.1

a. Trade within East Asia as a percentage of world trade.

b. East Asian economies' trade with members or signatories of the North American Free Trade Agreement as a percentage of world trade.

c. East Asian economies' trade with European Union members as a percentage of world trade.

Source: Author's computation based on the data compiled by Japan External Trade Organization (Jetro).

2001.[16] The share of intra-NAFTA trade in world trade also increased over the same period, but the share was slightly lower, at 10 percent in 2001. The corresponding share for the European Union was significantly higher, at 22 percent in 2001, although the share declined sharply from 29 percent in 1990.

Intra–East Asian trade increased its importance for East Asia's total trade (exports plus imports) over time, as shown in the increase in the relative measure from 43 percent in 1990 to 52 percent in 2001. Intraregional trade as a percentage of total regional trade also increased for the members of

16. Although not shown in Table 1.7, the absolute measure for East Asia declined slightly in the late 1990s after the financial crisis. See Kawai and Urata (2004).

NAFTA from 38 to 48 percent during the same period, but it declined for the European Union from 66 percent to 61 percent.

An analysis of the relative measures computed for exports and for imports shows that intra–East Asian trade is more important as a source of imports than as a destination for exports. This trading pattern reflects the behavior of multinational corporations. Many MNCs use East Asia as an export platform where they assemble export products for sale in regions outside of East Asia by importing parts and components from within the region. In contrast, intra-NAFTA trade is more important for NAFTA members' exports than for their imports.

The formation of trading patterns in East Asia mentioned above appears to indicate the emergence of a regional production system (Urata 2001). To analyze the production system in the region (Table 1.8), we utilize international input-output tables constructed by the Institute of Developing Economies (IDE) in Japan. The institute's data cover East Asian economies and the United States for 1985, 1990, and 1995, although Table 1.8 presents data from 1985 and 1995 only. The international input-output tables are based on input-output tables of the individual economies. The import sources and export destinations of the products are explicitly specified. The international input-output tables show the sources of inputs for production (inputs from the domestic market and imported inputs from other economies) and destinations of outputs (outputs sold in the domestic market and outputs exported to other economies). Below we focus on the sources of inputs for production by East Asian economies because our main interest here is to examine the interindustry, intraregional production relationship in East Asia.

The upper portion of Table 1.8 shows inputs from East Asian economies as a share of total inputs (intermediate inputs plus value added) for the nine economies included in the table and for East Asia as a whole. Two sets of figures are shown in the table. One is the share of inputs from East Asian economies including those from the economy itself, and the other is the share of inputs from East Asian economies excluding the economy itself. For example, the share of inputs in total inputs for Indonesia in 1985 was 0.372 if inputs from Indonesia are included, and 0.020 if inputs from Indonesia are excluded. The column on the far right of Table 1.8 indicates that for East Asia as a whole dependence on East Asia for the procurements of inputs increased from 1985 to 1995. In other words, intraregional dependence in production grew. Specifically, for East Asia the share of inputs from East Asia (excluding those from the economies themselves) in total inputs increased from 0.042 in 1985 to 0.058 in 1995. Examining the changes for

Table 1.8. *Regional Production Systems in East Asia, 1985 and 1995*
(Inputs from East Asian economies as a share of total inputs)

Effect	*Year*	*Indonesia*	*Malaysia*	*Philippines*	*Singapore*	*Thailand*	*China*	*Taiwan, China*	*Rep. of Korea*	*Japan*	*East Asia*
Direct effect (Input-output coefficients)[a]											
East Asia	1985	0.372	0.405	0.404	0.442	0.446	0.512	0.494	0.479	0.483	0.449
	1995	0.414	0.448	0.389	0.498	0.439	0.574	0.444	0.512	0.446	0.463
East Asia excluding the inputs from the	1985	0.020	0.069	0.020	0.144	0.039	0.012	0.033	0.036	0.009	0.042
economy itself	1995	0.022	0.111	0.051	0.155	0.067	0.019	0.057	0.034	0.006	0.058
Direct and indirect effects (Leontief inverse)[b]											
East Asia	1985	1.665	1.682	1.682	1.830	1.806	1.935	1.844	1.783	1.912	1.793
	1995	1.621	1.764	1.638	1.869	1.711	2.227	1.795	1.747	1.838	1.801
East Asia excluding the output induced in the country	1985	0.062	0.210	0.063	0.299	0.102	0.039	0.080	0.086	0.035	0.108
itself	1995	0.053	0.317	0.153	0.360	0.142	0.066	0.153	0.092	0.022	0.151

a. The proportional share of inputs from East Asian economies in total inputs (intermediate inputs plus value added).
b. The amount of output induced by an increase in one unit of final demand in East Asian economies.
Source: Author's computation based on data taken from Asian International Input-Output Tables, 1985 and 1995. Those tables were constructed by the Institute of Developing Economies (IDE) in Japan.

East Asian economies individually, one finds that intraregional dependence increased for all of the economies except Korea and Japan.

In order to investigate the extent of interindustry relationships in production in East Asia, we computed the amount of output induced by a change in final demand in East Asia by explicitly taking account of interindustry linkages. The results of the computation are presented in the lower portion of Table 1.8, and again two sets of data are shown. One set is the induced level of outputs in East Asia including the economy itself, and the other is the induced level of outputs in East Asia excluding the economy itself. For example, for 1985 a one unit increase of final demand in Indonesia induces 1.665 units of output in Indonesia and in other East Asian economies combined, while it induces 0.062 unit of output in East Asian economies excluding Indonesia. The last column shows that a one unit increase of final demand in East Asia led to a 1.793 unit increase in output for East Asia as a whole in 1985 and a 1.801 unit increase in output for East Asia as a whole in 1995. A similar increase can be found if the impacts on the economies themselves are excluded. The level of output induced in East Asian economies excluding the impact in the origin of the change in final demand increased from 0.108 to 0.151 for the period. These findings clearly indicate the deepening of the intraregional production relationship in East Asia.

Intraregional trade and intraregional dependence in production both increased, reflecting the emergence of a regional production system in East Asia. The emergence of a regional production system in several machinery sectors including electronics and automobiles (not shown in the table) appears to be attributable to the active operation of multinational corporations in East Asia.

Conclusions

This chapter examined recent FDI flows in East Asia and the factors that have influenced them. One important determinant of FDI flows is the policy framework for FDI. The effects of FDI on the economic growth of East Asian economies are discussed since FDI appears to have contributed to the formation of regional trade and production systems in East Asia.

FDI inflows to East Asia began to decline around 2000 after experiencing a steady and notable increase in the 1990s. One exception is China. Its FDI inflows continued to increase in the twenty-first century after a slight decline in 1999. Two new developments are worth noting. One is an increase in reinvested earnings, reflecting successful operations, and the other is a rapid expansion of mergers and acquisitions, partly because of relaxed regulation of M&As and the reduced value of assets resulting from the depreciation of some Asian currencies. The implications of these developments warrant scrutiny.

Most East Asian developing economies liberalized their FDI policies during the 1990s. Policymakers recognized the importance of attracting FDI for economic growth. However, further liberalization for many East Asian economies is still needed.

A regression analysis of the determinants of FDI inflows indicated the importance of the following factors in attracting foreign direct investment: a large and/or growing market, educated low-wage workers, a stable macroeconomic performance, well-developed infrastructure, and an open economic system. Policymakers should improve upon these aspects by formulating and implementing appropriate policies. Although the FDI policy framework certainly plays an important role in attracting FDI, our regression analysis did not support this point, probably because of the difficulty of quantifying an economy's FDI policy framework. Further studies are needed on this issue.

The last part of the chapter examined the impact of FDI on regional trade and production systems in East Asia. FDI appears to have contributed significantly to the creation of a regional production network linked by trade. A regional production network enables multinational corporations to achieve efficient production by locating particular production processes in the country or region where they may be performed most efficiently. Such a system was created largely because of liberalization in trade and FDI policies. A liberalized business environment has enabled MNCs to make business decisions on the basis of comparative and competitive advantages. For FDI recipients, exploiting the benefits of hosting the subsidiaries of multinational corporations can promote economic growth since multinational corporations have firm-specific advantages such as technology, management know-how, and well-developed procurement and distribution systems. These advantages contribute to the economic growth of the recipient economies. Several crosscountry statistical studies have found that the availability of well-educated workers helps assimilate technology in the recipient countries. The issue of how to make the best use of the presence of MNCs is very important, and further analysis is needed.

Appendix Table A1.1. *FDI Inflows to East Asian and Other Economies, 1990–2002*
(US$billions)

Economy	*1990*	*1991*	*1992*	*1993*	*1994*	*1995*	*1996*	*1997*	*1998*	*1999*	*2000*	*2001*	*2002*
World	208.67	158.82	166.97	225.50	255.90	333.81	384.96	481.91	686.03	1,079.08	1,392.96	823.82	651.19
Developing countries	36.96	43.29	55.30	81.49	104.29	114.88	149.76	193.22	191.28	229.30	246.06	209.43	162.15
East Asian developing countries	21.63	21.49	29.37	52.55	64.21	73.63	85.04	94.80	86.54	102.20	135.55	93.60	83.94
NIEs4	10.97	8.36	7.70	13.12	18.56	21.05	23.95	29.99	27.99	50.08	88.61	42.36	24.79
Hong Kong, China	3.28	1.02	3.89	6.93	7.83	6.21	10.46	11.37	14.77	24.58	61.94	23.78	13.72
Korea, Rep. of	0.79	1.18	0.73	0.59	0.81	1.78	2.33	2.84	5.41	9.33	9.28	3.53	1.97
Singapore	5.57	4.89	2.20	4.69	8.55	11.50	9.30	13.53	7.59	13.25	12.46	10.95	7.65
Taiwan, China	1.33	1.27	0.88	0.92	1.38	1.56	1.86	2.25	0.22	2.93	4.93	4.11	1.45
ASEAN5	7.01	8.51	10.32	11.72	11.59	15.59	19.25	18.73	13.27	10.45	5.22	3.37	5.06
Indonesia	1.09	1.48	1.78	2.00	2.11	4.35	6.19	4.68	–0.36	–2.75	–4.55	–3.28	–1.52
Malaysia	2.61	4.04	5.14	5.74	4.58	5.82	7.30	6.32	2.71	3.90	3.79	0.55	3.20
Philippines	0.55	0.56	0.78	1.24	1.59	1.58	1.62	1.26	1.72	1.73	1.35	0.98	1.11
Thailand	2.58	2.05	2.15	1.81	1.37	2.07	2.34	3.88	7.49	6.09	3.35	3.81	1.07
Vietnam	0.18	0.38	0.47	0.93	1.94	1.78	1.80	2.59	1.70	1.48	1.29	1.30	1.20
Other ASEAN	0.17	0.25	0.22	0.20	0.26	1.14	1.66	1.83	1.55	1.33	0.94	0.89	1.24
Brunei Darussalam	0.00	0.00	0.00	0.01	0.01	0.58	0.65	0.70	0.57	0.75	0.55	0.53	1.04
Cambodia	—	—	0.03	0.05	0.07	0.15	0.29	0.17	0.24	0.23	0.15	0.15	0.05
Lao People's Democratic Rep.	0.01	0.01	0.01	0.03	0.06	0.09	0.13	0.09	0.05	0.05	0.03	0.02	0.03
Myanmar	0.16	0.24	0.17	0.10	0.13	0.32	0.58	0.88	0.68	0.30	0.21	0.19	0.13
Other East Asia	3.49	4.38	11.14	27.51	33.79	35.85	40.19	44.24	43.73	40.33	40.77	46.98	52.85
China	3.49	4.37	11.16	27.52	33.79	35.85	40.18	44.24	43.75	40.32	40.77	46.85	52.70
Macao	0.00	0.01	–0.02	0.00	0.00	0.00	0.01	0.00	–0.02	0.01	0.00	0.13	0.15
South Asia													
India	0.24	0.08	0.25	0.53	0.97	2.15	2.53	3.62	2.63	2.17	2.32	3.40	3.45

— Not available.
Note: FDI flows have three components: equity capital, reinvested earnings, and intracompany loans.
Source: United Nations Conference on Trade and Development (UNCTAD), Foreign Direct Investment database on line.

Appendix Table A1.2. *M&A Transactions in East Asian and Other Economies, 1990–2001*
(US$billions)

Economy	*1990*	*1991*	*1992*	*1993*	*1994*	*1995*	*1996*	*1997*	*1998*	*1999*	*2000*	*2001*
World	150.6	80.7	79.3	83.1	127.1	186.6	227.0	304.8	531.6	766.0	1,143.8	594.0
Developing countries	16.1	5.8	8.2	14.3	15.0	16.5	35.7	67.0	82.7	74.0	70.6	85.8
East Asian developing countries	4.0	2.1	3.4	7.1	4.3	5.9	8.4	16.7	13.1	27.4	19.9	31.7
NIEs4	3.8	1.5	2.0	5.7	2.0	3.2	4.5	9.1	5.4	19.0	13.4	21.4
Hong Kong, China	2.6	0.6	1.7	5.3	1.6	1.7	3.3	7.3	0.9	4.2	4.8	10.4
Korea, Rep. of	—	0.7	0.0	0.0	0.0	0.2	0.6	0.8	4.0	10.1	6.4	3.6
Singapore	1.1	0.2	0.3	0.4	0.4	1.2	0.6	0.3	0.5	3.0	1.5	4.9
Taiwan, China	0.0	—	0.0	0.0	0.0	0.0	0.0	0.6	0.0	1.8	0.6	2.5
ASEAN5	0.2	0.4	1.2	0.9	1.6	2.3	2.0	5.5	6.9	5.9	4.2	8.0
Indonesia	—	0.1	0.2	0.2	0.2	0.8	0.5	0.3	0.7	1.2	0.8	3.5
Malaysia	0.1	0.1	0.0	0.5	0.4	0.1	0.8	0.4	1.1	1.2	0.4	1.4
Philippines	0.0	0.1	0.4	0.1	0.8	1.2	0.5	4.2	1.9	1.5	0.4	2.1
Thailand	0.1	0.1	0.5	0.0	0.1	0.2	0.2	0.6	3.2	2.0	2.6	1.0
Vietnam	—	—	—	—	0.0	0.0	0.0	0.1	—	0.1	0.0	0.0
Other ASEAN	0.0	0.0	0.0	0.0	0.0	0.0	0.0	0.3	0.0	0.0	0.0	0.0
Brunei Darussalam	—	—	—	0.0	—	—	—	—	—	—	—	—
Cambodia	—	—	—	—	—	—	—	0.0	—	—	—	—
Lao People's Democratic Rep.	—	—	—	—	—	—	—	—	—	—	—	—
Myanmar	—	—	—	0.0	—	0.0	—	0.3	—	—	—	—
Other East Asia	0.0	0.2	0.2	0.6	0.7	0.4	1.9	1.9	0.8	2.4	2.2	2.3
China	0.0	0.1	0.2	0.6	0.7	0.4	1.9	1.9	0.8	2.4	2.2	2.3
Macao	—	0.0	—	—	—	—	—	—	—	—	—	—
South Asia	0.0	0.0	0.0	0.0	0.0	0.0	0.0	0.0	0.0	0.0	0.0	0.0
India	0.0	—	0.0	0.1	0.4	0.3	0.2	1.5	0.4	1.0	1.2	1.0

— Not available.

Source: United Nations Conference on Trade and Development (UNCTAD), Foreign Direct Investment database on line.

Appendix Table A1.3. *M&A Transactions as a Share of FDI Inflows to East Asia and Elsewhere, 1990–2001*
(Percent)

Economy	*1990*	*1991*	*1992*	*1993*	*1994*	*1995*	*1996*	*1997*	*1998*	*1999*	*2000*	*2001*
World	72.2	50.8	47.5	36.8	49.7	55.9	59.0	63.3	77.5	71.0	82.1	72.1
Developing countries	43.4	13.4	14.8	17.5	14.4	14.4	23.9	34.7	43.2	32.3	28.7	41.0
East Asia	18.3	9.5	11.4	13.6	6.6	8.0	9.9	17.6	15.1	26.8	14.7	33.9
NIEs4	34.4	17.7	25.4	43.3	10.6	15.1	18.7	30.2	19.3	38.0	15.1	50.5
Hong Kong, China	80.0	55.6	43.1	76.6	20.5	27.4	31.2	64.5	6.4	17.0	7.7	43.6
Korea, Rep. of	—	57.1	0.0	0.3	0.1	10.8	24.3	29.4	73.4	107.8	69.5	103.4
Singapore	20.5	4.9	12.5	7.7	4.2	10.8	6.4	2.2	6.2	22.3	12.3	44.5
Taiwan, China	0.8	—	0.3	1.7	1.2	2.7	2.7	26.7	10.7	62.8	13.1	60.7
ASEAN5	2.4	4.9	11.4	7.4	13.5	14.6	10.4	29.5	52.0	56.7	80.7	237.4
Indonesia	—	10.1	13.1	8.5	9.8	18.6	8.6	7.1	–191.7	–42.4	–18.0	–107.7
Malaysia	3.3	3.2	0.9	9.0	9.7	1.7	10.5	5.5	40.4	29.9	11.6	261.5
Philippines	2.7	11.4	52.1	11.0	52.0	76.6	28.5	329.7	110.9	88.3	27.2	210.1
Thailand	2.7	3.9	23.1	2.3	6.5	7.8	10.0	16.3	42.8	33.0	76.7	25.1
Vietnam	—	—	—	—	0.1	0.0	0.3	2.4	—	4.0	1.5	0.3
Other ASEAN	0.0	0.0	0.0	6.0	0.0	0.8	0.0	14.2	0.0	0.0	0.0	0.0
Brunei Darussalam	—	—	—	15.0	—	—	—	—	—	—	—	—
Cambodia	—	—	—	—	—	—	—	0.6	—	—	—	—
Lao People's Democratic Rep.	—	—	—	—	—	—	—	—	—	—	—	—
Myanmar	—	—	—	9.6	—	2.8	—	29.6	—	—	—	—
Other East Asia	0.2	3.5	2.0	2.0	2.1	1.1	4.7	4.2	1.8	5.9	5.5	4.9
China	0.2	2.9	2.0	2.0	2.1	1.1	4.7	4.2	1.8	5.9	5.5	5.0
Macao	—	265.9	—	—	—	—	—	—	—	—	—	—
South Asia	—	—	—	—	—	—	—	—	—	—	—	—
India	2.1	—	13.8	18.0	39.5	12.8	8.2	42.0	13.7	48.2	52.6	30.5

— Not available.

Source: United Nations Conference on Trade and Development (UNCTAD), Foreign Direct Investment database on line.

Appendix Table A1.4. *FDI Outflows to East Asian and Other Economies, 1990–2002*
(US$billions)

Economy	*1990*	*1991*	*1992*	*1993*	*1994*	*1995*	*1996*	*1997*	*1998*	*1999*	*2000*	*2001*	*2002*
World	242.49	198.04	201.53	244.25	287.18	356.57	395.73	476.93	683.21	1,096.55	1,200.78	711.45	647.36
Developed countries	225.75	186.10	176.15	204.23	239.25	304.77	333.33	396.06	630.89	1,021.31	1,097.80	660.56	600.06
United States	30.98	32.70	42.65	77.25	73.25	92.07	84.43	95.77	131.00	209.39	142.63	103.76	119.74
Japan	48.02	30.73	17.22	13.71	17.94	22.63	23.43	25.99	24.15	22.74	31.56	38.33	31.48
Developing countries	16.68	11.90	25.31	39.71	47.47	51.11	61.14	76.66	49.84	72.79	99.05	47.38	43.09
East Asian developing countries	11.90	8.21	17.78	30.42	39.52	41.34	48.91	49.20	29.78	36.98	80.26	36.10	33.80
NIEs4	10.78	6.89	12.70	23.82	31.12	34.53	41.28	43.05	25.94	33.37	77.14	28.79	29.34
Hong Kong, China	2.45	2.83	8.25	17.71	21.44	25.00	26.53	24.41	16.99	19.36	59.38	11.34	17.69
Korea, Rep. of	1.05	1.49	1.16	1.34	2.46	3.55	4.67	4.45	4.74	4.20	5.00	2.42	2.67
Singapore	2.03	0.53	1.32	2.15	4.58	3.00	6.23	8.96	0.38	5.40	6.06	9.55	4.08
Taiwan, China	5.24	2.06	1.97	2.61	2.64	2.98	3.84	5.24	3.84	4.42	6.70	5.48	4.89
ASEAN5	0.29	0.40	1.08	2.15	6.41	4.79	5.48	3.57	1.20	1.81	2.05	0.39	1.55
Indonesia	–0.01	0.01	0.71	0.48	3.28	1.32	0.60	0.18	0.04	0.07	0.15	0.13	0.12
Malaysia	0.13	0.18	0.12	1.06	2.33	2.49	3.77	2.68	0.86	1.42	2.03	0.27	1.24
Philippines	0.02	0.03	0.10	0.37	0.30	0.10	0.18	0.14	0.16	–0.03	–0.11	–0.16	0.09
Thailand	0.15	0.18	0.15	0.23	0.49	0.89	0.93	0.58	0.13	0.35	–0.02	0.16	0.11
Vietnam	—	—	—	—	—	—	—	—	—	—	—	—	—
Other ASEAN	0.00	0.00	0.00	0.05	0.00	0.02	0.04	0.01	0.01	0.02	0.16	0.01	0.07
Brunei Darussalam	—	0.00	—	0.05	—	0.02	0.04	0.01	0.01	0.02	0.00	0.01	0.01
Cambodia	—	—	—	0.00	—	—	—	—	—	—	—	—	—
Lao People's Democratic Rep.	—	0.00	0.00	0.00	0.00	0.00	0.00	0.00	0.00	0.00	0.17	0.00	0.06
Myanmar	—	—	—	—	—	—	—	—	—	—	—	—	—
Other East Asia	0.83	0.91	4.00	4.40	2.00	2.00	2.11	2.56	2.63	1.78	0.92	6.90	2.85
China	0.83	0.91	4.00	4.40	2.00	2.00	2.11	2.56	2.63	1.78	0.92	6.88	2.85
Macao	—	—	—	—	—	—	—	—	—	—	—	0.02	—
South Asia													
India	0.01	–0.01	0.02	0.00	0.08	0.12	0.24	0.11	0.05	0.08	0.34	0.76	0.43

— Not available.

Note: FDI flows have three components: equity capital, reinvested earnings, and intracompany loans.

Source: United Nations Conference on Trade and Development (UNCTAD), Foreign Direct Investment database on line.

Appendix Table A1.5. *Investment Regimes and Individual Action Plans*

Economy	*Right of establishment (10)*			*Examination procedure (1)*			*MFN treatment (1)*			*Profit repatriation (1)*			*Work permit (1)*			*Taxation (1)*		
	1996	*1999*	*2000*	*1996*	*1999*	*2000*	*1996*	*1999*	*2000*	*1996*	*1999*	*2000*	*1996*	*1999*	*2000*	*1996*	*1999*	*2000*
Brunei Darussalam	4	4	4	6	6	6	0	0	0	10	10	10	8	8	8	10	10	10
China	4	5	5	6	6	6	10	10	10	6	6	6	7	7	7	6	8	8
Hong Kong, China	8	10	10	10	10	10	10	10	10	10	10	10	8	8	8	10	10	10
Indonesia	5	5	7	6	7	7	10	10	10	0	10	10	6	6	6	8	8	8
Korea, Rep. of	7	7	9	7	7	9	10	10	10	8	10	10	8	8	8	10	10	10
Malaysia	6	6	6	8	8	8	10	10	10	8	8	8	8	8	8	10	10	10
Philippines	7	7	8	8	8	8	0	10	10	9	9	9	6	6	6	8	9	9
Singapore	8	8	8	10	10	10	10	10	10	10	10	10	8	8	8	10	10	10
Taiwan (China)	7	7	8	9	9	9	8	8	8	9	10	10	8	8	9	8	10	10
Thailand	7	7	8	9	9	9	8	8	8	9	9	9	9	9	9	8	8	8
Average	6.3	6.6	7.3	7.9	8.0	8.2	7.6	8.6	8.6	7.9	9.2	9.2	7.6	7.6	7.7	8.8	9.3	9.3
Japan	8	8	9	8	8	8	10	10	10	10	10	10	8	8	9	10	10	10
United States	9	9	9	10	10	10	8	8	8	8	8	8	8	8	8	10	10	10

Economy	*Performance requirement (1)*			*Protection of investors (1)*			*Dispute settlement (1)*			*Investment incentives (1)*			*Capital exports (1)*			*FDI liberalization (Total)*		
	1996	*1999*	*2000*	*1996*	*1999*	*2000*	*1996*	*1999*	*2000*	*1996*	*1999*	*2000*	*1996*	*1999*	*2000*	*1996*	*1999*	*2000*
Brunei Darussalam	10	10	10	0	0	0	0	0	0	0	0	0	10	10	10	47	47	47
China	8	8	8	8	10	10	8	9	9	7	7	7	6	7	7	56	64	64
Hong Kong, China	10	10	10	0	10	10	10	10	10	10	10	10	10	10	10	84	99	99
Indonesia	8	8	9	8	8	8	8	10	10	6	6	6	0	0	0	55	62	72
Korea, Rep. of	10	10	10	8	10	10	10	10	10	6	6	6	8	10	10	78	81	92
Malaysia	9	9	9	8	10	10	10	10	10	6	6	6	10	10	10	74	75	75
Philippines	6	8	8	8	9	9	8	10	10	8	8	8	0	8	8	66	78	83
Singapore	10	10	10	8	9	9	8	9	9	8	8	8	10	10	10	86	87	87
Taiwan (China)	8	9	9	8	8	8	8	8	8	6	8	8	8	8	8	75	78	84
Thailand	6	8	9	8	9	9	8	8	8	10	10	10	8	8	8	77	78	84
Average	8.5	9.0	9.2	6.4	8.3	8.3	7.8	8.4	8.4	6.7	6.9	6.9	7.0	8.1	8.1	69.6	74.7	78.5
Japan	10	10	10	8	9	9	10	10	10	8	8	8	10	10	10	86	87	92
United States	9	9	9	8	8	8	10	10	10	8	8	8	10	10	10	90	90	90

Note: Scores range from 10 (full liberalization) to 0 (not mentioned in the sources used for the analysis). The highest possible score is 100. The right of establishment has a weight of 10; all other items have a weight of 1. The FDI liberalization total is obtained by summing all the scores.

Source: The information that was used to construct the figures for 1996 and 1999 is from APEC's *Investment Guidebook* 1996 and 1999, respectively; the information for 2000 is from Individual Action Plans 2000, plans that were submitted to the Asia-Pacific Economic Cooperation forum.

References

Borensztein, Edward, Jose de Gregorio, and Jong-Wha Lee. 1998. "How Does Foreign Direct Investment Affect Economic Growth?" *Journal of International Economics* 45: 115–35.

Chia, Siow Yue. 2000. "Regional Economic Integration in East Asia: Developments, Issues, and Challenges." In K. Hamada, M. Matsushita, and C. Komura, eds., *Dreams and Dilemmas: Economic Friction and Dispute Resolution in the Asia-Pacific*, 19–50. Center for Asian and Pacific Studies, Seikei University, Japan, and Institute of Southeast Asian Studies, Singapore.

International Monetary Fund. 2002. *Balance of Payments Statistics Yearbook*. Washington, D.C.

Japan National Committee for Pacific Economic Cooperation Council. 2002. *An Assessment of Impediments to Foreign Direct Investment in APEC Member Economies*. Tokyo, Japan.

Kawai, Hiroki, and Shujiro Urata. 2003. "Competitiveness and Technology: An International Comparison." In Sanjaya Lall and Shujiro Urata, eds., *Competitiveness, FDI and Technological Activity in East Asia*, 57–82. Cheltenham, U.K.: Edward Elgar.

Kawai, Masahiro, and Shujiro Urata. 1998. "Are Trade and Direct Investment Substitutes or Complements? An Empirical Analysis of Japanese Manufacturing Industries." In H. Lee and D. Roland-Holst, eds., *Economic Development and Cooperation in the Pacific Basin: Trade, Investment and Environmental Issues*, 251–93. Cambridge, U.K.: Cambridge University Press.

———. 2004. "Trade and Foreign Direct Investment in East Asia." In G. de Brouwer and M. Kawai, eds., *Exchange Rate Regimes and East Asia*, 15–102. London: Routledge Curzon.

Ministry of Economy, Trade, and Industry. 2003. *2003 Report on the WTO Consistency of Trade Policies by Major Trading Partners*. Tokyo: Industrial Structure Council.

United Nations. 1998. *World Investment Report 1998*. New York.

———. 1999. *World Investment Report 1999*. New York.

———. 2001. *World Investment Report 2001*. New York.

———. 2002. *World Investment Report 2002*. New York.

———. 2003. *World Investment Report 2003*. New York.

Urata, Shujiro. 1998. "Foreign Direct Investment and APEC." In Vinod K. Aggarwal and Charles E. Morrison, eds., *Asia-Pacific Crossroads: Regime Creation and Future of APEC*, 87–111. New York: St. Martin's Press.

———. 2001. "Emergence of an FDI-Trade Nexus and Economic Growth in East Asia." In Joseph E. Stiglitz and Shahid Yusuf, eds., *Rethinking the East Asian Miracle*, 409–59. New York: Oxford University Press.

Urata, Shujiro, and Hiroki Kawai. 2000. "The Determinants of the Location of Foreign Direct Investment by Japanese Small and Medium-size Enterprises." *Small Business Economics* 15: 79–103.

World Bank. 2002. *Global Economic Prospect 2003*. Washington, D.C.

Yamazawa, Ippei, and Shujiro Urata. 2000. "Trade and Investment Liberalization and Facilitation." In Ippei Yamazawa, ed., *Asia Pacific Economic Cooperation (APEC): Challenges and Tasks for the Twenty-first Century*, 57–97. London: Routledge.

2

Japanese Manufacturing FDI and International Production and Distribution Networks in East Asia

Fukunari Kimura and Mitsuyo Ando

Although Japanese firms have had a long history of foreign direct investment (FDI), their substantial commitment to an outward orientation did not begin until the mid-1980s.[1] By then Japanese firms had become successful exporters of their products and had gained enough confidence to go abroad. The sharp appreciation of the yen after the Plaza Accord in 1985 was a trigger for Japanese exporting firms to seriously consider the relocation of production plants to foreign countries. During this same period, East Asia was becoming a great attractor of FDI. The forerunners of ASEAN (Association of Southeast Asian Nations) switched development strategies in order to utilize incoming FDI more aggressively after economic slumps in the mid-1980s. China followed with open door policies in the first half of the 1990s.[2]

1. Before World War I, most of the foreign investment by Japan and the United States was direct investment rather than portfolio investment; for other developed countries, most of the foreign investment was portfolio investment (Wilkins 1986). Although all investment stock abroad was lost due to World War II, Japanese firms started investing again in the 1960s. The major focus of FDI, however, was on resource exploration and unskilled-labor-intensive manufacturing until the 1970s (conforming to the Kojima hypothesis), and the amount of FDI was also limited.

2. In this chapter East Asia includes ASEAN plus three Northeast Asian countries (Japan, the Republic of Korea, and China), except in some special cases that are mentioned.

Active Japanese investors in East Asia were manufacturing firms, particularly in machinery industries (general machinery, electric machinery, transport equipment, and precision machinery). Since products of these industries consist of many parts and components, managerial coordination of vertical production chains from upstream to downstream, in addition to maintenance of the high technical quality of parts and components, were crucially important for international competitiveness. Japanese firms excelled in these areas. Their management of production systems as well as the favorable policy environment in East Asia allowed Japanese machinery manufacturing firms to be key players in the formation of international production/distribution networks.

In domestic politics and in the Japanese press, the voice of large manufacturing companies represented by business associations such as Keidanren was always dominant. Domestic concern about outgoing investment, potentially causing the "hollowing out" of domestic industries, was relatively weak, at least until the mid-1990s, because of the shared strong confidence in the competitiveness of Japanese firms. The Japanese people expected large benefits from going abroad, and they optimistically believed that some of the high-value-added portion of the production process would remain inside Japan. Globalization of corporate activities provided good opportunities for Japanese firms to reformulate their corporate structure. The old type of interfirm relationship—for example, subcontracting arrangements (*shitauke*) and *keiretsu* relationship under the main bank system—gradually lost its competitive edge throughout the 1980s and 1990s. Outward FDI by large assemblers activated a self-selection mechanism for smaller size suppliers of parts and components, forcing them to decide whether to go abroad with large assemblers. Through such a mechanism, FDI by competitive Japanese small and medium-size enterprises (SMEs) became an essential part of East Asia's international production/distribution networks.

This chapter focuses on the formation of international production/distribution networks in East Asia and discusses the role of Japanese firms. We claim that the economic logic of new international trade theories—namely, fragmentation, agglomeration, and the internalization theory of "firm"—dictates the mechanics of international production/distribution networks in East Asia. We also emphasize the importance of the policy environment. Supportive policies for Japanese SMEs to invest abroad are reviewed in particular. From the viewpoint of East Asian countries as host countries, proper development strategies were crucial, and transparency, fairness, and predictability are the key for FDI-related policies.

The chapter begins with an overview on trade and FDI between Japan and other East Asian countries. The economic rationale for the formation of international production/distribution networks is then presented as well as evidence from the micro data of Japanese corporate firms. We summarize Japan's policy environment for outward FDI and discuss policy issues with regard to hosting East Asian countries. The chapter ends with our conclusions.

Overview of Trade and FDI between Japan and Other East Asian Countries

East Asia has increasingly become an important economic partner of Japan. During the 1990s, more than 30 percent of Japan's trade was with East Asia (China, NIEs4, and ASEAN4).[3] By 2000 that share reached almost 40 percent in terms of both exports and imports (Table 2.1). Between 1991 and 2000, China more than doubled its shares for both exports and imports (from 2.7 percent to 6.3 percent for exports and from 6.0 percent to 14.5 percent for imports).

Trade intensity indices confirm this picture of an economic partnership gaining strength. Table 2.2 presents trade intensity indices for exports and imports between Japan and other East Asian countries in 1990 and 2000.[4] In almost all cases, the indices are much greater than one. The intensity tended to become stronger from 1990 to 2000, particularly for exports. Trade between Japan and China is a typical case; the indices for both countries in terms of both exports and imports became larger, implying that the intensity between the two countries grew stronger.

As shown in Figure 2.1, machinery trade, particularly trade in machinery parts and components, is significant in East Asian countries including Japan.[5] Machinery goods, here defined as HS 84-92, include general machinery, electric machinery, transport equipment, and precision machinery.

---

3. NIEs4 refers to these newly industrializing economies: Hong Kong, China; Taiwan, China; the Republic of Korea; and Singapore. ASEAN4 refers to these members of the Association of Southeast Asian Nations: Indonesia, Malaysia, the Philippines, and Thailand.

4. The trade intensity index in terms of exports of A to B is calculated as follows:

$$\frac{\text{Exports of A to B}}{\text{Total exports of A}} \Big/ \frac{\text{Total imports of B}}{\text{Total imports in the world.}}$$

The trade intensity index in terms of imports of B from A is calculated as follows:

$$\frac{\text{Imports of B from A}}{\text{Total imports of B}} \Big/ \frac{\text{Total exports of A}}{\text{Total exports in the world.}}$$

5. To show the relative significance of trade in machinery parts and components, Figure 2.1 organizes countries from left to right, beginning with the one with the highest share of exports of machinery parts and components.

Table 2.1. *Japanese Exports to and Imports from East Asia, 1991–2000*

	1991	*1992*	*1993*	*1994*	*1995*	*1996*	*1997*	*1998*	*1999*	*2000*
(a) Total exports and imports of Japan (million JPY)										
Exports	42,359,893	43,012,281	40,202,449	40,497,553	41,530,895	44,731,311	50,937,992	50,645,004	47,547,556	51,654,198
Imports	31,900,154	29,527,419	26,826,357	28,104,327	31,548,754	37,993,421	40,956,183	36,653,647	35,268,008	40,938,423
(b) Share in total (%)										
Exports										
East Asia	32.1	33.0	36.1	38.6	42.1	42.4	40.6	33.2	35.8	39.7
China	2.7	3.5	4.8	4.7	5.0	5.3	5.2	5.2	5.6	6.3
NIEs	21.3	21.4	22.3	23.6	25.0	24.7	24.0	20.2	21.5	23.9
ASEAN4	8.1	8.1	9.0	10.3	12.1	12.4	11.4	7.8	8.6	9.5
Imports										
East Asia	28.9	30.1	31.7	32.9	34.4	35.2	34.7	34.9	37.6	39.6
China	6.0	7.3	8.5	10.0	10.7	11.6	12.4	13.2	13.8	14.5
NIEs	11.5	11.2	11.2	11.3	12.3	11.7	10.4	10.2	11.6	12.2
ASEAN4	11.3	11.6	12.1	11.6	11.4	11.9	12.0	11.4	12.1	12.8

Note: NIEs stands for newly industrializing economies. ASEAN is an acronym for the Association of Southeast Asian Nations. East Asia in this table includes NIEs (Republic of Korea; Taiwan, China; Hong Kong, China; and Singapore), ASEAN4 (Indonesia, Thailand, Philippines, and Malaysia), and China.

Source: METI (2003).

Table 2.2. *Trade Intensity Indices for Japan and East Asian Countries, 1990 and 2000*

	Exports		*Imports*			*Exports*		*Imports*	
	1990	*2000*	*1990*	*2000*		*1990*	*2000*	*1990*	*2000*
Japan					NIEs				
NIEs	3.95	4.10	2.84	2.42	Japan	2.14	1.73	2.68	2.48
Hong Kong	1.94	1.76	0.38	0.14	China	0.98	2.26	2.20	1.72
ASEAN4	2.79	3.07	4.07	3.10	NIEs (region)	1.32	1.94	1.39	1.34
China	1.40	1.86	2.76	3.71	Hong Kong	2.55	2.16	0.76	0.51
					ASEAN4	4.27	4.87	4.10	3.73
China									
Japan	2.19	2.91	1.67	2.46	ASEAN4				
NIEs	1.15	1.98	1.74	4.94	Japan	3.64	2.84	2.75	2.49
Hong Kong	18.46	5.54	11.14	1.32	China	1.35	1.03	1.38	0.97
ASEAN4	1.05	1.21	1.58	1.71	NIEs	4.80	4.67	5.00	4.44
					Hong Kong	1.44	1.34	0.77	1.02
Hong Kong					ASEAN4 (region)	1.51	2.31	1.51	2.12
Japan	0.85	0.97	1.89	1.60					
China	16.18	10.14	19.80	11.00					
NIEs	2.53	1.51	4.90	3.47					
ASEAN4	1.44	1.06	1.43	1.38					

Note: See Table 2.1 note for definitions. NIEs in this table, however, does not include Hong Kong.

Trade intensity index in terms of exports of A to B is calculated as follows:

$$\frac{\text{Exports of A to B}}{\text{Total exports of A}} \Big/ \frac{\text{Total imports of B}}{\text{Total imports in the world.}}$$

Trade intensity index in terms of imports of B from A is calculated as follows:

$$\frac{\text{Imports of B from A}}{\text{Total imports of B}} \Big/ \frac{\text{Total exports of A}}{\text{Total exports in the world.}}$$

Source: METI (2003).

Figure 2.1. *Trade in Machinery Goods and Machinery Parts and Components in East Asia and Latin America as a Percentage of Total Exports and Imports, 2000*

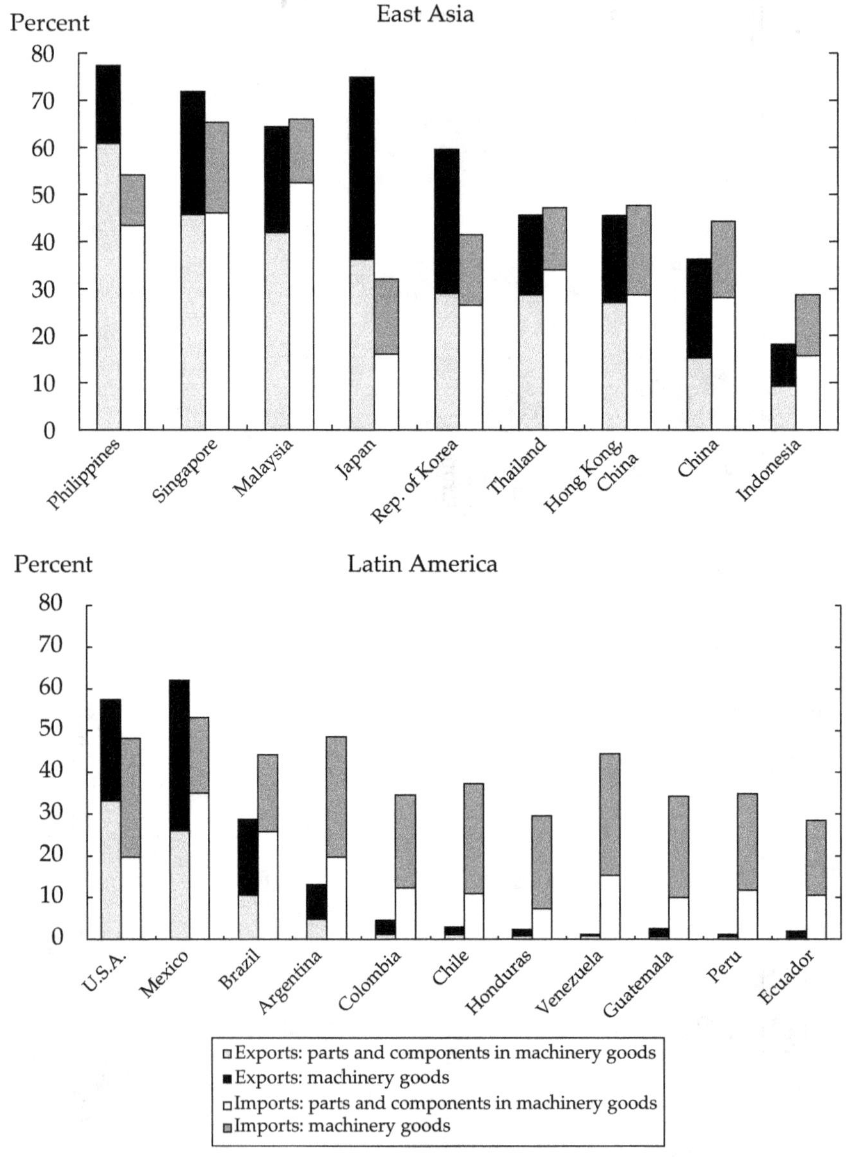

Note: Machinery goods, defined as HS 84-92, include general machinery, electric machinery, transport equipment, and precision machinery. The figure for Latin America includes the United States.

Source: Ando and Estevadeordal (2003).

Trade in machinery goods as a share of each East Asian country's total exports and imports is high with few exceptions.[6] Moreover, the share of trade in machinery parts and components is also high for both exports and imports in each East Asian country. Combined with large trade intensity indices, this indicates many back-and-forth transactions of parts and components (intermediate goods) of manufactured products among countries in the region. Clearly, trade integration, particularly intraregional trade of manufactured goods such as machinery parts and components, has developed in East Asia, and East Asian countries have become more important as trading partners for Japan during the 1990s.[7]

East Asian countries have also become important economic partners for Japan as locations of international corporate activities through FDI. Table 2.3 shows Japanese FDI outflows, by sector, to the world and to East Asia. The data are presented in terms of (a) number of cases and (b) values determined on the reporting basis. Figure 2.2 presents the values of Japanese FDI to China, NIEs4, and ASEAN4 on both the reporting basis and the balance-of-payment (BOP) basis.[8] Note that the data in both Table 2.3 and Figure 2.2 are flow data.

(*Text continues on page 77.*)

6. The machinery export share for the Philippines is surprisingly large, even larger than Japan's share. The 77 percent for 2000 is not exceptional, however. The machinery export share for the Philippines rapidly increased in the last half of the 1990s, from 59 percent in 1996, to 66 percent in 1997, to 73 percent in 1998, to 79 percent in 1999. Most of the Philippines' machinery exports are of electric machinery, equipment and parts; the country does not have any strong exported commodities other than those.

7. Figure 2.1 presents percentages for Latin America as well as East Asia. Countries in Latin America, with Mexico as a notable exception, present much lower shares of machinery exports than those observed for countries in East Asia. This indicates that Latin American countries are not forming networks yet (except the networks between the United States and Mexico). In addition, the shares of machinery imports are much higher than those of exports in Latin American countries. This suggests that their manufacturing production activities are of an import-substituting type.

8. The newly industrializing economies (NIEs) include the Republic of Korea; Taiwan, China; Hong Kong, China; and Singapore; ASEAN4 includes Thailand, the Philippines, Indonesia, and Malaysia. The Ministry of Finance data are presented on the reporting basis; that is, the actual investment may not be made in the year reported. The Bank of Japan data are on the BOP basis; that is, actual investment is recorded although the data present net investment.

Table 2.3. Japanese Outward Direct Investment by Case and by Value, Fiscal Years 1989–2002

	1989	*1990*	*1991*	*1992*	*1993*	*1994*	*1995*	*1996*	*1997*	*1998*	*1999*	*2000*	*2001*	*2002*
(a) **Total number of cases**														
FDI to the world	6,589	5,863	4,564	3,741	3,488	2,478	2,863	2,501	2,495	1,616	1,729	1,701	1,768	2,144
FDI to East Asia	1,707	1,499	1,277	1,269	1,478	1,305	1,629	1,233	1,157	545	534	459	504	534
(as % of total)	(25.9)	(25.7)	(28.0)	(33.9)	(42.4)	(52.7)	(56.9)	(49.3)	(46.4)	(33.7)	(30.9)	(27.0)	(28.5)	(24.9)
FDI to the world by sector (%)														
Manufacturing sector	27.8	26.1	29.3	35.2	39.9	49.8	55.5	49.1	43.2	36.8	35.6	31.3	30.0	29.7
Nonmachinery sectors	17.4	17.5	20.6	25.4	27.9	33.3	34.7	30.2	26.7	18.1	18.2	13.8	13.6	13.9
Textile	2.6	3.4	5.3	8.3	9.6	14.9	13.1	8.4	5.6	1.9	0.9	0.6	1.3	1.5
Other	14.8	14.1	15.3	17.1	18.2	18.5	21.6	21.8	21.2	16.2	17.4	13.1	12.3	12.5
Machinery sectors	10.3	8.6	8.7	9.8	12.0	16.4	20.8	19.0	16.5	18.6	17.4	17.5	16.5	15.7
General	3.5	2.3	2.8	3.4	4.3	3.2	5.7	5.2	4.6	5.3	4.3	3.1	3.4	3.4
Electric	4.6	4.6	4.6	4.8	5.4	8.4	10.4	8.9	7.5	7.9	8.2	9.8	8.3	5.5
Transport	2.2	1.7	1.3	1.6	2.4	4.9	4.8	4.8	4.4	5.5	4.9	4.6	4.8	6.9
Nonmanufacturing sector	71.1	73.1	70.1	64.1	59.2	48.7	43.3	50.1	56.3	62.9	64.0	68.5	69.6	70.0
Agriculture, fishery, forestry, and mining	3.0	3.4	4.7	4.3	3.9	3.3	3.2	4.9	5.6	5.6	3.5	1.2	1.1	0.7
Trade	13.6	13.7	16.3	15.4	14.8	8.2	8.3	10.6	11.5	12.1	11.5	8.9	7.8	5.8
Finance and insurance	4.8	4.0	3.7	5.2	5.4	6.2	4.3	4.5	6.9	19.6	25.0	39.9	44.7	51.2
Other	49.7	52.0	45.5	39.2	35.1	31.0	27.5	30.1	32.3	25.6	24.1	18.5	16.0	12.4

FDI to East Asia by sector (%)														
Manufacturing sector	52.4	50.6	56.3	60.4	64.7	72.2	76.6	67.0	60.9	59.8	60.5	67.1	66.5	72.1
Nonmachinery sectors	35.6	36.7	41.5	46.9	48.4	51.6	49.2	43.4	40.2	29.4	30.7	29.2	29.8	38.0
Textile	6.6	9.1	14.0	19.9	20.3	26.4	20.8	13.5	8.9	3.5	2.1	1.5	2.8	4.3
Other	29.0	27.6	27.5	27.0	28.1	25.2	28.4	29.9	31.3	25.9	28.7	27.7	27.0	33.7
Machinery sectors	16.8	13.9	14.8	13.6	16.4	20.6	27.4	23.6	20.7	30.5	29.8	37.9	36.7	34.1
General machinery	6.0	3.5	3.8	4.3	5.3	3.4	6.6	5.8	4.8	6.6	5.4	5.0	6.7	7.1
Electric machinery	9.0	8.1	9.4	7.5	8.1	11.8	14.0	11.3	9.4	14.3	15.5	27.2	19.8	13.9
Transport equipment	1.8	2.3	1.6	1.8	3.0	5.4	6.8	6.6	6.5	9.5	8.8	5.7	10.1	13.1
Nonmanufacturing sector	46.8	48.8	42.9	38.2	33.6	25.1	21.9	31.9	38.4	39.1	38.4	32.7	32.3	26.8
Agriculture, fishery, forestry, and mining	4.0	5.3	4.5	4.2	3.5	2.6	2.9	3.6	3.9	2.4	1.7	0.2	1.0	0.9
Trade	11.2	12.9	12.6	12.1	11.9	6.4	6.4	8.9	11.1	14.7	14.8	12.2	11.3	8.8
Finance and insurance	3.8	3.1	3.8	3.5	3.6	3.5	2.2	3.4	5.2	5.5	6.9	3.9	6.3	5.1
Other	27.8	27.6	22.0	18.4	14.6	12.6	10.4	15.9	18.2	16.5	15.0	16.3	13.7	12.0

(*Table continues on following page.*)

Table 2.3. (continued)

	1989	1990	1991	1992	1993	1994	1995	1996	1997	1998	1999	2000	2001	2002
(b) Total value (100 million JPY)														
FDI to the world	90,339	83,527	56,862	44,313	41,514	42,808	49,568	54,095	66,236	52,413	74,703	53,854	39,923	44,175
FDI to East Asia	11,003	10,343	8,107	8,316	7,672	10,084	11,921	13,083	14,954	8,449	8,053	6,626	8,029	6,768
(as percentage of total)	(12.2)	(12.4)	(14.3)	(18.8)	(18.5)	(23.6)	(24.1)	(24.2)	(22.6)	(16.1)	(10.8)	(12.3)	(20.1)	(15.3)
FDI to the world by sector (%)														
Manufacturing sector	24.1	27.2	29.8	29.4	30.8	33.7	36.8	42.2	35.8	30.0	63.2	24.0	44.4	40.2
Nonmachinery sectors	11.8	11.4	16.4	17.4	17.3	18.4	18.8	17.6	15.7	15.8	30.2	8.4	14.9	12.3
Textile	0.8	1.4	1.5	1.3	1.4	1.6	2.0	1.3	1.8	0.8	0.4	0.5	0.6	0.5
Other	11.0	10.0	14.9	16.1	15.9	16.8	16.7	16.3	13.9	14.9	29.8	8.0	14.2	11.7
Machinery sectors	12.3	15.8	13.4	12.1	13.5	15.3	18.0	24.6	20.2	14.2	33.1	15.6	29.5	27.9
General machinery	2.6	2.6	3.1	3.2	3.3	4.0	3.7	3.0	2.4	1.9	1.5	2.9	3.8	3.6
Electric machinery	6.6	10.0	5.5	5.3	7.5	6.4	10.5	13.6	12.4	8.4	24.4	6.3	12.1	10.8
Transport equipment	3.0	3.3	4.8	3.5	2.6	5.0	3.9	8.1	5.4	3.9	7.1	6.4	13.6	13.6
Nonmanufacturing sector	74.8	71.4	69.1	69.5	68.5	65.4	61.3	55.7	63.1	69.1	36.5	75.5	54.7	58.9
Agriculture, fishery, forestry, and mining	2.2	2.7	3.2	4.3	3.0	2.0	2.5	3.8	5.3	2.3	1.5	1.6	1.7	1.1
Trade	7.6	10.8	12.6	10.8	14.3	10.7	10.4	10.0	8.1	9.4	5.9	7.0	8.2	9.1
Finance and insurance	22.6	14.1	12.0	13.5	17.5	16.1	10.6	16.2	22.2	40.0	14.8	17.3	33.7	35.3
Other	42.5	43.7	41.3	40.9	33.7	36.6	37.8	25.8	27.5	17.4	14.2	49.5	11.1	13.4

FDI to East Asia by sector (%)														
Manufacturing sector	39.5	43.5	49.4	48.0	54.5	53.5	65.5	57.1	60.0	56.5	60.9	61.4	66.1	68.7
Nonmachinery sectors	22.2	22.6	27.2	33.6	30.7	31.1	32.2	29.7	33.8	29.9	34.8	24.4	33.6	30.5
Textile	2.4	4.2	3.7	3.5	4.5	5.1	6.1	3.1	3.5	3.4	3.2	2.3	1.5	1.9
Other	19.8	18.4	23.5	30.1	26.1	25.9	26.1	26.6	30.3	26.4	31.7	22.1	32.1	28.6
Machinery sectors	17.3	20.9	22.3	14.4	23.8	22.5	33.4	27.4	26.2	26.6	26.1	37.0	32.5	38.2
General machinery	4.3	3.7	4.3	3.4	6.6	4.1	6.5	4.8	4.3	4.3	4.6	3.6	4.6	4.3
Electric machinery	11.3	11.8	14.8	8.4	13.3	14.3	20.0	15.7	14.9	10.2	13.1	23.9	19.8	16.2
Transport equipment	1.7	5.3	3.2	2.7	4.0	4.1	6.9	6.9	7.0	12.1	8.4	9.6	8.1	17.8
Nonmanufacturing sector	59.3	55.2	48.6	49.3	43.8	43.5	30.0	36.3	37.8	41.9	37.7	34.8	30.1	28.7
Agriculture, fishery, forestry, and mining	3.1	4.0	5.2	7.0	4.7	3.7	2.8	4.8	9.4	4.5	1.9	0.1	0.3	0.2
Trade	8.0	17.2	12.0	11.9	10.7	6.2	6.6	6.8	6.4	17.4	13.1	13.4	5.6	6.9
Finance and insurance	12.9	9.1	13.4	10.7	10.4	12.0	6.2	6.8	4.7	6.7	10.7	7.9	12.3	10.5
Other	35.3	24.8	18.0	19.7	18.0	21.6	14.4	17.9	17.3	13.2	11.9	13.4	11.9	11.2

Note: FDI in this table is based on the flow data on the reporting basis. Cases show new transactions only. The shares of branches are excluded since most of them are less than 2 percent regardless of whether the measure is number of cases or values.

Source: Authors' calculation, based on MOF (2003).

Figure 2.2. *Japanese Direct Investment in China, NIEs, and ASEAN4, 1996–2002*

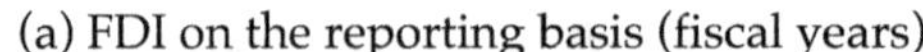

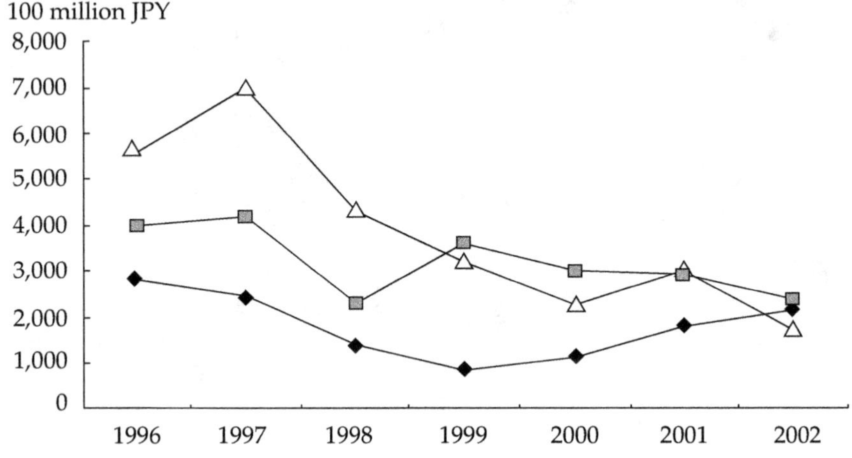

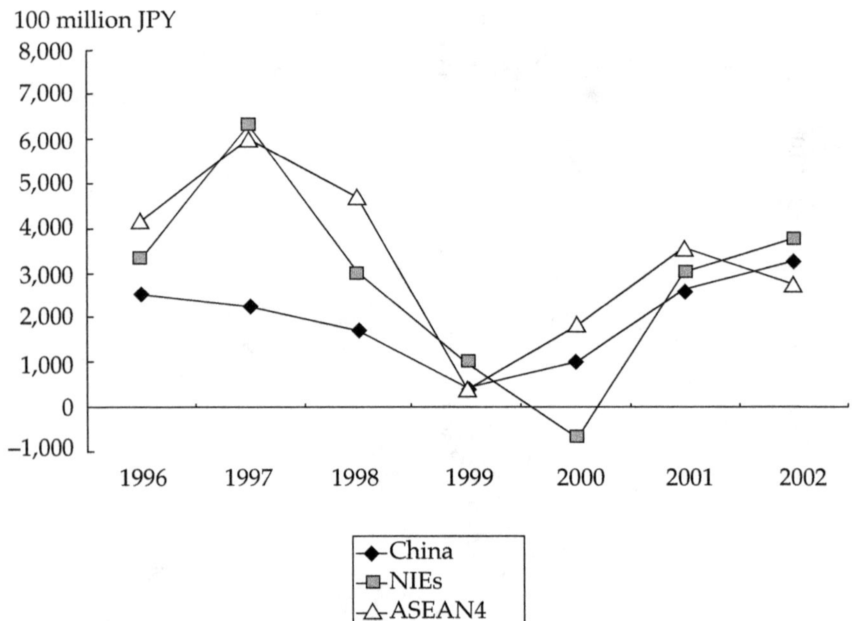

Note: See Table 2.1 note for an explanation of NIEs and ASEAN4.
Source: MOF (2003) for FDI on the reporting basis; BOJ (2003a) for FDI on the BOP basis.

Table 2.3 and Figure 2.2 provide several interesting insights. First, the share of East Asia in total Japanese FDI has increased in terms of cases and in terms of value. This increase was particularly notable from the late 1980s to the mid-1990s (Table 2.3). Fifty-seven percent of the total Japanese FDI in terms of cases went to East Asia in 1995 compared with only 26 percent in 1989. In the manufacturing sector, Japanese FDI to East Asia in 1995 reached 77 percent (cases) and 66 percent (value), up from 52 percent (cases) and 40 percent (value) in 1989. Japanese FDI to East Asia started to expand in the latter half of the 1980s and accelerated in the first half of the 1990s, concentrating in the manufacturing sector, in particular the machinery sector, where Japanese firms are competitive internationally.

Second, the sectoral pattern of Japanese FDI to East Asia differs markedly from the sectoral pattern of Japanese FDI to the world: for both number of cases and value, manufacturing shares are much greater for Japanese FDI to East Asia. In 2002, for instance, the manufacturing sector had 72 percent (cases) and 69 percent (value) of the Japanese FDI to East Asia but only 30 percent (cases) and 40 percent (value) of Japanese FDI to the world. Roughly speaking, half of the manufacturing shares are in the machinery sector such as general machinery, electric machinery, and transport equipment in the case of Japanese FDI to East Asia. Nonmanufacturing shares, in particular finance and insurance shares, are much smaller; in 2002, for example, the finance and insurance sector had only 5.1 percent (cases) and 11 percent (value) of Japanese FDI to East Asia, although 51 percent (cases) and 35 percent (value) of Japanese FDI to the world. Besides the significance of machinery parts and components trade in East Asia, these figures confirm the importance of Japanese FDI to East Asia in the manufacturing sector, particularly in the machinery sector.

Third, as Figure 2.2 suggests, Japanese FDI to China has gradually increased; the amount has been close to the amount of FDI to NIEs and even exceeded the amount to ASEAN4 in 2002.[9] Although flow data are widely fluctuating and the values of flow data are different on the reporting and

9. From 1989 to 2001, the accumulated value of Japanese FDI to China was about half of the value of Japanese FDI to ASEAN4. Moreover, the accumulated FDI to China was concentrated in the electric machinery sector, while accumulated FDI to ASEAN4 covered a wide range of sectors such as electric machinery, transport equipment, and chemicals (Marugami et al. 2003). Japan's direct investment position (assets) at the end of 2002 indicates that the FDI stock in China is still lower than that in NIEs or ASEAN4; 1481.2 billion Japanese yen (JPY) in China, 2975 billion JPY in NIEs, and 2242.1 billion JPY in ASEAN4 (BOJ 2003b).

BOP basis, China has indisputably become an important economic partner for Japan as the location of international corporate activities through FDI.

International Production and Distribution Networks in East Asia

International production and distribution networks formed in the 1990s in East Asia were unprecedented in their vertical division of labor across numerous countries.[10] To understand the pattern of production and trade in the twenty-first century, one must consider the addition of new theoretical flavors to the traditional international trade theory. In some circumstances the theory of comparative advantage based on the relative advantages in autarky (no trade situation) is still valid; technological gap and factor price differences explain where industries locate to some extent. In the globalization era, however, at least three new lines of thought must be incorporated into our analytical framework.

New Thinking about International Trade

The first line of thought is the fragmentation (or crossborder production sharing) theory.[11] It is a powerful tool for analyzing patterns of FDI going to developing countries and the formation of international production and distribution networks. The traditional international trade theory primarily explains industry-related location patterns. In East Asia, however, product-related and process-related location patterns across countries are often observed. A typical example is the semiconductor-related electronics industry. This industry as a whole is capital intensive or human capital intensive, but its production activities are finely segmented and located in various places. The fragmentation theory neatly explains this location pattern.

Deardorff (2001) defines fragmentation as "the splitting of a product process into two or more steps that can be undertaken in different locations but that lead to the same final product." Suppose a big factory located in

10. Ando and Kimura (2004) emphasize that international production and distribution networks in East Asia, mainly in the machinery sector, are distinctive in three respects: (1) their significance in the regional economy, (2) their geographical reach involving numerous countries in the region, and (3) their degree of sophistication in terms of intrafirm and arm's-length relationships across different firm nationalities.

11. On the fragmentation theory, see Jones and Kierzkowski (1990), Deardorff (2001), and Cheng and Kierzkowski (2001).

Japan handles all of the production activities from upstream to downstream. A careful look at individual production blocks may reveal that certain production blocks require close watch by technicians while others are purely labor intensive. Then the production activities in each production block separately located in Japan, Malaysia, and China, for instance, may contribute to savings in the total production cost.

Fragmentation becomes economical when the cost of service links (SL) connecting production blocks (PB) is sufficiently low. The SL cost includes transport costs, telecommunication costs, and various coordination costs between production blocks. The SL cost heavily depends on the nature of the technology in each industry. For example, a full-scale iron mill plant cannot be economically fragmented because of its energy efficiency. Globalization, however, reduces the SL cost and enables firms in many industries to fragment their production blocks further and locate them not only within a country but also across countries to reduce the total production cost. Since service links tend to carry strong external economies of scale, globalization may accelerate concentration and fragmentation at the same time, which may result in a situation where some countries (such as the East Asian countries) significantly enjoy the fruit of globalization, while others do not.

The second line of thought is the agglomeration theory.[12] It extends international trade theory with external economies of scale and introduces the concept of "space" from city planning and other fields. Although the microfoundation of spatial agglomeration has not yet been fully explored, the importance of agglomeration as a source of location advantage is increasingly recognized in the empirical and theoretical literature. The traditional comparative advantage theory defines comparative advantage based on relative production costs between two locations in autarky. Economies of scale or agglomeration effects, however, do not necessarily depend on the initial condition under autarky; in an extreme case, a country begins agglomeration purely by chance. In this sense, the source of gains of trade in the "new" international trade theory is different from those in the traditional theory of comparative advantage; the "new" theory generates the possibility of multiple equilibria as well as taking into account the new role of government.

Among the factors that generate location advantage for multinational enterprises (MNEs) to invest, agglomeration is one of the most important,

12. On the agglomeration theory, see Krugman (1991, 1995) and Fujita, Krugman, and Venables (1999).

particularly in developing countries. Governments in East Asia are conscious of the potential role they can play in promoting agglomeration. There are several types of agglomeration or industrial clusters. In cases of East Asian agglomeration observed so far, vertical link along the value chain is crucial; the cluster of producers of copy machines and printers in Guangdong, the agglomeration of Taiwanese computer producers also in Guangdong, and the cluster of automobile producers along the eastern seaboard of Thailand are examples of agglomeration.

The third line of thought is the internalization theory of "firm." A firm typically does not do everything from upstream to downstream. It sets its upstream-side boundary by purchasing materials or parts from other firms, and it determines its downstream-side boundary by selling its products to other firms or consumers. Boundary setting is an "internalization decision." In addition, a firm cuts its internalized activities into thin slices and places these slices at appropriate places (the "location decision"). A firm does make internalization decisions and location decisions at the same time, considering its own firm-specific assets such as technology and managerial know-how.

In East Asia various kinds of internalization patterns with innovative interfirm relationships emerge in the effort to concentrate on core competencies. Such sophistication is particularly salient in machinery industries and in the textiles and garment industry. Technological progress in the line of developing "module" accelerates the formation of sophisticated interfirm relationships. The international trade theory has not yet fully embraced the ownership advantages and internalization advantages that Dunning's OLI (ownership, location, and internalization) theory presents.[13]

Empirical Observations

This section provides some empirical observations based on the micro data of Japanese corporate firms. The tables in this section are constructed from two sets of micro data gathered by the Ministry of International Trade and Industry (MITI) of the Government of Japan (GOJ): the Fiscal Year 2001 Basic Survey of Business Structure and Activity[14] and the Fiscal Year 1999 Survey (the 27th Basic Survey) of Overseas Business Activities of Japanese

---

13. On the OLI theory, see Dunning (1993). Kimura (2000, 2001) analyzes the micro data of Japanese manufacturing firms and claims that corporate structure and interfirm relationships are jointly chosen with the location of activities.

14. The Basic Survey of Business Structure and Activity (*Kigyo Katsudo Kihon Chosa* in Japanese) was first conducted for fiscal year 1991, then for fiscal year 1994, and annually since then. The Basic Survey has several attractive features. First, the

Companies.[15] Tables 2.4 to 2.6 are constructed from the first database, in which foreign affiliates are defined as those with no less than 20 percent Japanese ownership. In Table 2.7, obtained from the second database, foreign affiliates include "affiliates abroad" with no less than 10 percent ownership by Japanese parent firms and "affiliates of affiliates abroad" with more than 50 percent ownership by such "affiliates abroad." Hereafter we call both types of affiliates "Japanese affiliates abroad." [16]

Table 2.4, part (a), presents the number of parent firms with foreign affiliates and the number of foreign affiliates, and part (b) the number of parent firms with affiliates in East Asia and the number of affiliates in East Asia. Both parts of Table 2.4 show the data by the industry classification of parent firms and by the industry classification of affiliates. In 2000, 3,773 out of 27,655 firms located in Japan (in the data set) had 18,943 foreign affiliates.[17] Among them, 2,994 firms had 10,224 affiliates in East Asia. In other words,

---

samples in the survey are comprehensive, covering firms with more than 50 workers, capital of more than 30 million yen, and establishments in mining, manufacturing, wholesale/retail trade, and restaurants. Second, the rate of return of the questionnaires is high although not disclosed (about 90 percent to 95 percent). Statistics collected by the government of Japan are legally classified into two categories: designated statistics (*shitei tokei*) and approved statistics (*shonin tokei*). The Basic Survey is the first type, and thus firms in the survey must return the questionnaires under the Statistics Law. Third, the Basic Survey provides firm-level data rather than establishment-level data. Although establishment-level data are useful in analyzing production activities, firm-level data are much more appropriate to examine corporate activities as a whole.

15. The Survey of Overseas Business Activities of Japanese Companies has been conducted annually since fiscal year 1970. Firms targeted by the survey are those with Japanese affiliates abroad, except firms in finance, insurance, or real estate. This survey is of the approved type, so the return ratios tend to be as low as 60 percent.

16. All sectors except manufacturing and wholesale trade are characterized in this chapter as "other" because most Japanese firms investing abroad are in the manufacturing and wholesale trade sectors. Although the industry classification of the Survey of Overseas Business Activities is different from that of the Basic Survey of Business Structure and Activity, the former industry classification is matched with the latter to make them comparable. See Appendix Table A2.1 for the industrial classification.

17. Because foreign affiliates covered in the Basic Survey are defined as those with no less than 20 percent Japanese ownership, there is a possibility of double counting the number of parent firms and their affiliates abroad. For instance, when Japanese firms have domestic and foreign affiliates and the domestic affiliates have foreign affiliate(s), both parent firms and the affiliates might be covered in the survey and might be reported as parent firms with foreign affiliates. When several Japanese firms together establish a foreign affiliate, each firm might report the foreign affiliate as its own firm (in reporting the number of foreign affiliates).

as much as 80 percent of the Japanese firms going abroad had at least one affiliate in East Asia, and 54 percent of the affiliates of Japanese firms were located in East Asia. Close to 70 percent of the parent firms with affiliates in East Asia were in the manufacturing sector (industries 120 to 340), and half of them were in the machinery sector (industries 290 to 320). (See Appendix Table A2.1 for the industry classification of the manufacturing and non-manufacturing sectors.) The sectoral composition by the industry of affiliates reveals some interesting differences. The pattern observed for the affiliates in East Asia is different from the pattern for all foreign affiliates: around 60 percent of the affiliates in the region are in the manufacturing sector, regardless of the industries of their parent firms, while the share for all foreign affiliates is much lower (47 percent).[18] These figures clearly show how dominant manufacturing activities are in East Asia.[19]

Japanese SMEs, defined as firms with fewer than 300 regular workers, have contributed to this concentration of manufacturing activities in East Asia by Japanese firms.[20] Table 2.5 presents the number of Japanese parent firms with affiliates in East Asia by the size of parent firms (the number of regular workers) and by the number of affiliates of each firm in 2000. Japanese firms investing in East Asia vary in domestic employment size: 13.7 percent of the firms have 50 to 99 workers, 19.5 percent have 100 to 199 workers, 11.9 percent have 200 to 299 workers, 14.9 percent have 300 to 499 workers, 16.8 percent have 500 to 999 workers, and 23.2 percent have 1,000 workers or more. This means that more than 40 percent of the Japanese firms going to East Asia are SMEs. In addition, a considerable number of firms, including SMEs, have more than three affiliates in East Asia. Active foreign direct investment by Japanese SMEs in East Asia, which mainly supply intermediate goods in the vertical production chains, has contributed to the formation of a critical mass of industrial clusters.

As suggested by Table 2.4, Japanese parent firms do not necessarily establish affiliates in their own industries where they have their main activ-

18. Considering that more than half of all of the affiliates are located in East Asia, the percentages of manufacturing affiliates are much lower in other regions.

19. See Kimura and Ando (2003, 2004) for a comparative study of Latin America and East Asia based on the micro data of Japanese corporate firms.

20. Statistical analysis on the characteristics of Japanese parent firms going abroad, based on logit estimation, also confirms that firms going to East Asia are relatively small in size at home, compared with firms going abroad in general or firms going to Latin America. See Appendix Table A2.2 for the results of logit estimation for Japanese parent firms in fiscal year 1995.

Table 2.4. *Japanese Parent Firms and their Foreign Affiliates by Industry, Fiscal Year 2000*

	By industry of parent firm				By industry of affiliate	
Industry	Number of parent firms	%	Number of affiliates	%	Number of affiliates	%
(a) Japanese parent firms with foreign affiliates						
Manufacturing sector						
Nonmachinery sectors						
120-280, 340	1,259	33.4	4,779	25.2	4,427	23.4
Machinery sectors						
290	378	10.0	1,821	9.6	961	5.1
300	489	13.0	2,608	13.8	2,024	10.7
310	283	7.5	1,526	8.1	1,168	6.2
320	96	2.5	426	2.2	292	1.5
Subtotal	**2,505**	**66.4**	**11,160**	**58.9**	**8,872**	**46.8**
Nonmanufacturing sector						
480	864	22.9	6,460	34.1	5,790	30.6
Others	404	10.7	1,323	7.0	4,281	22.6
Subtotal	**1,268**	**33.6**	**7,783**	**41.1**	**10,071**	**53.2**
Total	**3,773**	**100.0**	**18,943**	**100.0**	**18,943**	**100.0**
(b) Japanese parent firms with affiliates in East Asia						
Manufacturing sector						
Nonmachinery sectors						
120-280, 340	1,038	34.7	2,910	28.5	3,198	31.3
Machinery sectors						
290	286	9.6	810	7.9	543	5.3
300	429	14.3	1,598	15.6	1,475	14.4
310	222	7.4	752	7.4	664	6.5
320	75	2.5	226	2.2	202	2.0
Subtotal	**2,050**	**68.5**	**6,296**	**61.6**	**6,082**	**59.5**
Nonmanufacturing sector						
480	697	23.3	3,350	32.8	2,627	25.7
Others	247	8.3	578	5.7	1,515	14.8
Subtotal	**944**	**31.5**	**3,928**	**38.4**	**4,142**	**40.5**
Total	**2,994**	**100.0**	**10,224**	**100.0**	**10,224**	**100.0**

Note: Number of affiliates for the cases (a) and (b) are the (a) number of foreign affiliates as a whole and (b) number of affliates in East Asia, respectively. The industry classification is explained in Appendix Table A2.1.

Source: Ando and Kimura (2004).

Table 2.5. *Foreign Affiliate Ownership Patterns of Japanese Parent Firms, Fiscal Year 2000*
(Number of parent firms)

Number of regular workers of	*Number of affiliates in East Asia*												
parent firm	*1*	2	3	4	5	6	7	8	9	10	*More*	*Total*	%
50 to 99	301	67	25	12	1	2	1	—	—	—	1	410	13.7
100 to 199	413	101	34	23	7	1	2	—	2	—	—	583	19.5
200 to 299	196	92	30	12	8	10	3	2	1	—	1	355	11.9
300 to 499	242	99	36	28	18	8	6	4	2	—	4	447	14.9
500 to 999	209	117	65	42	27	20	5	2	4	2	10	503	16.8
1,000 or more	136	107	77	54	55	45	27	38	16	19	122	696	23.2
Total	1,497	583	267	171	116	86	44	46	25	21	138	2,994	100.0

— Not available.
Source: Ando and Kimura (2004).

ities.[21] Parent firms tend to have various activities across industries, and they establish foreign affiliates in order to conduct a subset of those activities abroad. Table 2.6 provides detailed information on sector switching between parent firms and their affiliates in East Asia; the first part of the table includes all Japanese firms with affiliates in East Asia, while the second part focuses on SMEs with affiliates in East Asia. The rows show the industry of the parent firms; the columns show the industry of the foreign affiliates. Diagonal cells of the table indicate the number of non-sector-switching affiliates; nondiagonal cells denote the number of sector-switching affiliates.

In East Asia 75 percent of the affiliates owned by manufacturing parent firms of all sizes are in the manufacturing sector. Among them, manufacturing parent firms have many sector-switching manufacturing affiliates (observed in nondiagonal cells for industries 120 to 340 in both rows and columns), in particular sector-switching machinery affiliates (nondiagonal cells for industries 120 to 340 in rows and industries 290 to 320 in columns). Even manufacturing SMEs have sector-switching manufacturing affiliates, particularly sector-switching machinery affiliates. For either large parent firms or SMEs, such behavior is typical in manufacturing activities aimed at supplying intermediate goods for other firms or for their own affiliates. An important role has been played by Japanese firms in developing vertical production networks in the region, particularly in machinery industries.[22]

Moreover, manufacturing parent firms also have nonmanufacturing affiliates, particularly in the wholesale trade sector. Sector-switching nonmanufacturing affiliates with manufacturing parent firms (cells for industries 120 to 340 in rows and industries 480 and others in columns) make up 25 percent of the affiliates owned by manufacturing parent firms of all sizes. This suggests that another strategy in East Asia is to establish global production and distribution networks by internalizing wholesale trade activities.

Let us turn now to the performance of Japanese affiliates abroad. Table

---

21. A firm usually conducts various activities at the same time. The industrial classification of a firm located in Japan is determined by the activity conducted by the firm that is the largest in terms of the value of sales.

22. As discussed above, parent firms tend to have various activities across sectors. Foreign affiliates, however, tend to pursue a narrower range of activities. Foreign affiliates are more likely to be involved in activities related to the production and distribution networks in East Asia even if these activities are not the main activities of the parent firms. Thus, one can observe many cases of sector-switching machinery affiliates with the parent firms mainly involved in sectors other than the machinery sector.

Table 2.6. *Sector Switching between Parent Firms and their Affiliates, Fiscal Year 2000*

(Number of affiliates in East Asia)

(a) Industries of Japanese parent firms and their affiliates in East Asia

Industry of parent firm	*Industry of affiliate in East Asia*																							
	120	130	140	150	160	170	180	190	200	210	220	230	240	250	260	270	280	290	300	310	320	340	480	Others	Total
120	145	1							2														20	15	183
130	5	28							12														19	10	74
140			70	7			2				2								1	2		2	10	0	96
150			5	73				2			2								1				12	1	96
160					14	1																1	2	0	18
170					2	25																1	8	0	36
180							45				2							1					5	3	56
190								63													1	6	4	7	81
200	9	2	43	4	1		1	3	520	3	15	2		4		4	7	6	8	1	3	10	174	47	867
210									2	2	4								1				9	18	36
220									7		184	6		1		1	2	2	8	1		5	33	4	254
230		1							1		3	89					2	1		4	1	3	15	8	128
240													6									1		0	7
250			1						1		4			87		1	7	1	3	1	4	2	21	26	159
260														1	51	3	10	2	8	4			7	29	115
270									1		2	1		1		161	14	3	30	14		2	30	23	282
280	1		1		2			1			4			2		14	161	7	27	5	1	8	34	9	277
290	4								10		4			1	8	1	15	362	65	20	18	15	214	73	810
300			2	2		1		1	5		12			5	1	3	6	79	1009	6	17	9	308	132	1598
310						1					2			2	5		9	22	25	569		3	59	55	752
320			1						2		1			3			1	6	14		131		56	11	226
340			1					1			10	1					2		2		3	66	48	11	145
480	115	11	83	157	13	8	14	9	142	11	60	22	3	70	47	32	63	39	266	34	22	56	1516	557	3350
Others	5	0	1	15	6	1	1	0	4	1	2	0	2	2	1	2	4	12	7	3	1	9	23	476	578
	284	43	208	258	38	37	63	80	709	17	313	121	11	179	113	222	303	543	1475	664	202	199	2627	1515	10224

(b) Industries of Japanese parent SMEs and their affiliates in East Asia

Industry of parent firm	*Industry of affiliate in East Asia*																							
	120	*130*	*140*	*150*	*160*	*170*	*180*	*190*	*200*	*210*	*220*	*230*	*240*	*250*	*260*	*270*	*280*	*290*	*300*	*310*	*320*	*340*	*480*	*Others*	*Total*
120	41								1														4	3	49
130		2																						0	2
140			29	2																			6	0	37
150			4	43				2															5	1	55
160					7	1																1		0	9
170					2	15																1	5	0	23
180							12				1							1					4	0	18
190								18													1	5	4	4	32
200								1	80	1	1			1		1	6	2					8	3	104
210										1													3	0	4
220									2		72	2				1	1	2	3	1			9	2	95
230												22										1	2	0	25
240													6									1		0	7
250														23			1					2	4	0	30
260															12		1	1		1			2	1	18
270																58			2			1	3	1	65
280			1					1			4						72	4	1	1			7	0	91
290	2										2			1	1	1	8	109	10	4	4	7	23	7	179
300			1					1			5					2	5	1	232		4	5	37	10	303
310											1			2			1	3	3	45		2	3	1	61
320			1											1					5		34		5	1	47
340			1								7						1		1		3	24	4	0	41
480	22	1	18	57	4	3	5	8	23	3	24	9	2	8	2	14	17	14	40	10	10	18	401	61	774
Others	1	0	1	0	0	0	0	0	2	0	0	0	2	1	0	1	1	3	4	3	0	1	6	70	96
	66	3	56	102	13	19	17	31	108	5	117	33	10	37	15	78	114	140	301	65	56	69	545	165	2165

Note: SMEs are small and medium-size enterprises having fewer than 300 regular workers. The industry classification is explained in Appendix Table A2.1.
Source: Ando and Kimura (2004).

2.7 presents by-destination sales and by-origin purchases by Japanese affiliates in East Asia. Most of the goods and services produced by Japanese affiliates in East Asia go to the local market (49.6 percent), to Japan (21.9 percent), or to countries within the region other than the local market and Japan (21.2 percent).[23] The pattern of by-origin purchases by Japanese affiliates in East Asia is also noteworthy. It shows that they purchase most goods and services from the local market (41.1 percent), or import them from Japan (33.4 percent), or import them from other East Asian countries (20.7 percent).[24] Japan's share in terms of by-origin purchases is slightly higher than the share in terms of sales, probably due to the supply of complicated machinery parts and components produced in Japan. These figures reveal that more than 90 percent of both sales and purchases by Japanese affiliates are transactions among East Asian countries, and suggest the presence of strong intraregional production networks in East Asia through back-and-forth transactions of intermediate goods.

In order to quantify the importance of transactions and confirm the magnitude of Japanese firms' activities in exporting from Japan and producing in East Asia and who is trading with whom, we now consider the concept of value added contents. This is useful since intermediate inputs embodied in traded commodities may be counted multiple times in the amount of gross sales. Figure 2.3 shows the estimated Japanese value added contents of each transaction added at the starting point of the corresponding arrow in 2000. The figure illustrates the three-country setting of the firm nationality approach.[25] The three geographical locations are Japan, Asia,[26] and the rest of the world (ROW), and the three nationality groupings are the Japanese, Asians, and foreigners (the national of ROW). "Japanese" includes Japanese-owned firms located in Japan, households and governments located in Japan, and foreign affiliates of Japanese firms (FAJFs) located in Asia and in ROW.[27] Asians and foreigners are defined in the same way. The three

23. Contrary to popular belief, sales to North America by Japanese affiliates in East Asia are small (3.4 percent), except in the leather and leather products sector.

24. The share of purchases from North America is quite small.

25. Baldwin and Kimura (1998) and Kimura and Baldwin (1998) propose the firm nationality approach in a two-country setting, and Kimura (1998) extends it to a three-country setting. See Kimura (1998) and Ando and Kimura (2004) for a detailed explanation of how the data in Figure 2.3 are estimated.

26. Asia refers here to Asian countries east of Pakistan.

27. In this definition of "Japanese," we treat foreign affiliates of Japanese firms as controlled by the Japanese, and we regard all of the activities of FAJF as activities by the Japanese.

Table 2.7. *Intraregional Production Networks: Sales and Purchases by Japanese Affiliates in East Asia, Fiscal Year 1998*

			Sales								Purchases							
					Share in total sales								Share in total purchases					
							Third countries (total)								Third countries (total)			
Industry	Number of affiliates	%	Total sales (million JPY)	%	Local	Japan		East Asia	North America	Europe	Total purchases (million JPY)	%	Local	Japan		East Asia	North America	Europe
Manufacturing sector																		
120+130	162	2.6	343,929	1.5	69.1	16.2	14.7	6.4	3.3	3.5	137,424	0.9	78.8	6.6	14.6	8.0	0.4	0.5
140+150	399	6.4	503,397	2.2	43.6	30.2	26.1	12.2	4.9	7.4	254,218	1.7	54.0	26.6	19.4	13.1	2.3	0.8
160	23	0.4	17,204	0.1	15.3	56.3	28.3	24.0	0.9	0.1	7,818	0.1	94.0	2.7	3.3	0.0	0.0	3.3
170	14	0.2	7,073	0.0	52.8	34.3	12.9	8.8	4.0	0.0	4,821	0.0	75.2	13.8	11.0	7.9	0.0	3.0
180	36	0.6	50,256	0.2	74.2	12.5	13.3	9.0	3.5	0.0	15,328	0.1	62.5	20.5	17.0	14.1	1.8	1.1
190	27	0.4	27,536	0.1	77.8	0.4	21.8	11.5	0.4	5.5	2,694	0.0	73.7	16.6	9.8	0.0	1.9	7.8
200	529	8.5	1,414,684	6.1	69.8	6.7	23.5	15.7	5.0	1.5	579,333	3.8	53.6	19.4	27.0	13.3	6.8	1.9
210	17	0.3	36,418	0.2	21.2	65.7	13.1	2.9	0.0	10.2	32,061	0.2	21.7	18.0	60.4	45.4	10.3	3.9
220	109	1.8	92,230	0.4	64.7	20.1	15.2	9.7	1.7	2.9	38,584	0.3	68.0	25.7	6.3	5.1	0.2	0.5
230	54	0.9	107,614	0.5	41.4	34.3	24.3	13.2	4.9	5.1	24,259	0.2	57.4	23.6	19.0	17.1	0.3	1.6
240	16	0.3	7,196	0.0	4.5	21.2	74.3	22.5	44.0	7.8	5,282	0.0	10.0	6.8	83.2	41.2	9.8	3.2
250	160	2.6	334,130	1.4	69.7	17.2	13.2	8.8	3.5	0.8	140,533	0.9	41.3	31.5	27.2	23.1	3.3	0.5
260	166	2.7	423,491	1.8	85.4	2.9	11.7	6.5	2.6	0.1	229,136	1.5	19.2	70.0	10.8	10.4	0.0	0.2
270	110	1.8	281,041	1.2	55.9	15.6	28.6	26.3	0.9	1.0	155,313	1.0	44.1	31.7	24.2	19.0	0.3	1.1
280	121	1.9	97,240	0.4	70.9	13.4	15.7	11.9	1.9	1.4	47,014	0.3	67.8	29.0	3.2	1.7	0.3	1.1
290	315	5.1	688,971	3.0	32.4	40.7	27.0	14.8	5.5	4.6	400,705	2.6	57.7	32.2	10.1	8.8	0.8	0.4
300	916	14.7	5,191,673	22.3	32.3	32.9	34.8	24.9	5.3	3.0	3,711,079	24.4	35.8	37.0	27.2	26.3	0.4	0.2
310	478	7.7	2,140,129	9.2	81.0	11.1	7.9	2.2	3.5	1.5	1,380,996	9.1	53.4	37.2	9.4	6.1	2.5	0.7
320	100	1.6	464,375	2.0	27.2	45.9	26.9	23.1	1.5	2.0	271,580	1.8	40.2	41.2	18.6	14.5	2.6	1.5
330+340	83	1.3	95,985	0.4	22.3	63.6	14.1	2.8	7.5	2.9	63,645	0.4	55.1	37.7	7.1	5.9	0.4	0.7
Nonmanufacturing sector																		
480	957	15.4	8,524,268	36.7	41.3	19.4	39.3	33.0	2.2	2.8	6,333,657	41.6	28.4	35.2	36.4	28.3	1.5	2.7
Others	1,421	22.9	2,386,309	10.3	77.7	11.2	11.1	8.0	1.5	1.2	1,387,281	9.1	72.7	19.5	7.8	5.5	1.1	0.6
Total	6,213	100.0	23,235,149	100.0	49.6	21.9	28.4	21.2	3.4	2.6	15,222,761	100.0	41.1	33.4	25.5	20.7	1.5	1.3

Note: The industry classification is explained in Appendix Table A2.1.
Source: Ando and Kimura (2004).

nationality groupings reside in three different locations, and so nine blocks are drawn in Figure 2.3. Although transactions within a block and between blocks conceivably could consist of 81 (9 times 9) arrows, 14 arrows of transactions are filled out because only statistical data from the Japanese side are readily available.

Although Figure 2.3 presents rough estimates and we have a number of reservations about the data set, the value added account provides useful insights into the activities of Japanese MNEs such as intrafirm relationships and arm's length relationships. When value added in exports by the Japanese in Japan to Asians (Asian firms) and foreigners (MNEs other than Japanese) in Asia is compared with value added in exports to Japanese (Japanese affiliates) in Asia, the former is larger than the latter. Also, when value added in sales by Japanese affiliates in Asia to Asians (Asian firms) and foreigners (MNEs other than Japanese) in Asia is compared with that to Japanese-owned firms in Japan, the former is larger than the latter. Thus, it is not true that the activities by Japanese firms are solely based on subcontracting relationships or intrafirm relationships between Japanese parent firms and Japanese affiliates in East Asia; rather the activities do include transactions with indigenous firms and MNEs in Asia. In other words, the strong intraregional production networks in East Asia include not only Japanese firms but also a mixture of firms of different nationalities.

The empirical observations we have made may not directly indicate the applicability of the three lines of new thought (fragmentation theory, agglomeration theory, or the internalization theory of "firm"). However, the validity of these theories with regard to the development of international production and distribution networks in East Asia is supported by the following: active FDI by Japanese SMEs, the existence of many sector-switching manufacturing affiliates, and intraregional trade and production activities by Japanese firms (including their affiliates) with indigenous firms and MNEs in Asia.

The Policy Environment in Japan and in Hosting East Asian Countries

The policy environment in Japan and in developing East Asian countries is an important determinant of FDI patterns. The Japanese government, both explicitly and implicitly, has consistently supported outward FDI by Japanese firms. FDI facilitation measures for SMEs have been particularly important because they had not necessarily been experienced players in the arena of global operations. When big assemblers decided to relocate their plants

***Figure 2.3.** Japanese Value Added Embodied in Sales to Asians and Foreigners by the Japanese, 2000*
(Million Japanese yen)

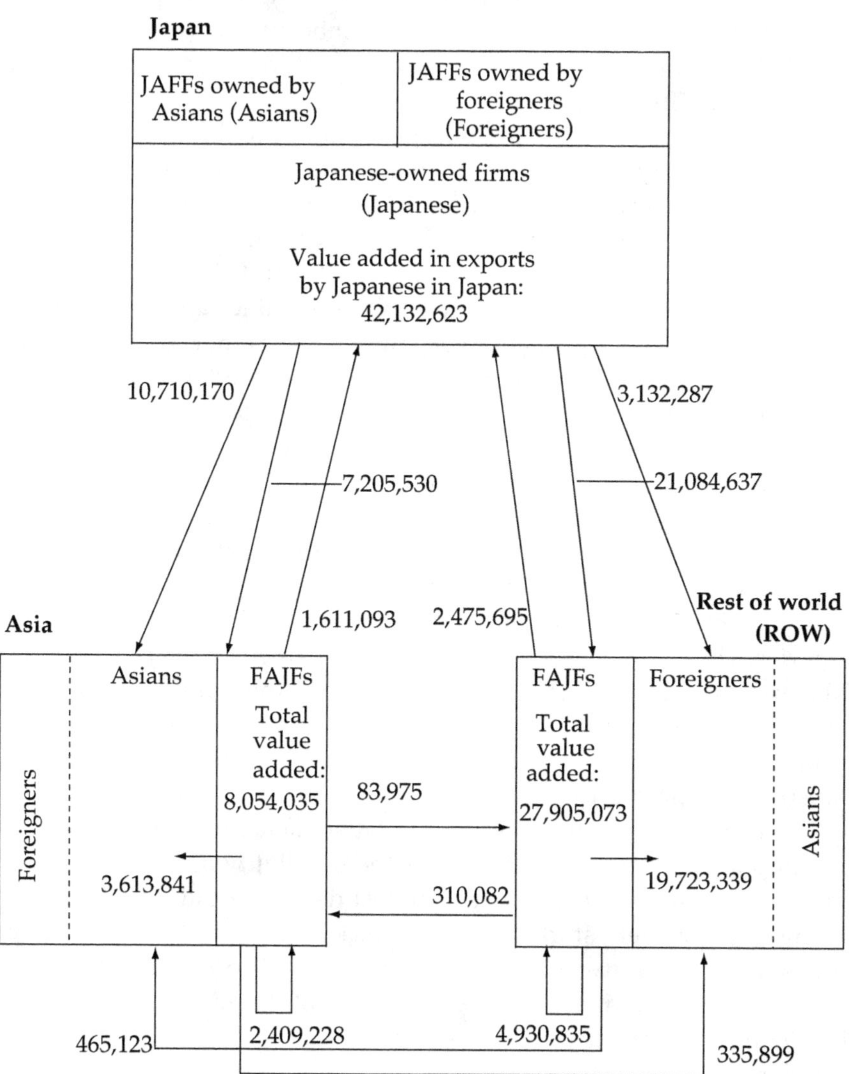

Note: JAFFs and FAJFs stand for Japanese affiliates of foreign firms and foreign affiliates of Japanese firms, respectively.

Source: Ando and Kimura (2004).

to East Asian countries, small-scale parts suppliers, initially connected with assemblers in the long-term subcontracting system, had to decide whether to go abroad with their clients or stay in disarray. Competitive SMEs decided to go abroad, while weak ones stayed. Going abroad provided good opportunities to nullify old and inefficient subcontracting systems and to construct new and efficient interfirm relationships. As a result, efficient turnovers of SMEs accelerated.

The government of Japan supported FDI outflows in three ways. First, it provided mildly concessionary financing arrangements for outward FDI through governmental financial institutions such as the Export-Import Bank (currently the Japan Bank for International Cooperation, JBIC) and the Japan Finance Corporation for Small Business. The concessionarity itself, which conformed to OECD guidelines and other international norms, was not probably very important; rather, such financing, which reduced information-gathering costs, was used to encourage private financial institutions to co-finance the main portion of the investment. Second, the Japan External Trade Organization (JETRO) and industrial organizations helped investing firms gather necessary local information, and they played a key role in facilitating investment. Although not in the governmental sector, general trading companies (GTCs) also worked as important channels to facilitate investment; sometimes they even constructed and managed industrial estates in East Asian countries. Third, Japanese FDI was indirectly helped by the Japanese Official Development Assistance (ODA) program, although it was not necessarily planned and implemented on purpose, and by other initiatives that promoted economic and technical cooperation in fostering supporting industries in host countries.

Policy makers as well as the press in Japan have provided strong positive support for outward FDI; initially, the possibility of "hollowing out" did not cause much concern. After the lost decade of the 1990s, the "hollowing out" problem started to be discussed more seriously. However, criticism against outward FDI remains weak. The declining location advantages of Japan is the issue at the center of discussion. The virtue of globalizing corporate activities has barely been challenged in Japan.

Hosting countries' policy environment is also a crucial factor in the formulation of international production and distribution networks. The manufacturing sector in Southeast Asian countries, particularly Malaysia, Thailand, the Philippines, and Indonesia, consists of import-substituting industries and export-oriented industries, and the governments apply different policy packages for these two groups of industries. This is the so-called "dual track approach" taken since the 1970s.[28] The balance between import-substituting industries and export-oriented industries, however, has changed over time. From the 1970s to the mid-1980s, these countries applied selective introduction of FDI primarily in import-substituting industries. Although FDI for export promotion was also invited at that time, competing domestic industries were typically protected by a policy that limited the activities of export-oriented FDI (for example, to geographically segregated export-processing zones). After the mid-1980s, these countries switched their FDI hosting policy from a selective acceptance policy to (basically) an "accept everybody" policy. While keeping trade protection for limited import-substituting industries, they tried to host as many foreign companies as possible and to formulate industrial clusters.

The dual track approach requires delicate policy manipulation in order to offset negative policy biases against export-oriented industries caused by protection of import-substituting industries. The duty drawback system—that is, the system of refunds of duties and indirect taxes on imported inputs in export production—is one of the effective policy arrangements to partially neutralize intermediate input procurement. In fact, MNEs in export-oriented industries are now paying very low tariffs in these countries.[29] Such a policy package allows them to attract both import-substituting FDI and export-oriented FDI.

Various measures to facilitate foreign direct investment are also crucial. These countries concentrated their public resources on the development of economic infrastructure including roads, ports, electricity and water supply, telecommunications, and industrial estate services. In addition, the upgrading services provided by FDI-hosting agencies yielded considerable benefits. For example, though its inefficiency has often been harshly criticized, the Board of Investment (BOI) of the Thai government worked hard to attract FDI just after the Asian currency crisis began by establishing itself as a "one-stop shop for services." Thanks in part to these efforts, FDI inflows to Thailand

---

28. Pangestu (2003) provides an excellent review of industrial policies in East Asia from the 1950s to the 1990s as well as policies and measures for promoting exports in East Asia.

29. Due to the duty drawback system as well as extensive tariff removals for IT-related parts and components, customs duty as a percentage of c.i.f. import value is pretty low: 0.3 percent in Singapore, 3.8 percent in Thailand, and 7.1 percent in the Philippines for 2000; 1.7 percent in Indonesia for 1999; 2.8 percent in China for 1998; and 4.3 percent in the Republic of Korea and 3.4 percent in Malaysia for 1997. See Kimura (2003) and Ando and Estevadeordal (2003) for the details.

recorded the highest levels in 1998; crossborder mergers and acquisitions (M&As) contributed to this increase as well. During the economic crisis, Malaysia imposed temporary restrictions on capital outflows starting in September 1998. The international community initially criticized this policy, which was expected to have a strongly negative impact on FDI activities. In fact, however, very few withdrawals of foreign affiliates from Malaysia were observed while new investment stagnated. One of the untold background stories was the close communications between government officials and foreign affiliates. Government officials made a great effort to frequently visit foreign affiliates and their industrial associations, and officials asked whether they were experiencing any inconvenience in sending money back and forth.

Before presenting our conclusions, we briefly consider Japanese manufacturing firms' assessment of East Asia as a potential destination of their FDI and what they regard as impediments in such countries for their FDI. Each year the JBIC conducts a survey of Japanese manufacturing MNEs; survey respondents are asked to list countries that they think are prospective destinations of their FDI in the short run (the next three years) and to provide the reasons for their choice as well as the strong and weak points of such countries.[30] Marugami et al. (2003) present the results of the survey in fiscal year 2002 (Table 2.8). Countries as possible destinations for FDI are ranked by Japanese manufacturing firms as follows: China (1st, selected by 373 firms); Thailand (2nd, 118 firms); United States (3rd, 108 firms); Indonesia (4th, 63 firms); Vietnam (5th, 62 firms); India (6th, 54 firms); the Republic of Korea (7th, 34 firms); Taiwan, China (7th, 34 firms); Malaysia (9th, 33 firms); and Brazil (10th, 19 firms). Many of the top ten destination countries are East Asian countries, although they follow China at quite a distance in terms of the number of firms making the selection.

What explains Japanese manufacturing firms' choices about prospective destinations for their FDI? As Table 2.8 makes clear, "market potential" and "inexpensive labor" are important conditions that attract incoming FDI in most of the East Asian countries. More interestingly, some other conditions are related to vertical production chains or intraregional trade. Many firms in most of the countries list as the strong points "to supply intermediate goods for assemblers," "to export to the third countries," and "to export to Japan."[31]

30. The fiscal year 2002 survey was of Japanese firms with three or more foreign affiliates, including at least one manufacturing foreign affiliate at the end of November 2001; 508 of 812 firms returned effective answers.

31. For instance, "to supply intermediate goods for assemblers" is selected as a strong point by 29 percent of the firms that list China as a prospective destination for

(*Note 31 continued on p. 98.*)

Table 2.8. *Strong and Weak Points of Prospective Destination Countries for Japanese Manufacturing FDI*
(Percent unless otherwise indicated)

	Ranking [a]									
	1	2	3	4	5	6	7	8	9	10
No. of firms	373	118	108	63	62	54	34	34	33	19
Strong and weak points / *Country*	*China*	*Thailand*	*U.S.A.*	*Indonesia*	*Vietnam*	*India*	*Rep. of Korea*	*Taiwan, China*	*Malaysia*	*Brazil*
Strong points[b]	373	112	108	61	54	50	32	32	30	19
Market potential	86.3	54.5	39.8	47.5	55.6	84.0	53.1	53.1	33.3	73.7
Inexpensive labor	68.9	48.2	0.9	73.8	70.4	60.0	12.5	15.6	40.0	26.3
To supply intermediate goods for assemblers	28.7	33.0	26.9	21.3	9.3	16.0	25.0	37.5	23.3	26.3
Present market size	17.2	9.8	62.0	9.8	1.9	14.0	28.1	43.8	10.0	10.5
To export to the third countries	25.2	32.1	2.8	36.1	24.1	16.0	6.3	21.9	30.0	5.3
Inexpensive parts and components/raw materials	30.0	9.8	2.8	16.4	11.1	16.0	12.5	9.4	10.0	15.8
To export to Japan	26.8	21.4	—	24.6	7.4	16.0	15.6	12.5	13.3	—
Human capital	11.0	8.0	16.7	—	33.3	6.0	25.0	25.0	10.0	—
R&D for the local market	9.9	6.3	27.8	4.9	5.6	30.0	6.3	9.4	3.3	15.8
Development of infrastructure	5.6	7.1	9.3	1.6	3.7	10.0	9.4	18.8	13.3	—
Investment incentives/ deregulation measures	7.2	11.6	—	1.6	3.7	6.0	3.1	9.4	13.3	5.3
Investment by other firms in the same industry	9.1	7.1	4.6	4.9	3.7	—	3.1	9.4	10.0	—
Advancement of regional integration	1.3	5.4	—	6.6	—	4.0	—	—	13.3	10.5

(*Table continues on following page.*)

Table 2.8. *(continued)*

	Ranking [a]									
	1	*2*	*3*	*4*	*5*	*6*	*8*	*7*	*9*	*10*
No. of firms	*373*	*118*	*108*	*63*	*62*	*54*	*34*	*34*	*33*	*19*
Country	*China*	*Thailand*	*U.S.A.*	*Indonesia*	*Vietnam*	*India*	*Rep. of Korea*	*Taiwan, China*	*Malaysia*	*Brazil*
Weak points[c]	356	89	73	60	43	43	28	31	28	15
Insufficient infrastructure	24.4	12.4	—	26.7	41.9	44.2	—	—	14.3	20.0
Underdevelopment of legal system	46.3	4.5	—	8.3	46.5	32.6	—	—	7.1	—
Nontransparency in the legal system	55.6	10.1	—	23.3	27.9	20.9	—	6.2	3.6	6.7
Frequent and sudden changes in institutional arrangements	51.7	4.5	—	10.0	11.6	7.0	3.6	3.2	7.1	6.7
Complicated taxation system	17.7	5.6	6.8	10.0	11.6	9.3	3.6	—	3.6	20.0
Nontransparency in the implementation of taxation system	37.4	10.1	—	10.0	9.3	16.3	3.6	—	—	20.0
Frequent and sudden changes in taxation system	36.5	3.4	—	3.3	11.6	2.3	3.6	3.2	—	13.3
High import tariffs	19.9	13.5	2.7	8.3	11.6	9.3	3.6	—	—	33.3
Insufficient deregulation for foreign capital	27.5	11.2	—	5.0	20.9	11.6	14.3	—	25.0	13.3
Complicated administrative procedure	41.0	7.9	1.4	13.3	16.3	11.6	3.6	3.2	3.6	6.7
Political and social environment	27.8	11.2	2.7	81.7	32.6	55.8	3.6	12.9	28.6	40.0

Instability of local currency	8.7	46.1	9.6	58.3	27.9	20.9	17.9	16.1	17.9	46.7
Difficulty in purchasing raw materials and parts and components in local market	20.5	20.2	5.5	18.3	25.6	18.6	10.7	6.5	7.1	6.7
Underdevelopment of indigenous supporting industries	10.1	7.9	—	15.0	20.9	9.3	—	3.2	10.7	6.7
Difficulty in local financing	15.4	10.1	8.2	13.3	11.6	14.0	14.3	3.2	7.1	—
Harsh competition with other firms in the local market	27.5	25.8	68.5	23.3	9.3	18.6	64.3	54.8	25.0	6.7
Insufficient human capital for managerial positions	25.8	30.3	24.7	30.0	16.3	16.3	17.9	16.1	25.0	6.7
Low level of local labor	12.9	9.0	9.6	11.7	2.3	11.6	3.6	6.5	3.6	13.3
Rising labor costs in host country	16.0	25.8	20.5	20.0	4.7	4.7	21.4	32.3	21.4	6.7
Local labor problems	11.8	7.9	16.4	25.0	7.0	14.0	25.0	—	7.1	13.3
Insufficient information on the host country	9.6	5.6	—	5.0	18.6	32.6	3.6	3.2	7.1	40.0

— Not available.

a. The ranking is based on the number of Japanese manufacturing firms that chose the country as a prospective destination for their FDI in the short run.

b. The figures to the right are the number of Japanese manufacturing firms that answered the question on strong points among those that chose the country as a prospective destination for their FDI.

c. The figures to the right are the number of Japanese manufacturing firms that answered the question on weak points among those that chose the country as a prospective destination for their FDI.

Note: This JBIC 2002 F/Y questionnaire survey was conducted for Japanese manufacturing firms with three or more foreign affiliates including at least one manufacturing foreign affiliate at the end of November 2001, in which 508 firms out of 812 returned effective answers. Multiple listings of destination countries are allowed.

Source: Marugami et al. (2003).

These conditions show that many Japanese manufacturing firms are involved in vertical production activities and form industrial clusters in East Asia, contributing to the formation of international production and distribution networks.

Table 2.8 also presents what Japanese manufacturing firms view as weak points in each prospective destination for FDI.[32] Many firms cite "insufficient infrastructure," "non-transparency in the legal system," "political and social environment," and other conditions as weak points of destination countries, particularly China, Vietnam, and India. Although Vietnam and India have been listed in the top ten of prospective destinations in the surveys in the last few years, they have received a small amount of FDI from Japan. The survey confirms that the development of economic infrastructure, transparency, fairness, and predictability are the key for hosting FDI as discussed above.

Conclusion

FDI is surely an important channel for supplying capital, transferring technology, and providing links with the world market. Overcoming the instinctive fear of strong foreign companies is not easy, but successful developing countries are beginning to realize the benefits of being host countries. Japanese firms are not the only active players in East Asia, but they have contributed greatly to the industrialization of the region. In particular, they have played a crucial role in the formulation of international production and distribution networks in East Asia, largely because of their competitive edge in machinery industries. The networks are an open system that is not limited to intrafirm transactions or arm's length transactions among Japanese firms. The system is open to firms with different nationalities. In order to fully capture the benefits of international production and distribution networks, countries need supporting industry and, ultimately, human capital. Government policies are important in investing countries and in hosting countries in order to take advantage of globalizing corporate activities.

---

their FDI. The percentages for other East Asian countries listed in Table 2.8 are as follows: 33 percent for Thailand, 21 percent for Indonesia, 25 percent for the Republic of Korea, 38 percent for Taiwan, China, and 23 percent for Malaysia.

32. For more details on trade and FDI-related policies abroad, see "Issues and Requests Relating to Foreign Trade and Investment in 2002," published by the Japan Business Council for Trade and Investment Facilitation (BCTIF). It is available at http://www.jmcti.org/mondai/top_e.html.

Japan gave financial and nonfinancial support to SMEs to invest abroad, which was particularly effective. Foreign direct investment by SMEs has played a crucial role in formulating international production and distribution networks. It was wise that the Japanese government was not overly concerned about "hollowing out," but recent location disadvantages of Japan are serious problems that the government now must consider.

In hosting East Asian countries, the new role of government was seriously considered.[33] The majority of developing countries in the rest of the world also admit the importance of hosting FDI, but their policy package is still only for the import-substitution-type FDI. A different set of policies for industrial promotion is required in the globalization era. East Asia provides an important model of development strategies for developing countries in other regions.

33. As Lipsey (2004) and Kimura and Ando (2004) discuss, the behavior of Japanese firms and U.S. firms in East Asia is similar in many points, which confirms that the environment of host countries/regions seems to be very important.

Appendix Table A2.1. *Industry Classification*

Manufacturing sector		*Nonmanufacturing sector*	
120	Food processing	480	Wholesale trade
130	Beverages, tobacco, and animal feed	Others	Services and others
140	Textiles		
150	Apparel		
160	Wood and wood products		
170	Furniture and fixures		
180	Pulp, paper, and paper products		
190	Publishing and printing		
200	Chemicals		
210	Petroleum and coal products		
220	Plastic products		
230	Rubber products		
240	Leather and leather products		
250	Ceramics, clay, and stone products		
260	Iron and steel		
270	Nonferrous metal		
280	Metal products		
290	General machinery		
300	Electric machinery		
310	Transport equipment		
320	Precision machinery		
330	Arms		
340	Other manufacturing		
290+300+ 310+320	Machinery sector		

Appendix Table A2.2. *Logit Estimation: Japanese Parent Firms, Fiscal Year 1995*

Independent variables	*Dependent variables*: *Foreign affiliates with= 1; without= 0* (1)		*Affiliates in East Asia with= 1; without= 0* (2)		*Affiliates in Latin America with= 1; without= 0* (3)	
Constant	–5.547	***	–5.713	***	–11.107	***
	(–42.82)		(–42.77)		(–30.53)	
Number of regular workers (log)	0.694	***	0.693	***	1.075	***
	(31.00)		(30.22)		(20.90)	
Tangible assets per regular workers	0.010	***	0.003	*	0.007	***
	(6.55)		(1.66)		(2.81)	
Foreign sales: ratio to total sales	7.132	***	5.146	***	3.942	***
	(25.06)		(22.84)		(12.86)	
R&D expenditure: ratio to total sales	9.565	***	6.160	***	1.774	
	(8.50)		(6.02)		(0.93)	
Advertisement expenditure: ratio to total sales	–0.122		–1.546		–1.837	
	(–0.14)		(–1.19)		(–0.45)	
Log likelihood	–5,948.385		–5,425.176		–898.884	
Number of observations	13,623		13,623		13,623	

* Significant at the 10 percent level.
** Significant at the 5 percent level.
*** Significant at the 1 percent level.
Note: Numbers in parentheses are t-statistics.
Source: Kimura and Ando (2004).

References

Ando, Mitsuyo, and Estevadeordal, Antoni. 2003. "Trade Policy Formation in Latin America and Asia-Pacific: A Comparative Analysis." Presented at the Latin American/Caribbean and Asia Pacific Economics and Business Association (LAEBA) panel in the 11th FIEALC (Federación Internacional de Estudios sobre Ame´rica Latina y el Caribe) 2003 Osaka "Globalization in Asia and Latin America: Trade, Investment, and Finance."

Ando, Mitsuyo, and Kimura, Fukunari. 2005. "The Formation of International Production and Distribution Networks in East Asia." In Takatoshi Ito and Andrew Rose, eds., *International Trade* (NBER-East Asia Seminar on Economics, Volume 14). Chicago: The University of Chicago Press. See also *NBER Working Paper 10167.*

Baldwin, Robert E., and Kimura, Fukunari. 1998. "Measuring U.S. International Goods and Services Transactions." In R. E. Baldwin, R. E. Lipsey, and J. D. Richardson, eds., *Geography and Ownership as Bases for Economic Accounting*, 9–48. Chicago: The University of Chicago Press.

BOJ (Bank of Japan). 2003a. "Long-term Time-Series Data: Regional Balance of Payments." November. See http://www.boj.or.jp/en/type/stat/dlong/index.htm.

———. 2003b. "Statistics: Balance of Payments." November. See http://www.boj.or.jp/en/type/stat/boj_stat/bop/index.htm.

Cheng, Leonard K., and Kierzkowski, Henryk. 2001. *Global Production and Trade in East Asia*. Boston: Kluwer Academic Publishers.

Deardorff, Alan. V. 2001. "Fragmentation in Simple Trade Models." *North American Journal of Economics and Finance* 12: 121–37.

Dunning, John H. 1993. *Multinational Enterprises and the Global Economy*. Wokingham: Addison-Wesley.

Fujita, Masahisa, Krugman, Paul, and Venables, Anthony J. 1999. *The Spatial Economy: Cities, Regions, and International Trade*. Cambridge: The MIT Press.

Jones, Ronald W., and Kierzkowski, Henryk. 1990. "The Role of Services in Production and International Trade: A Theoretical Framework." In Ronald W. Jones and Anne O. Krueger, eds., *The Political Economy of International Trade: Essays in Honor of Robert E. Baldwin*, 31–48. Oxford: Basil Blackwell.

Kimura, Fukunari. 1998. "Japanese Multinationals and Regional Integration in Asia." In Kiichiro Fukasaku, Fukunari Kimura, and Shujiro Urata, eds., *Asia and Europe: Beyond Competing Regionalism*. Brighton: Sussex Academic Press.

———. 2000. "Location and Internalization Decisions: Sector Switching in Japanese Outward Foreign Direct Investment." In Takatoshi Ito and Anne O. Krueger, eds., *The Role of Foreign Direct Investment in East Asian Economic Development*. Chicago: University of Chicago Press.

———. 2001. "Fragmentation, Internalization, and Interfirm Linkages: Evidence from the Micro Data of Japanese Manufacturing Firms." In Leonard K. Cheng and Henryk Kierzkowski, eds., *Global Production and Trade in East Asia*, 129–52. Boston: Kluwer Academic Publishers.

———. 2003. "Development Strategies for Economies under Globalisation: Southeast Asia as a New Development Model." In Tran Van Hoa and Charles Harvie, eds., *New Asian Regionalism: Responses to Globalisation and Crises*. London: Palgrave.

Kimura, Fukunari, and Ando, Mitsuyo. 2003. "Fragmentation and Agglomeration Matter: Japanese Multinationals in Latin America and East Asia." *North American Journal of Economics and Finance* 14 (3): 287–317.

———. 2004. "The Economic Analysis of International Production/Distribution Networks in East Asia and Latin America: The Implication of Regional Trade Arrangements." *Business and Politics* 7 (1): 1100.

Kimura, Fukunari, and Baldwin, Robert E. 1998. "Application of a Nationality-Adjusted Net Sales and Value Added Framework: The Case of Japan." In R. E. Baldwin, R. E. Lipsey, and J. D. Richardson, eds., *Geography and Ownership as Bases for Economic Accounting*, 49-82. Chicago: The University of Chicago Press.

Krugman, Paul. 1991. "Increasing Returns and Economic Geography." *Journal of Political Economy* 99: 183–99.

———. 1995. *Development, Geography, and Economic Theory*. Cambridge: The MIT Press.

Lipsey, Robert E. 2004. "U.S. Firms and East Asian Development since 1990." Paper presented at the second workshop on "Foreign Direct Investment and Economic Development: Lessons from East Asian Experience" sponsored by World Bank Institute (WBI) under the Brain Trust Program (funded by the Government of Japan) held in Bali, Indonesia, on November 30 and December 1, 2003.

Marugami, Takashi, Toyoda, Takeshi, Kasuga, Tsuyoshi, and Suzuki, Mayumi. 2003. "2002 nendo Kaigai Chokusetsu Toshi Ankeeto Chosa Kekka Hokoku (dai 14 kai) (The Report on the 14th Questionnaire Survey of Foreign Direct Investment in the 2002 F/Y)." *Journal of Research Institute for Development and Finance* 14 (January): 4–82. In Japanese.

METI (The Ministry of Economy, Trade, and Industry), Government of Japan. 2003. *White Paper on International Trade 2002*. Tokyo: Ministry of Finance Printing Office.

MOF (The Ministry of Finance), Government of Japan. 2003. "Statistics: Outward and Inward Foreign Direct Investment." November. See http://www.mof.go.jp/1c008.htm.

Pangestu, Mari. 2003. "Industrial Policy and Developing Countries." In Bernard Hoekman, Philip English, and Aaditya Matto, eds., *Development, Trade, and the WTO: A Handbook*. Washington, D.C.: World Bank.

Wilkins, Mira. 1986. "Japanese Multinational Enterprises before 1914." *Business History Review* 60: 199–231. Boston : Harvard Graduate School of Business Administration.

3

U.S. Firms and East Asian Development in the 1990s

Robert E. Lipsey

Traditionally, most of U.S. firms' overseas manufacturing activity has been in developed countries. From 1950 to 1990, about 25 percent of this activity was in developing countries. Then, in the 1990s, a shift toward developing countries occurred. The size of the shift depends on the measure used to judge it. The developing-country shares of worldwide U.S. affiliate activity increased during this decade by amounts ranging from almost half to two thirds for affiliate sales and employee compensation and by around 20 percent for employment and gross product (Table 3.1).

Of all these measures, the one showing the largest developing-country share of U.S. FDI activity in manufacturing is the number of employees, which reached over 40 percent in 2000. The difference between the large developing-country share of employment and the much smaller shares of employee compensation reflects the fact that the average wage of affiliate employees in manufacturing in developing countries is less than half the average wage in developed countries.

The Location of U.S. Firms' Overseas Manufacturing

Fifty years ago, almost all of U.S. affiliate manufacturing activity in developing countries was in Latin America. Latin America, and Canada and the

I am grateful to participants at the meetings in Fukuoka, Japan, and Bali, Indonesia, and particularly to Mitsuyo Ando, Fukunari Kimura, and Shujiro Urata for helpful comments and suggestions and to Hengyong Mo for research assistance.

Table 3.1. *Developing-Country Share of U.S. Affiliate Activity, 1989 and 2000*
(Percent)

Activity	*Manufacturing* 1989	*Manufacturing* 2000	*Other industries* 1989	*Other industries* 2000
All nonbank affiliates				
Sales	17	26	18	27
Employment	37	44	23	30
Employee compensation	14	20	14	19
Majority-owned nonbank affiliates				
Sales	15	25	18	26
Gross product	17	21	18	27
Employment	34	42	23	27
Employee compensation	13	19	14	17

Source: Mataloni and Goldberg (1994); Mataloni (2003); and U.S. Department of Commerce, Bureau of Economic Analysis website.

United Kingdom among developed countries, were the main recipients of U.S. foreign direct investment (FDI) for many years (U.S. Department of Commerce 1953, Appendix Tables 6 and 7). Table 3.2 presents the main elements of the very different geographical distributions of output and employment in 1989 and 2000. In 1989, 12 percent of worldwide U.S. manufacturing affiliate output (70 percent of output in developing countries) took place in Latin America and only 4 percent in Developing Asia. By 2000, the Latin American share of affiliate output in all countries had fallen to 11 percent, while the Developing Asia share had doubled.

The largest gains in manufacturing affiliate output in the 1990s took place in Mexico (Table 3.3). Two other countries outside Asia had gains of $1 billion or more (Argentina and Israel), and one country experienced a loss of affiliate output by more than $1 billion (Brazil). But Singapore, China, Malaysia, the Republic of Korea, and Thailand all had gains of over $1 billion in U.S. affiliate output. Quite a few Asian countries shared in the shift of the U.S. multinationals' manufacturing output to developing countries.

U.S. manufacturing affiliate production in Latin America has been much more concentrated than in Asia. Eighty-five percent in 1989 and more than 75 percent in 2000 were in Brazil and Mexico; only one other country, Argentina, accounted for as much as 10 percent of Western Hemisphere affiliate production in 2000. In Asia, six of the eleven countries each accounted for half a percent of world affiliate manufacturing production, and two others came close to that level. Four countries each accounted for

Table 3.2. Shares of Developing Countries, Latin America, and Developing Asia in Worldwide Production and Employment of Majority-Owned Nonbank Affiliates of Nonbank U.S. Parents, 1989 and 2000
(Percent)

	Worldwide production (gross output)		*Employment*	
Country group	*1989*	*2000*	*1989*	*2000*
Manufacturing				
All countries	100	100	100	100
Developing countries	17	20	34	42
Latin America[a]	12	11	23	24
Developing Asia[b]	4	8	9	15
Other industries				
All countries	100	100	100	100
Developing countries	19	27	23	27
Latin America[a]	4	9	10	14
Developing Asia[b]	7	10	6	10

a. Latin America, excluding Other Western Hemisphere.

b. Asia and Pacific, except Australia, Japan, and New Zealand.

Source: Mataloni and Goldberg (1994); Mataloni (2003); and U.S. Department of Commerce (1992).

close to 10 percent or more of manufacturing affiliate production in Developing Asia.

There was a shift in manufacturing affiliate employment similar to that in production. The world share of Latin America increased slightly, but the share of Developing Asia grew by 47 percent. Almost all the employment gains took place in China, Malaysia, and Thailand (Table 3.4). China became the country with the largest affiliate employment in Developing Asia.

With respect to affiliate manufacturing employment in Latin America, there were large gains in Mexico and large losses in Brazil, but no other increases of more than 13,000 employees. In Asia, however, where the 1989 employment had been less than half that in Latin America, gains in affiliate employment were larger than any in Latin America outside Mexico. The gains were especially notable in low-wage countries (China, in particular, as well as India, Indonesia, Thailand, and Malaysia).

A shift in U.S. affiliate manufacturing activity toward developing countries in the 1990s is unmistakable, by whatever measure. This shift was more toward Asia than toward Latin America, except for the large gains for Mexico. Not only was the predominant movement of production and employment

Table 3.3. *Gross Product of U.S. Manufacturing Majority-Owned Foreign Affiliates by Country, 1989 and 2000*
(Millions of U.S. dollars)

Country	*1989*	*2000*	*Change*
All countries	172,008	315,597	143,589
Latin America and other Western Hemisphere countries	21,492	36,744	15,252
South America	16,886	19,709	2,823
Argentina	973	4,066	3,093
Brazil	14,167	12,830	−1,337
Chile	364	535	171
Colombia	650	777	127
Ecuador	37	88	51
Peru	90	94	4
Venezuela	509	1,083	574
Central America	4,606	16,098	11,492
Costa Rica	99	402	303
Honduras	105	221	116
Mexico	4,123	15,078	10,955
Panama	182	32	−150
Asia and Pacific, excluding Australia, Japan, and New Zealand	6,161	27,081	20,920
China	36	4,381	4,345
Hong Kong (China)	751	1,426	675
India	161	886	725
Indonesia	100	285	185
Korea, Republic of	463	2,505	2,042
Malaysia	477	3,098	2,621
Philippines	625	1,676	1,051
Singapore	1,453	9,030	7,577
Taiwan (China)	1,531	1,757	226
Thailand	476	1,916	1,440
Other	88	121	33

Source: U.S. Department of Commerce (1992); Mataloni and Goldberg (1994); Mataloni (2003); and U.S. Department of Commerce, Bureau of Economic Analysis website.

toward Asia, but many Asian countries shared in it, while the gains in Latin America were more concentrated.

In industries outside manufacturing, U.S. affiliates in Developing Asia had produced a larger share of the world output of U.S. affiliates than U.S.

Table 3.4. Employment in Nonbank Affiliates of Nonbank U.S. Parents, by Country, 1989 and 2000
(Thousands of employees)

	Manufacturing affiliates			*Nonmanufacturing affiliates*		
Country	*1989*	*2000*	*Change*	*1989*	*2000*	*Change*
All countries	4,191.1	5,124.4	933.3	2,431.0	4,588.6	2,157.6
Latin American countries	1,028.7	1,298.3	269.6	279.2	746.3	467.1
South America	542.1	405.1	−137.0	106.2	405.0	298.8
Argentina	46.4	45.4	−1.0	13.9	70.0	56.1
Brazil	407.6	267.7	−139.9	32.5	147.4	114.9
Chile	8.3	21.4	13.1	10.3	46.8	36.5
Colombia	22.9	18.5	−4.4	16.5	57.9	41.4
Ecuador	6.4	7.7	1.3	2.9	6.1	3.2
Peru	3.4	6.3	2.9	10.4	19.1	8.7
Venezuela	43.6	34.0	−9.6	16.5	46.7	30.2
Central America	470.3	868.0	397.7	143.2	302.4	159.2
Costa Rica	9.8	14.2	4.4	13.8	11.2	-2.6
Honduras	6.9	14.1	7.2	14.6	7.6	-7.0
Mexico	443.5	821.5	378.0	83.7	244.8	161.1
Panama	2.3	3.7	1.4	18.0	—	—
Asia and Pacific, excluding Australia, Japan, and New Zealand	454.0	816.9	362.9	157.3	429.7	272.4
China	9.5	222.8	213.3	1.1	69.8	68.7
Hong Kong (China)	50.0	39.9	−10.1	28.9	60.1	31.2
India	35.3	66.6	31.3	2.6	33.2	30.6
Indonesia	8.9	30.3	21.4	29.9	43.0	13.1
Korea, Republic of	59.6	58.3	−1.3	11.3	34.4	23.1
Malaysia	46.2	110.7	64.5	9.0	21.6	12.6
Philippines	81.9	61.1	−20.8	18.1	24.6	6.5
Singapore	59.9	72.0	12.1	18.5	51.4	32.9
Taiwan (China)	52.1	39.5	−12.6	13.7	48.0	34.3
Thailand	42.9	104.9	62.0	17.9	29.8	11.9
Other	7.6	10.8	3.2	6.2	13.8	7.6

— Not available.

Source: U.S. Department of Commerce (1992) and Bureau of Economic Analysis website (2000 revised estimates).

affiliates in Latin America in 1989. After that, both Latin America and Developing Asia increased their shares of U.S. affiliate output, with Latin America a little faster (Table 3.5). The gains in nonmanufacturing affiliate production were distributed quite differently from those in manufacturing. The absolute increase was greater in Latin America than in Asia, and Brazil, which lost heavily as a location for U.S. affiliate manufacturing output, gained substantially outside of manufacturing, even more than Mexico. Argentina and Venezuela in Latin America, and Hong Kong (China) and Indonesia in Developing Asia, also showed large increases in output, a mixture of oil and other industry gains.

The contrast between manufacturing and nonmanufacturing affiliates is even stronger in employment than in gross product, and the regional story is somewhat different. Employment in U.S. nonmanufacturing affiliates worldwide grew by almost 90 percent; in manufacturing the growth was only about 22 percent (Table 3.4). Affiliate employment in Latin America was larger than that in Developing Asia in 1989, even though gross output was larger in Asia, but the rates of growth were similar in the two regions. The absolute growth was larger in five Latin American countries than in any Asian country except China, and three Latin American countries had more nonmanufacturing affiliate employment in 2000 than any Developing Asian country. Thus, the shift in U.S. affiliate activity toward Asia was reflected in manufacturing activity and not in nonmanufacturing activity.

U.S. Affiliates in Host-Country Output

Since host countries vary enormously in size, the impact of the activity of U.S. affiliates on the host economies is likely to be related more to their shares in the total host-country economies than to the total size of the affiliates. One measure of this role is the share of affiliate output in total national output, as measured by gross domestic product (GDP). We can make that comparison only for majority-owned foreign affiliates (MOFAs) because the data necessary for the calculation of affiliate gross product are collected only for them. Another measure is the share of affiliate employment in total employment or labor force.

Table 3.6 shows U.S. affiliate shares of national output in 1989 and 2000 for developing countries in Latin America and Asia. There were some reductions in U.S. penetration in Latin America, but none in Asia. The unweighted average of the changes among the Latin American countries in the table was 0.2 percent of GDP. In the ten Asian countries, the unweighted

Table 3.5. *Gross Product of Nonbank Nonmanufacturing MOFAs of U.S. Nonbank Parents, by Country, 1989 and 2000*
(Millions of U.S. dollars)

Country	*1989*	*2000*	*Change*
All countries	147,986	288,549	140,563
Latin American countries	6,560	24,598	18,038
South America	4,957	18,852	13,895
Argentina	604	3,730	3,126
Brazil	2,451	6,679	4,228
Chile	317	2,226	1,909
Colombia	500	1,992	1,492
Ecuador	235	290	55
Peru	307	1,002	695
Venezuela	227	2,382	2,155
Central America	1,602	5,747	4,145
Costa Rica	109	127	18
Guatemala	89	—	—
Honduras	182	136	–46
Mexico	760	4,689	3,929
Panama	348	304	–44
Asia and Pacific, excluding Australia, Japan, and New Zealand	10,888	27,479	16,591
China	–28	1,118	1,146
Hong Kong (China)	2,175	6,817	4,642
India	–4	792	796
Indonesia	3,899	6,095	2,196
Korea, Republic of	263	1,889	1,626
Malaysia	1,272	1,825	553
Philippines	381	910	529
Singapore	900	2,855	1,955
Taiwan (China)	407	2,147	1,740
Thailand	1,339	1,890	551
Other	284	1,142	858

— Not available.

Source: U.S. Department of Commerce (1992); Mataloni and Goldberg (1994); and U.S Department of Commerce, Bureau of Economic Analysis website.

average was 0.8 percent, paced by the jump to 11.6 percent in Singapore, the highest U.S. penetration ratio among these countries.

The 2000 average for both sets of countries was about 3.5 percent. The lowest ratios were for Taiwan, Korea, China, and India, all lower than any

Table 3.6. Output and Employment of U.S. Affiliates Relative to Host-Country Economies, 1989 and 2000

Country	Gross product of MOFAs of nonbank U.S. parents as percentage of host-country GDP			Employment of U.S. nonbank affiliates as percentage of host-country labor force		
	1989	2000	Change	1989	2000	Change
Latin America						
Argentina	2.1	2.5	0.4	0.50	0.79	0.29
Brazil	3.7	3.3	–0.4	0.69	0.51	–0.18
Chile	2.5	3.9	1.4	0.38	1.09	0.71
Colombia	2.9	3.5	0.6	0.29	0.37	0.08
Costa Rica	4.0	3.3	–0.7	2.11	1.67	–0.47
Ecuador	2.8	2.8	0.0	0.27	0.27	0.00
Honduras	8.1	6.0	–2.1	1.33	0.89	–0.44
Mexico	2.2	3.5	1.2	1.77	2.60	0.83
Peru	1.9	2.1	0.2	0.19	0.26	0.07
Venezuela	1.7	2.8	1.1	0.86	0.82	–0.04
Asia						
China	0.0	0.5	0.5	0.00	0.04	0.04
Hong Kong (China)	4.4	5.1	0.7	2.74	2.90	0.16
India	0.1	0.4	0.3	0.01	0.02	0.01
Indonesia	3.9	4.2	0.3	0.05	0.07	0.02
Korea, Republic of	0.3	0.9	0.6	0.37	0.36	–0.01
Malaysia	4.5	4.9	0.4	0.80	1.31	0.51
Philippines	2.4	3.2	0.8	0.42	0.25	–0.17
Singapore	7.9	11.6	3.7	5.28	6.04	0.76
Taiwan (China)	1.3	1.3	0.0	0.78	0.88	0.10
Thailand	2.5	3.1	0.6	0.20	0.39	0.19

Source: World Bank (2002), Taiwan (China), National Statistics of Taiwan Database, under website for China, Republic of; Mataloni and Goldberg (1994); and U.S. Department of Commerce, Bureau of Economic Analysis website.

in Latin America. The penetration ratios for China and India, at around 0.5 percent, put the gains of the 1990s in perspective; these are countries where U.S. firms still play an exceptionally small role in the economy as a whole.

U.S. affiliate penetration in terms of employment was much lower than in production. The ratio was below 1 percent, on average, for Latin America, and only a little over 1 percent for Asian countries. The highest ratio was for Singapore (6 percent), followed by Hong Kong (about 3 percent) and Mexico (2.6 percent). The average increase for the Latin American countries was about 0.8 percent and among the Developing Asian countries, almost twice as high.

Determinants of World and U.S. Affiliate Production Location

The determinants of the location of FDI can be viewed from the home-country side or the host-country side. Firms in a home country are searching for the most profitable host-country locations for their foreign operations, or operations of various types or in various industries. Some of the characteristics of a host country are permanent or slowly changing such as its closeness to the home country or to other markets, its size (in population and area), its income level, and its social, political, and legal institutions. Other characteristics, such as rates of economic growth in the host country or its neighbors, can fluctuate rapidly. Host-country policies, such as rules for allowing inward investment or subsidizing it, discriminatory or national treatment of foreign firms, labor regulations, openness to trade, and membership in regional economic groupings, also are changeable.

From the perspective of the host country, which is seeking to encourage inward investment, or certain types of investment, or even to discourage it, the permanent characteristics, such as size, are of little interest. Furthermore, the impact of inward FDI on the host country depends on its size relative to the host-country economy, as measured by its GDP, population, or labor force.

Because there are these two points of view, we analyze the determinants of FDI in two ways. To represent the home-country view, we explain absolute levels of FDI production, employment, and fixed assets. To represent the host-country viewpoint, we explain levels of FDI relative to host-country GDP, population, or labor force.

Table 3.7 relates world direct investment stocks in and flows to all developing countries in the 1990s to a few explanatory variables. The novel variable here is the measure called residual openness. The standard measure of openness, used in many studies, is the ratio of trade (the sum of exports and imports) to output (GDP). That measure is defective as an indicator of policy because it is greatly affected by country size. In the case of two countries with similar trade regimes, the country that is larger, in terms of population and land area, will have a smaller ratio of trade to output. In order to remove this effect, and to come closer to a measure of trade policy, we calculate a measure described as residual openness.

Table 3.7. *Determinants of World FDI in Developing Countries*

Dependent variable	*Independent variables*							*Adjusted*		*No. of*
			Rate of GDP per capita growth			*Residual openness*[b]				
	GDP in 1990 in 1995 US$[a]	*Real GDP, 1995*[a]	*1986–90*	*1991–95*	*1996–2000*	*1990*	*1995*	R^2	*Prob. F*	*observations*
Absolute[a]										
FDI inflows, 1996–2000		5.0468***		0.0240			15.99***	0.7147	<0.0001	92
		(0.381)		(0.042)			(3.429)			
FDI inflows, 1991–2000	12.626***		–0.0423			31.5654***		0.6817	<0.0001	89
	(1.024)		(0.085)			(6.123)				
FDI inward stock, 2000		0.0903***			–0.0015		0.597***	0.5357	<0.0001	91
		(0.011)			(0.001)		(0.104)			
Relative										
FDI inflows, 1996–2000		–0.6751		0.0052			50.746***	0.2879	<0.0001	92
		(0.908)		(0.101)			(8.160)			
FDI inflows, 1991–2000	–0.0008		–0.0002*			0.0508***		0.2431	<0.0001	89
	(0.002)		(0.000)			(0.009)				
FDI inward stock, 2000		–8.5424			–0.3936		618.906***			
		(8.235)			(0.787)		(79.645)			

* Significant at the 10% level.
** Significant at the 5% level.
*** Significant at the 1% level.
a. Trillions of U.S. dollars.
b. See text for explanation.
Note: The numbers in parentheses are standard errors.
Source: Author's calculations.

We fit an equation relating the crude trade ratio to population and land area. We then take the residuals from this equation, the part of crude openness not explained by population and land area, as our measure of residual openness. Although we use residual openness in all the equations that follow, the crude openness ratio does almost as well in explaining FDI as the residual openness measure.

The first two equations explain the absolute level of FDI inflows to each of about ninety host countries in the 1990s as a whole and in the last half of the decade. More than two thirds of the differences in the size of the inflows are explained by the size of each host country at the beginning of the period, as measured by real GDP, and the openness of the host country, as measured by residual openness (Table 3.7). The growth rate of the country in the preceding five-year period, as measured by the growth in real GDP per capita, was not a significant influence on a period's FDI inflow.

Cross-country differences in the stock of inward FDI in 2000 were explained, to the extent of over 50 percent, by the same pair of variables. Thus, among all the world's developing countries, the main determinants of the destinations of FDI (both the stock and flow) were country size and the openness of the economy to trade.

FDI stocks and flows relative to GDP, variables more related to the impact on host countries, are harder to explain. As shown by the second group of equations in Table 3.7, country size is not a significant influence, and the growth rate of per capita GDP is marginally significant in only one equation. Only residual openness is consistently significant, and it explains about a quarter of the differences in inflows of FDI and 40 percent of the differences in stocks. A greater degree of openness to trade is associated with more inward FDI, relative to the size of the country's economy.

For the twenty-two countries in Table 3.8, the equations are similar to those for developing countries in general in Table 3.7, with one difference: growth in GDP and GDP per capita in the previous period are significant negative influences on inward stocks and inward stocks relative to GDP in 2000 for the twenty-two countries. The negative coefficient stems from the combination for Hong Kong of slow per capita GDP growth and a very high level of inward FDI, much of which probably ended up in China. Aside from Hong Kong, there is no evidence of a negative relation between GDP growth and later inflows or stocks of FDI. GDP growth, the level of GDP, and residual openness explain between 60 percent and two thirds of the variance in inward FDI flows and stocks for the twenty-two countries.

If we try to explain inflows, stocks, and stocks as shares of host-country economies for the Latin American and Developing Asian countries separately,

Table 3.8. *Determinants of World FDI in Twenty-two Asian and Latin American Countries*

	Independent variables						
		Rate of GDP per capita growth					
Dependent variable	*Real GDP, 1995*	*1991–95*	*1996–2000*	*Residual openness, 1995*	*Adjusted* R^2	*Prob. F*	*No. of observations*
Absolute[a]							
FDI inflows, 1996–2000							
Asia	4.8876***	0.6368		36.0220**	0.7650	0.0079	10
	(1.253)	(0.502)		(13.161)			
Latin America	4.8170*	0.0550		5.8340	0.1233	0.2832	12
	(2.278)	(0.318)		(48.017)			
22 countries[b]	4.6778***	0.1305		23.5885**	0.6552	<0.0001	22
	(0.915)	(0.240)		(9.400)			
FDI inward stock, 2000							
Asia	0.1068**		–0.0259*	1.6258***	0.6326	0.0290	10
	(0.033)		(0.012)	(0.418)			
Latin America	0.1764***		0.0010	0.0712	0.9437	<0.0001	12
	(0.014)		(0.002)	(0.238)			
22 countries[b]	0.0973***		–0.0167**	1.2319***	0.5957	0.0002	22
	(0.023)		(0.007)		(0.272)		

Relative							
FDI inflows, 1996–2000							
Asia	0.2601	–0.0642		53.1665***	0.7858	0.0060	10
	(0.879)	(0.352)		(9.228)			
Latin America	–0.7481	0.6453**		84.6797**	0.3819	0.0803	12
	(1.640)	(0.229)		(34.574)			
22 countries	–1.0663	0.0827		34.4602***	0.4446	0.0033	22
	(0.834)	(0.219)		(8.566)			
FDI inward stock, 2000							
Asia	8.5045		–13.4537**	949.5121***	0.7525	0.0092	10
	(14.249)		(5.071)	(181.868)			
Latin America	–11.3986		1.0708	331.5924	–0.1216	0.6315	12
	(19.583)		(3.417)	(329.462)			
22 countries[b]	–0.4395		–8.9013**	776.3065***	0.6644	<0.0001	22
	(10.024)		(3.267)	(120.560)			

* Significant at the 10% level.
** Significant at the 5% level.
*** Significant at the 1% level.
a. Trillions of U.S. dollars.
b. See Table 3.5 for a listing of the twenty-two countries in Latin America and Asia.
Source: Author's calculations.

some substantial differences emerge, despite the small numbers of observations. These standard variables explain the ratios of FDI flows and stocks to GDP far better for the Asian countries than for the Latin American ones. They explained over three quarters of the variance in flows to Developing Asia during the late 1990s, almost two thirds of the variance in inward stocks, and three quarters of the variance in inward stocks relative to GDP in 2000. For Latin American countries, none of the variables explained the stocks of inward FDI relative to GDP in 2000. The nominal stock in 2000 was almost completely explained by country size. And flows from 1995 to 2000 were explained slightly, but not to a significant degree, by growth in the previous five years. If the openness measure represents policy toward trade, variation among the countries in trade policies, often combined with other similar policies, determined the attractiveness of Developing Asian countries to direct investors but had no influence on investment in Latin America.

U.S. data on foreign direct investment provide much more information on the actual operations of affiliates than do the data available for the world's FDI, with the drawback that they represent only one country's choices of locations for its affiliate production. Table 3.9 relates two measures of U.S. affiliate activity—(1) employment and (2) property, plant, and equipment (PP&E)—to host-country characteristics. Both are pretty certain to be in the host country, unlike the world flow and stock data, which may represent production and employment in a different country.

The location of total U.S. affiliate employment within Asia and Latin America was determined mainly by the size of the host country, with residual openness also playing a role in Asia. The location of PP&E in Asia was not explained significantly by any of these variables, although openness was marginally significant, but country size almost totally explained location within Latin America. In manufacturing industries, again, country size determined employment, with no role for other factors. The location of PP&E in Asia was affected only by the rate of growth in the previous five years, while in Latin America, country size was the only significant influence. The generally stronger role of country size in determining location in Latin America, and of country openness in Developing Asia, suggests a different balance of motivations for investors in the two regions. Latin American affiliates were probably not selected with the ability of the affiliate to export as a major consideration. This factor was probably more important for investors in Asia. And U.S. affiliates in Asia are, in fact, much more export oriented than U.S. affiliates in Latin America.

The measures of employment and fixed capital relative to labor force and GDP (Table 3.10) should tell more about the impact of FDI on individ-

Table 3.9. *Coefficients of Equations Explaining Employment and Property, Plant, and Equipment (P.P.E.) of U.S. Affiliates in Latin America and Developing Asia, 2000*

Dependent variable	Independent variables: Real GDP, 1995[a]	Independent variables: Rate of GDP per capita growth, 1996–2000	Independent variables: Residual openness, 1995	Adjusted R^2	Prob. F	No. of observations
All industries						
Employment						
Asia	45.137**	–1.7324	365.9316*	0.5840	0.0415	10
	(12.671)	(4.509)	(161.729)			
Latin	469.6728**	40.2701	1806.6493	0.5109	0.0468	11
America	(178.625)	(30.333)	(3034.268)			
P.P.E.						
Asia	0.0013	–0.0003	0.0285*	0.1354	0.3142	10
	(0.001)	(0.000)	(0.014)			
Latin	0.0255***	0.0007	–0.0440	0.9117	0.0001	11
America	(0.003)	(0.001)	(0.050)			
Manufacturing industries						
Employment						
Asia	37.0197**	–0.7675	231.7432	0.3506	0.1456	10
	(14.290)	(5.085)	(182.393)			
Latin	367.6879**	30.0223	1884.6923	0.4796	0.0575	11
America	(145.787)	(24.757)	(2476.451)			
P.P.E.						
Asia	0.0005	0.0006**	0.0095	0.5873	0.0406	10
	(0.001)	(0.000)	(0.008)			
Latin	0.0141***	0.0006	0.0379	0.7802	0.0031	11
America	(0.003)	(0.000)	(0.047)			

* Significant at the 10% level.
** Significant at the 5% level.
*** Significant at the 1% level.
Note: The numbers in parentheses are standard errors.
Source: Author's calculations.

ual host countries. None of the variables explains the ratio of fixed capital to GDP, but the U.S. affiliate employment share of the labor force in Asian host countries in 2000 is explained, to the extent of over 90 percent, by real GDP in 1995, the rate of growth in real GDP per capita from 1995 to 2000, and residual openness. In this case, the coefficient for country size is negative;

Table 3.10. *Coefficients of Equations Explaining Employment Relative to Labor Force and Property, Plant, and Equipment Relative to GDP of U.S. Affiliates in Latin America and Developing Asia, 2000*

	Independent variables					
Dependent variable	*Real GDP, 1995*[a]	*Rate of GDP per capita growth, 1996–2000*	*Residual openness, 1995*	*Adjusted* R^2	*Prob. F*	*No. of observations*
All industries						
Employment relative to labor force						
Asia	–0.5594**	0.2384**	13.9335***	0.9223	0.0003	10
	(0.184)	(0.065)	(2.346)			
Latin America	–0.1473	0.1984**	13.4842*	0.5888	0.0262	11
	(0.397)	(0.067)	(6.740)			
P.P.E. relative to GDP						
Asia	–1.3518	0.0373	23.6424	0.3754	0.1307	10
	(1.043)	(0.371)	(13.318)			
Latin America	–3.8941	0.1545	28.3895	–0.0485	0.5111	11
	(3.038)		(0.516)		(51.610)	
Manufacturing industries						
Employment relative to labor force						
Asia	–0.3808**	0.1899***	6.8479***	0.9044	0.0006	10
	(0.122)	(0.044)	(1.562)			
Latin America	0.3063	0.1024	10.2240	0.3196	0.1375	11
	(0.394)	(0.067)	(6.687)			
P.P.E. relative to GDP						
Asia	–1.1158	0.5532**	10.2075	0.6359	0.0283	10
	(0.601)	(0.214)	(7.674)			
Latin America	0.9514	0.0568	36.2228**	0.4696	0.0612	11
	(0.712)	(0.121)	(12.096)			

* Significant at the 10% level.
** Significant at the 5% level.
*** Significant at the 1% level.
Note: The numbers in parentheses are standard errors.
Source: Author's calculations.

although larger countries attract more inward FDI, the affiliate share of the labor force is smaller in the larger countries. Among Latin American countries, size is not a significant influence, but the growth rate is significant and the degree of openness, marginally so.

In manufacturing industries, country size, again with a negative coefficient, and the rate of growth and openness, with positive coefficients, influence U.S. affiliate location in the Asian countries, and they explain almost all of the variation among them. None of them is significant for Latin America. The equations for PP&E in manufacturing affiliates are different; openness is a significant positive influence in Latin America, but not in Asia, where only the rate of growth appears significant.

The location of U.S. affiliate employment relative to the labor force in Asia is strongly and positively affected by the degree of openness of the economy; location in Latin America is influenced much less. Only in the location of plant and equipment, and only in manufacturing, is there a clear sign of the influence of openness in Latin American location decisions.

Latin America vs. Developing Asia as FDI Locations

The determinants of foreign direct investment by the United States appear to be different for Latin America and Developing Asia. Investment in Latin America is more affected by host-country size and rate of growth, and that in Asia more by the openness of the host economy. Furthermore, there has been a shift of U.S. direct investment in manufacturing toward Asia and away from Latin America other than Mexico. What characteristics of the two regions could account for the shift or the differences in determinants?

The political and economic institutions of the two regions differ. These differences, or the perception of such differences on the part of investors, could be a factor. Table 3.11 compares Latin America and Developing Asia with respect to business costs, governance indicators, and "doing business" indicators. Developing Asia excluding China is superior to Latin America on several measures. For example, among fifteen indicators of the cost of doing business, fourteen show an advantage for Developing Asia over Latin America. Other institutional comparisons give similar results.

These differences may help to explain why there has been a movement toward investment in Asia, but how might they account for apparent differences in determinants? A hint is provided in Table 3.12. It shows the correlation between the residual openness measure, which is supposed to represent trade policy, and various institutional indicators. In almost every case, residual openness is much more strongly correlated with the institutional indicators in

Table 3.11. *Business Costs, Governance Indicators, and "Doing Business" Indicators for Latin America and Developing Asia*

Indicator	*Latin America*	*Developing Asia, excluding China*	*China*	*Higher(+) or lower(–) favorable*[a]
Business costs indicators				
Soundness of banks	4.4	4.7	4.0	+
Regulatory obstacles to business	4.6	4.3	3.5	–
Hidden trade barriers	4.1	4.8	4.9	+
Cost of importing foreign equipment	3.0	2.1	2.3	–
Technological sophistication	3.3	4.3	3.9	+
Quality of scientific research institutions	3.5	4.5	4.4	+
Quality of math and science education	3.3	4.8	4.1	+
Efficiency of legal framework	2.8	4.3	4.4	+
Property rights	3.8	5.0	4.1	+
Intellectual property protection	3.1	4.1	3.6	+
Burden of regulation	2.2	3.2	3.3	+
Extent of bureaucratic red tape	2.8	3.0	3.0	–
Irregular payments in exports & imports	4.3	4.6	5.1	+
Frequency of payments or bribes	3.5	4.6	5.2	+
Business cost of corruption	3.9	4.7	4.4	+
Governance indicators				
Voice and Accountability 2000	0.2	0.2	–1.4	+
Political Stability 2000	–0.1	0.2	0.3	+
Government Effectiveness 2000	–0.1	0.7	0.2	+
Regulatory Quality 2000	0.5	0.7	–0.2	+
Rule of Law 2000	–0.2	0.6	–0.3	+
Control of Corruption 2000	–0.2	0.4	–0.3	+
"Doing business" indicators				
No. of procedures to start business	12.3	9.0	11	–
Duration of starting business	73.8	54.2	46	–
Employment Laws Index	66.3	45.4	47	–
Procedural Complexity Index	73.7	52.4	52	–
Creditor Rights Index	1.3	2.4	2	+
Goals of Insolvency Index	43.2	58.8	51	+
Court Powers Index	61.3	62.9	67	+

a. Given the way countries were ranked, (+) means that a higher value is favorable for inward FDI, and (–) means that a lower value is favorable for inward FDI.

Source: For business costs, World Economic Forum (2003); for governance indicators, Kaufmann, Kraay, and Mastruzzi, (2003); for "doing business" indicators, World Bank (2003).

Table 3.12. Correlation between Residual Openness and Host-Country Institutional Characteristics, Latin America and Developing Asia

Indicator	*Latin America*	*Developing Asia*
Business costs indicators		
Soundness of banks	0.3	0.8
Regulatory obstacles to business	–0.1	–0.2
Hidden trade barriers	–0.1	0.8
Cost of importing foreign equipment	–0.2	–0.7
Technological sophistication	0.0	0.5
Quality of scientific research institutions	0.1	0.2
Quality of math and science education	0.0	0.6
Efficiency of legal framework	0.3	0.8
Property rights	0.4	0.7
Intellectual property protection	0.2	0.7
Burden of regulation	0.1	0.9
Extent of bureaucratic red tape	0.0	–0.5
Irregular payments in exports & imports	–0.2	0.6
Frequency of payments or bribes	0.1	0.3
Business cost of corruption	0.3	0.8
Governance indicators		
Voice and Accountability 2000	0.4	–0.4
Political Stability 2000	0.5	0.7
Government Effectiveness 2000	0.2	0.8
Regulatory Quality 2000	0.3	0.8
Rule of Law 2000	0.1	0.8
Control of Corruption 2000	0.2	0.8
"Doing business" indicators		
No. of procedures to start business	–0.4	–0.8
Duration of starting business	–0.1	–0.6
Employment Laws Index	–0.1	–0.9
Procedural Complexity Index	0.0	–0.3
Creditor Rights Index	0.5	0.5
Goals of Insolvency Index	–0.5	0.5
Court Powers Index	0.4	–0.4

Source: For business costs, World Economic Forum (2003); for governance indicators, Kaufmann, Kraay, and Mastruzzi, (2003); for "doing business" indicators, World Bank (2003).

Asia than in Latin America, positively correlated with the indicators for which a high value was favorable for investment and negatively correlated with those for which a low value was favorable. The result of this relationship is that in the regressions among Asian host countries, higher openness

Table 3.13. Exports as Percentage of Sales in U.S. Majority-Owned Foreign Affiliates, 1977, 1989, and 2000

	All industries		Manufacturing	
Year	Developing Asia	Latin America	Developing Asia	Latin America
1977	60.9	36.8	57.0	9.7
1989	51.0	35.6	59.7	22.0
2000	43.1	35.9	57.3	38.6

Source: U.S. Department of Commerce (1992) and Bureau of Economic Analysis website.

represents not only trade policy, but also a combination of other institutional factors favorable for inward direct investment. In Latin America this relationship is much weaker; greater openness is less likely to be accompanied by institutional characteristics attractive to foreign investors. The close relationship between trade openness and favorable institutional characteristics makes it difficult to observe the effects of the latter.

The differences between Latin America and Developing Asia in trade policy are reflected in the exporting behavior of U.S. affiliates in these two groups of countries (Table 3.13). These differences were particularly large in 1977. Majority-owned U.S. manufacturing affiliates in Developing Asia exported 57 percent of their sales and those in Latin America, less than 10 percent. Since that time, manufacturing affiliates in Latin America have steadily become more export oriented, but in 2000 they were still making more than 60 percent of their sales in their host countries, while manufacturing affiliates in Developing Asia continued to export almost 60 percent of their sales.

Latin American affiliates in all industries combined were also less export oriented than those in Developing Asia, making about a third of their sales abroad throughout the period. Affiliates in Developing Asia made 60 percent of their sales abroad in 1977 and only 43 percent in 2000. Thus, there was some convergence between the two regions, but in this case it took place through changes in Developing Asia affiliates.

U.S. Foreign Direct Investment during and after the Crisis

U.S. FDI flows to Asian countries during and after the crisis remained positive. Unlike bank lending and portfolio flows, they did not turn negative in any year (Table 3.14). The inflow did decline sharply in 1998, but a year later it was above its previous peak. It has been on a rising trend since then,

Table 3.14. *U.S. FDI Capital Flows to and Operations in Developing Asia, 1996–2002*
(Millions of U.S. dollars unless otherwise indicated)

Year	*Total FDI flows* (1)	*FDI flows except retained earnings* (2)	*Sales by MOFAs* (3)	*Gross product of MOFAs* (4)	*Capital expenditures by MOFAs* (5)	*Employment in MOFAs (thousands)* (6)
1996	10,714	3,552	198,507	40,494	9,459	722
1997	11,038	4,790	219,577	42,362	10,635	841
1998	7,667	3,507	204,711	36,087	10,376	837
1999	15,468	12,064	237,988	49,276	11,311	1,021
2000	17,543	5,450	292,893	56,239	12,140	1,061
2001	12,562	3,667	292,130	52,339	12,083	1,074
2002	20,674	4,789	—	—	—	—

— Not available.

Source: Columns 1 and 2: for 1999–2002, U.S. Department of Commerce (2003, 122–25); for 1996–98, Bureau of Economic Analysis website. Columns 3–6: for 2000–01, Mataloni (2003); for 1999, Mataloni (2002); for 1996–98, U.S. Department of Commerce (1999, 2000, and 2002).

interrupted by the U.S. recession in 2001. By 2002 it was again well above the pre-recession level and almost double the flow in 1996.

In most established FDI locations, much of the FDI inflow is in the form of retained earnings. When these fall, as they did in the crisis, the inflows of FDI fall with it. Since the retained earnings for an individual year probably reflect host-country conditions more than any planned strategy of the investors, the flow of funds other than retained earnings is more revealing of investing firms' long-term intentions. These inflows did fall by more than a quarter in 1998, but they quickly recovered and surpassed their earlier levels until the 2001 recession. Thus, the more "discretionary" part of the U.S. FDI flow gave no indication of any long-term retreat of U.S. firms from Asia.

Whatever the measure of financial flows that is observed, it has no necessary relation to the activities of U.S. affiliates in the host countries. It is these activities—such as sales, production, employment, and capital expenditure—that impinge directly on host-country populations and host-country development. The financial flows could affect these real activities of the affiliates, but they may not. They may represent mainly changes in the way the multinational chooses to finance its activities, without affecting the activities themselves.

Sales by U.S. affiliates in Developing Asia fell by 7 percent between 1997 and 1998. By 1999 they were already above the 1997 level, and the growth continued into 2000. The U.S. recession in 2001 barely affected affiliate sales. The financial crisis thus brought only a pause in the long-term growth of affiliate sales. In 2001 sales by majority-owned foreign affiliates, measured in U.S. dollars, were more than a quarter larger than those in 1996 and 1998, despite the large fall in the value of the Indonesian currency.

Sales are not an appropriate measure of production because they include the value of goods bought from others, including U.S. parents and local suppliers. A better measure of production is the affiliate's gross product, essentially value added within the firm.

Gross product of U.S. affiliates in Developing Asia fell by 15 percent between 1997 and 1998, a sharper decline than for sales, to 10 percent below the 1996 level. After 1998, the lowest point, it recovered rapidly, by over a third in one year. By 2000 the gross product of these affiliates had reached almost 30 percent above the 1996 level. The U.S. recession in 2001 did bring a decline in gross product of 7 percent, much more than in sales, suggesting that either wages or profits must have declined.

All of these measures suffer from uncertainty about the effects of inflation and of currency fluctuations and translations into U.S. dollars. An alternative, not the most carefully reported by respondents but at least free of inflation and currency fluctuation problems, is employment in the affiliates. Their employment peaked in 1997 and dropped by only 1 percent the next year. It was above the previous peak by 1999 but then fell again and has been fluctuating around the 1997 level.

The best indicator of the future role envisioned by the U.S. multinationals in Developing Asia is the path of capital expenditures. Multinationals disillusioned with the future of a region could stop acquiring plant and equipment there. They could then continue the response by remaining content with their current capital stock or by trying to sell part of it off, although in an unfavorable market.

In fact, the affiliates, in the aggregate, did neither. Capital expenditures decreased by a very small amount in 1998 and then quickly resumed their rising trend. Affiliate capital expenditures in 2000 were almost 40 percent higher than in 1996, before the crisis.

The numbers for capital expenditures may understate the expansion of productive facilities in the Asian countries. In several of the countries, although not all, there were severe currency depreciations. The prices of capital goods, to the extent that they were purchased locally, must have fallen when they were expressed in U.S. dollars. Capital expenditures after the crisis must understate the amount of capital acquired by U.S. affiliates and the expectations of their parent firms.

Conclusions

During the 1990s, U.S. direct investment shifted to developing countries, and direct investment within the developing countries increasingly shifted to Developing Asia.

The location of direct investment flows and stocks from all investing countries seems to be determined mainly by two variables. One is the size of the country, and the other is its openness to trade. Flows and stocks relative to GDP are not related to country size but mainly to openness.

There are large differences between host countries in Latin America and those in Asia with respect to the determinants of inward FDI. The Asian countries' inflows seem to be related to their trade openness, while inflows to Latin American host countries are more frequently related to country size and the rate of growth. Openness in Asian countries is closely correlated with a wide variety of favorable institutional characteristics, making it difficult to distinguish the effects of these characteristics from those of openness itself. There is no similar close relationship in Latin America. The correlation between openness and other characteristics suggests, but does not prove, that openness in the Asian countries is part of a much broader program of institutional incentives aimed at attracting FDI, particularly export-oriented FDI.

There is probably a connection between the greater openness of developing economies in Asia and the shift of U.S. manufacturing investment toward them. Increased fragmentation of manufacturing production probably places a premium on a combination of openness, ease of both exporting and importing, minimal red tape, high-quality physical infrastructure, and high-quality governance. Most developing countries in Asia seem to rank higher on openness and these other characteristics than their competitors for FDI in other parts of the developing world. The higher ranking of the developing countries in Asia in these respects may account, at least partly, for the fact that U.S. affiliates in Developing Asia are more export oriented than those in Latin America.

While capital flows to Asia dropped sharply during the crisis, they recovered quite quickly, especially the flows other than retained earnings. Measures of affiliate activity (such as sales, gross product, and employment) fell by much less than the capital flows and recovered the next year. The strongest sign of a maintained interest in producing in Asia was the quick recovery in capital expenditures by U.S. affiliates, signaling a continuation of production shifts into the future. Even the U.S. recession in 2001 produced only a slight dip in affiliate capital expenditures.

References

Kaufmann, Daniel, Aart Kraay, and Massimo Mastruzzi. 2003. "Governance Indicators." See http://info.worldbank.org/governance/kkz2002/tables.asp.

Mataloni, Raymond J., Jr. 2002. "U.S. Multinational Companies: Operations in 2000." *Survey of Current Business*, vol. 82, no. 12 (December): 111–13. Washington, D.C.: Bureau of Economic Analysis.

———. 2003. "U.S. Multinational Companies: Operations in 2001." *Survey of Current Business*, vol. 83, no. 11 (November): 85–105. Washington, D.C.: Bureau of Economic Analysis.

Mataloni, Raymond J., Jr., and Lee Goldberg. 1994. "Gross Product of U.S. Multinational Companies, 1977-91." *Survey of Current Business*, vol. 74, no. 2, pp. 42–53.

Mataloni, Raymond J., Jr., and Mahnaz Fahim-Nader. 1996. "Operations of U.S. Multinational Companies: Preliminary Results from the 1994 Benchmark Survey." *Survey of Current Business*, vol. 76, no. 12 (December): 11–37. Washington, D.C.: Bureau of Economic Analysis.

Taiwan (China). See National Statistics of Taiwan Database under website for China, Republic of. See also http://www.stat.gov.tw.

U.S. Department of Commerce. 1953. *Direct Private Foreign Investments of the United States: Census of 1950*. Balance of Payments Division, Office of Business Economics, Washington, D.C.

———. 1992. *U.S. Direct Investment Abroad: Benchmark Survey, 1989*. Bureau of Economic Analysis, Washington, D.C. October.

———. 1997. "Detail for Historical-Cost Position and Related Capital and Income Flows, 1996." *Survey of Current Business*, vol. 77, no. 9, pp. 119–48.

———. 1999. *U.S. Direct Investment Abroad: Operations of U.S. Parent Companies and their Foreign Affiliates, Revised 1996 Estimates*. Bureau of Economic Analysis, Washington, D.C. July

———. 2000. *U.S. Direct Investment Abroad: Operations of U.S. Parent Companies and their Foreign Affiliates, Revised 1997 Estimates*. Bureau of Economic Analysis, Washington, D.C. August.

———. 2002. *U.S. Direct Investment Abroad: Operations of U.S. Parent Companies and their Foreign Affiliates, Revised 1998 Estimates*. Bureau of Economic Analysis, Washington, D.C. February.

———. 2003. "U.S. Direct Investment Abroad: Detail for Historical-Cost Position and Related Capital and Income Flows, 2002." *Survey of Current Business*, vol. 83, no. 9, pp. 96–149.

———. 2004a. *U.S. Direct Investment Abroad: 1999 Benchmark Survey, Final Results*. Bureau of Economic Analysis, Washington, D.C.

———. 2004b. *U.S. Direct Investment Abroad: Operations of U.S. Parent Companies and their Foreign Affiliates, Preliminary 2000 Estimates.* Bureau of Economic Analysis, Washington, D.C.

———. 2004c. *U.S. Direct Investment Abroad: Balance of Payments and Direct Investment Position Estimates, 1982-2001.* Bureau of Economic Analysis, Washington, D.C.

U.S. Department of Commerce. Bureau of Economic Analysis. website, http://www.bea.gov/bea/ai/iidguide.htm#SRVS.

World Bank. 2002. World Development Indicators CD-ROM. Washington, D.C.

———. 2003. "Doing Business Indicators." Rapid Response Unit, http://rru.worldbank.org/DoingBusiness.

World Economic Forum. 2003. *The Global Competitiveness Report, 2002–2003.* New York and Oxford: Oxford University Press.

4

Hong Kong as a Source of FDI: Experience and Significance

Edward K. Y. Chen

Hong Kong (China) was probably the first developing economy to undertake significant and sustained foreign direct investment (FDI) in other countries/economies. This should not be a surprise, however, since Hong Kong was the first developing economy to achieve successful industrialization through export-oriented strategies.

FDI from Developing Economies: The Case of Hong Kong

The emergence of developing-country FDI or transnational corporations (TNCs) is related to the Flying Geese Hypothesis (Akamatsu 1962; Chen 1991) that says that economies in a region will undertake a subregional industrial division of labor. More industrialized economies will pass on their mature industries to the next tier of economies via FDI in the face of changing comparative advantage. Japan was the first to pass on industries such as textiles and clothing and electronic and electrical products to the then newly industrializing economies of Hong Kong, Singapore, Taiwan (China), and the Republic of Korea. Hong Kong in the 1970s was the first developing economy to pass on its mature industries to other developing economies. Hong Kong manufacturing firms that undertook FDI in the 1970s were therefore among the first of the so-called third world TNCs (Chen 1981; Chen 1983b). Table 4.1 presents a rough estimate of Hong Kong's FDI as early as 1981.

Table 4.1. *FDI Outflows from Hong Kong to Developing Economies, 1981*
(US$millions)

Host economy	*Cumulated amount of FDI*
Indonesia	400
Malaysia	130
Taiwan (China)	280
China	280
Singapore	230
Other[a]	500
Total	1,820

a. Includes the Philippines, Thailand, Vietnam, Bangladesh, and Mauritius.
Source: Chen (1983b).

Foreign direct investment by Hong Kong was primarily in labor-intensive manufacturing, particularly in textiles and later in electronics. This was in line with the pattern of economic development in the Flying Geese Hypothesis: more advanced countries pass on their outdated (losing comparative advantage) industries to the next tier of countries via FDI and other forms of technology transfer. At that time, many indigenous labor-intensive industries were established in Hong Kong on the basis of technology acquired from Japan. Later, FDI from Japan, Western Europe, and the United States to Hong Kong became significant. Foreign investors in Hong Kong were also active in the hotel industry and the construction sector. With economic transformation, Hong Kong firms then began to engage in finance, retail, and other services domestically and overseas.

Hong Kong's FDI in China

Since the mid-1980s, the focus of Hong Kong's foreign direct investment has been in China, which began to open up in the late 1970s. The scope of this chapter is confined to China—with particular reference to the Guangdong Province and especially the Pearl River Delta (PRD) region that is adjacent to Hong Kong—because of the volume and significant host-country and home-country effects of Hong Kong's FDI in that country. Table 4.2 shows the rapid increase in Hong Kong's FDI in China during the first half of the 1990s.

From 1990 to 1996, more than 50 percent of FDI in China came from Hong Kong. The share began to decline as a result of China's increased openness to the world economy in trade and investment over time. China has increasingly become a major recipient of the world's FDI, at first among developing countries and now among all countries (Zhang 2001). It is estimated by the

***Table* 4.2.** *Hong Kong's FDI in China, 1990-2002*

Year	*Flows in millions of U.S. dollars*	*FDI from Hong Kong as a percentage of China's total FDI inflows*
1990	2,018	57.87
1991	2,444	55.98
1992	7,706	70.01
1993	17,609	64.00
1994	19,823	58.71
1995	20,185	53.80
1996	21,257	50.94
1997	20,632	45.59
1998	18,508	40.71
1999	16,363	40.58
2000	15,553	38.12
2001	16,955	36.23
2002	17,861	33.86

Source: State Statistical Bureau (various years).

United Nations Conference on Trade and Development (UNCTAD) that in 2005 China will overtake the United States and become the world's largest recipient of FDI (US$53 billion), accounting for 10 percent of the world's FDI inflows (compared to 8.2 percent for the United States).

China's FDI inflow statistics, however, may be exaggerated as a result of "round tripping." Because of the preferential tax treatment given by China to FDI, investment that originates from the Mainland is disguised as foreign capital and repatriated via Hong Kong and other tax havens to the Mainland. The International Finance Corporation (IFC) estimated that, in 2000, 30 percent to 50 percent of FDI in China was round tripping. It is believed that the extent of round tripping increased during the 1990s (Wu and Puah 2003). Since then round tripping may have declined. About 10 percent to 20 percent of FDI in China may be round tripping because the number of Mainland Chinese companies incorporated in Hong Kong and the tax havens have decreased significantly in the past few years (Bank of China 2003). After the Asian financial crisis, the Chinese government put in place strict and more effective measures to control unauthorized capital flows.

Hong Kong is a major intermediary for round tripping. Although the importance of Hong Kong as a source of foreign direct investment in China should be qualified by round tripping, the predominance of Hong Kong's FDI in China is unquestionable.

According to a survey conducted by the Federation of Hong Kong Industries, an estimated 63,000 companies representing 52 percent of all Hong Kong–based manufacturing and trading companies were engaged in some form of business activities in the Mainland in 2002 (Table 4.3). The economic activities of foreign companies in China can be divided into two types (Federation of Hong Kong Industries 2003). The first type is FDI. Foreign direct investment, in turn, can be classified as (1) equity joint ventures, (2) contractual joint ventures (flexibility in capital contribution, operational control, and profit sharing between the host and foreign partners), and (3) wholly owned foreign companies. The second type of economic activity is excluded from the FDI statistics. It is called other foreign investments (OFI), and it comprises "three forms of processing and assembly operations and compensatory trade" (FHKI 2003, 90) in which the foreign partner does not have legal ownership of the companies. Table 4.3 therefore goes beyond the conventional definition of FDI to show Hong Kong's business activities in China. In this chapter, the discussion (although not statistics) of Hong Kong's FDI in China generally includes OFI.

The three forms of processing and assembly operations are (1) processing with supplied materials, (2) assembly with supplied parts, and (3) processing in accordance with supplied samples. Compensation trade is an arrangement whereby a foreign company provides a loan (in money or in kind) to a Mainland Chinese enterprise to set up production. The loan is repaid by the products produced by the enterprise within an agreed period of time.

Hong Kong's FDI in China is not evenly distributed; it concentrates in the Pearl River Delta in the Guangdong Province (Figure 4.1).

Table 4.3. *Hong Kong's Manufacturing Activities in China, 2002*

Activity	*No. of companies*	*Percentage of all Hong Kong manufacturing and trading companies*
Some activities	63,000[a]	52.0
Equity controls	27,000	22.2
Management and operation controls	32,000	26.2
Subcontracted processing	28,000	23.2

a. Of the 63,000 Hong Kong companies engaging in manufacturing in China, 7,000 are manufacturing companies and 56,000 are trading companies.

Note: The total number of companies classified by type of activity is larger than 63,000 because some companies engaged in more than one type of activity.

Source: Federation of Hong Kong Industries (2003).

Figure 4.1. *The Major Cities and Counties in the Pearl River Delta in Guangdong Province, China*

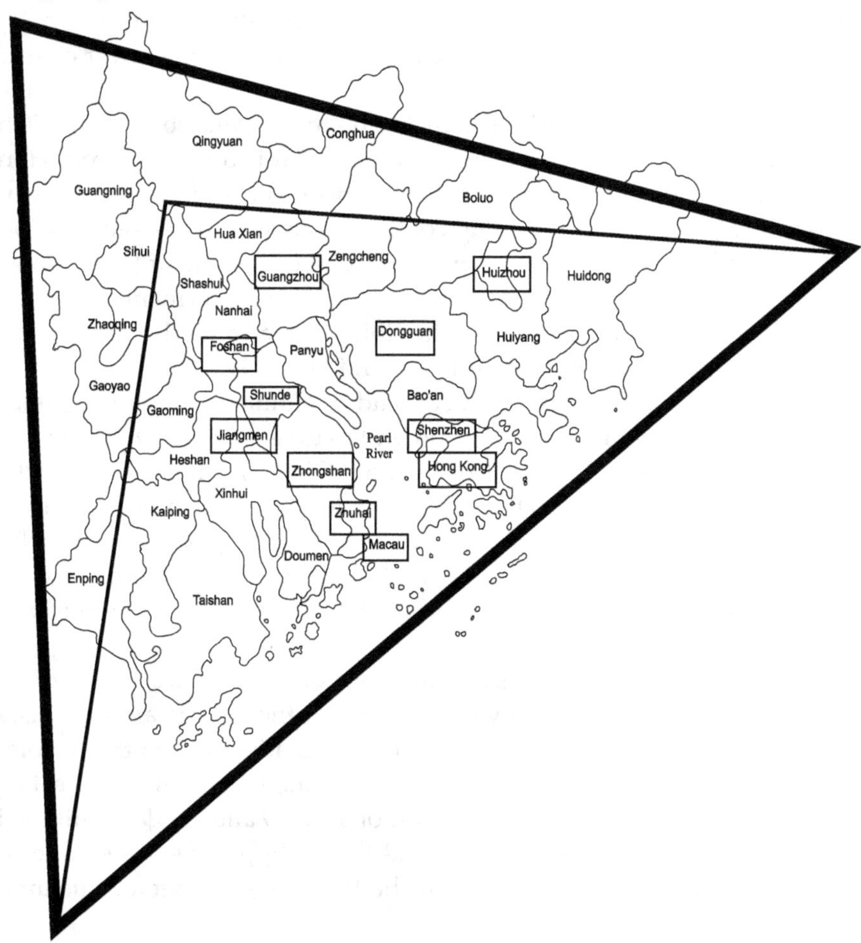

Source: Federation of Hong Kong Industries (2003).

Tuan and Ng (2003) give a detailed account of the development of this Hong Kong–PRD nexus. Of the 59,000 production facilities that Hong Kong companies have equity / management / operation controls in the Mainland, 53,300 (90.3 percent) are in Guangdong. Of these 53,300 in Guangdong, 21,300 (40 percent) are FDI and 32,000 (60 percent) are OFI. Geographically, these 53,300 enterprises are also highly concentrated.

Table 4.4 shows that Dongguan and Shenzhen are by far the most important locations for Hong Kong's foreign direct investment. Dongguan has become a major manufacturing center even though it is not a special economic zone enjoying tax and other concessions. But operating as it does on the fringe of special economic zones, Dongguan has the advantage of enjoying the infrastructural benefits of the region and yet having fewer controls imposed by the central government.

Although there are no official statistics on the original sources of FDI by Hong Kong in China, it is believed that most of it is originally from Hong Kong rather than from foreign companies incorporated in Hong Kong. Of course, many of those Hong Kong companies investing in China are joint ventures with foreign capital. As mentioned above, some of Hong Kong's FDI in China is the result of round tripping. The products manufactured by Hong Kong companies investing in China were made by Hong Kong though not made in Hong Kong (Bergen and Lester 1997).

The Pearl River Delta is the spearhead of China's economic development, and its success is largely attributed to Hong Kong's FDI. In 2001 the PRD accounted for 8.7 percent of China's GDP, and from 1995 to 2001 absorbed 24 percent of all FDI in China. In 2001 the PRD accounted for 34 percent of China's total exports—98 percent of China's exports of watches, 94 percent of China's exports of electric fans, 89 percent of China's exports of radios, 87 percent of China's exports of telephone sets, and 71 percent of China's exports of toys.

The growth of Hong Kong's FDI in other Asian countries, however, has slowed down. Hong Kong's investments in Southeast Asia after the Asian financial crisis drastically declined, as official statistics from the recipient countries reveal. Hong Kong's FDI in Indonesia, US$232 million in 1997, became a disinvestment of –US$144 million in 1999 and –US$122 million in 2000. Hong Kong's FDI in Thailand and the Philippines was less affected by the Asian financial crisis, though the trend has not been a sustained

Table 4.4. *Hong Kong's FDI in the Pearl River Delta, 2002*

City	*No. of companies*	*No. of employees (million)*
Dongguan	18,100	4.02
Shenzhen	15,700	2.58
Guangzhou	4,900	0.92
Huizhou	3,500	0.87
Zhongshan	3,000	0.61
Other	8,100	1.34
Total	53,300	10.34

Source: Federation of Hong Kong Industries (2003).

upward one. It is largely the case that Hong Kong's FDI in Asia is a zero-sum game, and China is Hong Kong's priority. The drastic increase in Hong Kong's foreign direct investment in China has been, to a large extent, at the expense of Southeast Asia. Wu and Puah (2003) argue, however, that the increase in FDI flow to China has not been at the expense of ASEAN countries in the past few years. But Hong Kong's FDI is probably different from that of other source economies. Because of geographical proximity, cultural affinity, and relatively predictable local government policies, China, especially the PRD, has been the main recipient of Hong Kong's FDI. FDI in China increased sixtyfold from 1981 to 2001.

Significant diversion of investment from China to Southeast Asia occurred immediately after the 1989 incident in Tiananmen Square. Once the political situation stabilized in China, however, Hong Kong's foreign direct investment in Southeast Asia contracted enormously. For example, Hong Kong's FDI in Thailand contracted from US$4,332 million in 1990 to only US$107 million in 1991; Hong Kong's FDI in Indonesia contracted from US$993 million in 1990 to US$278 million in 1991. By contrast, Hong Kong's FDI in China surged from US$3,680 million in 1990 to US$6,830 million in 1991.

Motivations and Determinants of FDI

In its analysis of the reasons for Hong Kong enterprises to invest in China and other host countries, this chapter relies on in-depth, unstructured discussions with the senior management of selected Hong Kong enterprises known to have made significant investments in China in the past ten to fifteen years, and in the survey results of Federation of Hong Kong Industries (2003). The management team of ten enterprises was interviewed in the following industries: electronic and telecommunications (2 enterprises); electric equipment and machinery (2 enterprises); metal products (1 enterprise), textiles (2 enterprises); garments (1 enterprise), plastics products (1 enterprise), and food processing (1 enterprise). These results are also discussed with reference to Chen (1983a and 1983b) and, of course, to the prolific literature on this subject as well.

Types of Motivations

In the literature, motivations can be divided into two groups. The first is cost minimization of production. However, the motives for cost minimization are different for export-oriented firms and import-substituting firms. For export-oriented transnational corporations, the major motive of FDI is to minimize the cost of production in every stage. As a result, production processes will take place in more than one host country depending on the maximum cost minimization that can be achieved in particular localities. The parts and semi-manufactures will then be transported to a hub for final assembly (again, the choice of location of this hub is dictated by costs) before exporting to the world (the source country itself included). This supply chain management has become a major activity of the logistics service that is now highly specialized, undertaken by a third party rather than in-house. This has been referred to as the vertical type of FDI (Shatz and Venables 2000). This type of FDI has become increasingly important because of cost reductions in transportation and communications, on the one hand, and drastic investment liberalization in many developing countries, on the other.

For import-substituting TNCs, cost minimization increases their competitiveness in the host countries, which are the final market. Cost minimization can take different forms: lower labor costs, greater accessibility to strategic resources (human capital, physical capital and technology, financial capital, natural resources), and lower transportation and distribution costs, for example. Most stages of production are, therefore, locally based for the most part. Of course, some TNCs may also export their products produced in their host countries. But today the Vertical Type of FDI with its high degree of division of labor among host countries prevails for import-substituting TNCs targeting the local market of the host country. This is because cost can be reduced by producing some of the parts and components in other host countries.

The second category of motivations is the search for markets in other parts of the world. The greatest attraction of a host country is its market size in terms of the potential purchasing power for the products the TNCs produce. There are, of course, many advantages of producing the products close to the consumers. Trade restrictions (tariff and nontariff barriers) are important considerations, especially in the past. But more important are product adaptation, customer relationship management, compliance with government regulations, taking advantage of local producer services, and achievement of dominant market shares. The primary consideration is lateral linkages in the host country.

In the case of Hong Kong's FDI in China in general and in Guangdong in particular, the predominant motivation has been the seeking of lower labor costs (Chen and Wong 1997). Hong Kong remains the location for regional headquarters responsible for product design, procurement, marketing, exporting, and financial management. Certainly, the vertical division of labor in the Hong Kong case is less sophisticated than in many developed-country

TNCs because the products are less sophisticated. But the basic pattern is the same. To a large extent, Hong Kong's FDI in China is export oriented. In 2002, on an average 71 percent of the output produced by Hong Kong's FDI and OFI was exported; 19 percent was for further processing in the Mainland; and only 10 percent was for domestic sales (Federation of Hong Kong Industries 2003). Also, it was estimated that about 50 percent of the Hong Kong TNCs in China exported 100 percent of their output. This pattern did not change much over time until very recently. The 2002 survey results were similar to those of Chen (1983b) and those of Chen and Wong (1995). Similar results are reported in Tuan and Ng (1995a and 1995b).

As discussions with the senior management of some Hong Kong enterprises suggest, this pattern may have begun to change. More and more Hong Kong TNCs in China have indicated that they will increase their domestic sales activities, move their procurement of materials to Guangdong, and also hire more local professional staff, especially engineers. In addition, some Hong Kong TNCs indicated that they will set up R & D departments in China and hire local scientific staff. It seems that Hong Kong's foreign direct investment in China has been gradually moving toward the Horizontal Type in which the TNCs try to increase their competitiveness in the host-country markets by exploiting the locational factors.

The OLI Framework

In the conventional OLI (Ownership Location Internalization) framework (Caves 1971 and Dunning 1981), the necessary condition for TNC activities is the possession of ownership advantages that can be internalized across borders. The sufficient condition is that a host country with the appropriate locational advantages is found. Otherwise, exports would be driven by the motivation of finding lower labor costs. The major reason Hong Kong selected China as a host for its FDI is the availability of labor at relatively low costs. This is not unexpected and has been confirmed by most studies. But what is debatable is the importance of such factors as cultural affinity, geographical proximity, host-government policies and incentives, and the quality of labor for the Hong Kong TNCs. In many cases, the differences in research results hinge on the sectoral differences between industries. Of course, research methodology and data sources are crucial.

Surprisingly, Cheng and Kwan (2000) find that the education variable (even if defined in different ways) is not a significant determinant of FDI flow in China. In most studies geographical proximity is a positive factor, but in one (Pan, Tse, and Li 1999), it is not significant. The reason for the difference in findings, however, is methodological. If an index were used of 1 for Hong Kong, 2 for Southeast Asia, 3 for Japan and Korea, 4 for North America, and 5 for Europe, the regression result would be distorted simply by Southeast Asian countries that are close to China but do not invest very much.

The importance of quality labor would depend on the type and nature of the industrial sector concerned. During the early period of Hong Kong's FDI and OFI in China, quality labor would understandably be of lesser importance because the industries concerned were of traditional, labor-intensive types. Similarly, cultural affinity would be more important for low-tech, small and medium-size enterprises. Hi-tech industries and enterprises would involve more formal and open transactions that count on enforceable contracts rather than relationships. Macroeconomic stability in the host country is a more important factor for large investors than for small investors. Government policy, however, is usually an important criterion for selecting a host country. A more predicable government is an advantage. But incentives are not always a major consideration.

Regions in China with Special Economic Zones (SEZs) tend to attract more FDI (Cheng and Kwan 2000). But it is difficult to delineate whether this is because of the investment incentives offered by the SEZs or because the physical infrastructure and institutions are better in those zones. Most agree that taking a developmental approach and creating an improved investment environment with better physical infrastructure and greater administrative efficiency is more of an attraction to investors than simply offering incentives (Chen 1998). In the study of FDI motivations and patterns, however, generalizations are dangerous because of the data sources and the complexity of socioeconomic variables under consideration.

American and Japanese TNCs have been compared (the Kojima-Ozawa hypothesis; see Kojima 1977 and Ozawa 1979). More recently developed-country (DC) transnational corporations and developing-country (LDC) transnational corporations have been compared in terms of motivations to invest abroad and behaviors in and therefore impacts on host countries (Chen 1983c). However, it has also been argued that the analysis of American versus Japanese TNCs or developed-country versus developing-country TNCs is not meaningful because the differences between these comparison groups are actually not the result of country-specific attributes. Rather the differences may reflect primarily the development stage of the source country, its development strategy (export-oriented or import-substituting FDI), the size of industries, the size of firms, and so on. For example, when Japan reaches the development stage of the United States, there should be little difference between Japanese and U.S. TNCs. On the basis of the above, Hong

Kong's FDI is discussed in the context of developing-country TNCs and in the context of Dunning's OLI framework/paradigm (Dunning 1981).

OWNERSHIP-SPECIFIC ADVANTAGES. Hong Kong's TNCs in China typically do not possess the whole package of ownership-specific advantages described by Kindleberger-Hymer (Hymer 1976). They usually possess only a partial package that does not include advanced technology but does include superior human resources (especially experience, skills, know-how, know-why, personal relationships that are not codified) and organizational resources (operational routine, corporate culture, organizational structure, corporate connections) (Chen 1983b; Shi 2001).

LOCATIONAL FACTORS. In most studies the gravity model applies. This is obviously true for Hong Kong's FDI in the PRD, which is adjacent to Hong Kong. The major pull factors are cultural affinity, geographical proximity, labor cost and availability, and market. The findings on the importance of labor quality are mixed. This is perhaps expected because of the heterogeneous nature of different industries and sectors. For TNCs in developed countries, it is often found that the general business environment, including the physical infrastructure and institutional advantage, is of paramount importance.

INTERNALIZATION. Internalization is less important for Hong Kong's TNCs and probably TNCs in other developing economies since these corporations usually do not engage in high-tech production involving intellectual property rights and/or contract enforcement issues. Internalization is nonetheless a consideration because in many cases the Hong Kong parent firm is engaged in product design and marketing. Internalizing these advantages is crucial for benefits derived from their FDI in China. The lesser importance of internalization is reflected in the entry mode or ownership structure or form of FDI preferred by Hong Kong's TNCs in China. The common entry mode is joint ventures (equity and contractual), although wholly owned subsidiaries are popular in some manufacturing activities. Also prevalent are new forms of FDI such as OFI, which is to say management and operation control and subcontract processing. These forms of ownership are more flexible and often mean lower risks. In 2001, 52 percent of Hong Kong's 122,809 manufacturing and trading firms had economic activities in the Mainland; of these 63,000, 43 percent had wholly owned or joint ventures, 51 percent had management and operation control, and 45 percent had made subcontract processing arrangements. The figures do not sum to 100 percent because 24.8 percent of the firms had two forms of activities and 7.1 percent had three forms.

As the lesser prevalence of wholly owned ventures and the existence of a looser vertically integrated structure suggest, the importance of internalization in the OLI framework is not as great for TNCs in Hong Kong (and perhaps for most developing-country TNCs) than it is for developed-country TNCs. These new forms of FDI were prevalent in sectors with higher business risks and in the traditional labor-intensive sectors for export processing.

Several trends are noteworthy. With the increasingly high technology and high value added production being undertaken by Hong Kong's foreign direct investors in the PRD (the production of lower market products having been relocated to north Guangdong and other adjacent lower-cost provinces), wholly owned ventures have become more prevalent, especially in export-oriented production. Vertical linkages have increased, and quality control has become of greater importance.

The Behavior of Hong Kong's TNCs

Obviously, the behavior of Hong Kong's TNCs in China is governed to a large extent by the motivations influencing Hong Kong's FDI in China. The primary motivation has been the search for lower costs of production for exporting to third markets on the basis of the ownership-specific advantages of Hong Kong companies that have a long experience in export-oriented industrialization.

Industry Clusters

Following Porter (1990, 1998), studies, both conceptual and empirical, have proliferated on industry clusters and the economic development of countries and regions (Birkinshaw and Hood 2000; Hill and Brennan 2000; Austrian 2000; Thompson 2002). Many of these studies actually are not breaking new ground but reflect a revival of location theory in economic development in general and with reference to FDI in particular.

The concept of industry clusters is relevant to economic development in the PRD. An industry cluster has been defined broadly as an aggregation of competing and complementary firms that are located in relatively close geographical proximity (Birkinshaw and Hood 2000). What is interesting in the case of the PRD is that industry clusters are found in small towns. Such clusters are highly concentrated, highly specialized, and highly successful. FDI plays a pivotal role in forming and developing such industry clusters, capitalizing on the experience, expertise, and entrepreneurial skills of enterprises. To maximize cost reduction, Hong Kong's FDI soon moved from the Special Economic Zone cities to the fringe of the zone, where both labor costs and the costs of compliance with government regulations were lower.

It must be a surprise to many that in the PRD small towns one can find the world's largest lighting production (in Zhongshan), the largest computer parts market (in Dongguan), and Asia's largest apparel wholesales center (in Dongguan). The existing literature postulates that TNCs attempt to "tap into" industry clusters in host countries in order to gain access to the leading-edge industries. But in the case of the PRD, TNCs have helped to create the leading-edge clusters in the first place. The establishment of clusters attracts more FDI, which explains the sustainability of the industry clusters. Their development enhances the region's and hence the nation's international competitiveness. The parent-subsidiary relationship is influenced by the industry cluster environment. The Hong Kong firms investing in the PRD industry clusters tend to let their subsidiaries enjoy more autonomy in decision making, and as a result the subsidiaries are more embedded in the local environment. This observation confirms many empirical studies of industry clusters in Western countries.

Linkages

The Hong Kong firms investing in the Pearl River Delta do not generally establish close vertical linkages with their subsidiaries in production. But the lateral linkages in the form of producer services are well established. This means that the subsidiaries depend to a large extent on their parent firms to source supplies (raw materials, parts, and components) and to export their products.

The following statistics from the Federation of Hong Kong Industries (2003) are revealing. It was estimated that 87 percent of the Hong Kong firms manufacturing in China exported to the world market via Hong Kong. In terms of value, 38.8 percent of these firms exported 99 to 100 percent of their Mainland factories' output via Hong Kong. With regard to sourcing of inputs, it was found that 49.7 percent of the value of inputs used by Hong Kong's TNCs in Mainland production was imported from Hong Kong and overseas, 33.6 percent was sourced from local suppliers, and 16.7 percent came from their other subsidiaries operating in China. An interesting research question is why linkages are limited despite the prevalence of industry clusters, a departure from the conventional wisdom. The answer seems to be found in the nature of the standardized industrial products produced by Hong Kong's TNCs in China during the earlier times. Quality control was less a concern; maximum cost reduction was to be achieved through the requisition of parts and components locally. Moreover, the indigenous firms caused little threat to Hong Kong's TNCs in China, and their headquarters in Hong Kong focused on producer support services rather than on production. In the course of time, this will change as TNCs from other economies (for example, Taiwan) become more prevalent, indigenous Chinese firms become more competitive, and (above all) the production and products of Hong Kong's TNCs in China become more sophisticated.

Technology Transfer

Technology is defined in a broad sense to include all knowledge that improves efficiency. Chen (1994) discusses the various aspects of technology transfer by TNCs to developing countries. Transnational corporations in Hong Kong and in developing countries in general have an important role in technology transfer in relation to the following:

(1) The transfer of "soft" technology, human resources, and organizational resources.
(2) The two-stage transfer of appropriate technology. (TNCs in the developing country serve as an intermediary. The technology for the local host-country environment is adapted before the transfer.)
(3) The form of technology transfer: patent technology, technological know-how, brand names, technological services, and so on.

Developing-country TNCs behave differently in technology transfer and technology development than do large TNCs in industrial countries because of the motivation factors discussed earlier. The different behaviors are related to the respective ownership-specific advantages they are exploiting and the location-specific advantages they are seeking when making FDI in China. Details about the extent and nature of technology transfer by Hong Kong TNCs to China will be provided in the next section.

The Impact of FDI on the Host Country

It has long been recognized that FDI has a vital role to play in the economic development of East Asia, although the earlier studies of Latin America point to the "exploitation" behavior of TNCs. There are a number of channels through which TNCs could have an impact on host countries. The first is the forward and backward linkages through which the TNC integrates or connects with the local firms. The second is the direct relationship between the TNC and the local firms that undertake subcontracting for the TNC. The third channel is the labor market in which professional workers move from TNCs to local firms. Usually, professional workers are from the host country, but they have gone through training and gained experience in TNCs. The fourth is the demonstrating effect of TNCs on local firms. Technologies or practices used by TNCs are replicated by the local firms because of their demonstrated success. This reduces the risks and uncertainties of adopting new technologies and practices. In some cases, local firms may use reverse engineering to acquire the technologies of TNCs.

Transnational corporations usually produce for the host country three positive effects in relation to export capability, technology transfer, and industrial transformation. The following is an analysis with reference to Hong Kong's FDI and OFI in China in general and in Guangdong in particular.

Export Capability

The export processing activities of Hong Kong firms in Guangdong were crucial for the province to build up its export capability. In 1986, soon after China started to promote FDI inflow actively, exports arising from processing and assembly were 16.6 percent of total exports. In 1984 many investment incentives were granted and laws were promulgated. Exports from processing went up from US$700 million in 1986 to US$6,794 million in 1987, accounting for 67 percent of total exports. The majority of FDI in Guangdong in the early years was from Hong Kong. The emergence of export growth in Guangdong was certainly created by Hong Kong's FDI. The success was almost predictable because such production under export processing combined Hong Kong's technological skills and marketing experience with China's extremely low labor costs. Today processing still accounts for 80 percent of total exports in Guangdong. For China as a whole, FDI accounts for about 50 percent of its exports.

There has been a change in the volume of exports, but more importantly there has been a change, especially after 1990, in quality or value added. The value added of processed exports can be illustrated by the ratio of processed exports to processed imports (Table 4.5). This is because processed exports depend on the import of parts and components, and equipment and machinery.

The development in Guangdong is a good illustration of the Vertical Type of FDI. Hong Kong's TNCs do not manufacture parts and components

Table 4.5. *Value Added, Guangdong's Exporting Industries, 1990–2001*

Year	Processing exports (a)	Processing imports (b)	Value added ratio a/b
1990	161.34	128.60	1.26
1995	423.69	323.93	1.29
1996	472.19	337.87	1.40
1997	548.86	389.51	1.41
1998	584.21	395.48	1.48
1999	604.27	420.52	1.44
2000	718.88	493.71	1.45
2001	765.09	504.71	1.52

Source: Guangdong Statistical Bureau (various years).

but procure them for their subsidiaries in China. Hong Kong's TNCs serve as regional quarters and are engaged in product development, financial management, and marketing. However, the linkages, backward and forward, have not been strong. The spillover effects on the local economy were limited for a long time. However, many state or collectively owned enterprises have recently arisen as dominant producers. The J learning curve effect has emerged. These enterprises at first sold in the domestic market, benefiting from the demonstration effect. After sufficient improvements in quality and productivity, they began to export their products and compete effectively with Hong Kong's TNCs.

Technology Transfer

Some macro studies have shown that significant technology change or total factor productivity (TFP) growth has taken place in Guangdong. Wu (2000) estimated that the TFP growth rate was 2.08 percent per annum for 1979 to 1983, 4.62 percent for 1986 to 1990, and 6.47 percent for 1993 to 1997 (assuming a capital share of 40 percent). The growth rate in recent years is truly phenomenal. This achievement is attributed to the integration of the Greater China region and the huge amount of FDI (particularly from Hong Kong) flowing into Guangdong. For the period from 1979 to 2000, Hong Kong's FDI accounted for 73 percent of total FDI in Guangdong. At the micro level, many interesting case studies have also been undertaken. Cheung and Lin (2003) show by regression analysis that FDI has a significant impact on innovation in Guangdong (as measured by the number of patent applications). The relationship between innovations and FDI is shown in Table 4.6.

Table 4.6. *FDI and Innovation in Guangdong Cities, 1996–2000*
(Percent)

City	*Share of FDI in Guangdong*	*Share of domestic patent applications in Guangdong*
Shenzhen	20.8	31.4
Guangzhou	21.8	18.4
Foshan	6.8	18.9
Dongguan	11.6	2.8
Huizhou	7.4	2.5
Zhuhai	7.2	6.6

Source: Guangdong Statistical Bureau (various years).

In cities / counties where FDI is significant, the propensity to innovate (as indicated by the patent applications of each city / county as a percentage of the total number of applications for the nation as a whole) is relatively high. Since the largest share of FDI in such cities is from Hong Kong, we can conclude that Hong Kong FDI has a significant impact on innovativeness and technological change in the PRD.

Thompson (2003) shows that Hong Kong's FDI in the garment industry does transfer significant technology to that industry in China. However, the significant technology transferred is "soft" rather than "hard." Soft technology refers to human-capital-intensive technology in management. A key factor that brings about the technology transfer is the high labor turnover rate in the industry in China. It was reported that the annual staff turnover was between 11 percent and 20 percent. Labor turnover, of course, is particularly important for the transfer of management and entrepreneurial skills. Hong Kong's TNCs employ relatively high levels of hard technology, usually levels higher than those of local firms. As far as Hong Kong's TNCs are concerned, they are using hard technologies that are slightly more advanced than those used by the parent firm in Hong Kong. Because of competitiveness and changing circumstances, China no longer serves as a dumping ground of Hong Kong enterprises for outdated capital goods. Nevertheless, the managers interviewed did not think that their hard technology had contributed much to upgrading the technological level in China in the traditional industries such as textiles, garments, and electrical / electronic appliances.

Shi (2001) compares the nature and type of technology transfer to local firms in China by Hong Kong's TNCs and large TNCs from developed countries (Table 4.7). The results are similar to those of Chen (1984), who studies the nature of technology exports by Hong Kong's TNCs.

Table 4.7. *Technology Transfer by Transnational Corporations in Hong Kong, Newly Industrializing Economies, and Industrial Countries*
(Percent of firms)

Type of transfer	*Hong Kong TNCs*	*NIE TNCs*[a]	*Industrial-country TNCs*
Percent of firms undertaking formal technology transfer	36.2	55.9	100.0
Patent	12.1	23.5	90.2
Know-how	20.7	17.6	100.0
Brand names	15.5	41.2	25.6
Technological services	25.9	47.1	100.0

a. The newly industrializing economies here include Taiwan (China), Singapore, the Republic of Korea, and Thailand.
Source: Shi (2001).

Compared to TNCs of developed countries and even of newly industrializing countries, Hong Kong's TNCs have not been formally transferring a high percentage of technology to local firms. Very few patents and brand names have been transferred. In contrast, all developed-country TNCs in the survey sample have transferred know-how and technological services to local firms, and 90 percent have transferred patents in product technology and process technology. TNCs in NIEs, notably in Taiwan, have often transferred brand names for the sake of capturing the local market in services and in manufacturing such as food and transport equipment. The extent of technology transfer seems to be related to the type of FDI. More technology transfer occurs when the FDI aims at domestic market sales. Hong Kong's TNCs aim largely at using China as an export platform; their transfer of hard technology is rather limited.

Earlier studies (for example, Chen and Wong 1995) showed that little in-house R&D activities were undertaken. For small firms, the machinery used in the subsidiary was transferred directly from the parent firm without much modification. For large TNCs in Hong Kong, technological modification took place in Hong Kong and was tested in China. However, in the past few years, significant changes have taken place. The R & D expenditure ratio is higher for firms in Guangdong than for firms in Hong Kong. The reason is simple: government support is lacking in research and development in Hong Kong, and the private sector is relatively shortsighted in the Hong Kong business environment where long-term commitment is not prevalent. However, in the business environment of China, where competition from local firms and other TNCs is keen, Hong Kong's

TNCs must maintain their technology at a relatively high level via in-house R&D.

Most important, in the 1990s the government policy of China changed; instead of concentrating R&D at the state level, China decentralized it to the enterprises. Incentives were also given to R&D activities in the form of tax concessions to enterprises engaged in technological improvement and in technology trade. In 1997 the establishment of R&D centers with foreign investment was allowed and promoted. In the past few years the ratio of R&D to GDP of Guangdong has increased significantly from below 0.5 percent to more than 1 percent since 2000. In Guangdong, R&D activities are concentrated in two major manufacturing industries: electronics and telecommunications, and electrical equipment and machinery. In 2001 these industries accounted for 76 percent of total R&D expenditures and 86 percent of the total number of invention patent applications. R&D activities are mostly undertaken by medium and large manufacturing enterprises, most of which are developed-country TNCs. In this regard, Hong Kong's TNCs have not played an important role. Nonetheless, we have to bear in mind that hard technology must be supported by soft technology. From this point of view, we can say that transnational corporations of Hong Kong have indeed made a significant contribution to technological improvements in China since they transfer soft technology to local firms.

Industrial Transformation and Enterprise Development

Hong Kong's TNCs have played a vital role not only in building up the export capability of Guangdong but also in effecting its industrial transformation. In the past few years Hong Kong/Macao/Taiwan FDI in the Pearl River Delta still accounted for a significant percentage of the total industrial output (Table 4.8) despite the rapid industrial transformation to high-tech and new industries. This suggests that Hong Kong's FDI is also involved in the transformation process. Some of the manufacturers who were interviewed talked about their investment in the new industries. In processed exports, Hong Kong's FDI prefers to operate on a wholly owned basis. However, in the new industries Hong Kong firms investing in China prefer equity or contractual joint ventures with local and overseas partners so that risks are lower.

Industrial development in Guangdong went through different stages. In the 1980s, Hong Kong's FDI was instrumental in developing processed exports in traditional industries such as textiles, garments, footwear, toys, watches and clocks, food, and plastics. This was basically a relocation of Hong Kong's

Table 4.8. *Industrial Production in the Pearl River Delta, 1998–2001*
(Percent of total industrial output)

Year	*Hong Kong FDI*[a]	*Other FDI*
1998	43.4	18.5
1999	42.9	19.8
2000	41.2	22.5
2001	41.4	24.2

a. Including Macao and Taiwan (China).
Source: Guangdong Statistical Bureau (various years).

outdated traditional industries to China so that their business could continue. In the late 1980s, Hong Kong's foreign direct investors began to invest substantially in the production of durable consumables, mainly household electrical appliances. This later made the Pearl River Delta the biggest producer of household electrical appliances in China. In the 1990s, some higher technology industries emerged, with the participation of Hong Kong's FDI in such industries as information technology, electrical machinery, and petrochemicals. These three industries have become the major newly emerging industries in Guangdong.

Table 4.9 shows the fall of traditional industry and the rise of new industries. The establishment of new industries was closely related to FDI. Inasmuch as most FDI in Guangdong is from Hong Kong, Hong Kong's FDI has been a driving force for industrial development and transformation in this province.

Table 4.9. *Industrial Production in Guangdong, 1995, 2000, and 2001*
(Percent)

	1995		*2000*		*2001*	
Major industry	*Production*	*Production by FDI*	*Production*	*Production by FDI*	*Production*	*Production by FDI*
New						
IT	13.4	82.9	19.4	75.4	22.2	78.3
Electrical machinery and equipment	10.5	41.7	13.0	56.6	13.1	54.7
Petrochemical	9.0	43.6	10.9	43.5	10.2	49.9
Traditional						
Textiles and garment	12.5	60.7	9.8	61.5	8.9	67.0
Food and beverages	9.8	41.0	6.4	47.0	6.2	48.1
Building materials	6.3	27.7	5.0	28.2	4.6	30.1

Source: Guangdong Statistical Bureau (various years).

The Impact of FDI on the Home Country

Whether the outward flow of FDI to relocate industrial activities will hollow out the domestic industry (deindustrialization) is a controversial issue. It seems that the phenomenon of hollowing-out cannot be generalized across countries. Two main types of resources—capital and labor—are released for relocation. Whether the domestic industry will be hollowed out depends on its restructuring capability to make the best use of the released resources.

In the case of Hong Kong, the massive relocation of labor-intensive manufacturing operations to southern China in the 1980s changed both the "nature" and "approach" of its manufacturing production. In the past two decades, industrial restructuring occurred rapidly. Since the market mechanism was working fairly well in Hong Kong and its work force was flexible, the physical and human resources released from relocation were able to find their way to even more productive uses, especially to services. Because of government facilitation, the hollowing-out effect on Hong Kong's industry leveled off so quickly that it was hardly discernible up to the mid-1990s.

In Hong Kong, industrial restructuring has been occurring at the interindustry and intrafirm levels. Interindustry restructuring occurs when investment in sunset industries is diverted to services. According to the Hong Kong Labor Department, from 1987 to 1992 almost 400,000 manufacturing jobs were lost in Hong Kong, whereas 450,000 jobs in the services sector were created. The challenge is to help displaced manufacturing workers get jobs in services sector. Workers forty-five to sixty years of age are suffering the most from structural unemployment because they are too young to retire but too old to be retrained. The Hong Kong Employees Retraining Board (HKETB) was established in 1992 to address this problem. Considerable emphasis has been placed on helping displaced workers to secure employment by providing them with retraining in vocational skills. In addition, assistance has been offered to workers who are still employed but may be displaced if their skills are not upgraded. Special attention has been given to middle-age workers, as noted earlier. Although the HKETB has a short history, it has been able to tackle the problem in an effective way. Nevertheless, the capacity to retrain workers remains limited relative to the number of workers who have been displaced.

Intrafirm restructuring has two related aspects. First, after relocation, the parent firm in Hong Kong has changed its production structure from manufacturing to manufacturing-related. Furthermore, the company's approach is to move toward high value added, design, management, and consumer-oriented production. Our interviews confirm the prevalence of this type of intrafirm restructuring in Hong Kong. Second, the relocated manufacturing activities are able to provide strong support to the parent company. According to the Hong Kong Census and Statistics Department, 72 percent of total imports from China and 74 percent of total domestic exports to China were related to outward processing in the Mainland in 1992. Apparently, the parent company and its subsidiary are maintaining close ties via intrafirm trade. This intrafirm bond has forward linkages affecting other sectors of the Hong Kong economy and its export potential that should not be overlooked.

Instead of hollowing-out, the relocation of manufacturing activities to Mainland China may have a "technology stagnation effect" on Hong Kong's industry. Earlier studies show that, for various reasons, the technology transferred from Hong Kong to China did not embody much new knowledge and skills. In this connection, the rate of technical progress and the technological capacity of the subsidiary would be low. If the technology of the supporting activities conducted by the subsidiary is stagnant, it can hardly serve as a stimulus for further technological change at home.

But in later years (after, say, 1995), Hong Kong's FDI did have a significant impact on industrial change in China. Hong Kong's FDI has been expanding to newer and more high-tech industries using imported technology. Also the transfer of soft technology has been shown to be significant. Soft technology has produced forward and backward linkages at home. Over time, these developments have led to the emergence in Hong Kong of producer services (supply chain management, customer relationship management, transportation and storage, product design and promotion) in support of Hong Kong-based enterprises operating in China.

The recent economic recession in Hong Kong should not be related to the hollowing-out effect. It is largely related to the property bubble (which, in turn, is related to Hong Kong's controversial land policy) and the outbreak of the Asian financial crisis. In fact, the relocation of Hong Kong industries to China has had a positive impact on Hong Kong's economic transformation from a manufacturing base, to a financial and commercial center, to a logistics hub.

Conclusion

The experience of transnational corporations in Hong Kong confirms conventional arguments about TNCs in industrial and developing countries. Compared to developed-country TNCs, Hong Kong's TNCs have less vertical integration with their subsidiaries despite the prevalence of industry clusters, transfer more appropriate technology and more "soft" or human resources–intensive technology, and tend to be more export oriented.

Hong Kong's FDI also has had a significant impact on industrial transformation and enterprise development in China. However, such features of Hong Kong's TNCs or developing-country TNCs, in contrast to those of TNCs in industrial countries, reflect Hong Kong's prevailing economic and industrial structure and development rather than Hong Kong-specific characteristics. Indeed, the characteristics of TNCs differ from one developing country to the next and over time.

Hong Kong's FDI in China in general and in Guangdong in particular demonstrates a successful experience in fostering economic growth and development in the host country and in facilitating the economic transformation of the source economy. A number of factors can be identified. Flexibility is the key word.

First, the form of organization and ownership was flexible and diverse from the very beginning. Different forms of export processing (OFI) and different forms of foreign ownership (FDI) have given a wide range of choices to suit the purposes of different industries and enterprises of different sizes and technological capabilities.

Second, the foreign investment policy was flexible. The central government promulgates a set of overarching rules and regulations, while individual provinces, counties, and cities can enjoy some degree of freedom to work with FDI. Incentives were given, but at the same time a development-oriented policy of creating a better business environment was also in place.

Third, China is huge, and the government has chosen an appropriate policy in selecting some coastal regions to be designated as SEZs for the process to start, allowing the contagion effect to take place later. The SEZs are not just export processing zones or industrial parks but comprehensive development areas.

Fourth, the promotion of processed exports at the very beginning has proved to be the right policy choice. Export-oriented FDI tends to have created more growth and employment for China than the import-substituting type at the early stage of development. Although it can be argued that such export-oriented FDI could also retard technological development and bring about a low level of value added because of the labor-intensive nature of such industries (Sung 2000), the experience of Hong Kong's foreign direct investment in China does not seem to confirm this.

Lastly, the Chinese success story must be related to the presence of Hong Kong as a source economy investing significantly in China. Hong Kong has achieved a high level of economic development already, and its traditional industries are awaiting opportunities for relocation through FDI. Despite the fact that Hong Kong is just a city economy with 6.7 million people, the size of its economy is relatively big, and its outward FDI accounts for a significant share of outward FDI from developing economies. In 2001 Hong Kong's GDP was US$164 billion, while Guangdong's was only US$129 billion, despite its population of almost 78 million. During the period 1985 to 2002, Hong Kong's outward FDI accounted for about one-third of all outward FDI from developing economies (UNCTAD 2003). While some of these investments can be attributed to Hong Kong as an intermediary in capital flows and M & A activities and to round-tripping of China's capital, a major part of FDI in official statistics was of Hong Kong origin. Above all, the cultural affinity and geographical proximity between Hong Kong and the Mainland must have been positive factors despite the contrary results of some econometric studies. In this regard, the Hong Kong factor is unique and generalization is perhaps difficult.

References

Akamatsu, K. 1962. "A Historical Pattern of Economic Growth in Developing Countries." *The Developing Economies,* Preliminary (1): 1–23.

Austrian, Ziona. 2000. "Cluster Case Studies: The Marriage of Quantitative and Qualitative Information for Action." *Economic Development Quarterly* 14(1): 97–110.

Bank of China. 2003. "Foreign Direct Investment in China." *Economic Review,* January.

Bergen, Suzanne, and Richard Lester. 1997. *Made by Hong Kong*. Hong Kong: Oxford University Press.

Birkinshaw, Julian, and Neil Hood. 2000. "Characteristics of Foreign Subsidiaries in Industry Clusters." *Journal of International Business Studies* 31(1): 141–54.

Caves, Richard E. 1971. "International Corporations: The Industrial Economics of Foreign Investment." *Economica* 38 (1): 1–27.

Chen, Edward K. Y. 1981. "Hong Kong Multinationals in Asia: Characteristics and Objectives." In K. Kumar and M. G. McLeod, eds., *Multinationals from Developing Countries.* Lexington, Mass.: D.C. Heath.

———. 1983a. *Multinational Corporations, Employment and Technology.* London: Macmillan.

———. 1983b. "Multinationals from Hong Kong." In S. Lall, ed., *The New Multinationals: The Spread of Third World Enterprises.* London: Wiley.

———. 1983c. "Factor Proportions of Foreign and Local Firms in Developing Countries." *Journal of Development Economics* 12(1/2): 267–74.

———. 1984. "Hong Kong." *World Development* 12(5/6): 481–90 (Special Issue on Exports of Technology by Newly Industrializing Countries).

———. 1991. "Economic Restructuring and Industrial Development in the Asia-Pacific: Competition or Complementarity?" *Business and the Contemporary World* 5(2): 67–88.

———. 1994. *Transnational Corporations and Technology Transfer to Developing Countries.* London: Routledge.

———. 1998. "Policy Competition and FDI in China: The Case of Three Provinces." Paris: Organization for Economic Cooperation and Development.

Chen, Edward K. Y., and Teresa Y. C. Wong. 1995. "Economic Synergy: A Study of Two-way FDI Flow between Hong Kong and Mainland China." In *The New Wave of Foreign Direct Investment in Asia.* Tokyo: Nomura Research Institute.

———. 1997. "Hong Kong: Foreign Direct Investment and Trade Linkages in Manufacturing." In Wendy Dobson and Chia Siow Yue, eds., *Multinationals and East Asian Integration.* Ottawa: International Development and Research Center.

Cheng, Leonard K., and Y. K. Kwan. 2000. "The Location of FDI in Chinese Regions: Further Analysis of Labor Quality." In Takatoshi Ito and Anne O. Krueger, eds., *The Role of Foreign Direct Investment in East Asian Economic Development.* Chicago: University of Chicago Press.

Cheung, K. Y., and Ping Lin. 2003. "Spillover Effects of FDI on Innovation in Guangdong, China." Paper presented at a Lingnan University workshop, Hong Kong, October 31.

Dunning, John. 1981. *International Production and the Multinational Enterprise.* London: Allen and Unwin.

Federation of Hong Kong Industries. 2003. *Made in PRD: The Changing Face of Hong Kong Manufacturers.* Hong Kong.

Guangdong Statistical Bureau. various years. *Guangdong Statistical Yearbook.* Beijing: China Statistical Publishing House.

Hill, Edward W., and John F. Brennan. 2000. "A Methodology for Identifying the Drivers of Industrial Clusters: The Foundation of Regional Competitive Advantage." *Economic Development Quarterly* 14(1): 65–96.

Hymer, Stephen H. 1976. *The International Operations of National Firms: A Study of Direct Foreign Investment.* Cambridge, Mass.: MIT Press.

Kojima, K. 1977. "Transfer of Technology to Developing Countries: Japanese Type versus American Type." *Hitotsubashi Journal of Economics* 17 (February): 1–14.

Ozawa, T. 1979. "Multinationalism, Japanese Style: The Political Economy of Outward Dependency." Princeton, N.J.: Princeton University Press.

Pan Yigang, David K. Tse, and Xiaolian Li. 1999. "The Inflow of FDI in China: The Impact of Country-Specific Factors." Chinese Management Centre (University of Hong Kong) Working Paper, March.

Porter, Michael E. 1990. *The Competitive Advantage of Nations.* New York: Free Press.

———. 1998. "Clusters and the New Economics of Competition." *Harvard Business Review* 76(6): 77–91.

Shatz, H., and A. J. Venables. 2000. "The Geography of International Investment." *World Bank Policy Research Working Paper 2338.* Washington, D.C.

Shi, Yizheng. 2001. "Technological Capabilities and International Production Strategy of Firms: The Case of FDI in China." *Journal of World Business* 36(2): 184–204.

State Statistical Bureau. various years. *China Statistical Yearbook.* Beijing: China Statistical Publishing House.

Sung, Yun-wing. 2000. "Costs and Benefits of Export-oriented Foreign Investment: The Case of China." *Asian Economic Journal* 14(1): 55–56.

Thompson, Edmund R. 2002. "Clustering of FDI and Enhanced Technology Transfer: Evidence from Hong Kong Garment Firms in China." *World Development* 30(5): 873–89.

———. 2003. "Technology Transfer to China by Hong Kong's Cross-Border Garment Firms." *The Developing Economies* 41(1): 88–111.

Tuan, C., and Linda Ng. 1995a. "Hong Kong's Outward Investment and Regional Economic Integration with Guangdong: Process and Implications." *Journal of Asian Economics* 6(3): 385–450.

———. 1995b. "Manufacturing Evolution under Passive Industrial Policy and Cross-border Operations in China: The Case of Hong Kong." *Journal of Asian Economics* 6(1): 71–88.

———. 2003. *A Miracle via Agglomerations: The HK-PRD Connection* (in Chinese). Hong Kong: The Chinese University of Hong Kong, Faculty of Business Management.

UNCTAD (United Nations Conference on Trade and Development). 2003. *World Investment Report.* New York: United Nations.

Wei, Xiangdong. 2003. "The Determinants of FDI Distribution in Guangdong: A Quantitative Analysis" (in Chinese). Paper presented at a Lingnan University workshop, Hong Kong, October 31.

Wu, Friedrich, and Puah Kok Keong. 2003. "FDI to China and Southeast Asia: Has Asean Been Losing Out?" *Journal of Asian Business* 19(1): 89–105.

Wu, Yanrui. 2000. "Productivity, Growth and Economic Integration in the Southern China Region." *Asian Economic Journal* 14(1): 39–54.

Zhang, Kevin H. 2001. "China's Inward FDI Boom and the Greater Chinese Economy." *The Chinese Economy* 34(1): 74–88.

5

The Role of Inward FDI: A Case Study of Foreign Firms in the Republic of Korea

Taeho Bark and Hwy-Chang Moon

The purpose of this chapter is to explain the factors that contributed to the expansion of inward foreign direct investment (FDI) in the Republic of Korea and to describe the impacts of inward FDI on the competitiveness of the country's economy in recent years. A deeper analysis of this issue is critical in order to identify the economic effects of inward FDI for host economies. This chapter hypothesizes that inward FDI has positive impacts on host economies. From this perspective, governments of host economies are encouraged to establish policies conducive to inward FDI.

The sluggishness of FDI in Korea until the early 1990s is mainly attributable to strict regulations against inward FDI by the government of Korea. However, with the introduction of the comprehensive five-year FDI liberalization plan in June 1993, the Korean government began to actively promote FDI and inflows started to increase. Then, when Korea joined the Organization for Economic Co-operation and Development (OECD) in December 1996, the Korean FDI regime was adjusted in line with international norms and standards, resulting in a surge of FDI.

FDI in Korea in Recent Years

After the 1997 financial crisis, the Korean government, following recommendations from the International Monetary Fund (IMF), further liberalized FDI policy as a means to overcome the crisis as quickly as possible. As a result, FDI flowing into Korea dramatically increased, amounting to $51.9 billion during the four years from 1998 until 2001.

According to the *World Investment Report* (UNCTAD 2003), the average annual flow of inward FDI from 1990 to 1995 was US$978 million, and it surged up to US$9.4 billion in 1999. The inflow as a percentage of gross fixed capital formation also increased, from an average of 0.8 percent during the 1990–95 period to 7.1 percent in 2000. (Figure 5.1). As the figure shows, FDI decreased both in amount and as a percentage of gross fixed capital formation in 2001 and 2002.

There are two types of FDI: crossborder mergers and acquisitions (M&As) and greenfield investments. Shortly after the crisis, there were "fire sales" of many domestic firms because of management failure or bankruptcy, and eventually these companies were acquired by multinational firms. This explains the surge in crossborder M&As compared to greenfield investments during the crisis years of 1997 and 1998. It should be noted that crossborder M&As were under 20 percent until the year 1997 (Bank of Korea 2003). In 1998, FDI inflows were almost equally divided between greenfield investments and crossborder M&As.

However, when the shockwave of the crisis subsided after 1999, greenfield investments as a percentage of all investments increased again to

Figure 5.1. *Inflow of FDI in the Republic of Korea, 1990–2002*

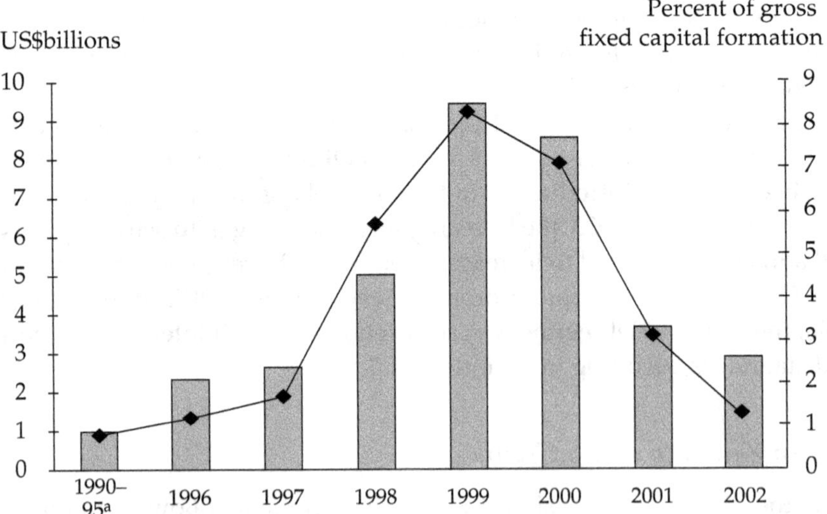

a. Annual average.
Source: UNCTAD (2003).

approximately 80 percent in 2002. Consequently, the proportion of "fire sale" M&As to greenfield investments decreased. During the short period from 1997 to 2000, immediate acquirable assets were mostly sold. The decreased availability of acquisitions resulted in a decline of inward FDI. Moreover, external factors such as the September 11 incident in 2001 in the United States affected the inflow of FDI in recent years (Ministry of Commerce, Industry, and Energy 2001, 2002). Although the impact of inward FDI on a host economy may differ depending on the mode of entry, inward FDI is usually beneficial to the host economy regardless of the type of FDI.

Source Economies

The major sources of FDI in Korea have been the United States, Japan, and the European Union (Ministry of Commerce, Industry, and Energy various years). In the crisis year of 1997, these three major economies accounted for about 80 percent of all inward FDI in Korea (Table 5.1). Although other countries increased their investments after 1997 up to almost 40 percent of all investments in 2000, the three major countries made a comeback to 80 percent in 2001. In 2002, however, there was an increase in China, Hong Kong (China), and Singapore. After the financial crisis, between 1998 and 1999, the percentage of FDI from the European Union increased. This can be explained by the policy focus on the region by the Kim administration (Kang 2001).

According to one report on FDI in Korea (KPMG Consulting 2001), the proportion of U.S. investment has decreased since 1997, while that of Japan has risen significantly. Japanese investment increased threefold in 1999 compared to the year before. This is viewed to be the result of greenfield investments and strategic alliances between Korean and Japanese companies during 1999. Also, according to a report by the Ministry of Commerce, Industry, and Energy (2001), big contracts between U.S. companies and Korean companies were either postponed or cancelled after the September 11 incident in 2001. Examples include the cancellation of purchasing shares of SK Telecom (US$2.9 billion) and Korea Exchange Bank (US$450 million), and the postponement of purchasing shares of Hyundai Securities (US$800 million) and Kookmin Bank (US$300 million).

FDI by Industry

During the 1990s, inward FDI was concentrated in the manufacturing and services sectors. On average, the manufacturing industry had a 55 percent

Table 5.1. *Inflow of FDI in the Republic of Korea, by Selected Economies, 1990–2002*
US$ million (percent)

Economy	*1990*	*1991*	*1992*	*1993*	*1994*	*1995*	*1996*	*1997*	*1998*	*1999*	*2000*	*2001*	*2002*
EU	200.5	678.9	290.9	251.3	366.6	437.8	861.5	1,735.9	2,690.1	5,104.8	3,093.2	2,571.7	1,559.5
	(22.4)	(57.7)	(36.2)	(34.5)	(37.0)	(32.1)	(37.3)	(56.2)	(51.0)	(47.3)	(30.4)	(52.9)	(42.4)
USA	265.1	262.0	268.0	303.3	222.9	340.6	392.9	390.9	1,486.1	2,002.3	1,762.1	839.4	567.9
	(29.6)	(22.3)	(33.3)	(41.7)	(22.5)	(25.0)	(17.0)	(12.7)	(28.2)	(18.5)	(17.3)	(17.3)	(15.4)
Japan	365.9	203.8	174.3	157.4	340.1	337.8	279.7	236.1	424.7	837.3	1,102.9	480.8	568.9
	(40.9)	(17.3)	(21.7)	(21.6)	(34.3)	(24.8)	(12.1)	(7.6)	(8.1)	(7.8)	(10.8)	(9.9)	(15.5)
Major 3[a]	831.5	1,144.7	733.2	712.0	929.6	1,116.2	1,534.1	2,362.9	4,600.9	7,944.4	5,958.2	3,891.9	2,696.3
	(92.9)	(97.2)	(91.2)	(97.8)	(93.7)	(81.9)	(66.4)	(76.5)	(87.3)	(73.6)	(58.6)	(80.1)	(73.3)
Canada	7.2	1.0	3.0	1.6	0.3	0.7	9.9	183.3	61.6	343.0	288.1	26.8	10.6
	(0.8)	(0.1)	(0.4)	(0.2)	(0.0)	(0.1)	(0.4)	(5.9)	(1.2)	(3.2)	(2.8)	(0.6)	(0.3)
China	0.5	0.6	2.8	1.5	2.1	7.0	3.4	2.7	2.7	13.1	57.9	47.1	80.8
	(0.1)	(0.0)	(0.3)	(0.2)	(0.2)	(0.5)	(0.1)	(0.1)	(0.1)	(0.1)	(0.6)	(1.0)	(2.2)
Hong Kong	19.0	6.1	9.0	6.2	13.4	27.7	15.2	23.7	9.8	181.9	129.0	61.0	99.9
	(2.1)	(0.5)	(1.1)	(0.9)	(1.4)	(2.0)	(0.7)	(0.8)	(0.2)	(1.7)	(1.3)	(1.3)	(2.7)
Singapore	12.6	2.8	2.3	2.5	6.8	69.8	39.5	39.4	181.8	522.1	118.2	54.3	169.4
	(1.4)	(0.2)	(0.3)	(0.3)	(0.7)	(5.1)	(1.7)	(1.3)	(3.4)	(4.8)	(1.2)	(1.1)	(4.6)
Total	895.4	1,177.4	803.6	728.1	992.0	1,363.6	2,310.1	3,089.7	5,269.9	10,798.8	10,172.5	4,858.8	3,680.3
	(100)	(100)	(100)	(100)	(100)	(100)	(100)	(100)	(100)	(100)	(100)	(100)	(100)

a. European Union, United States, and Japan.
Source: Ministry of Commerce, Industry, and Energy (2003).

share, and the services industry had a 42 percent share. This is mainly due to the relatively higher concentration of FDI in the manufacturing industry from 1996 to 1999. However, with the recovery of the Korean economy and the opening of the services industry to overseas competitors after the 1997 crisis, investment in the services industry picked up. It has increased steadily since 1999 (Table 5.2).

Following the sharp slow-down in the domestic economy in 1998, FDI in market-sensitive industries such as construction and lodging decreased dramatically. On the other hand, the financial services and insurance sectors experienced a sharp increase in FDI due to the further liberalization of FDI in those sectors and restructuring activities that were then under way. Investment in financial and insurance services continued to grow until 1999, but with the completion of the restructuring process, they slowed down after 2000. An increase in domestic demand, however, brought about another increase since 1999 in investment inflow to wholesale/retail, lodging, and various other service industry segments.

From 1998 to 2000, investment in the manufacturing industry was largely focused on major domestic industries such as electrical/electronics, machinery, and chemicals. The Korean government sought foreign investment in these industries as a means of restructuring in order to ensure their continued competitiveness. The 1999 joint venture between Philips and LG Electronics worth US$2.7 billion is a good example of such investments. In 2000, investment in the electrical/electronics industry became dominant, reflecting the attraction of information technology (IT) businesses as investment targets. Investment in the machinery industry also increased greatly, while investment in the petrochemical and food industries declined.

A Review of FDI Policy

Chang and Chun (2000) describe the FDI policy of the Korean government in four stages.

The first stage (1962–83) was an "investment restriction" stage. Although FDI in Korea was permitted after 1962, actual FDI inflow was limited to the minimal level since the Korean government chose the economic development strategy of relying on commercial loans and loans from multilateral organizations such as the World Bank. In fact, FDI was restricted to protect domestic firms. For the most part, technology was imported through licensing or by foreign technicians. This stemmed from the fear of foreign control of Korean industries and heavy reliance on foreign capital. As Korea defaulted on foreign debts in the 1980s, policies were amended to attract

Table 5.2. *Inflow of FDI in the Republic of Korea, by Industry, 1990–2002*
US$thousands (percent)

Industry	*1990*	*1991*	*1992*	*1993*	*1994*	*1995*	*1996*	*1997*	*1998*	*1999*	*2000*	*2001*	*2002*
Agriculture, livestock and fisheries	774	197	2,309	117	26,879	2,614	215,745	5,643	27,754	7,640	4,583	159	1,126
	(0.1)	(0.0)	(0.3)	(0.0)	(2.7)	(0.2)	(9.3)	(0.2)	(0.5)	(0.1)	(0.0)	(0.0)	(0.0)
Manufacturing	526,828	428,780	465,951	324,484	375,571	656,662	1,229,680	1,790,346	2,982,246	6,823,847	5,883,005	2,373,842	1,459,250
	(58.8)	(36.4)	(58.0)	(44.3)	(37.8)	(48.2)	(53.1)	(57.9)	(56.5)	(63.2)	(57.8)	(49.1)	(39.7)
Services	367,574	744,830	332,933	406,770	582,932	656,944	818,608	1,250,970	2,260,468	3,568,856	4,046,344	2,384,743	2,151,596
	(41.1)	(63.3)	(41.4)	(55.6)	(58.7)	(48.2)	(35.4)	(40.5)	(42.8)	(33.0)	(39.7)	(49.3)	(58.5)
Electricity, gas, water supply	0	0	0	0	0	0	65	0	36	378,696	201,023	75,189	44,023
	(0.0)	(0.0)	(0.0)	(0.0)	(0.0)	(0.0)	(0.0)	(0.0)	(0.0)	(3.5)	(2.0)	(1.6)	(1.2)
Construction	221	3,638	2,416	695	7,729	47,379	51,438	42,757	8,992	25,996	50,949	5,089	24,277
	(0.0)	(0.3)	(0.3)	(0.1)	(0.8)	(3.5)	(2.2)	(1.4)	(0.2)	(0.2)	(0.5)	(0.1)	(0.7)
Total	895,397	1,177,445	803,609	732,066	993,111	1,363,599	2,315,536	3,089,716	5,279,496	10,805,035	10,185,904	4,839,022	3,680,272
	(100)	(100)	(100)	(100)	(100)	(100)	(100)	(100)	(100)	(100)	(100)	(100)	(100)

Source: Ministry of Commerce, Industry, and Energy (2003).

FDI rather than loans (KPMG Consulting 2001). However, the FDI policy regime of Korea was still very restrictive.

The second stage (1984–92) focused on establishing a more stable institutional infrastructure. The government no longer imposed a 50 percent ownership ceiling on foreigners in limited sectors, but it still protected major domestic firms rather than promoting competition in the domestic economy by attracting FDI. Consequently, during this second stage, the change in policy did not bring about an actual increase in FDI.

The third stage (1993–97) was characterized by liberalization. Regulations were further relaxed, and Korea's market was opened up to foreign investment. This deregulatory policy was adopted to improve the country's industrial structure and to attract foreign investment in high-tech sectors. In 1993, a comprehensive five-year FDI liberalization plan was introduced and FDI inflows were allowed on a notification basis rather than an authorization basis. Specifically, 132 out of the remaining 224 restricted industrial sectors were opened in 1993 with conditions. In 1994, notification procedures for FDI were delegated to foreign exchange banks. The banks drastically reduced the processing period for notification from a period of twenty to thirty days to no more than three hours. In April 1995, the Korean government established a One-Stop Service System for FDI in Seoul and other provinces. This system helped resolve grievances of foreign-controlled firms, arranged linkages to joint venture partners, and provided comprehensive information and administrative services to foreign investors. With Korea's accession to the OECD in 1996, and the partial liberalization of crossborder M&As (permission for nonhostile cross-border M&As), the government increased its effort to match the practices of other developed countries (KPMG Consulting 2001). One of the incentives in this stage was an exemption of rents for high-tech investments over US$20 million and for investments in the manufacturing sector over US$200 million.

During the fourth stage (1998–2003), Korea underwent the most dramatic change, considerably relaxing restrictions on FDI. In November 1998, as part of the reform program agreed with the IMF, the Korean government enacted the Foreign Direct Investment Promotion Act, with a view to create a much more investor-friendly policy environment. Currently, foreign investors and foreign companies enjoy the same rights and privileges as local residents or local companies, as long as such investments do not violate national security, public health, and conservation of the environment. Also, the government permitted all types of FDI including hostile crossborder M&As. Two important aspects are nondiscrimination when purchasing real estate and an unconditional guarantee of international remittances by foreign investors. A recent revision of the Foreign Direct Investment Promotion Act is summarized below (Ministry of Commerce, Industry, and Energy 2003).

Cash grants: cash grants will be given to all new greenfield investments. In addition to tax exemptions, the Korean government will provide cash grants starting from January 1, 2004, to foreign high-tech and industrial support service businesses that invest US$10 million or more in building a new factory or expanding current production facilities, or invest US$5 million or more in R&D facilities.

Foreign investment reward: rewards will be given to employees of local governments, or public services, who make contributions to the inducement of FDI in Korea.

Public industrial complex included for government support: public development complexes will now be eligible for government support in order to provide benefits to foreign investing companies. (Currently, only the foreign investing companies moving into the government-managed complexes are eligible for support.) Also, incentives will be given on the lease of the land, which is part of the local industrial complex owned by the government. (Currently, there are no benefits given on the lease for local industrial complexes jointly owned by the state and the local government.)

One-stop service: the government will establish FDI promotional offices in central administration organizations and other local government organizations to reinforce one-stop services for foreign investors.

Investment Incentives and Administrative Support

In order to promote foreign investment, the Korean government provides a string of incentives and benefits such as tax and rent reduction or exemption. National property rent reduction or exemption applies to foreign industrial complexes, national industrial complexes, and government properties in Foreign Investment Zones. Rent reduction ranges from 50 percent to 100 percent depending on the investing company, the amount of investments, and the type of business. The deduction for purchasing or leasing private contracts for state or public assets currently given only to foreign investing private corporations will also be given to foreign investing public institutions such as schools and hospitals.

The Korean government provides a variety of supports through the provision of funds to small and medium-size venture businesses that possess technological skills and creativity. Its purpose is to enhance competitiveness and realize the growth potential of such businesses. Local and foreign companies are equally eligible for these benefits once the company's technological capabilities and business potential are assessed and found to satisfy basic requirements (KPMG Consulting 2001).

To simplify investment procedures, the Korean Trade-Investment Promotion Agency (KOTRA) established the Korea Investment Service Center in 1998 as the one-stop center to provide administrative support, consultative services, and postinvestment services. In addition, the Office of the Investment Ombudsman was established under article 15 of the Foreign Direct Investment Promotion Act of 1998 as a means to resolve difficulties experienced by investors in Korea and to enhance the overall business climate (UNCTAD 2002). The system has formed teams, grouped by region and by language, to provide a one-on-one service to foreign investors. The Ombudsman works jointly with local governments and foreign associations located in Korea (for example, the Seoul Japan Club, the European Chamber of Commerce, the American Chamber of Commerce, and the Korea Foreign Company Association) to attain effective and efficient problem solving. To protect the trademark rights of exported and imported goods, the Ombudsman suggested in 2001 that the Customs Office implement a computerized system to cover relevant trademarks and introduce various scientific measures. As a result, the Customs Office signed a contract with a subcontractor for developing a trademark-rights management system and embarked on implementing a pilot operating system (UNCTAD 2002).

Conceptual Framework

While this chapter's focus is the impact of inward FDI on the host economy, foreign direct investors' motivations influence that impact (UNCTAD 2001). In addition to the initial intentions of the transacting entities, there are unexpected results that affect the host economy as well. Thus, there is a need to provide a comprehensive framework incorporating both the motivation and impact of FDI.

This chapter highlights the studies of FDI motivations by Dunning (2000), UNCTAD (2000, 2001), and Moon and Roehl (2001), and the studies of FDI impacts by UNCTAD (2000, 2001) and Dunning (2003). As noted earlier, a single framework is needed that can incorporate and evaluate the motivation *and* impact of FDI. Building on the diamond dimensions of Porter (1990), we therefore present in this chapter a new model, which will be explained in detail below. Compared with the diamond dimensions of Porter (1990), all three typologies mentioned above—namely, Dunning (2000), Moon and Roehl (2001), and UNCTAD (2000, 2001)—have limitations in the sense that there is room to consider other dimensions regarding

Box 5.1. *FDI-Friendly Policies in the Republic of Korea*

Some 13,228 overseas companies had invested in the Republic of Korea as of March 2003. They include 45 percent—223 companies in total—of the Fortune Global 500 and all of the world's top twenty corporations. Moreover, the ratio of net profit to sales among foreign companies in Korea is far higher than that of domestic companies. In fact, the Korean branches of international companies are often among the top earners (if not the top earners) within their groups.

Foreign Investment Zones

In an effort to foster the development of foreign businesses, the government will endorse the business area of a single company or a consortium of foreign companies as a Foreign Investment Zone (FIZ). FIZ designation allows a company to take advantage of free land subsidies and 10-year tax reduction and exemption incentives, and it requires that more than the minimum investment amount be put into the business.

As of January 1, 2004, eligibility requirements for a FIZ designation will be relaxed. A foreign business or consortium of businesses then may combine their individual investments to satisfy the lowered minimum investment hurdles. Previously, a FIZ designation was only available for single corporations. The minimum investment amount for a FIZ designation will be reduced from US$50 million to US$30 million for manufacturing businesses, from US$30 million to US$20 million for tourism businesses, and from US$30 million to US$10 million for logistics businesses. Although the scope of eligible beneficiaries will be increased, the incentive period will be reduced a year later, on January 1, 2005, from ten to seven years. Throughout 2004 foreign investors not only could take advantage of free land subsidies and lowered FIZ eligibility investment hurdles; they also could seize the opportunity for a ten-year incentive period before it was lowered to seven years.

Foreign-Exclusive Industrial Complexes

Small-size foreign companies have not been ignored by Korea's FDI efforts. Rental discount incentives are available for small businesses that are established within any of the six government-designated Foreign-Exclusive Industrial Complexes (FEICs). Manufacturing businesses investing a minimum of US$10 million can enjoy a rental discount of 75 percent, while high-tech companies investing a minimum of US$1 million are eligible for a rental discount of 100 percent. Before the end of 2003, the government planned to expand the Jinsa and Ohchang Industrial Complexes by 171,900 and 330,578 square meters respectively, bringing the total FEICs space in Korea to 4.23 million square meters. The government also planned to offer the same FEIC benefits to foreign companies establishing themselves in any of the country's forty-eight privately developed industrial complexes.

Cash Grants for Greenfield FDI

To bolster greenfield FDI, the Korean government plans to give cash grants to foreign direct investors on a case-by-case basis. The grants will be aimed at investors in high-demand fields such as high technology, parts and materials, as well as at R&D center–related investors. The size of the cash grants will depend on the size of the investment and its anticipated effect on the domestic economy—provided that one of the following requirements is met: US$10 million or more is invested in a "high-tech and industrial support service business" for building a new factory or expanding current production facilities; or US$10 million or more is invested into a "parts and materials company" for building a new factory or expanding current production facilities; or US$5 million or more is invested in "R&D" facilities.

Source: http://www.investkorea.org.

the motivations of FDI. The *World Investment Report* (UNCTAD 2000, 2001) explains the effects of inward FDI on the host economy in terms of seven determinants: investment, financial resources, employment/skills, technology, export competitiveness, market structure, and competition. This typology, however, also is limited. Dunning (2003) has suggested the need to integrate Porter's (1990) diamond model in his OLI paradigm to have a better understanding of the L factor. This revised model cleverly integrates the important variables determining a nation's competitiveness (Cho and Moon 2000).

Porter's diamond model is somewhat ambiguous with regard to the enhancement of competitiveness through multinational activity. Porter (1990) argues that the most effective global strategy is to concentrate as many activities as possible in one country and to serve the world from this home base. Thus, Porter's global firm is primarily an exporting firm, and his methodology does not take into account the organizational complexities of true global operations by multinational firms. Moreover, sustainable value added in a specific country may result from domestically owned and foreign owned firms. Porter, however, does not incorporate foreign activities into his model. Therefore, Porter's single diamond model has been extended to the generalized double diamond model (Moon, Rugman, and Verbeke 1995, 1998), including multinational activity as an endogenous variable rather than an exogenous variable (Bark and Moon 2002).

The model presented in the following section is unique. Within a comprehensive framework it extends Dunning (2000, 2003), Moon and Roehl (2001), Porter (1990), and Moon, Rugman, and Verbeke (1995, 1998). It also reveals the limitations of the existing literature. This new framework helps explain the impact of inward FDI on the competitiveness of Korea.

Multinational Firms' Motivations to Invest

In order to understand the impact of FDI by multinational firms on host economies, one first must understand firms' motivations to invest. There is growing evidence that multinational firms are now dispersing their value chain activities across different economies. This is to take advantage of different locational advantages and thus optimize efficiency for the company as a whole. In order to effectively conduct these activities, the firms are transferring necessary resources to host economies. This transfer can enhance the competitiveness of the investing firm and the host economy as well along the diamond model's four determinants: factor conditions, demand conditions, related and supporting sectors, and business context (Table 5.3).

Factor Conditions

According to the product life cycle model, many manufactured goods go through a product cycle of introduction, growth, maturity, and decline. Thus, comparative advantage in the production of these goods shifts over

Table 5.3. *Explanatory Variables for FDI*

The Diamond Model		*Dunning (2000)*	*UNCTAD (2000)*	*UNCTAD (2001)*	*Moon & Roehl (2001)*	*Dunning (2003)*[a]
Factor conditions	Basic factors	√	√√	√√	√	√
	Advanced factors	√	√	√√	√	√
Demand conditions	Size	√	√	√	√	√
	Quality				√	√
Related & supporting sectors		√	√√		√	√
Business context	Strategy					√
	Structure		√√	√		√
	Rivalry			√	√	√

a. FDI regarded as an exogenous variable.
Source: The authors.

time from one economy to another. As the market matures in developed economies, the product becomes more standardized, and price becomes the main competitive weapon. At this stage, the locus of production shifts to developing economies to take advantage of cheap labor. In moving production, the investing firm trains workers in the host economy with technology transfer. Types of these technologies that are transferred to the affiliates include product technology, process technology, and managerial know-how. Investing firms can benefit from more productive labor in the host economy with more efficient technology transfer.

Multinational firms can also seek advanced factors, such as technology and skilled labor, across the globe. For example, some firms from developing economies such as Korea and Taiwan (China) invest in California's Silicon Valley, although they do not have any significant advantages relative to firms there. The traditional paradigm of FDI stipulates that a firm goes abroad when it has a significant ownership advantage, but the paradigm governing this new type of FDI states that firms use FDI to acquire access to new advanced advantages. FDI can thus be a learning mechanism.

Demand Conditions

Firms achieve competitive advantage through innovation in product, process, and management; but this is not enough. They also must find new markets. As industries become more global and fixed costs for developing new technologies increase and become huge, there is a growing need for expanding markets. When the domestic market is saturated, firms have to turn to international markets, and they often introduce new products simultaneously in the global market. In the past, firms did so mainly through exports, but nowadays they do so increasingly through FDI. Foreign subsidiaries in host economies produce and serve the local markets. In order to produce good quality products, investing firms have to transfer process technology and management skills to the workers in their host economies. By transferring technologies, the firms can increase their market share.

Related and Supporting Sectors

If related and supporting sectors are located near one another, firms can get easy access to components and machinery as needed. However, what is more significant is the advantage that related and supporting industries provide in innovation and upgrading. Suppliers and end-users located near one another can take advantage of short lines of communication, quick and constant flow of information, and ongoing exchange of ideas and innovations. Firms have the opportunity to influence their suppliers' technical efforts, and they can serve as test sites for R&D work, accelerating the pace of innovation. A clustering of related sectors also increases the likelihood that companies will embrace new skills, and it provides a source of entrants who will bring a novel approach to competing.

Business Context

New information and communication technologies intensify competition while allowing firms to manage widely dispersed international operations more efficiently. Since innovation-intensive industries and their business environments tend to be increasingly global, multinational firms have to be more innovative to maintain their competitiveness. The globalization of technologies and the competitiveness of firms are complementary. Innovation also leads to changes in the characteristics of technology transfer, with advanced technology-intensive activities growing faster than less technology-intensive activities. The increased technology intensity of products reduces the importance of primary and simple low-technology activities in FDI, while raising the importance of skill-intensive activities. Although the main motive of firms is "profit maximization," they would not try to deteriorate the situation of the host country. On the contrary, firms see that activities such as improvement of corporate governance or training actually increase efficiency and can enable them to maximize their profits. In addition, there can be an unintentional positive impact on the host country, such as improving the work ethic and thus contributing to a decline in the number of strikes.

Different economies embody different capabilities. A firm can gain cost advantages or differentiation advantages or both by configuring its value chain so that each activity is located in the economy where the activity can best be performed. This is the key concept of comparative advantage-based competitive advantage. Many activities in globally integrated production systems are technology intensive and dynamic. Their location in appropriate host economies can significantly transform the competitive situation of the firm, and the firm will further benefit by transferring state-of-the-art technologies to the host economies of its activities. Therefore, the global industrial structure will also become more competitive and efficient.

Understanding the motivations of FDI is useful for analyzing the impacts of inward FDI on host economies. As mentioned earlier in this chapter, it is important to give an integrated analysis of the motivations and impacts of FDI. The diamond model, a comprehensive framework, was used to explain the motivations of FDI. In the next section, the case of Korea will be introduced based on the four determinants of the diamond model.

FDI Impacts on Host Economies: The Case of Korea

Although Korea was struck hard by the economic crisis in 1997, the country has been determined to bounce back, and it has actually regained a sound economy. Many scholars and journalists have applauded Korea's policies toward reform and globalization (*The Economist* 2002). The article states that among the five major countries hit by the crisis (Korea, the Philippines, Malaysia, Indonesia, Thailand), Korea had the most drastic comeback in terms of GDP per capita from 1996 to 2001. How could Korea bounce back successfully in such a short time? Has the business sector, especially regarding the foreign firms in Korea, played any role in Korea's recovery? What are the impacts of inward FDI after the crisis? To determine the fundamental sources of Korea's success in the late 1990s, we need to look upon each determinant of the diamond.

Factor Conditions

With respect to factor conditions, there have been significant inflows of investment and technology into Korea, especially after the 1997 crisis. Since then, foreign firms have contributed to job creation (Table 5.4). In 1998, employees of foreign-owned firms in Korea represented only 5.9 percent of the employees of domestic firms; by 2001, this share had increased to 8.3 percent. This suggests that inward FDI has a positive effect on job creation.

FDI inflows were geared toward labor-intensive industries in the 1970s and capital-intensive industries in the 1980s. Beginning in the 1990s, investments were concentrated in technology-intensive industries. In fact, many

Table 5.4. *Employment by Firms in the Republic of Korea, 1998–2001*
(Thousands of persons)

Year	*No. of employees*		*Percent*
	Domestic firms	*Foreign firms*	
1998	2,323.9	136.2	5.9
1999	2,507.7	200.3	8.0
2000	2,653.0	193.0	7.3
2001	2,648.0	219.0	8.3

Source: Chang (2001).

of the IT ventures boomed in the mid-1990s with the help of inward FDI. Here, two aspects are noticeable. First, there may be a correlation between inward FDI flows and the contribution of foreign firms to the production output of Korea. Second, although inward FDI flows as a percentage of gross fixed capital formation was only 5.7 percent in 1998, the production performance of foreign firms was relatively high. From this we can infer that there has been an efficiency increase among the foreign firms in Korea. Technology may have been transferred to foreign affiliates and domestic firms as well. A survey was carried out in 2000 on technology transfer to foreign affiliates (Chang 2002). The foreign affiliates in Korea replied that their firms had experienced positive technology transfers in terms of core technology, managerial skills, and operational skills. Overall, the Korean work force has been transformed from a basic factor to an advanced factor with acquisition of new technologies from foreign firms.

Demand Conditions

Several capable domestic firms may become global suppliers by promoting exports. Acquiring and advancing technologies can enlarge domestic demand and improve the trade balance by means of import substitution and export promotion (Bark and Moon 2002). With their increased income, Korean consumers are spending more and thus enlarging the size of demand. In addition, demand is increasing for higher quality and more sophisticated goods as a result of world-competitive foreign firms that supply world-class products.

With respect to demand size, the domestic market share of foreign-owned firms has been on the rise. The proportion of sales by foreign firms, 6.1 percent in 1997, rose to 18.5 percent in 2000 (Han 2000), while the proportion of value added was 5.2 percent and 18.5 percent, respectively. Exports from foreign firms in Korea also have been on the rise since the crisis, increasing from 13 percent of total exports in 1997 to 18.1 percent in 2000 (Bank of Korea 2003).

By introducing various products in Korea, foreign-owned firms have also raised the sophistication of demand. In fact, with regard to 422 firms surveyed in 2000, 94.9 percent of the technology transfer was made by foreign companies and only 5.1 percent was made by domestic companies (Chang 2002). Furthermore, 36 percent of the R&D activities by foreign firms was geared to new product design.

Bosch Korea, a world leader in electronic home appliances and tools, is a good example of how foreign-owned companies can raise consumers' demand for sophisticated products. Maintaining its reputation as the market leader in Korea, the company not only introduced new products, but it also provided twenty-four-hour repair service and achieved a 99 percent success rate of completed repairs. These accomplishments set the standard of after-sales service in the electric tool industry of Korea. Finally, foreign-owned companies' track record with regard to customer satisfaction is noteworthy. From 1998 to 2003, more than 70 percent of the winners in each industry of the National Customer Satisfaction Index of Korea have been foreign firms. The quality of products and services are represented in this index. Clearly, foreign firms have led the way in expanding the frontier of demand sophistication in Korea. Another example of the impact of FDI on demand sophistication is LG-Philips (Box 5.2).

Related and Supporting Sectors

Foreign firms do not just transfer technologies to Korean workers; they also establish R&D centers in Korea, thereby developing and deepening regional clusters of related-sector and supporting-sector firms. More than 500 R&D centers have been established by foreign firms, about 10 percent of all the centers in Korea. Multinational firms such as Intel, IBM, Maxon Telecom, and Agilent Technologies have invested in R&D centers. IBM, for example, has signed a contract with the Ministry of Information and Communication to invest US$16 million in the creation of IBM Ubiquitous Computing Laboratory, which will develop software adapted to the wireless communication environment (*The Digital Times* 2003). Further efforts by the Korean government to attract R&D centers in cooperation with multinational firms are expected to eventually reform the nationwide science and technology system.

The strengthening of suppliers can lead to various indirect effects and spillovers for the rest of the host economy. Spillovers can take place through demonstration effects, mobility of trained labor, enterprise spin-offs, and competition effects. Strong linkages can promote production efficiency, productivity growth, and technological capabilities. Linkages can be categorized as backward and forward. Backward linkages exist when foreign firms purchase goods and services from domestic firms, and forward linkages occur when foreign firms sell goods and services to domestic firms. Technology transfers by foreign firms can have positive impacts on both kinds of linkages (Bark and Moon 2002). Domestic suppliers linked with foreign firms can have substantially higher sales and export contributions than suppliers that are not linked. GM Daewoo has initiated a "Buy Korea" policy; auto parts are purchased mainly from domestic suppliers such as Inzi Controls,

Box 5.2. *The Commitment of LG-Philips to the Korean Market*

As the result of two major joint venture formations with LG Electronics amounting to US$2.7 billion, Philips has become one of the largest foreign investors in Korea. LG-Philips LCD and LG-Philips Displays are global producers in the highly competitive fields of Thin Film Transistor–Liquid Crystal Displays (TFT-LCDs) and Cathode Ray Tubes (CRTs). Korea represents a vast market for Philips appliances and lighting products.

LG-Philips LCD was created in 1999 when Philips invested a record US$1.6 billion into LG LCD's Gumi plants. In October 2000, the company became the first in the industry to ship more than 1 million 15.1-inch TFT-LCD monitors. Exactly one year later in October 2001, the Gumi operation produced its 4-millionth 15.1-inch TFT-LCD for desktop monitor applications since shipments started in December 1997. The company in 2001 also shipped more than 3.2 million LCDs for monitors, setting an annual record for this segment, and it recorded a 148 percent increase in shipments from 2000 compared to overall industry growth of 142 percent. In the same month, the company unveiled its 29-inch unit for use in high definition televisions, the largest of its kind in the world.

The joint venture succeeded because Philips combined two highly complementary companies. It focused on the strengths of both companies and subsequently built on them to become number one in the TFT-LCD industry. Over 95 percent of production is for integrated users like LG IBM PC, but most customers in this category are based in overseas markets such as Taiwan (China), China, and Japan. Apple and Dell are also the company's corporate clients.

The merger of the displays businesses of Philips Electronics and LG Electronics on July 12, 2001, created LG-Philips Displays. Philips invested US$1.1 billion in this company for a 50-percent stake. With 36,000 employees, 34 factories worldwide, and annual sales of more than US$5 billion, LG-Philips Displays instantly became the world's largest supplier of television and monitor tubes. The merger puts in place all the ingredients required to maintain its number one position in the CRT industry—namely, unmatched technology, manufacturing excellence, and a profound and practical understanding of Western and Asian markets. Although 2001 was a difficult year, the company got off to a good start in 2002 and was on track to increase its world market position to over 30 percent by 2005.

In 2003, one out of four television sets or computer monitors had an LG-Philips Displays tube inside. It was the company's goal to make it one out of three by 2005. Although the company closed its Canadian and Austrian operations and moved production to its new Chinese, Mexican, and Czech factories, LG-Philips Displays remains committed to the Korean market for the long term. Philips has thus cemented its position in two major industries of the future by close association with Korea and a Korean corporation of world-class technologies. Philips is actively driving industry developments. It was the first to generate leading-edge technologies, and it has enabled customers to deliver services tailored to market expectations and aspirations. Because of the vision and commitment of companies such as Philips, Asia/Pacific can no longer be regarded as simply a low-cost production area. Rather it is a global engine of growth fired by key technologies.

Source: Korea Investment Service Center (2003).

Dong Yang Mechatronics, Halla Climate Control Co., and Samlip Industrial Co. Contracts since 2002 have totaled US$420 million under this initiative. Not only does this policy encourage direct exports of products from Korean subcontractors to the GM global network, but it also attracts direct assistance for the development of small and medium-size enterprises.

Business Context

FDI in Korea has enhanced the quality of its business climate. Numerous domestic firms on the verge of bankruptcy have been acquired and upgraded by multinational firms, thus enhancing the efficiency of their operations and their strategic decision making. An atmosphere of willingness to match the global standard was established even among domestic firms. Improving corporate governance was viewed as a means to enhance the competitiveness of firms, and foreign-owned firms were the first movers to pursue that target. More specifically, stakeholders among the firms in Korea have emphasized two major concepts, particularly after the 1997 crisis: transparency and ethics.

In addition to numerous small and medium-size enterprises, leading conglomerates in Korea's economy (Hanbo Steel, Jinro Co., and Daewoo Automobile, for example) have declared bankruptcy mainly because of liquidity trouble. These firms had maintained a super-high debt-to-equity ratio that normally would indicate nontransparent management procedures. Even though foreign firms had high debt-to-equity ratios during the crisis, the ratios still were lower than those of domestic firms in any year in the 1990s. In recent years, foreign firms have substantially reduced their debt-to-equity ratios, indicating that foreign firms have a different structure and strategy from domestic firms. In 1996, the debt-to-equity ratio of domestic firms was at an average of 310.7 percent, declining to 224.1 percent in 2002 (Bank of Korea 2003). In contrast, foreign firms started the debt-to-equity ratio at 229.0 percent in 1996 and significantly reduced the ratio to 62.5 percent in 2002. Foreign firms have paved the way for Korean firms to change their governance structure.

Compared to domestic firms, foreign firms in Korea have fewer labor disputes, even when controlling for relative size of employment (Table 5.5). The main reason for labor disputes among employees of domestic firms was unethical management procedures such as accounting fraud resulting in bankruptcy. Domestic firms are now learning from foreign firms' management procedures that emphasize transparency and ethical practices, essential attributes of competitive firms.

Table 5.5. *Labor Disputes in the Republic of Korea, by Type of Firm, 1996–2000*

	Domestic firms		*Firms with FDI*	
Year	*No. of disputes*	*No. of employees involved in dispute*	*No. of disputes*	*No. of employees involved in dispute*
1996	85	4,725,000	2	246,000
1997	78	4,537,000	5	250,000
1998	129	3,917,000	2	231,000
1999	198	4,027,000	9	640,000
2000	250	4,293,000	31	830,000

Source: Chang (2001).

Figure 5.2 summarizes the impact of FDI in Korea on the country's competitiveness. The determinants of the effects of inward FDI are shown in the figure at the four points of the diamond. The *basic factors* are the effects that appear in Stage 1 when FDI initially begins to flow: capital inflow, employment and production; market share and export; increase in R&D centers and spillovers; debt-to-equity ratio and labor disputes. As a host economy further lowers its barriers to FDI, businesses accumulate knowledge about how to strategically affect the *advanced factors*: technology transfer and efficiency; differentiated products and product quality; linkages and synergy; transparency and competition in Stage 2.

The government can also direct its policy according to these two stages of FDI inflow. Namely, the "stage one" policy can be directed to induce the basic impacts from inward FDI, and the "stage two" policy can be directed to induce the advanced impacts. The Korean government has been successful in implementing the first stage policy and consequently in increasing its inflow of FDI in terms of amount. What has remained as a task for the government is to direct inward FDI to induce more advanced impacts by implementing the "stage two" policy.

Conclusion

The government policy regime regarding FDI was an important factor in explaining the overall trend of inward FDI in Korea. As is well known, in the early stage of Korea's economic development, the government restricted imports and FDI to protect domestic firms. As a result, the FDI inflows in Korea were limited until the early 1990s. The Korean government took a more liberal policy stance toward FDI in 1993, and in 1996 Korea joined the OECD. With these developments, FDI inflows started to show a substantial

Figure 5.2. *The Effects of FDI in the Republic of Korea*

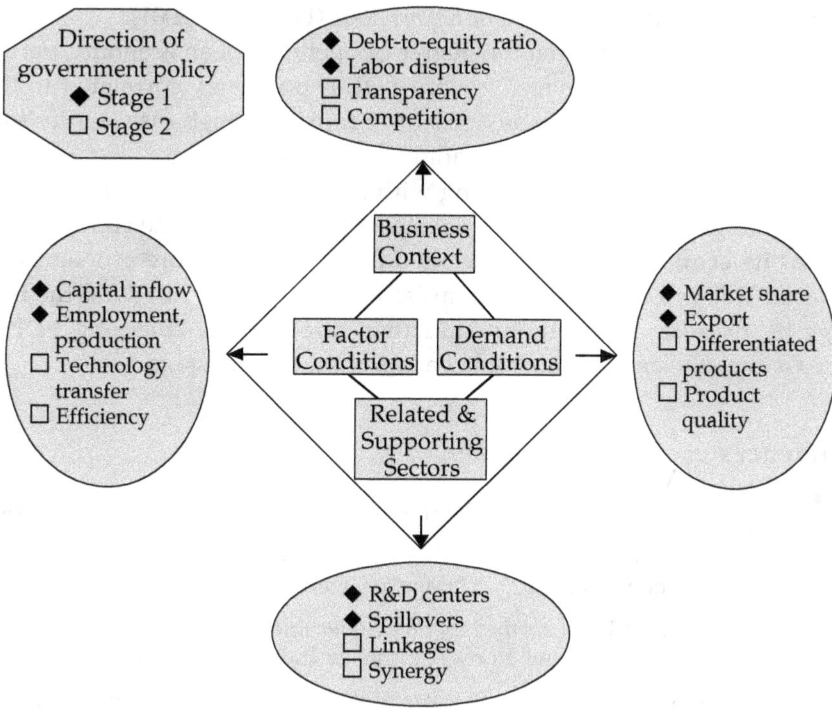

Source: The authors.

increase. After peaking during the postcrisis period of 1999–2000, FDI inflows slowed once again. This decrease in the FDI inflow in Korea may be partially explained by the world economic recession right after the September 11, 2001, incident. However, it also may be attributable to the unattractiveness of the FDI environment in Korea compared to the environment in other economies in East Asia such as China, Hong Kong (China), and ASEAN countries. In addition to FDI policies, domestic economic factors—such as industrial relations, corporate governance and accounting standards, and intellectual property rights protection—affect the FDI inflows.

This chapter has also examined how inward FDI affected the competitiveness of Korea through foreign firms. A rigorous analysis of the impacts of inward FDI on host economies requires a comprehensive analytical model. Throughout this chapter we have introduced the generalized double diamond model (Moon, Rugman, and Verbeke 1995, 1998; Bark and Moon 2002;

Dunning 2003), which extends the single diamond model (Porter 1990). This proves to be a more comprehensive and balanced model than the framework suggested by the *World Investment Report 2001* (UNCTAD 2001).

Our analysis showed that the degree of openness of an economy, particularly the degree of openness toward FDI, is positively correlated to the degree of economic performance. We have found through case studies that inward FDI benefits the host economy. Domestic firms can also upgrade their competitiveness by competing with and learning from foreign firms. Finally, the government should make efforts to improve the competitiveness of its economy by directing its policies toward more efficient FDI impacts. This can be achieved by initially inducing inward FDI at the first stage by opening its economy, and then strategically directing FDI to increase the efficiency of the impact areas at the second stage.

References

Bank of Korea. 2003. *Annual Statistics of Foreign Direct Investment* (in Korean). Seoul.

Bark, Taeho, and Hwy-Chang Moon. 2002. "Globalization of Technologies: The Role of Foreign Direct Investment." *Tech Monitor* (January-February): 20–25.

Chang, Yoon-jong. 2001. *An Analysis of Five Major Effects by Inward Foreign Direct Investment* (in Korean). Seoul: Korea Institute for Industrial Economics and Trade.

———. 2002. "A Study on the Effectiveness of R&D Activities of Foreign Firms and Technology Transfer in Korea (in Korean)." *Science Technology Policy* (July-August): 31–48.

Chang, Yoon-jong, and Joosung Chun. 2000. *Foreign Direct Investment Policy in a Global Economy* (in Korean). Seoul: Korea Institute for Industrial Economics and Trade.

Cho, Dong-Sung, and Hwy-Chang Moon. 2000. *From Adam Smith to Michael Porter.* Singapore: World Scientific.

The Digital Times. 2003. "IBM Establishes a Computing Research Center in Korea." October 24. http://dt.co.kr/content/2003102402019956609001.html.

Dunning, John H. 1958. *American Investment in British Manufacturing Industry.* London: Allen and Unwin.

———. 1977. "Trade, Location of Economic Activity and the Multinational Enterprise: A Search for an Eclectic Approach." In B. Ohlin, P. O. Hesselborn, and P. M. Wikman, eds., *The International Allocation of Economic Activity*, 395–418. London: Macmillan.

———. 1981. *International Production and the Multinational Enterprise.* London: Allen and Unwin.

———. 1988. *Explaining International Production*. London: Unwin Hyman.

———. 1993. *Multinational Enterprises and the Global Economy*. Wokingham, Berkshire: Addison-Wesley.

———. 1995. "Reappraising the Eclectic Paradigm in the Age of Alliance Capitalism." *Journal of International Business Studies* 26: 461–91.

———. 2000. "The Eclectic Paradigm as an Envelope for Economic and Business Theories of MNE Activity." *International Business Review* 9: 163–90.

———. 2003. "The Role of Foreign Direct Investment in Upgrading China's Competitiveness." *Journal of International Business and Economy* 4(1):1–13.

The Economist. 2002. "Five Years On." July 4. http://www.economist.com/.

Han, Ki-in. 2000. "A Study of R&D Activities among the Foreign Firms in Korea." *Korea Industrial Technology Association* (in Korean) 12: 2000–16.

Kang, Joongu. 2001. "Recent Trends of Foreign Direct Investment and Prospects (in Korean)." *Saegae Gyungjae* (September): 50–51.

Korea Investment Service Center. 2003. *Succeeding in Korea*. Seoul: KOTRA.

KOTRA (Korean Trade-Investment Promotion Agency). http://www.investkorea.org.

KPMG Consulting. 2001. *Foreign Direct Investment in Korea* (Summary Report): 12–19. Seoul.

Ministry of Commerce, Industry, and Energy. 2001. *Trends of Foreign Direct Investment in 2000 and the Forecast of 2001* (in Korean), *Annual Statistics.* http://www.mocie.go.kr.

———. 2002. *Trends of Foreign Direct Investment in 2001 and the Forecast of 2002* (in Korean), *Annual Statistics.* http://www.mocie.go.kr.

———. 2003. *Trends of Foreign Direct Investment in 2002 and the Forecast of 2003* (in Korean), *Annual Statistics.* http://www.mocie.go.kr.

Moon, Hwy-Chang, Alan M. Rugman, and Alain Verbeke. 1995. "The Generalized Double Diamond Approach to Global Competitiveness." In Alan Rugman, Julien Van Den Broeck, and Alain Verbeke, eds., *Research in Global Strategic Management: Beyond the Diamond,* 5, 97–114. Greenwich, Conn.: JAI Press.

———. 1998. "A Generalized Double Diamond Approach to the Global Competitiveness of Korea and Singapore." *International Business Review* 7: 135–50.

Moon, Hwy-Chang, and Thomas W. Roehl. 2001. "Unconventional Foreign Direct Investment and the Imbalance Theory." *International Business Review* 10: 197–215.

National Satisfaction Index. *Annual Report.* http://www.ncsi.or.kr.

Porter, Michael E. 1990. *The Competitive Advantage of Nations*. New York: The Free Press.

UNCTAD (United Nations Conference on Trade and Development). 2000. *World Investment Report 2000: Cross-border Mergers and Acquisitions and Development*. New York and Geneva: United Nations.

———. 2001. *World Investment Report 2001: Promoting Linkages*. New York and Geneva: United Nations.

———. 2002. *World Investment Report 2002: Transnational Corporations and Export Competitiveness*. New York and Geneva: United Nations.

———. 2003. *World Investment Report 2003: FDI Policies for Development: National and International Perspectives*. New York and Geneva: United Nations.

6

Inward FDI in Singapore: Policy Framework and Economic Impact

Chia Siow Yue

Singapore is a small island nation of 650 square kilometers and 4 million people. It achieved dynamic economic growth averaging more than 7 percent a year from the mid-1960s until the 1997–98 Asian financial crisis. By 1997 it had attained a per capita gross national product (GNP) of US$26,475. Singapore overcame its size constraint and achieved economic success by integrating into the global and regional economies through international trade and investment. Total merchandise and service trade is more than triple the GNP, reflecting not only a small resource base and domestic market but also the entrepot role and the free trade policy pursued by the Singapore government. Inward FDI stock ranks among the largest of the non-OECD economies. The high FDI penetration reflects the country's role as a global export manufacturing base and its integration into global production networks, as well as its role as a regional services hub in finance, trade, transportation, and logistics. Foreign multinational corporations (MNCs) are considered valuable partners in Singapore's economic development.

This chapter begins with an explanation of inward FDI trends and patterns, particularly since 1990. Singapore's economic strategy, its FDI locational advantages and policy regime, and the development of the electronics industry cluster are then examined. The chapter assesses the impact of FDI on economic growth and the development of the manufacturing sector, including exports, skills development, and technology development. The contribution of FDI to the development of Singapore's services is not covered. The chapter concludes with lessons from the Singapore experience.

Inward FDI Trends and Patterns

UNCTAD (2000b) uses the Inward FDI Performance Index to benchmark a country's success in attracting foreign direct investment. This index is the ratio of a country's share of global FDI flows to its share of global gross domestic product (GDP), and an index value larger than one means the country has attracted FDI that is disproportionately large compared to its GDP size. Singapore's Performance Index was exceptionally high at 13.8 during the 1988–90 period, the highest among the 140 countries in the UNCTAD sample. Although the ranking dropped to 18 a decade later in the 1998–2000 period, Singapore still ranks considerably above the global average.

Table 6.1 summarizes the stock, flows, and investment commitments for inward FDI. Despite the rapid growth of outward FDI since the early 1990s, Singapore remains a net FDI recipient, with inward FDI stock exceeding outward stock by a ratio of 1.7 in 2002. Inward FDI stock rose rapidly in the 1990s, from US$30.4 billion in 1990 to US$124.1 billion by 2002, equivalent to 137 percent of GDP. Balance-of-payments data show annual FDI inflows peaking in 1997 at US$13.5 billion. Inflows plunged 44 percent in 1998, reflecting the fallout from the Asian financial crisis. There was substantial recovery in 1999–2001, but another plunge took place in 2002, giving rise to concerns over loss of investment competitiveness. However, foreign net investment commitments in manufacturing continued to grow and reached new peaks in the 1999–2002 period. Over 90 percent of FDI is direct equity investment, with only minor net lending by parent companies. Singapore has become a mature host economy, welcoming more than 6,000 foreign MNCs and with reinvested earnings and expansion investments accounting for a growing share of FDI inflows. According to UNCTAD (2003, Table A.II.1, 225), reinvested earnings accounted for 28 percent of FDI inflows in 1999 and 75 percent in 2000. Economic Development Board (EDB) data on investment commitments in manufacturing for the period 1980 to 1990 showed expansion commitments exceeding new and diversification commitments; they rose from 51 percent of total commitments in 1980 to over 70 percent in 1989-90 (Low et al. 1993). Mergers and acquisitions (M&As) were not significant, since Singapore was not one of the East Asian "crisis countries." Instead, cash-rich Singapore firms were busy acquiring regional business assets as the crisis countries relaxed their foreign investment restrictions in efforts to recapitalize their distressed corporate and banking sectors (Freeman 2000).[1]

---

1. There is no comprehensive register of mergers and acquisitions in Singapore in the public domain. Therefore, the actual volume and profile of M&A activity in

Table 6.1. *Singapore's FDI Stocks, Flows, and Commitments*

FDI component	*1980*	*1985*	*1990*	*1995*	*2000*	*2001*	*2002*
FDI inward stock (US$m)	6,203	13,016	30,468	65,644	113,431	116,428	124,083
FDI outward stock (US$m)	3,718	4,387	7,808	35,050	53,104	67,255	71,336
Inward stock/GDP (%)	52.9	73.6	83.1	78.7	124.0	132.2	137.5
Outward stock/GDP (%)	31.7	24.8	21.3	42.0	58.1	76.4	79.1
	1991–96[a]	*1997*	*1998*	*1999*	*2000*	*2001*	*2002*
FDI inflows (US$m)	6,656	13,533	7,594	13,245	12,464	10,949	7,655
FDI outflows (US$m)	2,967	8,955	380	5,397	6,061	9,548	4,082
Inflows/GFCF (%)	28.8	37.0	24.7	47.6	45.6	43.8	n.a.
Outflows/GFCF (%)	11.6	24.5	1.2	19.4	22.2	38.2	n.a.
Crossborder M&A sales (US$m)	510	294	468	2,958	1,532	4,871	556
Crossborder M&A purchases (US$m)	966	2,888	530	4,720	8,847	16,516	2,946
Foreign net investment commitments in manufacturing (SGD$m)	3,878	5,964	5,214	6,257	7,235	6,609	7,039
United States	1,735	5,964	2,293	3,587	3,692	3,192	2,432
Europe	1,001	2,032	1,040	1,139	1,722	1,913	2,123
Japan	1,063	2,423	1,822	1,180	1,513	1,340	1,778
Others	79	86	58	352	309	165	706
	1991	*1997*	*1998*	*1999*	*2000*	*2001*	*2002*
Share of Singapore's GDP attributable to resident foreigners & foreign companies	33.8	34.1	34.9	39.2	38.9	41.6	40.4

GFCF gross fixed capital formation.
n.a. Not available.
a. Annual average.
Source: UNCTAD (2003), Department of Statistics, *Yearbook of Statistics* (various years).

Singapore since 1997 are uncertain. Rules and regulations governing mergers and acquisitions are contained in the Singapore Code on Takeovers and Mergers, the Companies Act, and the Singapore Exchange Listing Manual. M&A deals in the financial sector must conform with the Banking Act and receive approval of the Monetary Authority of Singapore.

Foreign ownership is very high in Singapore, reaching over one-third of shareholders' paid-up equity in the corporate sector in the 1990s (Table 6.2). For the manufacturing sector, the foreign ownership ratio rose from around 50 percent in the early 1990s to 62 percent by 2000. The foreign ownership ratios are lower in services, but they are still high compared to other East Asian economies, with the possible exception of Hong Kong, China. The sectoral distribution of FDI reflects Singapore's economic structure as well as the government's industrial policy to develop Singapore as a global manufacturing base and a regional services hub in finance, trade, transportation, and logistics. FDI is larger in services than in manufacturing, with financial and business services, commerce, and transport and storage services accounting for a 62.7 percent share in 2001. The manufacturing sector's share declined during the 1990s from 41.4 percent in 1990 to 36.5 percent in 2001.

As shown in Table 6.3, Singapore's sources of inward FDI are mainly from the advanced industrial economies. Europe leads with a 39.4 percent share. European investments are led by the Netherlands, Switzerland, and the United Kingdom, and they accounted for 53.9 percent of FDI in the manufacturing sector and 31.2 percent in the nonmanufacturing sector (mainly services) in 2001. The United States, the leading single-country investor, accounted for 17.2 percent of total FDI, 20.5 percent in manufacturing, and 15.3 percent in nonmanufacturing activities. Japan is the leading Asian investor. It accounted for 13.5 percent of total FDI, 32 percent in manufacturing and 68 percent in nonmanufacturing activities. ASEAN (the Association of Southeast Asian Nations) accounted for only 4.3 percent of total FDI; most of these investments (more than 90 percent) were in nonmanufacturing activities. From the Asian NIEs (newly industrializing economies), only Hong Kong (China) and Taiwan (China) have sizable FDI in Singapore, primarily in nonmanufacturing activities. Investments from the Caribbean and Latin America are mainly from tax havens and are concentrated in finance and insurance, although there are also sizable investments in manufacturing and commerce.

As shown in Table 6.4, FDI in manufacturing is heavily concentrated in two areas: electronic products and components (45 percent) and chemicals and chemical products (28 percent). Electronic products and components, more than 50 percent of net investment commitments in 2001–2, continue to dominate the manufacturing sector, which will be discussed later.

Table 6.2. *Sectoral Distribution of Foreign Equity in Singapore*

Shareholders' paid-up equity	*1990*	*1995*	*1996*	*1997*	*1998*	*1999*	*2000*	*2001*
All sectors, foreign and local (S$m)	68,139	119,160	138,926	166,792	208,885	242,026	230,326	—
Foreign-owned (S$m)	22,698	35,715	43,115	57,904	73,478	95,735	84,463	—
Foreign equity share (%)	33.3	30.0	31.0	34.7	35.2	39.6	36.7	—
Manufacturing sector, foreign and local (S$m)	10,228	15,415	18,363	21,396	25,475	29,402	28,674	—
Foreign-owned (S$m)	5,139	7,819	9,089	11,360	12,874	16,649	17,864	—
Foreign equity share (%)	50.2	50.7	49.5	53.1	50.5	56.6	62.3	—
Key service sectors, foreign equity share (%)								
Financial services	30.2	29.3	33.5	36.4	40.2	45.1	36.5	—
Commerce	34.7	34.2	33.5	37.4	34.6	39.2	40.6	—
Transport and storage	31.5	18.9	17.3	23.3	26.3	27.3	29.6	—
Insurance services	39.2	42.3	43.5	47.4	47.2	46.3	47.5	—
Foreign direct equity investment stock (S$m)	53,152	92,841	105,015	125,274	139,905	157,594	182,443	202,394
Percent distribution by sector	100.00	100.00	100.00	100.00	100.00	100.00	100.00	100.00
Manufacturing	41.36	38.25	37.56	37.58	37.83	36.50	37.23	36.54
Financial & business services	41.66	44.31	45.28	45.93	43.95	45.62	44.28	44.58
Commerce	12.82	13.18	12.78	12.24	13.62	14.06	13.83	13.94
Other services	4.15	4.27	4.38	4.26	4.60	3.82	4.66	4.94

— Not yet published.

Source: Department of Statistics, *Singapore's Corporate Sector, 1999–2000; Foreign Equity Investment in Singapore, 2000–2001.*

Table 6.3. *Singapore's Stock of Foreign Direct Investment by Country and Sector, 2001*

Country or economy	Total FDI	Manufacturing sector	Nonmanufacturing sector	Total FDI	Manufacturing sector	Nonmanufacturing sector	Manufacturing sector	Non manufacturing sector
	S$million			% distribution			Sectoral shares (%)	
Total foreign	217,282	78,386	138,896	100.00	100.00	100.00	36.08	63.92
Asia	51,098	11,396	39,701	23.52	14.54	28.58	22.30	77.70
ASEAN	9,369	709	8,660	4.31	0.90	6.23	7.57	92.43
Malaysia	5,883	655	5,228	2.71	0.84	3.76	11.13	88.87
Other ASEAN	3,486	54	3,432	1.60	0.07	2.47	1.56	98.44
Hong Kong, China	6,024	244	5,780	2.77	0.31	4.16	4.05	95.95
Japan	29,258	9,360	19,899	13.47	11.94	14.33	31.99	68.01
Taiwan, China	4,694	790	3,904	2.16	1.01	2.81	16.83	83.17
Other Asian	1,751	113	1,638	0.81	0.14	1.18	6.47	93.53
Europe	85,646	42,274	43,371	39.42	53.93	31.23	49.36	50.64
European Union	65,448	29,435	36,013	30.12	37.55	25.93	44.97	55.03
France	4,687	268	4,419	2.16	0.34	3.18	5.71	94.29
Germany	6,274	1,728	4,546	2.89	2.20	3.27	27.54	72.46
Netherlands	34,870	24,901	9,968	16.05	31.77	7.18	71.41	28.59
United Kingdom	14,392	1,114	13,278	6.62	1.42	9.56	7.74	92.26
Other EU countries	5,225	1,424	3,802	2.40	1.82	2.74	27.24	72.76
Switzerland	15,506	12,375	3,132	7.14	15.79	2.25	79.80	20.20
Other European countries	4,692	465	4,227	2.16	0.59	3.04	9.91	90.09
Americas	74,528	24,284	50,245	34.30	30.98	36.17	32.58	67.42
United States	37,300	16,047	21,253	17.17	20.47	15.30	43.02	56.98
Canada	3,086	271	2,815	1.42	0.35	2.03	8.79	91.21
Caribbean/Latin America	34,142	7,965	26,177	15.71	10.16	18.85	23.33	76.67
Australia & New Zealand	3,058	356	2,703	1.41	0.45	1.95	11.63	88.37
Other countries	2,953	76	2,877	1.36	0.10	2.07	2.57	97.43

Note: ASEAN refers to the Association of Southeast Asian Nations.
Source: Department of Statistics, *Foreign Equity Investment in Singapore, 2000–2001.*

***Table 6.4.** Singapore's Stock of Foreign Direct Investment in Manufacturing, 1986, 1990, and 2001*

Manufacturing industry	*1986*	*1990*	*2001*	*1986*	*1990*	*2001*
	S$million			*% distribution*		
Manufacturing sector total	12,194	19,760	78,386	100.00	100.00	100.00
Food, beverages, tobacco	120	296	516	0.98	1.50	0.66
Textiles, wearing apparel, leather	46	132	105	0.38	0.67	0.13
Wood, wood products	58	48	1	0.47	0.24	0.00
Paper, paper products, printing, publishing	136	319	1,430	1.12	1.61	1.82
Chemicals, chemical products	1,322	3,910	22,135	10.84	19.79	28.24
Petroleum, petroleum products	1,821	2,376	7,618	14.93	12.02	9.72
Rubber, plastic products	163	222	1,103	1.33	1.12	1.41
Basic metals	13	40	26	0.11	0.20	0.03
Fabricated metal products	253	453	1,199	2.08	2.29	1.53
Machinery & equipment	1,882	2,077	3,304	15.43	10.51	4.22
Electrical machinery & apparatus	—[a]	—[a]	1,801	—[a]	—[a]	2.30
Electronic products & components	4,483	7,386	35,004	36.76	37.38	44.66
Transport equipment	1,415	1,518	1,630	11.61	7.68	2.08
Instrumentation, photographic & optical goods	303	697	1,302	2.49	3.53	1.66
Others	180	287	1,211	1.47	1.45	1.54

a. For 1986 and 1990, the numbers for electrical machinery & apparatus were included in machinery and equipment.

Source: Department of Statistics, *Foreign Equity Investment in Singapore, 1990–1992; Foreign Equity Investment in Singapore, 2000–2001.*

FDI Determinants and the Policy Regime

Singapore's economic structure reflects its city-state status. In 2002 manufacturing accounted for 26.5 percent of GDP, while services accounted for 63.0 percent. Singapore embarked on industrialization in 1960 when the traditional services engines (entrepot trade and servicing the British military stationed in Singapore) faced gloomy prospects. With political independence in August 1965—and the stark reality of a small domestic market and a dearth of industrial expertise and entrepreneurship—Singapore abandoned the import substitution strategy adopted in 1960 in favor of export manufacturing spearheaded by FDI.

Export Manufacturing Base and Services Hub

Labor-intensive export manufacturing contributed to high economic and employment growth over the next decade. With the emergence of labor shortages by the late 1970s, Singapore's industrial strategy shifted toward higher skill and higher value added manufacturing as well as services.

The 1991 Strategic Economic Plan envisioned high-tech and high value-added manufacturing and services as the twin engines of growth. Manufacturing 2000 targeted manufacturing at not less than 25 percent of GDP. The planners sought to avoid the de-industrialization and hollowing out experienced by Hong Kong (China). They argued that industrial manufacturing capability is an essential component of an advanced economy, and a strong manufacturing base provides an anchor for other advanced capabilities in science and technology, logistics, and operations management.

Singapore's industrial strategy calls for the development of industry clusters, with each cluster having a complex of vertically and horizontally linked supporting industries and resources that collectively make the end-products or services competitive. The strategy seeks to upgrade capabilities across the entire value chain, including product and process development, production, engineering, and strategic marketing. The Economic Development Board established a Cluster Development Fund of S$1 billion (Singapore dollars) and Co-investment Programme to co-invest with foreign multinational corporations (MNCs) and local enterprises in joint ventures and strategic projects.[2]

As of 2002, the leading industry clusters in terms of output are electronics (42.0 percent of the manufacturing total), chemicals (22.8 percent), precision engineering (11.5 percent), transport engineering (7.2 percent), and biomed-

---

2. This co-investment with foreign MNCs is seen as necessary for capital-intensive and high-risk projects, where the standard tax incentive may be inadequate. The Co-Investment Programme involves government equity participation in joint ventures and supports cluster development in three areas. First, it addresses critical gaps in industry clusters with EDB co-investing in new capabilities and critical support industries. Second, it accelerates development of local enterprises. Third, the Co-Investment Programme supports government equity partnerships for strategic investments with local companies and MNCs going regional.

ical manufacturing (6.8 percent). The chemicals cluster had its origins in the petroleum refineries established in the 1960s and 1970s, using imported crude from the Middle East and leveraging on Singapore's role as a bunkering center. Singapore lost some of its competitive edge as a refining center in the 1980s with the emergence of new refineries in the petroleum-producing countries in the Middle East and Southeast Asia. As a result, it embarked on the downstream petrochemical complex using feedstock from the refineries.[3] The newest industry cluster is biomedical sciences, comprising the pharmaceutical, medical technology, biotechnology, and healthcare services industries. The EDB is targeting Singapore as a biomedical hub. Biomedical companies are locating their manufacturing, R&D, clinical development, and headquarters activities there. Specialized and integrated infrastructural complexes, including research and training institutes, have been developed to support the clusters. Foreign MNCs are encouraged to leverage on Singapore's rapidly growing scientific research base and intellectual property protection to develop and testbed new products and processes.

Table 6.5 shows the growth of the electronics industry, with its subsectors of consumer electronics, computers and peripherals, telecommunications, and electronic components. FDI has been crucial in the development of this cluster. In the late 1960s, an investment mission to the United States promoted Singapore as a location and leveraged on the emerging trend of U.S. MNCs seeking export platforms in East Asia to offset rising costs at home. This led to an influx of U.S. multinational corporations engaged in semiconductor assemblies for export. This influx was followed by similar investments from Japan and Europe (Chia 1989). Investments in consumer electronics and industrial electronics followed. Over the next decade, the Singapore industry underwent rapid structural change and upgrading in response to global competition, technological change, and shortening product cycles, as well as domestic labor shortages and rising wages. The responses of multinational corporations to the changing labor market in Singapore have been twofold: (1) process and product upgrading of Singapore operations into automated manufacturing, higher-end products, product design, and R&D or (2) relocation of labor-intensive operations and mature and lower-end product lines to countries with abundant low-wage labor.

---

3. An offshore island (Jurong Island) has been developed as the centerpiece of the chemical cluster and provided with world-class infrastructure and capabilities. The Singapore location provides communications, logistics, and financial infrastructure as well as connectivity to global markets to effectively and efficiently manage their Asian businesses.

Table 6.5. *Singapore's Electronics Industry*

Electronics industry, 1985–2002	*Establishment (No.)*	*Employment (No.)*	*Remuneration S$m*	*Manufacturing output S$m*	*Value added S$m*	*Gross fixed assets S$m*	*Direct exports S$m*
1985	167	65,917	960	9,014	n.a.	n.a.	n.a.
1986	159	68,763	976	11,183	n.a.	n.a.	n.a.
1990	240	122,797	2,160	27,878	n.a.	n.a.	24,027
1991	241	122,839	2,313	28,827	5,922	n.a.	23,676
1992	241	121,954	2,523	31,912	5,594	n.a.	26,312
1993	241	117,048	2,640	39,707	6,161	n.a.	32,964
1994	237	122,380	2,953	48,725	8,231	n.a.	39,830
1995	239	126,891	3,280	57,873	9,543	n.a.	45,162
1996	249	128,033	3,605	62,769	11,988	n.a.	n.a.
1997	236	123,835	3,641	62,904	11,583	n.a.	n.a.
1998	223	111,590	3,588	60,846	10,484	n.a.	n.a.
1999	205	105,826	3,386	68,718	12,321	23,102	53,125
2000	197	102,320	3,870	81,803	17,228	n.a.	n.a.
2001	190	98,012	3,686	60,514	11,615	32,462	46,800
2002	190	88,473	3,372	59,365	11,722	n.a.	n.a.

Breakdown of the electronics industry, 1999	*Establishment (No.)*	*Employment (No.)*	*Remuneration S$m*	*Manufacturing output S$m*	*Value added S$m*	*Gross fixed assets S$m*	*Direct exports S$m*	*Gross fixed assets/ worker S$000*	*Remuneration/ worker S$000*	*Value added/ worker S$000*	*Exports as a % of total sales*
Wafer fabrication	8	8,538	361	4,464	1,209	7,996	1,670	937	42.3	141.6	37.7
Other semiconductor devices	21	15,583	595	9,885	2,306	4,598	8,221	295	38.2	148.0	83.7
Capacitors and resistors	9	3,318	106	591	250	634	332	191	31.8	75.4	58.1
Printed circuit boards without electronic parts	22	5,029	161	1,045	347	1,052	583	209	31.9	69.0	56.3
Printed circuit boards with electronic parts	37	3,568	110	1,143	205	365	881	102	30.8	57.4	77.6
Contract manufacturers	15	7,442	189	2,817	379	451	631	61	25.4	51.0	22.7
Communications equipment	14	4,354	213	3,640	1,094	495	2,906	114	49.0	251.3	80.8
TV sets and other audio/ visual equipment	13	6,536	227	2,366	410	805	2,088	123	34.8	62.7	88.7
Computers and data processing equipment	11	4,944	185	10,221	2,556	674	8,112	136	37.5	517.0	79.6
Disk drives	7	29,324	682	18,924	2,812	2,657	15,982	91	23.3	95.9	84.4
Electronic security system	9	828	44	159	33	60	36	72	53.6	39.7	22.3
Other electronic products & components not elsewhere classified	39	16,362	513	13,464	3,633	3,316	11,683	203	31.3	222.0	86.6
Total electronic products & components	205	105,826	3,386	68,719	15,234	23,102	53,125	218	32.0	144.0	77.6

n.a. Not available.

Sources: Department of Statistics, *Yearbook of Statistics* (various years); Economic Development Board, *Report on the Census of Industrial Production 1999.*

By the mid-1980s, there was rapid growth in production of computers and data processing equipment, computer peripherals and disk drives, and telecommunications equipment. In the 1990s, Singapore invested heavily in semiconductor manufacturing, design, and development—wafer fabrication, IC-design houses, test and assembly facilities, and supporting industries. As shown in Table 6.5, the wafer fabrication industry has the highest gross fixed assets per worker. With the high capital intensity, co-investment by EDB was seen as necessary.[4] By 2002 the electronics cluster produced S$59 billion worth of output. There has been a shrinkage of the industry in terms of the number of establishments and total employment, since many labor-intensive operations relocated out of Singapore, remaining firms upgraded and reduced employment, and new firms became more capital intensive. Trade data show domestic exports reached S$34.1 billion for office machines and S$17.0 billion for electronic parts and components in 2002.[5] The cluster continues to attract the largest investment commitments in manufacturing because the EDB actively promotes investments to manufacture high value-added products, carry out R&D, create and manage intellectual property, and manage regional operations.

FDI and foreign MNCs have always dominated Singapore's electronics industry. A study by Chia (1997), using 1992 firm-level data, showed that the foreign equity share for the industry amounted to 88 percent. FDI penetration was highest in consumer electronics and industrial electronics. In consumer electronics, established international brand names and the technological superiority of foreign MNCs posed strong barriers to entry for local firms. In industrial electronics, foreign ownership was almost 100 percent in the subsectors of computers and data processing equipment, disk drives, and office machinery and equipment. The major computer companies included ALR International, Compaq, Digital Equipment, Apple, Hewlett Packard, and Siemens Nixdorf. Foreign dominance in communications equipment was less strong due to the presence of large state-owned enterprises. In electronic components, foreign equity was dominant in semiconductors and capacitors. Foreign electronics firms were mainly from Europe, Japan, and the United States. Japanese and American firms were dominant in different segments of the industry, with

4. For example, EDB—with Texas Instruments, Hewlett Packard, and Canon—co-invested in SemiTech to fabricate 16M-bit DRAMS.

5. Singapore also had a re-export trade in electronic parts and components that was sizable (S$37.5 billion in 2002).

the Japanese in consumer electronics and the Americans in industrial electronics, reflecting their respective strengths in the global market. Local firms were found mainly in the less scale-intensive, capital-intensive, and technology-intensive segments of the industry (resistors and printed circuit boards), with a proliferation of local firms undertaking contract manufacturing and becoming suppliers to the foreign MNCs. EDB actively promotes the local supporting industry through technical and financial assistance.

As with the continual upgrading and restructuring of the electronics cluster noted above, the Singapore manufacturing sector as a whole has been upgrading and restructuring as it loses comparative and competitive advantages in labor-intensive products and processes. However, Singapore still lacks the innovations and technologies to compete in the league of advanced industrial economies. The Economic Review Committee recommends that Singapore develop new capabilities to become an innovative creator of products and businesses (Ministry of Trade and Industry 2003). It recommends that Singapore identify and develop niche areas and new manufacturing clusters through technology, market, and enterprise development; strengthen interlinkages between industry, R&D, and intellectual property protection; and promote cooperation and co-development by research institutes and local enterprises of products and processes, thus bridging the gap between research and commercialization.

The 1991 Strategic Economic Plan includes not only Manufacturing 2000 but also International Business Hub 2000, a blueprint for the development of Singapore as a regional hub for trading, transport and logistics, telecommunications services, and financial services. Singapore's competitive advantages are numerous: strategic geographical location; well-developed physical infrastructure; expertise in commerce, finance, infrastructure management; a well-educated and English-speaking workforce; a conducive legal environment; minimal restrictions on right of establishment and national treatment in many areas; a favorable tax regime; no controls on capital flows and foreign exchange transactions; and political, social, and economic stability. The *Economic Review Committee Report* (Ministry of Trade and Industry 2003) recommends that Singapore further upgrade trading and logistics, information and communications technology, financial services, and tourism to remain competitive. It identifies new hub activities in healthcare, education, and creative industries. Recommended strategies include removing regulatory impediments and developing land and manpower resources for services.

Motivations: Why FDI?

Foreign direct investment provides in one package finance, technology, management, marketing, and integration into global production networks and supply chains. Unlike technology licensing, it enables continuous access to rapidly changing proprietary technologies. However, not all countries opt for a heavy dependence on FDI because of the costs they perceive (for example, loss of national sovereignty with large-scale foreign ownership and control of productive assets, crowding out of domestic enterprises, and vulnerability to trends in international investment flows). At the same time, some developing countries have been unable to attract FDI because of their negative investment environments.

FDI has played a critical role in Singapore's economic development since political independence in 1965 and for many years before that. Attracting FDI became a policy priority in the mid-1960s when the conventional wisdom among newly independent developing countries was to follow the Dependency School ideology of being hostile to FDI and MNCs.[6] Singapore's FDI strategy was motivated by pragmatism rather than ideology. The first mover advantage enabled Singapore to leapfrog into export manufacturing in the 1960s. The Singapore government viewed as too slow and uncertain the process of transforming domestic trading entrepreneurs into industrial entrepreneurs with international marketing capability (Chia 1989). Initial conditions for industrialization were different in Singapore than in Hong Kong, where an influx of Chinese industrialists and industrial capital fleeing communist China in the late 1940s and early 1950s enabled the transition from entrepot to manufacturing. Initial conditions were also different in the Republic of Korea and Taiwan. Those economies protected the domestic market to nurture domestic enterprise and develop technical and scientific manpower to license foreign technologies.

A moot point is why Singapore remains so dependent on FDI after almost four decades of rapid economic development and industrialization, particularly since it has been a capital exporter since the mid-1980s and is increasingly engaged in outward investment. Two explanations are posited. First, industrial restructuring has been very rapid for the small island nation; Singapore is continually in the "infant industry" mode, and com-

---

6. The Dependency School had a strong following in Latin America and Africa. The development literature of the 1950s and 1960s painted a highly negative picture of foreign investment. It accused foreign investors of political interference in host countries and of exploiting local resources, labor, and enterprises.

petitiveness can be more readily achieved by importing the necessary resources. Second, for most of the period from the 1960s to the 1980s, Singapore failed to develop a vibrant domestic entrepreneurial class with technological and international marketing capabilities.

FDI Determinants and Singapore's Locational Advantages

Dunning's OLI conceptual framework is useful in explaining foreign direct investment (Dunning 1993). Firms invest abroad because of ownership (O) advantages, which can be financial assets, knowledge and technologies, brand names, organization and management and marketing skills, and distribution networks. A firm with these assets can reap rents in foreign markets through overseas production by subsidiaries and joint ventures, or it can enter into licensing, franchising, management, marketing, and turnkey contracts. Firms may seek FDI to internalize (I) the benefits of exploiting the ownership-specific advantage in particular locations, such as to reap monopoly rents or because markets for assets and production inputs may be imperfect or nonexistent. Economies hosting FDI have locational (L) advantages that vary with the motivation of the investing firm. For resource-seeking investments, it is the possession of specific natural resources, labor, skills, technology, or physical infrastructure. For market-seeking investments, it is the size and growth potential of the host market, including preferential access to markets in regional trading arrangements.

For efficiency-seeking investments, it is the host economy's competitiveness and efficiency in producing for the export market. The ability to participate in global and regional production networks and supply chains has increasingly become an important locational advantage; multinational corporations locate different parts of the production processes and service functions across the globe to take advantage of the differences in costs, resources, logistics, and markets (UNCTAD 2002, 121). Three forces are driving the growth of international production systems: policy liberalization that opens up national markets to FDI and other nonequity arrangements; rapid technological change that forces firms to tap world markets and share the costs and risks, while falling transport and communication costs make it economical to integrate distant operations; and increasing competition that results in unexpected forms of relocation to new sites, with new ownership and contractual arrangements and involvement in new activities (Kaplinksy 2000).

Although some of Singapore's inward FDI includes resource-seeking and market-seeking investments, all foreign direct investments are efficiency-seeking since they are highly export oriented. In the 1960s and 1970s, geographical location was an advantage in the establishment of the petroleum refineries and the financial center; a large pool of trainable, low-wage labor was an important resource for labor-intensive manufacturing. For market-seeking investments, government policies have helped overcome the small size of the domestic market with extensive global transportation networks and regional and bilateral trading arrangements. Efficiency-seeking investments emphasize cost and productivity, which include labor and other production costs, procurement and distribution costs, efficiency for "just-in-time" manufacturing, and efficient transportation and logistics. Singapore is well integrated into the MNC international production systems and global supply chains.

Singapore's success in attracting FDI reflects the government's holistic approach: maximizing locational attractions, providing policy coherence, and conducting effective policy implementation. Components of that strategy are outlined below.

THE EDB AND INVESTMENT PROMOTION. The Economic Development Board was established in 1961 to spearhead Singapore's industrialization and FDI drive. The EDB is reputed to be one of the most effective investment promotion agencies in the world. "Professionalism, dedication and leadership all played a role in this success" (Hughes 1993, 15). The EDB works closely with an International Advisory Council that includes the global heads of leading multinational corporations.[7] The Council advises on international and regional strategies, and with various business networks. The EDB maintains a network of overseas promotion offices in North America, Western Europe, and Asia and targets sectors, activities, and firms for investment promotion in line with the government's overall economic and industrial strategies. It functions as an effective one-stop investment center. The Economic Development Board is known for speed in handling investment applications, an important consideration for time-sensitive products such as electronics. Notably, the EDB focuses not only on pre-investment but also on post-investment services, keeping existing investors satisfied so that they are encouraged to stay, reinvest, and expand. The satisfaction of investors is evident from the high proportion of foreign direct investments in Singapore each year that are reinvestment and expansion investments.

---

7. The 2003 Council includes the chairman of Agilent Technologies Inc., the chairman of Asahi Glass Co. Ltd., the chairman of BASF Aktiengesellschaft, a Board member of DaimlerChrysler AG, and the CEO of Exel plc.

FDI Policy Framework and Tax Incentives. Singapore has maintained an FDI policy regime since the mid-1960s characterized by three features. The first is the general absence of entry and ownership restrictions and performance requirements. Foreign investors are generally accorded right of establishment and national treatment (except for selected services), and they are represented on various national advisory and policymaking councils and committees together with their local counterparts. There are no performance requirements on joint ventures, local employment, local content, technology transfer, or exporting. There are no restrictions on foreign borrowings from the domestic capital market; no foreign exchange controls or limits are placed on repatriation of capital, dividends, interest, and royalties. The second feature is the provision of physical and human infrastructure and generous investment incentives. Singapore's attractiveness also is enhanced by its transparent and well-established legal framework. Third, the FDI regime is characterized by policy consistency over time and policy coherence. This provides predictability for investors and fosters effective policy implementation.

UNCTAD (1996) noted host country governments' increasing use of investment incentives to encourage inward FDI. These include fiscal incentives (such as tax holidays and tax concessions) and financial incentives (such as grants and preferential loans, land and factory site subsidies, credit subsidies, and training subsidies). In the developed countries the financial incentives are more common, while in developing countries, except for subsidies for infrastructure in industrial estates and export processing zones, tax holidays and other fiscal measures that do not require direct payments of scarce public funds are more common. However, the literature on investment incentives is highly critical of the use of the tax incentive. It is often argued that tax incentives are ineffective in attracting investments, distort resource allocation, and lead to loss of tax revenue; in addition, developing host economies compete unnecessarily with each other and raise the extent and cost of subsidies (Hughes and You 1969; Hughes 1993). Blomstrom and Kokko (2003) are more positive on tax incentives, making a case for them based on knowledge spillovers from FDI to local industry. For example, local firms may be able to improve their productivity as a result of forward or backward linkages with MNC affiliates; they may imitate MNC technologies or hire workers trained by MNCs. Foreign entry may also force local firms to introduce new technology and work harder. The authors caution, however, that such positive spillovers are not automatic, and potential spillover benefits can be realized only if local firms are able to absorb foreign technologies and skills.

Singapore makes extensive use of the tax incentive, in part to compensate for locational disadvantages (such as the high cost of land and labor and the small size of the domestic market) and in part to attract FDI to targeted sectors and activities that would promote Singapore's dynamic comparative advantage. The tax incentives were first introduced in 1959 for the purpose of encouraging the establishment and growth of new industries. The tax incentives now cover industrial expansion, use of foreign technology, skills development, industrial upgrading, innovation and R&D, and a growing range of service activities. There are also allowances to encourage capital investment and reinvestment and co-investments by the EDB and other government agencies for targeted capital-intensive strategic investments. A survey by Chng et al. (1986) covering the machinery, precision equipment, electrical, and electronics industries showed that investment incentives constituted an important factor motivating foreign investors. Indeed, investment incentives ranked second to political stability. Chia and Freeman (2000) surveyed ASEAN countries (including Singapore); 77 percent of the investors who responded to the survey said that incentive measures were important in the decision where to locate an investment.

It is difficult to estimate the quantity of FDI inflows to Singapore that would have occurred in the absence of tax incentives and the hypothetical fiscal revenue forgone. However, data are available on manufacturing establishments that have received the pioneer tax holiday at some time or other. Table 6.6 shows that they form a sizable segment of the manufacturing sector. By 2001, although they accounted for only 9.2 percent of total manufacturing establishments, they accounted for 67.1 percent of manufacturing gross fixed assets, 39.9 percent of manufacturing employment, 69.3 percent of manufacturing output, 64.0 percent of manufacturing value added, and 80.1 percent of manufacturing direct exports. The pioneer establishments are found to be larger than average in size, have higher output and value added per worker, and have higher export orientation.

The government is continuously introducing new tax incentives to promote new manufacturing and service activities or to improve the competitive edge of existing activities. This proliferation over the years has raised two issues: the constant need to fine-tune the tax incentives as new activities emerge and the growing burden on tax administration. The case for a low uniform corporate income tax, as pursued by Hong Kong, to replace the tax incentives has become more cogent. In an increasingly complex technological and business environment, industrial targeting in attempts to pick winners has become increasingly difficult. Moreover, Singapore's corporate tax regime has become the second lowest in East Asia (after Hong Kong). It fell progressively from 40 percent in the 1960s to 20 percent in 2003; in the process, the margin of preference provided by the tax incentive has fallen

Table 6.6. *Manufacturing Establishments in Singapore with Pioneer Status*

Indicator	*1990*	*1996*	*2000*	*2001*
Pioneer establishments				
Establishments (number)	415	397	362	373
Employment (number)	166,078	170,780	139,389	137,788
Manufacturing output (S$m)	43,435	82,418	113,656	92,129
Total output (S$m)	n.a.	83,356	116,613	94,788
Value added (S$m)	13,470	17,118	26,783	20,425
Remuneration (S$m)	3,308	5,352	5,841	5,817
Gross fixed assets (S$m)	20,308	36,115	54,199	61,779
Direct exports (S$m)	33,828	56,293	75,765	67,493
Pioneer extablishments/ total manufacturing (%)				
Establishments	11.2	9.8	9.0	9.2
Employment	47.2	46.4	40.4	39.9
Manufacturing output	60.9	68.8	71.6	69.3
Total output	n.a.	68.0	71.2	68.5
Value added	81.6	62.5	68.8	64.0
Remuneration	48.1	47.6	46.9	45.9
Gross fixed assets	61.9	63.6	66.2	67.1
Direct exports	72.0	77.2	80.7	80.1

n.a. Not available.
Source: Department of Statistics, *Yearbook of Statistics 2003.*

dramatically. Investors, local corporations and multinational corporations alike, may prefer a simple tax rate that is low and uniform since tax incentives are both selective and temporary.

CONDUCIVE BUSINESS ENVIRONMENT. Singapore's tax incentives are not the core locational attraction for FDI; rather, they are the "icing on the cake." The core locational attraction is Singapore's political, social, and legal institutions and governance, and its macroeconomic policies.

- Political and social stability and public governance. In a relatively turbulent region, Singapore has been an oasis of political and social stability. Industrial peace has prevailed since the early 1970s. Singapore's political leadership and bureaucracy are noted for integrity, probity, and competence, contributing to a positive business environment and low business transaction costs.

- Macroeconomic management. Singapore has one of the best-managed economies in East Asia. In addition to high growth and full employment, the country has had low inflation rates and stable exchange rates. The economy did not succumb to the contagion of the Asian financial crisis in 1997 because it had in place a sound financial system and prudent fiscal, monetary, and exchange rate policies.[8] Macroeconomic stability protected the asset values of foreign investors and contributed to cost predictability.
- Legal and regulatory framework. Singapore has a transparent legal and regulatory framework readily understood by the international investment community, and its enforcement record is strong. As Singapore has moved toward a high-tech and knowledge-based economy, it has put in place a strong intellectual property protection regime that has become critical for both FDI as well as the development of local innovation and R&D.[9]
- Industrial labor. Until the mid-1970s an abundant supply of low-cost industrial labor and an education system with improved technical education and industrial training contributed to the competitive edge for labor-intensive industries in Singapore. Since then, labor shortages have grown, and there has been industrial restructuring up the technology ladder. As a result, labor policy shifted its focus to upgrading the work force and relaxing immigration restrictions. Tertiary education expanded rapidly. By 2000, 60 percent of an age cohort was enrolled in polytechnics and universities compared to less than 5 percent in the mid-1960s. Scientific, engineering, and business education was emphasized. Inflows of foreign workers, particularly the skilled and professional, intensified to account for one quarter of Singapore's labor force. A tripartite system of indus-

---

8. Although Singapore was not one of the "crisis countries" suffering massive outflows of funds and plunging exchange rates, its growth performance after 1997 was affected by the meltdown of regional economies and the sharp fall in regional demand for its goods and services.

9. Singapore is a member of the Paris Convention, Berne Convention, Madrid Protocol, Nice Agreement, Patents Cooperation Treaty, Budapest Treaty, World Trade Organization Agreement on Trade-Related Aspects of Intellectual Property Rights (TRIPS), and the World Intellectual Property Organization (WIPO). Several multinational corporations have made Singapore, because of its intellectual property reputation, the launch pad for their IP activities in the region.

trial relations put in place since the early 1970s has helped ensure industrial peace.

- Physical infrastructure. Infrastructure-related bottlenecks and inefficiencies add to production and distribution costs. Singapore's physical infrastructure is planned way ahead and built in time to avoid supply bottlenecks. The country's physical infrastructure for business—industrial estates and science parks, sea and air transportation and telecommunications, and water and power supplies—is not only world class but readily available to meet business needs.
- Local suppliers. Since the mid-1980s, emphasis has been placed on developing a network of reliable and competent local suppliers for the electronics, chemicals, engineering, and precision industries. Such an availability has become an important selling point in investment promotion by the Economic Development Board.
- Market access and regional and global connectivity. Singapore is handicapped by a small domestic market. Therefore, access to wider markets and regional and global connectivity were keys to Singapore's success in attracting FDI. Under various free trade agreements, the global transportation and telecommunications connectivity is being reinforced by preferential market access to Southeast Asia, East Asia, and beyond.[10]

The Effects of FDI on the Economy

Foreign direct investment supplements as well as complements domestic resources. During the 1960s and 1970s, capital inflow from FDI helped to close the savings-investment gap and finance net imports of goods and services. By the mid-1980s, the national savings rate exceeded 40 percent of GNP, and Singapore had become a net capital exporter. Nonetheless, Singapore continues to rely heavily on FDI for other resources, in particular, technological and managerial know-how and links to global production and distribution networks.

---

10. By the end of 2003, Singapore was part of the ASEAN Free Trade Area and had negotiated or was negotiating free trade agreements with China, the Republic of Korea, and Japan in East Asia; Australia and New Zealand in Oceania; India and Sri Lanka in South Asia; the United States, Canada, and Mexico in North America; the European Free Trade Area; and Jordan in the Middle East.

GDP and Manufacturing Sector Development, Employment, and Exports

The Singapore economy has been growing at an average annual rate of over 7 percent since the mid-1960s. Foreign companies and foreign residents (managers, professionals, skilled and unskilled workers) have contributed sizably to that growth performance. Official statistics show that the share of Singapore's GDP attributable to resident foreign companies and resident foreigners rose from less than one-third of GDP in 1990 to over 40 percent in 2001–2 (Table 6.1).[11] The high GDP growth contributed by FDI has helped Singapore attain one of the highest per capita incomes in the world. It has also enabled Singapore to rapidly transit from a labor-surplus economy with near double-digit unemployment in the early 1960s to a labor-shortage economy by the late 1970s. Foreign labor composed one quarter of the work force by the turn of the twenty-first century.

Many studies (UNCTAD 2002 and others) have highlighted the contribution of FDI and MNCs to export performance and competitiveness, and in the process to the host country's income, employment, foreign exchange earnings, and economic efficiency. FDI contributes to the level and growth of exports and their diversification and technological and skill content. With the growth of international production systems and supplier networks, new forms of export competitiveness geared to international production systems enable host developing economies to enter techno-intensive activities and produce internationally branded products that otherwise could not have been created. In addition, local firms benefit from arm's length licensing and from contractual arrangements for original equipment manufacturers (OEM).

Since FDI in Singapore focuses mainly on export manufacturing and exportable services, it has made a vital contribution to the country's export performance and competitiveness. In 2002 exports of goods and services amounted to S$283 billion or 188 percent of GDP. Table 6.7 shows the growing sophistication of Singapore's nonoil domestic exports.[12] In 2002 the

---

11. Since the economy is heavily dependent on foreign capital, technology, and workers, a large share of the compensation of employees and of the operating surplus, as recorded in the national accounts, accrues to foreigners and foreign enterprises. The Department of Statistics computes the income accruing to foreign workers and foreign enterprises that reside in Singapore.

12. Total exports of goods includes both entrepot exports and domestic exports, the former being re-exports of imported goods and the latter being goods produced in Singapore. Domestic exports have been classified into oil and nonoil exports, the former comprising mainly refined petroleum and oil bunkers.

major nonoil exports were machinery and equipment (67.5 percent, mainly electronics) and chemicals (15.5 percent); in 1970 these two categories accounted for only 19.0 percent and 4.2 percent, respectively. The sophistication of Singapore's manufacturing sector is evident from Table 6.8. The major industries in Singapore in 2001, as measured by manufacturing output and value added, were electronic products and components, chemicals and chemical products, refined petroleum products, transport equipment, machinery and equipment, and pharmaceutical products. These are industries characterized by high gross fixed assets per worker, high value added per worker, high remuneration per worker, and high export levels.

Table 6.9 highlights the direct contribution of FDI to Singapore's manufacturing sector development. The sector is characterized by an exceptionally high level of foreign participation, particularly of firms with 100 percent foreign ownership. Foreign dominance has grown over time. In 2001 foreign firms (defined in the manufacturing census as those with at least 50 percent foreign equity) accounted for 78.7 percent of manufacturing output, 71.9 percent of manufacturing value added, 48.5 percent of manufacturing employment, and 88.0 percent of manufacturing direct exports. The 100 percent-foreign firms alone accounted for 72.0 percent of manufacturing output, 66.6 percent of manufacturing value added, 42.1 percent of manufacturing employment, and 83.3 percent of manufacturing direct exports. In contrast, although the 100 percent-local firms accounted for 41.2 percent of employment, they accounted for only 15.0 percent of manufacturing output, 19.9 percent of value added, and 7.0 percent of direct exports.[13] Among foreign firms, U.S. firms form the largest segment, contributing over half of the manufacturing sector's output, value added, and exports; the United States is followed by Europe and Japan. Comparing the 100 percent-foreign firms and the 100 percent-local firms, we find that the foreign firms have higher fixed assets per worker, higher value added per worker, and higher remuneration per worker, and they are much more export oriented (71.9 percent export ratio) than local firms (29.8 percent export ratio). The value added/employment ratio indicates the productivity of labor and inversely the labor intensity of production. While 100 percent-local firms have a ratio of 0.48, the 100 percent-foreign firms have a ratio of 1.57, with the joint ventures falling in between with a ratio of 0.7.

13. It should be noted that direct exports exclude sales of goods to domestic entities that are eventually exported.

Table 6.7. *Singapore's Domestic Exports*

Exports	*1970*	*1980*	*1990*	*1996*	*1997*	*1998*	*1999*
					S$million		
Total domestic exports	1,832	25,805	62,754	103,589	107,535	105,918	116,325
Oil exports	792	14,180	17,137	16,551	19,090	16,385	18,531
Nonoil exports	1,040	11,625	45,618	87,038	91,624	92,445	101,182
Food	105	601	958	1,259	1,275	1,221	1,237
Beverages & tobacco	12	103	386	494	407	393	263
Crude materials	30	152	460	495	562	549	498
Animal and vegetable oils	49	394	587	299	316	333	346
Chemicals	43	573	3,619	5,626	6,650	7,163	10,393
Medicinal products	8	258	251	298	282	383	1,291
Plastic materials	3	100	958	1,374	1,711	1,933	2,207
Manufactured goods	170	1,323	2,127	2,844	2,935	2,565	2,696
Veneer & plywood	41	334	94	21	13	12	9
Textile yarn & fabrics	23	262	193	282	289	263	330
Iron & steel	12	116	153	241	248	215	187
Machinery & equipment	198	6,567	32,352	70,288	72,845	72,428	76,363
Office machines	34	364	14,520	37,415	39,453	39,916	40,601
Industrial machines	2	126	512	659	746	879	745
Electric motors & resistors	6	346	1,004	2,287	2,400	2,441	2,828
Radio & TV receivers & parts	20	1,872	4,846	4,418	3,131	2,762	2,376
Electronic components & parts	n.a.	2,203	5,148	15,111	16,877	17,109	20,000
Ships, boats & oil rigs	10	588	303	435	238	599	429
Miscellaneous manufactures	145	1,887	4,866	5,176	6,017	7,005	8,522
Clothing	66	757	1,793	699	654	718	798
Optical & photographic equipment	0	154	146	279	342	445	490
Watches & clocks	3	143	184	243	303	236	236
Musical instruments	2	90	274	765	1,351	1,816	2,821
Miscellaneous	289	27	263	558	617	787	865

n.a. Not available.
Source: Ministry of Trade and Industry, *Economic Survey of Singapore*, various years.

2000	2001	2002	1970	1980	1990	2000	2002
			% distribution				
135,938	118,444	119,438	100.00	100.00	100.00	100.00	100.00
28,425	27,675	26,680	43.24	54.95	27.31	20.91	22.34
113,071	96,728	98,579	100.00	100.00	100.00	100.00	100.00
1,345	1,387	1,550	10.13	5.17	2.10	1.19	1.57
260	262	233	1.13	0.88	0.85	0.23	0.24
650	580	572	2.88	1.31	1.01	0.58	0.58
282	267	325	4.69	3.39	1.29	0.25	0.33
10,718	12,059	15,283	4.16	4.93	7.93	9.48	15.50
971	1,214	866	0.80	2.22	0.55	0.86	0.88
2,939	2,898	3,829	0.33	0.86	2.10	2.60	3.88
3,077	2,867	3,428	16.34	11.38	4.66	2.72	3.48
8	7	8	3.97	2.87	0.21	0.01	0.01
427	382	482	2.21	2.25	0.42	0.38	0.49
245	264	300	1.14	1.00	0.34	0.22	0.30
85,852	68,674	66,548	19.00	56.49	70.92	75.93	67.51
38,390	33,755	34,090	3.27	3.13	31.83	33.95	34.58
944	1,152	1,151	0.17	1.08	1.12	0.83	1.17
3,027	2,498	2,543	0.61	2.98	2.20	2.68	2.58
2,559	2,218	1,705	1.93	16.10	10.62	2.26	1.73
27,904	19,033	17,036	n.a.	18.95	11.29	24.68	17.28
925	654	324	0.96	5.06	0.66	0.82	0.33
10,068	9,840	9,743	13.89	16.23	10.67	8.90	9.88
872	707	689	6.30	6.51	3.93	0.77	0.70
558	600	600	0.02	1.32	0.32	0.49	0.61
233	249	214	0.28	1.23	0.40	0.21	0.22
3,548	3,430	3,102	0.21	0.78	0.60	3.14	3.15
819	792	899	27.77	0.23	0.58	0.72	0.91

Table 6.8. *Singapore's Manufacturing Sector by Industry, 2001*

Industry code	*Industry*	*Gross fixed assets %*	*Employ-ment %*	*Manu-facturing output %*	*Value added %*	*Direct exports %*	*Gross fixed assets/ worker S$000*	*Remuner-ation/ worker S$000*	*Value added/ worker S$000*	*Exports as a % of total sales*
31	Electronic products, components	35.3	28.4	45.5	36.4	55.6	331	37.6	119	76.5
24	Chemicals, chemical products	22.5	5.2	11.9	16.5	14.8	1,152	69.4	294	74.5
241	Petrochemicals, petrochemical products	13.8	1.3	5.0	2.9	4.5	2,943	95.0	215	57.9
242	Pharmaceutical products	2.8	0.7	3.8	8.8	7.1	1,096	67.2	1,178	99.1
243	Other chemicals, chemical products	5.9	3.3	3.1	4.9	3.2	478	60.0	138	64.7
23	Refined petroleum products	10.6	0.8	13.3	4.0	7.7	3,412	110.7	453	35.8
28	Fabricated metal products	5.1	10.9	4.6	5.5	2.4	124	29.5	46	33.4
29	Machinery, equipment	5.0	11.8	5.2	7.8	4.7	114	35.8	61	57.9
33	Transport equipment	4.1	11.4	5.3	9.1	4.2	97	35.8	74	51.5
15 & 16	Food, beverage, tobacco	3.3	4.7	2.5	3.1	1.5	189	30.7	62	37.2
22	Printing, reproduction of recorded media	2.9	5.3	2.0	3.9	0.7	143	39.2	68	22.4
25	Rubber, plastic products	2.6	6.1	2.0	3.0	1.2	116	27.9	46	39.6
30	Electrical machinery, apparatus	2.1	2.9	1.6	2.2	1.5	193	36.5	69	57.7
26	Nonmetallic mineral products	1.8	1.7	0.9	0.9	0.3	298	30.8	52	21.0
32	Medical, precision, optical instruments	1.6	3.0	2.2	4.2	3.1	138	36.8	62	37.2
21	Paper, paper products	1.0	1.3	0.6	0.8	0.3	209	33.2	55	34.2
27	Basic metals	0.4	0.4	0.4	0.3	0.2	270	44.9	63	30.1
18	Wearing apparel except footwear	0.3	2.3	0.6	0.7	0.8	33	18.5	26	87.3
20	Wood, wood products except furniture	0.2	0.5	0.2	0.2	0.1	96	26.7	40	34.2
17	Textile, textile manufactures	0.2	0.4	0.2	0.2	0.2	112	26.9	55	34.5
19	Leather, leather products, footwear	0.1	0.3	0.1	0.2	0.2	66	29.2	68	22.4
34	Other manufacturing industries	0.8	2.5	0.7	0.9	0.3	88	26.5	35	27.5
35	Recycling of waste and scrap	0.2	0.2	0.2	0.1	0.1	268	34.3	56	46.0
	Total Manufacturing	100.0	100.0	100.0	100.0	100.0	267	36.7	92	62.4

Source: Economic Development Board, *Report on the Census of Manufacturing Activities 2001.*

Table 6.9. *Singapore's Manufacturing Sector by Capital Structure*
(Percent)

Capital structure	*Total output*	*Value added*	*Employ-ment*	*Remun-eration*	*Direct exports*	*Direct exports to output ratio*
1975						
Wholly local	18.1	24.3	32.8	29.4	8.9	—
Over half local	10.7	13.0	15.2	15.6	7.0	—
Under half local	15.0	15.3	20.5	20.5	18.0	—
Wholly foreign	56.2	47.4	31.5	34.5	66.1	—
Total	100.0	100.0	100.0	100.0	100.0	—
1980						
Wholly local	15.6	19.1	28.1	26.3	7.1	—
Over half local	10.7	13.5	13.4	15.2	8.2	—
Under half local	15	13.3	18.5	17.6	13.2	—
Wholly foreign	58.7	54.1	39.9	40.9	71.5	—
Total	100.0	100.0	100.0	100.0	100.0	—
1990						
Wholly local	15.1	16.4	29.0	24.9	7.8	—
Over half local	9	10.9	12.0	13.8	6.4	—
Under half local	13.8	9.3	10.1	10.4	12.5	—
Wholly foreign	62.1	63.4	48.9	50.9	73.3	—
Total	100.0	100.0	100.0	100.0	100.0	—
2001						
Wholly local	15.2	19.9	41.3	31.9	7.0	29.8
Over half local	6.3	8.1	10.9	12.2	4.9	49.6
Under half local	6.6	5.4	6.3	7.3	4.7	43.5
Wholly foreign	71.9	66.6	42.2	48.5	83.3	71.9
Total	100.0	100.0	100.0	100.0	100.0	62.4
Local[a]	21.5	28.1	51.8	44.12	11.97	35.7
Foreign[a]	78.5	71.9	48.2	55.88	88.03	69.5
% distribution of foreign						
United States	53.2	53.4	41.2	43.2	61.3	80.9
Japan	17.1	16.9	31.2	27.2	14.0	57.0
Europe	21.2	23.7	18.3	21.3	19.2	61.3
European Union	19.8	21.8	15.7	18.1	17.8	60.4
United Kingdom	4.6	9.6	2.6	3.6	7.0	87.7
Netherlands	7.5	3.8	3.8	5.4	1.3	12.3
Germany	3.5	4.9	4.5	4.2	4.4	89.8
France	0.8	1.2	1.2	1.5	0.8	69.1
Other EU countries	3.3	2.3	3.5	3.2	4.4	91.2
Switzerland	1.2	1.5	2.0	2.5	1.2	79.1
Other European	0.3	0.4	0.6	0.7	0.2	63.4
Other foreign	8.5	6.0	0.4	8.2	5.5	44.5

— Not available.

a. Based on 50 percent of equity cut-off.

Source: Economic Development Board, *Report on the Census of Industrial Production* and *Report on the Census of Manufacturing Activities*, various years.

Contribution to Skills and Technology Development

Multinational corporations possess modern technologies, international brand names, and a global marketing presence. A key expectation of host countries is that some of these advantages will spill over to the domestic economy, work force, and firms. Positive spillovers take place through vertical linkages, horizontal linkages, labor turnovers, and labor spin-offs (Miyamoto 2003). Vertical backward and forward linkages occur when MNCs train or provide technical support to local firms that supply them with intermediate goods or buy their products. Horizontal linkages occur when domestic firms in the same industry gain skills through industry-wide or region-wide skills development institutions supported by MNCs. Labor turnover occurs when managers and workers in MNCs switch employment to local firms. Labor spin-offs occur when an MNC employee starts up a new firm based on the know-how gained from previous experience. All four spillovers have been evident in Singapore, but there are no quantitative estimates.

Wong (2003) has divided Singapore's technological development into four phases.[14] The first phase covers the early 1960s to the mid-1970s. This is the period of the industrial take-off; foreign MNCs transfer manufacturing technologies and skills development through the educational system and on-the-job learning among technicians and operators working for foreign MNCs. There were few innovation links between the foreign MNCs and the rest of the Singapore economy and few local supporting industries. The second phase spans the mid-1970s to the late 1980s. It is marked by local technological deepening with the rapid growth of local process technological development within MNCs and the development of local supporting industries. The third phase, from the late 1980s to the late 1990s, is characterized by the rapid expansion of applied R&D by foreign MNCs as well as by local firms and local public R&D institutes. The fourth phase, which began in the late 1990s, is marked by the emerging emphasis on high-tech start-ups and basic R&D development. Wong reckons that Singapore's ability to operate and adapt technologies is now close to the world frontier. Singapore's ability to innovate and pioneer new technologies, however, still lags considerably behind this frontier.

---

14. For a comprehensive discussion of Singapore's national innovation system, see Wong (2003).

Skills Development and Training. The availability of skilled labor is a key factor in attracting FDI, particularly in high-tech and high value-added industries. Skills development also is something a host developing economy expects from FDI. In Singapore the close cooperation between the government and multinational corporations promoted skills development.

Singapore started off with labor-intensive, low-skill industrialization in the early 1960s. As industries become increasingly sophisticated, skills and training requirements increase. During the late 1960s, the government began to reform the education and training system. It focused the curriculum on technical and vocational education and the development of the Institute for Technical Education (ITE). Tertiary education in polytechnical institutions and universities began to expand rapidly in the early 1980s. In particular, education in technology and engineering improved in an effort to meet the growing demand for advanced technicians and engineers. In the 1990s Singapore also sought to attract tertiary-educated professionals and managers. Wong (2003) notes that after the mid-1970s, local employees in MNCs were no longer just learning to use the technologies transferred from abroad; instead they began to adapt and improve upon them through on-the-job learning. Local employees also were increasingly mastering more sophisticated process technologies.

In addition to improving formal education, the government of Singapore sought to improve the labor supply in other ways. In 1979 it established the Skills Development Fund (SDF) through levies on employers (local and foreign). The Fund provides subsidies to train and upgrade the skills of the workers in both foreign and local enterprises. The levy on employers was 1 percent of the payroll of their employees earning not more than S$1,500 a month. SDF disbursements for training have grown over the years, and by 2001 the SDF had committed S$112 million for some 650,000 trainees to improve their productivity and quality-related skills, computer-related skills, technical production and engineering skills, technical service skills, management and supervisory skills, and trade and craft skills.

The government's commitment to industrial training can also be seen in the training centers and institutes established by the Economic Development Board in partnership with foreign multinational corporations and foreign governments. During the 1970s, three training centers were set up—in collaboration with India's Tata, Germany's Brown Boveri, and the Netherlands' Philips—to produce skilled craftsmen in tools and die making, precision machining, CNC machining, CAD/CAM, and advanced metrology. Craftsmen were given two years of intensive in-center training followed by two years of on-the-job training. The centers trained twice the number of workers required by the participating MNCs, with the rest of the trainees released to the labor market. Initially, the participating multinational corporations assumed 50 percent of recurrent expenditures, and the government bore the remaining 50 percent as well as the capital costs.

The Economic Development Board also established three institutes of technology in the 1980s in partnership with the governments of Germany, France, and Japan. The goal was to focus on the full-time training of technicians and technologists in precision engineering, factory automation, advanced manufacturing technology, mechatronics, and electronics. In 1993 the Tata and Brown Boveri centers were restructured and integrated into a single Precision Engineering Institute providing precision engineering labor and technical services to the tool and die industry. In the same year, EDB transferred the institutes to the Nanyang Polytechnic and the Institute of Technical Education. Other specialized technical training programs established in the 1980s included the Institute of Systems Science (ISS), the Information Communication Institute of Singapore (ICIS), the Japan-Singapore Artificial Intelligence Center (JSAIC), and the Automation Application Center (AAC). The Economic Development Board also established a Capabilities Development Division to fund new training programs to meet labor requirements of FDI projects in the pipeline. For example, in anticipation of FDI in the second half of the 1990s for semiconductor wafer fabrication, the EDB funded new programs for rapid training of wafer fab engineers in local universities and by attachment overseas.

The centers and institutes established under the EDB created teaching factories where real working conditions and operations of modern factories were simulated. They provided ready access to proven training systems, expertise, and state-of-the-art hardware and software. A steady stream of highly trained personnel was made quickly available to support the growth of specific sectors and facilitate quick factory start-ups and expansions. These training centers and institutes complement the efforts of other training organizations in Singapore to augment the pool of craftsmen, technologists, and engineers. Over the years Singapore has developed a strong reputation for technical training.

SPILLOVERS, LINKAGES, AND DEVELOPMENT OF LOCAL ENTERPRISES. Transfer of technology and know-how from parent MNCs and associates to their subsidiaries in host countries, and the promotion of linkages between foreign MNCs and local suppliers, are the most common spillover effects of FDI. Host governments use a range of investment incentives as well as performance requirements to induce such spillovers.

Chng et al. (1986) found that the turnkey method was the most common method of setting up factories in Singapore. Foreign training for local employees was also cited in the 1986 survey as well as visits by foreign experts and expatriate engineers stationed in Singapore on a contractual basis. Reliance on foreign experts and on residential engineers usually is greater when firms are newly established and not yet completely familiar with the technology. The new technology introduced may be relatively labor-intensive technology transferred from the home country, or it may be brand-new technology that is being tried out in Singapore for the first time. Dependence on technology from the turnkey phase may gradually lessen with localization of management and professional labor. All firms provide some form of on-the-job training for their workers; some have in-house training programs to enhance their capacity for technology absorption.

Positive spillover effects from joint ventures between foreign MNCs and local firms have not been substantial in Singapore since joint ventures have not proliferated. In 2001, of 4,041 manufacturing establishments employing at least 10 workers, there were only 401 joint ventures (both majority and minority foreign-ownership) as compared to 649 100-percent-foreign-owned establishments and 2,991 100-percent-local-owned establishments. The formation of joint ventures has been left entirely to market forces, and the market incentives are not strong. Export manufacturing obviates the need for local partners familiar with local market conditions; a transparent legal and regulatory framework and a noncorrupt and competent bureaucracy obviate the need for local partners to facilitate dealings with the government; and stable industrial relations anchored in institutionalized tripartism obviates the need for local partners to trouble shoot problems with unions and workers. More joint ventures could improve spillover effects. In recent years, matchmaking efforts by government agencies and chambers of commerce and industry have increased, including in product and process development and basic research. Through the Industry Cluster Development strategy, the EDB has facilitated joint ventures and technology alliances between Singapore firms and major MNCs in several high-tech industries, including semiconductor wafer fabrication and chemicals.

Local private enterprises in Singapore—unlike in Hong Kong (China), the Republic of Korea, and Taiwan (China)—have not played a significant role in the country's industrial takeoff and industrial upgrading. Until the late 1980s, local private enterprises remained weak. It took considerable time before a sizable local supporting industry emerged. Since FDI policy imposed no local content requirement, the MNCs had no incentive to source locally unless it was cost effective, and local firms did not meet technical standards in the early years. The emergence of local private enterprises was spurred by the requirements of the electronics industry for myriad parts and components, and by the Economic Development Board's active role in developing the technical and managerial capability of small and medium-size enterprises in Singapore. Local sourcing by multinational corporations contributed significantly to the technological development of local firms through exposure to their procedures and technologies in the buyer-supplier relationship. Long-term relationships helped reduce the suppliers' risk of investing in new technologies, contributing to greater technological effort by local supporting industries (Wong 2003). Linkages between MNC buyers and local suppliers also take place more frequently if buyers and suppliers operate in the same spatial and industrial area, and Singapore's cluster development promotes such interactions. In addition to learning from their MNC buyers, local firms invested in acquiring and exploiting imported technologies on their own, and such in-house product development capabilities in turn allowed the foreign MNCs to source more sophisticated components locally (Wong 2003).

An example of the EDB's role in facilitating ties between multinational corporations and local suppliers is the Local Industry Upgrading Program (LIUP) established in 1986. The participating MNCs provide assistance to their local vendor firms to help them improve their operational efficiency, develop new technical capabilities, and become more competitive. The program benefits the participating MNCs by giving them access to high-quality, cost-competitive products on a timely basis. The LIUP is implemented in three phases. Phase 1 attempts to improve overall operational efficiency through production planning and inventory control, plant layout, and financial and management control techniques, for example. Phase 2 involves introduction and transfer of new products or processes to the local enterprises. Phase 3 involves product and process research and development with MNC partners. By 2002 the Local Industry Upgrading Program had 124 multinational companies partnering more than 1,000 local companies.

RESEARCH AND DEVELOPMENT. Singapore has reached a stage of development where economic competitiveness must be based increasingly on innovation rather than cost efficiency. Since the early 1990s the industrial strategy has been emphasizing innovation and research and development.

Before then R&D activities in Singapore remained low for a number of reasons. Industrial growth in the 1960s and 1970s depended more on cost efficiency than on knowledge and innovation. The MNC subsidiaries in Singapore had ready access to processes and technologies from their overseas parents, and MNCs generally preferred to conduct R&D in their home base. Moreover, Singapore lacked a critical mass of scientists and researchers to provide a stimulating research environment. From their firm-level survey, Chng et al. (1986) found that most of the basic research, product design, product development, process development, and innovation technologies were done in the home base. Only process adaptation appeared to be a significant element in local R&D, with some MNC subsidiaries also involved in application technology. A firm-level study by Amsden et al. (2001) estimated that multinational corporations in Singapore accounted for more than 40 percent of Singapore's total R&D spending (an exceptionally high percentage for late-industrializing economies). However, the study also noted that the R&D activity in Singapore was less advanced than at corporate headquarters and rarely involved basic research or even applied research. In the early phase, the focus was on solving process and product design problems in manufacturing. Increasingly, in response to various government incentives, MNCs began to undertake more experimental development and applied research.

Since the early 1990s, the Singapore government has been pushing research and development using an array of institutional incentives, infrastructure and manpower support incentives, and financial and fiscal incentives. In 1991 the Strategic Economic Plan highlighted innovation as crucial for long-term competitiveness; the first National Technology Plan had a S$2 billion budget to promote R&D and related manpower and support infrastructure; and the National Science and Technology Board was established to oversee the development of science and technology in Singapore. The second National Technology Plan (1996) had a budget allocation (S$4 billion) that was twice as big as the budget for the first plan. This second plan emphasized the development of science in addition to technology. The third National Science and Technology Plan (2001) had an even higher budget allocation of S$7 billion, with a larger proportion earmarked for long-term strategic and basic research. In addition, new policy initiatives were announced in 1998 under Industry21, Manpower21, and Technopreneurship21. Reflecting the government's emphasis on the life sciences as a new growth sector, a US$1 billion Life Sciences Fund was announced in 2000 to accelerate the funding of R&D and technology commercialization in the life sciences.

In the new R&D environment, some large local firms also started to invest in applied R&D, the most well known being the government-linked companies under the Singapore Technology Group. There was also rapid establishment of public R&D institutes and expansion of R&D in tertiary institutions. Toh and Choo (2003) found that the research institutes in the public sector possess strategic basic research and applied research capabilities that complement the multinational corporations' product development expertise. These institutes deploy their personnel and resources in numerous collaborative efforts with industry, and they help the private sector deal with manufacturing-based problems that they could not solve themselves with experimental development. This collaboration is cited by many MNCs as an important factor in their establishment of R&D facilities in Singapore. With new waves of FDI and technological upgrading and deepening in the manufacturing sector, more and more MNCs began to establish R&D activities in Singapore. In addition, a growing number of MNC plants provide the engineering to develop new processes to support product launches and later to transfer them to other countries. Several MNCs—such as Philip consumer electronics and Hewlett-Packard ink-jet printers and hand-held computers—began to locate selected "world product charter" operations in Singapore, with full responsibility for product innovation from R&D and product launch to marketing and sales (Wong 2003).

As shown in Table 6.10, the *National Survey of R&D Expenditures in Singapore* conducted by the National Science and Technology Board (NSTB) and its successor, the Agency for Science, Technology and Research, records rising R&D activities from 1990 to 2002. The number of organizations engaging in research and development rose from 292 to 564. National gross expenditures on R&D (GERD) rose from 0.9 percent of GDP to 2.2 percent. The number of research scientists and engineers per 10,000 workers rose from 27.7 to 73.5, as the government encouraged local graduates to enter R&D careers and attracted foreign scientists and engineers to Singapore. The presence of a sizable and vibrant pool of local R&D personnel helps attract foreign talent. And the availability of R&D personnel has become a key factor in Singapore's ability to attract MNCs to transfer new processes and high-tech product lines. In 2002 Singapore citizens accounted for 81 percent of research scientists and engineers, the rest being permanent residents and other foreigners.

Survey data for 2002 show private sector GERD reached S$2.1 billion—more than 60 percent of total GERD. The bulk of private sector GERD is in manufacturing (72.4 percent). Research and development in the private sector is still predominantly in experimental development (62.6 percent), followed by applied research (33.0 percent), and basic research (4.4 percent).[15]

15. The survey defines "experimental development" as directed at producing new materials, products, and devices; installing new processes, systems, and services; or improving substantially those already produced or installed. "Applied research"

The cumulative number of patents owned reached 1,739, the number of patent applications for the year reached 936, and the number of patents awarded for the year reached 451. Although these numbers represent very fast growth in recent years, they are still very low when compared to those of the Republic of Korea, Taiwan (China), and the advanced industrialized economies.

Table 6.10 also shows R&D by foreign firms in Singapore in 2002. MNCs account for S$1.1 billion—52.9 percent of private sector GERD and 32.5 percent of national GERD. The MNC share of private sector GERD has been declining after peaking at 74.5 percent in 2002. The bulk of the GERD by MNCs is in experimental development (60.4 percent), with applied research accounting for 34.5 percent and basic research only 5.1 percent. At the national level, the MNCs account for 39.4 percent of experimental development, 32.3 percent of applied research, and 10.7 percent of basic research. The contribution of multinational corporations to manufacturing R&D appears to be lower than their contributions to manufacturing sector output, value added, and direct exports, as noted earlier. However, the data are not strictly comparable because the R&D survey defines a foreign firm as one with at least 70 percent foreign equity, and the industrial census uses a 50 percent equity cut-off. Even so, it would appear that many MNCs in Singapore still prefer to source their technologies from parent offices and affiliates elsewhere. Over half of GERD by MNCs is in electronics (mainly information-communications end products, computer peripherals, and semiconductors), followed by precision engineering, chemicals, and biomedical sciences.

Conclusion

Singapore has relied heavily on foreign direct investment as the driver of economic growth and economic restructuring since the early 1960s. It has succeeded in attracting a level of FDI far beyond its economic size. By 2002 the inward FDI stock had reached US$124 billion or 137.5 percent of GDP. FDI inflows rose progressively and reached US$13.5 billion by 1997. Since then, the effects of the Asian financial crisis and resultant economic recessions and

is to acquire new knowledge directed primarily toward a specific practical objective. The results of applied research are intended primarily to be valid for a single or limited number of products, operations, methods, or systems. "Basic research" is experimental or theoretical research to acquire new knowledge without any particular application or use in view.

Table 6.10. *Singapore's R&D*

Indicator	*1990*	*1991*	*1992*	*1993*	*1994*
Number of organizations performing R&D	292	331	354	436	454
Private sector	266	311	331	410	427
Public sector	26	20	23	26	27
Research scientists and engineers	4,329	5,218	6,454	6,629	7,086
Private sector	1,363	2,315	3,187	3,248	3,561
Public sector	2,966	2,903	3,267	3,381	3,525
RSE per 10,000 labor force	27.7	33.6	39.8	40.5	41.9
R&D expenditures (S$million)	572	757	950	998	1,175
As % of GDP	0.9	1.0	1.2	1.1	1.1
Public sector (S$million)	262	315	372	379	439
Private sector (S$million)	310	442	578	619	736
% share of GDP	0.5	0.6	0.7	0.7	0.7
% share of total R&D expenditures	54.1	58.4	60.8	62.0	62.7
% share by foreign companies	n.a.	n.a.	n.a.	67.6	74.5
Manufacturing (S$million)	n.a.	n.a.	n.a.	502	580
Nonmanufacturing (S$million)	n.a.	n.a.	n.a.	117	156
Basic research	n.a.	n.a.	n.a.	n.a.	n.a.
Applied research	n.a.	n.a.	n.a.	n.a.	n.a.
Experimental development	n.a.	n.a.	n.a.	n.a.	n.a.
R&D output					
No. of patents owned (cumulative)	n.a.	n.a.	96	200	204
No. of patents applied	n.a.	n.a.	n.a.	142	263
No. of patents awarded	n.a.	n.a.	20	52	58

R&D expenditures by foreign companies, 2002	*S$m*	*% distribution*	*% of private sector R&D*	*% of national R&D*
Total	1,106	100.0	52.9	32.5
Manufacturing	857	77.5	56.6	n.a.
Biomedical sciences	51	4.6	99.2	n.a.
Electronics	636	57.5	62.6	n.a.
Semiconductors	127	11.5	31.9	n.a.
Computer peripherals	158	14.2	71.4	n.a.
Information communication end products	304	27.5	88.5	n.a.
Other electronics	47	4.3	86.8	n.a.
Chemicals	55	5.0	68.6	n.a.
Specialty chemicals	32	2.9	70.9	n.a.
Other chemicals	23	2.1	65.6	n.a.
Precision engineering	89	8.1	38.4	n.a.
Transport engineering	14	1.3	15.1	n.a.
General manufacturing	12	1.1	28.4	n.a.
Services	246	22.2	52.4	n.a.
Basic research	56.4	5.1	61.2	10.7
Applied research	381.8	34.5	55.4	32.3
Experimental development	667.9	60.4	51.0	39.4
No. of patents owned (cumulative)	679	n.a.	47.7	n.a.
No. of patents applied	394	n.a.	59.7	n.a.
No. of patents awarded	138	n.a.	39.4	n.a.

n.a. Not available.
Source: Agency for Science, Technology, and Research (various years); Wong (2003).

1995	1996	1997	1998	1999	2000	2001	2002
470	526	543	604	624	582	558	564
440	496	508	571	593	539	513	519
30	30	35	33	31	43	45	45
8,340	10,153	11,302	12,655	13,817	14,483	15,366	15,654
4,163	5,085	5,792	6,573	7,502	7,997	8,389	8,598
4,177	5,068	5,510	6,082	6,315	6,486	6,977	7,056
47.7	56.3	60.2	65.5	69.9	66.1	72.5	73.5
1,367	1,792	2,105	2,492	2,656	3,010	3,233	3,405
1.2	1.4	1.5	1.8	1.9	1.9	2.1	2.2
485	659	790	956	986	1,144	1,188	1,314
881	1,133	1,315	1,536	1,671	1,866	2,045	2,091
0.7	0.9	0.9	1.1	1.2	1.2	1.3	1.3
64.5	63.2	62.5	61.6	62.9	62.0	63.3	61.4
64.3	67.0	61.2	55.8	55.8	na	57.6	52.9
730	1,000	1,110	1,335	1,336	1,512	1,625	1,515
152	133	204	201	335	354	420	577
n.a.	n.a.	n.a.	n.a.	n.a.	n.a.	n.a.	92
n.a.	n.a.	n.a.	n.a.	n.a.	n.a.	n.a.	689
n.a.	n.a.	n.a.	n.a.	n.a.	n.a.	n.a.	1,310
256	614	831	847	1,077	1,268	1,456	1739
242	316	490	579	673	774	913	936
51	91	132	136	161	239	410	451

uncertainties in the region, as well as the downturn of the global electronics cycle and weaker performance of the Singapore economy, have led to lower annual FDI inflows.

Singapore has been able to leverage on foreign finance, technology, entrepreneurship, and management expertise and integration into global production and distribution networks to achieve the growth in GDP, employment, and exports and the increasing technological sophistication of its manufacturing sector and export structure. Foreign companies and foreign workers contributed to over 40 percent of Singapore's GDP by 2001–2 and helped the country achieve a per capita GNP that is among the highest in the world. FDI contributed to the growth and export performance of Singapore's manufacturing sector. In 2001 firms with at least 50 percent foreign equity ownership accounted for 78.7 percent of manufacturing output, 48.5 percent of manufacturing employment, and 83.3 percent of manufacturing direct exports. Both the manufacturing output and manufactured exports of Singapore show increasing technological sophistication. With regard to the industrial upgrading over the decades, foreign MNCs have played a crucial role in introducing new technologies to Singapore and in the training and skill development of the work force and the local supporting industries. Since the early 1990s, foreign MNCs have been making significant contributions to Singapore's R&D activities.

Key components of Singapore's success with FDI and foreign MNCs suggest possible lessons for other host developing economies. Singapore had an early mover advantage since in the early 1960s few developing economies were keen to attract FDI for export manufacturing. Therefore, Singapore's locational advantages loomed large on the radar screen of potential investors. The radar screen has since become crowded. A growing band of countries vie with each other to host FDI. However, Singapore has been successful in building on its initial advantage to maintain its investment competitiveness through the years. It maximizes its locational advantages through a holistic approach and a comprehensive FDI policy package that includes the following: an efficient and honest government bureaucracy to facilitate business and keep transaction costs low; a transparent and well-established legal and regulatory framework, including intellectual property protection; macroeconomic stability and industrial peace; a highly effective investment promotion agency; an absence of entry and ownership restrictions and performance requirements combined with tax incentives and co-investment funds to induce FDI into targeted industries, services, and activities; partnership with MNCs to upgrade training facilities and government reform of the formal education system, which together produce a skilled and technologically oriented work force; provision of industrial estates and science parks and other physical infrastructure; and ready access to global markets and global sourcing of inputs through a free trade policy and world-class transportation and telecommunications networks.

The FDI policy package was effective because three conditions were present. First, there was political and social stability to minimize investors' risks. Second, there was policy coherence and consistency. For example, the offer of generous tax incentives was not negated by restrictive performance requirements that undermined efficiency. Policies were not subject to unpredictable and whimsical changes, and the government could keep faith with its investors over time. Third, there was successful policy implementation. Often countries put forward impressive programs, policies, and promises but fail on the delivery.

Enterprise and innovation are critical for the next phase of Singapore's economic development. The heavy dependence on FDI has an Achilles heel in the form of a weak local enterprise sector. Singapore's local enterprise sector is much weaker than the local enterprise sectors in Hong Kong (China), the Republic of Korea, Taiwan (China), and even in some of the ASEAN countries. Many factors contributed to this weakness. In the early phases of industrialization, local enterprises did not have a protected market and could not pass on the learning costs of local infant industries. Government policy failed to provide the necessary technical and financial assistance to help absorb some of these learning costs. There was no organization like the EDB with the mandate to develop local enterprise. Local small and medium-size enterprises also did not operate on a level playing field vis-à-vis the foreign MNC competitors since they lacked the same level of financial, technological, managerial, and marketing resources as well as international brand names. The foreign MNCs also had better access to local bank credit and were able to recruit the best local workers.

Official efforts to assist local private enterprises stepped up in the mid-1980s, but by then almost two precious decades had been lost. Initially, the policy focus was on developing local enterprises to be suppliers to the foreign MNCs in Singapore. Not until the 1990s was policy priority accorded to helping local enterprises become home-grown MNCs and to promoting indigenous innovations. This priority has been given greater emphasis in recent years with major revamps of the educational curricula and changes in government rules and regulations to promote a more creative and innovative society, local enterprise sector, and local work force in Singapore.

References

Agency for Science, Technology, and Research. various years. *National Survey of R&D Expenditures in Singapore*. Singapore.

Amsden, Alice, Ted Tschang, and Akira Goto. 2001. "Do Foreign Companies Conduct R&D in Developing Countries? A New Approach to Analyzing the Level of R&D, with an Analysis of Singapore." Institute Working Paper 14, March. Tokyo: Asian Development Bank.

Blomstrom, Magnus, and Ari Kokko. 2003. "The Economics of Foreign Direct Investment Incentives." Working Paper 168, January. Stockholm: European Institute of Japanese Studies.

Chia, Siow Yue. 1989. "The Character and Progress of Industrialisation." In Kernial S. Sandhu and Paul Wheatley, eds., *Management of Success: The Moulding of Modern Singapore*. Singapore: Institute of Southeast Asian Studies.

———. 1997. "Singapore: Advanced Production Base and Smart Hub of the Electronics Industry." In Wendy Dobson and Chia Siow Yue, eds., *Multinationals and East Asian Integration*. Canada and Singapore: International Development Research Centre and Institute of Southeast Asian Studies.

———. 2000a. *FDI Policy Regimes and Practices in ASEAN and their Applicability to Africa*. Report prepared for UNCTAD, August.

———. 2000b. "Singapore: Destination for Multinationals." In John H. Dunning, ed., *Regions, Globalization, and the Knowledge-Based Economy*. Oxford: Oxford University Press.

Chia, Siow Yue, and Nick Freeman. 2000. *Study on Investment Incentives and Impediments in the ASEAN Region: Policy Recommendations to Rebuild Investor Confidence and Attract Direct Investment Inflows*. Research consultancy monograph for the ASEAN Secretariat, September.

Chng, Meng Kng, Linda Low, Tay Boon Nga, and Amina Tyabji. 1986. *Technology and Skills in Singapore*. Singapore: Institute of Southeast Asian Studies.

Department of Statistics. *Foreign Equity Investment in Singapore, 1990–1992*. Singapore.

———. *Foreign Equity Investment in Singapore, 2000–2001*. Singapore.

———. various years. *Yearbook of Statistics*. Singapore.

———. 2002. *Singapore's Corporate Sector, 1999–2000*. Singapore.

Dunning, John H. 1993. *Multinational Enterprises and the Global Economy*. Wokingham: Addison-Wesley.

Economic Development Board. various years. *Report on the Census of Industrial Production*. Singapore.

———. various years. *Report on the Census of Manufacturing Activities*. Singapore.

Economic Review Committee. 2003. *Economic Review Committee Report*. Singapore: Ministry of Trade and Industry.

Freeman, Nick. 2000. *A Profile of Merger and Acquisition (M&A) Activity in Singapore since 1997*. Monograph prepared for the ASEAN Secretariat, September.

Guisinger, Stephen E., et al. 1985. *Investment Incentives and Performance Requirements.* New York: Praeger.

Hughes, Helen. 1993. "An External View." In Linda Low et al., eds., *Challenge and Response: Thirty Years of the Economic Development Board*. Singapore: Times Academic Press.

Hughes, Helen, and Poh Seng You, eds. 1969. *Foreign Investment and Industrialization in Singapore*. Canberra: Australian National University Press.

Kaplinsky, Raphael. 2000. "Spreading the Gains from Globalisation: What Can Be Learned from Value Chain Analysis?" *Journal of Development Studies* 37(2):117–46.

Lall, Sanjaya. 2000. "The Technological Structure and Performance of Developing Country Manufactured Exports." *Oxford Development Studies* 28(3): 337–69.

Low, Linda, Toh Mun Heng, Soon Teck Wong, Tan Kong Yam, and Helen Hughes. 1993. *Challenge and Response: Thirty Years of the Economic Development Board*. Singapore: Times Academic Press.

Ministry of Trade and Industry. 2003. *Economic Survey of Singapore 2002*. Singapore.

Miyamoto, Koji. 2003. "Human Capital Formation and Foreign Direct Investment in Developing Countries." Technical Paper 211, July. Paris: OECD Development Centre.

Oman, Charles. 2000. *Policy Competition for Foreign Direct Investment: A Study of Competition among Governments to Attract FDI.* Paris: OECD Development Centre.

Ritchie, Bryan K. 2002. "Foreign Direct Investment and Intellectual Capital Formation in Southeast Asia." Technical Paper 194, August. Paris: OECD Development Centre.

Toh, Mun Heng, and Adrian Choo. 2003. "Economic Contributions of Research and Development in Singapore." In *Economic Survey of Singapore 2002.* Singapore: Ministry of Trade and Industry. February.

UNCTAD (United Nations Conference on Trade and Development). 1996. *Incentives and Foreign Direct Investment*, Current Studies, Series A, No. 30. Geneva and New York: United Nations.

———. 1999. *World Investment Report*. Geneva and New York: United Nations.

———. 2000a. *The Competitiveness Challenge: Transnational Corporations and Industrial Restructuring in Developing Countries*. Geneva and New York: United Nations.

———. 2000b. *World Investment Report.* Geneva and New York: United Nations.

———. 2001. *World Investment Report.* Geneva and New York: United Nations.

———. 2002. *World Investment Report.* Geneva and New York: United Nations.

———. 2003. *World Investment Report.* Geneva and New York: United Nations.

Wong, Poh Kam. 1999. *The Dynamics of HDD Industry Development in Singapore.* Singapore: National University of Singapore, Centre for Management of Innovation and Entrepreneurship.

———. 2003. "From Using to Creating Technology: The Evolution of Singapore's National Innovation System and the Changing Role of Public Policy." In Sanjaya Lall and Shujiro Urata, eds., *Competitiveness, FDI and Technological Activity in East Asia.* Cheltenham: Edward Elgar.

7

Firm-Level Productivity and FDI in Taiwan

Bee-Yan Aw

One of the hallmarks of the decade beginning in 1985 is the significant increase in the international flow of long-term private capital, particularly of foreign direct investments (FDI). Feenstra (1998) documents the surge of investment into developed countries in the second half of the 1980s, followed, since 1990, by a rapid increase of investments into developing countries, especially China. More than one-third of the total inward flow of FDI has ended up in developing countries in recent years.

However, compared to international trade, the absolute magnitude of FDI in Taiwan (China) has been small. This is clear from the performance indicators of the economy. Between 1975 and 1985, the share of exports in gross domestic product (GDP) grew from 38.4 percent to nearly 50 percent a decade later, figures that are significantly higher than those in other developing countries. In contrast, the share of FDI in GDP hovered around 1.1–1.2 percent during the same period. However, beginning in the mid- to late 1980s, inflows of FDI surged. This surge reflected, in part, the rapid expansion of FDI into developing East Asia at a rate that exceeded that of world trade.

Formal FDI figures understate the importance of foreign firms in Taiwan. Many studies focusing on the industrial development of Taiwan conclude that FDI is one of the key sources of technology transfer. The transfer

I would like to thank Eric Ramstetter, Shujiro Urata, Mei Ling Sieh Lee, and participants at the FDI workshop in Bali, Indonesia, on November 30 and December 1, 2003, for very helpful comments.

of new technologies, managerial skills, marketing networks, and externalities associated with knowledge or technology spillover from the presence of FDI are of greater significance than the actual size of the capital inflow. Moreover, researchers have found that the extent of these benefits is highly dependent on the institutional framework under which FDI occurs. In particular, the higher the level of human skills, the greater the degree of interaction between domestic and foreign firms; the more outward-oriented the trade policy, the more likely are the growth-enhancing effects of FDI. All of these features are clearly present in Taiwan, suggesting that the bulk of the benefits from FDI in Taiwan, especially if spillovers are important, is likely to be grossly underestimated.

This chapter uses firm-level data from the Taiwanese Census of Manufactures to examine the changing trend and structure of inflows of FDI into Taiwan and the impact on overall productivity. In particular, the chapter focuses on the role of inward FDI in determining the productivity of firms with foreign ownership; the networks of subcontracting activities among Taiwan's manufacturing firms; and the extent to which FDI helps firms without any foreign ownership that are located in the same physical location or industry as those with FDI.

Trends in Foreign Direct Investment

In the 1970s, the growth in inward FDI lagged behind that of exports. Export growth was very rapid, averaging over 30 percent per year from 1970 to 1979, before declining to 18 percent annually in the 1980s, and eventually falling to single digit growth rates in the 1990s.

Table 7.1 shows the contrasting pattern in the growth rates of FDI, GDP, and exports. As export growth slowed between the 1970–79 period and the 1990–96 period, so did GDP growth, indicating the tight link between these two growth indicators. FDI growth was high in the 1980s. It slowed down significantly in the early 1990s before reaching over 38 percent annually between the onset of the Asian crisis in 1997 and 2000. This annual rate is more than five times the rate of export growth over the same time period. FDI inflows into Taiwan peaked in the 1987–89 and 1995–97 periods and again in 2000, when the rate of growth was almost 80 percent. These patterns reflect the general surge in FDI into East Asia beginning in the mid-1980s, a development that contrasts with declining growth rates in both exports and GDP over the same period.

However, unlike exports, the absolute magnitude of FDI in Taiwan is small, with the actual flows increasing from only 0.43 percent of GDP in 1986 to just above 1 percent of GDP in 1999. Table 7.2 presents the absolute

Table 7.1. *Average Annual Rates of Growth in Taiwan of FDI, GDP, and Exports*
(Percent)

Time period	*FDI growth*	*GDP growth*	*Export growth*
1970–79	16.7	10.2	31.7
1980–89	27.5	8.1	18.3
1990–96	6.8	6.7	8.0
1997–2000	38.5	5.7	7.5

Source: Council of Economic Planning and Development (2001).

figures of actual and approved inward FDI and its share of GDP. Although approved inflows of FDI have risen from an annual average of less than US$1 billion between 1980 and 1989 and US$2.6 billion between 1990 and 1999 to a peak of US$7.6 billion in 2000, the inward stock of FDI has remained relatively low by regional standards; it was around US$27.9 billion (or 9 percent of GDP) by the end of 2000 (UNCTAD 2001).

Table 7.2 also provides yearly flows of outward FDI. Starting in 1988, following the rapid expansion of foreign trade, actual flows of outward investments exceeded inward FDI flows, with the difference growing over time. In fact, since the early 1990s, Taiwan has become one of the leading exporters of capital. Outward FDI, the bulk of which is in mainland China, has grown from less than 0.1 percent of GDP annually in the 1980s to over ten times that magnitude in the 1990s. According to the International Financial Center's report in March 2002, the stock of outward FDI totaled US$49.2 billion in 2000, almost double the inward stock.

Nevertheless, inward FDI has displayed a strong pattern of resilience to the negative shock that hit many Asian countries following the 1997 financial crisis. FDI contributed about 2.5 percent of total domestic capital formation between 1984 and 1986 and about 3.5 percent between 1991 and 1996. This share rose to 6.3 percent in 1997, fell slightly to 5.1 percent in 1998, and rose again to 5.9 percent in 1999. As a share of GDP, approved FDI in Taiwan during 2000 reached almost 2.5 percent, the highest share in history. While the growth has slowed down since then, inward FDI flow as a share of GDP remains at a level significantly higher than in the 1990s (Ministry of Economic Affairs 2003).

This resilience of inward FDI, even during the period of economic turmoil in the region, stands in sharp contrast to growth rates in GDP and exports. This suggests that foreign direct investments, compared to portfolio investments and other forms of capital flows, are more sensitive to economic fundamentals in an economy.

***Table 7.2.** Inward and Outward FDI in Value and as a Percentage of GDP*
(US$millions and percent)

	Actual balance-of-payments FDI		*FDI approved by MOEA*	
Year	*Inward flows*	*Outward flows*	*Inward flows*	*Outward flows*
1959	3.8	n.a.	0.97	0.10
	(0.22)		(0.05)	(0.01)
1965	10.5	0.47	41.61	0.72
	(0.37)	(0.02)	(1.48)	(0.03)
1970	61.9	0.53	138.90	1.21
	(1.09)	(0.01)	(2.45)	(0.02)
1975	34	n.a.	118.18	4.46
	(0.22)		(0.76)	(0.03)
1980	166	42	465.96	10.76
	(0.40)	(0.10)	(1.13)	(0.03)
1986	326	65	770.38	56.91
	(0.43)	(0.09)	(1.02)	(0.08)
1991	1,271	2,055	1,778.42	1,656.03
	(0.71)	(1.15)	(0.99)	(0.92)
1996	1,864	3,843	2,460.84	2,165.41
	(0.67)	(1.37)	(0.88)	(0.77)
1997	2,248	5,243	4,266.63	2,893.83
	(0.78)	(1.81)	(1.47)	(1.0)
1998	222	3,836	3,788.76	3,296.30
	(0.08)	(1.44)	(1.42)	(1.23)
1999	2,926	4,420	4,231.40	3,269.02
	(1.02)	(1.54)	(1.47)	(1.14)
2000	n.a.	n.a.	7,607.7	5,077.06
			(2.45)	(1.64)
2001	n.a.	n.a.	5,128.5	4,391.65
			(1.78)	(1.53)

n.a. Not available.

Source: For actual FDI, Lim (2000, table on trends in Taiwan FDI); for FDI approved by the Ministry of Economic Activities and FDI as a percentage of GDP, Council of Economic Planning and Development (2002).

Since the early 1950s, the environment for inward FDI in Taiwan has been increasingly hospitable. Good infrastructure and attractive fiscal incentives have been coupled with increased inbound FDI, which took off in the early stages of export-oriented growth in the 1960s. The earliest inflow of FDI came from overseas Chinese investors; the bulk of the funds was channeled into export processing zones set up by the government. This inflow had a significant impact on the subsequent economic development of Taiwan (Schive 1990). Local manufacturers relied on the Chinese network to market their products in those countries throughout the 1970s. However, overseas Chinese investments diminished by the early 1980s as a percentage of the total value of inward FDI. Part of the explanation for this is that the average size of overseas Chinese investments is typically much smaller than the average size of nonoverseas Chinese investments.[1] Foreign investments from nonoverseas Chinese sources averaged 90 percent of Taiwan's total value of FDI from 1981 to 1996. This figure has increased to over 95 percent since 1997.

Traditionally, most overseas Chinese investments have been in industries oriented toward the domestic market. In particular, the service sector, nonmetallic minerals, construction, and the banking and insurance sectors have been major recipients of overseas Chinese funds. However, as high-technology sectors have succeeded over time, the overseas Chinese investors have joined investors from the United States, Europe, and Japan in the technology-intensive sectors.

Table 7.3 shows the principal source countries of foreign direct investment in Taiwan. From 1952 to 2000, about 25 percent of approved FDI in Taiwan originated from the United States, 21 percent from Japan, 13 percent from Europe, and 8 percent each from Hong Kong (China), and Singapore. After 1998, the share of FDI from both Europe and Singapore increased significantly. By the end of 2000, Europe and Singapore overtook the United States and Japan as the top two foreign investors in Taiwan with a combined share of over 50 percent of total FDI. Just over 25 percent (US$9.4 billion) of the FDI coming into Taiwan in the past four decades was channeled into the electric/electronics sector; the strongest growth was in the mid- to late 1990s, aided in part by liberalization and privatization of the financial service sector.

Table 7.4 displays the contribution of FDI in the manufacturing sector in terms of absolute and relative employment and sales in the sector. While the absolute and relative contribution of FDI to total manufacturing employment fell from 1986 to 1996, the contribution to total manufacturing sales kept up with the tremendous growth of the sector during that decade.

Despite the emphasis on developing the intricate networks created through foreign investors and overseas Chinese, the primary factor that

---

1. In 1987, the average overseas Chinese investment was $0.74 million, much smaller than the average non-Chinese investment of $2.6 million. The lower value of the average overseas Chinese investment was attributed to the investors' familiarity with the Taiwanese economy and their ethnic ties and family connections with the local population that facilitated their participation in many small ventures (Dahlman and Sananikone 1991).

Table 7.3. *Principal Sources of Overseas Chinese and Foreign Investment in Taiwan*

	1952–2000[a]			2000[b]		
Economy	*No. of cases*	*Amount in US$millions*	*Percent of total FDI*	*No. of cases*	*Amount in US$millions*	*Percent of total FDI*
United States	2,211	10,431	24.52	105	1,007	18.02
Japan	3,674	8,981	21.11	218	502	8.99
Europe	964	5,446	12.80	278	1,674	29.95
Hong Kong (China)	2.035	3,537	8.31	n.a.	n.a.	n.a.
Singapore	635	3,502	8.23	73	1,207	21.60
Netherlands	n.a.	n.a.	n.a.	13	269	4.81

n.a. Not available.
a. As of September 2000.
b. From January to September 2000.
Source: Huang (2001); Ministry of Economic Affairs.

Table 7.4. *Employees and Sales by Foreign-Owned Firms in Taiwan's Manufacturing Sector*

Indicator	*1986*	*1996*
Total employees (no.)	279,658	227,413
Percentage of total manufacturing employment	11.0	9.6
Total sales in US$millions	49,584,584	112,454,800
Percentage of total manufacturing sales	15.0	14.9

Source: Author's calculations from Taiwan, Director General of Budget and Statistics (1986 and 1996)

fueled Taiwan's economic growth was the private sector's engagement in the international market. In particular, small and large, foreign and domestic firms were drawn toward the rapidly expanding export market.

The Evolution of Policy toward FDI

Although the growth of FDI did not take off until the mid-1980s, the country's export-oriented trade strategy has been tightly linked with foreign investors since 1960 when the government announced three major reforms. Firstly, the Statute for the Encouragement of Investment became the foundation for investment incentives to both local and foreign investors. The statutes encouraged the growth of new enterprises backed with foreign capital by liberalizing ownership restrictions and granting various forms of tax credits. Secondly, the government dismantled the multiple exchange rate system and liberalized the foreign exchange allocation system that had limited imports during the earlier period. Finally, the effective rate of protection was lowered on various items to stimulate competition.

At first, foreign investment was slow in coming given the country's lack of natural resources, small domestic market, limited industry, and precarious political future. These drawbacks were offset by a cheap and disciplined labor force as well as solid infrastructure, thanks to Taiwan's Japanese colonial legacy. Gradually, as more and more foreign investors tested the Taiwanese market and were successful, word of their success attracted U.S., Japanese, and European electronics, textiles, and other industries that were looking to move their operations to Taiwan because of lower production costs.

To make Taiwan more attractive to foreign investors, the government in 1965 enacted the Statute for the Establishment and Management of Export Processing Zones (EPZs), which started operation in 1966. Combining the advantages of an industrial estate with those of a free port, the zones offered complete exemption from custom duties and commodity and sales taxes. EPZs also provided other incentives for export-oriented firms to set up in the zones. These EPZs had the effect of multiplying Taiwan's links with foreign firms through FDI and subcontracting. Typically, a large multinational corporation would invest in Taiwan, establish a large manufacturing plant, and generate a market for a host of small local suppliers and assembly operations.

During the 1960s and early 1970s, industries such as consumer electronics, various electronic components, synthetic fibers, and plastics were given priority in the zones. Through the 1970s, the Statute for the Encouragement of Investment was revised nine times to promote Taiwan as a destination for FDI. In 1979, the Statute for Investment by Foreign Nationals and the Statute for Investment by Overseas Chinese also underwent revision. Between 1970 and 1980, FDI increased by 700 percent, while FDI-financed firms accounted for 22 percent of exports (Ho 2003).

Since 1981, there has been keen competition from developing nations in the export of light industrial manufactures and increasing protectionism from developed countries. Therefore, Taiwan was compelled to develop capital-intensive and technology-intensive industries in order to remain internationally competitive. In the Eighth Four-Year Development Plan of 1982, the government identified four industries—electronics, general machinery, transport equipment, and precision instruments—as the "strategic industries" deserving of increased domestic and foreign investments.

The Statute for the Encouragement of Investment was amended in 1984 and then again in 1987. During this period, the government began a series of changes in policy to liberalize its goods and financial markets with the explicit goal of making Taiwan a more attractive destination for high-technology FDI. These moves included significant tariff reductions and the relaxation and abolition of nontariff barriers. By the end of the 1980s, import restrictions had become practically negligible in magnitude.

The most prominent government incentive for attracting FDI in high-tech industries was the establishment of science parks. These parks hosted both foreign and domestic enterprises. The objective was not only to attract more technologically sophisticated FDI, but also to broaden the industrial base and upgrade domestic skill development (Ho 2003).

The most well-known of the science parks was the Hsinchu Science-Based Industrial Park established in 1980. It has the physical infrastructure of a high-tech industrial city, and it benefits from the cooperation of two universities and the leading industrial technology research institute. In addition to these advantages, Hsinchu offers foreign investors generous financial and fiscal incentives through low-interest government loans and tax deferments on R&D investments. To qualify, firms must be involved in sophisticated and advanced technology, contribute to the local economy through local sourcing of their inputs, and have the export market as the destination of their output.

When Taiwan moved into the most sophisticated end of the technology sector in the 1990s, ethnic Chinese living in advanced developed countries began to invest in Taiwan; more importantly, they became a source of technical labor as they returned to work in high-tech corporations in Taiwan. The government has been very successful in luring back overseas Chinese with fiscal and financial incentives. Many of these returning nationals have received degrees in science and engineering from U.S. and Japanese universities, and they have assumed positions of leadership in large Taiwanese corporations. Recognizing the critical role that these returnees can play in the development of Taiwan's high-technology industry, the government has been very active in luring these R&D managers back to Taiwan to upgrade local technology.

At the Hsinchu Science-Based Industrial Park, the majority of computer corporations are owned by overseas Chinese or by Taiwanese who once worked overseas (Dahlman and Sananikone 1991). A group of returning executives have formed the Overseas Chinese Entrepreneurs Advisory Network Program to help returnees adjust to life in Taiwan, find business partners, and discuss business plans (Dahlman and Sananikone 1991).

In early 1988, the government replaced the "Positive Listing" of industries where FDI was permitted with a "Negative Listing Policy" for FDI applications. Under the "Positive Listing," industries permitted to welcome foreign shareholding were exceptions to the rule. With the "Negative Listing Policy," only pollution-causing industries and those in the banking and insurance industries as well as public administration were denied access by foreign investors. In April 1989, the government lifted the ban on foreign participation in the banking sector.

In 1991, the Statute for the Encouragement of Investment, which targeted specific "strategic industries," was replaced by the Statute for Upgrading Industries, which was designed to encourage both domestic and foreign investments in all industries. Similarly, the statutes for investments by foreign nationals and overseas Chinese were revised in 1997 to remove obstacles to investors and improve conditions for them. Perhaps as a direct result of all of these changes in policy toward foreign investors, total FDI in the 1990s nearly tripled the figures for the previous decade.

Taiwan's current policy toward FDI cannot be separated from its overall development policy that emphasizes the growth of high-technology industries in the 2000s. Preferential tax measures that included credits for R&D investments and five-year exemptions or shareholder investment credits for companies in high-technology industries were extended to 2009.

Finally, Taiwan's entry into the World Trade Organization (WTO) in 2002 and continuing liberalization of its domestic market are viewed as attractions for foreign direct investment in the country's manufacturing and service sectors. In 2003, the Negative List was further reduced to meet WTO rules. The List now contains only 10 prohibited and 25 restricted industries for investment by foreign nationals and only 8 prohibited and 22 restricted industries for investment by overseas Chinese.

Factors Contributing to the Growth of FDI

Described below are key factors influencing Taiwan's ability to use foreign investors to become more internationally competitive through exports and sustained economic growth.

Subcontractors

Multinational corporations were first attracted to Taiwan because of its cheap and disciplined labor force and its well-developed economic infrastructure. Local small and medium-size investors entered rapidly growing industries. These investors aggressively sought foreign partners or, with government assistance, entered into subcontracting arrangements with multinational companies (MNCs). During the start-up phase, many Taiwanese companies learned the art of manufacture by relying heavily on foreign firms for training and licensing agreements (Hobday 1995). Over time, the relationship between foreign investors and small-scale local suppliers developed into a viable, efficient, and dependable network of small subcontractors able and ready to act as local suppliers to foreign investors.

This pattern became established through the years. Foreign investors generated a dense network of small-scale local suppliers. The investors provided an important channel for the transfer of technology through their specification requirements. A study by Schive (1990) indicates that the degree of foreign capital involvement in a local company is linked to the application of foreign technology by that company. In addition, nearly all foreign-majority-owned companies in the electric/electronics industry received foreign technology from their foreign partners.

In exchange for the expertise of the foreign investor, the government ensured an efficiently run subcontracting network, a ready supply of relatively inexpensive and educated workers, and entrepreneurs with the strong potential to reduce the overall cost of production of the foreign enterprises. Most importantly, the creation of the Hsinchu Science-Based and Industrial Park, with its close proximity to major universities and the leading industrial technology research institute, enabled foreign investors, once located within the park, to benefit from the ready availability of skilled personnel in addition to generous financial and fiscal incentives.

Spillovers

Unlike other capital inflows, foreign direct investment is strongly associated with simultaneous technology and labor flows. Therefore, FDI is a potential source of spillover effects as a result of foreign investors' advanced techniques of production, organizational practices, new management, and marketing networks (Blomstrom and Sjoholm 1998). In Taiwan, FDI has helped upgrade the technological capabilities of the manufacturing sector through subcontracting and technical cooperation agreements between foreign and local producers. A fundamental purpose of Hsinchu Science-Based and Industrial Park is to capture the spillover from FDI, thus leading to technological upgrading as well as the necessary backward linkages in the local economy (Schive 1990).

Industry Associations

Foreign investors' links with local producers were further strengthened by pro-active industry associations. For example, the electronics industry association, TEAMA (the Taiwan Electric Appliances Manufacturers' Association), aggressively recruited members from both foreign and local producers and, with the support of the government, actively promoted the local content program. This program was instrumental in establishing the link between local producers and foreign direct investors (Kuo 1995). Local producers wanted to take advantage of the technology, management skills, and sales networks created as a result of FDI.

Local Content Requirements

Policies such as those related to local content requirements were used to generate backward linkages in the local economy and create a market for a host of small local suppliers and assembly operations. As noted earlier, foreign investors generated a dense network of small-scale local suppliers, boosting export production and channeling the transfer of technology through specification requirements. In addition, the growing number of local investors from small and medium-size enterprises (SMEs) constantly competed for orders with different foreign firms. The consequence was a highly competitive market structure in the domestic as well as international markets.

As long as local supplies met their quality standards, foreign producers stood to benefit from the local content program because it reduced labor and transportation costs. The response of foreign investors was enthusiastic. They began to train local technicians, provide technical know-how and management skills to suppliers, and cooperate with technical schools on internship programs. These links were further strengthened by production satellite systems that formally connected local producers and foreign investors as well as small producers of parts and components and large assemblers.

By subcontracting with foreign firms, local SMEs acquired the technology needed to produce goods of internationally competitive quality as well as gain a ready market for their output (Dahlman and Sananikone 1991). In this way foreign firms fueled the development of the intricate network of permanent linkages between the local economy and the international economic system. This strategy became even more crucial as Taiwan's FDI policy after the mid-1970s shifted from a concentration on labor-intensive manufactures toward more sophisticated, technology-intensive products and processes.

The Electronics Sector

The Taiwanese electronics and electrical appliance sector owes its early establishment and success to foreign multinational corporations such as RCA of America and Philips of Holland. The Taiwanese operations of both RCA and Philips, leading investors in the free trade zones in the late 1960s, changed with the growth of the export market. Both corporations upgraded their engineering facilities, engaged in the transfer of process and product technologies, and trained local engineers, technicians, and directors (Hobday 1995). In 1976, RCA began one of the first ventures to transfer chip technology to local firms; Philips followed suit in 1987. In both cases, the major technology spillover from these ventures came from the exposure and on-the-job training received by engineers and managers at RCA and Philips who later started their own businesses or moved to existing nationally owned firms. For instance, one of RCA's Taiwanese engineers later founded Winbond Corporation, which became by 1992 the second largest chip producer in Taiwan. The top executives of the local firm, GVC Corporation, a manufacturer of modems and notebooks and later cell phones, came from RCA and Philips.

Amsden and Chu (2003) trace the development of technological capability of firms in the Taiwanese manufacturing sector. They note that although the typical American investment in Taiwan, particularly in the electronics industry, was export-oriented and made by 100 percent foreign-owned firms, the typical Japanese investment was in joint ventures with Taiwanese firms; these investments were oriented toward the domestic market, utilizing local components in response to tariff protection policies and domestic content requirements.

Consequently, the Japanese investors have greater incentives than their American counterparts to transfer know-how to their joint venture partners as well as to their local suppliers of parts and components. In the case of TV manufacturing, "all local firms in Taiwan acquired their technology by proprietary transfer from foreign manufacturers, especially Japanese manufacturers, through the channel of joint ventures or technological contracts. Since TV manufacturers also produced other home electrical products, they chose their TV technology suppliers based on their cooperating experiences in manufacturing other products, or as sales agents of their technology suppliers. (For example, Sampo was the sales agent in Taiwan for Sharp TVs, and when Sampo decided to enter into the manufacture of TVs, the technology was provided by Sharp.) Finally, in the 1970s, exports of color TVs from Taiwan came under original equipment manufacture (or OEM) contracts which were mainly with Japanese firms" (Lin 1986, 98). Accordingly, technological learning in the electronics industry was strongly influenced by Japanese FDI in TV production. When growth in the demand for TVs slowed, the knowledge and experience accumulated from TV production aided manufacturers in the switch to monitors and terminals (Amsden and Chu 2003; Lin 1986).

As wages in Taiwan soared with rapid economic growth, U.S. as well as Japanese firms in the labor-intensive end of the electronics sector ceased to expand and gradually relocated some production to lower-wage countries in Asia. In their place, local Taiwanese companies filled the gap left by exiting foreign firms. These local firms, often labeled as Taiwan's high-technology start-ups, are owned and managed by individuals who once were employees of American firms in Taiwan. These local firms dominated Taiwan's electronics industry by the late 1990s.

Characteristics of Firms with FDI

This section on the characteristics of firms with foreign ownership and the following section on the productivity effects arising from FDI in the Taiwanese manufacturing sector are based on Census of Manufactures data as well as Survey of Manufactures data. Information on foreign ownership of firms in the Census data was collected only in 1986 and 1996. Panel data are available for all three years (1986, 1991, and 1996) in the Survey of Manufactures, comprising a random sample of large firms in all the industries. This data will be used to analyze the productivity of firms with FDI.

Table 7.5 indicates the incidence of firms with FDI and exports across six of the principal industries in the manufacturing sector of Taiwan. In 1986 and 1996, the chemicals and electric/electronics industries had the highest share of firms with FDI, followed by the transportation industry. The remaining industries had less than 1 percent of firms with FDI. Almost all firms with foreign ownership also export. For example in 1986, every firm with FDI in the clothing industry also exported. This is very likely the result of government incentives encouraging all firms with foreign ownership to export. In contrast to the low percentage of firms with FDI is the high percentage of firms in every industry involved in the export market.

How do firms with foreign ownership differ from domestic firms? Table 7.6 lists mean sales revenue, mean employment, and mean ratio of export to total sales for foreign-owned firms, non-foreign-owned firms, and exporting firms in six principal manufacturing industries. Several features of foreign-owned firms stand out in the table. First, while it is not surprising that firms with FDI are larger than domestic firms, the difference in the magnitude is quite startling. For all six industries in 1986, FDI firms are 7 (textiles) to 36

Table 7.5. *Firms in Taiwan that are FDI Firms, Exporting Firms, and Firms with both FDI and Exports, by Industry*
(Percent)

	1986			*1996*		
Industry	*FDI*	*Exports*	*FDI & exports*	*FDI*	*Exports*	*FDI & exports*
Textiles	0.74	34.0	0.70	0.68	20.1	0.64
Clothing	0.45	39.2	0.45	0.46	20.4	0.40
Plastics	0.59	28.4	0.53	0.52	13.7	0.41
Chemicals	4.90	24.1	4.20	4.80	29.0	3.90
Electric/ electronics	4.20	41.9	4.10	3.10	30.4	2.60
Transportation equipment	2.30	28.4	1.40	2.20	15.8	1.10

Source: Author's calculations from Taiwan, Director General of Budget and Statistics (1986 and 1996).

(transportation) times larger in sales revenue to 2 (plastics) to 5 (clothing) times larger in terms of employment. In three of the six industries, these size differences between FDI and non-FDI firms as well as FDI firms and exporting firms widen significantly ten years later.

Second, foreign-owned firms are, on average, many times more export oriented than are domestic firms, particularly those in the clothing and electric/electronics industries where the export to sales ratio in 1996 was 0.8 and 0.52, respectively. This feature is consistent with our earlier observation that, unlike domestic firms, most foreign firms engage in the export market.

Productivity of Firms with FDI

Table 7.7 summarizes the cross-sectional differences in average productivity of firms that have some foreign capital and those that are domestic owned. As explained in the Appendix, productivity is measured as total factor productivity (TFP). The intercept is the average TFP of the firms that have no foreign capital and coefficients in columns (2) and (4) represent the percentage difference in productivity between non-FDI firms and firms with FDI in 1986 and 1996, respectively.

Except for the textile industry in 1996, the coefficients of the FDI variable in the regression are all positive, implying that foreign firms are more productive than non-foreign-owned firms. However, only half of the coefficients in 1986 and one-third in 1996 are significantly different than zero.

Table 7.6. *Characteristics of FDI, Non-FDI, and Exporting Firms in Taiwan, by Industry*

	1986			1996		
Industry	*FDI firms*	*Non-FDI firms*	*Exporting firms*	*FDI firms*	*Non-FDI firms*	*Exporting firms*
Textiles						
Sales (billions of Taiwanese dollars)	567	82	215	1,431	104	407
Workers (number)	333	57	137	461	36	123
Export-sales ratio	0.54	0.23	—	0.40	0.09	—
Clothing						
Sales (billions of Taiwanese dollars)	386	38	84	356	43	120
Workers (number)	538	50	103	302	27	68
Export-sales ratio	1.00	0.34	—	0.80	0.16	—
Plastics						
Sales (billions of Taiwanese dollars)	412	40	120	3,219	33	225
Workers (number)	222	36	96	659	16	66
Export-sales ratio	0.70	0.22	—	0.42	0.08	—
Chemicals						
Sales (billions of Taiwanese dollars)	1,930	231	1,076	2,039	353	1,117
Workers (number)	207	60	222	170	53	148
Export-sales ratio	0.26	0.07	—	0.33	0.08	—
Electric and electronics						
Sales (billions of Taiwanese dollars)	1,132	58	226	1,493	200	654
Workers (number)	783	52	171	343	48	137
Export-sales ratio	0.77	0.27	—	0.52	0.16	—
Transport and equipment						
Sales (billions of Taiwanese dollars)	1,754	48	245	3,734	86	655
Workers (number)	422	38	115	449	32	143
Export-sales ratio	0.21	0.20	—	0.17	0.09	—

— Not applicable.
Source: Author's calculations from Taiwan, Director General of Budget and Statistics (1986 and 1996).

Table 7.7. *Productivity Difference between FDI Firms and Non-FDI Firms in Taiwan, by Industry*

	1986		1996	
Industry	*Intercept* (1)	*FDI* (2)	*Intercept* (3)	*FDI* (4)
Textile	0.049*	0.083	0.237*	–0.113
	(0.006)	(0.065)	(0.006)	(0.075)
Clothing	–0.069*	0.091	0.043*	0.164
	(0.007)	(0.103)	(0.008)	(0.122)
Chemicals	0.041*	0.184*	0.251*	0.040
	(0.010)	(0.044)	(0.011)	(0.051)
Plastics	0.254*	0.094*	0.313*	0.070
	(0.003)	(0.045)	(0.004)	(0.054)
Electric and	0.181*	0.020	0.407*	0.063*
electronics	(0.004)	(0.019)	(0.003)	(0.020)
Transport	0.056*	0.069**	–0.035*	0.134*
equipment	(0.006)	(0.037)	(0.006)	(0.041)

* Significant at the 5 percent level.
** Significant at the 10 percent level.
Source: Author's calculations from Taiwan, Director General of Budget and Statistics (1986 and 1996).

These coefficients range from 6.3 percent (electric/electronics industry in 1996) to 18.4 percent (chemicals in 1986). One possible reason for the weak correlation between foreign-ownership and productivity, particularly in 1996, is that the sample of domestic-owned firms, starting in 1991, includes Taiwanese MNCs with relatively high productivity. For evidence of this, see the large increase in outward FDI in the 1990s in Table 7.2.

Another indicator that these domestic MNCs are included in our sample of non-foreign-owned firms is the significant increase in the magnitude of the intercept term in 1996 compared to 1986 (except in the transportation industry). In the textile and electric/electronics industry, where outward investments by Taiwanese firms have been particularly active, the productivity of non-FDI firms increased by about 19 percent and 23 percent respectively during the ten-year period under study. Since most foreign-owned firms are exporting firms, the finding of higher productivity in foreign-owned firms is likely to be highly correlated with export activity. This feature implies that we need information on a distinguishing characteristic of the FDI activity to separately identify the productivity effect of FDI from that of exporting. A distinguishing characteristic of firms with FDI is their larger size (in terms of sales revenue and number of employees) relative to both non-FDI firms and exporting firms. Thus, we can use information on FDI intensity to see if the productivity differential between foreign-owned and non-foreign-owned firms is an increasing function of the share of a firm's total assets that is foreign owned. Such a pattern would allow us to attribute the observed higher productivity to foreign ownership.

Table 7.8 reports the results of regressions of firm productivity on year and FDI intensity dummies for each of the six principal manufacturing industries. The intercept represents the average TFP of firms with no FDI in the base year (1986), and the remaining coefficients measure the percentage difference in productivity between these firms with no FDI and firms with low FDI intensity (that is, firms with less than 25 percent of total assets that are foreign owned), moderate FDI intensity (25 to 75 percent), and high FDI intensity (more than 75 percent).

Table 7.8. *FDI Intensity and Firm Productivity in Taiwan, by Industry*

		FDI intensity			
Industry	*Intercept*	*Low*[a]	*Medium*[b]	*High*[c]	*Test results*[d]
Textile	0.049*	0.008	0.013	–0.037	2,3
	(0.006)	(0.094)	(0.081)	(0.081)	
Clothing	–0.069*	0.154	0.117	0.123	2,3
	(0.008)	(0.172)	(0.133)	(0.121)	
Chemicals	0.044*	0.057	0.139*	0.039	2,3
	(0.011)	(0.090)	(0.043)	(0.072)	
Plastics	0.254*	0.003	0.108	0.120	2,3
	(0.004)	(0.066)	(0.064)	(0.057)	
Electric and electronics	0.180*	–0.029	0.066*	0.055*	3
	(0.004)	(0.034)	(0.025)	(0.019)	
Transport equipment	0.055*	0.101	0.116*	0.097	2,3
	(0.007)	(0.056)	(0.039)	(0.063)	

* Significant at the 5 percent level.

Note: All regressions include year dummy variable; 1 if the year is 1996 and 0 for 1986. Standard errors are in parentheses.

a. FDI share of total assets is greater than 0 and less than or equal to 0.25.

b. FDI share of total assets is greater than 0.25 and less than or equal to 0.75.

c. FDI share of total assets is greater than 0.75.

d. Test results are coded as follows (all are for 5 percent level of significance): 1, do not reject the equality of all three FDI intensity coefficients; 2, do not reject the equality of the low and medium FDI intensity coefficients; and 3, do not reject the equality of the medium and high FDI intensity coefficients.

Source: Author's calculations from Taiwan, Director General of Budget and Statistics (1986 and 1996).

The positive coefficients of all but two of the coefficient estimates clearly indicate higher levels of productivity for foreign firms relative to non-foreign firms. There is no consistent movement in the level of average productivity across the intensity categories. In three of the six industries, none of the FDI intensity coefficients is statistically significant. With the exception of electric/electronics, where the coefficient of high FDI intensity is significantly positive, the coefficients for firms with low and high FDI intensity are not statistically different than zero in the remaining five industries. In three industries where the coefficients are statistically significant, the data indicate that firms with medium FDI intensity have average productivity levels that are between 6.6 percent (in electric and electronics) to 13.9 percent (in chemicals) higher than firms without any FDI.

Tests on the equality of the estimated coefficients suggest that, with the exception of the electric/electronics industry, we cannot reject the hypothesis that the low and medium FDI intensity *and* medium and high FDI intensity coefficients are equal. In the case of electric/electronics, we cannot reject the hypothesis that average productivity of the medium and high FDI intensity groups has equal average productivity.

Overall, the cross-sectional results in Tables 7.7 and 7.8 indicate that focusing only on the foreign-ownership of firms, foreign firms in some industries have higher productivity than do firms without any FDI. However, in many industries, this productivity difference is not statistically significant. This may be due, particularly in the 1990s, to a large number of highly productive Taiwanese MNCs included in the firms that are classified as firms without any FDI. Finally, the degree of FDI intensity appears to have little systematic effect on productivity for most of the industries under consideration.

FDI and the Role of Exports

To analyze the joint effect of foreign ownership and export activities on firm productivity, we present in Table 7.9 the results of the regression of firm productivity on dummies representing the presence of FDI only, exports only, or both FDI and exports. The intercept in the regression represents the productivity of baseline firms: those with no exports and no FDI. Three observations can be made about the table. First, across all six industries, average productivity of exporting firms exceeded that of firms without any FDI by between 4.6 and 15.6 percent. All of the differences in means are statistically significant. Second, only two of the six coefficients on the FDI dummy are statistically significant, with one of the two carrying a negative sign, suggesting that, in general, foreign ownership of firms has no significant impact on firm productivity. Finally, with the exception of the textile industry, firms in all the other industries that combine both export activity and FDI have significantly higher productivity than the baseline group of firms as well as firms that only export. The productivity premium from foreign ownership relative to the export-only firms ranges from 1.6 percent in the clothing industry to 7.6 percent in transport equipment.

The simple comparisons in Table 7.9 of average productivity of firms with various combinations of export and FDI indicate that the higher productivity observed among foreign-owned firms relative to non-foreign-owned firms is clearly linked with the export activity. At the same time, our evidence also suggests that when coupled with exports, firms' productivity is further enhanced by the presence of FDI. In the next section of this chapter, we exploit the time series aspects of the data from the surveys of the larger and more technologically advanced firms taken in 1986, 1991, and 1996 to show the importance of the export factor in the success of firms with FDI.

Table 7.9. *Productivity of FDI Firms and Exporting Firms, and Firms with Both FDI and Exports, by Industry*

		Investment activity		
Industry	*Intercept*	*Export*	*FDI*	*Both*
Textile	0.010	0.118*	–0.416*	0.051
	(0.006)	(0.009)	(0.196)	(0.051)
Clothing	–0.129*	0.156*	0.256	0.171*
	(0.009)	(0.012)	(0.289)	(0.084)
Chemicals	0.035*	0.046*	0.118	0.115*
	(0.012)	(0.018)	(0.084)	(0.038)
Plastics	0.226*	0.100*	0.004	0.121*
	(0.004)	(0.007)	(0.088)	(0.039)
Electric and electronics	0.150*	0.075*	–0.076	0.089*
	(0.005)	(0.006)	(0.042)	(0.015)
Transport equipment	0.038*	0.061*	0.102*	0.137*
	(0.008)	(0.011)	(0.043)	(0.039)

* Significant at the 5 percent level.

Note: All year dummy coefficients are significant at the 5 percent level.

Source: Author's calculations from Taiwan, Director General of Budget and Statistics (1986 and 1996).

The Timing of FDI

We focus our attention on the electric/electronics industry because it has the highest share of FDI among all the two-digit industries in Taiwan. Between 1990 and 1997, 42.4 percent of the total FDI in the manufacturing sector was in electronics. The chemical industry is a far second at 20.3 percent during the same time period.

In Table 7.10, firms in Taiwan's electric/electronics industry are viewed as those who participate (or do not participate) in two activities: firms that export and/or firms that receive foreign direct investment. They are classified into four separate categories: those with no exports and no FDI, those with only exports, those with only FDI, or those with both exports and FDI. The table reports the number of firms in each group in 1986, 1991, and 1996. In 1986, almost 20 percent of all firms in the survey had some foreign capital, and over 74 percent participated in the export market. Over the period covered by the panel, between 12 and 18 percent participated in both activities, and between 25 and 41 percent of the firms in each year did not participate in either activity. As shown earlier in the cross-sectional data in Table 7.5, the export activity was more prevalent among firms than was foreign ownership. While 46 to 56 percent of the firms in each year chose to only export, only 1.3 percent of firms have only FDI.

Although Table 7.10 summarizes the different combinations of FDI and export activities in each cross-section, it does not indicate how these combi-

Table 7.10. *The Incidence of FDI and Exports in the Electric/Electronics Industry in the 1986, 1991, and 1996 Surveys*
(No. of firms)

	Year		
Type of firm	*1986*	*1991*	*1996*
No exports and no FDI	224	641	453
	(24.6)	(41.2)	(34.9)
Only exports	507	717	677
	(55.8)	(46.1)	(52.1)
Only FDI	12	19	20
	(1.3)	(1.2)	(1.5)
Both exports and FDI	166	178	150
	(18.3)	(11.5)	(11.5)

Note: The numbers in parentheses are percent of column total.
Source: Aw (2002).

nations persist or change over time. To do this we focus on a balanced panel of firms that are observed in all three years of the survey.

Table 7.11 summarizes information about *changes* in firms' FDI/export status and illustrates how the initial state is related to the start or cessation of each activity. The table reports the number of firms and the share of firms that initiate or cease each activity in period *t+1*, conditional on each firm's initial state in period *t*. For example, column (1) reports the number and proportion of firms in each of the four initial states that began exporting five years later.

Two general transition patterns emerge from Table 7.11. First, regardless of the initial state of the firms, a higher proportion of them begin exporting than receive FDI. For example, of the 285 firms that did not participate in either activity in the initial period, 30 percent began exporting in the next period, whereas less than 2 percent had FDI five years later. Second, the FDI activity is more likely to proceed rather than precede the export activity. Comparing the first and second rows of the table, we find that 6.4 percent of firms with an export history receive FDI (row 2) compared to 1.8 percent without any export history (row 1). Of the total of 611 firms in the initial state, only 5 firms (less than 1 percent) are only-FDI firms.

Based on all of the evidence from simple counts of various activities in the panel data, we find that history substantially influences current engagement in either the exporting activity or FDI activity. In particular, export participa-

Table 7.11. *Transition Matrix for Continuing Firms in the Electric/Electronics Industry, 1986–96*

		Year t+1			
Type of firm in year t	*Number of firms in year t*	*Start exporting (1)*	*Stop Exporting (2)*	*Start FDI (3)*	*Stop FDI (4)*
No exports and no FDI	132 +153=285	44+42=86 (30.18)	—	1+4=5 (1.75)	—
Only exports	390+373=763	—	65+109=174 (22.80)	18+31=49 (6.42)	—
Only FDI	2+3=5	0+1=1 (20)	—	—	0+2=2 (40)
Both exports and FDI	87+82=169	—	1+7=8 (4.73)	—	23+24=47 (27.81)

— Not applicable.
Note: The percentages of the row total are given in parentheses.
Source: Aw (2002).

tion demonstrates more persistence than FDI. More importantly, firms tend to engage in exports prior to receiving FDI. These observations are consistent with our previous findings that exporting firms have higher productivity than nonexporting firms and / or non-foreign-owned firms. This observation is independent of the presence of FDI in the firm. In addition, firms that have an export history are more likely to receive FDI than are firms without any export history.

Spillovers and FDI

The share of foreign ownership of a firm's total assets may not be a complete measure of the benefits generated by foreign direct investment. Indeed, some of the key benefits of FDI are likely to arise from agents external to the firm.

Studies of the potential spillover effects from FDI have hypothesized that foreign firms import and demonstrate technologies that are useful to domestic firms. Recent work on the nature of spillovers suggests that the physical location of firms plays a significant role in the spread of ideas. Only a few studies have examined location spillover in developing countries. There is no evidence of any geographical spillover from FDI in Morocco (Haddad and Harrison 1993) or in Venezuela (Aitken and Harrison 1999), and there is no geographical spillover from export experience in Colombia, Mexico, and Morocco (Clerides, Lach, and Tybout 1998). These findings are not surprising. Foreign-owned firms have every incentive to minimize technology spillover to competitors, and therefore they restrict the mechanisms by which it can occur, such as imitation and labor mobility. However, in Taiwan interfirm linkages made possible by strong subcontracting relationships dominate. Thus, the potential for spillover benefits may be greater than in other developing countries. In their efforts to build efficient supply chains, foreign firms often share technical knowledge with their suppliers, enhancing their productivity in the process.[2]

Some evidence exists of indirect benefits generated by FDI firms in Taiwan's electronics industry for the period from 1986 to 1991. Aw (2002) focuses on three sources of new knowledge: FDI, exports, and R&D activities. All of these variables are measured at the firm-level using the same census data relied upon in this chapter. The empirical model answers two questions. First,

2. Blalock and Gertler (2003) find evidence of spillovers from FDI among Indonesian industries in regions with growing downstream FDI experiencing greater productivity growth.

do firms with positive investments in any one of these activities have higher productivity growth than other firms where these activities are absent? Second, do firms that are located in the same industry or geographical region or county, and that have greater intensity of investments in FDI, R&D investments, and exports, benefit from the diffusion of new knowledge associated with these activities? We quantify this "spillover" of foreign technology by taking the ratio of the sum of FDI (or export activity or R&D) of other firms to total revenue within each of the 193 counties or four-digit industries. Table 7.12 reproduces the results that are relevant for this analysis.

The results indicate that the firm's own investments in the three activities are positive and statistically significant. Given Taiwan's status as a technology

Table 7.12. *Coefficient Estimates of TFP Growth Regression and Survival Regression in the Electronics Industry*

Factor	*Value*
Constant	–0.965 (0.311)**
R&D	0.094 (0.029)**
Exports	0.051 (0.021)*
FDI	0.113 (0.044)*
County-wide TFP	–0.062 (0.049)
County R&D	–0.014 (0.013)
Industry R&D	–0.035 (0.015)*
County exports	0.010 (0.022)
Industry exports	0.059 (0.020)**
County FDI	0.015 (0.007)*
Industry FDI	–0.005 (0.013)
County-industry R&D	
County-industry Exports	
County-industry FDI	
Rho	0.848 (0.018)**
$\chi 2a$	837.18**
Survival equation:	
TFP	1.162 (0.076)**
R&D	0.280 (0.071)**
Exports	0.235 (0.048)**
FDI	0.307 (0.118)**
Constant	–0.470 (0.031)**

* Statistically significant at the 5 perccent level.
** Statistically significant at the 1 percent level.
Note: The dependent variable is TFP growth.
Source: Aw (2002).

latecomer, it is not surprising that productivity growth rates are positively and significantly correlated with the firm's own investments in R&D, FDI participation, and exports. However, only three of the six spillover variables are statistically significant. The coefficient of the variable measuring the degree of spillover benefits generated by export activities located in specific four-digit industries is positive (.059) and statistically significant. In addition, there are positive externalities generated by firms with FDI to other firms located within the same county, although the magnitude of this coefficient is small at .015.[3] The coefficient of the variable measuring the degree of spillover benefits generated by R&D investments located in specific four-digit industries is also statistically significant but negative in magnitude.

Table 7.12 also reports the determinants of survival rates of firms. Initial firm TFP has the biggest and most pervasive effect on firm survival into the next time period. This result is consistent with the predictions of recent theory of industry evolution that more efficient firms have the highest probability of survival. Of the three investment activities, FDI has the highest impact on firm survival rate. Firms with FDI have a 31 percent higher survival rate than those without any FDI.

While the results presented earlier in this chapter suggest that the relationship between FDI and TFP is mixed unless FDI is coupled with exports, the results from Table 7.12 show that FDI in a firm has a large and significant effect (11.3 percent) on its TFP growth and a strong positive and significant effect on the firm's survival rate over time. More importantly, FDI firms appear to benefit neighboring firms, especially small firms (fewer than 100 workers).

Summary and Conclusions

The earliest and most common source of new technology for Taiwan, like for many other developing countries, was foreign firms operating within its borders. In sheer volume, the direct contribution of FDI to Taiwan's economy has not been significant. Since the first inflows of FDI into Taiwan in the early 1960s, FDI's share of gross investment in the manufacturing sector ranged from 5.56 percent from 1962 to 1969 to 11 percent in the period from 1973 to 1994. The bulk of this investment (80 to 90 percent) came from foreign (non-Chinese) investors and went into electrical/electronic and

---

3. The same regression was run for small firms (fewer than 100 workers) and large firms. The result indicates that all the benefits reflected in the coefficient on the FDI spillover variable are those accruing to small firms.

machinery industries. The average annual rate of growth of FDI fell from 27.5 percent in the 1980s to 6.8 percent from 1990 to 1996. A high of 38.5 percent was reached from 1997 to 2000. With the development of Taiwan into a mature, advanced economy, it is not surprising to witness the rising importance of outward FDI as well as the increasing share of industrial output from domestically owned firms.

The small amount of foreign direct investment in Taiwan, compared to investment in Hong Kong (China) and Singapore, understates the contribution of FDI to the economy's industrial progress, technological capability, and export success. Many of the investments concentrated in leading export sectors, generating new export industries and facilitating the transfer of new technology. Foreign direct investments in Taiwan have fostered the start-up of many of Taiwan's electronics enterprises since numerous local companies grew up to supply these foreign firms with parts, components, subsystems, and services, leading to a dense network of subcontractors and the OEM system.

Empirical evidence in the literature on the role of FDI in Taiwan's economic development has been very mixed. There are two studies based specifically on data on FDI in Taiwan's manufacturing sector. Chen, Hsu, and Chen (1999), using cross-sectional 1986 and 1991 survey data, find that the effect of FDI on labor productivity is not significantly different than zero. Using the standard Granger causality tests to prove causality among variables, Chan (2000) concludes that there is a causal relationship between FDI and economic growth through improving technology rather than through increasing total capital accumulation or exports.

The findings of this chapter are fourfold. First, the benefit to Taiwanese firms from foreign ownership in terms of a higher level of TFP is very strongly linked with export activity. In fact, there is little evidence that FDI on its own directly leads to greater productivity. In part this may be attributable to the lack of observations of firms that only have FDI and no exports. Second, the direct benefits from FDI accrue to firms with an export history. In other words, firms with FDI that are in the export market tend to have higher productivity levels than do firms without any export history. Third, FDI has large and significant effects on the firm's TFP growth and future survival. Finally, there is some evidence that the presence of foreign firms indirectly benefits other firms, especially small ones that are in close physical proximity.

The first finding of this chapter is consistent with the view that for Taiwan, exports and FDI are complementary. Evidence of this was apparent as early as the 1970s and continued through the 1990s. Export-oriented foreign investors have arrived in Taiwan in response to the well-developed economic infrastructure and environment conducive to foreign investments.

For Taiwanese firms that succeeded in attracting foreign investors, FDI became more than an important source of superior management skills and new technology. FDI supported already developed marketing links with the rest of the world. Urata (2001, 451) refers to this FDI-trade nexus in the countries of East Asia: "The economies that succeeded in expanding exports attracted FDI, because they were seen as capable of providing an environment conducive to competitive production. In this way, virtuous spirals of export expansion and FDI expansion, or the FDI-trade nexus, were formed." Micro-level evidence from Taiwan strongly supports this view of how the economy grew and developed over the ten-year period from 1986 to 1996.

The second finding that the benefits from FDI accrue to firms with an export history is interesting from a policy perspective. Although no "magic" attends the export activity of firms, the evidence is very clear that once a firm is in the export market, FDI brings additional benefits that are not reaped by firms lacking export market penetration. This suggests that for Taiwanese manufacturing firms, the timing of investment activities may be crucial. This finding is consistent with empirical evidence in numerous studies using data from both developed and developing countries. These studies indicate that productive firms self-select into the export market.[4] It follows that these firms are more likely to attract FDI or have incentives to invest in other activities (such as R&D) to improve their productivity in order to stay competitive in the international market place.

According to Levy (1991), the simultaneous proliferation in Taiwan of a sophisticated network of subcontractors and export traders implies that the transaction costs of entering the export market may be lower in Taiwan than in many other countries, enabling higher than average participation by small firms in the export market. In developing countries entry into the export market may require firms to establish marketing channels, learn bureaucratic procedures, and develop new packaging or product varieties. Thus, lowering these barriers may be an important first step in encouraging productive firms to export and potentially benefit from any transfer of new technology.

---

4. Clerides, Lach, and Tybout (1998) use data from Colombia, Mexico, and Morocco; Bernard and Jensen (1999) study U.S. manufacturing firms; Aw, Chung, and Roberts (2000) use data from Taiwan (China) and the Republic of Korea; Bernard and Wagner (1997) use data from Germany; Liu, Tsou, and Hammitt (1999) use data from Taiwan (China); Delgado, Farinas, and Ruano (2002) use data from Spain. All the authors find evidence that efficient producers self-select into the export market. Aw, Chung, and Roberts (2000) also find evidence of productivity improvements following entry into the export market for a few Taiwanese industries.

Appendix A

The Measurement of Firm-Level Total Factor Productivity

Using the manufacturing data for Taiwan, we construct an index of total factor productivity (TFP) for each plant in each census year for which we have FDI information (1986 and 1996).[5]

A multilateral index that is useful for measuring TFP in firm-level panel data sets was developed by Caves, Christensen, and Diewert (1982). The TFP index is constructed as the log of the firm's output minus a revenue-share weighted sum of the log of the firm's inputs. In order to guarantee that comparisons between any two firm-year observations are transitive, each firm's inputs and outputs are expressed as deviations from a single reference point. As the reference point the Caves, Christensen, and Diewert multilateral index uses a hypothetical firm with input revenue shares that equal the arithmetic mean revenue shares over all observations; output and input levels equal the geometric mean of output and the inputs over all observations.

Therefore, each firm's output, inputs, and thus productivity in each year is measured relative to this hypothetical firm. Good, Nadiri, and Sickles (1996) discuss an extension of the multilateral index that uses a separate hypothetical-firm reference point for each cross-section of observations and then "chain-links" the reference points together over time in the same way as the conventional Tornqvist index of productivity growth. This productivity index is useful in our application because it provides a consistent way of summarizing the cross-sectional distribution of firm TFP. It only uses information specific to that time period and information about how the distribution moves over time.

Let $Y_{f,t}$ be the value of the output of firm *f* in time *t*. Let $S_{f,t}$ be firm *f*'s input share of input *i* and $X_{i,f,t}$ be firm *f*'s use of input *i*. An upper bar denotes the average across all firms in the industry in a given period. The natural log of firm *f*'s TFP in time *t* is calculated as:

$$\ln TFP = \left(\ln Y_{f,t} - \overline{\ln Y_t}\right) + \sum_{s=2}^{t}\left(\overline{\ln Y_s} - \overline{\ln Y_{s-1}}\right)$$

$$-\left[\sum_{i=1}^{n}\frac{1}{2}\left(S_{i,f,t} - \overline{S_{i,t}}\right)\left(\ln X_{i,f,t} - \overline{\ln X_{i,t}}\right)\right]$$

$$+\left[\sum_{s=2}^{t}\sum_{i=1}^{n}\frac{1}{2}\left(\overline{S_{i,s}} - \overline{S_{i,s-1}}\right)\left(\overline{\ln X_{i,s}} - \overline{\ln X_{i,s-1}}\right)\right].$$

5. Tybout (1996) discusses alternative productivity measures based on econometric estimation of production functions and summarizes the literature on the sources of productivity differences across producers.

The first line of the formula measures plant output and consists of two parts. The first part expresses the firm's output in year *t* as a deviation from the reference point, the geometric mean output over all firms in year *t*, thus capturing information on the cross-sectional distribution in output. The second part sums the change in the output reference point across all years, effectively capturing information on the shift of the output distribution over time by chain-linking the movement in the reference point. The remaining two lines of the formula perform the same operation for each input X_i. The inputs are then summed using a combination of firm factor shares S_{ift} and average factor shares S_{it} in each year as weights. The index provides a measure of the proportional difference in TFP for plant *f* in year *t* relative to the hypothetical plant in the base year. In our application we use 1981 as the base year for Taiwan.

References

Aitken, Brian, and Ann E. Harrison. 1999. "Do Domestic Firms Benefit from Direct Foreign Investment?" *American Economic Review* 89(3): 605–18.

Amsden, Alice H., and Wan-wen Chu. 2003. *Beyond Late Development: Taiwan's Upgrading Policies.* Cambridge, Mass.: The MIT Press.

Aw, Bee-Yan. 2002. "Accumulating Technology and Location Spillovers among Firms in Taiwan's Electronics Industry." *Journal of Development Studies* 39(1): 94–117.

Aw, Bee Yan, Sukkyun Chung, and Mark J. Roberts. 2000. "Productivity and Turnover in the Export Market: Micro-Level Evidence from Taiwan (China) and the Republic of Korea." *World Bank Economic Review* 14(1): 65–90.

Bernard, Andrew B., and J. Bradford Jensen. 1999. "Exceptional Exporter Performance: Cause, Effect, or Both?" *Journal of International Economics* 47(1): 1–25.

Bernard, Andrew B., and Joachim Wagner. 1997. "Exports and Success in German Manufacturing." *Weltwirtschaftliches Archiv* 133, pp. 134–57.

Blalock, Garrick, and Paul Gertler. 2003. "Technology Diffusion, Competition, and Welfare Gains from Foreign Direct Investment." Working paper. Ithaca, N.Y.: Cornell University.

Blomstrom, Magnus, and Fredrik Sjoholm. 1998. "Technology Transfer and Spillovers: Does Local Participation with Multinationals Matter?" NBER Working Paper 6816. Cambridge, Mass.: National Bureau of Economic Research.

Caves, Douglas W., Laurits R. Christensen, and W. Erwin Diewert. 1982. "Multilateral Comparisons of Output, Input, and Productivity Using Superlative Index Numbers." *Economic Journal* 92(365): 73–86.

Chan, Vei-Lin. 2000. "Foreign Direct Investment and Economic Growth in Taiwan's Manufacturing Industries." In *The Role of Foreign Direct Investment in East Asian*

Economic Development, edited by Takatoshi Ito and Anne O. Krueger. Chicago: National Bureau of Economic Research.

Chen, Been-Lou, Mei Hsu, and Jing-Yi Chen. 1999. "Technology Adoption and Technical Efficiency in a Developing Economy: Foreign Investment Led versus Export Performance Promoted." In *Economic Efficiency and Productivity Growth in the Asia-Pacific Region*, edited by Tsu-Tan Fu, Cliff J. Huang, and C.A. Knox Lovell. Cheltenham, England: Elgar.

Clerides, Sofronis K., Saul Lach, and James R. Tybout. 1998. "Is Learning by Exporting Important? Micro-dynamic Evidence from Colombia, Mexico, and Morocco." *Quarterly Journal of Economics* 113(3): 903–47.

Council of Economic Planning and Development. various years. *Taiwan Statistical Data Book*. Taipei, Taiwan (China).

Dahlman, Carl, and Ousa Sananikone. 1991. "Technology Strategy in the Economy of Taiwan: Exploiting Foreign Linkages and Investing in Local Capability." Mimeo. Washington, D.C.: World Bank.

Delgado, Miguel A., Jose C. Farinas, and Sonia Ruano. 2002. "Firm Productivity and Export Markets: A Nonparametric Approach." *Journal of International Economics* 57, No. 2, 397–422.

Feenstra, Robert C. 1998. "Facts and Fallacies about Foreign Direct Investment." Working Paper. Department of Economics, University of California, Davis.

Good, David H., M. Ishaq Nadiri, and Robin C. Sickles. 1997. "Index Number and Factor Demand Approaches to the Estimation of Productivity." In Hashem Pesaran and Peter Schmidt, eds., *Handbook of Applied Econometrics*, Vol. 2: Microeconometrics. London: Basil Blackwell.

Haddad, Mona, and Ann Harrison. 1993. "Are There Positive Spillovers from Direct Foreign Investment? Evidence from Panel Data for Morocco." *Journal of Development Economics* vol. 42, pp. 51–74.

Ho, Ming-Yu. 2003. "In Service of Growth: Legal Regimes, FDI and Taiwan's Economic Development." *IIAS Newsletter*, no. 32.

Hobday, Michael. 1995. *Innovation in East Asia*. Edward Elgar Publishing Limited, U.K.

Huang, Chih-peng. 2001. *Global Trends in Cross-Border Investment and Promotion of Taiwan's Two-Way Investment*. Director General, Industrial Development and Investment Center, Ministry of Economic Affairs, Taipei, Taiwan (China).

Kuo, Cheng-Tian. 1995. *Global Competitiveness and Industrial Growth in Taiwan and the Philippines*. University of Pittsburgh Press.

Levy, Brian. 1991. "Transactions Costs, the Size of Firms and Industrial Policy." *Journal of Development Economics* 34, pp. 151–78.

Lim, Bert J. 2000. "Taiwan at the Gate of Globalization." Paper presented to the Offshore 2000: Premier Offshore Conference in Asia, Taipei, Taiwan (China).

Lin, Y. 1986. "Technological Change: A Microeconomic Study of the Consumer Electronics Industry in Taiwan." Ph.D. dissertation. Economics Department, Northwestern University, Evanston, Ill.

Liu, Jin-Tan, Meng-Wen Tsou, and James K. Hammitt. 1999. " Export Activity and Productivity: Evidence from the Taiwan Electronics Industry." *Weltwirtschaftliches Archiv* 35, 675–91.

Ministry of Economic Affairs. various years. Report of the Ministry of Economic Affairs Investment Commission. Taipei, Taiwan (China).

Schive, Chi. 1990. *The Foreign Factor: The Multinational Corporation's Contribution to the Economic Modernization of the Republic of China.* Hoover Institution, Stanford University Press.

Taiwan, Director General of Budget and Statistics. various years. *The Report on Industrial and Commercial Census.* Taiwan-Fukien Area, The Republic of China.

———. various years. *The Report on Industrial and Commercial Survey.* Taiwan-Fukien Area, The Republic of China.

———. 1986. *Census of Manufactures.* Taiwan-Fukien Area, The Republic of China.

———. 1996. *Census of Manufactures.* Taiwan-Fukien Area, The Republic of China.

Tybout, James R. 1996. " Heterogeneity and Productivity Growth: Assessing the Evidence." In *Industrial Evolution in Developing Countries: Micro Patterns of Turnover, Productivity, and Market Structure,* edited by Mark J. Roberts and James R. Tybout. New York: Oxford University Press.

UNCTAD 2001. *World Investment Report 2001.* New York: United Nations.

Urata, Shujiro. 2001. "Emergence of an FDI-Trade Nexus and Economic Growth in East Asia." In *Rethinking the East Asian Miracle,* edited by Joseph E. Stiglitz and Shahid Yusuf. New York: Oxford University Press.

8

Foreign Investment and Development: Indonesia's Experience

Mari Pangestu and Titik Anas

This chapter analyzes foreign direct investment (FDI) and its impact on Indonesia's development prior to the Asian financial crisis, during the crisis, and in its nascent recovery process. The analysis has a twofold purpose: to identify the factors that explain the observed trends in FDI and to assess the impact of FDI inflows on the host economy in terms of employment generation, trade expansion, developing networks (production and other types of networks), and technology upgrading. Sector studies and cases also are examined in order to gain useful insights or lessons.

The chapter is divided into four main sections. We begin by assessing overall trends in FDI from the 1980s to the early years of the twenty-first century. In the subsequent section the policy and institutional factors behind these trends are analyzed. We then look at the impact of FDI on a number of economic indicators and describe the experiences in various sectors and case studies. The chapter closes with our conclusions and policy recommendations.

Trends in Foreign Direct Investment in Indonesia

In the boom years of the early 1990s, Indonesia attracted considerable FDI interest and inflows, but the situation reversed sharply after the 1997 crisis

The authors acknowledge the excellent research assistance provided by Imelda Madir in the preparation of this chapter.

(Table 8.1). Our findings are based on two data sources: (1) approved FDI through the Board of Investment (*Badan Koordinasi Penanaman Modal*, BKPM), which excludes the financial services and oil and gas sectors[1] and (2) FDI data reported in the balance of payments.[2]

Given the limitations we have described in our data sources, we observe the following trends in FDI in Indonesia. Approved FDI steadily increased from 1993 onwards, tripling at $33.8 billion by the time it peaked in 1997. The crisis began toward the end of 1997, and approved and implemented FDI plummeted during the worst crisis year of 1998 and into 1999. In 2000 and 2001 approved investment rose slightly to reach half of the peak level at around $15 billion. A sharp dip to around $10 billion occurred in 2002. Sim-

Table 8.1. *FDI Trends in Indonesia, 1990–2003*
(US$billions)

Year	*Approved FDI*	*Implemented FDI*	*Approved domestic investments*
1990	9.64	2.81	30.96
1991	9.03	2.33	20.69
1992	10.47	3.95	14.26
1993	8.15	2.90	18.82
1994	27.05	5.94	24.36
1995	39.89	6.40	30.26
1996	29.94	8.15	40.87
1997	33.79	3.07	25.78
1998	13.65	4.79	7.22
1999	10.88	5.79	7.56
2000	16.08	8.71	9.79
2001	15.06	2.79	5.66
2002	9.80	9.52	2.82
2003	13.21	4.97	5.74

Note: The data exclude the financial services and oil and gas sectors.
Source: BKPM.

1. In the absence of more detailed and accurate data on realized investments, approved investments, although much higher, can be used to gauge investment interest. BKPM data on realized investments are based on investors' reports that are not provided on a regular basis.

2. The accuracy of these data is also questionable. Apparently, the data are estimated based on a debt equity ratio of 30 percent and applied to the amount of external debt recorded.

ilar trends can be observed with implemented and approved domestic investments. The figures on implemented investments must be interpreted with some caution since they are based on reporting by companies.

The trend observed from balance of payments data is similar to the trend observed from data on approved investments. Inflows of around $2 billion in the early 1990s peaked at $6 billion in 1996; since the crisis they declined and turned to net FDI flows. Negative net FDI flows need to be interpreted carefully and should not be interpreted as divestments because a large percentage of these outflows, categorized as other capital, are debt repayments by foreign-owned companies (Table 8.2). In Indonesia, like other crisis countries, such as the Republic of Korea, an increase in mergers and acquisitions (M&As) has somewhat offset the outflows or lack of inflows of FDI. The amount of M&A increased from negligible amounts to $3 billion in 2001 and 2002.

Mergers and acquisitions include the purchase of distressed assets under the Indonesian Banking Restructuring Agency (IBRA), privatization of state-owned companies, private placements in both state and nonstate companies through the capital market or directly, and acquisitions of domestic

Table 8.2. *FDI and Mergers and Acquisitions in Indonesia, 1988–2002*
(US$millions)

		Breakdown of FDI		
Year	*M&A*	*Equity capital*	*Other capital*	*Total FDI*
1988	100	247	329	576
1989	150	308	374	682
1990	0	433	660	1,093
1991	149	589	893	1,482
1992	233	747	1,030	1,777
1993	169	887	1,117	2,004
1994	206	1,024	1,085	2,109
1995	809	1,793	2,553	4,346
1996	530	2,447	3,747	6,194
1997	332	3,001	1,676	4,677
1998	683	2,097	–2,453	–356
1999	1,164	1,111	–3,856	–2,745
2000	819	892	–5,442	–4,550
2001	3,529	687	–3,965	–3,278
2002	2,790	1,051	–2,565	–1,513

Source: FDI flows and the breakdown of FDI are from IMF (various years); mergers and acquisitions data are from UNCTAD (2003).

companies unrelated to IBRA sales. The Indonesian Banking Restructuring Agency, which closed in February 2004, was set up in 1999 for a fixed period of five years as part of a program to restructure the banks. The agency held a significant number of assets. These included major private banks that had been taken over (such as BCA, Niaga, and Danamon) and nonbank assets (companies in various sectors pledged by bank owners to repay their debt or as part of the loans taken over). After delays in implementing its tasks because of operational, institutional, and political interference, IBRA achieved a large amount of sales in the 2001–3 period as the deadline for closure approached.

Several factors appear to explain the trend in mergers and acquisitions. First, foreign companies were used as a vehicle by former owners to reacquire their assets. The second factor to consider is strategic motivation. Companies could enter Indonesia without setting up new operations. They took over existing operations, gaining access to their resources, and they took over companies with established market presence and/or brand.[3] In fact, the Singapore government's investment companies have been aggressive strategic investors as evident in the acquisition by SingTel of PT Telekomunikasi Sellular and STT Telemedia of Indosat as part of the divestment of state-owned enterprise shares. There is also the case of Temasek Holdings in partnership with foreign banks, such as Deutche Bank, to acquire Bank Danamon, which prior to the crisis was the second biggest private bank in Indonesia. More recently, Temasek Holdings bid for Bank International Indonesia, another large Indonesian private bank. Malaysian investors also have been active; Commerz Bank acquired Bank Niaga, and the Guthrie Group acquired palm oil plantations. One could argue that investors from Singapore and Malaysia, because of their geographical proximity and links, have been better placed to assess the high risk of investing in Indonesia and therefore have been able to be more aggressive than countries outside the region.

There is a third motivation behind the FDI trend. Foreign partners could take a greater share of the joint venture when the local partners experienced financial distress and debt restructuring problems. (For example, Yakult Indonesia Persada was acquired by Yakult Honsha Co., Japan; PT Astra Isuzu Motor was acquired by Toyota; and Mercedez Benz Indonesia was acquired

3. For example, Cemex acquired Semen Gresik; Heinz acquired the ABC group (leading local brand in soy sauce and other sauces); Danone, France, acquired Aqua (leading local brand in mineral water); and Reckitt Benckiser acquired Mosquito Coil Group (leading brand for mosquito repellant in the form of a coil).

by Daimler Chrysler.) Financial investors coming in with the hope of selling the company at a capital gain have not been prevalent in Indonesia.

Based on the BKPM data, the main sector (outside of financial services and oil and gas) receiving investment from 1990 to 1997 was manufacturing. The share of approved FDI going to manufacturing was around 60 percent up until the crisis (Table 8.3a), but after 1997 the share going to the services sector increased, and the share going to manufacturing between 1998 and 2003 was only 53 percent (Table 8.3b). During the 1990–97 period, the main subsectors in the manufacturing sector receiving investments were the paper industry, the chemical industry, and the metal goods industry. In the 1980s, however, a greater amount of FDI went to the more labor-intensive and export-oriented sectors such as textiles and footwear.

Prior to the crisis, around 30 percent of approved FDI went to the services sector, and in the 1990–94 period the important subsectors were electricity, gas and water, hotel, and transportation services. In the period immediately before the crisis, one of the main subsectors receiving investments was the more risky sector of housing and real estate. The other was electricity, gas, and water services related to the privatization of public utilities. The private power agreements that the government signed with a number of foreign joint ventures proved to be problematic after the crisis.

In the postcrisis period, more approved investments went to the services sector than during previous periods; the share of FDI in the services sector went up slightly over 40 percent. The following sectors—hotel, transportation, and electricity, gas, and water—received the bulk of the increase in FDI.

What about the major source countries? Based on the stock of investment, East Asian countries have been the most important source country, with Japan accounting for 15 percent of cumulative investment from 1990 to 2002, and the newly industrialized economies (NIEs) in East Asia (Taiwan, China; the Republic of Korea; Singapore; and Hong Kong, China) accounting for about 28 percent. The European Union accounted for 18 percent of FDI, with the United Kingdom being the most important investor, and the United States accounted for 4 percent during this 1980–2002 period. An interesting phenomenon is the increased importance of other developing countries in East Asia as investors in Indonesia; together they accounted for 10 percent of FDI, with China and Malaysia emerging as the most important investors.

There is a sharp distinction between precrisis and postcrisis trends with respect to the major source countries for FDI (Table 8.4). The dominant investor in Indonesia in the 1980s and first half of the 1990s, Japan invested much less after the crisis. Its share declined dramatically from 17 percent in

Table 8.3a. *Foreign Investment Approval by Sector, 1990–97*
(US$millions)

	1990–94				*1995–97*			
	No. of projects	*Value*	*Value/ projects*[a]	*Sectoral share (%)*	*No. of projects*	*Value*	*Value/ projects*[a]	*Sectoral share (%)*
Agriculture	39	1,744	45	2.7	105	3,369	32	3.2
Food crops & plantations	14	1,414	19	81.1	67	2,759	81	81.9
Livestock	6	123	20	7.0	8	137	17	4.1
Fishery	22	93	4	5.3	29	338	12	10.0
Forestry	–3	114	–38	6.5	1	135	135	4.0
Mining	1	3,626	3,626	5.7	5	1,698	340	1.6
Manufacturing	1,196	38,931	33	61.1	1,362	65,981	48	63.6
Food	94	2,167	23	5.6	100	2,596	26	3.9
Textiles	242	3,306	14	8.5	145	1,358	9	2.1
Wood	70	371	5	1.0	102	434	4	0.7
Paper	35	7,129	204	18.3	46	10,801	235	16.4
Pharmaceuticals	–1	–33	33	–0.1	9	117	13	0.2
Chemical	247	15,258	62	39.2	295	39,069	132	59.2
Nonmetallic mineral	43	2,400	56	6.2	65	2,536	39	3.8
Basic metal	43	2,700	63	6.9	44	1,300	30	2.0
Metal goods	357	5,307	15	13.6	529	7,528	14	11.4
Other	66	327	5	0.8	27	243	9	0.4
Services	528	19,414	832	30.5	1,047	32,629	681	31.5
Electricity, gas, water	8	5,103	638	8.0	22	9,198	418	8.9
Construction	36	384	11	0.6	163	809	5	0.8
Trade	137	1140.39	8	1.8	157	85	1	0.1
Hotel	86	6,574	76	10.3	91	3,178	35	3.1
Transportation	36	1,181	33	1.9	82	506	6	0.5
Housing/ real estate	69	4,104	59	6.4	81	17,218	213	16.6
Other	156	929	6	1.5	451	1,635	4	1.6
Total	1,764	63,715	36	100.0	2,519	103,679	41	100.0

a. The average value in U.S. dollars of projects in each sector.
Source: BKPM.

Table 8.3b. *Foreign Investment Approval by Sector, 1998–2003*
(US$millions)

	1998–2003				2003[b]			
	No. of projects	*Value*	*Value/ projects*[a]	*Sectoral share (%)*	*No. of projects*	*Value*	*Value/ projects*[a]	*Sectoral share (%)*
Agriculture	205.0	2,865.0	20.1	4.4	14	92.4	6.6	1.5
Food crops & plantations	120.0	2,413.2	7.5	3.7	6	23.2	3.9	0.4
Livestock	24.0	179.8	14.6	0.3	4	11.6	2.9	0.2
Fishery	8.0	116.7	2.9	0.2	7	26.2	3.7	0.4
Forestry	53.0	155.3	2.5	0.2	1	31.4	31.4	0.5
Mining	170.0	417.4	16.3	0.6	7	14.8	2.1	0.2
Manufacturing	2,106.0	34,276.4	13.7	52.6	216	2,474.6	11.5	40.2
Food	173.0	2,369.8	3.0	3.6	18	202.2	11.2	3.3
Textiles	334.0	989.2	3.2	1.5	27	113.0	4.2	1.8
Leather goods & footwear	112.0	353.6	2.6	0.5	8	27.8	3.5	0.5
Wood	124.0	324.8	32.5	0.5	10	168.1	16.8	2.7
Paper & printing	70.0	2,274.7	110.4	3.5	8	798.3	99.8	13.0
Chemicals & pharmaceuticals	187.0	20,637.1	5.5	31.7	17	204.4	12.0	3.3
Rubber & plastic	180.0	991.7	10.0	1.5	21	70.1	3.3	1.1
Nonmetallic mineral	49.0	488.3	8.6	0.7	5	507.1	101.4	8.2
Metal goods, machinery, & electronics	474.0	4,083.0	7.9	6.3	72	231.3	3.2	3.8
Precision instruments, watches	20.0	158.0	8.9	0.2	4	4.8	1.2	0.1
MV and other transport equipment	148.0	1,311.6	1.3	2.0	11	94.4	8.6	1.5
Other	235.0	294.6	7.4	0.5	15	53.1	3.5	0.9
Services	3,751.0	27,575.2	222.9	42.3	489	3,575.6	7.3	58.1
Electricity, gas, water	19.0	4,235.3	4.9	6.5	2	362.9	181.5	5.9

(Table continues on following page.)

Table 8.3b. (continued)

	1998–2003				2003[b]			
	No. of projects	Value	Value/ projects[a]	Sectoral share (%)	No. of projects	Value	Value/ projects[a]	Sectoral share (%)
Construction	133.0	655.6	2.0	1.0	22	360.8	16.4	5.9
Trade & repair	1,911.0	3,740.2	30.3	5.7	286	367.4	1.3	6.0
Hotel & restaurant	268.0	8,107.9	17.6	12.4	42	313.5	7.5	5.1
Transport, storage, & communication	307.0	5,394.3	16.0	8.3	35	1,979.1	56.5	32.1
Real estate, industrial estate	119.0	1,899.8	3.6	2.9	3	9.4	3.1	0.2
Other	994.0	3,542.1	10.5	5.4	104	182.5	1.8	3.0
Total	6,232.0	65,134.0	10.5	100.0	726	6,157.4	8.5	100.0

a. The average value in U.S. dollars of projects in each sector.
b. The first three quarters of 2003.
Source: BKPM.

the 1995–97 period to 8 percent in the 1998–2002 period. Nevertheless, Japan remains the most important investor in terms of the stock of investment. The share of U.S. investment also declined over time: 10 percent during the 1990–94 period, 4.8 percent in the 1995–97 period, and only 2.7 percent in the 1998–2002 period. In contrast to this decline, the European Union increased its share from around 12 percent in the 1990–94 period to 21 percent in the 1998–2002 period. The most important European investor, the United Kingdom, in fact increased its share of FDI from 8 percent in the 1990–94 period, to 13 percent in the 1995–97 period, to 16 percent in the 1998–2002 period. In the period just before the crisis, the increase appears to have been related to large-scale projects in the chemical subsector.

As for the East Asian NIEs, they became an important source of investment in the 1980s as they faced rising costs and appreciating currencies and relocated to Indonesia. During the 1980s these countries together accounted for around 22 percent of FDI; Hong Kong (China) accounted for 10 percent of FDI, followed by Taiwan (China) and the Republic of Korea at 5 and 4

Table 8.4. *Foreign Investment Approval by Country of Origin, 1990–2002*
(US$millions)

	1990–94				1995–97				1998–2002				1990–2002	
	No. of projects	Value	Value/projects[a]	Sectoral share (%	No. of projects	Value	Value/projects[a]	Sectoral share (%)	No. of projects	Value	Value/projects[a]	Sectoral share (%)	Value	Sectoral share (%)
America	112	6,732	75.3	10.6	145	5,035	44.7	4.8	295	1,513.3	7.1	2.3	13,280.3	6
United States	98	6,624	67.6	10.4	114	5,014	44.0	4.8	220	1,489	6.8	2.3	13,127	6
Canada	14	108	7.7	0.2	31	21	0.7	0	75	24.3	0.3	0	153.3	0
EU	156	7,479	160.9	11.8	229	21,548	313.1	20.8	771	13,838	52.5	21.2	42,865	18
United Kingdom	62	4,974	80.2	7.8	90	13,931	154.8	13.4	349	10,323	29.6	15.8	29,228	13
Netherlands	45	1,341	29.8	2.1	59	2,397	40.6	2.3	184	1,947	10.6	3.0	5,685	2
France	22	933	42.4	1.5	30	992	33.1	1	95	372	3.9	0.6	2,297	1
Germany	27	231	8.5	0.4	50	4,228	84.6	4.1	143	1,196	8.4	1.8	5,655	2
Asia														
Japan	405	11,401	28.1	17.9	350	17,774	50.8	17.1	419	5,208	12.4	8.0	34,383	15
NIEs	1,057	28,036	111.6	43.9	880	22,785	100.3	21.9	2,350	13,399	50.4	20.5	64,220	28
Hong Kong (China)	221	11,403	51.6	17.9	76	1,893	24.9	1.8	72	2,483	34.5	3.8	15,779	7
Rep. of Korea	234	4,603	19.7	7.2	152	3,558	23.4	3.4	1,116	1,870	1.7	2.9	10,031	4
Taiwan (China)	262	5,571	21.3	8.7	290	5,938	20.5	5.7	355	1,908	5.4	2.9	13,417	6
Singapore	340	6,459	19	10.1	362	11,396	31.5	11	807	7,138	8.8	10.9	24,993	11
ASEAN	77	973	29.4	1.5	163	6,542	245.3	6.3	408	3,992.6	18.4	6.0	11,507.6	5
Malaysia	56	854	15.2	1.3	148	4,848	32.8	4.7	365	3,827	10.5	5.8	9,529	4
Thailand	17	81	4.7	0.1	8	1,655	206.9	1.6	22	25.6	1.2	0	1,761.6	1
Philippines	4	38	9.5	0.1	7	39	5.6	0	21	140	6.7	0.2	217	0
China		61		0.1		161		0.2		6,377		9.7	6,599	3
Australia	52	948	18.2	1.5	128	6,480	50.6	6.3	288	3,080	10.7	4.7	10,508	5
TOTAL	1,764	63,715	36.1	100	2,519	103,679	41.2	100	6,229	65,456	10.5	100	232,850	100

a. The average value in U.S. dollars of projects in each sector.
Source: BKPM.

percent each; Singapore accounted for the remaining 3 percent. In the pre- and postcrisis periods, there has been a significant decline in the share of the NIEs investment in Indonesia except Singapore. Only Singapore maintained its share: 10 percent in the 1990–94 period, 11 percent in the 1995–97 period, and 11 percent in the 1998–2002 period. In addition, Singapore has been an aggressive player in mergers and acquisitions.

The other interesting development is the increase in the FDI share of other developing countries in Asia. Their share, negligible in the 1980s, increased in the 1990s, especially toward the end of the decade. The two notable investors were Malaysia and China; they accounted for 6 percent and 10 percent respectively of the share of FDI in the 1998–2002 period, reflecting a substantial increase in value and share compared with the previous periods (Table 8.4).

During the worsening investment climate in Indonesia, developing countries in the region continued and increased their investments. The reasons for this trend will be explored below. Although there has been no major divestment from major investors, the amount of new investment from the United States declined from 4.8 percent in the 1995–97 period to 2.3 percent in the 1998–2002 period. Japan's share declined as well, from 17.1 percent in the precrisis period to 8 percent in the postcrisis period. Whereas there has been some increase by European investors, this appears to be related to large-scale investments in the chemical sector.

Factors Underlying the Trends in FDI

What factors explain the ups and downs in foreign direct investment and other capital flows in Indonesia? As we will show, the factors include not only the host country's FDI policies. Macroeconomic fundamentals, infrastructure, and policy implementation were influential factors as well.

First Period of FDI Liberalization, 1986–89

There were two main periods of FDI liberalization in Indonesia prior to the 1997 crisis. The first was the deregulation of the mid-1980s in response to the fall in oil and commodity prices.[4] In addition to macro stabilization measures (such as depreciation of the rupiah, fiscal consolidation, and initial reforms in the financial sector), deregulation of trade and FDI policies

4. For a more detailed analysis of this precrisis period, see Hal Hill (1988), Pangestu (2000a, 2000b, and 2001), and Thee and Pangestu (1998).

occurred. The measures were aimed at switching from an import-substitution to an export-oriented regime in order to diversify the export and fiscal revenue base of Indonesia away from oil and primary commodities. A number of significant steps were taken, including revamping the corrupt and lengthy procedures at customs; implementing duty drawback schemes for exports and major deregulation of tariff and nontariff barriers; and removing various restrictions on FDI linked to export orientation. Minimum capital requirements were lowered, foreign ownership caps were increased, divestment requirements were relaxed, and allowances were made for national treatment (Box 8.1).

Box 8.1. *Summary of Deregulation in Indonesia, 1986–89*

Limits on foreign ownership. The maximum limit of foreign ownership increased from 80 percent to 95 percent for "high-risk," high-technology, and export-oriented companies (initially defined as 100 percent exports, later relaxed to 85 percent and then 65 percent); East Indonesia location and large capital expenditures (that is, project costs above $10 million). In 1989 full foreign ownership was allowed in Batam Economic Zone.

Minimum capital requirement. The minimum capital investment was lowered from $1 million to $250,000 for FDI that created employment and exports or went to supporting industries.

National treatment. National treatment means a company receives the same incentives as domestic companies. It was defined as at least 75 percent Indonesian owned (state and/or private); 51 percent of the company's shares had to be traded in the capital market. Later it was defined as 51 percent Indonesian owned (still later 45 percent); at least 20 percent of the company's shares had to be traded in the capital market.

Divestment requirements. The phase down to 51 percent foreign owned extended from ten to fifteen years; in 1989 for 100 percent foreign-owned investments in Batam, divestment to 95 percent in five years, and no further divestment requirement if FDI companies exported 100 percent of their products.

Overhaul of positive list. The positive list of priority sectors open to FDI was significantly expanded and made more transparent. In 1989 the positive list was changed to a negative list of sectors closed for FDI.

Relaxation of licenses. Product definition and capacity limitations were relaxed for licenses enabling broad banding measures, including diversification of up to 30 percent of existing capacity without obtaining a new license. FDI companies were also allowed to export their own products, purchase and export products of other Indonesian companies, and form new joint ventures in export trade.

These policy changes coincided with the outward movement of FDI from Japan and the newly industrializing economies of Singapore, Hong Kong (China), Taiwan (China), and the Republic of Korea in response to appreciation of their currencies, rising labor and other costs, and increased problems with labor (especially in Korea).[5] The spurt in foreign direct investment in the mid-1980s to early 1990s was motivated by export orientation. FDI policies had the desired outcome of increasing export-oriented FDI, and they also contributed to the diversification of exports away from oil. Nonoil exports as a share of total exports increased from 20 percent to 60 percent during this period, with manufactured exports (such as garments, footwear, and electronics) increasing in importance.

Foreign investment liberalization efforts experienced a lull after 1989, but approvals continued to rise as the economy strengthened; the average growth rate in the 1989–91 period was 7 percent.

Second Period of Liberalization, 1992–94

An apparent decline in foreign investors' interest beginning around 1992 led to a number of significant steps to relax restrictions on foreign ownership. These steps culminated in a bold move of allowing 100 percent foreign ownership with no explicit divestment requirements and allowing 95 percent foreign ownership in strategic sectors such as shipping (Box 8.2). The dramatic package in 1994 seems to have been driven by a number of factors: increased competition for trade and investment, deceleration in the growth of nonoil exports, a decline in foreign investment approvals in 1993, and the fact that Indonesia was host to APEC in 1994, and it wanted to champion the concerted unilateral liberalization process.

This dramatic policy change was a main factor behind the rise in investment approvals in the 1995–97 period, and it was not marred by the national car case whereby local content rules were in favor of a newly established automotive company owned by the president's son.[6] In this period FDI was

5. Indonesia probably also benefited as the logical alternative to China after the Tian An-Men incident, which increased foreign investors' cautiousness toward China. Of course, this situation changed in the mid-1990s. In the years prior to the crisis, Indonesia continued to attract FDI since it was seen as the alternative to China for locating labor-intensive operations as part of the diversification of risks strategy pursued by large multinational companies.

6. The automotive company had links with Kia of the Republic of Korea. It was allowed duty-free imports of components for assembly of its cars, and this was linked to fulfillment of local content. Not only was the company allowed three years to fulfill

Box 8.2. Summary of Liberalization in Indonesia, 1992–94

1992. A decree in 1992 permitted 100 percent foreign ownership for certain types of investment (over $50 million, in Eastern Indonesia, or bonded zone with 100 percent export), and the divestment requirement was extended to twenty years. The divestment requirement was relaxed to 5 percent within five years and then to 20 percent within twenty years. The decree lowered minimum capital to $250,000 for export-oriented and labor-intensive exports.

1993. The October 1993 deregulation package decentralized authority from the state level to the regional level for granting permits and licenses for land, building, operation, and environment. The 1992 package was reversed by making the divestment requirements more restrictive.

1994. The June 1994 package of liberalization measures was bold. It included almost full liberalization of foreign ownership, phase down requirements, and divesting foreign ownership; elimination of the minimum capital requirements; and automatic renewal of the license for foreign investment as long as deemed "beneficial." Foreign investments were no longer required to be located in designated Industrial Estates. Nine strategic sectors previously closed for foreign investment were opened for foreign ownership up to 95 percent (ports, production and generation of electricity, telecommunications, shipping, air transport, drinking water, railways, automatic energy generation plants, and mass media).

not motivated only by export orientation. Companies wanted to enter into the services sector and to serve the domestic market. The possibility of 100 percent foreign ownership is dramatic given the nationalist sentiments that underlie the restrictions and divestment requirements that existed since the early 1970s. These restrictions and divestment requirements helped explain companies' hesitancy to transfer technology, and they contributed to the uncertainty in the investment environment that was not conducive to long planning horizons by investors.

The Deterioration of the Investment Climate

Compared to Thailand and the Republic of Korea, Indonesia made a less rapid recovery from the crisis, and FDI played only a minimal role. The main reason was the worsening of all of the fundamental indicators that make up the broad investment climate faced by investors.

---

domestic content requirements, but no other company was given this privilege, including the established Japanese auto makers. Japan, the United States, and the European Union brought the case to WTO Dispute Settlement and won the case in 1998.

The rapid depreciation of the rupiah and confidence, capital outflows, and bank runs led Indonesia to turn to the International Monetary Fund for a bail out in October 1997. The crisis culminated in the resignation of President Suharto in May 1998. Unstable leadership and unpredictable policy followed. Upon the resignation of Suharto, President Habibie became president for about one year. The elections in June 1999 put President Abdurrahman Wahid in office. Under the latter's leadership, there were frequent changes in decision making as well as in institutional structures. Thus the period from August 1999 to October 2001 was marked by unpredictability. President Wahid was voted out in a no confidence motion, and President Megawati took over in July 2001. The process of regional autonomy and decentralization, which began in 2001, added to the uncertainty affecting investors at the local and regional levels.

Under the leadership of President Megawati, there have been fewer changes in policies, decision makers, and institutional structures. Despite having an open FDI regime after the IMF reform program, Indonesia has witnessed only a slight improvement in the investment climate. This is due to the lack of improvement in various basic indicators of interest to investors (such as growth, governance, law and order), and to problems that investors have faced with regard to labor, taxes, and decentralization, as will be explained below.

AN OPEN FDI REGIME ON PAPER. The crisis that hit Indonesia began in the last quarter of 1997, and thus approvals still peaked in 1997. As part of entering into the IMF program and having to sign on the Letter of Intent, the government agreed to remove the remaining restrictions on FDI (Table 8.5). Foreign investment in palm oil plantations and in the retail, wholesale trade was no longer restricted. The 85 percent cap on foreign ownership in banks was removed, and a number of restrictive trade practices were ended that constrained the operations of foreign companies in certain sectors. On paper, Indonesia appears to have one of the most open FDI regimes in the world.

A draft investment law was introduced in Parliament to enhance legal certainty and combine the laws governing domestic and foreign investment, thus ensuring national treatment. The law was also intended to guard against nationalization or acquisition of any foreign company, minimize the negative list, and clarify the role of the central government and regional governments in dealing with investments. FDI can come in only through the central government, while domestic investment can be made directly via local governments. The law also regulates the institutional set-up for investment services. For example, it revived the "one stop investment service" under BKPM.

Table 8.5. *Postcrisis Reforms in FDI Policies in Indonesia*

Policy action	*Target date*	*Status*	*Note*[a]
Remove 49 percent limit on foreign investment in listed companies.	September 1997	Completed	MEFP January 1998
Issue a revised and shortened negative list of activities closed to foreign investors.	June 30, 1998	Reduced from 35 to 9 to 7 sectors	MEFP January 1998
Remove restrictions on foreign investment in palm oil plantations, retail, and wholesale trade.	1998	Completed	MEFP January 1998
Dissolve restrictive marketing arrangements for cement, paper, and plywood.	1998	Completed	MEFP January 1998
Cement: remove price controls, allow exports.	1997, 1998	Completed	MEFP January 1998
Free up trade across region, including trade in cloves (eliminate marketing board), cashew nuts, vanilla.	1998	Completed	MEFP January 1998
Enforce prohibition of provincial and local-export taxes.	1998	Completed	MEFP January 1998
Remove monopoly in imports of wheat, wheat flour, soybeans, garlic; sale of wheat flour; import and marketing of sugar. Farmers no longer forced to plant sugar cane.	1998	Completed	MEFP January 1998
Simplify licensing procedures; reintroduce one-stop service at the Board of Investment; allow embassies abroad authority to approve application of FDI; permit approval of less than $100 million without signature of president; introduce fiscal incentives (pioneer industries, location; size; no. employed).	1998, 1999		Not LOI
Decentralization: regional offices of Board of Investment to approve; plan to make BOI more promotion oriented and less focused on licensing.	2000, 2001		Not LOI

a. MEFP refers to the Memorandum of Economic and Financial Policy. LOI refers to Letter of Intent.
Source: Adapted from International Monetary Fund website (www.imf.org).

At least on paper, FDI policies are on track. However, questions remain with regard to implementation, leadership, and political will. BKPM continues to suffer from leadership problems, ineffective streamlining, bureaucratic licensing procedures, and minimal efforts to promote investment. There is also no coordinated response to complaints by foreign investors. Several attempts to create a forum for businesspeople to channel their complaints have not been effective. Whether the BKPM can effectively deliver on the one-stop service is questionable without greater authority and political will. The requirements that investors must meet to obtain approval fall under different technical ministries/departments. Furthermore, the investment climate continues to deteriorate.

INDICATORS OF A DETERIORATING INVESTMENT CLIMATE. Table 8.6 shows the deterioration of the investment climate in Indonesia due to the worsening of country risk and governance. Although one can question the reliability of the survey-based information,[7] all indicators point to a worsening of the investment climate. This picture is consistent with the concerns raised by investors from various other surveys. In fact, the depreciation of the rupiah had made Indonesia's exports competitive, but inflation and the rapid rise in minimum wages offset this gain. Political pressure has led to minimum wages rising in dollar terms back up to precrisis levels, without a commensurate increase in productivity (as measured by the increase in value added per worker). These developments have hurt the labor-intensive and export-oriented segments of Indonesia's industry, sectors that had previously attracted relocation by NIEs in search of a lower cost base. Now some of these investors in the footwear and garment industries have closed down their companies or are thinking of relocating to lower-cost options such as Vietnam and Cambodia.

Foreign investors, in response to survey questions about the major issues facing them, reported concerns in the following areas: breakdown of law and order, security issues, and lack of legal certainty; labor issues; taxes and customs; and the high-cost economy because of corruption and local levies (see Table 8.7). Japanese investors also cited numerous concerns: security, social and political instability and recurring violence, poor infrastructure, labor problems, smuggling, difficulties in obtaining work permits, and restrictions preventing foreign firms from acting as importers or from investing and participating in domestic retail operations despite the deregulation measures (*Jakarta Post*, April 2002).

---

7. The reliability of these surveys can be questioned, especially the unexpected result of improvement in bureaucracy in 1998 and 1999.

Table 8.6. *Indicators of the Investment Climate in Indonesia, 1995–2002*

Indicator	*1995*	*1996*	*1997*	*1998*	*1999*	*2000*	*2001*	*2002*
Private investment as a percentage of gross domestic investment	73.0	77.3	79.4	71.0	61.0	40.6	35.5	32.7
ICRG Composite Risk Rating	69.5	70.0	60.3	41.0	51.8	54.8	56.3	58.5
Governance index[a]								
ICRG corruption rating	3	3	2	1	2	1	1	n.a.
ICRG bureaucratic quality rating	2	2	2	2	3	3	2	n.a.
ICRG law and order rating	5	4	4	2	2	2	2	n.a.
Wages and productivity[b]								
Minimum wage	552	608	541	181	267	317	338	497
Labor cost per worker in manufacturing	1,452	2,596	2,537	694	915	992	999	n.a.
Value added per worker in manufacturing	7,146	8,633	7,461	3,590	5,410	6,128	5,769	n.a.

n.a. Not available.

a. On a scale of 1 (bad) to 6 (good).

b. In U.S. dollars per year.

Source: World Bank (various years); the data on International Country Risk Guide (ICRG) indicators are from Transparency International, Heritage Foundation.

Security Concerns of Foreign Investors. The postcrisis period has been marked by increased security concerns. The security apparatus broke down under decentralization, and leadership from the top was not strong enough. There have been recurring riots and conflicts stemming from ethnic, religious, and political issues; separatist movements in Aceh; terrorist attacks; and a breakdown of law and order due to socio-economic needs (leading to pilfering that affected plantations, for instance). Decentralization has added to the complexity of the problem-solving challenges.

Foreign investors have experienced various problems related to security and safety (for example, the Exxon case in Aceh and the killing of Freeport employees in Timika, Irian Jaya). Exxon facilities in Aceh supply gas to the Arun LNG plant. These facilities have been under constant attacks since 2001 and have had to intermittently stop production. This disrupts exports of LNG to Japan and to the Republic of Korea, countries that are under long-term contracts. Foreign investors also have had to face the misuse of the legal system as shown by the Manulife case, for example (Box 8.3). Detainment and harassment of foreign personnel was evident in this case. The GM of Samsung received death threats after complaining about corruption in the Customs Department. In 2001, police in Surabaya threatened to imprison two foreign Cargill Inc. employees in a dispute over a grain shipment.

Table 8.7. *Concerns of Foreign Investors*

Association	*Issues raised*
Indonesian Chamber of Commerce	1. Ambiguous law on labor issues (Law No.13/2003) regarding outsourcing labor, regulation on overtime work and wages, structure and scale of wages, and subcontracting wages (room for conflict of interest and negotiations with stakeholders). 2. Plethora of business-distorting local regulations (1006 listed from its survey). 3. Low quality of government services and lack of legal certainty. 4. Illegal levies as a significant percentage of levies. 5. Investment-distorting policies.
International Business Chamber	1. Uncertainty in laws and regulations and unpredictable outcomes. For instance, new investment law reinforces concept of approval, which is bureaucratic control of power. Instead the law should have supported registration process. 2. Lack of infrastructure: roads, water and waste, transportation, and telecommunications.
Japan Club[a]	1. Taxation administration: low rate of compliance; delays in refund of value added tax that tie up companies' cash flow and increase documentation work. 2. Custom clearance service. 3. Public service related to taxes and customs.
Group of domestic industry associations and SMEs	1. Bureaucratic licensing requirements for SMEs should have one-stop service. 2. Treatment of import duty and luxury taxes needs to be rationalized; there is bias against manufacturing in Indonesia. 3. Price check and refund procedures are burdensome on cash flow and create a greater burden for SMEs. 4. Simplify tax audit and simplify appeal procedure to minimize interpretation of "gray areas" being used by tax officials and help firms avoid penalties with refund being withheld. 5. Simplify requirements for SMEs to access bank loans, including collateral procedures. 6. Local tax and retributions.

JETRO, Jakarta[b]	1. Taxation. 2. Manpower management. 3. Customs clearance and import/export duties. 4. Costs to obtain approvals and license from central and local governments. 5. Inconsistent government regulations.
CSIS[c]	1. Smuggling and high-cost economy. 2. Export procedures. 3. Labor law and labor issues. 4. Availability of working capital. 5. Tax issues. 6. Tariff and nontariff barriers.
LPEM[d]	1. Around 75 percent of respondents identify corporate tax and local charges as high or moderate obstacles to doing business. 2. 56 percent of respondents say license processing takes longer than expected. 3. "Extra costs" were close to 10 percent of cost on Java and over 11 percent outside Java.

a. Japanese companies in Indonesia.

b. Japan External Trade Organization. From survey of Japanese firms outside Jakarta, September 2003.

c. Centre for Strategic and International Studies, Jakarta. From survey of export-oriented foreign and local companies.

d. Lembaga Penyelidikan Ekonomi Masyarakat. From survey of the cost of doing business for local companies in several regional cities.

Source: Indonesian National Economic Recovery Committee; various media sources; Centre for Strategic and International Studies, Jakarta; and Lembaga Penyelidikan Ekonomi Masyarakat Universitas Indonesia.

Box 8.3. *The Manulife Case: An Example of the Uncertainties Facing Foreign Investors in Indonesia*

In June 2000, after a lengthy court case, a Jakarta commercial court declared PT Dharmala Sakti Sejahtera (DSS), part of the Dharmala group of Suyanto Gondokusumo, bankrupt. It was one of the few cases a debtor has lost in the bankruptcy court. A court-appointed receiver auctioned off the company's assets to reimburse creditors, including the Indonesian Banking Restructuring Authority.

In October 2000, there was an auction of 40 percent of the shares in the joint venture PT Asuransi Jiwa Manulife belonging to DSS. Its partner in the joint venture, the Canadian firm Manufacturers Life Insurance Co. (Manulife), was the only one that put in a bid for $18.5 million, thereby increasing its share to 91 percent. During the auction, Roman Gold, a firm registered in the British Virgin Islands, claimed that it had purchased the shares through a series of transactions dating back to 1996, when Gondokusumo supposedly sold them to Harvest Hero International, a firm based in Hong Kong (China).

The court did not accept the challenge since the sale was not registered in the company's records or with the Ministry of Finance, as required by law. The remaining 9 percent share is owned by the World Bank's financial arm, the International Finance Corporation (IFC). Roman Gold then filed a police report alleging the shares held by Manulife (91 percent of the shares) were forged. Thereafter, Manulife's senior vice-president, an Indonesian, was arrested and held for three weeks. He was released only after an intervention by the president, amidst concerns raised by the Canadian prime minister. The court receiver was also detained. Police froze the proceeds from the sale, pending further investigations. Manulife executives reported receiving threats.

Manulife filed a criminal suit against Roman Gold and the chairman of Dharmala Sakti, Suyanto Gondokusumo. In May 2001, Indonesian President Abdurrahman Wahid declared that Manulife was innocent of any wrongdoings. He said that the Manulife issue had affected Indonesia's relationship with Canada and with the International Monetary Fund in the United States. President Wahid ordered the country's attorney-general to drop the case. Only after an international outcry and pressure from the Canadian government was the ruling overturned.

Source: Asiaweek, February 16, 2001; Reuters, May 21, 2001; *Toronto Star*, May 29, 2001; and *The Economist*, October 23, 2003.

Regional Autonomy and Nationalism. In addition to security issues, foreign investors in the natural resource and agriculture sectors face regional autonomy issues. Local governments want bigger and bigger shares. For instance, Rio Tinto, a British/Australian mining company, is locked in a bitter legal battle with a provincial government over control of Kaltim Prima Coal. Cemex from Mexico has been unable to increase its 25 percent stake in

Box 8.4. *The Cemex Case: An Example of the Conflict between Privatization and Nationalism in Indonesia*

The Mexican firm Cemex, the third biggest cement producer in the world, put in a bid to get a majority share in PT Semen Gresik and its three subsidiaries in 1999. After protests from DPR, Cemex was allowed to purchase only 14 percent of the company. With shares it purchased from the stock market, Cemex ended up with a 25.5 percent stake.

In mid-2000, Cemex made a bid to increase its shares so it would own a majority of the stock. The bid has been blocked because of protests from West Sumatra at Gresik's Semen Padang unit. It opposed majority foreign ownership. Semen Padang contributed 36 percent of Semen Gresik's total sales volume and contributed the most to its exports. The Indonesian government is working on a compromise that would entail taking out Semen Padang before allowing Cemex to acquire a majority share. However, Cemex has refused to accept such a spinoff because of its original understanding in 1999 that it was buying Semen Gresik with three of its subsidiaries, including Semen Padang. Cemex threatened to pull out of Semen Gresik if the government changed the original deal by taking out Semen Padang. It would also then change its plan to base its Southeast Asian operations in Indonesia. The standoff and the change in the agreement after the investor had already invested are sending negative signals on privatization and the role of foreign investors. The issues are still not resolved, and Cemex is considering using international arbitration.

Semen Gresik because of squabbles between local government and central government officials.

Labor and Tax Issues. Among other concerns of foreign and domestic investors is the spate of labor disputes over workers' compensation. These disputes have led to conflicts and several months of halted production. New employment regulations continue to concern the business community as it increases severance pay obligations to workers whose employment has been terminated, even for those resigning voluntarily or dismissed for misdemeanors. Foreign investors have also complained about harassment by tax officials.

A NOT ENTIRELY GLOOMY PICTURE. Despite the lack of new investments and the deterioration of the investment climate, there have been no major divestments. The pull-out by some firms (for example, Sony and Procter and Gamble) has been highly publicized, but the reasons warrant closer examination. The worsening investment climate was not the only factor. Procter and Gamble closed down its hair care and health care products operations in Indonesia and relocated hair care to Thailand and health care products to the Philippines to consolidate the production base in response to the removal of tariffs for intra ASEAN trade under the ASEAN Free Trade Agreement (AFTA). The choice of Thailand and the Philippines over Indonesia, according to Procter and Gamble, was because the raw materials and supply industries were more developed in these countries than in Indonesia. In the case of Sony's relocation of its audio equipment production from Indonesia to Malaysia, there were several reasons. Labor disputes played a part. However, Sony wanted to consolidate its production in one center for exports as well as service the ASEAN market through the AFTA based on cost considerations (including existence of supplier industries). In addition, Sony was having its own internal problems and needed to consolidate and increase efficiency.

Once companies can sell to Indonesia without producing in Indonesia, the choice of production location is not influenced only by the policy factors mentioned above, but also by fundamental weaknesses in Indonesia's industrial structure, mainly the lack of supporting industries and quality infrastructure, including physical and human resources. This is not a new problem for Indonesia. Earlier studies have also pointed to the lack of supporting industries as a major problem for Indonesia in terms of building up its technological capability, graduating to higher value added industries, and deepening its industrial structure. On the electronics, textile, and motorcycle industries, see Thee and Pangestu (1998) and on Indonesia's competitiveness, see Lall (1998).

Established foreign companies, especially in the consumer goods industry, continue to locate in Indonesia because of the size of the market and their established position, as well as other factors such as availability of raw materials and labor. For instance, Unilever, a major consumer goods company operating in Indonesia since 1924, decided to increase its investment in Indonesia by $500 million over the next ten years. Because of AFTA and cost considerations, it relocated its factories from Australia and Singapore to centralize its production base for supplying the rest of the region. Indonesia was chosen as a location to supply Southeast Asia and Asia Pacific because of the large size of the Indonesian market, Unilever's already dominant position in the Indonesian market, low labor costs, and the supply of raw materials (*Jakarta Post*, June 16, 2003).

The Impact of FDI on Indonesia's Manufacturing Sector

Various studies, based on survey data from the Central Bureau of Statistics (CBS) and case studies, have explored the impact of FDI on the Indonesian economy. In this section, we confine our summary of these studies to the manufacturing sector.[8]

Analysis Based on CBS Data

Multinational companies usually possess firm-specific assets (such as production technology, management know-how, and marketing networks) that are superior to the assets of locally owned companies. Consequently, multinational companies are expected to be more efficient than the local companies, and positive productivity spillovers are expected as well.

FDI AND RELATIVE LABOR PRODUCTIVITY. Takii and Ramstetter (2000 and 2003) assessed the impact of FDI on labor productivity by using data from the CBS industrial surveys. Their study was conducted over a long period of time (1975 to 2000). They measured labor productivity as value added per worker and controlled for variation in size and vintage of the plant. Takii and Ramstetter found that foreign multinationals have significantly higher labor productivity than domestic firms, especially in the chemical industry and the electric and precision machinery industry. (Foreign multinationals employed one seventh of the total number of workers in the manufacturing industry and produced more than a quarter of the manufacturing industry's total output.) Less difference in labor productivity was found in the apparel, footwear, and transportation machinery industries.

Takii and Ramstetter (2000 and 2003) also found that the employment and production of foreign MNCs continued to increase in absolute and relative terms after the crisis. The authors also attempted to compare labor productivity differentials among MNCs. They classified foreign companies into three major groups: heavily foreign (with foreign share higher than 90 percent), majority foreign (with foreign share greater than 50 percent and less than 90 percent), and minority foreign (with foreign share between 10 and 50 percent). Companies classified as *majority foreign* exhibited the highest average labor productivity in the 1975–91 period and in 1997; in the 1992–96 and 1998–2000 periods, companies classified as *minority foreign* showed the highest labor productivity. Takii and Ramstetter also suggested that the three groups of companies (heavily, majority, and minority foreign) experienced a larger increase in nominal average labor productivity than local companies.

---

8. Obviously, FDI affected various service industries in Indonesia, notably financial services, oil and gas, and other natural-resource-based industries.

James, Ray, and Minor (2002), using the same data set, focused on competitiveness in the textile and garment industry. In the early 1990s, the labor productivity of locally owned apparel manufacturers was higher than the labor productivity of foreign companies; in the later period (from the mid-1990s to 2002), however, foreign manufacturers showed labor productivity and scale of productions that were higher due to a large increase in foreign firms in the apparel sector, especially Korean firms. These characteristics of foreign-owned establishments have become even more pronounced since 2002.

FDI AND PRODUCTIVITY SPILLOVERS. Takii (2001) examined the extent of productivity spillovers from foreign affiliated plants to locally owned plants. He found that the extent of the spillover was positively correlated with the share of foreign-owned plants in employment absorption. Spillovers tended to be smaller in industries where large technological gaps existed between foreign and locally owned plants.

FDI AND WAGES. Lipsey and Sjoholm (2001) compared the behavior of locally owned and foreign-owned firms in the Indonesian labor market and the effect of foreign-owned firms on Indonesian wages. Surveys of manufacturing establishments in 1996 showed that foreign firms paid workers more than locally owned firms. The greater the foreign presence was, the higher the wages in locally owned establishments. Since foreign establishments pay higher wages than do locally owned ones, that higher foreign presence raised the general wages level in a province and industry (Lipsey and Sjoholm 2001).

FDI AND TOTAL FACTOR PRODUCTIVITY. Aswicahyono (1998) tested the relationship between total factor productivity and ownership in the manufacturing sector using the same data set.[9] Foreign ownership was relatively large in the period from 1975 to 1985, about 26 percent as a result of the more

---

9. This study uses the growth accounting approach; TFP growth is calculated as the difference between output growth rates and cost-share-weighted input growth rates. The survey data from the Central Bureau of Statistics are classified in seven ownership categories: government (G), private (P), foreign (F), and the following four types of joint ventures: G-P, F-P, G-F, and G-F-P. Aswicahyono simplified these seven categories to government (G+GP), private (P), foreign (F+FP), and government joint ventures (GF+GFP). Some adjustments were made to the last category. The end result was three categories: government (in the sugar, fertilizer, cement, basic metals, and ship-building industries, government control was dominant), foreign (government is passive), and private.

open FDI regime following the liberalization in the late 1960s and early 1970s. Foreign ownership declined to 19 percent from 1985 to 1990 as a result of private investment being crowded out by government investments funded by oil revenues, especially in heavy industries. Note that the ownership concentration comes with a lag after the change in policy or approach. In the 1990–93 period, reforms taken in the mid-1980s to expand the role of private and foreign investors led to an increase of foreign ownership again to 22 percent. However, in this period the major change in ownership was from government to private. There were variations in foreign investors' shares; shares in chemicals, metal goods, and other industries were higher than in industries such as food, textiles, wood products, and paper products.

Aswicahyono (1998) went on to classify the twenty-eight industries in the Indonesian manufacturing sector according to the change in relative importance of each type of ownership. The relationship between TFP growth and ownership structure was assessed by comparing change in ownership structure, and its relation (not causality) to change in TFP. The results were not conclusive, and they were rather sector specific. For instance, TFP in the foreign ownership group was high in only two sectors: transport equipment and leather products. A positive association was found between TFP growth and the increasing importance of private firms during the 1984–93 period. The author's regression results (finding the determinants of TFP) also showed that the government and foreign ownership variables were insignificant. According to the theoretical literature, the sign of these variables is ambiguous. According to Aswicahyono (1998), the insignificant result may be due to the fact that ownership has no effect on TFP growth, or to the inaccuracy of the measurement of ownership.

Analysis Based on Case Studies

Studies over the years have examined differences in foreign and domestic firms' ability to weather the financial crisis and in their impact on technology and productivity. Since this chapter explores the role of foreign investment in Indonesia's recovery, we thought it would be illustrative to provide a summary of case studies on two industries in the manufacturing sector: electronics and automotive components. We compare these industries' pre- and postcrisis situations with respect to the role of foreign investment or linkages. The summary that follows is based on Feridhanusetyawan, Aswicahyono, and Anas (2000) and Feridhanusetyawan et al. (2001).[10]

10. Four major companies in the electronics sector and six companies in the automotive components subsector were interviewed by the CSIS research team.

ELECTRONICS INDUSTRY. Foreign firms tended to perform better than domestic firms prior to the crisis in the electronics sector. The consumer electronics industry is characterized by a dualistic structure: efficient foreign firms have an extensive trade network; inefficient domestic firms are mainly domestic oriented. CBS data from the industry survey reveal the following differences between foreign and domestic firms. During the 1990–96 period, wholly owned foreign firms and joint ventures in this industry exported an average of 46 percent of their output and experienced 78 percent capacity utilization; domestic firms exported on average 28 percent of their output and experienced 67 percent capacity utilization. Similarly, labor productivity (as measured by value added per worker) for foreign firms was more than three times higher than labor productivity for domestic firms. Another performance criterion, the average number of workers to represent economies of scale, was also much higher for foreign firms than domestic firms. Lastly, the import content of domestic firms was higher (84 percent) than that of foreign firms (79 percent).

The performance discrepancies between foreign and domestic firms in the electronic components subsector are less pronounced. In 1996, export/output ratios for foreign and domestic firms were 82 percent and 50 percent respectively. Capacity utilization, labor productivity, import content, and average number of workers for foreign and domestic firms did not differ much.

The crisis negatively affected the electronics industry because the sharp depreciation of the rupiah led to a sharp increase in the cost of imported inputs, which comprised 90 percent of the cost of production. Even domestic suppliers quoted the price of inputs in U.S. dollars. The collapse of the domestic market and a worsening of smuggling as security controls became lax led to a significant reduction in output. The crisis affected the consumer electronics subsector more than the electronic components subsector. While it is a fact that the latter sector had more foreign firms, the main explanatory factor for the differential impact appears to be that foreign firms tended to be more export oriented and were able to easily shift sales to export markets. In 1996, 34 percent of firms in the electronic components subsector exported 100 percent of their output; 10 percent of firms in the consumer electronics subsector exported all their products.

Interviews with companies in the electronic sector also showed the importance of being part of a network. The companies that were interviewed tended to engage in trade, production, and technology networks. Only one of the companies was part of an ownership network. Thus, it was found that companies with a trade network could switch their output from the domestic market to exports relatively easily. Most of these companies were foreign owned. The domestic-owned companies often did not have access to export markets. Companies with a flexible production network could switch from relatively expensive suppliers to cheaper suppliers of input; however, the impact on cost was slight since the rupiah depreciation meant that the cost of inputs went up considerably whichever the supplier.

The companies that were interviewed engaged in several types of technology networks: technical assistance, licensing agreement, and turnkey arrangements. Initially, the company received technical assistance, especially in the case of Japanese companies. Over time the technology network evolved; some companies went from one technology network to developing their own domestic technology capability. Others went from one partnership to another to survive global competition. Those companies that were locked into an imported technology found it difficult to adjust to the financial crisis.

The formation of joint venture agreements became an important part of the crisis response for some companies; they found they could benefit from the bigger networks, better access to cheap sources of raw materials and intermediate inputs, and better access to export markets. A domestic counterpart in the joint venture company can purchase a small quantity of intermediate inputs through its counterpart, who buys the inputs in large quantity so it can get them at a lower unit price. Similarly, a firm that has an extensive trade network can tap the benefit of economies of scale from the larger market.

AUTOMOTIVE COMPONENTS INDUSTRY. The automotive components industry is essentially an import substitution industry that emerged as part of the local content program of the 1980s. Thus, it is mainly owned domestically and sells to the domestic market; only 3 percent of output was accounted for by export-oriented firms (CBS industry survey data) in 1996. In the same year foreign firms produced 54 percent of output. Other characteristics of the industry are its high import content of 86 percent and its relatively low capacity utilization of 60 percent (1990–96 average). Exporting firms in this industry also showed higher value added than the industry average, indicating that exporting firms performed better than domestic-oriented firms. However, comparisons of foreign and domestic firms showed mixed results, with foreign firms having higher import content and lower capacity utilization.

The automotive components industry was one of the industries badly affected by the crisis, especially companies supplying the domestic market—supplying either original equipment (OE) for new cars or auto parts for the after sales market. Automotive sales plummeted drastically during the crisis. However, some companies did gain from the depreciation of the rupiah, especially those that had trade networks and were able to switch to the export markets. Companies producing universal components not linked to certain auto manufacturers particularly benefited from the rupiah depreciation. Companies producing specific components for certain auto manufacturers could not easily switch to the other automotive manufacturers or assemblers. Thus, having a foreign network or link was not sufficient in the case of automotive components. However, companies (universal component and specific component producers) that were part of the ownership network of the principal automobile manufacturers found assistance in terms of financial or market access. The crisis caused domestically owned companies or majority domestic shareholders to look to foreign investors to rescue their companies.

The role of the production network varied depending on its type. Companies participating in a rigid network had to stick with their current suppliers even though these suppliers turned out to be more expensive. On the other hand, companies with a flexible production network could adjust their input supply more easily. They could import from Korea or Thailand and other countries that offered prices lower than Japan or the United States. However, the unreliability of the domestic supply still meant that inputs had to be imported and the higher cost due to the rupiah depreciation still had to be borne.

SUMMARY. In sum, the main results of the case studies in these two industries—electronics and automotive components—are worth noting. The impact of the financial crisis depended on a variety of factors: the industry's dependence on imported or domestic components; its reliance on domestic or export markets; the support of international networks in finance; and marketing. It appears that companies with strong links to international networks fared better during the crisis, and this would involve foreign affiliates as well as domestic companies, which were being subcontracted by foreign companies.

Conclusions and Recommendations

In the early phase of Indonesia's industrialization process and the move from import substitution to export-oriented industrialization, the removal of restrictions and deregulation of current FDI and real sector regimes were sufficient. In fact, Indonesia did not use tax incentives as a tool to attract investment at the time, and it did away with tax incentives all together in 1984. Instead it provided more liberal policies for the type of FDI it wanted to attract—namely, export-oriented FDI. Subsequent attempts to use tax incentives also have not worked. Separate policies governed the role of FDI in the financial and oil and gas sectors. However, Indonesia's export orientation led to a dualistic structure of export-oriented industries with high import dependency and, at the time of the crisis, continued failure to develop domestic supporting industries and an indigenous technological capability. This weakness will continue to be a major problem for Indonesia in the years ahead.

In the current, postcrisis situation, a country like Indonesia can no longer attract the right type of foreign direct investment simply by improving its FDI regime or giving tax incentives. It must first of all address the basic conditions of concern to foreign investors: safety, security, and law and order. Although there have been slight improvements under the Megawati government, obvious concerns about terrorism and basic security remain. These issues are not likely to go away in the short term. Indeed, they were center stage during the election process in 2004. A wait-and-see attitude prevails; the new president, Susilo Bambang Yudhoyono, was elected on September 20, 2004. The new government must make a concerted effort to address the major issues contributing to the country's negative investment climate.

Investors, including domestic investors, know that it will take time to improve the fundamental problems Indonesia faces. Institutional, infrastructural, and human resources need to be increased. Given the competition for investments that exists, the new president and cabinet ("United Indonesia") can spur the much-needed new investments only if there is a credible beginning to woo back investors and address their concerns. Only then will the process of restructuring and building up Indonesia's industrial base and capability proceed successfully. Although this chapter is about foreign direct investment, the role of domestic investors in Indonesia needs to be taken into account. Interviews have revealed that foreign investors look to the return of domestic investors (who have funds abroad to bring back to Indonesia) as an important signal of a healthier investment climate.

Beyond the short-term considerations of just improving basic conditions for investors, what should be the government's long-term policy toward FDI? In a nutshell, Indonesia needs to have a clear and comprehensive policy. To begin, it needs consensus on the role of FDI in Indonesia's economic development (Soesastro and Thee 2000). Otherwise, vacillations between efficiency considerations and nationalism will prevail. From an economic perspective, the traditional role of FDI (with regard to capital inflows, technology and management know-how, the development of spillovers in terms of supplier industries and human resource development, and improved market access) remains important. In addition, given technological developments and large multinational companies' tendency to outsource goods and services, developing countries are exploring how they can fit into the production network that is evolving within big firms and within regions. Increased specialization and discovery of a market niche is the name of the game today. The focus is no longer on large-scale production to lower costs (although still relevant for some industries) or on manufacturing everything from capital and intermediate goods to final goods. Countries or companies do not have to graduate in a stepwise fashion along the value chain anymore. They can leap frog or choose different parts of the value chain to specialize in. The emergence of China as a regional production and export center is extremely important. China has huge import demand to satisfy domestic demand as well as export production. The question is how countries and companies can be part of the regional production network of multinational companies or, independent of this, supply and be a part of China's huge production and export needs.

As others have recommended (Thee and Pangestu 1998), we concur that Indonesia and other developing countries need to adopt a comprehensive FDI policy. In the first place, an open FDI regime and open implementation (the latter is still a weakness in the current context) are needed. There must truly be a streamlining of licensing and administrative procedures, including by provincial governments. This requires clear and simple procedures with minimal approval processes and a clear mechanism for recourse. The Board of Investment needs to be restructured and tasked with true investment promotion. Instead of being another bureaucracy involved in the licensing process, it should be a Board that is committed to addressing investors' concerns. The process of ratifying the investment law needs to be accelerated to increase and enhance predictability. Of course, implementation will be watched carefully, and the resulting track record evaluated.

Investors will choose to locate where there is strong supplier industries and services, where there is supporting infrastructure (both physical and human), and where there is a market. Indonesia must look beyond manufacturing. It must look at the need for efficient supporting services whether in the backbone services, such as telecommunications and transport, or in other specialized services pertaining to the industry. Developing countries like Indonesia also need to consider whether they can participate as exporters of low-cost labor services such as data processing.

How can these goals be accomplished? Physical infrastructure can be developed through a combination of fiscal spending by the government and foreign investment by the private sector. Greater openness is needed, specifically clear domestic regulatory policies including the regulation of competition and the regulation of pricing; in some cases certain industries do tend to be natural monopolies. Strategic development of human resources can be accomplished with training and education programs on a continuous and regular basis since they will take a long time to produce fruit.

This question often arises: should industrial policy target the development of certain industries, including supporting industries? Past experience would suggest that this is not easy to do and that a general policy that will improve the policy environment without biasing a particular sector is preferable. Targeted interventions are difficult to implement in the world of imperfect information and imperfect governments. The creation of a cluster of supporting industries and services is difficult to create without the development of a dynamic final goods and services industry. For these reasons, the focus should be on providing a conducive policy environment, creating a sound financial sector as a source of financing, and ensuring an adequate physical and human resources infrastructure. Targeted interventions in R&D, training, education, specialized skills, and technology development should complement such policies but not be a substitute for them.

Finally, one must look beyond the economic objectives and address the noneconomic concerns that often arise—the forces of nationalism in particular. FDI also must be related to social objectives, such as employment creation. These noneconomic objectives of FDI must be recognized, and the most specific policy to address the concern should be pursued. For instance, in the case of privatization of so-called strategic industries, if the concern is dominance of ownership in the sector, then privatization can be designed so that there is divestment by the foreign acquirer to the capital market by a certain time period. The role of local governments and their shares of FDI also need to be addressed since current experience shows that this issue can be a real deterrent for investors. FDI is often also expected to contribute to social objectives. For example, it is expected to promote small and medium-size enterprises, cooperatives, and the creation of jobs. Satisfying these expectations cannot be forced upon foreign direct investors. Rather, incentive programs are needed or programs where contributions from FDI (possibly through the fiscal system) are pooled and administered in an efficient and transparent manner to achieve the objective (say training). As for the transfer of technology and indigenous technological capability development, past studies have shown that this responsibility also cannot be imposed on the foreign investor. Progress can occur only if the industries in question are required to be competitive in the global and/or domestic market so that ensuring technological capability becomes a necessity to compete. Progress also depends on the absorptive capacity of the domestic industries and players, whether the partner in the joint venture or the supplier industries. As noted throughout the chapter, a set of policies related to infrastructure, education, and human resources is essential. Governments can intervene, but targeted interventions, such as science parks or R&D assistance, must be seen as a complement to the other basic policies that need to be in place.

References

Aswicahyono, H. H. 1998. *Total Factor Productivity in Indonesian Manufacturing, 1975–1993.* PhD thesis, Australian National University, Canberra. Unpublished.

Feridhanusetyawan, Tubagus, et al. 2001. "Banking Industry during the Crisis: The Survival of Foreign Banks." Chiba, Japan: Institute of Developing Economies, Japan External Trade Organization.

Feridhanusetyawan, Tubagus, Haryo Aswicahyono, and Titik Anas. 2000. "Economic Crisis and Manufacturing Industry: The Role of Industrial Networks." Chiba, Japan: Institute of Developing Economies, Japan External Trade Organization.

Hill, Hal. 1988. *Foreign Investment and Industrialization in Indonesia.* New York: Oxford University Press.

IMF (International Monetary Fund). various years. Balance of Payments. Washington, D.C.

James, William, David Ray, and Peter Minor. 2002. *Indonesian Textile and Apparel Industry: Meeting the Challenges of the Changing International Trade Environment.* Technical report of the U.S. Agency for International Development and ECG. Jakarta, Indonesia.

Lall, S. 1988. "Technology Policies in Indonesia." In H. Hill and Thee Kian Wie, eds., *Indonesia's Technological Challenge.* Singapore: Institute of Southeast Asian Studies.

Lipsey, Robert, and Fredrik Sjoholm. 2001. "FDI and Wages in Indonesian Manufacturing." Working paper. Kitakyushu, Japan: The International Centre for the Study of East Asian Development (ICSEAD).

Pangestu, Mari. 2000a. "Foreign Investment Policy in Indonesia: Evolution and Characteristics." In Faroukh Iqbal and William James, eds., *Indonesia's Experience with Trade and Investment Policy: Distortions, Deregulation and Future Reforms.* Westport, CT.: Praeger, 2001.

———. 2000b. "The Potential Role of Foreign Direct Investment in Indonesia's Recovery." Paper presented at PAFTAD 26, *Globalization in the New Millennium,* Seoul, the Republic of Korea, June 14–16.

———. 2001. "New FDI Patterns and Economic Development." Paper presented at the APEC Investment Symposium, Cheju, Republic of Korea, March 20–21.

Soesastro, Hadi, and Thee Kian Wie. 2000. "Comprehensive Investment Policies in a Competitive Environment." Paper presented at the Faculty of Economics, University of Indonesia, 50th Anniversary Conference, Jakarta, Indonesia, October 4.

Takii, Sadayuki. 2001. "Productivity Spillovers and Characteristics of Foreign Multinational Plants in Indonesian Manufacturing 1990–1995." Working paper 2001-14. Kitakyushu, Japan: The International Centre for the Study of East Asian Development (ICSEAD).

Takii, Sadayuki, and Eric Ramstetter. 2000. "Foreign Multinationals in Indonesian Manufacturing, 1985–1998: Shares, Relative Size and Relative Labor Productivity." Working paper 2000-18 September. Kitakyushu, Japan: The International Centre for the Study of East Asian Development (ICSEAD).

———. 2003. "Employment, Production, Labour Productivity and Foreign Multinationals in Indonesian Manufacturing, 1975-2000." Working paper 2003-25 September. Kitakyushu, Japan: The International Centre for the Study of East Asian Development (ICSEAD).

Thee, Kian Wie, and Mari Pangestu. 1998. "Technological Dynamism and Export Performance in the Electronics and Textiles Sector in Indonesia." In Dieter Ernst, Tom Ganiatsos, and Lynn Mytelka, eds., *Technological Capability and Export Success in East Asia*. London and New York: Routledge.

UNCTAD (United Nations Conference on Trade and Development). 2003. *World Investment Report 2003*. Geneva and New York: United Nations.

9

FDI Inflows and Economic Development: The Postcrisis Experience of Malaysia

Sieh Lee Mei Ling

The development of Malaysia as an emerging economy, after attaining independence in 1957, has been heavily dependent on trade and foreign direct investment (FDI). Guided by continuous policy adjustments and strategy refinements over time according to changing needs and the economic environment, FDI channeled primarily through multinational corporations (MNCs) has contributed significantly to economic growth and the achievement of Malaysia's social goals by most standards of development. From an exporter of primary commodities and importer of consumer goods, Malaysia has become a manufacturer and exporter of final and intermediate industrial products with the help of foreign capital inflows. MNCs developed production capacity, introduced technology, opened markets, and created jobs. During the past decade, the services sector has also expanded with FDI support. In addition to MNCs from industrial economies, MNCs from newly industrializing economies (NIEs) in Asia have come onto the scene. The ASEAN (Association of Southeast Asian Nations) Free Trade Agreement may expand to include other East Asian economies; Malaysia then would see more traders and investors in the enlarged regional market. There have been some in the country who have pointed to the negatives of MNCs, such as limited technology transfer, while others fear being overdependent on foreign firms.

Since the Asian financial and economic crisis of 1997–98, the character and behavior of FDI in Southeast Asia generally and in Malaysia specifically have changed, some believe. The pattern of trade is also believed to have altered because of increasingly close links between trade and FDI attributable to structural changes in industrial production processes—changes caused in part by technological innovations and the forces of regionalism and globalization (Dobson and Chia 1997; Sieh 2000b). Measures taken by the Malaysian government to cope with the difficulties during the crisis have included actions that were different from the IMF-linked approach adopted by neighboring countries. Therefore, it is useful to examine the impact of some of the policy changes on FDI inflows into Malaysia after the crisis. This will enable a better understanding of the future role of MNCs in economic development against the backdrop of other changes that are taking place due to regional and global economic arrangements among governments.

This chapter examines the role of FDI inflows on the development of the Malaysian economy. Following are its specific objectives:

- to analyze FDI trends in terms of sectors or industry targeted by FDI and source countries, by paying close attention to the factors that attracted FDI inflows into Malaysia before and after the crisis,
- to analyze the recent economic effects of FDI on, for example, employment generation, sales, trade expansion, network creation, and technology-related issues,
- to study recent government policy changes pertaining to FDI and their impact on inflows, using examples especially from the electrical and electronics industries, and
- to draw conclusions and implications for appropriate policies and strategies regarding FDI and its role in the future development of the Malaysian economy.

This chapter relies on secondary data from government sources and is supplemented by information gained through in-depth discussions with officials who implement FDI policies. Meetings have been held with MNCs currently in Malaysia. Electronic firms have been selected as a focus in order to flesh out in greater detail issues pertaining to FDI within a specific industry.

FDI Trends in Malaysia before the Asian Crisis

Malaysia's FDI inflows since 1997 have differed somewhat from those in earlier periods. Three distinct periods were discernible before the crisis. The first began immediately after political independence in 1957. The import substitution period from 1957 to 1968 saw FDI channeled into consumer goods production; investors were attracted by the young growing market and by the advantages of overcoming high tariff rates then. During the 1960s, foreign direct investments were particularly focused on the electrical and electronics (E&E) sector, manufacturing relatively low-tech labor-intensive consumer products for the local market. FDI enabled Malaysia to save on foreign exchange, to generate domestic income, to create employment, to learn from foreign enterprises, and to achieve economic growth.

The second period started with the Investment Incentives Act of 1968. From 1968 to 1982, MNCs were encouraged to produce in Malaysia for export markets and to benefit from the country's low production costs. Numerous fiscal and nonfiscal concessions drew industries new to the country; they created jobs and dispersed industries within the domestic economy. Attempts were made to provide an attractive environment for FDI through infrastructure development and minimal bureaucratic difficulties. MNCs then regarded the political stability of Malaysia as the single most important factor for choosing the country as a low-cost production site (Sieh and Tho 1987). The 1970s saw E&E industries shifting toward export markets in the region. MNCs, especially from the United States and the United Kingdom, decided to relocate their production facilities from their home countries, in order to escape the inflationary pressures there, and to reap cost advantages as competition in export markets increased.

The third period, 1982 to mid-1997, was an integrative phase. Trade induced by FDI activities within and among several FDI recipient locations supported the same value chains. Before the eruption of the crisis, affiliates of E&E multinational corporations in Malaysia were part and parcel of powerful production and market networks within the east Asian region (Dobson and Chia 1997). During the decade before the Asian crisis, FDI stocks for all industries in Malaysia expanded rapidly. From 1988 to 1996, foreign equity stock increased from US$1.59 billion to US$9.21 billion. FDI inflow of US$0.11 billion equity in 1988 for all industries increased to US$1.38 billion in 1992 before declining to US$1.15 billion in 1995 (Table 9.1). The slight decline in 1993 was partly due to the fact that many MNCs had already rushed in before the 1990 deadline of equity relaxation, as will be explained. The mid-decade dip coincided with the generally weak global economic condition, particularly in the major advanced economies then. As discussions with businesses confirm, during this time of uncertainty regarding AFTA and WTO, foreign and local investors had a wait-and-see attitude.

The annual inward equity flow of FDI for manufacturing, which accounted for over 60 percent of that for all industries, increased from US$0.07 billion in 1988 to US$0.82 billion in 1995. The big leap that took place between 1989 and 1990 (Table 9.1) reflected the lifting of equity

Table 9.1. *Inward FDI Flows and Stocks from Foreign MNCs to Malaysia, 1988–98*
(US$billions)

Year	All industries		Manufacturing		Wholesale/retail	
	FDI equity flows	FDI equity stocks	FDI equity flows	FDI equity stocks	FDI equity flows	FDI equity stocks
1988	0.11	1.59	0.07	1.00	0.00	0.14
1989	0.76	2.35	0.38	1.38	0.06	0.21
1990	0.77	3.12	0.63	2.01	0.04	0.25
1991	0.84	3.96	0.70	2.71	0.06	0.31
1992	1.38	5.34	1.35	4.05	0.07	0.38
1993	0.80	6.14	0.64	4.70	0.01	0.39
1994	1.92	8.06	1.04	5.73	0.07	0.46
1995	1.15	9.21	0.82	6.55	0.02	0.47
1996	n.a.	n.a.	0.74	7.71	n.a.	n.a.
1997	n.a.	n.a.	–2.40	5.31	n.a.	n.a.
1998	n.a.	n.a.	0.84	6.15	n.a.	n.a.

n.a. Not available.
Source: For all industries, Malaysian Department of Statistics (various years); for manufacturing, MIDA (various years) and IMF (2003); for wholesale/retail, Malaysian Department of Statistics (various years).

conditions for foreign investors during the period. In 1995 the stock of foreign equity in manufacturing was valued at US$6.55 billion for plants that together employed 526.68 thousand workers and produced US$45.13 billion worth of gross output. The FDI equity stock for manufacturing was 70 percent of the foreign equity stock for all industries valued at US$9.21 billion in 1995.

FDI equity inflows into the tertiary sector can be estimated from the difference between equity data for all industries and for manufacturing firms, as the primary sector was reducing in relative share. In 1988 only US$0.04 billion was recorded for foreign services activities giving an FDI equity stock of US$0.59 billion, which is close to 60 percent of that for manufacturing. The figures rose to US$0.33 billion inflow for 1995, while FDI stock in services increased to US$2.66 billion. The stock of FDI equity in the services sector in 1995 just prior to the outbreak of the Asian crisis reached 29 percent of FDI sources for all industries and approximately 40 percent of the corresponding figure for manufacturing.

Table 9.1 also shows the steady rise in foreign investment interest in distributive services since the late 1980s. Given the fact that the distributive trades make up the largest services subsector, the role of FDI in wholesale and retail would have significant effects on the Malaysian economy. The stock of MNC equity in wholesale and retail trade grew to US$0.47 billion by 1995, and sales revenue approached US$10 billion. Although foreign involvement in such activities is not new to Malaysia, operators that have entered since the late 1980s differed significantly from earlier operators in terms of scale, format, and management strategies. Global economic forces backed by technological innovations are key contributory factors for the new genre of investors in the country's distributive trades (Sieh 2000a, 2003; Tay and Sieh 2000).

What drove foreign direct investors to Malaysia? Rapidly rising costs in home economies since the mid-1980s pushed MNCs, while the fast growth of Southeast Asian host economies pulled them. Malaysia experienced a gradually liberalizing trade environment, before the 1990s for manufacturing, and for services, such as distributive services, during the 1990s. In particular, MNCs took advantage of Malaysia's temporary suspension of equity conditions for FDI in the late 1980s—a key measure to check a shrinking economy in 1985. The New Economic Policy introduced in 1971, which limited foreign equity ownership to 30 percent, had a dampening effect on MNCs that sought 100 percent ownership of their foreign subsidiaries. The recession in the mid-1980s prompted the temporary lifting of the equity ceiling for FDI entry before 1991, hence the upsurge of arrivals. The timing also coincided with the business strategy of MNCs that were spreading different portions of their production processes among various locations, while linking their value chain through trade of intermediate goods and services; in other words, the trading of outputs across borders occurred within the same multinational corporate group (Dobson and Chia 1997; Sieh 2002a).

FDI inflows helped to restore the Malaysian economy. GDP growth averaged 8 percent per annum for nearly a decade after 1988. FDI pull factors then would have included political stability, a modern infrastructure and legal system, an educated and trainable workforce conversant in English, a host of fiscal and other incentives for MNCs, and the promising outlook of a young and growing regional ASEAN market with a free trade area arrangement in the making.

Within the manufacturing sector—the sector that had been considered the main "engine of economic growth" by the economic planners, particularly from the late 1970s to the early 1990s—fixed assets in foreign firms expanded from US$10.4 billion in 1988 to nearly US$40 billion in 1995. They were supported by foreign equity stock, which rose from nearly one billion dollars to six and a half billion dollars. Sales from FDI in manufacturing grew from US$9.5 billion to nearly US$50 billion during the period (Table 9.2).

The contribution of FDI to the Malaysian economy is also illustrated by its share of gross output and employment within the manufacturing sector. FDI accounted for 35.8 percent of the economy's gross manufacturing output in 1988 and 49.6 percent in 1992. In fact, just after the crisis, FDI's share exceeded half of all manufacturing gross output, accounting for nearly 54 percent in 1999. Furthermore, MNCs have been a significant provider of jobs in Malaysia. In 1988 they employed 36.4 percent of the workforce in manufacturing firms. The share increased to 45.5 percent—nearly half the total employment in the fastest growing sector. However, the share of employment dipped compared to the share of gross output. This was because of the gradual shift to more capital- and technology-intensive investment from labor-intensive type of work, partly in response to policy incentives to move up the technology ladder and partly because of the reality of labor conditions in the host economy.

The more capital-intensive investments in manufacturing suited the increasingly short supply of labor in Malaysia. They also resulted in higher productivity within the manufacturing sector as a whole. Total Factor Productivity rose from 0.3 percent in 1997–98 to 8.7 percent 1999–2000, according to the National Productivity Corporation. Output per thousand plant workers in MNCs almost doubled (from US$0.047 billion in 1988 to US$0.086 billion in 1995). During the Asian crisis of the late nineties, however, productivity rose only marginally. It stagnated around US$0.089 billion (Table 9.2).

FDI Trends in Malaysia after the Asian Crisis

FDI inflows accounted for about 4 to 5 percent of GDP in the "normal" (non-crisis) years of the 1990s (Figure 9.1). It is therefore important to understand the disruptions during and after the Asian crisis.

In dollar value, FDI inflows for all industries were depressed from 1998 to 2000. The drop in FDI was most obvious around the crisis period of 1996 to 1998. In 1997 a negative flow of US$2.4 billion foreign equity was recorded. For 1998 only US$0.84 billion worth of foreign equity was received into the manufacturing sector as divestment reverted to a positive level; only US$2.16 billion inflow of assets was recorded for the year. At its peak in 1996, the stock of foreign equity in manufacturing stood at US$7.71

Table 9.2. *FDI and the Malaysian Manufacturing Sector: Assets, Equity, Sales, Output, and Employment, 1988–99*
(US$millions)

				Plant gross output			*Plant employment*		
Year	*Value of fixed assets by firms with FDI*	*Foreign equity stock*	*Sales of firms with FDI*	*Total (local firms & firms with FDI)*	*Firms with FDI*	*FDI as a percent of total output*	*Total no. of workers (local firms and firms with FDI)*	*Firms with FDI*	*Percent of the work force employed by firms with FDI*
1988	10,393	999	9,460	28,339	10,136	35.8	595,646	216,922	36.4
1989	10,266	1,378	12,180	29,829	13,045	43.7	695,048	273,475	39.3
1990	13,112	2,006	15,610	35,426	16,141	45.6	841,768	358,649	42.6
1991	16,706	2,706	19,840	43,743	21,050	48.1	974,047	439,868	45.2
1992	22,142	4,053	25,060	52,662	26,101	49.6	1,031,286	469,284	45.5
1993	26,978	4,695	29,590	64,090	28,997	45.2	1,147,542	492,366	42.9
1994	30,780	5,732	39,480	75,034	36,657	48.9	1,222,075	529,168	43.3
1995	39,430	6,549	49,380	98,596	45,130	45.8	1,369,151	526,681	38.5
1996	n.a.	n.a.	n.a.	108,684	50,462	46.4	1,432,215	555,495	38.8
1997	45,448	n.a.	n.a.	105,620	50,070	47.4	1,398,170	558,441	39.9
1998	n.a.	n.a.	n.a.	n.a.	n.a.	n.a.	n.a.	n.a.	n.a.
1999	37,665	n.a.	n.a.	94,604	50,757	53.7	1,347,156	570,284	42.3

n.a. Not available.
Source: MIDA (various years); Malaysian Department of Statistics.

Figure 9.1. *FDI Inflows to Malaysia as a Percent of GDP, Selected Years, 1990–2001*

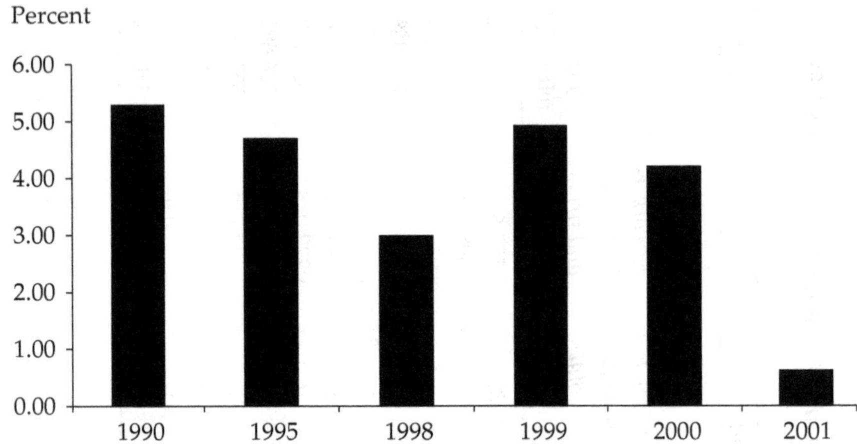

Source: For GDP figures at current market prices, Asia Development Bank; for FDI inflow data, International Monetary Fund.

billion. Two years later the equity stock of FDI in manufacturing industries had diminished to US$6.15, probably reflecting the mood of investors when living through and assessing the uncertain outcomes of the Asian crisis.

Just before the Asian crisis, FDI in the electrical and electronics industries, long the favorite for MNCs in Malaysia, started to drop. From US$0.72 billion in 1997, FDI in those industries further declined in 1998 to half a billion dollars. However, from 1999 to 2001, foreign investment for E&E improved markedly, rising to a high of US$2.69 billion approvals in 2000. Some MNCs were trying to seek advantages that matched their longer-term strategies when asset costs were relatively low in recessionary conditions. The behavior of electronic firms in Malaysia was more a function of business cycles within the global industry than fluctuating conditions of the host economy.

Malaysia's E&E sector has been and continues to be dominated by MNCs even after the crisis. In 1992 E&E contributed to one third (US$15.6 billion) of the output of the manufacturing sector and 31 percent (US$3.1 billion) of the value added generated by manufacturing. E&E employed 30 percent (282,000 persons) of the total labor force, and it paid 30 percent (US$1.3 billion) of the labor cost within the sector, while accounting for 23 percent (US$2.3 billion) of the fixed assets invested within manufacturing. Exports from the industry amounted to 65 percent (US$29.9 billion) of

Malaysia's manufactured exports in 1994—the largest foreign exchange earner for the economy. However, Malaysia's place as the world's largest exporter of semiconductors was gradually eroded by lower labor cost production sites in emerging economies in Asia and elsewhere (Sieh 1998).

Nevertheless, after the crisis, other FDI inflows into E&E could have resulted from the liberalization of government policies because changes in equity and market conditions were partly aimed at overcoming the gloomy investment environment. MNCs were exempted from the series of currency control measures taken by the government for alleviating the negative effects of the crisis (as will be discussed later). Clearly, the government had in view Malaysia's regional and multilateral trade commitments (its longer-term economic plans) and not just the short-term actions needed to solve the woes at hand. Unlike other Asian economies, Malaysia took exception to adopting the prescriptions of the International Monetary Fund for managing the economy during the crisis. Some of the key measures taken in response to the crisis (Box 9.1) include measures for rebuilding confidence in the economy that helped to boost FDI inflows. However, confidence in better economic performance was not restored until the year 2000.

MNCs in E&E activities in Malaysia quickly recovered in 1999–2000, but they slowed down again after 2001. This seems to suggest that electronic MNCs were affected by the crisis only in their short-term tactical decisions. Their long-term strategic decisions were not significantly altered. The fact that MNCs resumed their plans and continued with their networked production and marketing efforts among affiliates in the region and with their parent firms, especially in the case of U.S. firms, showed that other considerations were more pertinent. These considerations were as follows: first, global competitiveness; second, regional, subregional, or global intergovernmental economic arrangements (for example, free trade area agreements including AFTA, contractual commitments of WTO, even APEC influences); and third, worldwide business cycle effects that influenced inventory levels for the industry in the medium term. Such factors were probably more forceful than the crisis in driving the direction of FDI and in ascertaining detailed strategic decisions of MNCs and their affiliates along value chains. The interplay of short-term and long-term decision making by MNCs together with the policy measures taken gave rise to the net result, a shaky balance. The economic situation after the crisis was not altogether strong and yet not weak. Looking back, we can see that the decisions individually and collectively did help to support the recovery from the crisis.

However, within the first three years of the new century, FDI started tapering downwards again for all industries. Malaysia really began to feel

Box 9.1. *Measures for the Crisis in Malaysia*

The currency-financial-economic crisis that erupted in 1997 changed the entire economic scene. Industries that utilized imported inputs for producing outputs that were sold in the domestic market suffered the most (for example, consumer goods, automobiles). Industries that depended on local inputs but for outputs sold to foreign markets were spared (for example, palm oil, rubber, and wood-based products). Firms that were moderately affected were those that sold most of their output internationally even when their inputs were imported (for example, electronic components, industrial and consumer electronic goods).

The Malaysian ringgit depreciated sharply by 40 percent by August 1998 (compared with 54 percent for the Thai baht, 48 percent for the Korean won, and 83 percent for the Indonesian rupiah). The deflationary impact resulted in Malaysia's negative 7.5 percent GDP growth in 1998.

Contingency measures adopted by Malaysia differed from those in other Asian countries. The most important measures were as follows:

- currency control and pegging of the ringgit at 3.8 to one U.S. dollar (targeted at fund flows for portfolio investment and not for FDI or genuine trading activities or for living expenses)
- agency restructuring of corporate debts and recapitalization of the banking system
- close and constant monitoring by the National Economic Action Council
- corporate surveillance through improvements in corporate governance
- social safeguards for unemployment
- other steps to lift domestic demand.

the effects of competition for FDI from lower cost production sites in Asia, especially in China, which had gathered greater momentum in drawing in manufacturers. In an address in late 2002 to major electronics firms that operate in the country, the Malaysian minister of human resources noted that three dozen shoe manufacturers of international brand names had been uprooted from the outskirts of Kuala Lumpur and relocated in China within a period of three years and not a single facility remained. Competition also came from economies in south Asia (India), east Asia (the Republic of Korea), and Southeast Asia (other ASEAN members), economies that had rebounded from the Asian crisis. Worldwide FDI was also drawn to other economies that had become members of various regional economic arrangements located elsewhere (for example, eastern Europe, Latin America). The slower rate of investment was also known among domestic businesses in Malaysia. Commercial banks faced difficulties in establishing new loans for business projects, and the central bank had to set loan targets for the banking sector to achieve. Control of the outward flow of funds by Malaysians for foreign investment and other purposes was part of the package of measures to restore financial and economic stability after the crisis. As a result, liquidity began to build within the system since business confidence was not robust enough for investment.

It appeared that the precrisis economic expansion would unlikely be repeated in the near future. In 1999 GDP grew by 4.3 percent. Growth continued into 2002, but the trend was buckled by external developments in 2003, particularly the Iraq war and the SARS epidemic. In the first quarter of 2004, the government reported a 4.5 percent GDP expansion for 2003 and expected a 5 to 5.5 percent GDP growth for 2004. It was generally accepted that FDI had a role to play in helping the Malaysian economy out of the recession years, especially by exporting. Indeed, exports were aggressively sought. Even the second national car manufacturer, Perodua, sought and opened new export markets when domestic purchases were adversely affected. By the third quarter of 2004, it appeared likely that GDP for the year would reach 7 percent before declining to 6 percent for 2005 due to high oil prices. The relative strength of the economy since the Asian crisis was evident from the fact that expansionary measures were not included in the national budget proposed for 2005.

FDI as a Share of Total Investments

Around the mid-1990s, analysts thought that Malaysia's heavy dependence on FDI might become a phenomenon of the past. Between 1993 and 1998, domestic investments into approved manufacturing projects accounted for more than half of the annual total and had overtaken the contribution of FDI. However, after the crisis, the reverse occurred. In 1999 FDI accounted for 72.4 percent of the total investment in manufacturing industries approved (approved FDI is used to gauge recent FDI positions), and the dominance of FDI increased to nearly three quarters in 2001 (Table 9.3). Box 9.2 compares past approved FDI against different data sources of actual inflows. In spite of time lags, approved and actual FDI flows somewhat correlated. Had the Malaysian economy regained its attractiveness as an investment destination for FDI? Or had Malaysia managed to compete more effectively than neighboring or newer economies? An analysis of other economies shows that neither was the case.

FDI host economies (such as China, Brazil, Mexico, Argentina, Ireland, Singapore) were able to land more FDI in absolute value. Even ASEAN neighbors such as Indonesia and the Philippines attracted US$0.605 billion and about US$0.5 billion worth of FDI respectively in 2001 compared to Malaysia's US$0.5 billion, according to the Malaysian Industrial Development Authority (MIDA) data. In 1997, one fifth of FDI inflows were destined for expansion of existing projects or diversification rather than for new projects. This proportion rose to around half between 2000 and 2003. Clearly, convincing new entry of projects or new investors would be an uphill task.

A better explanation appears to be that Malaysia's domestic investment was weakening. From 1997 to October 2002, FDI in approved manufacturing projects valued at US$2.375 billion amounted to 64.5 percent of the total investment of US$3.68 billion; domestic investors accounted for only 35.5 percent. Domestic investment had dropped from its peak share of 56.2 percent of total investments in 1995.

The truth was that many large, state-nurtured and state-supported entrepreneurs had failed. Many of the Bumiputera high flyers who had projected a successful corporate image before the crisis were badly hurt by heavy indebtedness, and they were waiting for bail outs. Instead of being

Table 9.3. *Approved Manufacturing Projects and FDI Share of Investments, 1990–2002*

Year	*Approved foreign investment in manufacturing (US$billions)*	*FDI share of total investment in manufacturing (%)*
1990	0.652	62.6
1991	0.580	55.3
1992	0.698	64.0
1993	0.244	45.7
1994	0.432	49.4
1995	0.365	43.8
1996	0.678	49.8
1997	0.407	44.4
1998	0.332	49.6
1999	0.323	72.4
2000	0.522	58.9
2001	0.497	74.0
2002	0.294 (to Oct)	67.7

Note: See Box 9.2 on the relation between approved FDI and actual FDI.
Source: MIDA (various years).

Box 9.2. *Approved FDI and Actual FDI in Manufacturing, 1988–95*

Figure 9.2 compares approved FDI and actual investments. Despite the time lags between time of approval and time of implementation, the overall changes in direction correlate in a crude manner and do reflect the statistics for most of the period shown, especially after 1990.

Figure 9.2. *Foreign Investments in Malaysia, 1988–2001*

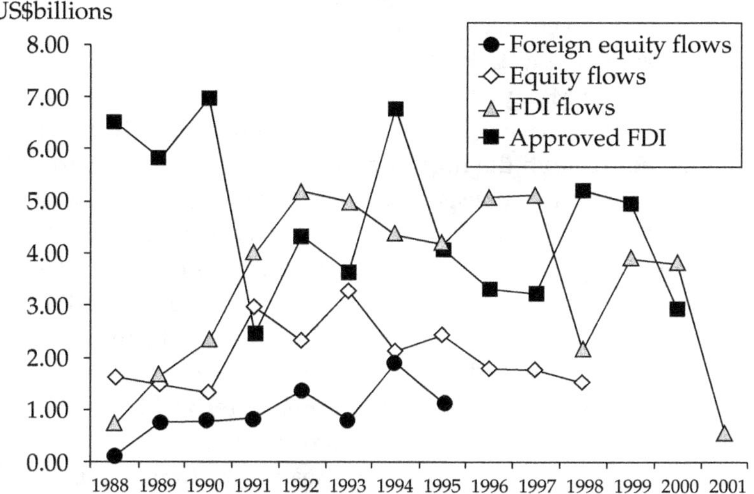

Source: For approved FDI, MIDA (various years); for FDI flows, IMF (2003); for equity flows, Bank Negara Malaysia; and for foreign equity flows, Malaysian Department of Statistics (various years).

the favorites for contracts, they were bombarded with calls for greater accountability, transparency, and exercise of corporate governance, particularly when their over-geared conditions were exposed. Chinese businesses that were subcontractors for Bumiputera firms also reduced investments because their secondary roles were adversely affected. To encourage loan creation by banks, the central bank relaxed its rules for MNC borrowing from local banks, permitting them up to 60 percent instead of 40 percent (with the balance from overseas). MNCs continued investing to keep going despite the difficult environment; most of the affected Malaysian firms, however, either restructured, merged, or were acquired.

FDI in Targeted Industries

Foreign participation in industries has changed over time, from primary sector activities before independence, to import substitution manufacturing of consumer goods, to labor-intensive goods, including electrical goods and low-end electronics for export markets. The late 1980s and early 1990s saw the gradual shift of FDI into higher technology industries that promised higher value added, particularly within the electrical and electronics subsector. By the time of the Asian crisis, the electrical and electronics industry had already been a choice focus for MNCs in Malaysia, receiving nearly half of all FDI in 1996 (Sieh and Loke 1998; Sieh 1998).

The E&E sector in Malaysia constitutes an important node in the global production-marketing network of MNCs in the industry. Backward linkages are achieved through the import of inputs by FDI projects from home countries as well as from overseas production facilities, either from affiliates or from unrelated producers. Forward linkages are achieved when E&E products from Malaysia are exported back to their home countries or to affiliates elsewhere. Trade with home countries that are industrial countries, such as the United States and Japan, is primarily in the form of electronics and electrical components and parts. Trade with the newly industrializing economies of Asia, especially Singapore, is characterized by trade of parts and components in two directions: through forward linkages, E&E parts and subassemblies are supplied to Singaporean firms for assembly and distribution; through backward linkages, Singaporean firms supply parts and components to production facilities located in Malaysia.

The E&E industry has always been the single most important employer in the Malaysian manufacturing sector. The socio-economic role and ensuing effects of FDI in the industry, a key job creator, have been immense. From a total employment of 81,900 workers in 1985, the E&E firms employed five times more workers fifteen years later. In 2000, employment in electronic firms stood at 401,700 workers. The Asian crisis appeared to have caused only a slight dent in the employment trend. Employment in the industry rose again as FDI inflows increased in 1999 and 2000. Subsequently, the reversal of the employment trend started as electronics facilities relocated outside the country, or reduced employment because of new activities that were more capital-intensive than labor-intensive.

Because the E&E subsector is in the forefront of rapid technological developments, Malaysia greatly benefited from the foreign direct investment that had been channeled into the economy through MNCs in the industry. Apart from contributing to employment in terms of quantity, the industry has also contributed toward skill and technological development of those engaged by the firms. Human development through elevating the quality of workers and improving managerial or supervisory personnel is of great importance for the Malaysian economy. Further, the E&E subsector accounted for nearly a third of the 1,162 technical agreements signed by the various industries in Malaysia between 1989 and 1997 (Sieh and Shen 1998). But more business linkages between Malaysian firms from the host economy and E&E multinational corporations should be developed. Then indigenous firms could participate actively in a bigger way in the production and market networks of MNCs within as well as beyond Malaysia.

Between 1997 and 2002, E&E continued as the leading FDI recipient industry, although it accounted for a smaller share of all FDI arrivals (42 percent). Long-established MNCs in the industry were contacted during this study. They reported that many of the relatively labor-intensive electronic products, such as electronic consumer goods, and components, such as assembly and testing of semiconductors, were diverted to Mainland China. The diversion was not unexpected; liberalization that would be brought about by China's World Trade Organization membership in 2001 was anticipated. China's emerging role and its effects on ASEAN economies, especially with the China ASEAN Free Trade Agreement, could not be disregarded (Sieh 2002b).

The petroleum and gas industry was the top FDI recipient in 1992 (representing 66 percent of FDI inflow). This industry fell into second place in 1997. The industry has maintained its leading position since the crisis. Investment by MNCs in chemical and chemical products, which rose in importance during the 1990s, has also remained important since the crisis. Table 9.4 reveals an interesting development during the period from 1997 to 2002. Food manufacturing attracted 2.8 percent of FDI within the manufacturing sector, nearly double the percentage for 1990 to 1997. A likely explanation is the deliberate curtailing of imported final goods and services to save foreign exchange immediately after the crisis. In addition, the entry of large-scale multinational food distributors and retailers, begun in the 1980s, continued after the crisis. Such retail services primarily distributed locally produced or processed goods. Many of the large retailers would have involved FDI, as alluded to above.

Other manufacturing industries with FDI interest have diminished post-crisis. They include textiles and textile products, and transport equipment. In these industries many of the firms had restructured their regional or global production networks to take advantage of new opportunities related

Table 9.4. *FDI in Approved Manufacturing Projects, by Industry, 1997–2002*

Industry	*Approved FDI (US$billions)*	*Percent of approved FDI*
Electrical and electronics	9.0	41.9
Petroleum and gas	3.0	14.0
Chemicals	1.8	8.4
Paper	1.4	6.4
Nonmetallic	1.1	5.0
Basic metals	0.8	3.6
Food	0.6	2.8
Other industries	3.8	17.9
Total	21.5	100.0

Note: The data cover through October 2002.
Source: MIDA (various years).

to cost or markets. Statements made by government leaders highlighted that labor-intensive businesses had re-sited in emerging locations in Vietnam or China as reforms take place in those countries. Investors' decisions were explained by long-term global production and marketing networks rather than the crisis. However, the crisis might have hastened their plans to depart. The rapid rise of FDI in China—from US$38.9 billion in 1993 to US$64.4 billion in 1997 and US$58.5 billion in 1998 before evening to US$52.6 billion in 1999—as reported by a senior Chinese government economist, tends to support this observation (Li 2002).

In 2001 and 2002 approved FDI manufacturing projects in Malaysia again were directed to electronics or related technologies. They included US$0.243 billion for fabricated wafer; US$0.092 billion for LED chips/devices and subassemblies and LED- based lighting products or systems; US$0.039 billion for 100-gigabyte thin film magnetic disks; US$0.025 billion for parts of computer peripherals; and US$0.014 billion for re-manufacturing of data storage devices and and other items. Other major FDI recipients included the manufacture and R&D of pharmaceutical products (US$0.079 billion) and medical devices (US$0.037 billion). There was also a project approved for producing synthetic rubber powder and thermoplastic elastomers.

It appears that Malaysia's traditional pull factors for FDI (such as political stability, modern infrastructure and legal system, an educated and trainable workforce conversant in English) continue to remain relevant for manufacturing industries that are inclined toward more sophisticated processes. After the crisis, there was an overall improvement in the performance of manufacturing output and exports and gradual improvement in Malaysia's global competitiveness. The opportunities of AFTA (ASEAN Free Trade Area) and the proposed enlargement of ASEAN to other East Asian economies also have drawn FDI applications for manufacturing and manufacturing-related services from MNCs. The shift to more capital-intensive and knowledge-intensive investments is evident from the average gross plant output per employee in the manufacturing sector. (Output doubled within a decade.) On average, gross plant output was US$89 million per employee in 1999 and US$45 million per employee in 1990. The vast improvement in productivity mirrors the higher investments in capital-intensive production processes. If expenditures for consultancy, training, and engineering services were included as investment in services (data are not available), FDI figures might be bigger than the data for conventional investments.

The increasing interest of foreign direct investors in Malaysia's growing services sector is not well documented, except for specific subsectors like finance, privatized utilities, and large trading activities for commodities and industrial goods. The role of FDI in nonmanufacturing activities, such as services, is probably best estimated by taking FDI in all industries less those in manufacturing. However, the different basis of the data sets causes difficulty. Table 9.1 shows FDI only in the distributive trade subsector, which has always been the largest single group of economic activities within the tertiary sector. The stock of FDI equity in distributive trades rose from US$0.14 billion in 1988 to US$0.46 billion in 1995. Foreign investment in wholesale and retail is not new to Malaysia, and recent trends seem to have started a restructuring process that will last for some time (Box 9.3).

FDI has introduced restructuring processes within the Malaysian economy's distribution system. MNCs brought in more than capital. MNCs have introduced new technologies, injected innovative management approaches, trained workers in new skills, and started modernizing the wholesale and retail trade. Consumers have benefited from the efficiencies of MNCs through lower prices, a more comfortable environment, better facilities, and more convenient multisited outlets. The wave of change invoked reaction from small, local distributors who had difficulty competing. In turn, the Malaysian government introduced new guidelines in 1995 and in 2002 to regulate the entry of large foreign hypermarkets. When the guidelines were implemented, confusion resulted. Partly as a political measure, the government, in October 2003, announced a freeze on new hypermarkets and branches for five years in the three most densely populated areas of the

Box 9.3. *Malaysia's Distributive Trades*

After the decline of British interests in Malaysia in the fifties and sixties (though some interests did remain to cater to expatriates and local elites), there were Singapore joint venture investments in "emporiums" in the seventies and Japanese supermarkets and department stores in the eighties. Also noteworthy are new large-scale wholesale and retail establishments such as supermarkets and hypermarkets (over 5,000 square meters for the trading floor area and more than 50,000 stock keeping units). Makro from the Netherlands was among the first of the new distributive formats to invest in Malaysia as a joint venture with the Selangor state development agency in the late 1980s. Carrefour of France, Dairy Farm of the Jardine Matheson Group in Hong Kong, and Dutch Ahold followed in rapid succession. The British Tesco arrived after the Asian crisis, implying that its plans to invest were not aborted by the difficulties.

country (Klang Valley, Penang, and Johore). The economic implications of such a move cannot be taken lightly because the reduction of competition would raise Malaysia's cost of doing business and the economy's competitiveness as a destination for FDI. The possibility of displeasure among fellow WTO partners and trading partners in regional arrangements may bring negative consequences. The disruption to the plans of MNCs for entry and growth may not be as serious as the effect of protecting large operators that are already established. The small local retailers, those whom the measure was probably intended to safeguard, may not gain as much.

Sources of FDI before and after the Crisis

Between 1985 and 1997 (before the crisis), Japan, Singapore, the United States, and Taiwan (China) were the main FDI sources; together they accounted for over half the FDI received by Malaysia. The only exception was Taiwan (China), topping the list in 1990. Since the early 1990s, other Asian investors have begun to break onto the scene, as FDI from traditional sources—namely, Japan, Singapore, and Taiwan—declined (Sieh and Shen 1998). The main industries that benefited from these sources were those linked with E&E activities.

In terms of equity from FDI, U.S. inflows rose from US$0.097 billion in 1991 to peak at US$0.5 billion in 1995; the equity inflows of Japanese MNCs dropped from US$0.6 billion to US$0.53 billion in the same period. However, FDI from both sources dropped significantly in 1996 and 1997 by about

40 percent. After the crisis, investments from the United States picked up, reaching US$0.46 billion equity inflow in 2000. But those from Japan continued to decline. This could be explained by the depressed sentiment of Japanese MNCs because of their home market difficulties, which were further aggravated by the crisis in east and Southeast Asia. In 2002, Japanese firms invested only US$0.18 billion in Malaysia compared with US$0.21 billion invested by U.S. firms.

But before the crisis, sales of the manufacturing sector attained by Japanese MNCs were more than twice those of U.S. firms, because of the stock of FDI already invested by the Japanese. During the crisis in 1998, and immediately after in 1999, sales by U.S. MNCs surpassed sales by Japanese MNCs (Table 9.5). By 2000 the position of Japanese MNCs appeared to have shifted back to the precrisis trend relative to multinational corporations in the United States. The higher employment by Japanese MNCs before and after the crisis tends to indicate that Japanese MNCs were more labor intensive than their U.S. counterparts in Malaysian manufacturing, probably due to differences in the way work was organized. U.S. MNCs were quicker than the Japanese to uproot their facilities and relocate in countries where labor costs were lower and conditions more favorable for their investments. Many Japanese MNCs originally came to Malaysia to take advantage of the lower labor costs in the earlier years. They are less footloose than the U.S. MNCs. Therefore, it is not surprising that they remain more labor intensive by comparison. This does not mean that Japanese MNCs have not been restructuring. Within the ASEAN region, resiting of manufacturing facilities has been taking place. More labor-intensive production has shifted to Indonesia and elsewhere, while the Malaysian facilities of MNCs have moved up the technology ladder.

After the Asian crisis, only FDI inflows from the United States remained significant. FDI from other traditional sources shrank: Japan to 12 percent, Singapore to 19 percent, and Taiwan to 29 percent of their respective 1996 precrisis levels. Germany, a previously insignificant source of foreign direct investment in Malaysia, increased FDI flows by 34 times, and the Netherlands by 8 times, when comparing their 1996 and 2002 levels. Perhaps of greater interest is the emergence of a very new Asian source of FDI, namely China. China recorded over a seventyfold increase between 1996 and 2001, from US$10.61 million to US$769.13 million. In addition, toward the end of the crisis period, Pakistan showed up as an investor. The interest shown by these nontraditional FDI sources may partly be attributed to the relaxation of equity since July 1998. Foreign investors could have wholly owned projects irrespective of the export levels of those investments. It is interesting that these new FDI sources came in with projects that were few in number

Table 9.5. *FDI Inflows to Malaysia from U.S. and Japanese Multinational Corporations: Sales and Employment in the Manufacturing Sector, 1991–2002*
(US$millions)

	U.S. MNCs			*Japanese MNCs*		
Year	*Total equity flows*	*Manufacturing sector sales*	*Employment in manufacturing sector (no. of persons)*	*Total equity flows*	*Manufacturing sector sales*	*Employment in manufacturing sector (no. of persons)*
1991	97.283	3,932	68,200	600.348	8,477	109,870
1992	179.173	4,954	72,700	290.102	8,159	105,670
1993	195.817	5,480	72,200	227.653	11,573	147,490
1994	391.016	6,857	111,400	390.967	16,742	182,930
1995	500.393	8,544	125,700	532.263	20,137	190,470
1996	384.737	9,933	100,100	329.102	23,427	208,390
1997	289.062	12,462	117,200	392.082	22,080	203,370
1998	306.842	14,522	109,200	303.743	12,787	174,980
1999	358.947	17,736	106,300	205.263	16,862	209,690
2000	462.368	19,579	104,500	240.526	21,300	233,100
2001	189.331	n.a.	n.a.	142.200	n.a.	n.a.
2002	213.853	n.a.	n.a.	181.135	n.a.	n.a.

n.a. Not available.

Source: Malaysian Central Bank, U.S. Bureau of Economic Analysis, Japanese Ministry of Trade and Industry.

but large in scale when compared to the medium-scale Japanese and Singapore investments. Many were probably government-initiated projects that were indirectly linked to the need to diversify FDI sources on the part of Malaysia and the need for palm oil on the part of China and Pakistan. However, European investors from Germany, the Netherlands, and Switzerland were also sufficiently confident about the Malaysian economy to invest in large-scale projects.

Existing foreign firms were accorded the same equity conditions for expansion or diversification projects. The equity conditions were to be reviewed after December 31, 2003. For the period 1996 to 2002, the main FDI contributors were the United States, Japan, Singapore, Germany, the Netherlands, Taiwan (China), the United Kingdom, the Republic of Korea, and so on in that order (Table 9.6). Data on the E&E sector for 2001 show

Table 9.6. *Sources of FDI in Approved Projects in Malaysia, 1996–2002*
(US$millions)

Economy	*1996*	*1997*	*1998*	*1999*	*2000*	*2001*	*2002*[a]	*Total*
Netherlands	29.42	11.92	160.08	203.23	572.31	18.15	152.36	1,147.46
Japan	1,831.26	769.32	475.96	264.77	758.04	885.82	150.11	5,135.29
Republic of Korea	256.08	240.92	19.38	9.29	190.22	448.23	96.87	1,260.99
Pakistan	—	—	11.65	258.68	—	—	—	270.33
Singapore	1,894.15	455.49	246.70	237.47	468.02	586.27	233.20	4,121.30
Switzerland	750.24	44.65	36.09	186.20	23.91	22.31	6.69	1,070.09
Taiwan (China)	308.32	478.13	255.02	70.26	241.07	299.95	59.68	1,712.43
United Kingdom	151.30	73.47	122.16	50.63	203.04	32.39	40.38	673.37
United States	1,149.97	852.04	1,639.30	1,357.60	1,971.56	897.80	692.68	8,560.96
Germany	58.91	643.65	38.69	49.25	435.77	685.07	1,324.57	3,235.91
China	10.61	0.77	91.97	3.04	8.88	769.13	10.64	895.03

— Negligible.
a. To October 2002.
Source: MIDA (various years).

that the four major foreign sources of investment in the industry were the United States, Japan, Germany, and Singapore.

It is difficult to discern any clear pattern of FDI changes by home countries that could be linked specifically to the Asian crisis. Clearly, Taiwan (China) and the Republic of Korea were hit hard by the crisis and had reduced their FDI outflows. Singapore was also affected by the crisis, and Japan was indirectly affected through affiliates in the rest of Asia. Nevertheless, these two countries (Japan, the second largest FDI source, and Singapore, ranking third) continued investing in Malaysia, although a clear downward trend was observed. In the case of Singapore manufacturers, investing in Malaysia was probably a strategy to lower production costs further; other cash-rich Singapore corporations, which were not adversely affected by the financial crisis, grabbed the opportunity to invest overseas by acquiring cheap assets, such as in banks of other ASEAN countries. For Japanese firms, the Asian crisis added to the problems of the prolonged recessionary condition in their home economy. Their continued FDI flows to Malaysia were to support existing investments as well as to meet longer-term plans that had already been decided.

MNCs from Germany and the Netherlands could have been attracted by possible opportunities in crisis-hit Malaysia when deflated asset values were attractive on the one hand and by push factors in their home economies on the other. China appeared to have started to embark on a longer-term strategy that takes into account economic linkages with the Southeast Asian region.

The trends discussed above suggest that when home economies were affected by crisis, FDI outflows were curtailed, as seen among Asian investors from Taiwan (China), the Republic of Korea, and to some extent Singapore and Japan. The reverse appears to be the case for FDI from home economies that were crisis free (for example, the United States and Europe). But the global bursting of the technology bubble in 2000 could have affected FDI outflows from the United States, as shown by the Malaysian data.

Malaysia's FDI inflows have been moving toward capital-intensive, higher-tech, and knowledge-intensive activities. During the crisis years from 1997 to 1998, the average size of new investment projects was bigger than that of re-investment, possibly to take advantage of deflated assets and lower costs. But the trend reversed for two years after that. Between 1999 and 2000, the average re-investment was larger than that for new projects, probably reflecting upward technology shifts in existing FDI facilities. Some MNCs were converting existing facilities to manufacture new or different products rather than keeping their old product mix; others were expanding to achieve scale economies possibly incorporating technological improvements. This reversal was particularly prominent in 2000, a year when expansion or diversification projects surpassed new ones. This augured well for the host economy as MNCs were either preparing for, or responding to, competition from elsewhere by moving up their value chains.

China's open door policy led the Chinese economy toward greater global economic integration. MNCs anticipated fundamental changes when operating within Asia's new economic and business environment. After China's admission to the WTO and the liberalization of trade and investment that followed, MNCs were offered a huge labor market as well as a large consumer market to tap into. A number of labor-intensive E&E productions from Malaysia were reported to have re-located in China to take advantage of lower costs and market opportunities. According to industry sources, suppliers of electronic and electrical parts and components are end-customer driven. They re-locate to follow the re-siting of other manufacturers along the value chain who are their major buyers.

Some claim that Malaysia is losing its advantage as a low-cost production site compared to China and other emerging Southeast Asian economies. Malaysia recognizes that in the medium to long term, higher level knowledge-intensive activities must be pursued and the upgrading must be fast enough to stay ahead. Fiscal incentives are already in place to do the following: move from design and development to R&D, begin OBM (own brand manufacturing) while producing for OEM (original equipment manufacturing), move into technology clusters up and down value chains, and engage MNCs in various ways, from back room service work to marketing and sales liaisons. Malaysia further encourages attempts to join in with the Chinese in their home markets (for example, room air-conditioner production), and in other niche production activities. However, Malaysia may require a more concerted and focused strategy than the strategy undertaken until now. Malaysian firms are small in absolute size compared to other foreign investors in China and to Chinese domestic firms. Mechanisms are needed to "gather" interested parties into consortiums that share information, technology, contracts, and markets in order to truly engage China as a partner to the benefit of the Malaysian economy. Partners may come from the ASEAN region, from MNC affiliates that are already in Malaysia, or from the host economy. Malaysia must work on a deliberate strategy for outward investment and plug into the greater regional economy. Some of the apprehensions and hopes faced by Southeast Asian businesses because of the China threat have been discussed elsewhere (Sieh 2002b).

After the crisis, Malaysia did experience some FDI inflows, but they were for activities that differed from before, especially in the electrical and electronics sector. In 2001, U.S. MNCs remained the largest source of FDI in the E&E sector. But they have shifted their focus to producing advanced electronic components and parts, mainly for the information and communication technology industries as well as data storage and telecommunication industries. New investments from Japan have also shifted direction. Instead of traditional consumer electrical and electronic products, investors are turning to industrial electronics components and parts. In the consumer electronics industry, Japanese MNCs have restructured to concentrate on higher-end digital products such as DVD and VCD players, digital video cameras, home theater systems, and audio products (MIDA 2002). Singapore firms continue to concentrate on small and medium-scale production of electronic parts, components, and subassemblies. But some newer Singapore investments have shifted toward higher-value consumer electronics such as cellular phones, digital video and audio products, as well as game consoles and peripherals. Germany, a nontraditional source of FDI in the E&E sector, has started to invest heavily in Malaysia. In 2001 US$0.55 billion of the total investment of US$0.68 billion from Germany was for a new single project to produce semiconductor devices (MIDA 2001).

It appears likely that the shift in focus of multinational corporations' investment in the E&E industry was not because of the Asian crisis, even though the crisis may have hastened or delayed their plans to restructure. The more probable cause was their need to adopt new strategies in anticipation of regional and international environmental changes for long-term competitive reasons. Electrical and electronic MNCs in Malaysia had already developed well-established intracompany production and production-related trading networks as part of their global strategies. Since their production value chains were increasingly located in different countries to achieve a cost advantage, intrafirm trading with the parent company in the home country as well as with overseas subsidiaries or affiliates had already become common.

Changes in FDI Policy after the Asian Crisis and their Impact

Policy shifts in Malaysia after the crisis reflect attempts to pursue new strategic approaches. Malaysia is seeking new industries, new forms of existing industries, as well as niches where Malaysia can compete effectively. However, such attempts have not swayed the country from the longer-run strategy of following a cautiously liberal direction, although impacts of the crisis would have been factored into the changes in a tactical manner. The key policy areas include direct measures that affect FDI and indirect ones.

Direct Measures

First, a Cabinet Committee on National Competitiveness was formed in 2003 to review policies and procedures that impede national competitiveness, to provide policy direction, and to monitor implementation of initiatives at a high level.

Second, equity conditions and the controversial Industrial Coordination Act of 1976 and the Promotion of Investments Act of 1968 are being reviewed to ensure that the pull factors remain attractive to foreign direct investors. (Specifically, in 2003 only the 30 percent equity for Bumiputera condition remained.)

Third, a manufacturing services sector division was established in the Malaysian Industrial Development Authority to develop and strengthen R&D, design capability, integrated support industries, packaging, and distribution and marketing activities connected with manufacturing industries.

Fourth, in January 2003 a fast-track mechanism for approval of manufacturing licenses within seven days began as well as media promotions and exhibitions to promote foreign and domestic investments.

Fifth, Malaysia currently emphasizes promotion of high-technology, capital-intensive, and knowledge-driven industries; manufacturing industries that produce intermediate goods that will help reduce importation of components and parts for other industries; advanced electronics, optics and photonics, wireless technology, display technology design, biotechnology, petrochemicals, chemical pharmaceuticals, and resource-based industries; parts and components that are export oriented are also encouraged. Apart from ASEAN-level promotions, incentives are provided to MNCs to begin regional manufacturing-related services such as the following: Operational Headquarters (OHQ), International Procurement Centers (IPC), Representative Offices (RE), Regional Office (RO), Regional Distribution Centre (RDC), Integrated Logistic Services (ILS), Integrated Market Support Services (IMSS), and Integrated Central Utility Facilities (CUF). Incentives include more expatriate posts, significantly reduced market performance conditions, relaxed local content conditions, financial control measures, and fiscal incentives such as tax exemption and the exemption of import duty and sales tax.

Indirect Measures

Other policies not specifically targeted for FDI will influence decisions by MNCs (for example, policies on human resources, education and training, technology development, especially in information and communication technologies, and finance and banking). Malaysia is shifting from a production-based economy to a knowledge-based economy and seeking higher value-adding activities by focusing on services sector development and trade. It also has hopes of becoming a center of quality tertiary education as well as training/re-training. Emphasis has been placed on English as an international medium of communication, and the use of English in the teaching of mathematics and science has started in all schools. Measures are already in place to push Malaysia toward becoming a regional and global player in tertiary education and professional training.

Effects of the Policy Changes on FDI Inflows

FDI inflow is not solely dependent on policy measures. But the FDI policies incorporated in the crisis management program have been somewhat effective. After the direct and indirect measures were introduced, FDI inflows returned and rebounded. With regard to the sustainability of inflows, it appears that policies, although crucial and relevant, are not the only determinants of inward and outward movements of FDI. The competitiveness of the host economy in the long term—vis-à-vis neighboring economies within the region and other regions in the wider global context—must be reckoned with. Policy makers must continue nurturing the positive factors within the underlying economy to ensure that the economic structure enables a competitive environment that draws MNCs to Malaysia. The conditions of political, economic, and financial stability, transparent processes of a clean government and administration, are as relevant as the availability of infrastructure, educated labor, and reasonable facilities and conditions for foreign investors. But new considerations related to long-term geo-political developments, such as security threats linked to religious movements, also require attention. Those managing the socio-economic order must be willing to try new approaches.

As far as FDI is concerned, certain seemingly short-term factors may be as devastating as long-term factors. The Asian crisis is one example. Other short-term factors include the outbreak of diseases and wars. The "lingering effects" of short- and medium-term events can jeopardize long-term FDI inflows. Medium-term factors that may impact FDI include intra-industry considerations such as business cycle effects, demand conditions, and inventory levels. As Malaysian industries and other east Asian industries, especially in the electrical and electronics sector, have shown, activities along different parts of the value chain are affected by medium-term market factors. Closer monitoring of short-term interruptions and medium-term intra-industry factors that affect FDI flows is needed in the future. Developing early warning systems may help to dampen the negative effects on host economies of investment flow changes. Long-term plans to compete may also require more effort directed to outward investment by Malaysia.

Conclusions

The following conclusions may be drawn from the preceding analysis. First, future FDI inflows into the Malaysian economy will depend on a host of factors. Policy direction plays a major role in MNC decisions in normal as well as abnormal economic conditions. While most of the traditional factors known to draw FDI in host economies remain important, global developments in the early twenty-first century in terms of international security, political changes, and intercountry relations appear to be influencing business paths as much as economic rationale. In Malaysia, the industries targeted by investors before the crisis continue to be important, particularly those in the manufacturing sector where their dominance in the electrical and electronics firms has not changed. However, product diversification toward capital- and knowledge-intensive activities has been reported, both by the approving authority and by industry players. Policy changes that inclined to more deregulation and greater liberalization of markets have contributed to the rapid rebound in FDI inflows after the crisis-affected years of 1997 and 1998. But the trend of receiving FDI for expansion or diversification rather than for new projects needs to be closely monitored by policy makers. The rise of FDI in the services sector such as in distributive trades is expected to improve the economy's competitiveness if intervention by the regulators is kept minimal.

Second, the major sources of FDI—the United States, Japan, Singapore, and Taiwan (China)—have continued after the crisis despite the slight change in the ranking of those home countries. North American investors have taken over the lead from Japan for annual FDI inflows. But the stock of Japanese FDI accumulated over the years has enabled Japanese firms in Malaysia to maintain the major role in production output and trade. However, their higher employment indicates their use of more labor-intensive technologies than their American counterparts in Malaysia. Notwithstanding the entrance of new FDI sources (such as China and Pakistan) and renewed interest from European investors, much of the impact of FDI on Malaysia's economic growth, output, trade, employment, technology development, markets, and social development has come from the stock of FDI assets that exists already.

Third, FDI flows are also determined by a combination of short-term, medium-term, and long-term considerations. Long-term factors, such as those brought about by fundamental policy shifts or through regional and global economic arrangements, are generally more relevant for setting major corporate-wide FDI directions. As a consequence of long-term factors, it is not uncommon to see MNCs engaging in internal product rationalization as they restructure their regional value chain. Some E&E firms in Malaysia think that the industry is lagging too far behind China and other countries in terms of cost and productivity. As with most economies in ASEAN, Malaysia has its fears, doubts, and hopes as China emerges as an economic force that will alter the economic position of Southeast Asia. However, adjustments to the changes up and down the value chains are taking place in schools and educational institutions, in research and technology agencies, and in financial institutions. However, more coherent plans are needed to integrate Malaysian firms and organizations, which are small and disconnected, compared to the large-size companies in China and global competitors elsewhere, even if a niche strategy is pursued by Malaysia.

Fourth, long-term strategic factors are usually not regarded as being as disruptive as short-term upheavals and medium-term disruptions because strategic elements are usually mulled over with careful analysis of various aspects of change. Short-term factors that impinge on FDI flows include unpredictable and unforeseen circumstances (such as the Asian crisis), deadly diseases (such as SARS), and conflicts of short duration (such as the first Gulf War). With short-term factors many questions arise. How long will they last and to whose detriment? What will be the extent of economic and psychological damage for future investments? A "dent" effect on investment could be expected only if the disruptions were short-lived and if economic institutions and social structures remained intact and running after the upheavals. However, past experience shows that short-term factors may be as disastrous as long-term factors as far as FDI is concerned, especially factors stemming from war. Both short- and medium-term events (business cycle and inventory conditions) may negatively affect long-term FDI inflows. This means that all time frames must be taken into consideration when hosting FDI, so that steps are ready to cushion the undesirable effects of these investments

Implications for the Future

The first few years after the Asian crisis were difficult for businesses in Malaysia as a whole. Amid the regional restructuring of production and business strategies, there were changes in product and resource markets that were particularly challenging for FDI projects in the electrical and electronics sector. Multinational corporations began to take new strategic directions in response to an increasingly competitive global environment and new markets in the Asia Pacific region. Malaysia recognized the need to continue forging new partnerships with MNCs in order to benefit from their vast economic power in the long term. In the medium term, Malaysia's electrical and electronics sector—which has been heavily reliant on FDI for technology, capital, and markets—would continue to be affected by the waves of new technology as the new millennium unfolds. Furthermore, recent economic and political developments in the world have brought great uncertainties to the global investment outlook in the short term, and they cannot be ignored.

In response to these threats, Malaysia has overhauled its industries. In the case of the E&E industry, it has positioned itself away from competing directly with East Asian markets for FDI. Malaysia will increasingly focus on attracting quality-oriented FDI in the production of advanced electronics, telecommunications components, wireless technology, and supporting services (such as R&D, design, prototyping, testing, regional logistics, and distribution of E&E products). Malaysia will need to further exploit its geographical advantage between the Western and Eastern hemispheres by strengthening trade linkages with both sides. The government has invested heavily to improve its port facilities in Port Klang and Tanjung Pelepas, Johore in order to meet international standards and requirements.

Malaysia will need to position its economy with respect to other ASEAN members and countries in the wider Asia Pacific region. One possibility is to take different positions along the value chain so as to complement, rather than compete with, each other. For example, Malaysia can concentrate on capital-intensive, automated manufacturing, and support services, while countries with larger populations can focus on labor-intensive production tasks besides providing large consumer markets for FDI outputs. Firms within the economy must also seek ways to form larger entities when dealing with large enterprises elsewhere. Security developments will affect future investment, trade, and economic relationships among countries and within regional groupings. Yet in Southeast Asia, spillover effects from international politics to economics may show up even in bilateral trade and investment arrangements, particularly since Malaysia is predominantly a Muslim country. International affairs may affect the decisions of MNCs about future investments and FDI destinations. As long as Malaysia continues to pursue trade agreements and other economic cooperation arrangements with its major trade and investment partner countries and act responsibly in the context of regional and multilateral economic platforms, hope for FDI and the countries it links will remain.

Malaysia as a FDI host economy provides many lessons for other developing countries, particularly those that have religious differences and other social differences with the home countries of MNCs. Through the use of rational economic management, Malaysia has successfully reaped considerable gains from FDI in the past, and it hopes to continue to do so in the future. Malaysia has always maintained an open economy, participated actively in regional and international economic forums, and earnestly pursued FDI, bearing in mind the interest of investors as well as its own economic welfare. Malaysia's approach has been characterized by a readiness to adjust to changing circumstances in the short term and to follow medium-term developments of businesses. However, developing countries, including Malaysia, must be cautioned against schemes such as future investment agreements that are not in their best interest from an economic development perspective—especially with the rejection of the Multilateral Framework on Investment in WTO. In particular, the demands made by parties from more advanced economies may limit the authority and policy space of governments of developing countries. Malaysia will need extreme care when taking on obligatory commitments that may impede the economic, social, and human development of its people and the generations to come.

References

Dobson, Wendy, and Chia Siow Yue, eds. 1997. *Multinationals and East Asian Integration.* Ottawa and Singapore: International Development Research Centre and Institute of Southeast Asian Studies.

IMF (International Monetary Fund). 2003. International Financial Statistics CD ROM. April. Washington, D.C.

Li, Shantong. 2002. "China's WTO Entry: Impact on China." Paper presented at the Fourth Asia Development Forum on Trade and Poverty Reduction, November 3–5. Seoul.

Malaysian Department of Statistics. various years. *Report on the Financial Survey of Limited Companies* (no longer published).

MIDA (Malaysian Industrial Development Authority). various years. *Statistics on the Manufacturing Sector.* Kuala Lumpur.

———. 2001. *MIDA Annual Report 2001.* Kuala Lumpur.

———. 2002. *Malaysia Investment in the Manufacturing Sector: Policies, Incentives and Facilities.* Kuala Lumpur.

———. 2003a. *Electronic Industry—Business Opportunities in Malaysia's Electronic Industry.* Kuala Lumpur.

———. 2003b. *Report on the Performance of the Manufacturing Sector 2002.* Kuala Lumpur.

Montes, M. F. 1998. *The Currency Crisis in Southeast Asia.* Singapore: Institute of Southeast Asian Studies.

Sieh, Lee Mei Ling. 1998. "Malaysia's Electronic Industry." In *The Effects of Liberalization on Asia's Textiles, Clothing and Electronics Industries, Studies in APEC Liberalization,* chap. 6. Canberra: Australian Department of Foreign Affairs and Trade.

———. 2000a. "Asian Retail and Distribution System in a Globalised Environment: Recent Developments in Malaysia." In *Proceedings of the Asian Retail and Distribution Forum 2000: Entering a New Millennium,* 98–123. Kobe.

———. 2000b. *Taking on the World: Globalization Strategies in Malaysia.* Kuala Lumpur: McGraw-Hill.

———. 2002a. "AFTA in the Globalization Processes: Perspectives from Industries in Malaysia." *Japan Foreign Direct Investment and the East Asian Industrial System.* Springer.

———. 2002b. "The Economic Impact of Sino-U.S. Relations on ASEAN: Apprehensions, Aspirations and Adjustments." Paper presented at the Fourth International Conference on Sino-American Economic Relations under the World Trade Organization, Hong Kong, May 6–7.

———. 2003. "Is WTO a Boon or Bane for Shoppers and Retailers in Malaysia?" Inaugural Lecture, University of Malaya, Kuala Lumpur, October 17.

Sieh, Lee Mei Ling, and Loke, Wai Heng. 1998. "FDIs in Malaysia: Firm Level Characteristics." *Papers and Proceedings of International Symposium, Foreign Direct Investment in Asia.* Department of Research Cooperation, Economic Research Institute, Economic Planning Agency, Government of Japan.

Sieh, Lee Mei Ling, and Shen Tzong Ruey. 1998. *Strategic Alliances for Third Markets: Firms from Malaysia and Taiwan.* Taipei: Chung Hwa Institute of Economic Research.

Sieh, Lee Mei Ling, and Tho Lai Mooi, Susan. 1987. *Malaysia Manufacturing Futures Survey Report 1987,* vols. 1 and 2. Kuala Lumpur: Faculty of Economics and Administration, University of Malaya.

Sieh, Lee Mei Ling, and Yew Siew Yong. 1997. "Malaysia: Electronics, Autos and the Trade-Investment Nexus." In Wendy Dobson and Chia Siow Yue, eds., *Multinationals and East Asian Integration*. Ottawa and Singapore: International Development Research Centre and Institute of Southeast Asian Studies.

Tay, Angeline, and Sieh, Lee Mei Ling. 2000. "Retail Investment in Malaysia: Local Responses and Public Policy." In R. Davies and T. Yahagi, eds., *Retail Investment in Asia/Pacific: Local Responses and Public Policy Issues*, 145–59. Oxford: The Oxford Institute of Retail Management, Templeton College, University of Oxford.

Yeow, Teck Chai. 2002. "Economic and Investment Outlook." *Malaysia Strategic Outlook 2002 Conference*. Kuala Lumpur: Malaysian Industrial Development Authority.

10

FDI and Economic Development: The Case of the Philippines

Myrna S. Austria

Industrialization has always been a major development goal for the Philippines since its independence. This goal was carried out through trade and investment policies. The country has, in fact, undergone several trade and investment policy regimes in its pursuit of industrialization. Over the years, the government has gradually opened up the economy by removing barriers to trade and investment. The more liberalized environment increased the country's participation in international trade and in the activities of multinational companies through increased foreign investment flows to the country. Because of the high degree of linkage between trade and foreign direct investment (FDI), the trade structure of the Philippines has also significantly changed over the years. An exporter of primary commodities until the 1980s, the country during the 1990s became an exporter of manufactures.

The shift to exports of manufactures and the increasing presence of FDI in the country have not been accompanied by a rapid growth of the manufacturing sector, however. The contribution of the sector to the country's domestic product remained steady at 25 percent over the past two decades.

The author would like to acknowledge the valuable comments and suggestions of Professor Shujiro Urata, Professor Fukunari Kimura, Professor Chia Siow Yue, and Dr. Nagesh Kumar on earlier drafts of this chapter. The author would also like to acknowledge the excellent research assistance provided by Mr. Jitendra Mojica.

This contrasts sharply with the experience of other countries in East Asia that are pursuing the same development strategy. Concern about the effects of the Asian crisis on domestic economic stability has sparked a debate concerning the country's reliance on foreign capital flows to aid economic development. These issues raise the need to examine the role of FDI in the country's economic development in the 1990s.

The objectives of this chapter are twofold: (i) to analyze the country's FDI flows, trends, and patterns; and (ii) to examine the factors that affect FDI flows and the mechanisms through which FDI contributes to the country's economic development. The chapter begins with a review of the current literature on the relationship between foreign direct investment and economic development. FDI trends and patterns are then discussed as well as the factors driving and inhibiting FDI in the country. Policy reforms made in the 1990s are highlighted. Next, the channels through which FDI affects economic development are examined. The chapter concludes with a summary of the findings and their policy implications.

Foreign Direct Investment and Economic Development

Foreign direct investment has become an important source of private capital for developing countries since the mid-1980s. However, the question of whether or not FDI generates positive effects for the host countries has been the subject of debate in recent years. The common benefits associated with FDI to a host country's economic development include access to world markets, employment generation, high wages and benefits to workers, high levels of research and development, sophisticated managerial and marketing techniques, and the spillover effects to the rest of the economy (Moran 1998; Lim 2001; Stein and Daude 2001).

There are various channels by which FDI can generate positive spillovers. One common channel is through the linkage between the affiliates of multinational companies (MNCs) and their local suppliers. MNCs can help prospective local suppliers set up their production facilities, provide technical assistance or technology transfer to improve the product, and assist in finding additional customers, including their affiliates in other countries (Lim 2001). Spillovers are also generated when workers trained by MNCs are later hired by domestic firms. These workers bring with them the skills, knowledge, and experience they acquired from the MNCs. This, in turn, can improve the productivity and efficiency of domestic firms.

In the 1990s, FDI in East Asia was more associated with the establishment of international production networks of MNCs (Kawai and Urata

2001). Under this integrated production system, labor-intensive segments of technologically complex production processes of MNCs are first separated from the capital-intensive and the skill-intensive segments and then relocated in labor abundant countries. This type of FDI integrated developing countries into the multinational companies' international production networks through exports. To enhance their overall competitive position in the international markets, parent MNCs provide their local affiliates with newer technology, more rapid technological upgrading, and greater attention to quality control, cost control, as well as human resource development. They also attract other foreign investors, including their competitors and foreign suppliers, to cluster in the same area. The combination of these factors (cutting-edge technology, exporting into competitive world markets, and clustering of foreign investor activity) generates substantial spillovers and externalities that far exceed the standard positive effects of FDI (Moran 1998).

However, FDI may also generate negative spillovers detrimental to a host country's development. Foreign firms may displace domestic firms, especially when the latter have little access to capital. The cost of factors of production may also increase as a result of FDI (Stein and Daude 2001).

The benefits of FDI to host countries may depend on the manner in which FDI is attracted to a country. Prior to the 1990s, when tariffs and other barriers to trade were relatively high, MNCs located in developing countries to overcome the trade barriers. However, FDIs of this type generate the usual list of inefficiencies and misallocation of resources and leave the host economy worse off than if it had never received the investment in the first place (Moran 1998). Developing countries also aggressively compete to attract FDI by offering fiscal incentives and subsidies to potential investors. Studies have shown that these locational factors have the same effect as trade restrictions in reducing allocative and dynamic efficiency (Brewer and Young 1999; World Trade Organization 2000). Furthermore, when intense competition leads to a race to the bottom, the potential benefits generated by FDI will be competed away, and they will accrue to foreign investors (Stein and Daude 2001). A restrictive investment environment (with conditions such as mandatory joint partnership, licensing, and domestic resource requirements) tends to attract FDI that is less efficient, exhibits older technology and business practices, and lags in technology upgrading (Moran 1998).

With trade and investment barriers rapidly receding in the 1990s, new factors became important for attracting FDI. These include the quality of institutions, labor force, and infrastructures of host countries. Corruption, inefficient bureaucracy, and an unstable regulatory environment have been shown to have negative effects on FDI (Stein and Daude 2001; Lim 2001). On the other hand, a sound infrastructure and logistics that lower production costs and facilitate easy supply chain management—from the procurement of inputs (whether local or imported) to the export of output—attract large FDI, particularly investments in the international production networks.

In recent years, the growth of regional trading arrangements (RTAs) also has affected the location of FDI. Lower barriers to trade and investment, reduced transaction costs, and harmonized standards and legal norms often characterize free trade areas (FTAs). These factors increase the likelihood of FDI source countries selecting host countries that are linked to the same free trade agreements as them (Stein and Daude 2001). In addition, the rules of origin (ROR) in free trade areas encourage multinational companies to locate in countries where the source countries belong to the same FTA in order to overcome the ROR. The ROR determine how much domestic content a product must have to qualify as an internal product in a preferential trade agreement.

FDI Trends and Patterns in the Philippines

Foreign direct investment in the Philippines grew very little in the 1980s. (For an explanation of how FDI in the country is measured, see Box 10.1.) Although the FDI stock in 1990 was almost three times larger than the stock in 1980, the increase was much larger during the 1990s (Table 10.1). The FDI stock in 2000 was almost four times higher than in 1990.

The Philippines missed an opportunity in the 1980s to become a favorable site for investment when Japanese FDI grew rapidly following the appreciation of the yen. This lost chance can be attributed primarily to the political uncertainty at that time, including the EDSA revolution in 1986 and the series of coups during the Aquino administration. The effect of this instability can be seen in the smaller share of Japanese FDI the Philippines attracted compared to Singapore, Thailand, and Malaysia (Austria 1998). Labor-intensive and highly competitive electrical appliances and electronics, food, and textile industries were the largest recipients of FDI in these countries in the late 1980s (Takeuchi 1995). However, as wages increased in these countries in the 1990s, there was a shift in their FDI orientation. They moved from labor-intensive industries to higher value added industries or high-technology industries. The rise in the labor cost opened opportunities for the Philippines and other developing countries (like China, Indonesia, and Vietnam) as alternative investment locations for labor-intensive industries.

Table 10.1. *FDI Inward Stock, by Selected Economies, 1980, 1985, 1990, 1995, 2000, and 2001*

Host region/economy	*1980*	*1985*	*1990*	*1995*	*2000*	*2001*
A. Amount (US$millions)						
World	635,534	913,182	1,871,594	2,911,725	6,258,263	6,845,723
East Asia	160,156	197,200	280,641	513,126	1,151,380	1,225,898
China	6,251	10,499	24,762	137,435	348,346	395,192
Hong Kong, China	124,286	129,750	148,183	174,063	42,9036	451,870
India	1,177	1,075	1,668	5,652	18,916	22,319
Indonesia	10,274	24,971	38,883	50,601	60,638	57,361
Korea, Rep. of	1,372	2,160	5,864	9,991	62,786	47,228
Laos	2	1	13	205	550	574
Malaysia	5,169	7,388	10,318	28,732	52,748	53,302
Myanmar	746	746	913	1,831	3,191	3,314
Philippines	1,281	2,601	3,268	6,086	12,440	14,232
Singapore	6,203	13,016	28,565	59,582	95,714	104,323
Taiwan, China	2,405	2,930	9,735	15,736	27,924	32,033
Thailand	981	1,999	8,209	17,452	24,468	28,227
Vietnam	9	64	260	5,760	14,623	15,923
B. Percent distribution,						
East Asia	100.0	100.0	100.0	100.0	100.0	100.0
China	3.9	5.3	8.8	26.8	30.3	32.2
Hong Kong, China	77.6	65.8	52.8	33.9	37.3	36.9
India	0.7	0.5	0.6	1.1	1.6	1.8
Indonesia	6.4	12.7	13.9	9.9	5.3	4.7
Korea, Rep. of	0.9	1.1	2.1	1.9	5.5	3.9
Laos	0.0	0.0	0.0	0.0	0.0	0.0
Malaysia	3.2	3.7	3.7	5.6	4.6	4.3
Myanmar	0.5	0.4	0.3	0.4	0.3	0.3
Philippines	0.8	1.3	1.2	1.2	1.1	1.2
Singapore	3.9	6.6	10.2	11.6	8.3	8.5
Taiwan, China	1.5	1.5	3.5	3.1	2.4	2.6
Thailand	0.6	1.0	2.9	3.4	2.1	2.3
Vietnam	0.0	0.0	0.1	1.1	1.3	1.3

Source: UNCTAD (various years).

FDI annual flows accelerated beginning in 1993 (Figure 10.1). The favorable performance continued, with an increase from $1.2 billion in 1993 to $1.5 billion in 1996. A decline then occurred with the onset of the Asian financial crisis in 1997, but FDI returned to the 1993 level during the year. It made a rebound in 1998, reaching $1.8 billion, and then suffered a massive contraction

Box 10.1. *Measuring Foreign Direct Investment in the Philippines*

Comprehensive data on FDI in the Philippines are lacking. Data from the principal government agencies in charge of FDI data collection, namely the Board of Investment (BOI) and the Bangko Sentral ng Pilipinas (BSP), are not comparable because of differences in definitions, coverage, and collection methodology. The BOI defines FDI as equity acquired by nonresidents and nonresident nationals. Only those approved by the Board of Investment under the investment incentive laws or the Omnibus Investment Code (OIC) are included in the data (that is, those registered with the BOI). The data reflect approved FDI rather than investment actually implemented. The data also do not include FDI in the export processing zones.

Unlike the Board of Investment, the BSP defines FDI as equity acquired by nonresidents only. All corporations and partnerships with foreign equity are required to register with the BSP. The BSP data include foreign equity registered with the BSP, including investment not registered with the BOI because investors did not avail themselves of the fiscal incentives under the Omnibus Investment Code.

This chapter uses the BSP data to analyze the sectoral composition of FDI and the sources of FDI. However, data from the *World Investment Report* is used when FDI in the Philippines is compared with FDI in other countries.

in 1999. (The $0.6 billion flow in 1999 was only one-third of the 1998 amount.) FDI flows recovered beginning in 2000, and by 2001, they had reached $1.8 billion—higher than the country's pre-crisis trend levels. In general, except for the decline in the FDI flows in the immediate aftermath of the Asian financial crisis, serious disruptions in FDI in the country did not occur. This suggests that foreign investors had a relatively optimistic view of the long-run economic prospects of the Philippines in the 1990s.

Despite the increase in foreign direct investment in the 1990s, FDI flows in the Philippines remained small by international standards (Table 10.2). The country accounted for a lower share of the total FDI flows in East Asia compared to Thailand, Singapore, Malaysia, and China. Having missed the opportunity in the 1980s, the country in the 1990s was confronted with much greater competition, especially from China.

The behavior of FDI during the Asian financial crisis was strikingly different when compared with other sources of foreign capital. FDI registered a net inflow of $2,127 million in 1998. Although the amount declined to $632 million in 1999, it increased to $1,348 million in 2000 and US$1,953 million in 2001. On the other hand, portfolio and other investment flows suffered a combined net outflow of $1,644 million in 1998, US$1,567 million in 1999, $7,845 million in

Figure 10.1. *FDI Inflows, Philippines, 1990–2001*

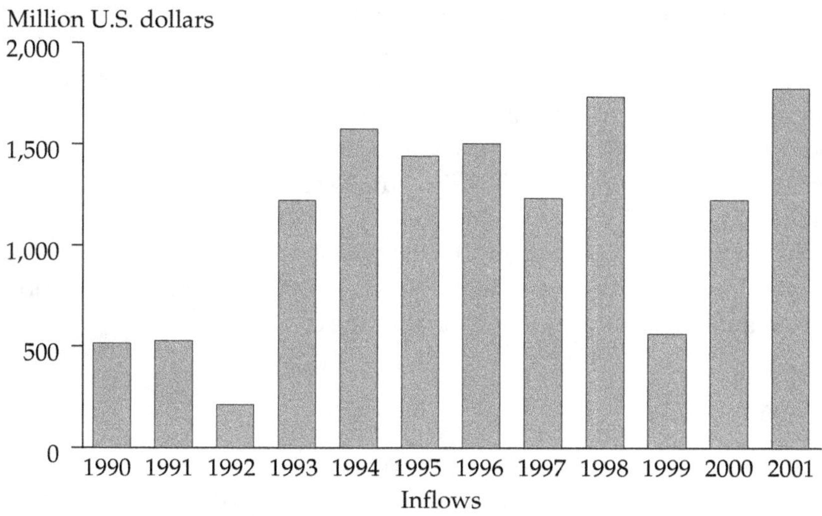

Source: UNCTAD (various years).

Table 10.2. *Average Annual Distribution of FDI Inflows, by Host Economy, East Asia, 1985–90, 1990–95, and 1995–2001*
(Percent)

Economy	*1985–90*	*1990–95*	*1995–2001*
China	22.0	40.2	45.3
Hong Kong, China	13.3	7.7	21.2
India	1.4	1.3	2.9
Indonesia	4.6	5.5	1.2
Korea, Rep. of	5.9	2.9	4.9
Laos	0.0	0.1	0.1
Malaysia	8.7	12.7	5.0
Myanmar	0.2	0.4	0.3
Philippines	3.4	2.3	1.5
Singapore	24.5	16.1	9.5
Taiwan, China	7.3	2.6	2.6
Thailand	8.4	6.6	3.6
Vietnam	0.2	1.7	2.0

Source: UNCTAD (various years).

2000, and $6,270 million in 2001. The trend shows that FDI is more resilient in the wake of the Asian crisis and hence a more stable source of capital.

Another striking feature of FDI during the 1990s in the Philippines is the increase in crossborder merger and acquisition (M&A) after the crisis. M&A sales registered an average of $445.1 million per year during the 1990–96 period and went up to $2,002.8 million per year during the 1997–2001 period. However, unlike the other crisis-hit countries that adopted policy changes in FDI in response to the crisis, the Philippines did not adopt any shift in policy toward FDI, even in the area of M&A. While corporate distress has been the major reason driving M&A in other countries, in the Philippines M&A has been associated with consolidating market positions and streamlining operations in response to the crisis.

Sectoral Allocation

FDI is highly concentrated in the manufacturing sector, which received an average of 45.3 percent of the total annual inflows during the period from 1990 to 2001 (Table 10.3). However, the share has noticeably been going down. Banks and other financial institutions were the second largest recipient of FDI in the 1990s. The surge in FDI started in 1996 as foreign financial institutions established their presence in the country due to the liberalization of the banking industry. By 2001, the sector accounted for more than 50 percent of total FDI.

Public utilities, particularly in communications, is another sector that received a chunk of FDI in the 1990s. The dramatic increase in the first half of the 1990s was caused by the boom in infrastructure investment due to the overvaluation of the peso that increased the price of the nontradable sector, as will be explained in the next section.

The share of the mining industry in the 1990s fell relative to the second half of the 1980s. Several mining companies have stopped operations in the more recent past because of the industry's deteriorating price competitiveness in the international market. Some companies also have closed due to environmental concerns. These developments lessened the attractiveness of the industry to FDI.

Within manufacturing, the share of machinery, appliances, and supplies increased strongly over the past decade (Table 10.4). The industry includes electronics, particularly semiconductors, which constituted the largest exports of the country in the 1990s. The industry also accounted for the largest share (73 percent) of investment in the export processing and special economic zones. On the other hand, the shares of chemical and chemical

Table 10.3. *Distribution of Inflows of Foreign Equity Investment, by Industry, 1985–90 and 1990–2001*
(Percent)

Industry	*1985–90 (average)*	*1990*	*1991*	*1992*	*1993*	*1994*	*1995*	*1996*	*1997*	*1998*	*1999*	*2000*	*2001*
Total foreign equity investments	100.0	100.0	100.0	100.0	100.0	100.0	100.0	100.0	100.0	100.0	100.0	100.0	100.0
Banks and other financial institutions	10.2	12.5	7.4	11.1	13.0	3.9	11.0	40.1	21.5	21.8	12.3	34.6	55.5
Manufacturing	49.8	55.7	72.0	55.4	67.9	77.2	41.5	37.3	16.3	27.7	49.8	12.3	30.6
Mining	24.7	15.4	7.4	3.7	0.5	4.6	5.1	0.3	0.3	18.2	1.3	17.1	7.7
Commerce	6.9	10.0	5.4	5.5	2.8	0.8	11.6	6.6	7.4	18.3	7.9	4.5	2.7
Services	4.7	2.5	7.1	21.2	2.7	7.6	3.7	2.7	3.2	1.4	0.8	0.4	1.0
Public utility	1.0	0.6	0.3	1.4	12.9	5.8	26.8	9.4	28.3	7.7	26.2	30.3	2.4
Agriculture, fishery, and forestry	2.6	3.1	0.1	0.1	0.1	0.0	0.0	0.1	0.0	0.0	0.0	0.0	0.0
Construction	0.1	0.1	0.4	1.5	0.2	0.2	0.3	3.5	23.0	0.7	0.1	0.1	0.0
Others	0.0	0.0	0.0	0.0	0.0	0.0	0.0	0.0	0.0	4.1	1.6	0.8	0.0

Source: Bangko Sentral ng Pilipinas.

Table 10.4. *Selected Manufacturing Industries as a Share of Total FDI, 1985-2000*
(Percent)

Sector	*1985*	*1986*	*1987*	*1988*	*1989*	*1990*	*1991*	*1992*	*1993*	*1994*	*1995*	*1996*	*1997*	*1998*	*1999*	*2000*
Chemical and chemical products	11.1	26.2	19.5	13.7	9.9	8.4	10.8	8.7	9.2	3.6	4.4	4.1	2.4	4.9	0.7	4.2
Food	24.0	0.2	5.4	2.5	3.7	8.0	2.1	6.7	4.7	1.4	1.3	1.5	1.3	3.5	40.5	5.6
Textiles and garments	1.2	1.6	2.0	5.8	4.1	4.8	3.5	5.1	1.7	0.5	1.5	0.2	0.2	0.2	0.3	0.0
Transport equipment	9.6	n.a.	3.6	0.0	2.7	3.8	5.2	12.2	3.6	0.6	6.5	2.8	2.2	0.7	1.0	0.4
Petroleum and coal	0.9	2.1	1.1	0.0	0.0	0.0	3.0	0.0	34.2	63.7	5.4	0.0	0.0	1.5	0.0	0.0
Machinery, apparatus, appliances, & supplies	1.8	1.4	5.3	3.7	23.9	13.1	40.7	16.6	6.8	4.3	16.3	12.3	6.5	6.0	3.9	1.3

n.a. Not available.
Source: Bangko Sentral ng Pilipinas.

products, food, and textiles and garments decreased substantially. These industries were largely protected until the late 1980s. The changes in shares largely reflect changes in competitiveness as tariff protection has been progressively removed. The declining share of textiles and garments indicates that this sector remains uncompetitive. It is incapable of drawing in large amounts of FDI and driving export growth as has happened in other East Asian economies. The large share of petroleum and coal in 1993 and 1994, however, was due to the privatization of Petron, an oil company that had been government-owned.

Sources of FDI

The United States is the dominant source of FDI in the Philippines (Table 10.5). However, its share has substantially declined from an average of 54 percent per year during the 1985–90 period to 16 percent per year during the 1990–2001 period. Two significant factors that caused the decline are the US-Caribbean Base Initiative (CBI) and the North American Free Trade Agreement (NAFTA) that resulted in the diversion of investment away from the Philippines. This is particularly true in the garments industry where the United States is the country's major export market (Austria 1996, 2003b). U.S. foreign direct investment used to take advantage of the Philippines' low wage rate, with the objective of re-exporting production to the United States. However, the rules of origin under NAFTA and the US-CBI (allowing a duty-free arrangement on garments from Mexico that used U.S. pre-cut fabrics) restricted exports of garments from the Philippines. The result was the decline in U.S. FDI.

Japan ranks second to the United States in terms of contribution to foreign direct investment in the Philippines. Japan's share increased considerably from an annual average of 18 percent per year from 1985 to 1990 to an annual average of 25 percent from 1990 to 2001. The increase stems primarily from the rapid appreciation of the yen, the shortage in labor, the surge in wage rates, and continued high cost structures that pushed Japanese firms to operate overseas (Urata and Tullao 1995; DFAT 1998). As discussed earlier, the Philippines became a favorable alternative investment location when labor costs rose in the NIEs during the 1990s. However, the prolonged recession in Japan is taking its toll, as the share of Japan in the annual flows has been declining since the latter half of the 1990s. Among European countries, the Netherlands, the United Kingdom, Switzerland, and Germany accounted for the largest share of FDI in the country.

During the 1990s, nontraditional sources of FDI (for example, Singapore, Malaysia, Taiwan, and the Republic of Korea) made a significant contribution

Table 10.5. *Distribution of FDI, by Source Economy, 1990–2001*
(Percent)

Economy	*1990*	*1991*	*1992*	*1993*	*1994*	*1995*	*1996*	*1997*	*1998*	*1999*	*2000*	*2001*
Total foreign equity investments	100.0	100.0	100.0	100.0	100.0	100.0	100.0	100.0	100.0	100.0	100.0	100.0
United States	26.9	18.1	17.1	9.4	8.6	6.8	22.9	11.1	27.5	4.0	17.5	22.5
Japan	27.7	45.4	47.1	12.2	7.9	30.0	36.8	31.4	17.0	14.4	7.2	22.5
Hong Kong, China	7.8	7.9	11.5	5.7	5.5	28.9	6.0	5.7	2.4	1.0	1.2	0.5
Netherlands	1.7	0.9	1.6	3.6	62.1	3.7	4.1	3.9	9.6	18.3	12.1	15.4
United Kingdom	4.4	3.7	0.6	40.6	3.9	6.5	4.9	1.7	1.4	0.4	25.8	0.1
Switzerland	3.7	2.0	2.5	4.0	0.1	0.0	0.6	0.9	0.4	36.5	0.1	0.0
Australia	3.9	0.4	1.0	0.1	0.6	2.4	0.2	1.2	0.4	1.1	0.0	0.0
Canada	1.7	0.2	0.3	0.0	0.2	0.1	0.1	0.1	0.1	0.0	2.6	0.2
France	0.5	0.2	1.7	0.1	0.3	0.8	0.8	0.3	1.6	0.6	0.0	0.9
Republic of Nauru	0.0	0.0	0.5	0.0	0.0	0.2	0.0	0.0	0.0	0.0	0.0	0.0
Germany	1.1	1.3	2.3	2.2	0.2	2.0	2.2	6.9	4.8	1.1	1.1	0.2
Sweden	3.3	1.2	0.4	0.2	0.0	0.1	0.0	0.6	0.0	0.0	0.0	0.0
Panama	1.2	0.0	0.0	0.3	0.1	0.0	0.0	0.0	2.7	0.0	0.0	0.0
Austria	0.0	2.3	0.0	0.0	0.0	0.0	0.0	0.0	0.0	0.0	0.0	0.0
Singapore	3.2	2.1	2.6	2.5	6.8	9.3	1.5	6.4	5.8	1.7	23.3	20.3
Denmark	0.4	0.1	0.0	0.6	0.1	0.0	0.0	0.2	0.0	0.0	0.0	2.8
Luxembourg	0.0	0.2	0.2	2.1	0.0	0.0	0.0	0.1	0.0	1.4	0.2	0.0
Malaysia	0.2	0.1	0.1	0.5	0.0	3.3	1.4	1.1	0.2	1.2	3.8	0.4
Bahamas	0.0	0.0	0.0	0.0	0.0	0.0	0.0	0.0	0.0	0.0	0.0	0.0
New Hebrides	0.0	0.0	0.0	0.0	0.0	0.0	0.0	0.0	0.0	0.0	0.0	0.0
Bermuda	0.1	0.2	0.0	0.9	0.3	0.3	0.0	3.1	0.9	10.1	0.0	0.1
Republic of Korea	3.9	8.6	4.0	0.9	0.7	1.0	2.3	1.7	1.4	0.7	0.6	0.0
Taiwan, China	3.9	1.5	0.9	1.1	0.3	0.9	3.7	1.9	5.8	0.7	0.1	5.7
British Virgin Islands	0.0	0.3	1.3	0.0	0.0	0.0	8.3	16.8	6.1	0.1	0.6	5.8
Other countries	4.4	3.4	4.5	12.9	2.2	3.7	4.3	5.0	11.9	6.6	3.6	2.6

Source: Bangko Sentral ng Pilipinas.

to foreign investment in the Philippines, their shares increasing continuously during the decade. The increases can be attributed to the rising domestic labor cost in these countries relative to the Philippines. They had to relocate the labor-intensive segment of their production processes to the low-wage ASEAN economies, like the Philippines (Austria 2003b). FDI from these countries was not affected by the financial crisis (with the exception of the Republic of Korea, which suffered a massive contraction from 1996 to 2001).

Factors Driving FDI

Foreign direct investment in the Philippines has been driven by numerous factors, including the country's FDI policy, investment incentives, trade liberalization, exchange rate deregulation, deregulation in other areas, monetary policy, and the labor force.

FDI Policy

During the 1990s, the government expanded areas and industries open to foreign investors. The Republic Act (RA) 7042, known as the Foreign Investment Act of 1991, liberalized foreign investment by allowing foreign equity participation of up to 100 percent in all areas, except those specified in the Foreign Investment Negative List (FINL)—the list of areas restricted to foreign investment. By disclosing the restricted areas, the law provided transparency into the investment regime (Aldaba 1994). It also removed bureaucratic discretion arising from the need to seek government approval of foreign equity above 40 percent. In 1996, further legislation shortening the foreign investment negative list was passed.[1] The liberalized investment environment increased business confidence and the attractiveness of the country to foreign investors. Therefore, FDI inflows starting in 1993 increased, as discussed in the previous section.

The services sector was also opened to foreign investors. In 1993, Executive Order (EO) 215 opened investment in the energy sector to private investors,

---

1. Restrictions on foreign direct investment now include only two areas: Negative List A and Negative List B. Negative List A includes areas (such as the mass media, cooperatives, and small-scale mining) reserved for Filipino nationals by virtue of the Constitution or specific legislation. Negative List B includes areas related to defense, risk to health and morals, and protection of local small and medium-size enterprises. Examples of these investment areas are the manufacture of firearms and gunpowder, and sauna and steam bath houses.

including 100 percent foreign-owned companies, through build-operate-transfer schemes. The Build-Operate-and-Transfer Law (RA 6857) allowed private sector participation in infrastructure and development projects ordinarily undertaken exclusively by the government. In 1994, Republic Act 7721 liberalized the entry of foreign banks. The reform resulted in the entry of ten new foreign banks, thus increasing FDI in the sector. The insurance sector was also liberalized in 1994; it allowed up to 100 percent foreign ownership.

Land ownership, however, is still restricted to Filipinos and corporations that are at least 60 percent Filipino-owned. Foreign investors can only lease commercial land for their operations for fifty years, renewable for an additional twenty-five years.

Investment is promoted through bilateral and regional investment agreements. In 2002, the government signed thirty-four bilateral investment agreements with other countries.[2] The Philippines is also a signatory to the ASEAN Investment Area (AIA) and the Non-binding Investment Principles (NBIP) of the Asia-Pacific Economic Cooperation Conference (APEC).[3]

It is noteworthy that, as part of the efforts to manage the Asian financial crisis in 1997–99, the country's FDI policies were not revised.

Investment Incentives

The government also implements a comprehensive incentive system to encourage foreign investors to locate in the country, although the same incentives are available to local investors. The locational incentives have strategic-trade properties. They are meant to promote exports and encourage use of domestic labor as well as indigenous raw materials. To be eligible for the incentives, an enterprise must meet certain requirements on export-performance, domestic-content, and capital-labor ratio.

The investment incentives include those under the Omnibus Investment Code (OIC) or under the export processing zones (EPZs) and special eco-

---

2. These agreements cover, for example, reciprocal protection and nondiscrimination of investment; free transfer of capital, payments, and earnings; freedom from expropriation and nationalization; and recognition of the principle of subrogation.

3. The AIA requires members of the Association of Southeast Asian Nations to gradually eliminate investment barriers, liberalize investment rules and policies, grant national treatment, and open industries to ASEAN investors by 2010 and to all investors by 2020. The Non-binding Investment Principles of APEC affirm the need to strengthen the efficiency of investment administration, eliminate investment obstacles, and establish a free and open investment in the APEC region.

nomic zones (SEZs).[4] The fiscal incentives include an income tax holiday for a specified number of years, tax and duty exemptions on imported capital equipment and accompanying spare parts, and tax credits and nonfiscal incentives that include employment of foreign nationals in certain positions. Additional incentives are given to firms located in the EPZs and SEZs, like exemptions from payment of local taxes and licenses, except real estate taxes, contractor's taxes, wharfage fees, and export tax. These firms also can deduct from their taxes labor training expenses and organizational and operating expenses.

The investment incentives did not have a significant statistical effect in attracting FDI inflows (Aldaba 1994). However, they did increase the bias toward capital-intensive industries for BOI-approved projects (Austria 1998; Medalla 2002). Nonetheless, the net economic impact of the export processing zones and economic zones was positive (World Bank 1997). This was primarily due to the increased involvement of the private sector in the development of the zones and, hence, lower government expenditures in the zones. During the 1990s, the number of firms operating in the zones and the value of investments generated dramatically increased (Austria 1998).

Trade Liberalization

Tariffs and other barriers to trade were substantially lowered in the 1990s following a three-track approach involving unilateral, regional, and multilateral modalities toward freer trade. Unilateral reform came through the Tariff Reform Program (TRP), which progressively reduced tariffs with the objective of a uniform tariff rate of 5 percent by 2004, and the Import Liberalization Program (ILP), which progressively reduced quantitative restrictions (Table 10.6).

Regional trade liberalization is being accomplished through the ASEAN Free Trade Area (AFTA) and Asia-Pacific Economic Cooperation. AFTA's Common Effective Preferential Tariff (CEPT) scheme of reducing intraregional tariffs to 0 to 5 percent beginning in 1993 enhanced the country's trade policy thrust since the country's CEPT commitments are lower than TRP (Table 10.6). Almost 99 percent of the country's tariff lines were already included in the CEPT in 2001 (Austria 2003b). The country's tariff

4. Export processing zones are owned and operated by the government; production is solely for export. Special economic zones are privately owned industrial estates; production is either for export or the domestic market.

commitments in APEC are the same as its applied tariff rates at the World Trade Organization (WTO).

As discussed earlier, industries that once received high protection registered a decline in their shares in total FDI. Although it was an important factor in attracting FDI during surges in the 1980s, tariff protection was not important in the following decade.

The study by Austria (2003b) shows that the trade policy reforms improved domestic resource allocation, increased productivity, increased the competitiveness of manufacturing industries, increased exports, and increased the integration of the economy in the global market. More significantly, the trade reforms, together with the liberalization of investment, enabled the country to participate in the global production network of multinational companies (MNCs). By lowering barriers to trade and investment, the policy reforms created an environment in which MNCs are freer to choose their crossborder base and conduct their investment activities; they now can exploit factor price differences between the Philippines and other countries in the region.

Table 10.6. *MFN and Preferential Tariff Rates, Philippines, 1993–2001*
(Percent)

	TRP[a]	*WTO*[b]		*APEC*[b]	*AFTA-CEPT*
Year	*Unilateral*	*Bound*[c]	*Applied*[d]	*Applied*[d]	*Preferential*[e]
1993	23.50	n.a.	n.a.	n.a.	n.a.
1994	19.72	n.a.	n.a.	n.a.	n.a.
1995	15.87	n.a.	n.a.	n.a.	n.a.
1996	15.55	n.a.	n.a.	n.a.	n.a.
1997	13.43	32.50	12.11	12.11	9.07
1998	10.69	31.85	9.44	9.44	7.34
1999	9.98	30.05	9.05	9.05	6.83
2000	8.06	27.59	6.92	6.92	4.53
2001	7.71	27.53	6.70	6.70	3.87
2002	6.03	26.74	5.27	n.a.	3.67
2003	6.19	25.80	5.31	n.a.	3.56

n.a. Not available.
a. Based on average nominal tariff rate.
b. Based on Most Favored Nation (MFN) rates.
c. Based on simple average bound tariff rate.
d. Based on simple average applied tariff rate excluding sensitive agricultural products.
e. Based on simple average applied preferential tariff rate.
Source: Tariff Commission.

Exchange Rate Deregulation

The government lifted several restrictions on foreign exchange. Prior to the foreign exchange deregulation in 1992, exporters were required to remit their foreign exchange earnings through the domestic banking system and could retain only 2 percent of their export receipts. After deregulation, exporters could retain 100 percent of their export receipt. Moreover, foreign exchange can now be freely sold and purchased outside of the banking system in the parallel foreign exchange market.

Trade reform in the country had one major shortcoming, however: the lack of adjustment of the exchange rate in the face of trade liberalization. Reductions in tariff protection and import restrictions have not been complemented by a consistent exchange rate policy that favors (or is neutral to) exports. From 1990 to 1996, the real exchange rate continuously appreciated by as much as 25 percent. This prolonged appreciation led to the overvaluation of the currency.

The real appreciation and overvaluation of the currency affect the competitiveness of the tradable and nontradable sectors because they increased the domestic price of nontradables relative to tradables. This had two consequences for the economy. First, it was not consistent with the adjustment called for by trade liberalization. It penalized exports and encouraged the growth of imports. Second, it made investment in the nontradable sector more attractive. As explained in the previous section, the appreciation of the peso prior to the Asian crisis increased investment in public utilities and infrastructure.

The major depreciation experienced during the crisis in 1997 and 1998 was a long overdue correction of the appreciation of the peso. The depreciation of the peso lowers domestic production costs, thus making foreign investment profitable. The continuous depreciation of the peso in the 2000–03 period could increase foreign investment flows into the country.

Deregulation and Privatization

In addition to liberalization of the banking and insurance industries and the opening up of the energy sector to the private sector as discussed earlier, deregulation occurred in the telecommunication sector, maritime industry, and the civil aviation industry. In 1993, the monopoly held by the Philippine Long Distance Telephone (PLDT) company was abolished. In 1994, the entry of operators in the maritime industry was also liberalized, and shipping rates were deregulated. In 1995, restrictions on entry in domestic routes in the civil aviation industry were eliminated, including government controls on airfares and charges. The flag carrier Philippine Airlines (PAL) was also privatized. In 1997, the Metropolitan Waterworks and Sewerage System (MWSS) was privatized.

These reforms in the services sector, together with the opening up of public utilities and infrastructure to private sector investment, helped create an environment conducive to growth and investment. In particular, the reforms in the civil aviation and shipping industries increased competition and efficiency in the industries (Austria 2002b and 2003a).

Macroeconomic Fundamentals

The inflation rate in the Philippines declined from 1990 to 2002 because of tight monetary policy (Figure 10.2). On average, the inflation rate went down from 14.2 percent per year during the 1981–90 period to 8.3 percent per year during the 1990–2002 period. In addition, the interest rate declined from an average of 18.1 percent during the 1981–90 period to 14.1 percent from 1990 to 2002 (Figure 10.2).

Figure 10.2. *Inflation Rate and Interest Rate, Philippines, 1981–2002*

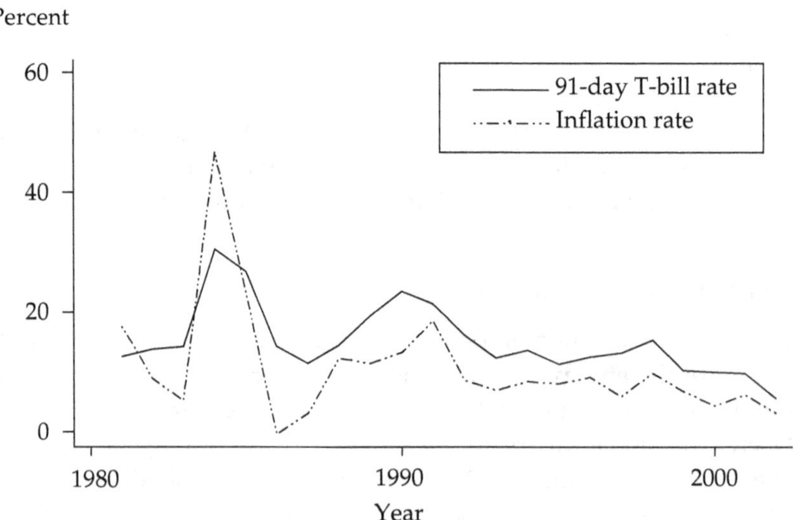

Source: Website of the Bangko Sentral ng Pilipinas.

Labor Force

The country is well known for the positive features of its labor force: high literacy, good quality of secondary education, easy to train, and the ability to speak English. The compensation package is also relatively low for mid-level management and skilled workers. Because of these factors, several surveys have ranked Filipino workers higher than their counterparts in other Asian economies.

Japan's Fujitsu Ltd. has located its hard disk drive assembly plant in one of the export processing zones in the Philippines since 1995; one reason is the availability of skilled workers on a three-shift, twenty-four-hour basis (Kimura 2001). These workers (engineers) command salaries much lower than their counterparts in developed countries. The assembly process is very capital intensive, and given rapid product innovation, quick depreciation of capital is necessary. The availability of cheap skilled labor in the country, however, makes the capital-intensive activity profitable.

Factors Inhibiting FDI

Factors inhibiting FDI in the Philippines include certain aspects of the labor force, the country's logistics, infrastructure, and utilities; supplier industries; the political situation and rule of law; and the legal system and bureaucracy.

Labor Force

The militancy of the labor unions, inadequate technical and vocational skills of the labor force, and the high cost of unskilled labor relative to other countries inhibit the flow of FDI into the country. These factors lessen the attractiveness of the country as an investment site for labor-intensive export-oriented industries This problem is compounded by the fact that labor productivity fails to keep pace with wage increases—unlike in other ASEAN economies where productivity outstrips wage increases (Takeuchi 1995). An important factor contributing to this phenomenon is minimum wage setting, a long-time practice that is becoming more politicized.

In recent years, some shortages in local skills are appearing in the faster growing industries, like electrical machinery (DFAT 1998). The many regulations and laws on labor also restrict FDI.

Logistics, Infrastructure, and Utilities

Infrastructure and utilities in the 1990s improved significantly compared to the 1980s (Serafica 2002). The liberalization and deregulation of the services sector and the opening up of infrastructure to private sector investment are the primary reasons for the notable change. Reforms in the shipping and air transport industries also improved competition and efficiency in these sectors, although much is still desired (Austria 2002b, 2003a).

While much has been achieved, the country's current state of logistics and infrastructure compares poorly with other countries in East Asia. The high infrastructure costs and delays arising from poor logistics lessen the profitability and competitiveness of the country in terms of the global production network of multinational companies. As trade protection has declined drastically worldwide, logistics and infrastructure in the Philippines are becoming even more crucial in determining the attractiveness of the country as an investment site in the region.

Supplier Industries

Local supplier industries in the Philippines are few and still immature. This reduces the local components used by multinational companies and forces them to import their intermediate inputs (Urata and Tullao 1995; Austria and Medalla 1996). For example, Japanese firms procure fewer inputs locally in the Philippines than in any other ASEAN country where they operate (Tecson 1995). This practice makes foreign investors more vulnerable to import price changes induced by exchange rate volatility, and hence can make production costs higher. Over the past few years, attempts were made to overcome this constraint through supplier clustering in the export processing zones and industrial parks. However, the clustering is still limited to foreign suppliers of parts and components. A case study by Kimura (2001) shows that a large number of upstream suppliers from Japan and other developed countries have established their affiliates in the country. However, much is still desired (Box 10.2).

Political Situation and Rule of Law

Throughout the 1990s, the political climate in the Philippines was relatively stable. Starting with the Ramos administration, the political stability improved the business climate and increased the confidence of foreign investors in the economy. However, the EDSA II and III uprisings in 2001

***Box 10.2.** Supplier Clustering in the Philippines*

Wistron Infocom (Philippines), formerly ACER International, is located at the Subic Bay Industrial Park with an investment of US$105 million and total employment of 3,500. The company manufactures motherboards and computer notebooks solely for export. The excellent infrastructure of the industrial park attracted the company's suppliers originally located in Taiwan (China) to also locate in the park. This enabled the company to overcome the nonavailability of local suppliers for its parts and components. The suppliers include the following:

- Catcher Technology Philippines, Inc.—manufacturer of computer and notebook casings and peripherals.
- Comoss Electronics Philippines—manufacturer of cable assemblies, peripherals for computers and computer tables.
- Golden Net International Company, Inc.—printing, designs, binding, packaging, and assembly of manuals.
- Sanyo Denki—manufacturer of cooling systems for computers or micro fans.
- Sankyo Seiki—manufacturer of micromotors for disk drives.
- Shan Soong—manufacturer of plastics moldings.
- Win Cross—manufacturer of di-casting.

These foreign suppliers form an agglomeration inside the park to the advantage of Wistron. When the demand from Wistron is low, they also supply the parts and component requirements of other companies in the country, particularly those located in other industrial parks. The proximity of foreign suppliers to Wistron and other companies in the country not only reduces production costs, but it also increases the value added of exports.

The foreign suppliers have also established ties, through outsourcing, with local suppliers within the vicinity of the industrial park. This linkage, however, is still minimal for two reasons: the poor quality of the output of local suppliers and the more expensive cost of production because of outsourcing. A firm located inside the industrial park is exempted from paying the local taxes, but local suppliers are not exempt. Thus, when part of the production chain is contracted or outsourced to local suppliers, the local taxes are passed on to foreign suppliers in higher prices.

Source: Author's interview with officials of the Subic Bay Metropolitan Authority.

created instability.[5] Political instability hinders FDI, since foreign investors will not risk their capital in an environment that is perceived to be unstable (Aldaba 1994).

5. EDSA stands for Epifanio Delos Santos Avenue. It is the main road that passes through major cities in Metro Manila and the venue of the uprising in 1986 and 2001.

Foreign investors also are scared by problems in the southern part of the country caused by the MILF and the Abu Sayyaf. This is an urgent situation that needs to be addressed.

Legal System and the Bureaucracy

The Philippines ranked very low in the Berlin-based Transparency International corruption index for 2003. The index is based on perceptions by business leaders, academics, and risk analysts of the degree to which corruption exists among public officials and politicians. The maximum possible score is 10 points ("highly clean"), and the lowest score is 0 ("highly corrupt"). The score for the Philippines went down from 2.9 in 2001, to 2.6 in 2002, to 2.5 in 2003 (Doronila 2003). The trend indicates a perception of worsening corruption in the country.

The Philippines is also considered a heavily regulated country by a recent World Bank report (Doronila 2003). It takes fifty days and eleven procedures to start a business, in contrast to the two days required to register a business in developed countries like Australia.

The regulatory environment, particularly with regard to enforcing investment contracts in private infrastructure projects, is highly vulnerable to changes in government administration. For example, the suspension of the nearly completed Ninoy Aquino International Airport 3 (NAIA) is a classic case of market failure due to imperfect contracts (Box 10.3). The case is yet to be resolved. Who wins the case in the end may matter less than the negative message the controversy is sending about the country. The fact that the case arose when the project was nearly complete raises a question about the stability of the country's regulatory environment. By meddling with agreements that were approved by previous administrations, government authorities put investment agreements at risk (Moran 1998). The vulnerability of investment contracts drives investors away.

Impacts of FDI on Economic Development

Foreign direct investment made a significant contribution in Philippine economic development, specifically in capital formation and access to world markets. However, its impact on technology transfer, productivity, domestic linkages, and employment fell short of expectations.

Capital Formation

FDI has contributed to domestic capital formation in the Philippines. The share of FDI in gross fixed capital formation has been increasing, and this has not

Box 10.3. *NAIA 3 and the Philippine Legal System*

The construction of the nearly completed airport terminal NAIA 3 was suspended in November 2002 after President Macapagal-Arroyo declared null and void the contracts granted to Philippine International Air Terminals Co. (Piatco), the company that won the contract to build and operate the airport. The German airport operator Fraport AG and the Filipino Cheng Family are the major investors in Piatco. The nullification is based on the grounds that the contracts contained onerous provisions.

The NAIA 3 project was approved during the Ramos administration, and the contracts awarded to Piatco were modified during the Estrada administration. Fraport alleged that the Macapagal-Arroyo administration demanded changes to the concession agreements that would have impeded the drawdown of long-term financing that it had arranged. Fraport further alleged that when the government did not get what it wanted, it went to the Supreme Court to have the contracts nullified. Fraport is now asking for $425 million in compensation for unrecovered investment and damages from the government for the unfair, arbitrary, and inequitable treatment that resulted in the company's expropriation of its money when the government nullified Piatco's contracts.

Source: Philippine Daily Inquirer, various issues.

been disrupted by the crisis. The average share at 8 percent per year during the 1997–2000 period is higher than the pre-crisis (1991–96) average share at 7.5 percent.

Market Access and Exports

FDI markedly changed the composition of the country's exports in the 1990s. The export performance requirement as a strategy to attract FDI succeeded. Industries that received the bulk of FDI, in particular electrical machinery, apparatus and appliance (SITC 77), have become the country's leading exports. These products increased their share in the country's total exports from an average of 13.2 percent per year during the period 1991 to 1995 to 40.4 percent during the period 1995 to 2000. Office machines and automatic data processing machines (SITC 75) also have made a significant contribution to exports since 1996. On the other hand, the industries that experienced a drop in foreign investment, like garments (SITC 84), registered a decline in their shares in the country's total exports. The share of garments went down from an average of 9.9 percent per year during the period 1991 to 1995 to 7.9 percent per year during the period 1995 to 2000.

The big shift in the composition of exports was driven by intra-industry trade. As pointed out earlier, the country played an important role during the 1990s in the global/regional production network of multinational companies, particularly in the labor-intensive assembly stage of the production process. The country's participation in the global activities of MNCs is also reflected in the increasing intra-industry trade index for manufactures, the index that measures the amount of trade within a commodity (Austria 2003b). The increase in the index between the country and East Asian economies between 1990 and 1999 was highest in the Republic of Korea, Taiwan (China), China, Singapore, and Malaysia. Except for China, these countries registered large increases in their investment in the Philippines in the 1990s.

The country's participation in the global/regional production network of the MNCs increased its market share in the world market in the very same industries and products where FDI was high. The country's market share in the world market for electrical machinery, apparatus, and appliances went up from less than 1 percent during the first half of the 1990s to almost 3 percent from 1995 to 2000 (Austria 2003b). The country's world market share in office machines and automatic data processing machines also improved from less than 1 percent in the 1990–95 period to almost 2 percent in the 1995–2000 period. Even during the Asian crisis, the country's share went up for both groups of products.

Multinational companies generated the bulk of exports from the export processing and special economic zones. The share of exports originating from the zones increased remarkably from 7.1 percent of the country's total exports in 1990 to almost 61 percent in 2001 (Figure 10.3).

Technological Spillover

Although the Philippines has been involved in the global production network of MNCs, technology transfer has been limited. The country's role has been restricted to the labor-intensive, low-skill assembly stages of the production chain of otherwise high-technology products. High-technology manufactures accounted for only 27.6 percent of the country's merchandise exports, a share that was one of the smallest in the region (World Investment Report 1999).

The limited technology transfer, however, is not surprising. The linkage of MNCs to their local suppliers serves as a channel through which technological spillover is achieved. Given the lack of local supplier industries in the country, the opportunity for technology transfer is restricted. The clustering of local suppliers around MNCs is yet to be developed.

Figure 10.3. *Exports and Imports, Export Processing and Economic Zones*

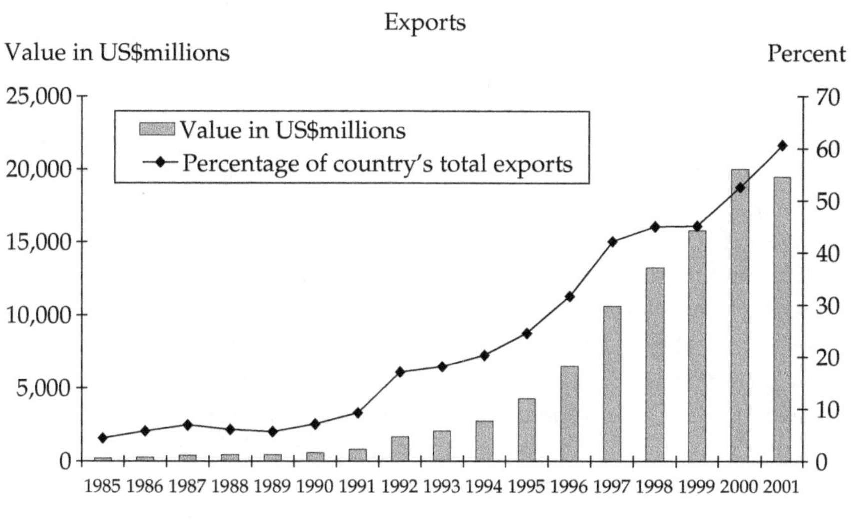

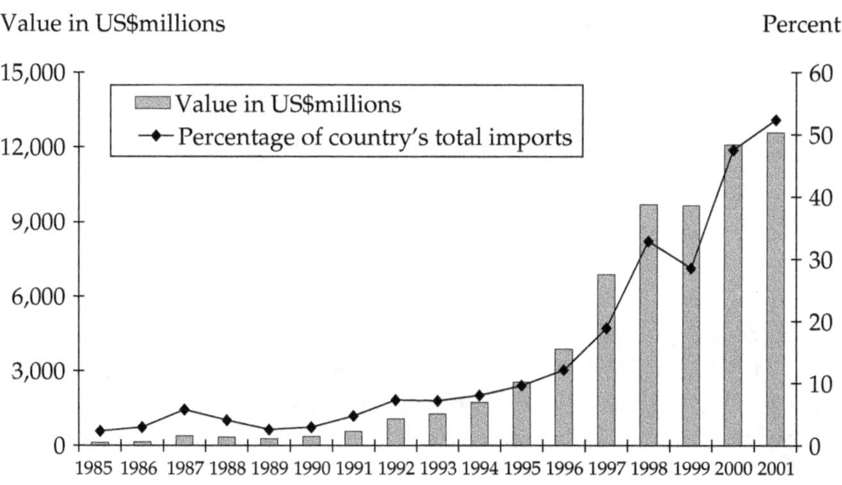

Source: Websites of the Philippine Economic Zone Authority (PEZA), Bangko Sentral ng Pilipinas (BSP), and the Philippine Institute for Development Studies (PIDS).

The limited technological spillover illustrates the differences in expectations of the host country on the one hand and the actual behavior of the MNC on the other. While the Philippine government expects MNCs to bring in technologies with the hope of upgrading the country's technological capability, the MNCs operating in the country, constrained by the lack of supplier industries, are only interested in its cheap skilled labor

Productivity

The study by Austria (2002a) on the determinants of total factor productivity (TFP) in the Philippines for the period from 1960 to 1996 shows mixed results on the role of FDI. FDI has a positive but insignificant effect on the growth of TFP. While it is argued that it takes some time before FDI brings about productivity increases, the inclusion of a one-year lagged FDI as one of the determinants yields a positive, though weak, effect. However, including both total FDI and FDI in manufacturing as determinants results in a significant positive effect of total FDI to TFP growth but a significant negative effect of FDI in manufacturing. For the latter outcome, the paper argued that to the extent that MNCs are oriented toward global rather than local profits, there may be less room for adaptation of technology to the local environment. Likewise, the limited effect of FDI on technology transfer, as discussed above, may help explain the weak effect of FDI on productivity. A study by Okamoto (1996) also showed that the spillover gains on productivity from FDI in the country tended to be weak.

Domestic Linkages

The type of FDI that the country is attracting has given rise to manufacturing exports that are labor-intensive and highly import-dependent and hence no backward linkages occur. There has been a marked increase in the country's imports of electrical machinery, apparatus and appliances from an average of 9.2 percent per year in 1991–95 to 24.3 percent per year in 1995–2000. This is also reflected in the remarkable increase in imports of the export processing zones and economic zones as a share of the country's total imports (Figure 10.3).

The kind of FDI the country is attracting may well be a response to the kind of infrastructure the country has. Poor infrastructure and logistics (particularly in transport, ports, power, and communication) limit FDI to industries that do not have strong linkages with the rest of the economy, since poor infrastructure raises the cost of production, making industries uncompetitive in the world market.

There are risks with continuing the existing pattern of production, investment, and trade—that is, with continued reliance on the low-skill, labor-intensive production segment of the international production chain of multinational companies. First, it necessitates the type of FDI that is highly mobile, since cost advantages can be easily lost due to wage increases or to the emergence of more attractive locations. There will always be competing locations for these types of products if labor in the country becomes relatively more expensive than labor elsewhere. (This is already evident among the country's competitors like China, India, and Vietnam.) Indeed, wage rates in the Philippines are becoming less and less attractive given developing countries' increasing ability to attract this type of FDI. Second, there is the risk of being locked into the current structure if technological upgrading is not pursued. Being involved in labor-intensive production does not automatically result in a spillover of the technology that is required to be able to move up in the production chain. This could hinder the long-term development of the domestic supply capability and hence limit the country's long-term competitiveness.

By developing local supplier industries, the country can make its participation in the international production network more beneficial for the economy. This not only will open channels for technological spillover, but it also will raise the value added of exports.

Employment and Income Distribution

The rapid growth of labor-intensive exports from the export processing and economic zones was accompanied by a concomitant increase in employment. Direct employment from the zones has been continuously growing since 1990. From 35,200 in 1990, it reached 328,400 by 2002 (Figure 10.4).

Nonetheless, as a percentage of total employment in the country, employment in the zones has remained small, contributing less than 1 percent throughout the 1990s (Figure 10.4). The share improved a little in 2000–2, reaching 1 percent.

Trade liberalization in the country caused an increase in the incomes of all resource owners (Lanzona 2002). However, the returns to unskilled labor were lower than to the skilled. This meant that wage inequality widened in recent years, even though all resource owners were actually better off.

Given the close linkage between trade and investment in the country, FDI may have similarly widened the country's income distribution, putting unskilled workers at a greater disadvantage. This is supported by the study of te Velde and Morrissey (2002) of African and East Asian countries, including the Philippines. They concluded that FDI increased wages but more so for skilled workers, thereby expanding wage inequality.

In the Philippines, the problem is that it has a large pool of educated and skilled unemployed workers who compete with the unskilled in

Figure 10.4. *Employment, Export Processing and Economic Zones, 1985–2002*

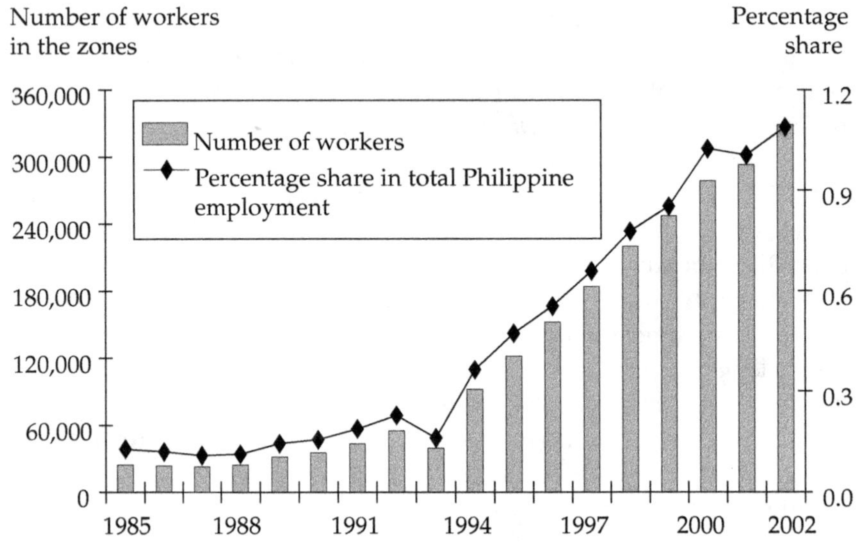

Source: Philippine Economic Zone Authority (PEZA).

labor-intensive industries. Thus, the exports of labor-intensive products keep the unskilled marginalized.

Summary and Conclusions

Foreign direct investment in the Philippines grew much faster in the 1990s than it did in the 1980s. To attract FDI, the government liberalized its investment policies by opening more sectors to foreign investors, and it offered fiscal incentives to investors that met certain requirements on export performance, domestic content, and the capital-labor ratio. Substantial trade policy reforms were also undertaken to improve efficiency in resource allocation and increase the overall competitiveness of the country.

Liberalized policies concerning trade and investment encouraged the establishment of export-oriented operations that are an integral part of multinational companies' international sourcing and production networks. The outcome has been the rapid growth of exports and an increase in the country's world market share but only for selected manufactures (electrical machinery, and office machines and automatic data processing machines). This FDI-induced trade, however, gave rise to exports that are labor-intensive, highly import-dependent, and lack backward linkages with the rest of the economy. In short, the link of MNCs to domestic economic activity is limited. Thus, the value added of the country's major exports is very low.

The apparent lack of local suppliers and poor logistics and infrastructure have been the major impediments to FDI. The lack of local suppliers increases production costs since industries must rely on imported inputs, which are subject to exchange rate volatility. More importantly, the lack of local suppliers limits the channel by which technology can create spillover effects in the rest of the economy. Poor logistics and infrastructure limit FDI to industries with weak linkages with the rest of the economy. They also increase production costs, making industries less competitive in the world market.

The country's experience shows that removing barriers to trade and investment is not enough. For FDI to have a greater impact on the country's economic development, the government needs to adopt an activist approach by addressing the above constraints. In particular, the government needs to develop local supplier industries to increase the domestic content of the operations of MNCs. This will require a package of technical assistance and specialized training to develop skills of local suppliers. In addition, the availability of and access to financing must be ensured.

Likewise, given the regional or global orientation of the operations of MNCs, it is crucial that infrastructure and logistics in the Philippines are oriented to the world-wide management of the value chain. This means reducing power and communication costs, providing adequate port systems, cutting travel time, and offering travel and shipment options. Opening up infrastructure and services to private sector investment is a step in the right direction since the huge budget deficit limits the ability of the government to invest in physical infrastructure and utilities. However, the regulatory and legal environment must reinforce the longer-term stability of investment agreements in private infrastructure projects so as to strengthen the credibility of the policy environment and increase the confidence of foreign investors in the economy. Addressing these issues not only will increase the attractiveness of the country to FDI, but it will also make FDI have a greater impact on the country's economic development.

References

Aldaba, Rafaelita. 1994. "'Foreign Direct Investment in the Philippines: A Reassessment." PIDS Research Paper Series No. 94-10. Makati: Philippine Institute for Development Studies.

Austria, Myrna S. 1996. "The Effects of the MFA Phase Out on the Philippine Garments and Textile Industries." In P. Intal, ed., *The Emerging World Trading Environment and Developing Asia: The Case of the Philippines.* Manila: Asian Development Bank.

———. 1998. "The Emerging Philippine Investment Environment." *Journal of Philippine Development* 24(1): 79–126.

———. 2001. "APEC's Commitments on Investment." In Richard Feinberg and Ye Zhao, eds., *Assessing APEC's Progress: Trade, Ecotech and Institutions*, chap. 3. Singapore: Institute of Southeast Asian Studies.

———. 2002a. "Productivity Growth in the Philippines after the Industrial Reforms." In Josef Yap, ed., *The Philippines beyond 2000: An Economic Assessment*, chap. 6. Makati City: Philippine Institute for Development Studies.

———. 2002b. "The State of Competition and Market Structure of the Philippine Air Transport Industry." In E. Medalla, ed., *Towards a Rational Philippine Competition Policy.* Makati: Philippine Institute for Development Studies.

———. 2003a. "Philippine Domestic Shipping Transport Industry: State of Competition and Market Structure." Research Paper Series No. 2003-02. Makati: Philippine Institute for Development Studies.

———. 2003b. *The Philippines in the New Global Trading Environment: Looking Back and the Road Ahead*. Makati: Philippine Institute for Development Studies.

Austria, Myrna S., and Erlinda Medalla. 1996. *The Study on Trade and Investment Policies in Developing Countries: The Case of the Philippines.* Tokyo: Institute of Developing Economies.

Bautista, Romeo. 2002. "Exchange Rate Policy in Philippine Development." Paper presented during the PIDS-PES Distinguished Speakers' Lecture, Makati, 29 August.

Brewer, Thomas, and Stephen Young. 1999. "Investment Policies in Multilateral and Regional Agreements: A Comparative Analysis." In Thomas Brewer, ed., *Trade and Investment Policy,* vol. 2. Northampton, Mass.: Edward Elgar Publishing, Ltd.

DFAT (Department of Foreign Affairs and Trade of Australia). East Asia Analytical Unit. 1998. *The Philippines beyond the Crisis.* Canberra, Australia.

Doronila, Amando. 2003. "Perceptions of Corruption." *Philippine Daily Inquirer* 15 October 2003. Manila.

Kawai, Masahiro, and Shujiro Urata. 2001. "Trade and Foreign Direct Investment in East Asia." Paper presented during the APEC roundtable, APEC at the Dawn of the 21st Century, organized by the Institute of Southeast Asian Studies, Singapore, 8–9 June.

Kimura, Fukunari. 2001. "Intrafirm Fragmentation: Fujitsu, Ltd.'s Production of Hard Disk Drives." In Leonard K. Cheng and Henryk Kierzkowski, eds., *Global Production and Trade in East Asia,* 289–93. Norwell: Kluwer Academic Publishers.

Lanzona, Leonardo. 2002. "Analysis of Globalization and Wage Inequality in the Philippines: An Application of the Stolper-Samuelson Theory." In Leonardo Lanzona, ed., *The Filipino in a Global Economy.* Makati: Philippine APEC Study Center Network and the Philippine Institute for Development Studies.

Lim, Ewe-Ghee. 2001. "Determinants of, and the Relation between, Foreign Direct Investment and Growth: A Summary of the Recent Literature." IMF Working Paper WP/01/175. Washington, D.C.: International Monetary Fund.

Medalla, Erlinda. 2002. "Trade and Industrial Policy beyond 2000: An Assessment of the Philippine Economy." In Josef Yap, ed., *The Philippines beyond 2000: An Economic Assessment,* chap. 3. Makati City: Philippine Institute for Development Studies.

Moran, Theodore. 1998. *Foreign Direct Investment and Development: The New Policy Agenda for Developing Countries and Economies in Transition.* Washington, D.C.: Institute for International Economics.

Okamoto, Yumiko. 1996. "FDI, Employment and Production Efficiency in the Philippines: Does APEC Liberalization Matter?" Working Paper Series No. 13. Tokyo: Institute of Developing Economies.

Serafica, Ramonette. 2002. "An Assessment of Infrastructure Policies." In Josef Yap, ed., *The Philippines beyond 2000: An Economic Assessment,* chap. 9. Makati City: Philippine Institute for Development Studies.

Stein, Ernesto, and Christian Daude. 2001. "Institutions, Integration, and the Location of Foreign Direct Investment." Paper presented during the 2001 annual meeting of the Boards of Governors, Inter-American Development Bank, and Inter-American Investment Corporation, Santiago, Chile.

Takeuchi, Junko. 1995. "Trends and Prospects for Foreign Investment in ASEAN Countries in the 1990s." *RIM Pacific Business and Industries,* vol. 1, no. 27, pp. 22–41.

Tecson, Gwendolyn. 1995. *Desiderata for Future Philippine-Japan Economic Relations.* Quezon City: School of Economics, University of the Philippines.

UNCTAD (United Nations Conference on Trade and Development). various years. *World Investment Report.* Geneva and New York: United Nations.

Urata, Shujiro, and Tereso Tullao. 1995. *Foreign Direct Investment: Gearing Towards Stronger Philippine-Japan Economic Relations in the 90s and Beyond.* Manila: Yuchengco Center for East Asia, De La Salle University.

te Velde, Dirk Willem, and Oliver Morrissey. 2002. *Foreign Direct Investment: Who Gains?* Briefing Paper. United Kingdom.

World Bank. 1997. *Philippines: Managing Global Integration.* Washington, D.C.

World Trade Organization. 2000. *Report of the Working Group on the Relationship between Trade and Investment to the General Council.* Geneva.

11

The Experience of FDI Recipients: The Case of Thailand

Peter Brimble

It is generally recognized that foreign direct investment has long played an important role in Thailand's economic development. Although several researchers have examined the impact of FDI on levels of investment, long-term capital inflows, exports, and employment generation, very few have looked at the broader effects on human resource development and technology transfer.[1] Even less attention has been given to the effect of FDI on poverty alleviation and community development per se.

Foreign firms often undertake micro-level efforts to provide training, undertake technology transfer, or carry out corporate philanthropy. If these efforts go beyond the basic training or technology transfer that is necessary to enable the foreign company to operate effectively, then they are likely to have a broader positive impact on the country and on the communities in which they are involved. This chapter attempts to go beyond the traditional examination of FDI impacts. It examines the innovative kinds of programs that foreign companies have carried out that go beyond the basic required levels of training or technology transfer. It is with these types of programs that FDI can play a significant catalytic role, from creating stronger linkages with local educational institutes to generating incomes in rural villages through the development of rural industries.

1. Brimble (2003) and Somkiat, Nikomborirak, and Krairksh (2003) represent recent exceptions to this pattern.

Following an overview of the global and national trends that are shaping the business climate for Thailand, the chapter examines recent FDI trends and policies. Findings on the various effects of FDI are then presented. The chapter concludes with recommendations and lessons learned.

Global Trends and Challenges

From both the business and policy perspectives, any strategy toward FDI must be designed to respond to current global and regional trends in economics and business. The following assessment of the most influential global and regional business-related trends attempts to identify the factors that are shaping the environment within which Thailand and Thai firms will need to operate in the future.

Globalization and rapid changes in global markets are forcing Thai-based businesses to increase the scope, pace, and intensity of global business linkages in order for them to maintain their competitiveness and market position. Liberalization is bringing both expanded market opportunities and new sources of technology. Increased FDI has brought greater competition in domestic markets. It also has forced domestic Thai firms to become more competitive or risk losing their market position to foreign firms and products. The rise of global supply chains is drawing Thai firms more closely into international production networks. And finally, the emergence of the knowledge-based economy is creating a new breed of foreign investors. They demand much higher levels of skills and related assets when seeking new investment locations (Box 11.1). Even relatively simple labor-intensive activities require new technologies and upgraded skills with the reorientation of production toward more sophisticated markets and consumers. This means greater challenges for the Thai public and business sectors alike.

The Macroeconomic Picture

Before the economic crisis in 1997, Thailand's economy experienced an average economic growth rate of nearly 8 percent per year from 1960 to 1996. This rapid growth, driven largely by expanding FDI inflows and exports, was accompanied by a shift of the economy toward manufacturing. The manufacturing share of total GDP had reached almost 30 percent by 1995, up from 11.6 percent in 1960.

Table 11.1 shows Thailand's recent key macroeconomic indicators. The 1997 East Asian financial crisis involved the collapse of the financial sector and

Box 11.1. *New Forms of FDI in the Knowledge-based Era*

At the global and regional levels there is a growing segment of "higher quality" FDI for which knowledge-based assets are specifically valued when corporate decisions are made about a range of key issues. These new forms of FDI:

- are increasingly significant in influencing corporate decisions on start-up of production via initial investment in countries like Thailand at the present time; and
- are probably even more important in influencing later decisions on whether to expand and stay in particular countries, to upgrade activities, or to move elsewhere.

In both cases it is evident that corporate decisions are strongly shaped by the extent to which subsidiaries of transnational companies (TNCs) fully utilize strong local bases of skill and knowledge resources, along with associated structures of knowledge-centered institutions—training centers and colleges, knowledge-intensive service suppliers, universities, research institutes, and so forth.

More generally, cutting across locally owned and foreign-owned enterprises, this knowledge-centered resource base is a critically important component of a wider package of assets and resources that contributes to the localized agglomeration of production around particular sectors and supply chains. Whether undertaken by locally owned or foreign-owned firms (and it is frequently a combination of both), these clustered patterns of production are becoming important bases for competitiveness in the global knowledge-economy.

In this context of clustered production and knowledge systems, the "higher quality" forms of FDI differ from those of the past in one fundamentally important respect. Traditional forms of FDI typically employed local labor and exploited local natural resources without adding very much to those traditional determinants of competitiveness. "Higher quality" FDI obviously does draw on the existing local resource-base of skills and knowledge, but it strengthens and extends these knowledge-centered resources—building and renewing the basis for future competitiveness. However, the extent to which this happens varies. It depends partly on differing company-specific strategies and partly on policy measures in host countries.

New forms of FDI that are more knowledge-based and technology-based will undoubtedly demand sophisticated infrastructure and institutional support, not least in the area of information and communications technology. As a result, these forms can only be attracted by countries that have devoted significant attention to developing the "knowledge" sector and its related elements.

Source: Derived from Bell et al. (2003).

an immediate reversal of the high levels of economic growth of the earlier period. GDP fell by 1.4 percent in 1997 and by a further 10.5 percent in 1998.

The economy returned to 4.4 percent growth in 1999, albeit with continuing low capacity utilization and significant disruptions in the real sector,

Table 11.1. *Thailand's Key Macroeconomic Indicators, 1995–2003*

Indicator	*1995*	*1996*	*1997*	*1998*	*1999*	*2000*	*2001*	*2002*	*2003*[a]
GDP at current prices (US$billions)	167.7	181.6	150.3	111.8	122.5	122.6	115.4	126.9	148.5
Real GDP growth rate (%)									
Overall	9.2	5.9	−1.4	−10.5	4.4	4.8	2.1	5.4	6.2
Agriculture	4.0	4.4	−0.7	−1.5	2.3	7.2	3.5	3.0	6.8
Manufacturing	11.9	6.6	1.4	−10.9	11.9	6.1	1.4	6.8	10.2
Construction	6.7	7.0	−25.6	−38.3	−6.8	−9.5	0.3	5.7	3.4
Services and other	8.7	5.4	−0.4	−9.4	0.8	4.1	2.5	4.9	4.3
Sectoral shares of GDP (%)									
Agriculture	9.5	9.5	9.4	10.8	9.4	9.0	9.1	9.4	9.8
Manufacturing	29.9	29.7	30.2	30.9	32.7	33.6	33.4	33.9	35.2
Construction	7.2	7.4	5.7	3.9	3.6	3.1	3.0	3.0	2.9
Services and other	53.4	53.4	54.6	54.5	54.4	54.3	54.5	53.7	52.1
Consumer prices (% change)	5.8	5.9	5.6	8.1	0.3	1.6	1.6	0.7	1.8
Exports									
Value (US$billions)	55.7	54.7	58.4	52.9	56.8	67.9	63.1	66.1	78.4
Growth (%)	24.8	−1.9	3.3	−6.8	7.4	19.5	−7.1	4.8	18.6
Total debt service ratio (%)	11.4	12.3	15.7	21.4	19.4	15.4	20.8	19.6	15.8

a. Preliminary data for the year.
Sources: National Economic and Social Development Board and Bank of Thailand.

and continued to grow by 4.6 percent in 2000. In 2001 GDP growth slowed to 2.1 percent largely as exports fell by 7.1 percent in the face of the global slowdown, especially in electronics products.

In 2002 the economy bounced back impressively with growth of 5.4 percent on the back of strong growth in private sector consumption, private investment, and exports, and in 2003 the economy performed even better (preliminary growth estimates of 6.2 percent). This reflected improved growth in the global economy and stronger commodity prices. Much of the growth of the past few years has been driven by the strong performance of the manufacturing sector, which increased its share of GDP to over 35 percent in 2003. Continuation of the strong performance of the economy will depend to a great extent on the willingness of banks to expand corporate sector lending and whether investors will be attracted by the available returns on investment.[2] Economic growth has been accompanied by price stability and controlled levels of debt.

Given the strong recent performance of the Thai economy and the need for enhanced corporate performance to maintain the economic recovery—not to mention the high growth rates targeted by the present government—FDI remains critical. It is expected to bring in new technologies, to stimulate competitiveness through greater training and domestic capacity development, and to help generate employment and incomes.

The New Industrial Crossroads: Coping with the Knowledge-based Economy

Since the first development plan was implemented in the early 1960s, the Thai government has supported private enterprise and limited government involvement in the economy to the key utility and infrastructure sectors and to maintaining an incentive structure to encourage the private sector. Box 11.2 summarizes five phases of Thailand's industrial development.

Thailand's 9th Economic and Social Development Plan in 2002 identified competitiveness as one of the main pillars; it emphasized the return to longer-term issues. The administration of Prime Minister Thaksin has given increasing attention to industrial development and competitiveness. In early 2002 a high-level National Competitiveness Committee was established to spearhead the government's policy efforts across a wide range of related areas; the Office for the Promotion of Small and Medium-Size Enterprises (SMEs) also was created.

The economic crisis revealed Thailand's deficiencies in research and development, science and technology, and in its overall education system. The focus on developing competitiveness in Thailand is shifting more and more from macroeconomic to microeconomic factors. Thailand is forced to contend with industry's heightened demands for knowledge-based resources. In this climate, the critical challenge will be to develop the innovative capacity to support and commercialize new technologies, products, and processes.

While many factors influence the competitiveness of firms, industries, and economies, knowledge-based capabilities are playing increasingly important roles.[3] Technology is being used more efficiently and creating

---

2. See World Bank (2003) for a discussion of these issues.
3. This section draws on Bell et al. (2003).

Box 11.2. *Phases of Thailand's Industrial Development*

Phase 1 1960s	• Pursued traditional import-substitution strategy; imposed tariffs on imports, particularly on finished products. • Greatly reduced the role of state enterprises and raised investment in infrastructure. • Nurtured the institutional system necessary for industrial development.
Phase 2 Late 1960s to early 1970s	• Experienced balance of payments problems resulting from import-substitution policies. • Imported most components, raw materials, and machinery to support finished product production. • Shifted policy toward export promotion but with continued protection of domestic industry.
Phase 3 Late 1970s to early 1980s	• Continued emphasis on export industries but kept high tariffs on import-competing industries well into the 1990s. • Shifted toward resource-based and labor-intensive industries, as well as toward the promotion of regional industries. • Passed New Investment Promotion Law in 1977 that gave the Board of Investment more power to promote regional industries and address problems faced by investors.
Phase 4 Late 1980s to mid-1990s	• Attempted to promote openness and competitiveness, with progressive liberalization of import tariffs. • Experienced boom conditions, which led to carelessness and complacency in industrial policy making.
Phase 5 After 1997	• Focused initially on short-run financial restructuring and corporate restructuring of the large distressed companies. • Became increasingly aware of the importance of competitiveness and of Thailand's declining position. • Developed the industrial base and exports, largely by supporting the development of various sector and functional institutes.

Source: Author's research.

new products, processes, and organizational systems. Knowledge-based capabilities can be categorized in three ways:

- Technical and managerial/organizational knowledge and skills.
- Design, engineering, and associated managerial capabilities.
- Research capabilities required to underpin technology acquisition, implementation, and development efforts by acquiring or generating new knowledge and understanding.

Bell et al. (2003) conclude that Thailand lags significantly in the knowledge-based assets area. The country's key science, technology, and innovation indicators not only lag behind certain major East Asia competitors, such as Taiwan (China), Singapore, and the Republic of Korea; they also lag behind the levels of indicators for those economies when they exhibited a general economic structure similar to that of Thailand today. Table 11.2 presents a set of selected knowledge-related indicators for Thailand and some regional neighbors. Thailand lags well behind Malaysia in most indicators, particularly R&D and information and communications technology.

Thailand is at a critical crossroads in its quest to build back the competitiveness of its industrial base and cope with the increasingly knowledge-based global environment. The investments in human resources and technology that are required to build the foundations for innovation involve a significant "public good" element, are relatively bulky (or indivisible), and require a long time for the results to become evident. This provides clear economic rationale for a strong government commitment to supporting programs to develop higher quality manpower in science and technology and increased attention to innovation and R&D, both in the public and private sectors. It also places pressures on policy makers to seek ways in which FDI can be leveraged more strongly to support these objectives.

Trends in FDI

FDI inflows into Thailand, as shown in Figure 11.1, were relatively insignificant in the period before 1980. They increased slightly in the early 1980s, but it was not until 1988 that FDI jumped over US$1 billion for the first time following the Plaza Accord, which resulted in currency appreciation in Japan and the newly industrializing economies (NIEs) such as Taiwan (China), Hong Kong (China), and the Republic of Korea. From 1990 to 1996, FDI averaged around US$2 billion per year. In the aftermath of the economic crisis in 1997, FDI increased dramatically as large amounts of FDI flowed in to take over distressed companies. FDI continued to average around US$3 billion until 2001. The year 2002 saw a dramatic fall in FDI to just over one billion in U.S. dollars—the lowest level since 1987. This fall was due in part to the overall decline in global FDI activities and in part to rather large repatriations of funds that were invested following the crisis in 1997 to shore up Thai-based operations. Data from 2003 show a recovery in FDI inflows to US$1.5 billion.

The growth of FDI in the postcrisis period was characterized by a dramatic increase in mergers and acquisitions (M&As) as foreign firms took

Table 11.2. *Selected Knowledge, Technology, and ICT Indicators for Thailand and Regional Neighbors*

Indicator	*Basis*	*Thailand*		*Singapore*		*Malaysia*		*Philippines*		*Vietnam*	
		Score	*Rank*	*Score*	*Rank*	*Score*	*Rank*	*Score*	*Rank*	*Score*	*Rank*
R&D indicators, 2002[a]											
Total expenditure on R&D	% of GDP	0.258	57	2.154	17	0.711	44	0.078	58	n.a.	n.a.
Total expenditure on R&D per capita	US$	5.2	55	455.7	18	27.5	43	0.7	58	n.a.	n.a.
Business expenditure on R&D per capita	US$	2.18	53	279.5	18	18.06	39	0.28	56	n.a.	n.a.
R&D personnel in business per capita[b]	Hard data	0.114	47	2.747	19	0.259	44	0.023	52	n.a.	n.a.
Technology perceptions[c]											
Technological sophistication[d]	Business perceptions	4.1	36	5.8	6	4.7	22	3	70	2.9	71
FDI and technology transfer[e]	Business perceptions	5.2	24	6.3	2	5.8	4	5.4	14	5.3	19
Quality of scientific research institutions[f]	Business perceptions	4.2	43	5.4	10	4.3	36	3	89	4.4	35
Company spending on R&D[g]	Business perceptions	3.6	36	4.8	10	4	25	2.9	68	3.7	30
University/industry research collaboration[h]	Business perceptions	4	25	5.3	3	4	26	2.7	72	3.5	40
S&T manpower[i]											
Quality of the educational system[j]	Business perceptions	3.8	41	6	2	4.5	22	3	65	3.2	62
Quality of math and science education[k]	Business perceptions	4.5	42	6.5	1	4.4	47	2.8	89	3.9	57
Availability of scientists and engineers[l]	Business perceptions	4.4	63	5.7	16	4.4	65	4.1	72	5.3	32
Tertiary enrollment[m]	Hard data	35.27	41	43.82	32	28.16	50	31.21	43	9.73	75
Quality of management schools[n]	Business perceptions	4.6	36	5.7	9	4.2	46	4.8	32	3.2	85

ICT Indicators[o]											
Cellular telephones, 2002[p]	Hard data	26.04	47	79.14	17	37.94	39	17.77	57	2.34	85
Internet users, 2002[q]	Hard data	776	49	5,397	4	3,078	26	438	61	185	76
Internet hosts, 2002[r]	Hard data	11.75	60	479.18	16	31.1	48	3.94	70	0.06	95
Telephone lines, 2002[s]	Hard data	10.5	66	46.36	26	19.16	52	4.17	78	4.51	77
Personal computers, 2002[t]	Hard data	3.98	58	50.83	8	14.77	34	2.75	67	0.98	81
Internet access in schools[u]	Business perceptions	4.6	30	6.6	2	4.3	37	3.5	53	2.9	71

n.a. Not available.
a. Sixty countries are ranked.
b. Full-time work equivalent (FTE) per 1,000 persons.
c. One hundred and two countries are ranked.
d. Your country's position in technology (1 - generally lags behind most other countries, 7 - is among those of the world leaders).
e. FDI in your country (1 - brings little new technology, 7 - is an important source of new technology).
f. Scientific research institutions in your country (1 - nonexistent, 7 - the best in their fields).
g. Companies in your country (1 - do not spend money on R&D, 7 - spend heavily on R&D relative to international peers).
h. In R&D activity, business collaboration with local universities (1 - minimal or nonexistent, 7 - intensive and ongoing).
i. One hundred and two countries are ranked.
j. The educational system in your country prepares for coping with the needs of a competitive economy (1 - clearly no, 7 - clearly yes).
k. Math and science education in your country's schools (1 - lags far behind that of most other countries, 7 - is among the best in the world).
l. Scientists and engineers in your country (1 - nonexistent or rare, 7 - widely available).
m. Gross tertiary enrollment rate, 2000 or most recent year available.
n. Management or business schools in your country (1 - limited or of poor quality, 7 - the best in the world).
o. One hundred and two countries are ranked.
p. Cellular mobile subscribers per 100 inhabitants, 2002.
q. Internet users per 10,000 inhabitants, 2002.
r. Internet hosts per 10,000 inhabitants, 2002.
s. Main telephone lines per 100 inhabitants, 2002.
t. Personal computers per 100 inhabitants, 2002.
u. Internet access in schools (1 - very limited, 7 - pervasive, most children have frequent access).

Source: For R&D indicators, IMD (2004); for technology perceptions, S&T manpower, and information and communications technology (ICT) indicators, World Economic Forum (2003–4).

Figure 11.1. *Thailand's Net FDI Inflows, 1970–2003*

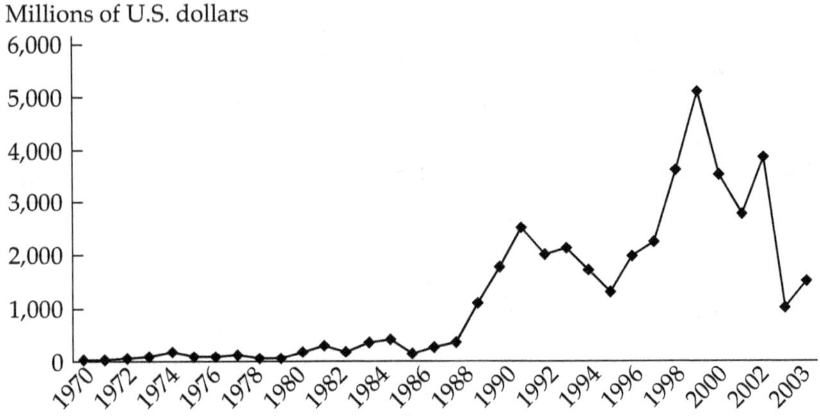

Source: Bank of Thailand.

over Thai companies that faced severe debt and liquidity problems. UNCTAD's *World Investment Report 2000* reported that cross-border M&A sales or M&A FDI in Thailand was about US$0.6 billion in 1997, US$3.2 billion in 1998, US$2.0 billion in 1999, and US$2.6 billion in 2000. These orders of magnitude were confirmed by a firm-level survey on M&A (Brimble and Sherman 1999) that found that a large part of the so-called M&As involved existing foreign investors, mainly Japanese, taking up increasing shares in their local affiliates. Foreign ownership limits were progressively relaxed. This explains, to some extent, the subsequent drop-off of FDI inflows. The contribution of M&A transactions to total net FDI flows has increased from around 50 to 60 percent in 1998–99 to 90 percent in 2000. This massive shift to M&A activities fell almost as quickly as it rose, with much fewer deals and estimated values in 2001 and 2002.

Another casualty of the East Asian financial crisis was Thai outward investment, which had grown strongly in the mid-1990s to peak at almost US$800 million in 1996. It has steadily dropped off to under US$100 million per year in 2001, 2002, and 2003. This is a lost opportunity for Thai firms to enhance competitiveness by taking advantage of more favorable business conditions in other countries.

Table 11.2 shows flows and shares of FDI by sector since 1991. The manufacturing sector has consistently been a large recipient of FDI with a generally increasing share in net FDI flows. The trade sector has also gained share but at a lower magnitude. FDI in financial institutions went up significantly in 1998 to over 16 percent as a result of the increase in limits of foreign participation in the banking sector; in the two previous years, the financial sector accounted for only 3 percent of FDI. Once the banking sector essentially reached its limits for foreign participation, FDI dropped to 7 percent and 5 percent in 1999 and 2000, respectively, and saw net outflows from 2001 to 2003. FDI in real estate peaked at 33 percent of FDI in 1996, but once the property bubble burst in 1996 and 1997, the inflows almost completely dried up before staging a recovery in 2003.

Within the manufacturing sector, the electronics industry consistently attracts large volumes of FDI, amounting to 17.6 percent in 2001. In 2002 and 2003, however, the sector unexpectedly showed net outflows, despite indications that electronics activities as a whole staged a recovery in the early 2000s. For the period from 1998 to 2000, electronics was overtaken by machinery and transport equipment, deriving mainly from the automotive industry; many Japanese automotive parent companies injected capital to assist their subsidiaries and suppliers in Thailand following the crisis. The chemical industry surged in 2000 as a number of local producers restructured; the chemical industry accounted for 13.6 percent of FDI, before completely dropping off in 2001. Some recovery occurred in 2002 and 2003.

Source countries for FDI in Thailand have traditionally included Japan, the United States, Europe, Taiwan (China), Hong Kong (China), and Singapore (Table 11.3). Japan was the largest source of FDI with the exception of 1999 when the United States was number 1, and 2001 and 2002, when large inflows from Singapore dominated FDI inflows. High-profile Singaporean investments took place in banking, telecommunications, and other sectors, and certain foreign investors used their Singapore-based affiliates as vehicles for activities in Thailand. Following a decline in 1999, Japanese FDI increased again in the early 2000s, partly as Japanese firms increased equity shares in local subsidiaries. European investment rose strongly in 1998 and 1999, led by the Netherlands, but fell off rapidly after 2000. FDI by the United States fell dramatically to only 1.5 percent of the total in 2001; net outflows in 2002 and 2003 were substantial.

Investors' interest in Thailand declined following the crisis in 1997 (Tables 11.4 and 11.5). The total planned investment of foreign projects approved by the Board of Investment dropped from almost US$10 billion in 1997 to US$2.3 billion in 2002, the lowest level in many years. The increase in BOI approvals in 2000 and 2001 to around US$5 billion in both years was largely due to an increase in expansion investments of Japanese export-oriented projects that performed well after the baht devaluation. The year 2003

(*Text continues on page 368.*)

Table 11.3. *Net Flows of Foreign Direct Investment in Thailand, by Sector*

Sector	*1991–95*	*1996*	*1997*	*1998*	*1999*	*2000*	*2001*	*2002*	*2003*[a]
A. Flows in millions of U.S. dollars									
Industry	2,836	709	1,818	2,209	1,269	1,813	2,223	514	548
Food & sugar	233	45	226	74	94	94	108	–72	97
Textiles	166	49	41	125	21	29	55	25	31
Metal & nonmetallic	387	113	216	342	262	93	354	91	116
Electrical appliances	1,022	241	602	264	425	298	662	–72	–117
Machinery & transport equipment	352	109	396	661	393	667	433	222	114
Chemicals	544	183	164	225	8	383	57	77	60
Petroleum products	–226	–250	10	329	9	30	277	32	5
Construction materials	55	4	–10	24	38	58	–3	22	–39
Other industries	304	216	173	165	20	161	280	189	281
Financial institutions[b]	664	72	112	842	247	134	–209	–291	–253
Trade	1,591	545	1,035	1,052	1,042	68	956	491	412
Construction	964	70	164	192	–152	–3	–3	0	31
Mining & quarrying	439	19	20	22	–42	–275	518	–97	–14
Agriculture	34	2	1	1	2	0	2	0	16
Services	312	125	292	275	485	449	166	628	13
Investment	59	–22	26	364	571	99	–50	–657	25
Real estate	2,547	753	112	28	149	70	111	25	119
Other industries	–202	–3	47	161	–9	458	159	410	629
Total	9,245	2,271	3,627	5,143	3,562	2,813	3,873	1,023	1,526

B. Flows as a percentage share									
Industry	30.7	31.2	50.1	42.9	35.6	64.5	57.4	50.2	53.6
Food & sugar	2.5	2.0	6.2	1.4	2.6	3.3	2.8	–7.0	9.5
Textiles	1.8	2.2	1.1	2.4	0.6	1.0	1.4	2.4	3.0
Metal & nonmetallic	4.2	5.0	6.0	6.6	7.4	3.3	9.1	8.9	11.3
Electrical appliances	11.0	10.6	16.6	5.1	11.9	10.6	17.1	–7.0	–11.4
Machinery & transport equipment	3.8	4.8	10.9	12.9	11.0	23.7	11.2	21.7	11.1
Chemicals	5.9	8.1	4.5	4.4	0.2	13.6	1.5	7.5	5.9
Petroleum products	–2.4	–11.0	0.3	6.4	0.2	1.1	7.2	3.1	0.5
Construction materials	0.6	0.2	–0.3	0.5	1.1	2.1	–0.1	2.2	–3.8
Other industries	3.3	9.5	4.8	3.2	0.6	5.7	7.2	18.5	27.5
Financial institutions[b]	7.2	3.2	3.1	16.4	6.9	4.8	–5.4	–28.4	–24.7
Trade	17.2	24.0	28.5	20.4	29.3	2.4	24.7	48.0	40.3
Construction	10.4	3.1	4.5	3.7	–4.3	–0.1	–0.1	0.0	3.0
Mining & quarrying	4.8	0.9	0.6	0.4	–1.2	–9.8	13.4	–9.5	–1.4
Agriculture	0.4	0.1	0.0	0.0	0.1	0.0	0.1	0.0	1.6
Services	3.4	5.5	8.1	5.3	13.6	16.0	4.3	61.4	1.3
Investment	0.6	–0.9	0.7	7.1	16.0	3.5	–1.3	–64.2	2.4
Real estate	27.6	33.2	3.1	0.5	4.2	2.5	2.9	2.4	11.6
Other industries	–2.2	–0.1	1.3	3.1	–0.2	16.3	4.1	40.1	61.5

a. Preliminary data for the year.

b. The nonbank sector only.

Note: Direct investment is equity investment plus loans from related companies.

Source: Bank of Thailand, Economic Research Department.

Table 11.4. *Net Flows of Foreign Direct Investment in Thailand, by Country*

Country	*1991–95*	*1996*	*1997*	*1998*	*1999*	*2000*	*2001*	*2002*	*2003*[a]
A. Flows in millions of U.S. dollars									
Japan	1,942	524	1,348	1,485	488	869	1,377	632	687
United States	1,401	429	781	1,283	641	617	57	–239	–179
European Union	998	168	360	912	1,368	507	188	–440	50
United Kingdom	399	57	124	102	186	401	329	223	–78
Germany	150	42	60	100	288	104	33	11	76
France	304	30	3	279	240	27	103	–11	33
Netherlands	149	–41	155	332	643	–73	–375	–744	–12
Newly industrializing economies	3,250	653	877	1,115	899	845	1,928	1,378	802
Republic of Korea	62	25	30	73	6	–5	23	43	27
Taiwan (China)	424	138	134	106	122	159	116	77	83
Hong Kong (China)	1,832	215	442	394	234	333	162	24	131
Singapore	932	275	271	542	538	358	1,627	1,234	561
ASEAN (excluding Singapore)[b]	56	33	27	28	32	29	22	–11	47
Other countries	1,597	464	234	320	134	–54	301	–297	119
Total	9,245	2,271	3,627	5,142	3,562	2,813	3,873	1,023	1,526

B. Flows as a percentage share									
Japan	21.0	23.1	37.2	28.9	13.7	30.9	35.6	61.8	45.0
United States	15.2	18.9	21.5	25.0	18.0	21.9	1.5	–23.4	–11.7
European Union	10.8	7.4	9.9	17.7	38.4	18.0	4.9	–43.0	3.3
United Kingdom	4.3	2.5	3.4	2.0	5.2	14.3	8.5	21.8	–5.1
Germany	1.6	1.8	1.6	2.0	8.1	3.7	0.9	1.1	5.0
France	3.3	1.3	0.1	5.4	6.7	1.0	2.7	–1.1	2.2
Netherlands	1.6	–1.8	4.3	6.5	18.1	–2.6	–9.7	–72.7	–0.8
Newly industrializing economies	35.2	28.8	24.2	21.7	25.2	30.0	49.8	134.7	52.6
Republic of Korea	0.7	1.1	0.8	1.4	0.2	–0.2	0.6	4.2	1.8
Taiwan (China)	4.6	6.1	3.7	2.1	3.4	5.7	3.0	7.5	5.4
Hong Kong (China)	19.8	9.5	12.2	7.7	6.6	11.8	4.2	2.3	8.6
Singapore	10.1	12.1	7.5	10.5	15.1	12.7	42.0	120.6	36.8
ASEAN (excluding Singapore)[b]	0.6	1.5	0.7	0.5	0.9	1.0	0.6	–1.1	3.1
Other countries	17.3	20.4	6.5	6.2	3.7	–1.9	7.8	–29.0	7.8

a. Preliminary data for the year.
b. The Association of Southeast Asian Nations.
Note: Direct investment is equity investment plus loans from related companies. The data cover investment in the nonbank sector only.
Source: Bank of Thailand, Economic Research Department.

Table 11.5. *Foreign Investments in Thailand Approved by the Board of Investment*
(US$millions)

Country	*1997*		*1998*		*1999*		*2000*		*2001*		*2002*		*2003*[a]	
	No. of projects	*Total investment*	*No. of projects*	*Total investment*	*No. of projects*	*Total investment*	*No. of projects*	*Total investment*	*No. of projects*	*Total investment*	*No. of projects*	*Total investment*	*No. of projects*	*Total investment*
Total foreign investment[b]	516	9,614	485	6,161	517	3,599	761	5,290	575	4,711	483	2,317	563	5,123
Foreign-owned investment[c]	188	1,175	204	1,932	264	2,043	380	3,065	315	2,397	273	1,243	305	2,518
Share of total[d]	36.4%	12.2%	42.1%	31.4%	51.1%	56.8%	49.9%	58.0%	54.8%	50.9%	56.5%	53.6%	54.2%	49.1%
Asia														
Japan	220	4,706	158	1,307	188	715	282	2,671	257	1,873	215	893	260	2,376
Asian NIEs														
Taiwan (China)	56	380	69	242	86	209	120	439	50	153	41	63	57	327
Hong Kong (China)	9	44	16	122	25	50	31	155	20	218	5	37	14	87
Rep. of Korea	20	126	13	44	19	26	17	35	21	32	33	75	40	84
Singapore	43	1,882	49	257	52	185	84	495	51	202	40	305	36	162
China	1	1	2	2	7	15	8	9	12	195	7	9	11	35
Malaysia	33	150	21	100	27	90	43	152	29	627	23	39	30	105
Indonesia	3	18	2	12	5	30	4	32	2	8	2	3	2	13
Philippines	0	0	0	0	1	2	0	0	0	0	1	0	3	16
India	5	6	10	245	6	36	11	253	12	44	5	2	11	85

North America	61													
United States	4	2,817	62	450	53	1,226	72	939	40	902	37	258	40	592
Canada	6	10	9	64	3	688	6	27	5	8	2	2	2	6
Australia	16	151	13	67	10	31	21	67	21	136	11	17	9	120
All Europe	95	2,831	123	3,245	83	900	144	775	87	585	78	475	70	682
United Kingdom	24	907	33	758	17	104	38	145	18	109	15	261	14	494
Germany	19	300	22	208	12	49	39	159	24	308	19	50	12	10
Switzerland	10	29	11	37	10	84	10	57	7	57	12	87	7	22
France	9	54	12	4	11	75	13	27	11	29	9	13	13	32
Belgium	3	55	8	23	7	23	2	8	7	9	3	2	5	11
Italy	7	30	4	19	3	3	9	11	2	14	2	15	3	2
Netherlands	12	136	22	2,127	18	595	21	157	10	83	10	20	5	20
Exchange rate:														
Baht/US$		31.37		41.40		37.80		40.20		44.50		43.00		41.50

a. Preliminary data for the year.
b. Projects with FDI of 10 percent or more.
c. Projects with FDI of 100 percent (totally foreign owned).
d. Projects with FDI of 100 percent as a share of total projects with FDI of 10 percent or more.
Note: Firms with investment from more than one country are double counted. Foreign projects are those with a foreign component of 10 percent or more.
Source: Board of Investment. Exchange rate: Bank of Thailand.

also saw a resurgence in investors' interest; BOI approvals jumped back to US$5 billion, largely reflecting an increase in investment project proposals from Japan.

The Evolution of Thailand's FDI Policy

Foreign direct investment policies in Thailand date back more than three decades to a time when there was very little industry, primarily simple assembly activities, and the domestic marketplace was relatively small. Therefore, capital goods had to be imported, as did many raw materials and components, with the obvious exceptions of agriculture and minerals. The result was foreign exchange losses and balance of trade deficits.

The revisions to Thai investment promotion schemes corresponded closely with changes in the nation's overall macroeconomic situation and responded to the national development objectives outlined earlier. Although the Board of Investment is the agency responsible for attracting FDI, other government agencies periodically influence the investment environment. The era of investment promotion started in the early 1960s when the BOI was established under the Investment Promotion Act B.E. (Buddhist Era) 2499. BOI policies evolved from import substitution in the early 1960s, to promotion of manufactured exports from the early 1970s to the late 1980s, to industrial decentralization beginning in the early 1990s.

Investment promotion policy remained relatively unchanged from 1993 until the 1997 financial crisis. To restore the lost confidence of investors, the government worked hard to increase revenues, reduce spending, strengthen the country's legal and regulatory framework, and reduce foreign currency losses. In 1997 and 1998, the BOI adopted a number of short-term measures to stimulate investment and exports of Thai-manufactured goods. It relaxed zoning requirements for export projects, permitted duty-free imports of replacement machinery used by exporters, and allowed projects to increase their production capacities more easily so that they could achieve economies of scale and find new markets. Existing joint venture projects could, with the Thai partners' consent, raise capital to ease financial difficulties and become majority or 100 percent foreign-owned companies.

In August 2000 the BOI introduced a new incentive package that continued to emphasize industrial decentralization. The new policies allowed foreign investors to own a majority of shares, or all of the shares, in manufacturing projects, lifted local content and export requirements to comply with World Trade Organization (WTO) rules, and required ISO 9000 certificates to be obtained within two years of start-up for projects with investment capital over 10 million baht (excluding cost of land and working capital) to promote efficiency and competitiveness. In addition, promoted projects were required to prove that they had complied with the promotion conditions before enjoying tax holidays. In December 2002 the Investment Promotion Law was revised to limit the amount of tax holidays enjoyed by each project to the amount of investment capital. These "control" type of measures were aimed at minimizing tax losses from investment promotion to strengthen the country's fiscal position.

Thailand's Current FDI Policy

The Board of Investment in 2003–4 introduced the following new measures to enhance the competitiveness of Thai industries. First, the BOI relaxed location conditions attached to the list of activities eligible for investment promotion in order to encourage cluster development. With the exception of six activities that have perceived environmental problems, investors can locate new facilities or expansion projects anywhere in the country.

Second, the BOI identified the need for customized incentive packages to create a more suitable balance between the needs of investors and their economic contribution to the country. In this regard five industries have been targeted for "aggressive promotion": the agro-industry, the fashion industry, the automotive industry, the information and communications technology (ICT) industry, including electronics, and high value-added services.

The BOI recently offered the agro-industry these incentives: exemption from corporate income tax for eight years and exemption from import duty on machinery for activities that enhance the capabilities of companies across the agro-industry supply chain, including postharvest and farm management activities, regardless of their locations. The BOI aims to support activities that will build off the existing strengths of the agricultural sector. The Board wants to help the sector move to higher value-added agro-processing by improving product quality, yields, and sustainability.

To help Bangkok achieve its goal of becoming a fashion city, the BOI added design services and design centers as activities eligible for investment promotion; maximum tax incentives encourage foreign investors to help Thai artisans develop their design skills and the quality of their products and break into international markets. Thai craftspeople are well respected for their artisanship, yet there are more opportunities to improve product design and build up Thai products and brands in leather, garments, and jewelry.

The automotive industry is one of Thailand's fastest growing sectors. Thailand is now home to 15 assemblers, and there are 2,000 automotive parts companies currently located in Thailand, including 400 first-tier component manufacturers. A special tax incentive package has been introduced by the BOI to support this industry and promote automotive clusters. Extra tax incentives are offered to projects, with investment of at least 10 billion baht, that are submitted by a group of investors comprising vehicle assembly and manufacturing of vehicle parts and engines.

With respect to information and communications technology, the BOI recently announced new policies to promote the entire electronics supply chain, not only contract manufacturing. Many transnational corporations have subcontracted manufacturers in Thailand to produce brand-name goods. The BOI aims to encourage them to further invest in R&D, engineering, training, and marketing. The goal is to increase local value added and to improve the capabilities of local firms with whom multinational companies have subcontracting relationships. Companies that do so and that have total annual sales of at least 2.5 billion baht will receive the same incentives as their contract manufacturers. In 2004 the BOI introduced a new incentive package for the computer hard disk drive industry. In addition, the BOI is in the process of revising incentives and conditions for the software industry, including facilitating foreign information technology (IT) personnel to come to work in Thailand.

The last target industry is a collection of service activities that are considered to be high value-added industries. They include regional operating headquarters, the entertainment industry, the printing and publishing industries, healthcare / long stay, call centers, etc.

Regional Operating Headquarters (ROH) can receive considerable tax and nontax incentives. The term *Regional Operating Headquarters* is defined as a company legally registered in Thailand that provides managerial, administrative, and technical services to its affiliates, with paid-up capital of at least 10 million baht, with overseas services and subsidiaries in at least three countries, and with overseas earnings of at least 50 percent of total revenues. Incomes from their services to affiliates will be subject to a corporate income tax rate of 10 percent instead of a normal rate of 30 percent, with no time limits, and expatriates working for ROHs will pay a personal income tax rate of 15 percent for the first two years instead of a much higher progressive schedule. The nontax incentives, such as eligibility to own land, repatriate foreign currency, and bring in foreign experts, also are considerable.

In order to make Thailand a center for printing and publishing industries in ASEAN (the Association of Southeast Asian Nations), the Board of Investment intends to promote printing and publishing industries as a cluster. It has established a printing / publishing industrial zone; projects related to printing and publishing—such as advertising, artwork, architecture services, and music—will be promoted and will receive special tax incentives as a package in order to create stronger linkages between these industries.

Although there are specific policies for the above activities, the BOI's overall FDI policy will remain the same. Nontargeted sectors will not see any backtracking, nor are there any plans to reduce incentives. The intention apparently is to augment existing policy, not replace it. However, there was, for the first time, a systematic attempt at investor targeting, both at the sector and at the firm levels. At the sector level, previous efforts had focused only on the production of sector-specific investment promotion materials and sector workshops in the investing countries. Now, prompted by the focus of the government on the five sectors noted earlier (the agro-industry, the fashion industry, the automotive industry, the ICT industry, including electronics, and high value-added services), the BOI is moving much more aggressively to develop customized packages for the targeted sectors. Since late 2003 the BOI has pursued a new approach at the firm level with regard to these sectors. It involves the appointment of senior executives to cover the major investing countries and the recruitment of investment consultants in the major countries to identify and target key potential investors in the five sectors. It is too early to judge the effectiveness of this new approach.[4] The approach reflects global tendencies in best-practice investment promotion agencies[5] and also the advice of many former advisors to the BOI.

On the technology front, in a welcome departure from existing policies, the BOI has recognized that skill development, technology transfer, and innovation (STI) are critical to Thailand's industrial competitiveness. Previously, foreign investors were required to register technology transfer agreements with the Bank of Thailand to be able subsequently to make the payments abroad called for in the agreements. But liberalization of the capital account rendered that policy obsolete. The BOI itself had discussed the possibility of introducing technology requirements in the late 1980s and early 1990s, but, in the face of strong opposition from industry associations, these plans were shelved.

---

4. One of the new sectors targeted for special treatment is the hard disk drive industry. This follows years of relatively passive government attention to the industry. In the second quarter of 2004, following the introduction of a new incentive package, the three major producers in Thailand—Seagate Technology, Hitachi Global Storage Technologies, and Western Digital —announced expansion projects totaling more than US$600 million (*Bangkok Post* 2004). While the causality is not solid, company interviews indicate that the industry appreciates the recent attention given to it by the government, not to mention more generous tax incentives.

5. See UNCTAD (2002) for more details.

In early 2004, the BOI adopted a series of "carrot" rather than "stick" measures to promote investment in skill development, technology transfer, and innovation. First, the BOI will offer additional tax incentives to activities with STI elements that need to innovate in order to remain competitive in global markets. The STI criteria include:

- R&D or design expenditures of not less than 1 to 2 percent of annual total sales in the first three years;
- recruitment of not less than 1 to 5 percent of the total workforce, within the first three years, of S&T personnel with a minimum of a bachelor's degree in science, engineering, or other technology, R&D, or design-related fields;
- training expenditures for staff of not less than 1 percent of total payroll within the first three years; and
- cost of programs to develop vendors or to support related educational institutes of not less than 1 percent of annual total sales within the first three years.

Projects that meet each of these criteria will receive one additional year of a corporate income tax holiday. The cap on the total amount of tax incentives will not apply. The total corporate income tax holiday cannot exceed eight years. In addition, machinery imported for use in these projects will be exempt from import duty.

Second, projects in eight activities that directly support the development of STI in Thailand will be treated as priority activities and will receive maximum incentives regardless of location. Benefits for these projects will not be subject to the cap on incentives, and imports of machinery will be duty-free. The eight activities are as follows:

- manufacture of medical supplies or medical equipment;
- manufacture of scientific instruments;
- electronic design;
- research and development (R&D);
- scientific laboratories;
- calibration services;
- human resources development (HRD); and
- manufacture and repair of aircraft.

Third, in order to promote STI infrastructure and support facilities, science park projects will be treated as priority activities and will receive maximum incentives, including:

- eight-year corporate income tax holiday, with no cap on benefits;
- 50 percent reduction of corporate income tax for an additional five years after the expiration of the income tax holiday;
- duty-free import of machinery; and
- maximum tax incentives for S&T activities that are located in the promoted science parks.

Apart from promoting FDI, the BOI has recognized the need to create new small and medium-size enterprises (SMEs)—majority Thai-owned companies with fixed assets not exceeding 200 million baht or employees not exceeding 200 persons—and to strengthen the existing SMEs. Special incentives have been offered to those in agro-industry and the manufacturing of creative or lifestyle products (products intensive in design). The minimum capital requirement has been reduced from one million baht to half a million baht, and maximum tax incentives are given with no cap on benefits.

The Effects of FDI

This section considers the quantitative and qualitative effects of FDI under the following broad headings: conventional impacts, employment and poverty alleviation, skills and technology development, and corporate philanthropy and related activities.

Conventional Impacts

A number of studies have considered the impacts of FDI on key macroeconomic variables of the Thai economy. The effects on growth, exports, productivity, wages, and business practices are described below.

Somkiat, Nikomborirak, and Krairksh (2003) cite two studies that indicate the positive impacts of FDI on the growth of the Thai economy. Archanun (2003) confirmed that FDI had a positive influence on growth in the presence of an open trade regime. Kinoshita (2001) went further and showed that a 10 percent increase in FDI will generate an increase of 44.3 percent in fixed capital formation, an increase of 2.0 percent in imports, and an increase of 2.3 percent in exports in the peak period. This, in turn, would yield an increase in GDP of 1.6 percent, indicating that FDI is a major driver of economic growth in Thailand.

Since the early 1980s, FDI has been a major contributor to exports, especially in the higher technology product areas such as electronics. Sibunruang (1986) and more recent studies indicate that foreign firms play a major role in manufactured exports, accounting for more than 30 percent of the total and a much larger share in certain high-technology sectors. Few researchers have examined this issue in recent years. However, using estimates of TNC shares of plant-level output and of company sales presented in Ramstetter (2003), it is possible to make some estimates of the dominant role played by foreign investment in generating exports from Thailand (see Table 11.6).

Transnational corporations contributed around 60 percent of total manufacturing exports before the financial crisis and roughly 70 percent after the crisis in the year 2000. The contribution of TNCs to exports is higher than the overall TNC share in output or sales in 2000. The Electric, Office and Computing Machinery category has become more and more important. It includes the high-technology and high-growth sectors of computer disk drives, integrated circuits, and consumer electronics, all of which are dominated by foreign investors.

With regard to productivity, the evidence is mixed. Ramstetter (2001) shows that differences in productivity levels between FDI and local firms were not as great as might have been expected. According to Dollar et al. (1998), foreign firms utilized labor and capital 50 percent more efficiently than Thai firms on average, although there was a group of highly productive Thai firms that did perform as well as their foreign counterparts.

Significant wage differentials existed between foreign and local companies both before and after the economic crisis, with the magnitude of the difference increasing over time (Matsuoka 2001). Foreign firms paid nonproduction workers 20 and 28 percent higher wages in 1996 and 1998 respectively, and production workers 8 and 12 percent higher wages.

The rapid influx of FDI in the period following the economic crisis brought with it significantly improved governance and business practices in certain sectors. In the banking sector, for example, the newly formed foreign banks brought with them better prudential practices with regard to the extension of loans, better procedures for extending loans to projects based on income projections rather than the simple asset-based lending of the past, and much better practices with regard to servicing clients. In the retail sector, although the influx of foreign players after the crisis created serious tensions with the local retailers, the price and quality of products provided to Thai consumers greatly improved.

Employment and Poverty Alleviation

The rate of unemployment and percentage of population living under the poverty line move in line with each other; when one goes down so does the

Table 11.6. *Transnational Corporations' Contribution to Exports from Thailand*

	Share of foreign TNCs				*Export values (US$millions)*		
	Plant gross output		*Large-firm sales*				
Sector	*1996*	*2000*	*1996*	*2000*	*1996*	*2000*	*2003*
Total manufacturing	56.79	59.93	51.65	61.01	45,646	59,673	68,853
Food and beverages	27.88	36.84	20.83	22.03	3,617	3,282	3,721
Textiles and apparel	54.10	49.95	43.44	47.38	5,471	5,597	5,470
Chemicals	56.16	59.40	62.61	57.98	1,265	2,851	2,847
Electric, office and computing machinery	90.68	93.49	86.00	92.32	18,652	26,848	29,160
General and transportation machinery	84.41	91.53	74.49	87.99	747	2,535	4,137
Other manufacturing	42.81	50.81	41.25	50.41	15,893	18,560	23,518

	1996		*2000*		*2003*[a]	
Estimates of TNC exports (US$millions)	*Plant gross output*	*Large-firm sales*	*Plant gross output*	*Large-firm sales*	*Plant gross output*	*Large-firm sales*
Total manufacturing	29,027	27,076	42,549	41,401	48,792	47,478
Food and beverages	1,008	753	1,209	723	1,371	820
Textiles and apparel	2,960	2,377	2,796	2,652	2,732	2,592
Chemicals	711	792	1,693	1,653	1,691	1,651
Electric, office and computing machinery	16,914	16,041	25,100	24,786	27,262	26,921
General and transportation machinery	630	556	2,320	2,231	3,787	3,640
Other manufacturing	6,804	6,556	9,430	9,356	11,949	11,855
TNC share of total manufacturing exports	63.6%	59.3%	71.3%	69.4%	70.9%	69.0%

a. Based on foreign TNC shares of 2000.

Note: See the discussion of plant gross output and large-firm sales in Ramstetter (2003). These in-sample shares are probably much larger than foreign TNC shares of all firm revenues in Thailand because these samples exclude many small firms that are predominantly non-TNCs. It is likely, however, that the smaller firms do not export that much.

Sources: For shares of foreign TNCs, Ramstetter (2003, Table 3); for export values, Bank of Thailand. Plant gross output is based on data from the National Statistical Office.

other. Accordingly, FDI can have a direct impact on poverty by increasing the total number of employed persons and by concentrating those jobs in areas of mass unemployment or low incomes. However, FDI can also have an indirect effect on poverty alleviation through indirect employment generation. Indirect employment is created through vertical or horizontal linkages, and, in certain sectors or activities, one direct job may generate many more indirect jobs.

Foreign direct investment may play a significant role in generating both direct and indirect employment opportunities, and hence in reducing poverty. Foreign investors' decisions on location and on technology (that is, how labor-intensive a production method to use) are determined largely by profit motives, however. The decisions represent a response to the cost and incentive structure of a particular investment climate; the impact on poverty is incidental to the decision to invest. The impacts of FDI on poverty are likely to be greater when regional poverty implies lower wages, and therefore lower costs of production, and when government subsidies to help poor regions affect incentives positively.

Direct employment by foreign investors in the manufacturing sector alone amounted to almost 800,000 persons in 1997.[6] Between 1985 and 1997, foreign investors directly accounted for 607,000 additional manufacturing jobs of a total increase of 2.6 million manufacturing workers over the same period. This amounts to 24 percent of the additional industrial sector labor force. Clearly, foreign investors played a major role in bringing Thailand's labor force to higher levels of sophistication and productivity.

With regard to the distribution of employment by location over time, there was a steady move over time from Bangkok and the surrounding provinces to Zone 2 in the 1971–80 period and then on to Zone 3 in subsequent years.[7] The share of Zone 1 in the employment generated by foreign

---

6. This section draws on Brimble et al. (1999). In order to measure the contribution of FDI to employment in Thailand, a database of 1,901 foreign firms in the manufacturing sector was constructed from a variety of sources: the project-level database of the BOI, a factory directory with comprehensive employment and location information, and a database on firms operating in the Eastern Seaboard of Thailand compiled for the BOI. Information on employment in foreign-owned service firms and other nonmanufacturing firms was difficult to obtain, so these firms were not included in the analysis. It was deemed unlikely that they generated significant employment, in any case.

7. See the BOI website for the definitions of the Zones. Zone 1 is Bangkok and the five surrounding provinces; Zone 2 is the provinces around that; and Zone 3 is the rest of the country.

firms declined sharply from 97.1 percent for those starting up before 1970 to 26.9 percent for those starting up in the 1991–98 period. Conversely, the employment share of Zone 3 increased from 2.9 percent to 37.4 percent for the same time periods. The generation of numerous relatively high-paid jobs by foreign investors in Zone 3 will have affected the poverty levels in those areas, both in terms of direct income generation and the additional spillover effects.

The indirect employment effects were examined in principle by estimating indirect employment multipliers from an input-output table. In 1997 the direct employment of 789,736 persons resulted in the additional employment of around 1.6 million persons. Overall, the employment effects of FDI, including direct and indirect employment, accounted for around 7.4 percent of the total labor force in Thailand in 1997 of around 32 million persons.

Of the total nationwide employment in manufacturing in 1997 of around 4.644 million persons,[8] direct employment by foreign firms covered in the database accounted for 17 percent. This represented a considerably more dominant position in manufacturing by foreign firms than in 1985, when they accounted for only 8.8 percent of total manufacturing sector employment.[9]

The rapid surge of FDI in the late 1980s and early 1990s is reflected in the FDI employment figures of 1997. Foreign investors accounted for a much greater relative percent of additional manufacturing employment than did local firms. Of an increase of 2.577 million manufacturing workers over the 1985–97 period, FDI directly accounted for 24 percent or 607,000 workers. FDI was clearly a driving force in the industrialization of the Thai labor force.

Skills and Technology Development

While less easy to measure quantitatively, there are numerous indications that foreign investors have made a contribution, and probably an increasing contribution in recent years, to the levels of skills and technology in the Thai industrial sector. The International Drive Equipment and Manufacturers' Association (IDEMA) and its high-technology training programs have brought together the computer disk drive industry and the Asian

---

8. These data are derived from the National Statistical Office Labor Force Surveys of February 1997 and August 1997.

9. See Sibunruang and Brimble (1988). In 1985 direct employment by foreign firms amounted to 182,655 persons and indirect employment 408,048 persons for a total employment of 590,703 workers.

Institute of Technology; state-of-the-art Certificates of Competence in Storage Technology are now awarded. The Board of Investment's innovative programs have leveraged engineering resources from selected foreign investors to develop curricula for certain electronics and automotive training courses at the Department of Vocational Education. The Ayutthaya Technical Training Center (ATTC), a joint venture of the Hi-tech Industrial Estate and the King Mongkut Institute of Technology North Bangkok (KMITNB), has facilitated the recruitment of skilled workers of industries in the Hi-tech Industrial Estate and nearby and provided training. And, to cite a final example, the Thai-German Institute (TGI), with funding from both governments, has been active in operating a training facility in the Eastern Seaboard area. German companies, which have sent experienced staff to help develop a core group of permanent trainers, donate most of the modern equipment used in TGI.

At the firm level, there are also a number of positive stories. Toyota Motor Thailand (TMT) has been very active in the development of corporate training programs and linkages with local universities. AMD in the integrated circuit industry has funded the development of a Bangkok primary and secondary school near its factory. In addition, the company has provided more than fifty scholarships to technical institutes in Thailand. Seagate Technology has developed an extremely ambitious program of cooperation with local universities. A customized automation training program at a number of local universities trains automation engineers as part of Seagate's drive toward automation. Working with two Thai-based institutions, Seagate Technology is developing curricula for new courses and then providing instructors to teach these courses. It also is donating a research laboratory to Khon Kaen University.

In technology development and technology transfer, positive activities include:

- foreign investor participation in the Board of Investment's BUILD program, where a number of major TNCs have played an important role in strengthening links with Thai suppliers through the BOI's vendor-meet-supplier activities; and
- vendor development programs in the automotive industry, especially among the major Japanese assemblers.

According to a recent survey of R&D and innovation expenditures by Thai-based firms (Brooker Group 2003), the levels of "knowledge-expenditure intensity" did not differ substantially between foreign controlled firms and locally controlled firms. Table 11.7 presents a tabulation of knowledge intensities by ownership and size of firm. Overall the ratios are rather similar. Foreign controlled firms report a slightly higher level than locally controlled firms (0.97 compared to 0.87), while exhibiting certain differences according to firm size: small Thai-controlled firms undertake much greater levels of knowledge expenditures, while medium-size firms show much higher levels for foreign controlled firms. Because of the small sample sizes (around eighty-eight firms), strong conclusions cannot be made about the role of foreign firms in the knowledge resources area, although the results in Table 11.7 do not indicate a very strong role.

A recent survey of the computer hard disk drive (HDD) industry also generated mixed indications with regard to the technology activities of foreign owned firms in Thailand. [10] Figure 11.2 is based on the technology capability definitions in Table 11.8 and on detailed interviews with ten major companies in the HDD sector. The research exercise measured the technological capabilities in five broad areas and at three different levels.

The firms exhibited strong capabilities in investment, process development, and industrial engineering, areas that are required to support their manufacturing operations in Thailand. The firms showed much weaker capabilities in product engineering and innovation, with some indications that American firms had gone much further in building these capabilities in their Thai operations than had firms that were not American. The firms' capabilities in linkage development were very weak; interest was strong in

Table 11.7. *Average Knowledge Expenditures/Sales Ratios*

No. of employees	*Local companies*[a]	*Foreign companies*[b]	*Total*
Fewer than 50 employees	1.38	0.33	0.98
Between 50 and 200 employees	0.83	1.71	1.21
More than 200 employees	0.81	0.78	0.80
Total	0.87	0.97	0.91

a. With Thai ownership of 70 percent or more.
b. With foreign ownership of more than 30 percent.
Note: Knowledge expenditures are the sum of spending on R&D and innovation activities.
Source: Calculated from the 2002 R&D/Innovation Survey.

10. This section is based on work by Asia Policy Research and the Asian Institute of Technology being carried out for the Thai National Science and Technology Development Agency.

Figure 11.2. *Technological Capabilities in Thailand's Hard Disk Drive Industry*

Level of technological capability	Type of technological capability					
	Investment	Manufacturing: Process engineering	Manufacturing: Product engineering	Manufacturing: Industrial engineering	Innovation	Linkages[a] ■ ■
Basic	2	■	4		5	■ ■ ■ ■ ■
Inter-mediate	3	■	4	6	3	■
Advanced	5	8	2	4	2	■ ■

a. Single cases because the scoring was less consistent for this type of technological capability. Two have a level of technological capability that is even less than the basic level.

Note: The boxes and the number in the boxes refer to the number of firms out of ten.

Source: Afzulpurkar and Brimble (2004).

developing better linkages if the support infrastructure was in place. Concerted efforts from both industry and the government are needed to build an environment that is conducive to linkage development.

Most companies are linked to a certain degree into the vertical supply chain of the Thai HDD cluster and share related information with regard to specific product-related issues, especially for new products (Figure 11.3). But only a few firms co-operate closely with either Thai-based suppliers or customers in broader product, process, or human resource development related activities, indicating rather weak innovation-related vertical links. And even fewer companies have horizontal linkages to universities, R&D institutions, service providers, or competitors. This suggests that innovation-related horizontal links are weak. The main reasons for this derive from the supply and the demand sides. On the supply side, there are relatively few firms or academic institutions that have capabilities or resources of interest to the industry; on the demand side, many of the foreign investors do not appear to have the strong desire to take the time and devote the resources required to build the linkages.

Figure 11.3. *The Nature of Linkages*

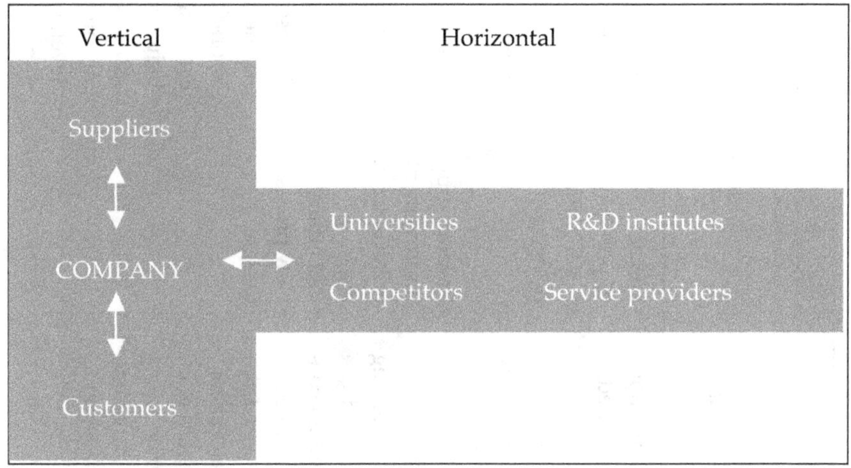

Source: Afzulpurkar and Brimble (2004).

Community Development

A path-breaking (and still unique) study of corporate contributions in Thailand (Pongsapich and Kataleeradabhan 1997) analyzed the community development activities and philanthropy of over fifty multinational firms. Foreign firms were asked in the survey carried out in 1991 whether they had allocated a portion of their budget to community development activities. Out of fifty-three firms, twenty-five responded that they had not, and another eighteen stated that the budget was not specified. Only nine firms had allocated a portion of their budget to community development programs, with the amount varying from under US$50,000 to over US$1 million.

Although nearly all of the multinational firms surveyed had contributed to philanthropic causes, only a minority of programs were directed toward community and social development. Nearly 65 percent of the total amount of support was provided for education, research, and publication projects. Forty percent of the firms supported sport, music, and art and culture programs. Another 40 percent of firms supported projects geared toward religion. The types of projects that firms supported less frequently were those concerned with politics, science and technology, and social welfare. Indeed, only 8 percent of the fifty-three multinationals surveyed had maintained any social welfare or science and technology programs.

Table 11.8. *Technological Capabilities in Thailand's Hard Disk Drive Industry: A Unified Framework*

Level of technological capability	*Type of technological capability*					
	Investment	*Manufacturing*			*Innovation*	*Linkages*
		Process engineering	*Product engineering*	*Industrial engineering*		
Basic	• Feasibility studies • Site selection • Project preparation	• Scheduling • Maintenance • Quality management	• Understanding basic product design • Adapting minor product changes	• Optimization based scheduling • Basic skill upgrading programs	• Process improvement • Local parts development	• Local supplier base development • Subcontracting to technological service providers
Intermediate	• Technology selection • Contract negotiation • Technology transfer agreements • Recruitment and initial training project execution	• Process optimization • Process adaptation for product variations • Introduction of TQM/Kanban techniques	• Technology transfer for new products	• Productivity analysis • Benchmarking • Advanced inventory control (JIT etc.) • Advanced skill development • Logistics management • Supply chain management	• Product support improvement (packaging, testing) • R&D transfer • New process design	• Process/product upgrading in collaboration with suppliers and R&D institutes • Reverse system engineering in collaboration with external partners • Industry networking and collaboration for competitive development

Advanced	• Organization management using ISO and BS standards • Ability to develop own turnkey projects • Export of project know-how	• Implementation of MRP ERP systems • Process standardization using ISO and BS standards	• Tracking global product changes • New product design	• Long-term HR development programs • Supply chain development (cluster based)	• New product innovation • Organization set-up for innovation	• Long-term linking with R&D institutions and universities • Licensing new technology to partners and suppliers • Strategic alliances with academic institutes and R&D agencies to open new product markets and services

Source: Afzulpurkar and Brimble (2004).

The study further showed that firms would increase their level of support if the government or other organizations played a more active role as facilitators of philanthropic activities. This foundation approach, respondents stated, would allow corporations the ability to fund projects without having to spend the time and resources to administer specific projects.

The study identified two key issues. First, many firms had not broadened their current understanding of philanthropic activities and continued to donate money and other resources to traditional philanthropic activities. One main reason for this was the lack of viable alternatives to traditional forms of developmental linkages. Second, firms felt that they were often unable to establish the forms of community programs that they would like to establish. Instead of creating innovative forms of community linkages (which are likely to take significant time and financial resources), firms opted for traditional philanthropy, a less time-consuming and expensive choice. Within the context of a group or foundation where the government was somewhat involved, firms said they would be more willing to participate, both financially and in other ways.

Indeed, a number of group initiatives involving foreign investors have been successful in community development and philanthropic activities. The Thai Business Initiative in Rural Development (TBIRD) was established in 1998 by the Population and Community Development Association (PDA), a large nongovernmental organization. TBIRD has facilitated corporate involvement in rural development over the past fifteen years. It offers two methods of establishing community development programs. The first of these is village adoption. Corporate sponsors normally adopt a village for a specific time period and during this period actively support its development through funding. The corporate sponsors often introduce cottage industry aimed at sustainable income generation for the village. Examples of foreign firms that form the core sponsors of the TBIRD program are Singer Thailand, Mobil Oil Thailand, Bristol-Myers Squibb (Thailand), and 3M Thailand.

The second form of corporate sponsorship involves the establishment of income-generating rural industries in local villages. Working in conjunction with the Ministry of Industry, TBIRD has helped facilitate the relocation of manufacturing plants from Bangkok to rural villages. For example, Bata Shoes launched a village shoe manufacturing plant in Buriram province. Although TBIRD has not directly targeted foreign interests, more than 30 of the 115 sponsors that had participated in the programs as of the late 1990s were foreign. After the financial crisis, the village adoption program faced serious problems in locating new corporate sponsors. However, no companies presently involved have withdrawn their participation.

A good example of an FDI-supported nonprofit organization is the Thailand Business Coalition on AIDS (TBCA). It was founded in 1993 by two expatriate American businessmen to address business concerns related to HIV/AIDS. TBCA provides training courses for executives and managers on effective management of HIV/AIDS in the workplace and AIDS education for company employees. It also offers consultancy services to managers and acts as a catalyst for fundraising for other AIDS organizations. TBCA is funded by membership fees, donations, and project financing from funding institutions and more than 100 corporate members. Most emphasize that their interest in participating is partly because they can benefit from the services of TBCA and at the same time support a worthwhile cause.

Another American initiative, the U.S.-Thai Development Partnership, uses funding resources from USAID, the Thai government, and the Kenan Charitable Trust of North Carolina. It has provided small amounts of value-added selective support for partnerships between U.S. and Thai firms or institutions that address environmental or HIV/AIDS development problems in Thailand. In the late 1990s, the project spread its coverage a bit further through the American Corporations for Thailand (ACT) initiative. It receives financial support from a number of major American firms active in Thailand. The ACT initiative supports selected training activities in areas of critical need (such as internal auditors and logistics specialists). It also supports programs that provide Internet access to poor rural schools and computer graphics skills to disabled persons.

Innovative programs in human resources development areas and employment practices have strong demonstration effects and provide useful models for other firms to imitate. A major American consumer products company offers safety and health programs; an American airline firm develops corporate policies on sexual harassment; and a Dutch retail chain gives special training programs and employment arrangements for part-time employees.

In addition, several foreign chambers of commerce have carried out community development activities, harnessing the resources of their members and providing administrative support.[11] For example, the Australian Chamber constructed a school library. The British and Thai-Canadian Chambers raise funds for Thai charities each year. The Thai-Hong Kong Chamber has provided scholarships for local technical students and donated playgrounds to local schools, and the Japanese Chamber has given

11. See Brimble et al. (1999) for a more complete listing of the kinds of activities carried out by various chambers of commerce in Thailand.

scholarships to students in northeast provinces. Finally, in order to mitigate the effects of the crisis on small-scale businesses, the Thai-Canadian Chamber of Commerce launched a revolving loan fund to finance potential entrepreneurial activities.

Recommendations

Thailand needs to become much more proactive in creating an investment environment that encourages ongoing high levels of investment from both the domestic and foreign business communities. The comments below suggest directions to take if the country is to compete in the increasingly competitive global marketplace, and in particular with the emergence of China as an economic powerhouse in the region. [12]

First, the full potential of FDI has not been realized in Thailand. The typology employed by Sanjaya Lall (2003) puts Thailand at the passive end of the spectrum. Thailand receives billions of dollars worth of FDI, and the impact on the economy, growth, and employment is substantial. However, linkages between foreign and domestic firms, technological capacity building, and knowledge and skills transfer have received insufficient attention. In addition, more targeted investment promotion activities to fill technology gaps and meet technology needs have not been sufficiently pursued.

Second, Thai policy makers in general, and in the investment promotion arena in particular, need to recognize that the challenge in the global knowledge-based economy of today is to build knowledge, not just buildings and machines. Most incentives, especially investment incentives, primarily support capital investments of one kind or another. The knowledge economy and the value of information have been widely discussed, and the BOI has introduced recently a set of measures to promote science, technology, and innovation activities. Nevertheless, these measures remain strictly limited to basic tax incentives, and innovative FDI policies to support the domestic acquisition, utilization, and development of such assets remain to be developed and implemented. Turpin et al. (2002) conclude that the incentives in place to support skill and technology development at the firm level remain highly fragmented and relatively ineffectual. They call for a significantly enhanced role for "grant-based" incentives and much stronger coordination of support mechanisms for skill and technology upgrading.

Third, Thailand needs to actively enhance the broad effects of foreign direct investment. The perception prevails that the domestic strategies of

---

12. This section develops the ideas presented in Brimble (2003).

transnational corporations are completely determined by the head office, with little input from domestic TNC affiliates. However, international evidence shows that TNCs are increasingly giving greater autonomy to their affiliates in developing countries; they are allowing them to make decisions on allocating resources to a range of activities that support technological development, from technical training to R&D activities (Arnold et al. 2000). This trend is also becoming increasingly evident in Thailand and needs to be exploited.

It is imperative that government and private industry better understand the potential spillover benefits from FDI, particularly how they help increase the country's and firms' competitiveness. The government needs to put forth a platform of policies designed to specifically enhance competitiveness, restructure the industrial base, strengthen the legal and regulatory frameworks that support business, and support closer interface among the government, foreign investors, and the domestic business community. Moreover, the government will need to explore selective interventions to encourage innovative programs with foreign investors—such as linkages with local firms, academic institutions, and communities. For its part, the local private sector will need to develop strategies to harness the technical and managerial capabilities of foreign firms, establish greater forward linkages with foreign firms, and discern ways of increasing their competitive position in global markets.

The importance of "facilitators" should be recognized.[13] Facilitating organizations or networks—be they chambers of commerce, nongovernmental organizations, or groups of private sector players—can encourage innovative activities with strong positive externalities. In many cases, ambitious efforts to create strong linkages with local institutions and communities fell short of their potential. One reason was the absence of, or weaknesses in, facilitating programs and networks. The various models implemented to date in Thailand with regard to facilitators and group initiatives merit closer scrutiny so that lessons can be derived. Lastly, the tax laws of Thailand provide very little incentive for charitable donations. To facilitate the flow of resources from companies and individuals to develop institutions and to support charitable activities, more generous tax deductions should be considered.

Fourth, the government, in considering policy measures to enhance industrial competitiveness, must carefully distinguish between welfare

13. See Brimble, Sherman, Sibunruang, and Ratchatatanun (1999) for more details on the importance of facilitators in stimulating greater spillover benefits from FDI.

objectives and competitiveness objectives. A common perception in Thailand is that large or foreign firms are capable of helping themselves and do not require assistance from the government. Public sector incentives can "encourage good firms to do good things better and with more spillovers" if the true externalities are correctly evaluated and the programs are implemented fairly and efficiently. The critical lesson for Thai policy makers is to create an environment that stimulates the private sector to devote greater resources to technological development activities, especially those that lead to spillovers. They should not feel threatened by the resulting "dynamism" generated by the business sector. Indeed, if channeled properly, this private sector dynamism will drive Thailand to higher levels of competitiveness.

Fifth, the government should strengthen investment promotion activities and make them more proactive as tools of competitiveness policy, responding to the technological, managerial, marketing, and financial needs of industry. Efforts to date have been relatively extensive but not well coordinated or monitored. A more strategic approach to industrial development is needed. So-called "created assets" are becoming more important in the increasing competition for FDI. A more proactive role of the public sector is called for in facilitating joint activities with foreign investors, as well as domestic investors, to stimulate the growth of competitiveness-enhancing networks and services.

Lessons Learned from the Thai Experience

From the Thai experience can be derived a number of key lessons of relevance for other developing economies. Thailand has performed relatively well with regard to getting the macroeconomic environment right and providing reasonably good infrastructure. The importance of these factors should not be ignored by other developing economies. FDI policy making in Thailand, on the other hand, has tended to be determined in a reactive manner. Developing economies should proactively use FDI as an explicit tool to strengthen industrial competitiveness.

Although the outputs of FDI in Thailand have been judged primarily on the quantitative results (such as quantitative FDI inflows and exports generated by FDI), the qualitative impacts of FDI are becoming very important. In general, as the balance between investment promotion activities moves away from the provision of investment incentives, there is a strong need for better promotion activities and the use of a wider and richer range of policy tools than simple tax breaks. Investment promotion resources should increasingly focus on the strategic targeting of investment. This will maximize the efficiency of use of limited resources. Investment promotion should also extend to areas beyond the basic incentive package—such as the technology and human resource development needs of industry. It is important for developing economies to work closely with transnational corporations already in-country to maximize spillovers and enhance benefits to the domestic industry and community at large. Networks with all key players, domestic and international, must be built, maintained, and nurtured.

Finally, developing economies need a basic analytical capacity to relate FDI policies to broader policy issues. Related to this is the need for a firm-level tracking system to evaluate and improve promotion activities as well as enhance efforts to stimulate greater spillover activities of foreign investors.

References

Afzulpurkar, Nitin, and Peter Brimble. 2004. *Building a World-Class Industry: Strengthening the Hard Disk Drive Cluster in Thailand—A Blueprint from Industry/Government/Academia*. Report prepared for the National Science and Technology Development Agency. September.

Archanun, Kohpaiboon. 2000. *Foreign Trade Regimes and the FDI-Growth Nexus: A Case Study of Thailand*. Canberra: Australian National University.

Arnold, Erik et al. 2000. *Enhancing Policy and Institutional Support for Industrial Technology Development in Thailand: The Overall Policy Framework and the Development of the Industrial Innovation System*. Paper prepared for the National Science and Technology Development Board with support from the World Bank, Bangkok. December.

Bangkok Post. 2004. "Capital Investment: Thailand Set to Become Top Manufacturer of Hard Disks," by Sasiwimon Boonruang. June 23.

Bell, Martin et al. 2003. *Knowledge Resources, Innovation Capabilities, and Sustained Competitiveness in Thailand: Transforming the Policy Process*. Final report prepared for the National Science and Technology Development Board with support from the World Bank, Bangkok. January.

Board of Investment. 1999. "Hard Disk Drive Industry in Thailand." Paper prepared for workshop entitled "Thailand's Hard Disk Drive Industry: Future Developments in a Regional Context," Bangkok, July 16.

Brimble, Peter. 1999. *Building Partnerships for Better Development: Outlook for Partnerships in Thailand*. Conference Proceedings of the 1st International Outlook Conference on Community Development in Asia-Pacific, Bangkok, September 10.

———. 2002. "Foreign Direct Investment: Performance and Attraction: The Case of Thailand." Paper presented at the International Monetary Fund workshop entitled

"Foreign Direct Investment: Opportunities and Challenges for Cambodia, Laos, and Vietnam," Hanoi, August 16–17.

———. 2003. "Foreign Direct Investment, Technology and Competitiveness in Thailand." In *Competitiveness, FDI, and Technological Activity in East Asia,* edited by Sanjaya Lall and Shujiro Urata. Cheltenham, U.K.: Edward Elgar Publishing. June.

Brimble, Peter, and Chatri Sripaipan. 1994. *Science and Technology Issues in Thailand's Industrial Structure: The Key to the Future.* Report prepared for the Asian Development Bank, Manila. June.

Brimble, Peter, and J. Sherman. 1999. "Mergers and Acquisitions in Thailand: The Changing Face of Foreign Direct Investment." Paper prepared for the United Nations Conference on Trade and Development. Geneva and New York: United Nations. May.

Brimble, P., J. Sherman, A. Sibunruang, and W. Rachatatanun. 1999. "The Broader Impacts of Foreign Direct Investment on Economic Development in Thailand: Corporate Responses." Paper prepared for the High-Level Roundtable on Foreign Direct Investment and its Impact on Poverty Alleviation, Singapore, December 14–15, 1998; revised April 1999.

Brimble, P., C. Sripaipan, S. Vanichseni, and Y. Mukdapitak. 1997. "Towards a Technological Innovation Strategy for Thailand." Paper prepared for the First International Conference on Technology Policy and Innovation, Macau, July 2–4.

Brooker Group. 1996. *Modalities of University-Industry Cooperation in the APEC Region.* Bangkok: APEC Research Project prepared for the Thai Ministry of University Affairs.

———. 1999. *Thailand's Hard Disk Drive Industry: Future Developments in a Regional Context.* Summary of Findings of Workshop and the Elements of an Action Plan, Bangkok, July 16.

———. 2001. *NSTDA R&D/Innovation Survey 2000,* Final Report, September.

———. 2003. *NSTDA R&D/Innovation Survey 2002,* Final Report, August.

Dahlman, Carl, and Peter Brimble. 1990. "Technology Strategy and Policy for International Competitiveness: A Case Study of Thailand." Industry and Energy Department Working Paper, Industry Series Paper 24. Washington, D.C.: The World Bank. April.

Development Evaluation Division, National Economic and Social Development Board. 1998. "Poverty Profiles for Thailand." In *Indicators of Wellbeing and Policy Analysis,* vol. 2, no. 3, May.

Dollar, D. et al. 1998. "Short-term and Long-term Competitiveness Issues in Thai Industry." In *Competitiveness and Sustainable Economic Recovery in Thailand,* edited by J. Witte and S. Koeberle. Washington, D.C.: The World Bank.

Doner, Richard, and Peter Brimble. 1998. *Thailand's Hard Disk Drive Industry.* Information Storage Industry Center, Report 98-02. San Diego: University of California.

Foreign Investment Advisory Service (FIAS). 1991. *Backward Linkages of Foreign Direct Investment: Selected Countries' Experience and the Case of Thailand.* Washington, D.C.

IMD (International Institute for Management Development). 2004. *World Competitiveness Yearbook.* Lausanne.

Joint Foreign Chambers of Commerce in Thailand (JFCCT). 2001. "Toward Enhancing Thailand's Investment Climate: Progress Report and Recommendations." Paper presented to the Prime Minister, April.

Kaosa-Ard, M. 1991. "A Preliminary Study of TNCs' Hiring and Localization Policies in Thailand." *TDRI Quarterly Review*, vol. 6, no. 4, December.

Kinoshita, Soshichi. 2001. "East Asia Economic Growth and a Quantitative Model of Trade and FDI: The Case Study of Thailand." ICSEAD Working Paper Series Vol. 2001–27. International Centre for the Study of East Asian Development.

Lall, Sanjaya. 2003. "Foreign Direct Investment, Technology Development and Competitiveness: Conceptual Issues and Empirical Review." In *Competitiveness, FDI, and Technological Activity in East Asia*, edited by Sanjaya Lall and Shujiro Urata. Cheltenham, U.K.: Edward Elgar Publishing. June.

Matsuoka, Atsuko. 2001. "Wage Differentials among Local Plants and Foreign Multinationals by Foreign Ownership Share and Nationality in Thai Manufacturing." ICSEAD Working Paper Series Vol. 2001–25. International Centre for the Study of East Asian Development. September.

McKendrick, David, Richard Doner, and Stephan Haggard. 2000. *From Silicon Valley to Singapore: Location and Competitive Advantage in the Hard Disk Drive Industry.* Stanford, Calif.: Stanford University Press.

Nipon Paopongsakorn and Pawadee Tonguthai. 1998. "Technological Capability Building and the Sustainability of Export Success in Thailand's Textile and Electronics Industries." In *Technological Capabilities and Export Success in Asia*, edited by Dieter Ernst, Tom Ganiatsos, and Lynn Metelka.

Patarapong Intarakamnerd, Pun-arj Chairatana, and Tipawan Tangchitpiboon. 2001. "National Innovation System in Less Successful Developing Countries: The Case of Thailand." Paper presented at the Nelson-Winter Conference at Aalborg, Denmark, June.

Pongsapich, A., and N. Kataleeradabhan. 1997. *Thailand's Nonprofit Sector and Social Development.* Chulalongkorn University Social Research Institute.

Ramstetter, Eric. 2001. "Labor Productivity in Local Plants and Foreign Multinationals by Nationality in Thailand Manufacturing, 1996 and 1998." ICSEAD Working Paper Series Vol. 2001–31. International Centre for the Study of East Asian Development. November.

———. 2003. "Foreign Multinationals in Thailand after the Crisis: The Challenge of Measuring and Interpreting Recent Trends." Processed paper of International Centre for the Study of East Asian Development. March.

Siamwalla, A. 1997. *Why Are We in This Mess?* J. Douglas Gibson Lecture at Queen's University, Ontario.

Sibunruang, A. 1986. *Foreign Investment and Manufactured Exports from Thailand.* Bangkok: Chulalongkorn University Social Research Institute.

Sibunruang, A., and Peter Brimble. 1988. "The Employment Effects of Manufacturing Multinational Enterprises in Thailand." International Labor Office Working Paper No. 54, Geneva.

Somkiat Tangkitvanich, Deunden Nikomborirak, and Busaba Krairiksh. 2003. "Country Studies on Foreign Direct Investment: Thailand." Paper prepared for ADB RETA 5994: A Study of Regional Integration and Trade—Emerging Policy Issues for Selected Developing Member Countries, Asian Development Bank, Manila.

Somsak Tambunlertchai. 2002. "Tracking Manufacturing Performance." Paper prepared for UNIDO Project on Tracking Manufacturing Performance: Toward an Early Warning Mechanism Geared to the Real Economy. July.

Turpin, T., et al. 2002. *Improving the System of Financial Incentives for Enhancing Thailand's Industrial Technological Capabilities.* Report prepared for the World Bank and the National Science and Technology Development Agency. June.

UNCTAD (United Nations Conference on Trade and Development). 2000. *The Competitiveness Challenge: Transnational Corporations and Industrial Restructuring in Developing Countries.* New York and Geneva: United Nations.

———. 2002. *The World of Investment Promotion at a Glance: A Survey of Investment Promotion Practices.* UNCTAD Advisory Series No. 17. New York and Geneva: United Nations.

———. various years. *World Investment Report.* New York and Geneva: United Nations.

World Bank. 2003. *Thailand Economic Monitor.* Washington, D.C. October.

World Economic Forum. various years. *Global Competitiveness Reports.* Geneva.

12

FDI and Economic Development: The Case of Vietnam

Tran Van Tho

As a strategy of transition from a socialist economic system to a market economy, the shock-therapy approach is well known. Vietnam, however, can be considered a gradualist in many respects. The gradualist approach or the two-track approach is characterized by the postponement of reforms of politically sensitive sectors, typically the state-owned enterprises (SOEs). On the other hand, this approach promotes the development of non-SOE sectors.

The transition from a socialist country to a market economy usually involves the privatization of economic activities, but in the case of SOEs, the privatization of ownership is postponed due to social and political considerations. Instead, reforms of SOEs are gradually conducted through the provision of autonomy to the management and the hardening of budget constraints in order to improve the efficiency of the SOEs. In that process, it is essential to promote the development of the private sector, which can generate new employment and fiscal resources for the government to conduct further reforms in the future. In a word, the efficient development of the (new) private sector is essential for the success of gradualist reforms.

In that process, the role of foreign direct investment (FDI) is particularly important. FDI has a dynamic impact on the economy in transition at least in two aspects. First, FDI generates new financial, managerial, and technological resources that push forward the production possibility frontier (PPF) of the economy. If there were no distortions due to wrong policies, such expansion of PPF would be expected to favor the comparatively advantaged industries. Thus, along with the inflows of FDI in a labor-surplus economy such as Vietnam, increase in employment and exports is expected, and this will facilitate the transition toward a market economy even though the reforms of inefficient SOEs are postponed.

Second, FDI not only generates new private firms (foreign-owned firms) in the economy, but through linkage effects and other transactions, it may also transfer know-how and technology to SOEs and domestic private firms. With the expansion of FDI inflows, we may expect that the increasing interplay among FDI firms, SOEs, and domestic private firms will promote the efficient development of the economy. Of course, the extent of such effects depends on many factors, including host government policies and the behavior of multinational corporations (MNCs).

Vietnam's Record as a Transition Economy

Among transition economies, Vietnam may be considered one of the successful cases so far in terms of economic growth and stability during the transitional process. The reform strategy was adopted in late 1986, and reform measures have been comprehensively implemented since 1988. After several years of trial and error, the Vietnamese economy since the early 1990s has grown at a high rate. In the period from 1993 to 1997, the average annual growth rate was 8.5 percent. After the Asian financial crisis, the growth slowed, but Vietnam still maintained 6 to 7 percent growth per year from 1998 to 2003. In terms of macroeconomic stability, Vietnam has also performed well. Consumer price indices turned from three-digit to two-digit figures in 1989 and have declined further to one-digit figures since 1996. The exchange rates of the *dong* have generally been stable since the mid-1990s.

The Effects of Reforms

Three factors account for this good performance. First, reforms that emphasized the supply side of the economy led to the expansion of investment and output. This strategy was applied to the agricultural sector and later to the industrial sector. Second, reforms promoted the inflows of foreign financial and managerial resources (official development assistance, FDI, and other resources). They made possible the expansion of investment and provided expertise to facilitate the reform process. Third, reforms helped integrate the country into world markets. The rapid rise of trade as a percentage of GDP is noteworthy. Particularly important was the integration of Vietnam into the dynamic Asian Pacific region.

The latter two factors reflect what may be called the "outward-looking policy." Probably because of the demonstration effect generated by neighboring countries, in Vietnam FDI has been emphasized since the beginning of *doi moi* (renovation). However, at least until the late 1990s, Vietnamese leaders appeared to have ambivalent feeling toward MNCs. On the one hand, they recognized the positive role of FDI for economic development; on the other hand, they worried that the expansion of FDI inflows would lead the economy toward capitalism. In fact, in 1994 the Vietnam Communist Party adopted the so-called socialism-oriented economic development strategy. This strategy emphasizes the role of SOEs and the need to achieve social equity in the development process. Both incentives and requirements have been applied to MNCs, but, as explained below, until 2000 the latter had been particularly severe.

The Legal Framework

In the context of *doi moi*, the Foreign Investment Law was promulgated in 1987, providing the legal framework for foreign firms to operate in the country. This law provided tax exemption and other incentives to attract foreign capital, but at the same time it imposed many regulations and requirements upon foreign investors. By the late 1990s, these regulations and requirements included the principle of unanimity (all members of the board of directors of the joint venture must agree on its decisions); requirements concerning local contents; and the dual pricing policy under which foreigners are charged much more (double) for utilities, housing, and transportation, for example, than locals are charged. In response to the requests and claims of foreign investors, the Foreign Investment Law has been revised many times since the early 1990s.

Despite these regulations and requirements, FDI flows to Vietnam have expanded since the early 1990s (Figure 12.1). The positive reaction of MNCs to the open-door policy of Vietnam may be attributed to three factors. First, because of Vietnam's sizable population, relatively high literacy rate of workers, and good location, its potential as an export base and as a market for manufactured products has been highly recognized. Second, Vietnam has increasingly received intellectual and financial cooperation from industrial countries and the international community. Their resources have helped build soft and hard infrastructure. Coupled with the macroeconomic stability since the early 1990s, such cooperation has reduced the uncertainties and risk of investment in Vietnam. Third, regulations and legal problems have been expected to improve as the economic reforms have

Figure 12.1. *FDI in Vietnam, 1988–2002*

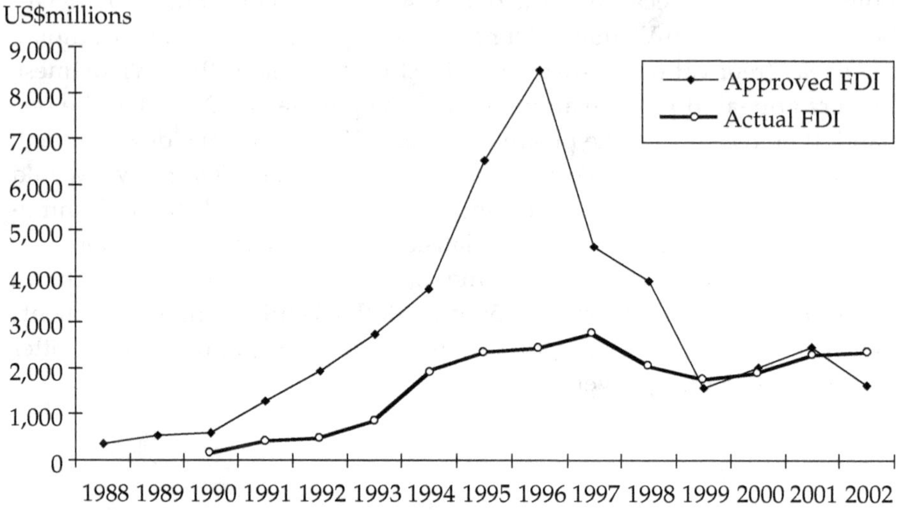
US$millions
9,000
8,000
7,000
6,000
5,000
4,000
3,000
2,000
1,000
0
Approved FDI
Actual FDI
1988 1989 1990 1991 1992 1993 1994 1995 1996 1997 1998 1999 2000 2001 2002

Source: Compiled from Tran (1996), Komh te va du bao (various issues), and data from the Ministry of Planning and Investment.

deepened and the confidence of the Vietnamese government concerning external economic relations has increased.

The annual survey by the Japan Bank for International Cooperation (JBIC) asks thousands of major Japanese manufacturing firms about their mid-term (three-year) plan for FDI and about potential investment sites. Vietnam has been among the top ten economies that receive the highest attention by Japanese firms (ranked 5 in 1992, 4 in 1993, 2 in 1994 and 1995, 3 in 1996, and 4 in 1997). After 1998, the rank of Vietnam turned down, but the country still maintained its position among the top 10. Vietnam ranked fourth in the 2003 survey.[1]

Overall Trends in FDI

In contrast to the continuing high evaluation of the economy's potential, approved FDI in Vietnam peaked in 1996 (Figure 12.1). The regulations governing investments and other legal problems have not been improved as expected. In addition, the complicated and inefficient bureaucratic adminis-

1. Before 1998 the survey was conducted by the Export-Import Bank of Japan. This bank merged in 1998 with the Overseas Economic Cooperation Fund (OECF) to form JBIC.

tration has disappointed foreign investors. Japanese and other foreign investors tried to diversify their investment sites from advanced ASEAN countries, such as Thailand and Malaysia, and they considered Vietnam as a potential site, but the FDI boom in Vietnam was short, lasting only three years (1994–96). Compared to Vietnam, China became much more attractive.

Confronted by difficult conditions brought about by the continued decline of FDI inflows and the downturn in exports following the financial crisis in Asia, the Vietnamese government began to propose reforms in 1998. In March 1999 a Prime Ministerial directive stipulated the implementation of a series of policies aimed at improving the investment environment. These policies included reductions in electricity and telephone charges and reductions in office-opening approval fees for foreign-affiliated businesses, and reductions in individual income tax for foreign residents. In May 2000 the Foreign Investment Law was amended.

Effective since September 2000, the law has made the FDI environment of Vietnam almost comparable with that of neighboring countries, at least in terms of the legal framework. Five features of the new law are explained below. Firstly, to facilitate the establishment of joint ventures by multinational corporations, all domestic companies (including small family-owned businesses) became eligible to participate as the Vietnamese partner in FDI projects. (The domestic partners in the joint ventures until then had virtually been limited to SOEs.) Secondly, the activities of foreign-affiliated companies became more advantageous with regard to value-added tax. For example, exemptions from value-added tax, which had formerly applied only to imported goods that could not be produced domestically, became applicable to all goods imported by FDI firms. Thirdly, regarding the investment registration regulations, the "negative list" was introduced. Under this new policy, investment fields were divided into areas for which inspection of applications was necessary, and those for which it was not. In the latter category, a certificate of approval was promptly issued after registration. Fourthly, whereas previously the collateral used by foreign-affiliated companies for bank loans was limited to actual real estate (such as structures), under the revised law, land usage rights could also be used as collateral. Fifthly, the scope of application of the principle of unanimity in joint venture decision making was reduced, from four items to two (appointment of president and vice president, and changes in the internal regulations of the joint venture).

The new law, however, was unable to reverse the trends in FDI (Figure 12.1). The implementation of laws is still not transparent, and frequent changes in industrial policies have made the investment environment unpredictable. The policy on the motorcycle industries in September 2002 is a typical example, as will be discussed later in the chapter. Since the beginning of 2003, the Vietnamese government has recognized the seriousness of the problem and has tried to improve the investment climate. It launched a new campaign for expanding FDI. The prime minister made a working visit to Japan in April, and the Investment Protection Pact with Japan was signed in November 2003.

Despite the current stagnation, FDI has been significantly important for the Vietnamese economy since the mid-1990s. As shown in Table 12.1, the position of FDI in Vietnam's major indicators has been quite high. For example, the share of FDI in total capital formation was about 19 percent, higher than Malaysia and China (about 15 percent) and comparable with Hong Kong and Singapore in 2000 and 2002. FDI has played a particularly important role in terms of output in the industrial sector of Vietnam. Table 12.1 also shows the increasing role of FDI in Vietnam's exports. However, the lower share of FDI in exports than in imports and in industrial output suggests that FDI has concentrated in import-substitution industries. We will return to this point later on in the chapter.

Excluding the projects that had been dissolved or fully localized, at the end of 2002, there were 3,711 FDI-related firms in Vietnam, with the cumulative approved investment of about US$38 billion (about US$21 billion had been disbursed or realized). Out of these disbursed investments, the exploration of oil accounted for 16.0 percent and other primary industries (agriculture, forestry, and fishery) accounted for 6 percent. The tertiary industries (mainly real estate such as hotels, offices, housing, building of

Table 12.1. *FDI as a Share of Major Indicators of the Vietnamese Economy, 1990–2002*
(Percent)

Economic indicator	*1990*	*1995*[a]	*1998*	*2000*	*2002*
GDP	n.a.	6.3	10.0	13.3	13.9
Capital formation	13.1	32.3	25.0	18.6	18.8
Industrial output	16.7	25.1	33.2	39.2	n.a.
Employment	n.a.	0.4	0.7	0.8	n.a.
Industrial employment	0.4	4.0	9.3	n.a.	n.a.
Exports[b]	n.a.	8.1	21.2	23.2	30.0
Imports	n.a.	18.0	23.1	28.6	n.a.

n.a. Not available.
a. The employment data are for 1996.
b. Excluding crude oil.
Source: Prepared from data provided by the General Statistical Office, the Central Institute of Economic Management, and the Ministry of Commerce of the Vietnam government.

export processing zones and industrial zones, and other service sectors such as telecommunications, tourism, finance, and banking) accounted for 29.4 percent. By the mid-1990s, a large number of FDI projects related to the exploration of oil and the building of real estate had been undertaken. Most of the FDI in real estate and the other tertiary industries had been essential for building business infrastructure. This facilitated the operation of manufacturing FDI projects in subsequent periods. Since the mid-1990s, FDI in the manufacturing sector has been substantial. By the end of 2002, the manufacturing sector (2,435 projects, cumulative approved investment US$17.8 billion, actual investment US$9.8 billion) accounted for two-thirds of FDI in terms of the number of projects and nearly 50 percent in terms of the cumulative approved investment and actual investment. It is this manufacturing sector that will be analyzed in more detail in the next three sections.

Features of Manufacturing FDI in Vietnam

The 2,435 FDI projects in the manufacturing sector of Vietnam will be broken down with regard to source countries, ownership, and industrial allocation.

Source Countries

In terms of approved cumulative investment as of December 2002, Taiwan (China) was the top investor in Vietnam's manufacturing sector (733 projects, approved investment US$3.5 billion, actual investment US$1.6 billion). However, in terms of cumulative actual investment in Vietnam, Taiwan fared much less well. Japan (261 projects, approved investment US$3.3 billion, actual investment US$2.1 billion) was the leader in actual FDI. It accounted for about 22 percent of the total. Also active in manufacturing FDI in Vietnam are the following economies: the Republic of Korea (411 projects, US$2.5 billion approved investment, US$1.4 billion actual investment), Singapore (133 projects, US$2.4 billion approved investment, US$1.4 billion actual investment), and Hong Kong, China (124 projects, US$1 billion approved investment, US$0.7 billion actual investment). The four Asian NIEs (newly industrializing economies) together accounted for about half of the actual investment stock at the end of 2002.

The strong presence of Asian NIEs in manufacturing FDI in Vietnam is noteworthy. Since the mid-1980s, Asian NIEs became net exporters of capital. As they began to lose their comparative advantage in labor-intensive industries due to rising labor costs and other factors in their home economies, they tended to invest in ASEAN countries.[2] Influenced by Vietnam's *doi moi* and the open-door policy, Asian NIEs found this newcomer of industrialization to be a promising location of production of labor-intensive industries. Until the early 1990s, the United States imposed economic sanctions on Vietnam, and firms from Japan and other industrial countries that had diplomatic ties with the United States could not make any substantial move to invest. Sanctions created much room for Asian NIEs to invest in this new market.

Because their share of FDI in Vietnam is very high, about 70 percent in terms of the number of projects and the actual investment value, this chapter focuses on the behavior of these five investors: Japan, Taiwan (China), the Republic of Korea, Singapore, and Hong Kong (China). Taiwan (China) and the Republic of Korea tended to undertake small-scale projects; Japan and Singapore, large-scale projects (Table 12.2). In terms of exports, Hong Kong's FDI projects ranked high, followed by Korea, while Singapore ranked low. The cumulative actual investment can be considered a proxy for capital

Table 12.2. *The Export Ratio and Factor Intensity in Manufacturing Industries of Top 5 Investors in Vietnam, 2002*

Economy	*Actual investment (US$ millions)* A	*Sales (US$ millions)* B	*Exports (US$ millions)* C	*Employees (thousands of persons)* D	*Export ratio (%)* C/B	*Factor intensity ($1,000 per person)* A/D
Japan	2,127	9,396	4,418	59	47.0	36.1
Taiwan	1,625	4,300	1,805	88	42.0	18.5
Republic of Korea	1,419	6,015	3,618	93	60.1	15.3
Singapore	1,366	4,307	701	17	16.3	80.4
Hong Kong	655	2,061	1,510	109	73.3	6.0
Total for 5 investors	7,192	26,079	12,052	366	46.2	19.7
Total	9,779	33,902	13,228	434	39.0	22.5
Share of top 5	73.5%	76.9%	91.1%	84.3%	—	—

— Not applicable.

Note: The economies are ranked by actual investment. The figures for actual investment, sales, and exports are cumulative figures for 1988 to 2002. The data on employees are from the end of 2002.

Source: Compiled from data from the Ministry of Planning and Investment.

2. Tran (1993b) analyzed in detail Asian NIEs as new suppliers of managerial resources in the Asian Pacific region.

stock. Calculating the average factor intensity of FDI projects by source country, we found that FDI by Hong Kong tended to concentrate in labor-intensive sectors, while FDI by Singapore focused on capital-intensive sectors.

The most labor-intensive FDI had the highest export propensity (Hong Kong, China) and the most capital-intensive FDI had the lowest export propensity (Singapore); Japan and Taiwan (China) were in between Hong Kong and Singapore in both export ratio and factor intensity (Table 12.2). This finding seems to be consistent with the Hecksher-Ohlin theorem since Vietnam is a labor-surplus economy. Keeping the OLI framework of Dunning (1993) in mind, we investigate whether the behavior of the five investors is related to ownership advantage. The breakdown of subsectors in manufacturing for each of the five investors is presented in Table 12.3. Hong Kong (China) and Taiwan (China) concentrate their investments in the two most labor-intensive industries, shoes and apparel, which are also highly export oriented. Japan and the Republic of Korea tend to invest in more capital-intensive subsectors, such as automobiles and motorbikes and metal mechanics; in Vietnam these industries are still import substitutes. Reflecting the upgrading of industrial structure in their respective economies, most firms in Japan and Korea appear to be large in size and have comparative advantage in capital-intensive areas. In contrast, Hong

Table 12.3. *FDI in Six Major Manufacturing Industries in Vietnam*

Manufacturing industry	*Capital/labor ($1,000 per person)*	*Export ratio (%)*	*No. of FDI projects*	*Top investor (no. of projects)*		*Second investor (no. of projects)*	
Shoes	4	98.9	175	Hong Kong	(7)	Rep. of Korea	(42)
						Taiwan	(37)
Apparel	6	82.2	226	Taiwan	(60)	Singapore	(8)
						Rep. of Korea	(46)
						Hong Kong	(28)
Textiles	30	51.5	114	Rep. of Korea	(20)	Taiwan	(28)
Electronics	25	68.5	286	Japan	(45)	Rep. of Korea	(17)
Automobiles/motorbikes	37	17.8	107	Japan	(26)	Rep. of Korea	(16)
Metal/mechanics	37	17.9	229	Rep. of Korea	(28)	Singapore	(13)
				Japan	(28)		

Note: The capital/labor ratio and export ratio are the average for all FDI projects in the industry. The investor ranking is based on realized capital.

Source: Compiled from data from the Ministry of Planning and Investment.

Kong and Taiwan are characterized by small and medium-size firms that tend to undertake FDI in labor-intensive industries.

Industrial Allocation of FDI Projects

We have broken down all 2,435 FDI manufacturing projects into 23 subsectors and created a ranking by cumulative actual investment at the end of 2002. The capital/labor ratio (capital stock per employee) at the end of 2002 and the export/sales ratio in 2002 have also been calculated. The top four industries (nonferrous metals, food and drinks, cars and motorcycles, and chemicals) accounted for 53 percent of total actual investment in the manufacturing sector. These industries are relatively capital intensive and inclined to import substitution (low export ratio). Of the 23 manufacturing subsectors, 11 are highly export-oriented industries (export/sales ratio higher than 50 percent). These industries account for 40 percent of total actual investment, but their share in total employees is as high as 89 percent. In fact, in terms of employment generation, the largest industries are leather products and apparel. Both industries are export oriented (export ratios are 99 percent and 77 percent, respectively) and labor intensive as well (the smallest capital stock per employee).

Figure 12.2 shows the export/sales ratio and the capital/labor ratio of each industry in the manufacturing sector. With few exceptions, FDI projects in export-oriented industries tend to be labor intensive. This finding is in line with Vietnam's comparative advantage.

FDI projects have been undertaken in both import-substitution and export-oriented industries in Vietnam. As expected, import-substitution industries are capital intensive, while export-oriented industries are labor intensive. The partial concentration of FDI in labor-intensive export industries can be viewed favorably since it generates employment and thus contributes to the achievement of equity in the growth process of a labor-surplus economy. It also combines the managerial resources of MNCs with the most abundant factor of Vietnam and thus reveals the potential comparative advantage of the country.

FDI also has concentrated in the import-substitution industries, and they are capital intensive and heavily protected by high tariff barriers.[3] The

3. For example, in the late 1990s the import tariff of metal products was 256 percent, plastics and plastic products was 185 percent, and paper was 118 percent (World Bank 2000, 25).

Figure 12.2. *Export Propensity and Factor Intensity of FDI Firms in Twenty-three Manufacturing Industries in Vietnam*

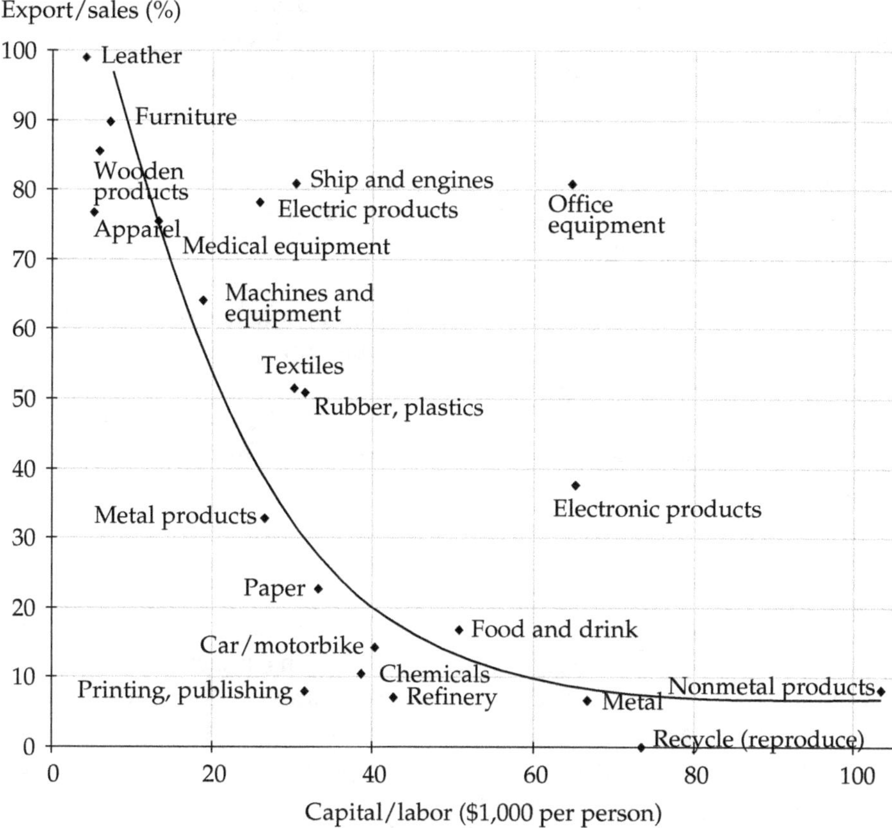

Note: The percentages are the average for all FDI projects in the industry.
Source: Compiled from data from the Ministry of Planning and Investment.

domestic market is expected to expand, given the steady and high growth of an economy in this country with 70 million people in the early 1990s and 80 million people in 2002. Not surprisingly, foreign firms have undertaken import-substitution FDI in Vietnam. If industry can shift from the import substitution to the export stage, or if industry can compete effectively with imported products without tariff and nontariff barriers in the future, the "nourishment policy," as well as foreign direct investment in such "infant" industries, can be viewed favorably. Given the relatively short history of manufacturing FDI in Vietnam, more time is needed before we can see whether import-substitution FDI brings about any successful cases of industrial development. However, if the operation of foreign firms in import-substitution industries generates positive linkage effects to domestic firms, such FDI may also prove to be useful.

In Vietnam too many workers are still concentrated in the agricultural sector, and the unemployment rate remains high. For these reasons Vietnam should have absorbed more labor-intensive export-oriented FDI. Even though the economy recorded high growth (the driving force was the industrial sector), the share of the agriculture sector in total employed labor remained as high as about 70 percent. From 1991 to 2000, the secondary sector (mainly industrial products) as a share in GDP rose from 23.5 percent to 36.9 percent, but its share in total employed labor showed only a slight increase (from 12.4 percent to 13.2 percent). Due to this weak absorption of employment, the living standard of most rural people has been low. Moreover, the gap between rural income and urban income is expanding. For instance, in 1993 the per capita expenditure of urban people was 80 percent higher than that of rural people; in 1998 it rose to 2.2 times. Based on the preceding evidence, it appears that FDI in labor-intensive industries has so far been insufficient.[4]

Ownership of Firms Receiving FDI

Under the Foreign Investment Law of Vietnam, FDI can be of four types: joint ventures (JV), 100 percent foreign-owned firms, business cooperation contract (BCC) between foreign and local firms, and build-operation-transfer (BOT) projects. The last two types are not involved in the establishment of foreign-affiliated firms in Vietnam. The pattern of ownership is thus related to the first and the second types.

Many studies have discussed the preference of multinational corporations in the choice of ownership in their FDI activities. MNCs usually prefer full ownership if the technology to be transferred is new and sophisticated, and if it should not be leaked to the third party. On the other hand, if the technology is standardized, a joint venture is also accepted by MNCs. Many other factors may cause MNCs to choose joint ventures instead of full ownership. Park and Lee (2003, 72) identify three main factors that influence the choice of ownership structure: (1) acquisition of the partner firm's resources—for example, firm-specific technologies or know-how and capital; (2) acquisition of host-country specific skill or know-how—for example, economic, political,

4. Sachs et al. (1997) also point out that FDI in Vietnam should move away from import substitution to export-oriented industries.

and cultural information for the home country; and (3) host-government restrictions. For Vietnam and other developing host countries, the third factor may be the most important. The first and second factors with some modifications are also relevant in the case of Vietnam. In an environment characterized by many regulations and frequent changes in policies, obtaining the partner firm's resources may help reduce transaction costs.

Preference for a particular ownership mode also depends on the motivations of MNCs. If the FDI project is export oriented, particularly if that project forms an integral part of MNCs' international value-added chain, MNCs will prefer to command tight control over their subsidiaries to ensure close coordination (Dunning 1993; Park and Lee 2003). On the other hand, if the FDI project is import substituting in host countries, joint ventures are preferred to obtain local skills and information on local markets.

Compared to studies of the motivations of MNCs, fewer studies have been conducted on the behavior of host countries with regard to the ownership of FDI projects. Kojima (1977) argues that joint ventures are preferable for developing countries since this type tends to promote transfer of technology from MNCs to the host country. If technology is defined in a broad sense to include management, marketing, and administration know-how, that argument seems convincing since local managers can absorb managerial know-how from MNCs through their participation in the management of joint ventures. In many developing countries, host governments, because of nationalism, tend to permit only joint ventures in the FDI projects. From the viewpoint of technology transfer, however, it is the behavior of local partners in the joint venture that is most relevant. Some prefer maximizing dividends to acquiring management know-how; some local partners may not show interest in management and localization of technology at various levels.[5]

Until the mid-1990s, foreign investors, except in special cases, were not allowed to set up full ownership subsidiaries in Vietnam. Since then, however, the government has removed the restriction on the ownership of FDI projects in order to improve Vietnam's investment environment.

During the period from 1988 to 1992, 100 percent foreign-owned projects accounted for around 12 percent of approved FDI projects. This share rose to 38 percent in the period from 1993 to 1996 and to 64 percent in the 1997–2000 period. Between 1997 and 2000, the number of 100 percent foreign-owned projects was more than double that of joint ventures. For the

---

5. The Republic of Korea, however, exemplifies a strong effort to absorb technology and management know-how from joint ventures (Tran 1988).

year 2000 alone, there were 4.5 times more 100 percent foreign-owned projects than joint ventures.

Since around 1997 foreign companies have tended to view joint ventures as undesirable. Not only have full foreign-owned projects come to account for most new investment projects, but some joint ventures have switched to 100 percent foreign ownership. According to the report from the Ministry of Planning and Investment (MPI), the demand for conversion from joint ventures to 100 percent foreign ownership began in 1997; by April 1999, approval had been granted for thirty-nine ventures to become 100 percent foreign owned.

This phenomenon is probably due to a desire on the part of foreign companies to switch to full ownership in order to avoid inefficiency and risk resulting from the management problems experienced by partners on the Vietnamese side. In most cases of joint ventures in Vietnam, local partners are SOEs. Therefore, members of the board of management in the joint ventures include the people sent from SOEs or from the ministries to which the SOEs are affiliated. In many cases these people behave more like bureaucrats than entrepreneurs. In addition, the principle of unanimity in joint venture decision making induces foreign firms to choose wholly-owned subsidiaries to avoid complicated management problems.

FDI in Vietnam as a Means of Technology Transfer

The most important effect of FDI for host developing countries is technology transfer. The effective transfer of technology not only has a direct impact on the industry in which FDI is undertaken, but through vertical linkages it can generate spillover effects to other industries. The two concepts "technology" and "transfer" warrant clarification.

The Conceptual Framework

Technology in a broad sense includes not only production technology (defined as the scientific knowledge or methods used to realize or improve the production and distribution of commodities and service) but also management know-how, organization skills, and marketing capacity. Production technology is called "hard" technology, while management know-how and the like are called "soft" technology (Tran 1993a; Thompson 2003). Hard and soft technologies are both important but the latter can be more crucial, particularly if production technology has become standardized. The soft technology ensures that the hard technology is optimally used, as Thompson (2003, 90) notes.

The "transfer" can occur at three levels. One is the *intrafirm transfer*—the transfer of technology by an MNC to its subsidiary in the host country. Another level is the transfer from the subsidiaries of MNCs to domestic firms in the same industry of the host country. This may be called *horizontal interfirm transfer*. The third level is called *vertical interfirm transfer*, the spillover of technology from subsidiaries of MNCs to local firms in backward and forward industries.

Consider first the intrafirm transfer. Suppose an MNC undertakes an FDI project in a developing country to produce a manufactured good. A factory must be built. The factory is a form that embodies production technology, which is the combination of equipment and operators. The transfer of this technology requires the transfer of equipment as well as the transfer of the knowledge and method to operate it. Local operators must be trained. In the production process, there are many forms of administration: inventories, quality control, production scheduling, and so on. These types of administration are directly related to production and confined to the factory level. We may classify them as a part of production technology. The transfer of this type of technology involves the training and education of engineers and managers at the section chief level or mid-management.

In this example the MNC also has to set up the head office in the host country to manage the operation of the factory (or a number of factories) and conduct strategies related to planning, marketing, finance, and the like. Thus, the "soft" technology is embodied in this head office. High-level managers at the head office must follow the trends in product markets, technology, and other areas, and undertake strategies that handle new situations. The transfer of this soft technology requires the training of high-level managers, who are gradually allowed to occupy the top-class managerial posts initially held by staff dispatched from the MNC's home country.

The horizontal interfirm transfer of technology promotes the spillover of knowledge to local firms in the same industry. In this way the competitiveness of the industry is rapidly strengthened. This transfer of technology occurs along two channels (Tran 1992, chap. 3; Saggi 2002). One is the demonstration effect. Local firms through imitation may adopt technologies introduced by MNCs. From marketing and other activities of MNCs' subsidiaries, local firms also learn to improve their operations. Another channel is labor turnover. Workers previously employed and trained by MNCs may transfer know-how and information to local firms by switching employers, or they may contribute to technology diffusion by starting their own firms.[6]

6. See Saggi (2002, 211–12) for a more detailed discussion on this point.

Compared to horizontal interfirm transfer, vertical interfirm transfer of technology is much more important because of its extensive and intensive impacts on the host economy. However, government policies can have unintended consequences. Local content policy may aim at development of supporting industries, but if the supply side conditions (availability of competitive small and medium firms) are not fulfilled, the policy will result in an inefficient supply of inputs. This, in turn, weakens the international competitiveness of the final products. If the host government attempts to attract MNCs to invest in the import substitution up-stream sectors that are protected by tariff and nontariff barriers, the downstream firms will be adversely affected due to the high cost of intermediate goods. In this case, imports of cheap and high-quality upstream products are preferable to the *forced* forward linkage effects. Many studies show that good (not *forced*) linkages and other positive effects of FDI are stronger in the case of export-promotion regimes than in highly protected import substitution regimes (Balasubramanyam, Salisu, and Sapsford 1996; UNCTAD 2001). Export-oriented firms are sensitive to the cost and quality of intermediate goods since they ensure the competitiveness of final products. If such intermediate goods are not available due to weak supporting industries, export-oriented FDI operations tend to be enclaves in the host economy.

Technology Transfer by FDI Firms in Vietnam's Manufacturing Sector

Given the current structure and weaknesses of domestic firms (state-owned enterprises and domestic non-SOEs), the linkage effects brought about by FDI firms are particularly significant. They will strongly influence Vietnam's industrialization strategy. Before *doi moi*, the economy of Vietnam was run by three types of firms: SOEs (national ownership), cooperatives (collective ownership), and household units of production or service. Cooperatives were seen mainly in agriculture and, to a lesser extent, in traditional handicrafts and services. With *doi moi*, other types of firms (that is, private firms and foreign-owned enterprises) have emerged. Until the early 1990s such firms were small in number. Although FDI flows started in 1988, a substantial amount of disbursement has been recorded only since 1994. By the early 2000s, both domestic private firms and FDI firms had increased in number.

Table 12.4 breaks down the manufacturing sector into twenty-three subsectors and shows the shares of SOEs, domestic non-SOEs, and FDI firms in each subsector in 2000. As expected, FDI firms have a large share in cars and motorcycles, office equipment, and radio and television. In the labor-intensive industries, such as leather products, textiles, and clothes, the position

Table 12.4. *Three Types of Firms in Vietnam's Manufacturing Industry*

Manufacturing industry	*Production value in 2000 current prices (billions of Vietnamese dong)*	*Production value as a percent of the total for all manu-facturing industries*	*Shares (%)*		
			SOEs	*Non-SOEs (domestic firms)*	*FDI firms*
Food and drink	70,854	(28.9)	40.0	32.9	27.1
Cigarettes	5,136	(2.1)	97.8	0.8	1.5
Textiles	13,224	(5.4)	46.0	14.7	39.3
Clothes	11,704	(4.8)	46.0	19.9	34.1
Leather products	14,211	(5.8)	17.0	17.9	65.0
Wooden products	4,224	(1.7)	37.7	41.3	21.0
Papers	5,720	(2.3)	41.7	40.7	17.6
Printing, publishing	4,067	(1.7)	92.7	5.7	1.6
Oil refinery	1,158	(0.5)	0.0	23.3	76.7
Chemicals	18,596	(7.6)	48.8	12.0	39.2
Rubber and plastics	9,468	(3.9)	27.2	36.5	36.2
Nonferrous metals	18,710	(7.6)	56.7	13.6	29.7
Metals	8,459	(3.5)	33.7	14.7	51.6
Metal products	7,475	(3.1)	21.4	33.5	45.2
Machines, equipment	4,315	(1.8)	36.9	12.1	50.9
Office equipment	8,504	(3.5)	0.0	0.2	99.8
Electric, electronic products	7,085	(2.9)	30.6	12.9	56.5
Radio, television	7,394	(3.0)	18.7	2.9	78.4
Medical equipment	1,049	(0.4)	9.4	17.5	73.0
Cars and motorcycles	5,379	(2.2)	14.8	4.9	80.3
Other transport equipment	13,838	(5.6)	21.8	9.4	68.8
Furniture	4,424	(1.8)	8.4	39.7	52.0
Other industry	25	(0.0)	0.0	100.0	0.0
Total	245,017	(100.0)	37.2	21.2	41.6

Source: Calculated from General Statistical Office, the Result of the Enterprise Census at 1st April 2001, Statistical Publishing House, 2002.

of FDI firms also is strong. SOEs have large shares in capital-intensive products, such as cigarettes, nonferrous metals, and chemicals. Domestic non-SOEs are strong in the field of labor-intensive products (such as furniture, food and drink, plastics) usually run by household small businesses.

As Table 12.4 shows, food and drink as well as textiles and apparel are important for all three types of firms. We will consider the textile and apparel industry with respect to the horizontal as well as vertical transfer of technology from FDI firms to SOEs and domestic non-SOEs. Electronic products, office equipment, and cars and motorcycles are important for FDI firms but also for SOEs and non-SOEs. The production of these products heavily involves supporting industries. We will therefore choose one of these industries, the motorcycle industry, for studying the possible backward linkage effects of technology transfer from FDI firms.

A Case Study of the Textile and Apparel Industries

Textiles and apparel are among the major manufacturing industries of Vietnam. In 2001 the two industries combined accounted for 2.2 percent of GDP and about 11 percent of total value added of the manufacturing sector.

Since the early 1990s, apparel, which is a typical labor-intensive industry, has risen to be the most important exporting industry of Vietnam, a labor-surplus economy.[7] In the mid-1990s, the apparel industry accounted for as much as 15 percent of Vietnam's total exports, and approximately half the manufactured exports. Following the rise of shoes and other new export products, the share of apparel has declined, but it still maintained at about 10 percent in 2001.

Textiles (yarns, fabrics) are up-stream products or intermediate goods of apparel. This industry is composed of knitting, weaving, and spinning stages. Table 12.5 presents the number of firms in each stage of textile and apparel production. As a whole, the number of FDI-related firms is quite large, accounting for about one-third of the total number of firms in the textile and apparel industries. As expected, non-state-owned firms, which are usually small in scale, tend to concentrate in the apparel industry. SOEs and FDI firms are operating actively in the production of capital-intensive spin-

7. The wage cost of Vietnam is among the lowest in Asia. In 2002 the average wage for blue-collar workers in the textile and apparel industries in Vietnam was US$0.18 per hour. This can be compared to Indonesia, US$0.23 per hour, China US$0.34, the Philippines US$0.67, Thailand US$0.87, Hong Kong US$3.39, and Taiwan US$5.00 (Dang 2003, 6).

Table 12.5. *Textile and Apparel Firms in Vietnam by Type of Ownership*
(Number of firms)

Stage of production	*All ownership types*	*State-owned enterprises*	*Non-state-owned enterprises*	*FDI firms*
Spinning	99	42	17	40
Weaving	124	43	24	57
Knitting	54	26	9	19
Apparel	659	139	299	221
Others	150	60	65	25
Total	1,086	310	414	362

Source: Directory 2003 of the Vietnam Textile and Apparel Association.

ning and weaving textiles. However, compared to SOEs, FDI firms tend to concentrate in the apparel-making industry.

Asian NIEs, especially Taiwan (China), have used Vietnam as an export base of labor-intensive garments. Their export ratios are very high, and the average scale of operation is small. (Singapore is exceptional, with its low export ratio and large operation scale, but why this is the case unfortunately is unknown.)

Asian NIEs have undertaken FDI as an instrument to exploit the comparative advantage of Vietnam; France, Germany, Japan, and other industrial countries have preferred the so-called contractual arrangement. The trading firms or apparel firms of these countries supply fabrics and other materials for processing to Vietnamese firms and later buy the finished garments back for re-exporting. This type of contractual arrangement is called CMT (cutting, making, trimming), and it accounts for about 60 percent of garment exports from Vietnam (Dang 2003, 49).

How has technology transfer been conducted in the apparel industry? To answer this question we rely on existing literature as well as the results of our field survey in August 2003. (We interviewed fifteen apparel and textile firms in Hanoi and Ho Chi Minh City.)

First let us consider the intrafirm transfer of technology. The training of operators of machines and equipment at the beginning stage of production is essential. So is the localization of engineers and managers at the factory and the head office. In the early stage of the projects, senior managers at the office or supervisors at the factory were expatriates from the investing countries. It is interesting that most FDI firms from Taiwan and Hong Kong tended to hire experts from China since the wage cost was much cheaper. After three to four years of operation, these positions have been filled by

Table 12.6. FDI in Vietnam's Apparel Industry, 2002

Foreign partner	*Number of projects*	*Registered capital ($1,000)*	*Realized capital ($1,000)*	*Sales ($1,000)*	*Exports ($1,000)*	*Labor (no. of workers)*
Taiwan	60	152,440	99,996	140,168	120,596	18,477
Singapore	8	96,263	49,510	111,032	27,808	3,131
Rep. of Korea	46	75,561	34,317	43,468	39,366	14,212
Hong Kong	28	63,353	39,446	87,675	83,374	12,915
Japan	26	47,595	35,382	52,344	49,433	6,010
Total for 5 investors	168	435,213	258,651	434,686	320,576	54,745
Other/ unknown[a]	226	460,565	197,846	241,575	198,645	33,693
Total	562	895,778	456,497	676,262	519,221	88,438

Foreign partner	*Realization ratio (%)*	*Average scale ($1,000)*	*Export ratio (%)*	*Capital intensity ($1,000 per person)*
Taiwan	65.6	2,541	86.0	5
Singapore	51.4	12,033	25.0	16
Rep. of Korea	45.4	1,643	90.6	2
Hong Kong	62.3	2,263	95.1	3
Japan	74.3	1,831	94.4	6
Total for 5 investors	59.4	2,591	73.7	5
Other/unknown[a]	43.0	2,038	82.2	6
Total	51.0	2,274	76.8	5

a. This category includes projects that identified the foreign investor by name but not by nationality. Therefore, the data of countries specifed in the table may be slightly influenced. The unknown nationality projects accounted for approximately 34 percent of the total number of projects and 16 percent of the total registered.

Source: Prepared by the author with data from the Ministry of Planning and Investment.

Vietnamese employees to further reduce costs. The average wage of a Vietnamese engineer is about half that of a Chinese engineer and about one-fourth of a Taiwanese engineer.

Evidence on the horizontal interfirm transfer of technology is difficult to obtain. In the field survey several cases were reported in which senior staff of FDI firms left to set up their own businesses. The contractual arrangement of garment export (CMT) transfers hard and soft technology to local firms to ensure the quality of products that are mainly exported to advanced markets.

The issue of vertical interfirm transfer of technology is particularly important. We have to investigate whether the operation of FDI firms or the contractual arrangement in the apparel industry has generated backward linkages to weaving, spinning, and dyeing stages of the textile industry. In the case of the contractual arrangement, foreign firms tend to depend entirely on import sources of materials. According to the survey by Goto (2003), foreign firms do not tend to procure Vietnamese materials since domestic textile producers are not considered capable of supplying materials that meet international standards in terms of quality and timely delivery.

In the case of FDI firms in the apparel industry, local procurement of materials occurs more often, although the general situation is not very encouraging. For FDI firms in both the apparel and textile industries, more than two-thirds of material inputs have been imported (Table 12.7). In this table "intrafirm" refers to the inputs from foreign factories that are operated by the same parent (MNC) company. "Direct imported channel" refers to the import conducted directly by the FDI firm (in Vietnam); "consigned channel" refers to the indirect import made through intermediary trading

Table 12.7. *Sources of Inputs for Firms in Vietnam's Textile and Apparel Industry, 2002*
(Percent)

Industry and ownership type	*Percentage of inputs from*		*Domestic inputs*		*Imported inputs*		*Imported channel*	
	Domestic source	*Imported source*	*Intra-firm*	*Other*	*Intra-firm*	*Other*	*Direct*	*Con-signed*
Textile	45	55	15	85	70	70	57	43
State-owned enterprises	48	52	13	87	77	77	58	42
Non-state-owned enterprises	57	43	12	88	9	91	34	66
FDI firms	24	76	25	75	41	41	97	13
Apparel	48	52	5	95	16	84	58	42
State-owned enterprises	47	53	13	87	11	89	65	35
Non-state-owned enterprises	54	46	1	99	3	97	48	52
FDI firms	33	67	6	94	44	56	77	23

Source: The data are from the Central Institute of Economic Management. See Dang (2003).

firms. In particular, FDI firms with full foreign ownership appear to rely almost entirely on imports of material inputs. In the case of Company G, a Japanese fully-owned apparel maker, the local content of the major input (yarn) in 2003 was merely 3 percent, a low share even considering that the company had been in business seven years.

Joint ventures between foreign firms and SOEs may procure more local inputs since those inputs are usually produced by the SOEs themselves. Domestic procurement of material inputs in foreign affiliated firms tends to be confined to the supply by other FDI firms in the up-stream stage. In other words, with the increase in FDI in the up-stream stage, local procurement by FDI firms in the downstream stage is likely to increase. Since the mid-1990s, foreign direct investment in Vietnam's textile industry by the Republic of Korea, Taiwan (China), and other economies has increased. By the end of 2002, such projects had risen to a substantial number (Table 12.8).

Table 12.8. *FDI in Vietnam's Textile Industry, 2002*

Foreign partner	*Number of projects*	*Registered capital ($1,000)*	*Realized capital ($1,000)*	*Sales ($1,000)*	*Exports ($ 1,000)*	*Labor (no. of workers)*
Republic of Korea	20	675,866	211,540	120,101	57,123	5,820
Taiwan	28	365,298	240,598	135,123	80,590	8,778
Japan	8	38,888	23,464	12,487	9,296	773
Total for 3 investors	56	1,080,052	475,602	267,711	147,009	15,371
Other/unknown[a]	58	963,247	252,191	122,459	53,833	8,719
Total	114	2,043,299	727,793	390,169	200,842	24,090

Foreign partner	*Realization ratio (%)*	*Average scale ($1,000)*	*Export ratio (%)*	*Capital intensity ($1,000 per person)*
Republic of Korea	31.3	33,793	47.6	36
Taiwan	65.9	13,046	59.6	27
Japan	60.3	4,861	74.4	30
Total for 3 investors	44.0	19,287	54.9	31
Other/unknown[a]	26.2	16,608	44.0	29
Total	35.6	17,924	51.5	30

a. This category includes projects that identified the foreign investor by name but not by nationality. Therefore, the data of countries specifed in the table may be slightly influenced. The unknown nationality projects accounted for approximately 34 percent of the total number of projects and 16 percent of the total registered.

Source: Prepared by the author with data from the Ministry of Planning and Investment.

From this case study several general conclusions can be drawn. First, FDI firms have been active in training local workers and in the localization of senior staff (the intrafirm transfer of technology). This observation is in line with what we know about the behavior of multinational corporations and with other empirical studies.[8] Second, vertical interfirm transfer of technology has been very weak. FDI firms tend to rely on the imports of their inputs since local materials are not qualified in terms of quality and timely delivery. This situation stems from the fact that the industrial sector in Vietnam is still dominated by inefficient SOEs.

A Case Study of the Motorcycle Industry

The Vietnamese market for motorcycles in the early 1990s was small, and the growth of the market to that point had been slow. After 1992 GDP began to grow, and the market for motorcycles began to improve (Table 12.9).

Table 12.9. *Market and Production of Motorcycles in Vietnam, 1990–2002*
(1,000 units)

			Domestic production		
Year	*No. of motorcyles in use*	*Increase in motorcycles from the previous year*	*By local firms*	*By FDI firms*	*Total*
1990	2,770	n.a.	n.a.	0	n.a.
1991	2,806	36	n.a.	0	n.a.
1992	2,846	40	n.a.	0	n.a.
1993	2,901	55	n.a.	n.a.	n.a.
1994	3,275	374	n.a.	n.a.	n.a.
1995	3,678	403	n.a.	n.a.	n.a.
1996	4,209	531	n.a.	n.a.	n.a.
1997	4,827	618	n.a.	n.a.	n.a.
1998	5,206	379	n.a.	n.a.	n.a.
1999	5,549	343	343	212	555
2000	6,387	838	1,334	295	1,629
2001	8,359	1,972	1,884	285	2,169
2002	10,273	1,685	900	785	1,685

n.a. Not available.

Source: JICA-NEU (2003, 233, 245). Figures for 2002, however, have been estimated by the author.

8. Regarding this issue, Tran (1995) provides a conceptual framework and an empirical study on the synthetic fiber industry in Thailand.

During the 1980s, most new motorcycles were imported from the former Soviet Union, the former East Germany, and the former Czechoslovakia. From 1989 to 1997, trading companies, mainly state owned, were allowed to import used motorcycles from Japan. Since 1997 imports of used motorcycles have been prohibited, and since 1998 imports of new motorcycles have also been prohibited. These changes in policy were aimed at promoting import substitution.

Since the early 1990s, in addition to imports of used motorcycles, some domestic firms have imported parts and accessories for local assembly. There were two types of such imports: Complete Knocked Down (CKD) and Incomplete Knocked Down (IKD). The number of domestic firms that assembled CKD and IKD rose to approximately 100 in the early 1990s. Assembly of CDK is technically simple and does not require a large investment; this type of import substitution was therefore allowed for a few state-owned enterprises with limited quantity of production. In other words, only IKD assembly has been allowed for non-SOEs. Since the mid-1990s, entry of foreign firms has been substantial.

The first FDI project for assembling motorcycles in Vietnam was undertaken in 1993 by the Chinfon Corporation of Taiwan (China). The presence of foreign firms has been notable since the entry of Japanese firms in the mid-1990s. By June 2002, there had been seven FDI firms out of the total of fifty-two assemblers of motorcycles in Vietnam. Honda, with its good reputation, has grown fast. Its brand name, high price, and high market share have brought about a high profit rate for Honda. Honda was able to make a profit in 1999, only fifteen months after the start of operations in Vietnam. With news of the low prices of Honda motorcycles made in Thailand has come public criticism of the high prices of Honda motorcycles made in Vietnam.

At this time, domestic companies started to import IKD sets from China in order to produce cheap motorcycles to compete with Honda. These sets were mainly supplied to low-income consumers, particularly in rural areas. Motorcycles with Chinese inputs gradually eroded the market dominated by Honda. In January 2002, to change that trend, Honda introduced Wave Alpha, the new model. This model partially used the China-made IKD sets and supplied cheap motorcycles to the market.

In order to manage the imports of IKD as well as to speed up the localization of parts and accessories, the Vietnamese government in 1998 changed its policy. Each assembling company now faces different rates of tariffs on IKD sets imported (the higher the ratio of local content, the lower the tariff rates). At the beginning of the year, each firm registers with the government its planned ratio of local content and pays the corresponding tax when importing IKD. Adjustment of the paid tax is made at the end of each year, taking into account the actual ratio of local content of each firm.

The sharp increase in the supply of motorcycles since 2000 has been accompanied by an increase in the number of traffic accidents, a serious social problem. In 2002 the government limited the number of new motorcycles supplied to the market to 1.5 million units, fewer than the nearly 2 million units in the previous year (Table 12.9).[9] Of this number, 900,000 units have been allocated to domestic firms (taking into account their performance in 2001), and the rest were for FDI firms. In fact, the number allocated to FDI firms (600,000 units) was twice as big as the number produced in the previous year (Table 12.9). Most FDI firms had planned to expand production capacity to a level far surpassing the allocated volume. The government suddenly announced its decision and made it immediately effective. Therefore, it is not surprising that FDI firms complained strongly.

Honda, the biggest assembler in Vietnam, is a case in point. Honda's production in 2001 was 170,000 units, but its capacity was 400,000 units, and its plan for 2002 was 600,000 units. Under the new policy by the government, only 280,000 units were allocated to the firm. Honda, discouraged by the policy, decided to stop production beginning in September 2002. Later, at end of October 2002, the government decided to add 185,000 units (110,000 sets for Honda). In other words, it increased the amount of IKD sets that could be imported by FDI firms.

The sudden change in policy has made the market conditions of the motorcycle industry unstable and unpredictable. The government's policy hurt the investment environment and affected the long-term development of the supporting industries as well.

At the end of 2002, 110 firms supplied parts and accessories to 7 FDI firms and 45 local assemblers of motorcycles. Unfortunately, there is no detailed information on the development of supporting industries relating to the motorcycle industry. We therefore will observe the case of Honda, the largest motorcycle assembler in Vietnam. [10]

---

9. The restriction of production seems to be justified in terms of traffic safety. However, from the viewpoint of industrial development, direct control of production is not wise since it limits the discretion of firms in the market. The traffic problem should be addressed in other ways. Motorcycles can also be regulated by other measures. Direct control of production is not the best solution.

10. Honda Vietnam is a joint venture of Honda Motors (Japan, 42 percent ownership), Asia Honda (Asia-wide company of Honda, 28 percent ownership), and Vietnam Engine and Agricultural Machinery Corporation (30 percent ownership). The license was given in March 1996, and the operation started in 1997.

The ratio of local content of Honda was high from the beginning and it has risen very fast. This localization has been realized at a higher speed than the plan (see Table 12.10), and it was more progressive than the speed required by the government. According to the regulations applied to the motorcycle industry, FDI firms in the first year of operation must procure local parts and accessories with an amount equivalent to at least 10 percent of total inputs, and this ratio of local content must be raised to at least 60 percent by the sixth year of operation. Honda's behavior can be explained in part by its hope to expand production in the near future. Its production in 2001 was 170,000 units, far under its capacity of 400,000 units. The reason was competition from cheap China-made motorcycles. In 2002, with the expansion of sales of the new model (Wave Alpha), Honda raised capacity by changing the production system from two to three shifts. It planned to produce at full capacity of 600,000 units. (Due to the sudden changes in policy noted earlier, Honda production volume in 2002 was only 390,000 units.) If the original plan had been realized, Honda could have expanded its capacity in the future. The active behavior of Honda on the local content can therefore be understood in the context of its planned expansion of capacity.

Even though the localization of inputs has been undertaken at a fast rate, a closer look at the structure of firms supplying parts and accessories to Honda reveals that the linkages between Honda and local firms are still

Table 12.10. *Production of Motorcycles and Localization Performance of Honda Vietnam Corporation, 1998–2003*

	Production by Honda				*Number of suppliers*	
Year	*In thousands of units*	*As a percentage of total production*[a]	*As a percentage of production by FDI firms*	*Ratio of local content*[b]	*Total*	*Local suppliers*
1998	60	16	n.a.	44 (12)	16	5
1999	90	16	42	51 (17)	19	5
2000	160	10	54	51 (29)	28	8
2001	170	8	60	53 (44)	31	10
2002	390	43	63	66 (52)	32	11
2003	450	37	49	70 (71)	42	13

n.a. Not available.

a. Total production is domestic production of local and FDI firms.

b. Figures in parentheses are planned ratios registered in the license of the project.

Source: Author's survey data.

weak. There are three sources of parts and accessories: Honda's in-house production, FDI-related firms, and local firms. The first source has supplied engine parts and other technology-intensive sophisticated parts. By the end of 2002, Honda had six production lines of engines, built in the main factory, and these lines supplied about 30 percent of the engines of Honda assembly operations in Vietnam (the rest of the engines relied on imports).

At the end of 2003, twenty-nine FDI- related firms were producing various types of parts and accessories for Honda. Only thirteen local firms were in operation at the end of 2003 (Table 12.10). According to our survey, Honda has investigated and examined more than 100 Vietnamese firms, including SOEs and private enterprises. The thirteen local firms listed in the table met the requirement of Honda concerning the quality of inputs. This achievement is the result of transfer of technology from Honda. The number of local firms that have participated in the supply of parts and accessories for Honda can be considered too small if the Honda operation in Thailand is the benchmark. In Thailand, Honda produces about 1 million units a year, approximately twice as many units as Honda in Vietnam. In Thailand more than 100 local firms have supplied inputs for Honda operations. Of course, this comparison is for reference only since Honda has a much longer history in Thailand than in Vietnam.

Like in the textile and apparel industries, in the motorcycle industry the backward linkages between FDI firms and local firms have been very weak. Various policy measures should be adopted to strengthen such linkages. It is essential that Vietnam develop supporting industries through restructuring SOEs and other existing local firms as well as by providing incentives to develop new firms that can supply parts and other inputs on a competitive basis in terms of quality and cost.

Conclusion

FDI has played an important role in the development of the Vietnamese economy since the mid-1990s. FDI as a percentage of most macroeconomic indicators has been high in Vietnam compared to other economies in East Asia. So far, however, FDI firms appear to be enclaves in the Vietnamese economy. Their operations tend to depend largely on the imports of materials and other inputs. This has been true of wholly foreign-owned and highly export-oriented FDI firms such as those in the apparel industry. The dominance of inefficient SOEs largely explains this trend. Drastic reforms of SOEs and the nourishment of the private sector are essential for promoting the linkages between FDI firms and domestic firms.

The motorcycle industry is another case in point. Unlike the apparel industry, which is export oriented, the motorcycle industry is an import-substitute industry, and its success depends largely on the long-term development strategy of the government. Policies in recent years have tended to discourage FDI inflows and to retard the backward linkages in the industry. Heavy intervention in the operation of firms has occurred recently. The government set the ceiling on units produced and imposed the production quota allocated to firms that restrain the competition. In addition, there have been frequent changes in policies and lack of support for small and medium-size enterprises (SMEs) that can supply qualified parts and other inputs in terms of cost and quality. Halting intervention of this kind, instituting a longer-term policy, and promoting development of supporting industries are actions necessary for the successful development of the motorcycle industry and other import-substitution industries.

We recommend several policy measures to enhance the linkages between FDI firms and local firms. First, the government should conduct a comprehensive survey of all SOEs that are producing parts and other inputs for motorcycles, apparel, and other consumer goods. It then should list up the firms that are potentially competitive. Second, the government should set up an assistance scheme for strengthening those firms by providing technical support and information on markets, and by facilitating the access to capital for new investments. Third, the government should encourage the development of private SMEs in the supporting industries by providing special incentives related to tax and access to credit. Fourth, frequent communication between the government and FDI firms is useful. It enables the former to find out the problems faced by the latter and provide a timely solution. It also may reveal ways to enhance the linkages between FDI firms and local firms. Inappropriate implementation of tax policy and lack of information are common obstacles to vertical linkages between FDI firms and local firms. The implementation of value-added tax in Vietnam has been one impediment in recent years.[11]

In a word, to promote the needed linkages between FDI firms and local firms, Vietnam must develop supporting industries. At the same time, it must remove obstacles, such as the inefficient implementation of value-added tax, that prevent vital transactions between FDI firms and local firms.

---

11. Firms must pay value-added tax when purchasing local inputs, but the tax is supposed to be refunded if most final products are exported. In fact, however, the refund process is so complicated and time consuming that FDI firms avoid using local inputs and tend to rely on imports.

References

Balasubramanyam,V.N., M. Salisu, and David Sapsford. 1996. "Foreign Direct Investment and Growth in EP and IS Countries." *Economic Journal* 106 (January): 92–105.

Dang, Thi Dong. 2003. "Cong nghiep det may: Gia tri gia tang va chien luoc phat trien" (The Textile and Apparel Industries: Their Value-Added and Development Strategy). In JICA and NEU (2003, chap. 2).

Dunning, John H. 1993. *Multinational Enterprises and the Global Economy.* Wokingham: Addison-Wesley Publishers Ltd.

Goto, Kenta. 2003. "Sen-i Hosei Sangyou: Ryutsuu Mihattatsu no Kensho" (Textile and Apparel Industries: An Empirical Study on their Distribution Underdevelopment). In Ohno and Kawabata (2003, chap. 5).

Ito, Takatoshi, and Anne O. Krueger, eds. 1993. *Trade and Protectionism.* Chicago: University of Chicago Press.

JICA and NEU (Japan International Cooperation Agency and National Economic University). 2003. *Chinh sach cong nghiep va thuong mai cua Viet Nam trong boi canh hoi nhap* (Vietnamese Trade and Industrial Policies in the Era of Globalization), vol. 3. Hanoi: Nha xuat ban thong ke.

Kojima, Kiyoshi. 1977. "Transfer of Technology to Developing Countries: Japanese Type versus American Type." *Hitotsubashi Journal of Economics* 17, No. 2, pp. 1–14.

Lall, Sanjaya. 1978. "Transnationals, Domestic Enterprises, and Industrial Structure in Host LDCs: A Survey." *Oxford Economic Paper* 30, No. 2, July.

Minami, Ryoshin, et al., eds. 1995. *Acquiring, Adapting and Developing Technologies: Lessons from the Japanese Experience.* London: The Macmillan Press, Ltd.

Ohno, Ken-ichi, and Nozomu Kawabata, eds. 2003. *Betonamu no Kougyouka Senryaku* (Industrialization Strategy of Vietnam). Tokyo: Nihon Hyouronsha.

Park, Bohm, and Keum Lee. 2003. "Firms from South Korea, Hong Kong, and the United States in Shandong Province." *Journal of the Asia-Pacific Economy*, vol. 8, no. 1 (February): 57–84.

Sachs, Jeffrey, et al. 1997. *Development Strategies for Vietnam: Challenges to Prosperity.* Harvard Institute for International Development (HIID), Harvard University, September.

Saggi, Kamal. 2002. "Trade, Foreign Direct Investment, and International Technology Transfer: A Survey." *The World Bank Research Observer*, vol. 17, no. 2 (Fall): 191–235.

Thompson, Edmund R. 2003. "Technology Transfer to China by Hong Kong's Cross-Border Garment Firms." *The Developing Economies*, XLI-1 (March): 88–111.

Tran, Van Tho. 1988. "Foreign Capital and Technology in the Process of Catching up by the Developing Countries: The Experience of the Synthetic Fiber Industry in the Republic of Korea." *The Developing Economies*, vol. 26, no. 4 (December): 386–402.

———. 1992. *Sangyou Hatten to Takokusekigyou* (Industrial Development and Multinational Corporations). Tokyo: Toyo Keizai.

———. 1993a. "Japan's Technology Transfer in Thailand: Effective Transfer and Management Style." In Tran Van Tho, ed., *Japanese Management Style and Technology Transfer in Thailand*, Research Report No. 3, pp. 58–87. Tokyo: Japan Center for Economic Research.

———. 1993b. "Technology Transfer in the Asian Pacific Region: Implications of Trends since the Mid-1980s." In Ito and Krueger, eds., pp. 243–71.

———. 1995. "Japanese Technology and Industrial Development in Thailand: The Experience of the Synthetic Fiber Industry." In Minami et al., eds., chap. 12.

———. 1996. *Betonamu Keizai no Shintenkai* (New Development of Vietnamese Economy). Tokyo: Nohon Keizai Shimbun.

———. 2001. "Vietnamese Gradualism in Reforms of the State-Owned Enterprises." *Vietnam Socio-Economic Development*, No. 26, Summer, pp. 3–23.

UNCTAD (United Nations Conference on Trade and Development). 2001. *World Investment Report: Promoting Linkages.* New York and Geneva: United Nations.

World Bank. 1997. *Vietnam, Deepening Reform for Growth: An Economic Report*, October 31. Washington, D.C.

———. 2000. *Vietnam 2010: Entering the 21st Century* (Vietnam Development Report 2001). Hanoi: The World Bank, Asian Development Bank, United Nations Development Program.

13

The Experience of FDI Recipients: The Case of China

Yu Yongding

This chapter describes the value, sources, and sectoral as well as geographical distribution of foreign direct investment (FDI) in China. Also assessed are the factors determining FDI in China—the country's low-cost and skilled labor force, established infrastructure, stable macroeconomic environment, preferential policy toward investors, and huge domestic market. The chapter details the varied effects of FDI on the Chinese economy, and in the final section offers some general conclusions about the future.

FDI Trends in China

Foreign direct investment, as defined by the Organization for Economic Cooperation and Development (OECD), "reflects the objective of obtaining a lasting interest by a resident entity in one country ('direct investor') in an entity resident in an economy other than that of the investor ('direct investment enterprise'). The lasting interest implies the existence of a long-term relationship between the direct investor and the enterprise and a significant degree of influence on the management of the enterprise" (Lipsey 1999, 310). The key concept is that FDI is an ownership arrangement instead of a contractual arrangement. Quantitatively, FDI is understood as the purchase of at least 10 percent of the equity of a particular company by a foreign investor (Lipsey 1999, 311). In China, according to the "Law of China and Foreign Jointly-Owned Enterprises," a foreign investor's share of total investment in an enterprise should surpass 25 percent.[1] Otherwise, the investment will not be regarded as FDI, and the project invested or the enterprise established will not achieve the status of foreign funded enterprises (FFEs). Thus, it will not receive the preferential treatments FFEs enjoy (Wang 1997, 367).

Three Stages of FDI in China

Foreign direct investment in China can be divided into three stages: 1979 to 1991, 1992 to 2000, and 2001, the year of China's entry into the World Trade Organization (WTO), to the present. In 1979, when the policy of reform and liberalization began, FDI inflows into China were a negligible amount of US$0.08 million. Following the establishment of the four Special Economic Zones, and the opening up of more regions and cities to foreign investors, FDI inflows into China began to pick up. From 1984 to 1991, they grew annually at a rate of 20 percent (Chen 2002).

In 1992, after Deng Xiaoping's tours of South China, China's reform and opening up process intensified, and FDI inflows increased by leaps and bounds. From US$4.4 billion in 1991, they increased dramatically to US$11 billion in 1992, a jump of more than 150 percent. After that the increase in FDI inflows was rapid and steady until the Asian financial crisis struck in 1997. The economic turmoil caused the increase in FDI inflows to stall from 1998 to 2000.

No sooner had China finally sealed the deals for its entry into the WTO, than the momentum of FDI inflows into China picked up with a vengeance. In 2001 FDI inflows increased 12 percent over 2000, and the share of FDI in China's total fixed investment reached 10.5 percent. By the end of 2001, China's cumulative utilization of FDI had reached US$395.4 billion, and cumulative contracted FDI had reached US$745.1 billion. Some 400 companies on the Forbes 500 list have invested in some 2,000 projects in China, and major international manufacturers of computers, electronic products, telecom equipment, petrochemicals, and other products have extended their network into China (UNCTAD 2001). In 2002, with FDI inflows reaching US$52.7 billion, China surpassed the United States to become the largest FDI recipient country in the world. According to the Ministry of Foreign Trade and Economic Cooperation and Trade (MOFTEC),

1. As of April 1, 2003, a foreign funded enterprise that is formed through the merger and acquisition of Chinese enterprises is allowed to own less than 25 percent of the shares of the enterprise. Investment thus made by foreign investors is regarded as FDI. However, some preferential treatments will not apply to these investments. (For example, imported equipment and other objects will not receive tax reductions or exemptions.) See *Foreign Investment in China*, 2003, No. 5 and No. 8.

which is now the Ministry of Commerce, contracted foreign investment—an indicator of future trends—surged 19.6 percent to US$82.8 billion in 2002, compared with the growth rate of 10.4 percent in 2001 (Table 13.1).

Sources of FDI

In the 1980s, the single most important source of FDI in China was Hong Kong (China). In the 1990s, FDI from Hong Kong, Taiwan (China), Singapore, and other parts of East Asia, a region where there are large numbers of ethnic Chinese, still accounted for over 50 percent of total FDI in China. However, the relative importance of these sources has declined with the significant increase in FDI from the United States, the European Union, and Japan.

HONG KONG. During the 1980s and early 1990s, Hong Kong was by far the largest source of FDI in China. Up to 1992, the share of FDI in China from Hong Kong was almost 70 percent. Hong Kong contributed nearly half of the cumulated FDI in China during the past two decades. Currently, Hong Kong is still the most important source of FDI in China. However, since the second half of the 1990s, major industrial countries' contribution to China's

Table 13.1. *FDI in China, 1991–2002*
(US$billions)

Year	*Utilized FDI*	*Contracted FDI*	*FDI as a percentage of fixed capital formation*
1991	4.366	11.977	4.13
1992	11.008	58.124	7.51
1993	27.515	111.36	12.13
1994	33.767	82.680	17.08
1995	37.521	91.282	15.65
1996	41.726	73.276	15.10
1997	45.257	51.003	14.79
1998	45.462	52.102	13.23
1999	40.318	41.223	11.17
2000	40.715	62.380	10.32
2001	46.878	69.192	10.54
2002	52.700	82.768	15.00

Sources: Bureau of Foreign Capital, the Ministry of Foreign Trade and Economic Cooperation (the Ministry of Commerce since March of 2003).

FDI inflows has increased significantly. In 2001, Hong Kong's share in China's total FDI inflows dropped to 36 percent.

It is not surprising that, following China's success in industrial upgrading and greater openness to the outside world, the role of Hong Kong in providing and intermediating FDI inflows into China has decreased. This role will be further reduced in the future. It is well known that a very large proportion of Hong Kong's FDI is so-called round-tripping capital. However, no reliable estimates of the round-tripping capital are available.

THE UNITED STATES. During the 1980s, the share of foreign direct investment in China by the United States was relatively high but very unstable. In 1992, America's FDI in China was US$500 million, accounting for only 4.6 percent of China's total attraction of FDI in that year. However, in the next year, U.S. FDI in China shot up to US$2 billion, a fourfold jump, and accounted for 7.5 percent of China's total attraction of FDI. With the exception of 1997, FDI flows from the United States have been increasing gradually and steadily ever since. In 2001, FDI inflows from the United States reached US$4.4 billion and accounted for 9 percent of China's total attraction of FDI. The United States has been the second largest investor in China since 1998.

THE EUROPEAN UNION. FDI inflows into China from the European Union and from the United States are motivated by similar factors and followed a similar pattern. From 1987 to 1992, average annual FDI inflows into China from the European Union were very small, only about US$200 million. In 1986, FDI from the EU reached US$2.2 billion and accounted for 8 percent of China's total attraction of FDI that year. Thereafter, the growth rate of FDI from the European Union relative to other sources was slower, and so its share in China's total FDI inflows dropped quite dramatically. In 1992, its contribution accounted for only 2.2 percent of China's total FDI. From 1993 to 1996, FDI inflows from the European Union entered a fast-growing stage, increasing rapidly from US$671 million in 1993 to US$4.17 billion in 1997. The European Union's share in China's total FDI increased from 2.4 percent in 1993 to 9.2 percent in 1996. From 1997 on, FDI from the E.U. held stable at roughly US$4 billion a year. In 2001, E.U. direct investment in China increased to US$4.69 billion and accounted for 8.9 percent of China's total FDI inflows (Ming 2003, 78).

JAPAN. Japan is China's close neighbor. However, the Sino-Japanese relationship is complex and has been characterized by ups and downs over the past two decades. In 1992, Japan's direct investment in China was US$710 million, second only to direct investment by Hong Kong and 1.4 times as high as direct investment by the United States. Japan's FDI in China peaked in 1997.[2] Since then Japan's FDI in China has dropped dramatically, while other major investors have increased their investment in China. In 1998, Japan's direct investment in China was less than Singapore's. More worrying, from China's point of view, is the fact that Japan's direct investment in China as a share of Japan's overall overseas investment also diminished drastically. Japan's direct investment in China was US$4.47 billion in 1995, accounting for 8.8 percent of Japan's total overseas direct investment. However, in 1999, according to Japanese sources, Japan's direct investment in China accounted for only 1.1 percent of Japan's total overseas direct investment.[3] In the second half of 2000, Japan's FDI in China began to resurge. In 2001, FDI from Japan reached US$4.3 billion, which accounted for 9 percent of China's total FDI inflows in that year. The trends have continued ever since.

OTHER COUNTRIES AND REGIONS. In addition to the above-mentioned economies, Taiwan (China), the Republic of Korea, and many other economies have become important sources of foreign direct investment in China. In order of the magnitude of their investment, these sources are Hong Kong, the United States, Japan, Taiwan, Korea, Germany, the United Kingdom, France, Australia, and Canada. Figure 13.1 shows the regional distribution of FDI in China.

The Sectoral Distribution of FDI

In the past two decades, the sectoral distribution of FDI in China changed significantly. In the early periods of reform, FDI inflows, which were overwhelmingly from Hong Kong, were concentrated in the service sector, especially the real estate sector, and to a lesser degree in the labor-intensive manufacturing sector. In the 1990s, FDI inflows rapidly extended to almost all sectors of the economy. The manufacturing sector became the biggest recipient of investment, accounting for 60 percent of cumulated FDI in all sectors by the end of 1999, and the real estate sector remained a prominent recipient of FDI, accounting for 24.4 percent of cumulated FDI in all sectors. On the whole, the industry concentration of FDI in China is not very high

---

2. According to other studies, Japan's FDI to China peaked in 1995.
3. Lee (2001, 16). There may be some under-reporting by Japanese enterprises.

Figure 13.1. *Sources of China's FDI Inflows, 2001*

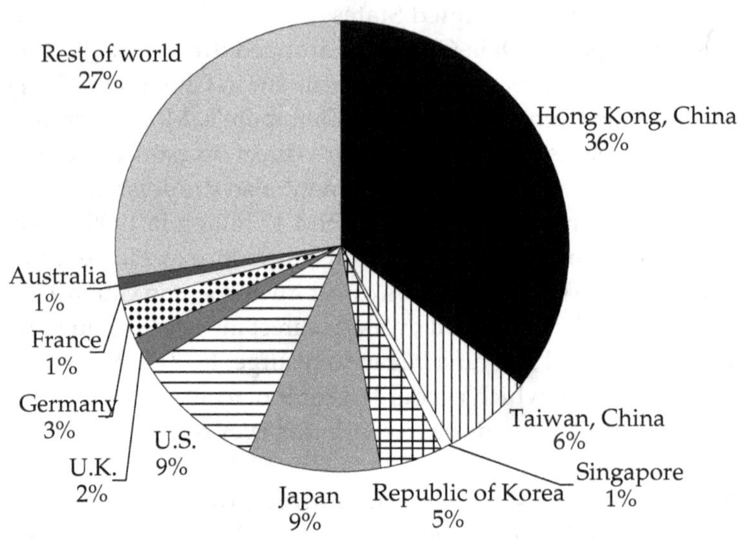

Source: Ministry of Commerce, Government of China, 2003.

compared with the industry concentration in other countries (IMF 2002). Since the late 1990s, FDI inflows into the manufacturing sector have shifted increasingly from labor-intensive industry to processing industry.

In recent years, the sectoral distribution of China's FDI inflows has resembled the pattern of the 1990s. FDI inflows into the manufacturing sector as a share of total annual FDI inflows increased from 56 percent in 1999 to 66 percent in 2001. At the same time, the share of FDI inflows into the service sector, including in real estate, decreased to a much weaker second place (Figure 13.2).

THE SERVICE SECTOR. The service sector has long been the most important area for FDI inflows in China. Since the beginning of opening up, more and more of China's service sectors have attracted foreign investors. In fact, one of the first three joint ventures ever made in China was Jianguo Hotel, a joint venture by Chinese and American investors. Only after 1993 did the relative importance of FDI in the service sector begin to decrease.

FDI in the real estate sector has accounted for the lion's share of FDI in the service sector. FDI in real estate has been biased toward speculative types of investment, which strongly correlated with the macroeconomic sit-

Figure 13.2. *Sectoral Distribution of FDI in China, 2001*

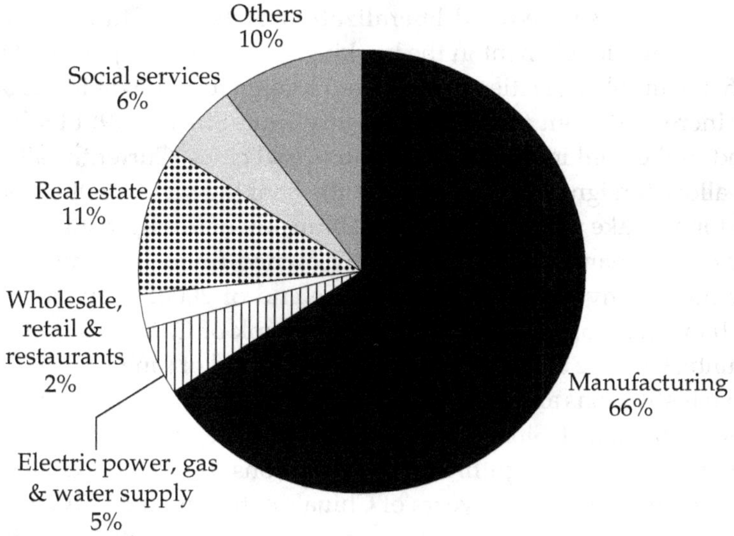

Source: Customs Statistics 2002.

uation and fluctuated widely in response to the acceleration and deceleration of the growth of the economy (Lai 2001). Currently, ethnic Chinese from Hong Kong and South East Asian countries still dominate FDI in China's service sector, especially in real estate. Their familiarity with local culture and social networks, and hence their ability to overcome bureaucratic hurdles and contend with corruption, placed them in an advantageous position compared to U.S. and European investors. However, China's entry into the World Trade Organization has begun to change the situation.

According to some estimates, from 2004 to 2008, the annual growth rate of real estate will be maintained at 7 percent, and the profit rate of housing construction will be as high as 25 percent. Since 2002, foreign investors in the real estate industry have been entering China in droves. So far foreign investors have been involved in more than 5,000 real estate companies in China; these companies account for 20 percent of China's real estate developers. In the first three quarters of 2002, the growth rates of real estate investment in Shanghai, Beijing, and Guangzhou, where real estate development is most prosperous, were 31.4 percent, 29 percent, and 30 percent, respectively. Foreign investors have made important contributions to the growth of China's real estate development.

So far, FDI inflows into sectors such as banking, insurance, wholesale, and retail trade are still limited, but they are expected to increase rapidly following China's scheduled liberalization. Actually, China had already allowed foreign investment in the banking sector on an experimental basis. In 1995, the number of cities that allowed foreign investment in the banking sector increased from thirteen to twenty-four. Since 1999, FDI has been allowed in the banking sector in all municipal cities. Currently, all cities in China allow foreign investors to enter the banking sector. FDI in the banking sector can take various forms: local branches of foreign banks, wholly or jointly owned banks, wholly or jointly owned financial companies, and jointly owned investment banks. By the end of 2000, thirty-two foreign banks had been approved by the People's Bank of China to conduct RMB (Renminbi, Chinese currency) business. By the end of June 2002, 167 foreign financial institutions and 233 resident offices of foreign financial institutions had been established. Since 2001, all geographical and customer restrictions on the activities of foreign financial institutions in foreign exchange dealings have lifted. Within five years of China's entry into the WTO in 2001, all geographical and customer restrictions on the activities of foreign financial institutions in RMB businesses are expected to be lifted (Sun 2002).

Since 1992, China has gradually opened its insurance markets. By the end of 2001, twenty-nine foreign insurance companies had entered China and established forty-four operational offices. Within two to three years of China's entry into the WTO, a much more relaxed regime has been adopted in regulating foreign insurance business. Foreign insurance companies are speeding up their entry into China's insurance markets.

Before 2001, foreign direct investment in China's telecommunications sector was prohibited. However, after WTO entry, restrictions on location, shareholding, and business sphere are being gradually eased. In 2002, American AT&T, Shanghai Telecom, and Shanghai Information Investment Company Limited jointly created the first telecommunications company to provide telecommunications services in China.

In 1992, China decided to allow foreign investors to establish one to two enterprises engaged in retail business jointly with Chinese partners in each of the following five cities: Beijing, Tianjin, Shanghai, Dalian, and Qingdao. Later, foreign firms were allowed to establish retail chain stores in Shanghai and Beijing. Since 1999, all provincial capitals and some major cities have opened to foreign retail businesses, and wholesale businesses are also opened on an experimental basis.

By 2000, there were forty-nine retail joint ventures and one wholesale joint venture with 482 branches, reflecting US$514 million FDI in China

(Sun 2002). The world's largest retail giant, Wal-Mart, established its global purchasing center in Shenzhen in February 2002 to take charge of US$200 billion worth of purchasing. Wal-Mart made China its regional purchasing center in Asia.

Since the 1980s, foreign investors have been allowed to establish international trade enterprises within the Free Tax Zones in Shenzhen, Shatoujia, Shantou, Xiamen, Haikou, Dalian, Tianjing, Qindao, Zhangjiagan, Waigaoqiao, Ningbo, Fuzhou, and Guangzhou. In 1996, foreign international trade companies were established to engage in exporting and importing businesses in the Pudong Economic Development Zone and the Shenzhen Special Economic Zone, and restrictions on foreign international trade companies' exporting and importing activities were eased significantly. Five foreign owned international trade companies have been established in China (Sun 2002).

Since the 1990s, foreign direct investments have been made in other areas in the service sector such as restaurants, tourism, transportation, parcel delivery, and airliners. McDonald's and Kentucky Fried Chicken have 700 Chinese restaurants between them, and they are opening scores more each year. So far there are ten foreign travel agencies, more than sixty joint ventures for domestic water transportation, sixty joint ventures for international maritime transportation, and 200 foreign international cargo agencies in China. UPS has become China's most important express parcel delivery enterprise. By the end of 2002, FDI in the airlines sector was US$420 million, with sixty-four foreign-owned or jointly owned enterprises (Sun 2002).

The liberalization following China's membership in the WTO is expected to lead to more FDI, especially more investment from industrial countries in the service sector. The greatest liberalization will be in financial services, telecommunications, and distribution. These subsectors in the service sector are expected to see rapid increases in FDI.

THE MANUFACTURING SECTOR. After 1986, the manufacturing sector's share of FDI increased rapidly. Its share reached 80 percent of total FDI inflows in 1991, decreased to 46 percent in 1993, and since 1994 has risen again. Over the past two decades, China's manufacturing sector saw a steady upgrading of FDI inflows from labor-intensive industries to capital- and technological-intensive industries and from traditional manufacturing industries to information technology (IT) related industries. By the end of the 1990s, IT related industries in China had become the most important beneficiaries of FDI inflows within the manufacturing sector (Table 13.2).

During the 1980s, FDI in the manufacturing sector, which was mainly funded by investors from Hong Kong, and, to a lesser extent, Macao and

Table 13.2. *FDI in China's Manufacturing Sector, 1997–99*
(US$billions)

Sector	*Value*	*FDI as a percentage of manufacturing sector FDI*
Manufacturing	76.305	100.00
Electronics, telecommunication equipment	8.237	10.79
Textiles	5.688	7.50
Chemicals	5.329	6.98
Machinery	3.705	4.86
Pharmaceuticals	1.808	2.37

Source: Yearbook of China's Investment (December 2001), vol. 1. Beijing: Xinhua Publishing House.

Taiwan, concentrated in traditional labor-intensive manufacturing industries, such as textiles, apparel, shoes, electronics, plastics, and leather products. After 1992, the bulk of FDI inflows into the manufacturing sector shifted to capital- and technology-intensive manufacturing sectors, such as electronics, automobiles, family appliances, office machines, measuring and checking instruments, telecommunications equipment, pharmaceuticals, and chemicals (Table 13.2). The shift was caused mainly by the increase in FDI by multinationals from industrial countries.

Utilized FDI in China's electronics and telecommunications equipment sector witnessed the most significant increase in dollar terms of any investment category. In the second half of the 1990s, especially from 1997 to 2000, the IT industry became the focus of FDI.[4] During this period, the amount of both contracted and actual FDI in electronics and telecommunications saw rapid expansion. The former increased from US$2.944 billion to US$11.36 billion, and the latter rose from US$2.659 billion to US$4.594 billion. In 2000, within electronics and telecommunications, the amounts of contracted investment in computers and electronic components rose by 80.06 percent and 64.63 percent, reaching US$0.87 billion and US$1.88 billion, respectively. A decade ago, China began attracting semiconductor manufacturers with tax breaks and cheap land. Today there are at least a dozen silicon-wafer fabrication plants in various stages of planning or construction in

4. The categories "IT" and "Electronics and telecommunication equipment" are used interchangeably in this chapter.

China. More are expected to come as Taiwan eases its rules barring investments in semiconductor manufacturing in the Mainland (Smith 2002). The commitment by NEC Electronics Inc. of US$300 million to its Shanghai Hua Hong semiconductor venture was among the largest investments in this subsector.

Since China's WTO entry in 2001, FDI from multinationals has increasingly concentrated in capital-intensive heavy chemistry, large-scale infrastructure, high-technology industry, and the service industry. It seems that the momentum of FDI in the manufacturing industry will be maintained in years to come. However, because of the liberalization of the service sector, the manufacturing sector's share in total FDI is likely to be stabilized and then to fall. Furthermore, the shift from labor-intensive industry to the processing industry, which became noticeable in the second half of the 1990s, probably will continue.

RESEARCH AND DEVELOPMENT. Since 1994, multinational corporations have begun to establish research and development centers in Beijing and other major cities in China. By the end of 2001, thirty-four research and development centers had been established in Beijing, forty-one in Shanghai, eighteen in Shenzhen, and seven in Suzhou. These centers concentrate in fields of information and communications, pharmaceuticals, chemicals, and transport equipment. Among the multinationals that have established research and development centers in China are Microsoft, Intel, IBM, Nokia, Motorola, Eriksson, Lucent, Fujitsu, LG, Colgate, Hewlett Packard, Sun Microsystems, General Electric, Volkswagen, National, Toshiba, Nortel, Bell, and Michelin. Multinational corporations—such as IBM, the U.S. computer giant; Microsoft, the U.S. software corporation; and Intel, the computer chip company—also increased the size of their research and development operations in China in 2002. Most of these research and development centers are either solely funded by the multinationals or controlled by multinationals as major shareholders (Jiang 2002).

Geographical Distribution of FDI in China

The geographical distribution of FDI in China is highly uneven.[5] In the early periods of opening up, FDI was concentrated in the Shenzhen Special Economic Zone. Later FDI spread into eastern coastal areas and some inland

5. This subsection draws on Lai (2001).

areas. The first four special economic zones were located in Guangdong Province (Shenzhen, Zhuhai, and Shantou) and Fujian Province (Xiamen). Foreign-funded enterprises inside these special economic zones were given preferential treatment. These FFEs were basically export oriented. In 1984 and 1985, the government decided to open fourteen coastal cities, including Shanghai, Tianjin, Dalian, Qingdao, and Guangzhou. At the same time, the government also authorized the Yangtze River Delta Area and the Xiamen-Zhangzhou-Quanzhou Delta Region in southern Fujian as open coastal economic zones. In 1988, the open coastal economic zones were further extended to Liaodong Peninsula, Shandong Peninsula, and some other coastal cities. By 1990, the central government had decided to develop and open the Pudong Area in Shanghai. By 2000, FDI could be seen in all provinces of China except Tibet.

After 1984, the concentration of FDI in the four special economic zones (especially, Shenzhen) gradually decreased. The actual investment share of the south coastal area decreased from a peak level of 81.7 percent in 1984 to 59.3 percent in 1991 to 38.8 percent in 2000. The share of the northern coastal areas increased from 7.1 percent in 1984 to 22.9 percent in 1991, before decreasing to 21.2 percent in 2000. The share of the middle coastal areas increased from 8 percent in 1984 to 10.3 percent in 1991 to 27.8 percent in 2000.

The change in the provincial distribution is directly related to change in the origin of investing countries/regions. In the initial investment period, most direct foreign investment came from Hong Kong. After 1992, the increase in FDI largely came from Japan, the Republic of Korea, Taiwan, Singapore, the United States, and the European Union. While investment from Hong Kong was heavily concentrated in the Pearl Delta, most of the increase in investment from other major sources flowed to other areas. The northern coastal areas attracted relatively more investment from geographically adjacent Japan and Korea. This explained the rise of the investment share of the northern coastal areas in the second half of the 1980s. For investors from Taiwan, Singapore, the United States, and the European Union, Jiangsu and Shanghai became the main destinations for investment. This explained the rise of the investment share of the middle coastal area in the 1990s. Jiangsu saw an especially fast growth of foreign capital inflows. Since 1994, Jiangsu has replaced Shanghai as the second largest recipient of foreign direct investment. In contrast, investment in Shanghai has fluctuated widely. Much of the investment in Shanghai was directed at speculative real estate, but investment in Jiangsu was concentrated in the manufacturing industry. The geographical distribution of FDI in China today also is the result of local governments' efforts to create a favorable investment environment, especially in fostering industrial clusters in their jurisdictions.

Empirical studies of the geographical distribution of FDI in China include Chen and Kwan (2000) and Hsiao and Shen (2003). Chen and Kwan's study is based on twenty-nine regions in China from 1985 to 1995. They found that large regional markets, good infrastructure, and preferential policy had a positive effect in attracting FDI (Chen and Kwan 2000). Using China's provincial and municipal data from 1996 to 1998, Hsiao and Shen regressed the FDI/GDP ratio on six explanatory variables. Their results support the argument that the development of cities and infrastructure and easy access to markets are two of the primary factors often determining multinational corporations' choice of where to invest (Hsiao and Shen 2003).

In recent years, the widening economic gap between the east coastal areas and western China has greatly concerned the central government. To narrow the gap, it has pursued a strategy of developing the West. Attracting FDI in western China is a key part of the strategy. There are three reasons why western China may look attractive to foreign investors. One is the diminishing return of investment in eastern coastal areas due to the increasing cost of production there (land prices, for example). Another is the government's preferential policy—tax exemptions, policy loans and commercial loans with favorable conditions, free technical assistance—and the government's own large-scale investment in infrastructures in the West. The third factor is the abundant cheap labor supply in the region. However, the policy of attracting more FDI into the West has not been as successful as expected, which may be attributable to the under-development of the areas in education, administrative efficiency of government, infrastructure, market mechanisms, business culture, and entrepreneurship. In other words, lack of human capital may be the single greatest obstacle to the development of western China. The diversification of FDI into the West will be a long and slow process.

Factors Contributing to FDI in China

The literature categorizes factors contributing to capital flows into developing countries as push (external) factors and pull (internal) factors. Push factors include economic conditions outside the host country, while pull factors include the economic conditions of the host country.[6] The focus of the chapter

6. Sammo Kang el (2002, 17).

will be on pull factors, although the separation of the two kinds of factors sometimes is impossible.

Low-Cost Skilled Labor

Low-cost skilled labor has long been regarded as China's most important advantage in attracting foreign companies to make goods in China (Table 13.3), especially in the early stage of China's liberalization.

Over the past two decades, the wage and salary levels of white-collar employees rose steadily in big cities such as Shanghai, Guangzhou, and Beijing. However, the wage levels of unskilled workers remained extremely low. As a matter of fact, over the past decade, the wage levels of unskilled workers (primarily migrant farmers) failed to change in any significant way. Take Guangdong Province as an example. Of all of China's provinces, it has attracted by far the largest proportion of FDI. The wage levels in the province are around $60 to $90 a month, virtually the same as they were ten years ago (Kuroda 2000). In China there are annually more than 20 million newly added workers in urban areas entering the labor market, and many

Table 13.3. *Wages and Unit Labor Costs in Manufacturing: China and Selected Developed and Developing Economies, 1998*

Economy	*Ratio to Chinese wage level*
United States	47.8
Sweden	35.6
Japan	29.9
Singapore	23.4
Taiwan (China)	20.6
Republic of Korea	12.9
Chile	12.5
Mexico	7.8
Turkey	7.5
Malaysia	5.2
Philippines (1997)	4.1
Bolivia	3.7
Egypt	2.8
Kenya	2.6
Indonesia (1996)	2.2
Zimbabwe	2.2
India	1.5

Source: UNCTAD (2002, 158).

times more rural migrants who are moving around the county to search for jobs. The Chinese government has adopted a policy of promoting urbanization. Many old decrees and systems that restricted farmers from leaving the countryside—such as "Hukou Zhidu" (the system of registered permanent residents) and Shourong Zhidu (the system of detaining migrants without proper identification)— have been abolished. To realize urbanization, cities and towns eventually must absorb several hundred million rural surplus laborers. It is expected that, in the next two decades, there will be at least 15 million farmers entering cities and towns to find work each year (Shen 2003). In other words, China's potential in labor supply is virtually unlimited, and it will remain so for many decades to come. Furthermore, Chinese workers are not only cheap, but diligent, motivated to improve, and good with their hands. These qualities of Chinese workers have been confirmed by multinational corporations (Kuroda 2000).

China's advantage in the supply of white-collar workers is also very great. China has always emphasized the importance of higher education and vocational education. Illiteracy is relatively low countrywide, and technical and managerial workers are being trained in large numbers. More than 1,000 Chinese universities turn out over 900,000 graduates every year (Table 13.4). Young Chinese technicians are better prepared for work than their foreign counterparts, and they make superior workers (Kuroda 2000). Chinese engineers are well trained in mathematics and in their specialties, although their English is not as good as their Indian counterparts. There is no doubt whatsoever that China will fully utilize its comparative advantage in having an abundant supply of skilled workers, technicians, and engineers as well as unskilled workers. It will make great inroads in the higher value chains of the global production networks. This trend has been borne out by China's success in upgrading its industrial and export structures, and the rapid increase in the number of R&D centers funded by multinational corporations in China.[7]

Highly Developed Infrastructure

To attract FDI, the Chinese government over the past two decades has spent billions of dollars on highways, ports, fiber-optic networks, and other infrastructure. Indeed, China's physical infrastructure has rapidly improved. Take highways, for example. In 1988, the mileage of China's expressways

---

7. In some empirical studies, wages were found to have a negative or insignificant influence in attracting FDI. See Chen and Kwan (2000) and Hsiao and Shen (2003).

Table 13.4. *Basic Statistics of Regular Schools in China by Level and Type, 2002*
(1,000 persons)

Level of education	*Graduates*	*Entrants*	*Enrolled students*
Graduate education	80.8	202.6	501.0
Undergraduate education	1,337.3	3,205.0	9,033.6
Secondary schools	26,013.3	33,712.2	94,152.1

Source: Ministry of Education, Government of China, 2002. See www:moe.edu.cn.

was just 147 kilometers. Ten years later, it was 8,733 kilometers. From 1998 to 2001, another 17,463 kilometers of expressways were built. By 1999, the total length of rail lines opened to traffic in China had reached 65,780 kilometers, including electrified lines of 8,988 kilometers.[8]

After spending two decades in building up its infrastructure, China has developed into a place for one-stop shopping. Companies can obtain everything in China, from raw materials to packaging, and get their products to customers anywhere in the globe almost as conveniently as in a developed country. China's infrastructure compares favorably with many other economies in the region. The importance of infrastructure in attracting FDI is confirmed by several empirical studies of the geographical distribution of FDI in China; the coastal regions that attract the largest sums of FDI have the best infrastructure.[9]

Preferential Policy toward FDI

China's preferential policy toward FDI is assumed to be another important factor contributing to China's attractiveness as a recipient of foreign direct investment. From the beginning of opening up, the Chinese government has made great efforts to formulate a set of policies that will attract FDI. These policies, roughly in order of implementation, include income tax exemption and reduction, tariff exemption and reduction, value-added tax rebate, preferential loans.

To what extent preferential policy has been effective in attracting FDI is a matter of debate. Experience seems to show that, at least in the initial stage, preferential treatment was effective in attracting FDI from Hong Kong and from other newly industrializing economies that were seeking to "hollow-out" their labor-intensive industries to the places that offered the

8. See www.chinaexcite.com/tradeguide/china_communication.htm.
9. IMF (2002). Also see Hsiao and Shen (2003).

best terms. However, solid conclusions on the effectiveness of preferential policy based on rigorous empirical studies are not abundant. Hsiao and Shen (2003) found that preferential policy represented by corporate tax indeed has a positive impact on FDI.

In recent years, more and more economists have raised doubts about the effectiveness of preferential policy. It has been pointed out that preferential policy might not be that important for foreign investors, especially for multinationals, which base their investment decisions on complex and long-term global strategies. Furthermore, excessive preferential treatment might offset to a very large extent the benefits obtained from FDI. In China the central government now has to deal with the question of how to restrict vicious competition between local governments offering concessions to foreign investors to attract FDI into the localities under their jurisdictions at the expense of others. For example, to compete with neighboring regions, some local governments even adopt a policy of zero rent for using land, which is the scarcest resource in China. Wasteful economic development zones are mushrooming (the number has reached 5,000), and the total size of the zones has surpassed 35,000 square kilometers. The artificially low factor prices not only have led to misallocation of resources, but they also have caused serious social tensions. Farmers are driven away from their lands. The so-called *new enclosures* have aroused the great concern of the Chinese government.

After China's entry into the WTO in 2001, the Chinese government began shifting its policy focus from providing preferential treatment to foreign investors to fulfilling its commitments of liberalization. The liberalization measurements include (1) relaxing local content requirements; (2) relaxing export requirements; (3) liberalizing the current account, which basically was done before China's entry into the WTO; (4) dismantling the requirement for self-balancing of foreign currency; (5) easing restrictions on foreign ownership; and (6) dismantling barriers to highly profitable and sensitive sectors, especially the four most important sectors: telecommunication, banking, insurance, and professional services. China's planned participation in Trade-Related Investment Measures (TRIMs) and Trade-Related Aspects of Intellectual Property Rights (TRIPs) will further improve China's investment environment. The liberalization policy is believed to be more important than preferential policy in attracting or, more precisely, facilitating FDI by multinationals from the United States, Japan, and the European Union. The liberalization policy that has exposed domestic enterprises to foreign competition has caused a great deal of concern about the survival of China's indigenous enterprises. Nevertheless, its positive impact on the reduction of X inefficiency via competition has been universally acknowledged. No matter how many questions are left unanswered, one thing is sure: high tariffs to protect monopolistic state-owned enterprises will result in nothing but an inability to compete, making these enterprises easy prey eventually for takeover by foreign companies.

Huge Domestic Market

Since the late 1990s, with China's persistent high growth rate and loosened restrictions on FDI, many multinationals have shifted their sights to China's domestic market, which has become more lucrative than one could possibly have imagined even a few years ago. Most Chinese, with per capita GDP US$1,000 in 2003, cannot afford even low-end foreign-made goods. The average annual income of people living in eastern China is much higher, with Shanghai, the richest region, attaining a per capita GDP reaching US$4,600. It is commonly assumed that the middle-class population accounts for 20 percent of China's total population. In other words, there is a huge middle-class population of 250 million in China.

Already China is the world's biggest cellular telephone market, and it is expected to surpass Japan as the second-biggest personal computer market this year. China buys more film than the Japanese, and as many vehicles as the Germans. China even ranks very high in high-end luxury durable markets. For example, China is the third largest market for Bentley in the world.

With an average annual growth rate of industrial product of more than 10 percent, China's industrial sector is expanding and becoming a major buyer of raw materials, machinery, and high-tech equipment. For example, China's electronics and telecommunications industry uses a skyrocketing number of computer chips—$12 billion worth in 2001. It is predicted that China will be the world's second-biggest consumer of computer chips by 2010, behind only the United States. Applied Materials, an industry leader in chip-making equipment, predicts that 20 percent of its revenue could come from China in the next ten years (Smith 2002).

Before China's WTO entry in 2001, given the huge domestic market, tariffs, quotas, and some other policies aimed at protecting domestic enterprises provided extra incentives for some multinationals to seek joint ventures and produce goods within China. After China's entry into WTO, to capture China's huge market rather than to avoid tariff and non-tariff barriers has become the most important incentive for multinationals to invest in China. To be near a market that is huge and expanding rapidly is certainly more advantageous than to produce for the same market in a distant place. However, markets per se perhaps are China's most precious resource. Many Chinese economists are worried about losing market shares to multinationals, which may have serious consequences for the future development of Chinese enterprises (Lu and Ling 2003).

Stable Macroeconomic Environment

Over the past two decades, China's average annual growth rate was above 9 percent, and the average annual inflation rate was kept below 3 percent. Three features characterize China's current economy as an open economy: a quasi-fixed exchange rate,[10] capital controls, and persistent "twin surpluses" (in the current account and capital account). The basic task of the government in the management of an open economy is to maintain the stability of the RMB, while preserving an independent monetary policy. The independence of monetary policy is a precondition for achieving the final objective of the Chinese government's macroeconomic management: non-inflationary economic growth. Under current economic and institutional constraints, the government must resort to capital controls. Having chosen to maintain a stable exchange rate and preserve the independence of monetary policy via increasingly costly capital controls,[11] the Chinese government has strived to maintain a balance of payments surplus to give credibility to the sustainability of the exchange rate.

A stable macroeconomic environment (a sustained high growth rate, low inflation, adequate liquidity, a strong balance of payments position, and a stable but slightly undervalued exchange rate) must contribute significantly to China's attractiveness as a recipient of foreign direct investment. Hsiao and Shen did a regression on the contribution of GDP growth to FDI. They found that the elasticity of a 1 percent increase in GDP raises FDI by 2.117 percent (Hsiao and Shen 2003). Unfortunately, more comprehensive econometric studies of a stable macroeconomic environment as a determinant of FDI in China are still unavailable.

10. China's exchange rate policy has gone through many stages of change. Officially, China's exchange rate regime is managed floating. In fact, it is pegged to the U.S. dollar with a narrow band. Dr. Zhang Zhichao has provided several excellent accounts and analyses of the evolution of China's exchange rate policy. For example, see Z. Zhang (2000, 1057–81).

11. Hong Kong Monetary Authorities maintain the dollar pegging but have given up an independent monetary policy. As a result, as long as the economy can withstand the instability caused by turbulent capital movements, capital control is not necessary.

The Effects of FDI on the Chinese Economy

This section explains the effects of FDI on the Chinese economy in the following areas: employment generation, trade expansion, technology upgrading, and growth.

Employment Generation

According to a study by the Development Research Center of the State Council (2001), foreign funded enterprises created 60,000 new jobs (less than one thousandth of the newly created jobs) from 1981 to 1985, 60,000 new jobs (0.43 percent of the newly created jobs) from 1986 to 1990, 3.75 million new jobs (9.26 percent of the newly created jobs) from 1991 to 1996, and 720,000 new jobs (6 percent of the newly created jobs) in the period from 1997 to 1999. According to the Ministry of Commerce, up to mid-2003, the total employment of foreign funded enterprises was 23 million workers. The net increase of the employment of foreign funded enterprises since 1997 has been 5.5 million workers.[12]

It should be noted that while creating new jobs, FDI could also destroy jobs by crowding out domestic enterprises via competition. The entry of Coca-Cola and Pepsi created many jobs, but it destroyed several times more jobs that were provided by indigenous soft drink enterprises. More careful studies are needed to determine the net contribution of job creation by FDI.

In light of the high share of FDI in China's capital formation, foreign funded enterprises' contribution to China's job creation is less impressive than expected. This point of view seems consistent with the following observation by UNCTAD (2001, 55): "Since foreign funded enterprises tend to use more capital-intensive techniques than local firms in similar industries, their contribution to job creation is modest. Their scope for absorbing workers released from SOEs in labor-intensive industries will be very limited." More importantly, even if FDI has a very big positive effect on job creation in absolute terms, compared with China's need for job creation of 20 million a year, FDI's contribution is relatively small.

Trade Expansion

When China opened up to foreign capital in earnest, the debt crisis of Latin American countries had just struck. The Chinese government realized that

12. See *Foreign Investment in China*, 2003, no. 5, p. 5.

while FDI was a preferable form of using foreign capital to debt borrowing, it would not preclude balance of payments problems. Therefore, from the start, China's policy toward FDI (characterized by tax rebates on exports, exemption of tariffs on imported parts and components that were used for processing) was biased in favor of exports, especially processing trade.

China's trade growth rate during the reform period has been about 4.5 times the world average, and foreign funded enterprises have played a key role in this achievement. Their share in exports rose from 1 percent in 1985 to between 45 and 50 percent in 2002 (IMF 2002). In 1991, exports by foreign funded enterprises were US$12 billion, 16.75 percent of China's total exports. In 2002, foreign funded enterprises' exports were US$275 billion, which represented about half of China's total exports.

The most important category of exports by foreign funded enterprises is manufacturing goods, both in terms of the absolute value of exports and relative to domestic enterprises. In 2000, while the value of exports by foreign funded enterprises was US$194.4 billion, accounting for 48 percent of China's total exports in the year, the value of manufacturing exports by foreign funded enterprises was US$99.1 billion, accounting for 82.99 percent of foreign funded enterprises' total exports and 40 percent of China's total exports in the year.

Because of the emergence of an international production network and China's policy in favor of processing trade, China's exports are dominated by processing trade. In 1980, China's total value of processing trade was US$1.66 billion. By 2001, the value was US$241.4 billion, a 145-fold increase. The share of processing trade in China's total trade increased from 4.4 percent in 1980 to 47.4 percent in 2001 (Development Research Center of the State Council 2003, 6). In the 1990s, China's foreign trade expansion relied mainly on processing trade. Since the second half of the 1990s, processing trade has already accounted for more than half of China's exports (Lemoine and Unal-Kesenci 2002, 13-14).

The close relationship between processing trade and FDI inflows is evident from China's trade structure. The fastest growth of exports came from machinery and electrical machinery, other transportation equipment, and instruments, which are sectors dominated by foreign funded enterprises. Correspondingly, imports of capital goods, semifinished goods, and materials for processing exports grew very fast. The fact that China runs a trade surplus primarily with the United States and a trade deficit with the East and South East Asian economies suggests that East Asian investors are using China as an export platform for the Western markets (UNCTAD 2002, 155). China became one of the most important participants of the international production network. The domination of processing activities in foreign trade activities shows that, for multinationals that are increasingly relying on outsourcing, China's attractiveness as a production base for exports is strong (UNCTAD 2002, 15). As a result, more and more foreign enterprises from industrial countries are boosting investment in China and importing cheap Chinese goods back home as a way to cut costs and raise profits.

Until 1997, however, foreign funded enterprises were creators of trade deficit, due to exports of foreign funded enterprises' high import contents. From 1991 until 2001, foreign funded enterprises' cumulated trade deficit was US$65 billion (US$760 – US$695).[13] Foreign funded enterprises ran a trade surplus of US$4.2 billion, US$2.7 billion, US$2.2 billion, and US$7.4 billion in 1998, 1999, 2000, and 2001, respectively. When China entered the WTO in 2001, restrictions on FDI (such as self-balancing of exchanges and local content requirements) began to be scrapped. Multinationals will produce goods solely or mainly for domestic markets, and imports of parts and components will increase. Consequently, FDI's overall impact on China's trade balance may turn negative again. The expansion of international trade may improve an economy's overall resource allocation and hence its efficiency (because of the role of preferential policy in FDI attraction and export promotion), but price signals are highly distorted. The extent to which China's FDI-led export drive has contributed to China's overall improvement in efficiency remains to be seen.

Technology Upgrading

During the 1980s and early 1990s, most of China's FDI came from the economies of Hong Kong, Macao, and Taiwan, and these investments were concentrated in labor-intensive sectors. The technology content of these FDI inflows was relatively low. However, since 1992, industrial countries have become more important sources of FDI, and the technology content of FDI inflows from those countries has been relatively high, concentrated in capital-intensive and technology-intensive sectors. The mainstream economists hold that FDI inflows have contributed significantly to the upgrading of China's industrial structure and have improved the quality of China's capital stock.[14] However, many economists tend to be suspicious. Kunrong Shen

13. Based on Customs Office figures. See Jiang (2002, 72).

14. The author is very grateful to Dr. Jiang Xiaojuan and Dr. Wang Chunfa for their kind permission to cite their research results.

(1999) did a cross-section analysis of the correlation between FDI and total factor productivity (TFP). He concluded that the elasticity of TFP with respect to the FDI/GDP ratio was 0.37 (Shen 1999, 5). Jinping Zhao (2001) also found the impact of FDI on domestic technical upgrading to be significant.[15] On the other hand, Jie He in his analysis implied that FDI enterprises had provided little help in improving China's overall resource utilization efficiency (He 2000, 12). Xiaoqi Xiong (2002, 9) reached a similar conclusion.

The available case studies are as controversial as empirical ones. According to Xiaojuan Jiang (2002), most multinationals have transferred most advanced or relatively advanced technology to their subsidiaries in China. In Jiang's sample, among 207 foreign funded enterprises, 86 percent transferred their technology in exchange for market access. Thirty-four percent of the foreign funded enterprises transferred advanced technology to their Chinese partners, and the remaining 66 percent transferred only matured technology (Development Research Center of the State Council 2003, 7). In Jiang's opinion, multinationals' investment in China has had a strong technology spillover effect on the rest of the Chinese economy. The spillover effect worked through the following channels: the flow of managerial personnel between domestic and foreign funded enterprises; the supply of parts and components by domestic enterprises to foreign funded enterprises according to the specification set by those enterprises and sometimes with technical assistance from them (backward linkages); technical exchanges between domestic and foreign funded enterprises; technical cooperation between multinationals and local research centers and universities; the creation of joint research centers and labs with Chinese enterprises and universities; exchanges between Chinese enterprises and multinationals in various forms, tangible and intangible; and competition pressures exercised by foreign funded enterprises on domestic enterprises.

Other economists reached different conclusions than Jiang (2002). According to R. F. Crow's survey of 150 American and Japanese companies that transferred technologies to Chinese enterprises, "50 percent of the American and Japanese enterprises felt that the technologies transferred by them were on a par with the current technical levels of China; only 32 percent of Japanese enterprises and 20 percent of American enterprises felt that the levels of technologies transferred by them were on a higher level. Twenty-one percent of American enterprises felt that the technologies transferred by

---

15. Development Research Center of the State Council, "Comprehensive Appraisal on the Role of Using Foreign Capital in Promoting Economic Growth," *DRC Report*, 2001, 1–30.

them to Chinese enterprises were at a lower level."[16] In his field study, Xie (2000) concluded that the spillover effects of foreign enterprises were not obvious, and the policy of internal control by foreign investors hindered Chinese enterprises' absorption and grasp of core technologies. Shengfu Liu (2003) also found that strict restrictions on technology diffusions and transfers by multinational corporations made Chinese enterprises incapable of commanding core technologies.

A field study team of the Institute of World Economics and Politics, led by Wang Chunfa (2003), conducted an analysis of questionnaires collected in Dongguan.[17] The team found three important features of foreign funded enterprises with respect to technology transfer and diffusion. First, the technology linkages between FDI enterprises and their parent companies are mainly embodied in machinery equipment. Second, the technology linkages between FFEs and their parent companies are maintained mainly by means of technology advisory services. Third, technological cooperation and exchanges between FFEs and Chinese university and governmental scientific research institutions are very limited. In Suzhou, Wuxi, and Changzhou Science and Technology Parks, researchers have also found similar results (Wu and Wu 2002, 155). Most case studies found that the technology upgrading effect of FDI on the host economy, to a very large extent, depended on the host country's R&D capability and its own efforts in creation and innovation.

In a recent study of China's automobile industry, Lu and Mu (2003) pointed out that, due to the government's overprotection against competition and enterprises' overreliance on multinationals in technology transfers, China's major carmakers have weakened their ability to conduct research and development, and they have been locked into a low rung of the ladder of division of labor in the global car manufacturing industry (Feng 2004).

Impact on Growth

Using the Harrod-Domar model as the framework for analyzing the impact of FDI on growth, we can see that FDI has raised GDP growth in two ways. One way is through higher capital accumulation. The other way is through higher productivity in the form of a lower capital-output ratio. Calculating the contribution of FDI to growth via a higher investment rate is not as easy as it seems to be. Besides the statistical problem, the most difficult part of

16. Quoted in Zhou (1998, 3).
17. The author is very grateful for Dr. Wang's contribution to this section.

the study is to estimate the net contribution after deducting the crowding out effect of FDI on domestic investment. As mentioned above, there are few solid econometric studies of the impact of FDI on China's economic growth.

The most reliable result in terms of methodology of econometrics perhaps is the one provided by Cheng Hsiao and Yan Shen (2003). They concluded that the short-run elasticity of a 1 percent increase in FDI raises the GDP by 0.0485 percent a year; in the long run, the impact of a 1 percent increase in FDI raises GDP by 0.296 percent. However, if one takes into consideration that an increase in GDP will lead to an increase in FDI, the long-run elasticity of a 1 percent increase in FDI raises the GDP by 5.4 percent in ten years. Most econometric studies on FDI's impact on economic growth in China reached similar results.

Conclusion

For developing countries, FDI has two major benefits. First, FDI allows developing countries constrained by the lack of loanable funds to maintain a higher growth rate than otherwise would be possible. Second, FDI provides finance as part of a package of technology and management, with the host country and foreign investors sharing both the risks and rewards of the ventures. On the whole, China's FDI policy has been successful, and FDI has played a significant role in China's economic development over the past two decades.

The contribution of FDI to China's employment is important in absolute terms but limited in relative terms, due to China's huge unemployment problem. The contribution of FDI to China's exports is the most obvious effect of FDI and the least controversial. While the impact of FDI on China's technological progress and managerial skill is significant, the long-term effects remain unclear.

To maintain sustainable growth, China needs to improve its ability to attract and use FDI. Otherwise, it will become the victim of its own success. Several conclusions are offered here. First, preferential policy for FDI and especially export-oriented FDI can create serious market distortions and lead to serious resource misallocations. This, in turn, can affect negatively the economy's overall efficiency.[18] Second, the overreliance on multinationals'

---

18. In many cases, enterprises that attract FDI do not want foreign currency to buy foreign equipment and machinery. What they really want are credits in RMB, which can be obtained by selling foreign exchanges that they obtained through

willingness to transfer technology may weaken indigenous enterprises and their independent ability to conduct research and development. As a result, indigenous enterprises may forever lose the opportunity to raise their status from Original Equipment Manufacturer (OEM) to Original Design Manufacturer (ODM), saying nothing of Original Brand Manufacturer (OBM). Some industries may have to be satisfied with being locked into a low rung of the ladder of division of labor in the value chain of the international production network. Third, FDI tends to have an asymmetrical income effect on the economy, socially and geographically. The income gap between different social stratum and localities created by FDI inflows may cause serious social tensions. Finally, following the accumulation of FDI, investment income received by foreign investors will accelerate rapidly. China will need a bigger and bigger trade surplus to balance the investment income outflows. At the same time, owing to the dismantling of foreign exchange self-balancing and local content requirements, FFE-related trade deficits would increase and hence would reduce China's overall trade surplus. The weakening of China's current account position in turn will produce a negative impact on China's capital account. As a result, China's international balance of payments may face more and more pressure in the future. There is no manna from heaven. The extra benefits enjoyed from FDI today must be paid back tomorrow.

In summary, over the past two decades, FDI has played a significant positive role in China's economic development. From a short-run perspective, the success of China's FDI policy is beyond doubt. However, compared with the experience of Japan, the Republic of Korea, and Taiwan (China), China perhaps may have paid a price too high for this success, and the long-term impact of China's success in attracting FDI has yet to be seen.

References

Chen, Chunlai. 2002. "Foreign Direct Investment: Prospects and Policies." In *China in the World Economy.* Paris: Organization for Economic Cooperation and Development, OECD-China Program.

Chen, L. K., and Y. K. Kwan. 2000. "What are the Determinants of Location of Foreign Direct Investment? The Chinese Experience." *Journal of International Economics* 51: 379–400.

---

attracting FDI. Because these enterprises used the RMB to buy domestic products, there was no increase in imports to mirror the FDI inflows. As a result, a current account surplus and a capital account surplus coexist. The increase in FDI ended up producing an increase in foreign exchange reserves. This phenomenon obviously is a reflection of the misallocation of resources caused by market distortion.

China Statistical Year Book. various issues. State Bureau of Statistics. Beijing.

Development Research Center of the State Council. Study Group. 2001. "Direct Contribution of FDI to China's Economic Growth." *JingJi CanKao ZiLiao*, September 17.

———. 2003. "Processing Trade: New Road to Industrialization under Globalization." *JingJi CanKao ZiLiao*, no. 11.

Gu, Shulin. 1998. "Some Conceptual Notes on the NSI Approach for Studies on Economic Development in Developing Countries." UNU/INTECH, October.

He, Jie. 2000. "Further Precise Quantification of FDI's Spillover Effects to China's Industrial Sectors." *World Economy*, vol. 12.

Hsiao, C., and Y. Shen. 2003. "Foreign Direct Investment and Economic Growth: The Importance of Institutions and Urbanization." *Economic Development and Cultural Change* 51,4 (July): 883–96.

IMF (International Monetary Fund). 2002. "Foreign Direct Investment in China: What Do We Need to Know?" Transcript of Economic Forum, Washington, D.C., May 2.

Jiang, Xiaojuan. 2002. *The Foreign Capital Economy*. Beijing: People's University Press.

Jiang, Xiaojuan, and Li Ru. 2002. "FDI's Contributions to China's Industrial Growth and Technical Advance." *China Industrial Economy*, 7.

Jin, Linzhu. 1998. *From Imitation to Innovation: Driving Forces of Korean Technology Learning*. Beijing: Xinhua Publishing House.

Kagami, M., and M. Tsuji. 2001. *The IT Revolution and Developing Countries: Late-Comer Advantage?* Chiba, Japan: Institute of Developing Economies.

———. 2003. *Industrial Agglomeration: Facts and Lessons for Developing Countries*. Chiba, Japan: Institute of Developing Economies.

Kuroda, Atsuo. 2000. "The Rise of China and the Changing Industrial Map of Asia." Tokyo: Japan Economic Foundation.

Lai, Pingyao. 2001. "Recent Trends in Foreign Direct Investment in China." Institute of World Economics and Politics, Chinese Academy of Social Sciences.

Lee, Chang-lae. 2001. *Rationale for Institutionalizing Northeast Asian Economic Cooperation and Some Possible Options*.

Lemoine, Francoise, and Deniz Unal-Kesenci. 2002. "China's Processing Trade." CEPII, Working Paper 2002-02. Paris: CEPII.

Lipsey, Robert E. 1999. "The Role of FDI in International Capital Flows." In *International Capital Flows*, ed. Martin Feldstein. Chicago: University of Chicago Press.

Liu, Shengfu. 2003. "Transnational Companies and Technical Advance of Chinese Enterprises." *Enterprise Technical Advance*, 1.

Lixin, Wang, and Jiang Cao. 2000. "Quantitative Analysis of FDI's Contributions to the Economic Growth of Shanghai." *Shanghai Economic Research*, 5.

Lu, Feng. 2004. *On the Policy Alternatives for the Development of China's Automobile Industry with Indigenous Property Rights*. Internal Document.

Lu, Feng, and Mu, Ling. 2003. "Indigenous Innovation, Capacity Building and Competitive Advantage." *Management World*, no.12.

Ming, Tian. 2003. "How to Attract Direct EU Investment." *Business World*, no. 3.

OECD (Organization for Economic Cooperation and Development). 1997a. *Benchmark Definition of Foreign Direct Investment*, 3d ed. Paris.

———. 1997b. *National Innovation System*. Paris.

Sammo Kang el. 2002. "Understanding the Determinants of Capital Flows in Korea." Korea Institute of International Economic Policy. December.

Shen, Kunrong. 1999. "FDI and China's Economic Growth." *Management World*, no. 5.

Shen, Kunrong, and Qiang Geng. 2000. "An Analysis of FDI's Spillover Effect." *Financial Research*, 3.

Shen, Shuisheng. 2003. "Theoretical Analysis and Policy Suggestions on Current Employment Policy." *Reference of Economic Studies*, no. 51.

Smith, Craig S. 2002. "China Makes Progress on Chips." *New York Times*, May 6.

Song, Hong, and Chai Yu. 1999. "Effect of FDI on Economies of Developing Host Countries: Theoretic Retrospect and Prospect." *World Economy and Politics*, 2.

Song, Jaeyong. 2001. "Sequential Foreign Investments, Regional Technology Platforms, and the Evolution of Japanese Multinationals in East Asia." Asian Development Bank Institute. Working Paper 22. July. Tokyo: ADBI Publishing.

Sun, Peng. 2002. "The Opening of China's Service Industry: Current State and Prospects." July 7. See the website of the Ministry of Commerce, May 2003.

Thomsen, Stephen. 1999. "Southeast Asia: The Role of Foreign Direct Investment Policies in Development." OECD, Directorate for Financial, Fiscal and Enterprise Affairs, Working Papers on International Investment. Paris: Organization for Economic Cooperation and Development.

Tian, Ming. 2003. "How to Attract Direct EU Investment." *Business World*, no. 3.

UNCTAD (United Nations Conference on Trade and Development). 1996. "Fostering Technological Dynamism: Evolution of Thought on Technological Development Processes and Competitiveness: A Review of the Literature." New York and Geneva: United Nations.

———. 2001a. *Trade and Development Report*. New York and Geneva: United Nations.

———. 2001b. *World Investment Report*. New York and Geneva: United Nations.

———. 2002. *Trade and Development Report*. New York and Geneva: United Nations.

———. 2003. *Trade and Development Report*. New York and Geneva: United Nations.

Wang, Chunfa. 2000. *Road of Technology Competition on a Background of Economic Globalization.* Beijing: Economic Science Publishing House.

———. 2003. "FDI, Technological Linkages, and Economic Growth in East Asia." Paper prepared for the Ford Foundation Conference on Vietnam, October, Hanoi.

Wang, Luolin, ed. 1997. *The Report on Foreign Investment.* Beijing: Economic Management Press.

Wu, Linhai, and Songyi Wu. 2002. *Discussions on Transnational Companies' Technology Transfers to China.* Beijing: Economic Management Press.

Wu, Xianming. 2001. *Transnational Companies and East Asian Economic Development.* Beijing: Economic Science Publishing House.

Xia, Jingwen. "Empirical Analysis on China's Using FDI and Its Economic Performance." *Industrial Technological Economy,* 4.

Xie, Fuji. 2000. "Countermeasure Study on Using FDI to Advance the Progress of Chinese Enterprises." *Management Modernization,* no. 3.

Xie, Fuji, and Rongfang Shen. 2002. "Analysis of Factors Affecting FDI's Role in Propelling the Technical Advance of Chinese Enterprises." *Technology and Management,* 1.

Xiong, Xiaoqi. 2002. "Transnational Companies' Controlling Core Technologies." *China Foreign Investment,* 9.

Yamazawa, I. 1990. *Economic Development and International Trade—The Japan Model.* Honolulu, Hawaii: East-West Center.

Zhang, Yangui. 2002. "Diffusion of Transnational Company R&D Centers to China." *International Economic Cooperation,* 12.

Zhang, Z. 2000. *Exchange Rate Reform in China: An Experiment in the Real Targeting Approach.* Oxford: Blackwell Publishers.

Zhao, Jinping. 2001. "Getting Started in a System: China's Strategic Adjustment on Using Foreign Capital in the New Period." *International Trade,* 2.

Zheng Gang. 1998. "Success and Failure of Asian Four Little Dragons' Technological Development Model and Its Revelations to China." *Scientific Management Research,* 6.

Zhou, Xiebo. 1998. "Factor Analysis and Countermeasure Study on China's Technology Introduction and Technology Diffusion." *Financial and Trade Economy,* 3.

14

Liberalization, FDI Flows, and Economic Development: The Indian Experience in the 1990s

Nagesh Kumar

Foreign direct investment (FDI) is now widely perceived as an important resource for expediting the industrial development of developing countries. FDI flows as a bundle of capital, technology, skills, and sometimes even market access. Therefore, most developing countries welcome the multinational enterprises (MNEs) that are usually associated with FDI. India's case is typical in this context. After following a somewhat restrictive policy toward FDI, India liberalized its FDI policy regime considerably in 1991. This liberalization has been accompanied by increasing inflows of foreign direct investment as well as changes in the sectoral composition, sources, and entry modes of FDI. In recent years multinational enterprises have increasingly recognized India's locational advantages in knowledge-based industries. To exploit these advantages, MNEs are concentrating their investments in software development and in global R&D centers.

This chapter begins with a review of the Indian government's policy toward FDI. Trends and patterns in FDI inflows to India as well as determinants of those inflows are then discussed. The impact of FDI in terms of

This chapter has benefited from the useful comments of Shujiro Urata, Yu Yongding, Chia Siow Yue, and K. J. Joseph. Jayaprakash Pradhan assisted with extracting a number of tables from the database of the Research and Information System (RIS) for Developing Countries. However, the views expressed are the author's and should not be attributed to either the World Bank Institute or RIS.

various parameters of development is also examined in detail. The chapter then describes MNE activities in two knowledge-based industries: information technology (IT) software and global R&D activities. In the chapter's conclusion, policy lessons based on the Indian experience are presented. Appendix A, entitled "India's FDI Inflows: A Comparative East Asian Perspective," compares FDI inflows in India and China in terms of magnitude and sectoral composition of FDI.

The Evolution of the Indian Government's FDI Policy, 1948–2003

The Indian government's policy toward FDI has evolved over time in tune with the requirements of the process of development in different phases (Kumar 1998b). Soon after independence, India embarked on a strategy of import-substituting industrialization in the framework of development planning. The focus was on encouraging and improving the local capability in heavy industries, including the machinery-manufacturing sector. Since the domestic base of "created" assets (technology, skills, entrepreneurship) was quite limited, the attitude toward FDI was increasingly receptive. FDI was sought on mutually advantageous terms, although majority local ownership was preferred. Foreign investors were assured of no restrictions on the remittances of profits and dividends and of fair compensation in the event of acquisition. The foreign exchange crisis of 1957–58 led to further liberalization in the government's attitude toward FDI.

The government adopted a more restrictive attitude toward FDI in the late 1960s. The local base of machinery manufacturing capability and local entrepreneurship developed, and the outflow from India of remittances of dividends, profits, royalties, and technical fees abroad on account of servicing of FDI and technology imports grew sharply. Restrictions were put on proposals of foreign direct investments unaccompanied by technology transfer and on investments seeking more than 40 percent foreign ownership. The government listed industries in which FDI was not considered desirable in view of local capabilities. The permissible range of royalty payments and the duration of technology transfer agreements with foreign collaborators were specified for different items. The guidelines evolved for foreign collaborations required exclusive use of Indian consultancy services wherever available. The renewals of foreign technical collaboration agreements were restricted. Since 1973, the further activities of foreign companies (along with those of local, large industrial houses) were restricted to a select group of core or high-priority industries. In the same year a new Foreign Exchange Regulation Act (FERA) came into force. It required all foreign companies operating in India with up to 40 percent foreign equity to register under Indian corporate legislation. Exceptions from the general limit of 40 percent were made only for companies operating in high-priority or high-technology sectors, tea plantations, or those producing predominantly for exports.

In the 1980s the attitude toward FDI began to change as a part of the strategy of modernization of industry. Imports of capital goods and technology were liberalized, exposing the Indian industry to foreign competition. MNEs acquired a greater role in the promotion of manufactured exports. The policy changes adopted in the 1980s covered liberalization of industrial licensing (approval) rules, a host of incentives, and exemption from foreign equity restrictions under FERA to 100 percent export-oriented units. Four more export processing zones (EPZ) were set up in addition to the two existing ones (Kandla, set up in 1965, and Santacruz, set up in 1974). The new zones were established to attract MNEs to create export-oriented units. A degree of flexibility was introduced in the policy concerning foreign ownership, and exceptions from the general ceiling of 40 percent on foreign equity were allowed on the merits of individual investment proposals. The rules and procedures concerning payments of royalties and lump-sum technical fees were relaxed, and withholding taxes were reduced.

India's growth performance during the 1980s (an average of nearly 6 percent) was respectable and much better than that achieved during the previous decades. However, it was fuelled by excessive reliance on short-term external borrowing. The accumulated debt servicing burden began to strain the balance of payment toward the end of the decade. This strain was accentuated by two major external shocks: the collapse in 1989 of the Soviet Union, India's major trading partner, and the Gulf War in 1990–91, leading to a rise in oil prices and adversely affecting the inflow of remittances by the nonresident Indians in the region. These developments pushed the country into a severe liquidity crisis. Foreign exchange reserves barely covered just a month's imports. As a result, the government had to negotiate a structural adjustment loan from the International Monetary Fund (IMF). As part of the conditionalities attached to the IMF's Structural Adjustment Program, a package of economic reforms was introduced in the middle of 1991 by the government. Among the reform measures implemented was a less restrictive policy toward FDI, a much more liberal trade policy, and reforms of capital market and exchange controls (see Kumar 2000c, among others, for details).

The New Industrial Policy (NIP) announced on 24 July 1991 marked this departure with respect to FDI policy. The NIP and subsequent policy amendments have liberalized the industrial policy regime in the country especially as it applies to foreign direct investments. The industrial approval system in all industries has been abolished except when needed on strategic or environmental grounds. In order to bring greater transparency to the FDI approval system and expedite approvals, automatic clearance was put into practice for FDI proposals fulfilling certain conditions, such as the ownership levels of 50 percent, 51 percent, 74 percent, and 100 percent foreign equity allowed in sectors specified for each limit. The cases other than those following the listed norms are subject to normal approval procedures. A new package for enterprises in EPZs and 100 percent export-oriented units was announced; it included automatic clearance for proposals fulfilling specified parameters on capital goods imports, location, and value addition, for example. The guidelines have been laid down for this approval process as well. The FERA of 1973 was amended in 1993; restrictions placed on foreign companies by the FERA were lifted.

New sectors—such as mining, banking, insurance, telecommunications, construction and management of ports, harbors, roads and highways, airlines, and defense equipment—have been thrown open to private companies, including foreign-owned companies. However, the extent of foreign ownership is limited in some of these service sectors. For example, it is limited to 49 percent in banking, 26 percent in insurance, 51 percent in nonbanking finance companies, 49 percent in telecommunications, 74 percent in internet service providers, 40 percent in airlines, 74 percent in shipping, 51 percent in export-oriented trading, 49 percent in broadcasting, 74 percent in advertising, and 51 percent in health and education services. Foreign ownership up to 100 percent is permitted in most manufacturing sectors, and in some sectors even on an automatic basis. The exceptions are defense equipment (limited to 26 percent) and items reserved for production by small-scale industries (limited to 24 percent). However, FDI above 24 percent is permitted in small-scale industries (SSI) for reserved items subject to a mandatory export obligation of 50 percent of annual production; this export obligation also applies to a large domestic enterprise. In 2000 the conditions related to dividend balancing and the related export obligation conditions on foreign investors, which applied to twenty-two consumer goods industries, were withdrawn (Ministry of Commerce and Industry 2000).

Liberalization and Trends and Patterns in FDI Inflows

The economic reforms in general and liberalization of FDI policy in particular have affected the magnitude and pattern of FDI inflows received by India. During the 1990s, they showed a marked increase until 1997, when they peaked at US$3.6 billion. After stagnating for a few subsequent years at around US$2.5 billion, they rose again to a level of about $3.4 billion in 2002 and $4.3 billion in 2003 (see Figure 14.1). The magnitude of these inflows would appear too small, especially if compared with inflows received by other countries in the region such as China (around $50 billion in recent years). However, the difference in the FDI to GDP ratio narrows if account is taken of underestimation of FDI in India and overestimation of FDI in China due to round tripping of Chinese capital (see Appendix A).

In an analysis of the role of liberalization in explaining the rising inflows of FDI until 1997, Kumar (1998b) found that only a part of the increase could be attributed to liberalization. A part of the rise was explained in terms of a sharp expansion in the global scale of FDI outflows during the 1990s. The decline in inflows since 1997, despite continued liberalization, suggests that policy liberalization is not an adequate explanation. Macroeconomic fundamentals of the host economies emerge as the most powerful explanatory variables in the intercountry analysis of FDI inflows; they also explain the year-to-year fluctuations in FDI, although with a lag. This becomes clear from Figure 14.2. It plots FDI inflows during the 1990s against the fluctuations in the annual rates of growth of industrial output. One finds a good correspondence between the industrial growth rate in a year and the FDI inflows in the following year. The industrial growth seems to signal to foreign investors the prospects of the economy. Therefore, it appears that policy liberalization may be a necessary condition but not a sufficient condition for FDI inflows.

Figure 14.1. *India's FDI Inflows, 1991–2003*

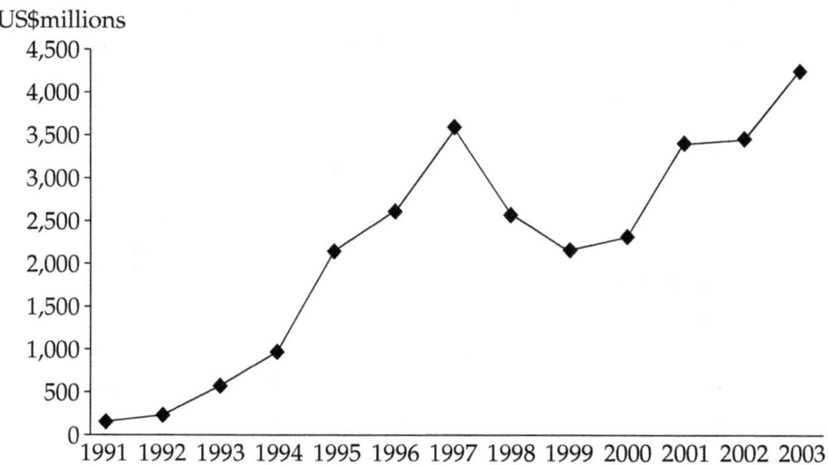

Source: UNCTAD (2004).

Figure 14.2. *Industrial Growth and FDI Inflows in India, 1991–2003*

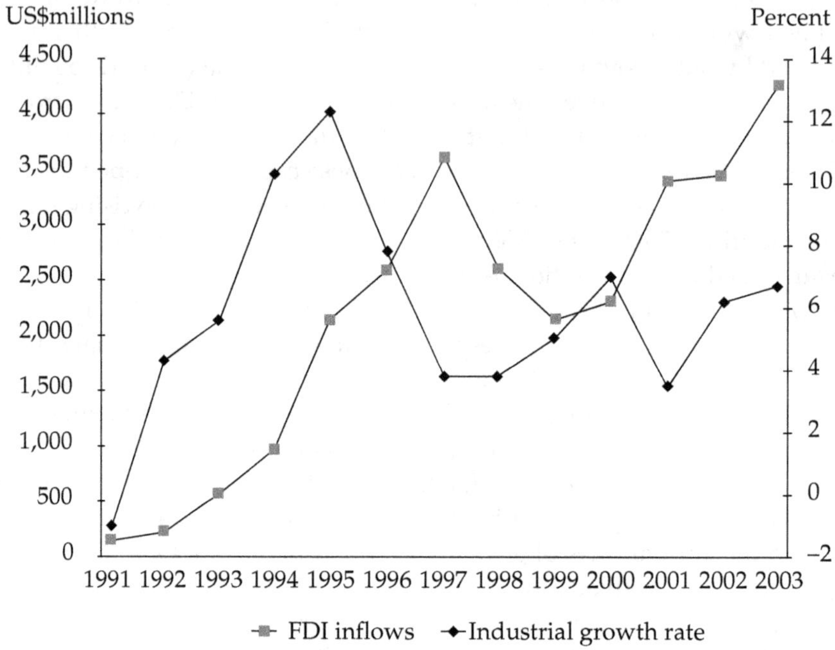

US$millions

Percent

4,500 4,000 3,500 3,000 2,500 2,000 1,500 1,000 500 0

14 12 10 8 6 4 2 0 −2

1991 1992 1993 1994 1995 1996 1997 1998 1999 2000 2001 2002 2003

FDI inflows — Industrial growth rate

Source: Author's calculations based on Figure 14.1 and Ministry of Finance (2004) data.

The Sectoral Composition of FDI in India

The sectoral composition of FDI in India changed significantly between 1980 and 1997 (Table 14.1). The combined share of the plantations, mining, and petroleum sectors fell markedly from 9 percent in 1980 to only 2 percent in 1997. The bulk of FDI inflows in the pre-liberalization era was directed to the manufacturing sector. Indeed, it accounted for the bulk of FDI stock. The nearly 87 percent share in 1980 declined marginally to 85 percent in 1990. However, with the liberalization of the FDI policy regime in the 1990s, FDI inflows shifted to the services and infrastructural sectors. This brought the share of manufacturing down to 48 percent in 1997. During the 1990s, services clearly emerged as a major sector receiving FDI. Power generation among other infrastructural sectors (the "Other" category in the table) also attracted substantial investments. From a marginal share in 1980 and 1990, "Other" increased to nearly 35 percent in 1997.

Among the manufacturing subsectors, FDI stock in 1997 was fairly evenly distributed between food and beverages, transport equipment, met-

***Table 14.1.** India's Inward FDI Stock, by Industrial Sector, 1980, 1990, and 1997*

	1980		*1990*		*1997*	
Industrial sector	*Value (Rs. million)*	*Percent of total FDI*	*Value (Rs. million)*	*Percent of total FDI*	*Value (Rs. million)*	*Percent of total FDI*
Plantations	385	4.13	2,560	9.46	4,310	1.18
Mining	78	0.84	80	0.30	410	0.11
Petroleum	368	3.94	30	0.11	3,330	0.91
Manufacturing	8,116	86.97	22,980	84.95	175,230	48.00
Food & beverages	391	4.19	1,620	5.99	24,310	6.66
Textiles products	320	3.43	920	3.40	10,390	2.85
Transport equipment	515	5.52	2,820	10.43	24,570	6.73
Machinery & machine tools	710	7.61	3,540	13.09	19,310	5.29
Metals & metal products	1,187	12.72	1,410	5.21	7,600	2.08
Electrical goods & machinery	975	10.45	2,950	10.91	29,400	8.31
Chemicals & allied products	3,018	32.34	7,690	28.43	32,530	8.91
Other manufacturing	1,000	10.72	2,030	7.50	27,120	7.43
Services	320	3.43	890	3.29	54,650	14.97
Other	65	0.70	510	1.89	127,170	34.83
Total	9,332	100.00	27,050	100.00	365,100	100.00

Note: The data are as of the end of March in 1980, 1990, and 1997.
Source: RBI Bulletin (April 1985, August 1993, October 2000).

als and metal products, electricals and electronics, chemicals and allied products, and miscellaneous manufacturing; this distribution contrasts with the heavy concentration of India's inward FDI stock up to 1990 in relatively technology-intensive sectors such as machinery, chemicals, electricals, and transport equipment. The infrastructural sectors, which commanded nearly half of the total approved investments in the 1990s, had not been open to inflows of foreign direct investment before and hence could be attributed to the policy liberalization.

It may be useful to look at the distribution of inward FDI within the services sector given its increasing importance in the FDI inflows during the 1990s. About 61 percent of approved FDI in this sector during the 1991–2000 period went to telecommunications; financial and banking services were the second most important recipient of FDI in the services sector (receiving nearly 14 percent of the total amount of approved FDI). Other important subsectors were hotels and tourism, and air and sea transport.

The Changing Sources of FDI in India

European countries were major sources of FDI inflows to India until 1990. However, their relative importance as sources of FDI to India has steadily declined in the post-liberalization period. The share of major European source countries (which include the United Kingdom, Germany, France, Switzerland, Sweden, Italy, and the Netherlands) declined from 69 and 66 percent of FDI stock in 1980 and 1990 respectively to just 31 percent by 1997. This decline became more prominent with diversification of sources of FDI to India during the 1990s.

The United States emerged as the most important source of FDI with nearly 19 percent of FDI inflows in 1992. In 1997 the share of the United States at 13.75 percent is, however, deceptive since a large proportion of the U.S. FDI is believed to be routed through Mauritius. Mauritius appears as the largest source of investments in India in 1997, with Rs. 65.46 billion or nearly 18 percent of total FDI stock in the economy (Table 14.2). The emergence of Mauritius as the largest source of FDI can be explained by the Double Taxation Avoidance Agreement signed between Mauritius and India during the 1990s. The agreement enables foreign investors to minimize their tax liability given the tax haven status of Mauritius. Hence, investors from other countries, principally the United States, route their investments through Mauritius to take advantage of the tax treaty.

The Mode of Entry of FDI in India

Mergers and acquisitions became an important channel of FDI inflows during the 1990s. During the period from 1997 to 1999, for instance, nearly 39 percent of FDI inflows into India took the form of M&As by foreign companies of existing Indian enterprises; in the pre-reform period, FDI entry was invariably in the form of greenfield investments (Table 14.3). Acquisitions, compared to greenfield entry, have limited potential to add to the stock of productive capital and to generate favorable knowledge spillovers and competitive effects.

The Impact of FDI Inflows on the Indian Economy

Given their intangible assets, MNE affiliates can contribute to their host country's development with generation of output, employment, balanced

Table 14.2. *India's Inward FDI Stock, by Source Economy, 1992 and 1997*
(Rupees Crores or ten million)

	1992		*1997*	
Economy	*Value*	*Percent*	*Value*	*Percent*
Mauritius	n.a.	n.a.	6,546	17.93
United States	713	18.57	5,019	13.75
United Kingdom	1,545	40.23	4,379	11.99
Germany	476	12.40	2,078	5.69
Japan	213	5.55	1,958	5.36
Netherlands	164	4.27	1,175	3.22
Switzerland	185	4.82	785	2.15
Singapore	n.a.	n.a.	449	1.23
Canada	108	2.81	367	1.01
Hong Kong, China	n.a.	n.a.	346	0.95
France	19	0.49	329	0.90
Sweden	93	2.42	328	0.90
Belgium	n.a.	n.a.	257	0.70
Iran	n.a.	n.a.	140	0.38
West Indies	n.a.	n.a.	78	0.21
Other	324	8.44	12,276	33.62
Total	3,840	100.00	36,510	100.00

n.a. Not available.
Source: RBI Bulletin (October 2002).

Table 14.3. *Mergers and Acquisitions as a Share of FDI Inflows in India, 1997–99*

Year	*FDI inflows (US$millions)*	*M&A funds (US$millions)*	*Share of M&A (percent)*
1997	3,200	1,300	40.6
1998	2,900	1,000	34.5
1999[a]	1,400	500	35.7
Total	7,100	2,800	39.4

a. January to March.
Source: Kumar (2000b).

regional development, technological capability, and export expansion, among other parameters. The lack of data on the economic activity of enterprises operating in India classified by nationality of ownership has constrained a fuller appreciation of the role played by FDI in the country's economic development.

Sales, Capital Formation, and GDP

The relative importance of FDI in India is suggested by output or sales of foreign affiliates as a percentage of total output or sales in Indian manufacturing. Foreign-controlled firms accounted for nearly 25 percent of output of large private-sector corporations in industry and 31 percent of output in the manufacturing sector in 1980–81 (Kumar 1990a). Arthreye and Kapur (1999), updating Kumar's estimates, found that foreign firms in 1990–91 accounted for about 26 percent of sales in manufacturing. The declining share of foreign-controlled enterprises reflects the restrictive attitude followed by the government with respect to FDI during the period. Similar estimates for the post-liberalization period are not available.

We computed the share of foreign firms in total value-added and total sales using a sample of large private-sector companies quoted on Indian stock exchanges and included in the RIS (the Research and Information System for Developing Countries) Database. The sample was compiled by extracting information on relevant companies from the Prowess (online) Database of the Centre for Monitoring Indian Economy (CMIE). Shares computed on the basis of a sample such as this one are useful only for observing trends over time; information is not available on the representativeness of the sample. The shares of foreign enterprises in both value-added and sales rose in the 1990s, particularly in the late 1990s (Table 14.4). Therefore, liberalization seems to have led to a greater role of foreign enterprises in Indian manufacturing.

The growing importance of FDI inflows in the Indian economy is also indicated by FDI inflows as a share of gross fixed capital formation. That share increased from 0.3 percent in 1990 to 3.2 percent in 2001. Moreover, inward FDI stock as a percentage of GDP rose from 0.5 percent in 1990 to 5.1 percent in 2002 (Table 14.5).

The Growth Rate and Domestic Investment

FDI inflows could contribute to the growth rate of the host economy by augmenting the capital stock as well as with infusion of new technology. However, high growth rates may also lead to more FDI inflows by enhancing the investment climate in the country. Therefore, the FDI–growth relationship is subject to causality bias given the possibility of a two-way relationship. What is the nature of the relationship in India? A recent study has examined the direction of causation between FDI and growth empirically for a sample of 107 countries for the 1980–99 period. In the case of India, the study finds

Table 14.4. *Value Added and Sales in Indian Manufacturing, by Foreign and Domestic Firms, 1990–2001*

Year	No. of sample firms			Foreign firms as a percentage of	
	Total	Foreign firms	Domestic firms	Total value-added	Total sales
1990	1,378	126	1,252	9.50	11.26
1991	1,754	149	1,605	9.77	11.77
1992	1,991	158	1,833	9.61	11.69
1993	2,381	171	2,210	9.77	11.88
1994	2,987	178	2,809	9.91	11.67
1995	3,500	190	3,310	9.25	11.03
1996	3,649	195	3,454	9.65	11.67
1997	3,695	208	3,487	10.77	12.64
1998	3,695	216	3,479	11.20	12.85
1999	3,716	225	3,491	12.12	13.66
2000	3,726	224	3,502	12.76	14.05
2001	2,959	193	2,766	12.63	13.77

Source: RIS database.

Table 14.5. *India's FDI Inflows as a Share of Gross Fixed Capital Formation and GDP, Selected Years, 1990–2002*

Indicator	1990	1995	2000	2002
FDI inflows as a percentage of gross fixed capital formation	0.3	2.4	2.3	3.2[a]
Inward FDI stocks as a percentage of GDP	0.5	1.6	4.1	5.1

a. For 2001.
Source: Author's calculations based on UNCTAD data.

a Granger neutral relationship since the direction of causation was not pronounced (Kumar and Pradhan 2002).

With the market power of their well-known brand names and other resources, FDI projects may actually crowd out or substitute domestic investments from the product or capital markets and may thus be immiserizing (Fry 1992; Agosin and Mayer 2000). Therefore, it is important to examine the effects of FDI on domestic investment to evaluate the impact of FDI on growth and welfare in the host economy. Our study, however, did not find a statistically significant effect of FDI on domestic investment in the case of India (Kumar and Pradhan 2002). It appears, therefore, that FDI inflows received by India have been of a mixed type; some inflows crowded in domestic investments, while others crowded them out, with no predominant pattern emerging.

Empirical studies suggest that the effect of FDI on domestic investment depends on host-government policies. Governments have extensively employed selective policies and imposed various performance requirements, such as local content requirements (LCRs), to deepen the commitment of MNEs to the host economy. The Indian government has imposed the condition of phased manufacturing programs (or local content requirements) in the auto industry to promote vertical interfirm linkages and encourage the development of the auto component industry (and crowding in of domestic investments). A case study of the auto industry shows that these policies (in combination with other performance requirements, viz. foreign exchange neutrality) have succeeded in building an internationally competitive vertically integrated auto sector in the country (see Box 14.1). The Indian experience in this industry, therefore, is in tune with the experiences of Thailand, Brazil, and Mexico (Moran 1998).

Exports and Balance of Payments

A number of developing countries have used FDI to exploit the resources of multinational enterprises (globally recognized brand names and best practice technology, for example) or to become integrated with their global production networks in order to expand their manufactured exports. Early studies analyzing the export performance of Indian enterprises in the preliberalization phase reported no statistically significant difference between the export performance of foreign and local firms (Kumar 1990a; Kumar and Siddharthan 1994). Sharma (2000), in a study using a simultaneous equation model examining the factors explaining export growth in India over the 1970–98 period, found FDI to have no significant effect on export performance, although its coefficient had a positive sign. Obviously, in a highly protected setting, both local and foreign firms found it more profitable to concentrate on the domestic market. For the postreform period, Agarwal (2002) found weak support for the hypothesis that foreign firms have performed better than local firms in India in the postreform period of 1996 to 2000, although the estimates were not robust across various technology groupings and the foreign ownership dummy turned out to be significant at ten-percent level only in the case of medium-high-technology industries. Controlling for several firm-specific factors, fiscal incentives, and industry characteristics, Kumar and Pradhan (2003) find that Indian affiliates of MNEs appear to be performing better than their local counterparts in terms of export orientation overall, although with some variation across industries. In light of the findings of earlier studies relating to the pre-liberalization period of no significant difference in the export orientation of foreign and local enterprises, it would appear that reforms have prompted foreign MNEs to begin to explore the potential of India as a base for export-platform production.

Studies have analyzed the determinants of the patterns of export-orientation of MNE affiliates across seventy-four countries in seven branches of industry over three points of time. These studies have shown trade liberalization to be an important factor in explaining the export orientation of foreign affiliates. Furthermore, in host countries with large domestic markets, the export obligations have been found to be effective for promoting the export orientation of foreign affiliates to third countries (Kumar 1998c). From that perspective, the liberalization of India's trade regime during the 1990s may have facilitated the export orientation of foreign affiliates.

Export obligations have also been employed fruitfully by many countries to prompt MNE affiliates to exploit the host country's potential for export platform production. In China, which has succeeded in expanding manufactured exports with the help of MNE affiliates, regulations stipulate that wholly owned foreign enterprises must export more than 50 percent of their output (Rosen 1999, 63–71). As a result of these policies, the proportion of foreign enterprises in manufactured exports steadily increased during the 1990s to 44 percent. MNE affiliates account for over 80 percent of China's high-technology exports (UNCTAD 2002, 154, 163). India has not imposed export obligations on MNE affiliates except for those entering the products reserved for SMEs. However, indirect export obligations in the form of dividend balancing have been imposed for enterprises producing primarily consumer goods. (This was phased out in 2000.) Under these policies, a foreign enterprise was obliged to earn the foreign exchange that it wished to remit abroad as dividend so that there was no adverse impact on the host country's balance of payments. Sometimes a condition of foreign exchange neutrality has been imposed under which the enterprise is required to earn foreign exchange enough to cover the outgo on account of imports.

Therefore, these regulations have acted as indirect export obligations prompting foreign enterprises to export to earn the foreign exchange required by them. Evidence suggests that such regulations have prompted foreign enterprises to undertake exports. To comply with the foreign

Box 14.1. *Performance Requirements and India's Auto Industry*

Like a number of other developing countries, India has used performance requirements (PRs) to build the domestic manufacturing capability of its auto industry. The Indian government entered into a joint venture agreement with Suzuki Motor Corporation (SMC) of Japan to set up a manufacturing facility in the early 1980s for the production of small passenger cars in Gurgaon near Delhi. In the Maruti-Suzuki joint venture, the government of India and Suzuki were equal partners. In this phased manufacturing program, local content had to be increased to 75 percent within five years.

In order to comply with this requirement, Suzuki started a program of vendor development in India. Indian manufacturers of auto components were assisted by Suzuki to produce components of its designs and specifications. Joint ventures with a number of them involved the transfer of technology. Furthermore, a number of Japanese OEM suppliers of SMC were prompted to license technology or set up joint ventures with Indian component manufacturers to be able to supply to its Maruti venture. As a result, a cluster of auto component manufacturers emerged around the Maruti plant in Gurgaon, and the proportion of local value added steadily increased. However, exports of cars or components were relatively insignificant. The government, as a part of its measures to deal with the foreign exchange crisis of 1991, imposed the condition of foreign exchange neutrality and dividend balancing on consumer goods industries (including passenger car manufacturers). These obligations pushed Maruti to obtain a product mandate from its Japanese partner for exporting compact cars to Europe following phasing out of the production of the Alto model by it in Japan.

An extensive network of auto component manufacturers was created as a result of the phased manufacturing programs imposed on Maruti. This has laid the foundations for an internationally competitive auto component industry as follows. The subsequent entrants to the industry, in the wake of liberalization of the FDI policy in the 1990s, not only found a good base for their indigenization efforts. They also were able to fulfill their export obligations easily as is evident from case studies of Ford, GM, and Daimler-Chrysler (Kumar and Singh 2002). The export obligations prompted them to consider buying some components from India for export to their operations in other countries. Ford management was initially hesitant to import components from India because it feared poor quality—apprehensions that were belied. Following a visit in 2000 by a Ford team to components suppliers in India, a joint program was launched with the Automotive Component Manufacturers Association (ACMA) for sourcing components from the country for Ford. Ford set up two dedicated ventures in India to handle component sourcing. Ford has also exported an increasing number of Ikon CKD kits to Mexico and South Africa. Thus, export obligations not only prompted Ford to discover an important sourcing base of quality components; from the host-country point of view, they helped the country's auto component manufacturers develop their linkages with one of the world's largest manufacturers of automobiles. Similarly, General Motors India (GMI) Ltd.

Box 14.1. *(continued)*

claims to have helped its parent source components from India including a major export order from GM Europe that in turn also helped GMI to fulfill its export obligation. GMI is also pursuing partnerships with Indian component suppliers for worldwide sourcing of components for GM overseas units from India. Daimler-Chrysler India has developed more than twenty joint ventures for manufacture and export of auto components to the Daimler-Chrysler plants in Germany to fulfill its export obligations.

The exports of components by these major producers has prompted interest by other auto producers in Indian supply capabilities, even though the performance requirements have been abolished. About fifteen of the top auto manufacturers have already set up international purchasing offices in India. In May 2003 CEOs of thirty Indian auto component producers were invited by Navistar, Caterpillar, Ford, and Delphi to visit the United States to discuss global outsourcing possibilities. The auto components exports from India fetched US$375 million in 2002–3. With the sudden interest of auto manufacturers in sourcing from India, exports were likely to increase nearly four times to $1.5 billion in 2003–4.

Therefore, PRs imposed on the auto industry in the form of export obligations and phased manufacturing programs until recently have been successful in meeting government policy objectives (namely, development of the local manufacturing base while preventing the heavy drain of foreign exchange on imports). Even though the PRs have been abolished, the export and import figures in the car industry in March 2002 were balanced at around Rs 21 billion. Also most manufacturers had achieved high levels of localization of production. For instance, as of March 2002, Ford had achieved a domestic content level of 74 percent; GM, 70 percent; Astra and Corsa, 64 percent; Mercedes and Toyota, close to 70 percent; and Honda, around 78 percent, given the development of the local base of OEM suppliers. Furthermore, the export obligations helped in overcoming the information asymmetry regarding the host country's capabilities and led to a fuller realization of the export potential through MNEs with establishment of vendor-OEM linkages between Indian component producers and global auto majors that would be of long-term value.

Source: Kumar (2003a).

exchange neutrality condition, foreign auto manufacturers have exported auto components from India; this not only opened new opportunities for Indian component manufacturers but also led to profitable opportunities for business (Box 14.1). Exports of auto components from India are now growing at a rapid rate that exceeds the obligations several times over. These regulations have acted to remove the information asymmetry existing in the minds of auto majors about the poor quality of Indian components. In that respect, India's experience is very similar to that of Thailand, which has emerged as the major auto hub of Southeast Asia (Moran 1998; Kumar 2003a).

Another case study of a consumer goods MNE is summarized in Box 14.2. Even indirect export obligations such as foreign exchange neutrality and dividend balancing can be effective in prompting MNEs to exploit opportunities for export-oriented manufacturing. In this case, Pepsi developed a model of contract farming in Punjab with new technology brought in for growing horticulture products of requisite quality and specifications in the country. This way the indirect export obligations have helped the country benefit from not only export earnings but also from the transfer and diffusion of new technology among farmers.

Box 14.2. *Export Obligations and Technology Diffusion: Pepsi Foods and Contract Farming in Punjab*

Pepsi Foods Limited was established in the late 1980s as a joint venture of PepsiCo Inc., USA, Voltas (a Tata group company, India), and the Punjab Agro Industries Corporation (PAIC). In addition to the joint venture requirement, the company was supposed to meet an export obligation as well as a dividend balancing requirement since it was a consumer goods producer. Subsequently, it became a wholly owned subsidiary of PepsiCo. It manufactures soft drinks and snack foods, and runs a few fast food restaurant chains with an approximate annual turnover of Rs. 40 billion and exports around Rs. 4 billion, according to company sources.

As per FDI approval terms, there was an export commitment of Rs. 2 billion in ten years besides other export obligations attached to capital goods imports. For a company whose main business was bottling soft drinks for the domestic market from imported concentrate, meeting the export obligations posed a formidable challenge. This challenge was turned into an opportunity with a pioneering approach to contract farming and a rewarding business proposition. Moreover, thousands of farmers were able to improve their earnings, as observed below.

Pepsi proposed to meet the export obligation by undertaking exports of tomato puree and other processed foods. In 1989, when Pepsi set up tomato and food processing plants in Punjab, it faced problems of raw materials supply. For example, Punjab had only table varieties (not processing varieties) of tomatoes available over a period of about twenty-five days—an inadequate amount in any case. Pepsi had a huge plant, and it needed tomatoes over a minimum time frame of fifty-five days. To resolve these problems, Pepsi thought of contract farming of improved varieties that would fit its quality requirements. An R&D team composed of three scientists brought by Pepsi from its headquarters and scientists from Punjab Agricultural University (PAU) was formed to develop

Box 14.2. *(continued)*

technology to improve productivity and decrease the cost of production of tomatoes. A Pepsi team, under the direction of PAIC, first educated farmers about the benefits of contract farming and then introduced it. Contracted farmers were provided seeds/plantlets at the doorstep with written instructions in the local language. These farmers were loaned some equipment and provided regular crop inspection and advisory services on crop management. They also were offered procurement of a certain quantum of output at a pre-agreed price. The tomato yield per hectare increased from 16 to 52 metric tonnes (MT) in Punjab over the 1989–99 period, according to the company.

Contract farming by Pepsi Foods—with initial R&D inputs and regular fine-tuning later in experimental trials—has now extended to other crops (potato, basmati rice, chilly, peanuts, garlic, groundnuts, etc.) and to several other states. The technology has also spread to non-Pepsi growers; they buy from the company's nursery and other extension services without any buy-back arrangement—implying benefits to a broad-based spectrum of users. Thus, the export obligation imposed on Pepsi has resulted in a mutually rewarding partnership among the farmer, PAU, PAIC, and Pepsi, and it has fueled a horticultural revolution in Punjab, with significant improvement in yields and technology. Although the export obligation was over by 1996, the company's exports have continued and are now booming. Indeed, exports have become a thrust area for the company with the company entering exports of other agricultural commodities such as rice.

Source: Kumar and Singh (2002).

R&D, Local Technological Capability, and Diffusion

Compared to local firms, foreign firms appear to have spent more on R&D activity in Indian manufacturing enterprises, although the gap between their R&D intensities had practically vanished by 2001 (Table 14.6). After controlling for extraneous factors, a study analyzing the R&D activity of Indian manufacturing enterprises in the context of liberalization has found that MNE affiliates reveal a lower R&D intensity compared to local firms, presumably on account of their captive access to the laboratories of their parents and associated companies. The study also observed differences in the nature or motivation of R&D activity of foreign and local firms. Local firms seem to be directing their R&D activity to absorption of imported knowledge and to backing up their outward expansion. MNE affiliates, on the other hand, focus on customization of their parents' technology for the local market or undertake R&D assignments for their parents (Kumar and Agarwal 2000).

Table 14.6. *R&D Intensity of Indian Manufacturing Enterprises, by Type of Firm, 1990–2001*
(Percent)

Year	*All firms*	*Foreign firms*	*Domestic firms*
1990	0.053	0.114	0.046
1991	0.082	0.086	0.082
1992	0.148	0.213	0.139
1993	0.201	0.365	0.178
1994	0.217	0.378	0.196
1995	0.272	0.377	0.259
1996	0.312	0.376	0.303
1997	0.413	0.447	0.409
1998	0.341	0.559	0.309
1999	0.352	0.477	0.332
2000	0.311	0.386	0.298
2001	0.343	0.320	0.346

Source: RIS database.

With respect to the contribution of FDI to local technological capability and technology diffusion, evidence is mixed. Fikkert (1994), a study of 305 private sector firms in India, showed that firms with foreign equity participation have an insignificant direct effect on R&D, but they tend to depend significantly more on foreign technology purchases, which in turn tend to reduce R&D. In view of these findings, Fikkert concludes that India's closed technology policies with respect to FDI and technology licensing had the desired effect of promoting indigenous R&D.

On the knowledge spillovers from foreign to domestic enterprises, the evidence suggests that they are positive when the technology gap between foreign and local enterprises is not wide. When the technology gap is wide, the entry of foreign enterprises may affect the productivity of domestic enterprise adversely (that is, there could be negative spillovers).

Some governments have imposed technology transfer requirements on foreign enterprises. Malaysia is one example. However, such performance requirements do not appear to have been very successful in achieving their objectives (UNCTAD 2003). Other performance requirements, such as local content requirements or domestic equity requirements, may be more effective in the transfer of technology. Local content requirements and export performance requirements have prompted foreign enterprises to transfer and diffuse some knowledge to domestic enterprises in order to comply with their obligations (Boxes 14.1 and 14.2). Similarly, domestic equity requirements may facilitate the quick absorption of the knowledge brought in by foreign enterprises. This is an important pre-requisite of the local technological capability, as is evident from the case studies presented in Box 14.3. Some believe that domestic equity requirements may adversely affect the extent or quality of technology transfer (Moran 2001). However, it has been shown that MNEs may not transfer key technologies, even to their wholly owned subsidiaries abroad, fearing the risk of dissipation or diffusion through mobility of employees. Furthermore, even if the content and quality of technology transfer are better in a sole venture than in a joint venture, from the host-country point of view, the latter may have more desirable externalities in terms of local learning and diffusion of the knowledge transferred (Kumar and Singh 2002).

A recent trend in FDI is that of globalization of R&D activity including other knowledge-based activities such as the development of custom software, business process outsourcing. Once India's potential as a competitive location for software development was established in the mid-1990s, MNEs began to set up their dedicated software development centers in the country, as will be discussed later.

Firm Size, Profitability, and Efficiency

Foreign affiliates have generally been larger than their local counterparts. This is because of their strategy to employ nonprice rivalry, such as product differentiation, which has substantial economies of scale (Kumar 1991). Table 14.7 indicates that the average size of foreign firms was larger than that of domestic firms from 1990 to 2001.

The early studies of profitability in the Indian industry suggested that foreign affiliates had higher profit margins on sales than did their local counterparts in most branches of Indian manufacturing (Kumar 1990a). A further analysis of the determinants of profit margins of foreign and local firms suggested that the higher profitability of foreign firms was attributable to their focus on the less price elastic upper ends of the market with product differentiation; they left more price competitive lower ends of the market to local firms. The study did not find any evidence that their higher profitability could be due to their better efficiency of resource utilization (Kumar 1990b). The trend of higher profit margins of foreign firms continues even during the postliberalization period (Table 14.7). The table also suggests that foreign affiliates not only have enjoyed consistently higher profit margins; their profit margins have been more stable than local firms'.

Box 14.3. *Local Learning in Joint Ventures: A Case Study of the Two-Wheeler Industry in India*

Joint ventures between MNEs and local enterprises in developing countries can be instrumental in learning and technology absorption by the local partners and hence can contribute significantly to the building of local technological capability. The evidence on learning and absorption of knowledge by local partners is clear from the following two cases. In both the cases, the local partners were able to put on the market new products developed by them after the joint venture ended, suggesting the absorption of knowledge during their involvement in the joint venture that led them to design and produce new models independently.

TVS Motor Company Ltd. (formerly Ind-Suzuki Motorcycles Ltd.) started as a joint venture between Sundaram Clayton Group and Suzuki Motor Corporation in 1982 to produce motorcycles. In 2000–1 it produced 1,39,000 scooters, 3,58,000 motorcycles, and 3,69,645 mopeds. During the past two decades, the local partners in the joint venture absorbed technology and knowledge brought in by Suzuki and built capability to design and develop new models of two-wheelers. In 2001 Sundaram Clayton and Suzuki disengaged in an amicable manner. The company, renamed TVS Motor Company, was run entirely by Sundaram Group. Subsequent to the departure of Suzuki, TVS launched its own, indigenously developed, 110 cc four-stroke motorcycle, TVS-Victor. Victor was developed completely by the company's in-house R&D team involving 300 personnel within 24 months with an investment of Rs. 250 million. The new product has been described as a "stunning success" by the business press. It captured a 16 percent share of the market and gave the company a new confidence in its ability to develop and market new products on its own. The company decided to double its R&D spending in 2002 to 3.6 percent of sales; it has a number of new product launches up its sleeve and an ambitious expansion plan that includes establishing its presence in Asian markets such as Thailand, Vietnam, and Indonesia.

The second case study concerns Kinetic Motor Company Ltd. (formerly Kinetic Honda Ltd.). It began as a joint venture between Kinetic group and Honda Motor of Japan in 1984 for the manufacture of advanced scooters in India. In 1998 the Honda partnership was realigned as a technical collaboration since Honda pulled out from the joint venture to launch its own wholly owned subsidiary. On the basis of the learning and knowledge it absorbed during the partnership with Honda, Kinetic has launched several new products. These include the recently launched Kinetic Nova, a four-stroke 115 cc scooter with a breakthrough design and best in class performance. It competes directly with the erstwhile joint venture partner's Honda Activa, a 102 cc auto geared scooter. It is also launching a 65 cc scooterette, Zing, which is custom designed for college goers. Like TVS, Kinetic is also planning a major export push with a 50 percent export growth in 2002.

These two cases suggest that joint ventures can provide opportunities for local partners to absorb knowledge brought in by the foreign partner and become technologically self-reliant.

Source: Kumar and Singh (2002).

Table 14.7. *Foreign and Domestic Firms in Indian Manufacturing, by Sales and Profit-to-Sales Ratio, 1990–2001*

	Average sales (Rs. Crores)			*Profit-to-sales ratio (%)*		
Year	*All firms*	*Foreign firms*	*Domestic firms*	*All firms*	*Foreign firms*	*Domestic firms*
1990	97.3	119.8	95.1	3.8	6.2	3.5
1991	90.3	125.1	87.0	3.7	7.0	3.3
1992	95.9	141.3	92.0	3.6	6.5	3.2
1993	92.8	153.4	88.1	3.4	6.0	3.1
1994	88.2	172.7	82.8	5.1	7.4	4.8
1995	94.3	191.6	88.7	6.7	9.0	6.4
1996	113.3	247.3	105.7	6.3	8.0	6.0
1997	119.8	269.0	110.9	4.6	7.8	4.1
1998	130.0	285.8	120.3	3.2	8.0	2.5
1999	134.9	304.3	124.0	1.6	7.6	0.7
2000	149.3	348.9	136.5	1.6	8.0	0.6
2001	187.5	395.6	172.9	1.4	7.9	0.3

Source: RIS database.

FDI and the Knowledge-Based Economy in India

This section discusses the role of multinational enterprises in the IT software and services industry in India as well as the country's position as a global research and development hub.

India's Software Industry

The rise of the IT software and services industry (henceforth software industry) during the 1990s represents one of the most spectacular achievements of the Indian economy (Kumar 2001a). The industry has grown at an incredible rate over the past few years, is highly export-oriented, has established India as an exporter of knowledge-intensive services in the world, and has brought in a number of other spillover benefits such as new jobs and the development of a new pool of entrepreneurs. The evolution of India as an exporter of these knowledge-intensive services has also created much interest in the development community worldwide. The Indian software industry has grown at a phenomenal compound annual rate of over 50 percent during the 1990s; modest export revenue of US$100 million in 1989–90 increased to nearly $10 billion in export earnings by 2002. The industry has set itself a target of $50 billion of exports by 2008 and is confident of achieving it despite a recent slowdown in technology spending in some of the key markets such as the United States.

The Indian export success in the software industry is primarily driven by local enterprise, resources, and talent. The role played by multinational enterprises in software development in India is quite limited. Although all the major software companies have established development bases in India, their overall share in India's exports of software is rather small (19 percent). MNEs do not figure among the top seven software companies in India in terms of overall sales or exports. Among the top twenty software companies, no more than six are MNE affiliates or joint ventures. Seventy-nine of the 572 member companies of Nasscom are reported as foreign subsidiaries. Some are actually subsidiaries of companies promoted by nonresident Indians in the United States; others were Indian companies to begin with but were subsequently taken over by foreign companies. The foreign subsidiaries include software development centers of software MNEs and subsidiaries of other MNEs that develop software for their parents' applications. Examples include subsidiaries of financial services companies (such as Citicorp and Deutsche Bank) and telecommunication MNEs (such as Hughes and Motorola). In addition, MNEs have set up sixteen joint ventures with local enterprises—British Aerospace with Hindustan Aeronautics, Bell South with Telecommunication Corporation of India, and British Telecom with the Mahindra Group, among others. In all, ninety-five companies have controlling foreign participation. The bulk of the entries took place after 1994; by then, India's potential as a base for software development had already been established.

Despite the entry of all major IT multinational enterprises into the country and the forming of subsidiaries and joint ventures for software development, the FDI inflow has not been substantial. The total subscribed capital of the seventy-nine foreign subsidiaries that had been set up in the country by 1999 is Rs. 4,713 million (or US$115 million at the exchange rate of Rs. 41 to a dollar). Therefore, the total inflow of FDI by the MNE subsidiaries in the past fifteen years was no more than $115 million, not a considerable amount compared to the inflow of about $3 billion worth of FDI that India received annually.

Gains from the activity of MNE subsidiaries in the software industry have been distributed much more to home countries than to host countries. Apparently, some of the MNE subsidiaries in software development are doing pioneering work for their parents. For instance, Oracle Software Development Center located in Bangalore has been responsible for designing the "network computer" introduced entirely by Oracle. SAP of Germany has recently launched its internet-enabled distributor reseller management (DRM) solutions for high-tech industry developed entirely at SAP Labs, India, a Bangalore-based subsidiary of SAP. Many other design centers of MNEs in India are doing highly valuable development work for them. However, the Indian subsidiaries of these MNEs do not share the revenue streams generated by their developments worldwide. MNEs tend to invoice the exports of their subsidiaries to them at cost plus 10 to 15 percent. Therefore, the distribution of gains is grossly in favor of the home country of the MNEs and against the host country, which is India in this case.

Most of the export-oriented software companies operate as "export enclaves" with few ties to the domestic economy, if any. MNE subsidiaries in software development, in particular, derive almost all of their income from exports to their parents. Hence, hardly any vertical linkages are developed with the domestic software market or the rest of the economy. The enclave nature of operation generates very few knowledge spillovers for the domestic economy. The bulk of the work done is also of a highly customized nature, having little application elsewhere. Given the high salaries and perks of foreign travel, the movement of personnel from these companies to domestic firms also does not take place. The employees of export-oriented firms are usually lured by foreign companies. However, there is considerable movement of personnel from domestic market-oriented firms to export-oriented firms or foreign subsidiaries. A survey of the software industry suggested that 45.6 percent of the professionals were recruited by software firms from other companies (Kumar 2001a). The domestic market also supports the exports of products that are first tried locally and are improved on the basis of feedback data generated before being exported. In terms of technological complexity and sophistication, some projects in the domestic market are more advanced and challenging than export projects.

Global R&D Activity in India

Although the R&D activity of domestic-market-oriented MNE affiliates is not high compared to their local counterparts as observed above, MNEs are increasingly looking to India because of her relatively well-developed scientific and technological infrastructure and resources for setting up global and regional R&D centers. They provide solutions to specific R&D problems for their global operations as well as research collaborations with Indian enterprises having complementary capabilities. This trend has been encouraged by the development of international communication and information technologies (ICT) that allow efficient communication between research groups based in different places across the continents through dedicated networks. This enables MNEs to fragment R&D projects into smaller subprojects, some of which can be subcontracted to units located in developing countries with particular skills in a particular branch of knowledge. The internationalization of R&D conducted in this manner involves little risk of dissipation or diffusion of technology to competitors because of the high specificity of the subproject.

A quantitative analysis of the factors explaining the locational pattern of overseas R&D by U.S. and Japanese MNEs suggests that countries that are characterized by a large scale of technological activity and abundant cheap but qualified R&D personnel are most likely to play host to MNEs' overseas R&D activity (Kumar 2001b). As observed earlier, the Indian government has invested cumulatively in building centers of excellence in different branches of science and technology. These centers, coupled with India's relative abundance in qualified but cheap R&D personnel, have begun to attract MNEs for the purpose of setting up global or home-base augmenting R&D centers. Since the late 1990s, nearly 100 MNEs have set up R&D centers in India. These include GE's $80 million technology center at Bangalore that is the largest outside the United States and employs 1,600 people. The list of MNEs that have set up global R&D centers in India includes Akzo Nobel, AVL, Bell Labs, Colgate Palmolive, Cummins, Dupont, Daimler-Chrysler, Eli Lilly, GM, HP, Honeywell, Intel, McDonald's, Monsanto, Pfizer, Texas Instruments, and Unilever, among many others.

According to some reports, the Indian R&D centers of the U.S. multinational enterprises have begun to generate substantial intellectual property for their parents and have filed more than 1,000 patent applications with the U.S. Patent and Trademark Office during 2002–3 alone. The Indian centers of multinational technology companies expect to double the number of their employees from 40,000 in 2003. The Indian R&D centers of MNEs have begun to play an important role in knowledge generation for their parents. For instance, 30 percent of all software for Motorola's latest phones was written in India (*The Hindu* 2003).

A look at the illustrative cases of global R&D centers and R&D joint ventures and contracts set up by MNEs in India suggests that most of the R&D centers have been motivated primarily by the abundance of highly talented R&D personnel in India at much lower cost than that prevailing in the Western world (Kumar 1999). The average annual salary of an Indian engineer is about $2,300 compared to $60,000 for a U.S. engineer.

A few internationally renowned and public-funded centers of excellence—for example, the Indian Institute of Science (IISc), the National Chemical Laboratory (NCL), and the Indian Institute of Chemical Technology (IICT)—have helped India to attract R&D investments from MNEs. Actually, the Indian research centers of Astra AB and Daimler-Benz were specifically attracted to Bangalore by the prospects of collaboration with IISc. Astra has endowed a chair at IISc to cement its relationship with the institute, and the Benz research center has contracted a project in avionics to IISc. Encouraged by its research contracts with IICT and NCL, Du Pont set up a separate India Technology Office at its headquarters to systematically target India for its technology research activity. These investments are concentrated in a few Indian cities, such as Bangalore or Hyderabad, because of the high concentration of innovative activities there. Bangalore has also been chosen by a number of ICT multinational enterprises as their base for software development, and it is widely referred to as India's Silicon Valley.

Summary

To sum up the foregoing discussion of the role of FDI in the software industry and R&D activity, we note that India's success owes largely to the cumulative investments made by the government over the past five decades in building what is now termed "national innovation systems." India has developed a system of higher education in engineering and technical disciplines, created an institutional infrastructure for S&T policy making and implementation, built centers of excellence and numerous other institutions for technology development, and pursued other initiatives. The Indian government recognized the potential of the country in computer software in the early 1970s and began building necessary infrastructure, particularly for training of personnel. The government also facilitated the building of technological capability by investing in R&D institutions and supporting their projects, by creating computing facilities, and by developing infrastructure for data transfer and networking. The clustering of software development activity and the case study of Bangalore support the contention that public-funded technological infrastructure has crowded in the investments from the private sector in skill-intensive activities such as software development. It would appear from this that investments made by governments in national innovation systems have substantial positive externalities.

Conclusion

This chapter has reviewed the evolution of the Indian government's attitude toward FDI, examined the trends and patterns in FDI inflows during the 1990s, and considered, from a comparative East Asian perspective, the impact of FDI on a few parameters of development. The Indian government's policy toward FDI has changed as the country's needs at different phases of development have changed. This changing policy framework has affected the trends and patterns of FDI inflows received by India. The magnitude of FDI inflows has increased. In the absence of policy direction, however, most of these inflows have gone into services industries and soft-technology consumer goods industries; the share of manufacturing and technology-intensive investments has declined, in sharp contrast to the East Asian countries. Although the importance of FDI as a source of capital and output has risen, the impact of FDI on direct investment and growth is mixed. Some FDI inflows possibly crowd in domestic investments, while some others crowd it out. Local content regulations, where they have been pursued (phased manufacturing programs in the auto industry, for example), have yielded desirable results.

Compared to East Asian economies, India has had less success fostering export-oriented industrialization with the help of FDI. However, recent analysis suggests that MNEs are beginning to take a serious look at India's potential as a base for export-oriented manufacturing. As in the East Asian countries, performance requirements such as export obligations have helped prompt MNEs to consider using India as a sourcing base, and they also have helped in obviating the perception gap on the country's potential.

In terms of technology and R&D, the manufacturing affiliates of MNEs in India, compared to domestic enterprises, seem to be spending a smaller proportion of their turnover on R&D activity after controlling for extraneous influences. It also appears that the R&D activity of MNE affiliates is geared to customization of their technology for local markets or to work on assignments by their parents. In contrast, the focus of R&D activity of local enterprises is on technology absorption and efforts to strengthen their external competitiveness. The case study evidence suggests that joint venture requirements and vertical interfirm linkages may facilitate diffusion of knowledge brought in by multinational enterprises.

India is also attracting increasing attention from MNEs as a base for their knowledge-based activities such as software development and global R&D activity. A case study of multinational enterprises' involvement in knowledge-based activities suggests that India's success owes largely to the cumulative investments made by the government over the past five decades in building national innovation systems.

MNE affiliates in India usually enjoy better and more stable profit margins than do local enterprises. The reason is not so much their greater efficiency per se. It is largely because of their ability to exploit economies of scale with their larger operations and their strategy to focus on less price sensitive upper segments of markets.

Clearly, government policies can play an important role in attracting FDI inflows for development. From the preceding analysis we may now draw a few policy lessons for India and other similarly placed developing countries.

First, liberalization of FDI policy may be necessary but not sufficient for expanding FDI inflows. The overall macroeconomic performance continues to exercise a major influence on the magnitude of FDI inflows; it signals to foreign investors the growth prospects for the potential host economy. Hence, paying attention to macroeconomic performance indicators (growth rates of industry, public investments in socio-economic infrastructure, and other supportive policies) and creating a stable and enabling environment will crowd-in FDI inflows.

Government policies influence the developmental impact of FDI and facilitate the exploitation by host countries of the potential benefits of FDI. Even with liberalized policy, it is desirable to give some policy direction to foreign direct investments, as the case of East Asian countries demonstrates.

One way to maximize the contribution of FDI to the host country's development is to improve the chances that FDI will crowd-in domestic investments and minimize the possibilities of it crowding-out domestic investments. In this context the experiences of Southeast Asian countries such as Malaysia, the Republic of Korea, China, and Thailand deserve careful consideration. Through selective policies and export performance requirements imposed at the time of entry, these countries channeled FDI into export-oriented manufacturing or to areas where local capabilities (pioneer industries) did not exist. Similarly, because MNE entry through acquisition of domestic enterprises is likely to generate less favorable externalities for domestic investment than greenfield investments, some governments discourage acquisitions by foreign enterprises (Agosin and Mayer 2000).

Another sphere where governmental intervention may be required to maximize gains from globalization is in diffusion of knowledge brought in by foreign enterprises. An important channel of diffusion of knowledge brought in by MNEs in the host economy is vertical inter-firm linkages with domestic enterprises. In the past, many governments—in developed as well as developing countries alike—have imposed local content requirements on MNEs to intensify generation of local linkages and transfer of technology. The host governments could also consider employing proactive measures that encourage foreign and local firms to deepen their local content as a number of economies—Singapore, Taiwan (China), the Republic of Korea, and Ireland—have done so successfully (Battat, Frank, and Shen 1996).

Investments made by governments in building local capabilities for higher education and training in technical disciplines, centers of excellence, and other aspects of national innovation systems have substantial favorable externalities. This is demonstrated by the case study of FDI in India's knowledge-based industries.

It is of critical importance that host governments preserve flexibility to pursue selective policies or impose performance requirements on FDI, if necessary. Some performance requirements (for example, local content requirements) have already been outlawed by the TRIMs (Trade Related Investment Measures) Agreement of the World Trade Organization (WTO); others, such as export performance requirements, can still be imposed. Attempts are being made by developing countries to expand the scope of international trade rules beyond what is covered under TRIMs and the General Agreement on Trade in Services (GATS) and further limit the policy flexibility available to developing countries by creating a WTO multilateral framework on investment (Kumar 2003b). Coordinated action by developing-country governments in the ongoing negotiations have helped in the exclusion of investment from the Doha Round as per the July Framework agreed by the WTO members. Similar coordinated action on their part to preserve their policy space will be useful in the future.

Appendix A
India's FDI Inflows: A Comparative East Asian Perspective

Although FDI inflows into the Indian economy increased considerably during the 1990s following the reforms, their magnitude was small, especially when compared with inflows to other countries in the region such as China. In 2001 India's reported inflows of about $3.4 billion represented a mere 1.7 percent of total inflows attracted by developing countries. In the same year, China received inflows of an estimated $46.8 billion, nearly 23 percent of the total inflows received by developing countries. Sectoral patterns and the acquisition modes differed across countries as well. Key differences and some possible explanations are offered below.

The Amount of FDI Inflows

India's US$3.4 billion in annual inflows of FDI is often compared to China's US$45 billion in annual FDI inflows. It has been pointed out, however, that FDI inflows in India and China are not comparable because of certain differences.[1] Firstly, the Indian data on inflows do not follow the International Monetary Fund's *Balance of Payments Manual* that is followed internationally. The principal difference is that India counts only the fresh inflows of equity and does not take into consideration the reinvested earnings by foreign affiliates in the country nor the intercorporate debt flows that are generally included when computing FDI data in accord with IMF guidelines. Therefore, the Indian figures tend to underreport the inflows. Secondly, FDI inflows in China are believed to be overestimating the real FDI inflows in view of round-tripping of Chinese capital to take advantage of more favorable tax treatment of FDI. Therefore, the data for India and China are not strictly comparable and tend to overplay the difference between the intensity of inflows between the two countries. Finally, the size of the Chinese economy is much larger than the Indian economy and hence the figures should be normalized.

Table A14.1 presents FDI inflows in India and China in a way that makes them comparable. FDI inflows in China in 2000 as a proportion of GDP is 3.6 percent compared to 0.5 percent in the case of India. However, when the data for India are revised by taking into account the reinvested earnings and intercorporate debt and when the data for China are revised by taking

1. This was first noted by the International Finance Corporation (2002). See Pfefferman (2002).

Table A14.1. *FDI Net Inflows in India and China, 2000*

	India		*China*	
Indicator	*Reported FDI*[a]	*Adjusted FDI*[b]	*Reported FDI*	*Adjusted FDI#*
Balance of payment, current US$billions	2.3	8.0	39.0	20.0
Percent of GDP	0.5	1.7	3.6	2.0

a. Published by official sources.

b. International Finance Corporation (2002). See Pfeffermann (2002).

Source: Srivastava (2003) based on World Bank (2002) and International Finance Corporation (2002).

into account possible round-tripping of FDI inflows (using the estimates provided by the IFC), the gap in the FDI/GDP ratios narrows to 1.7 to 2.0 for India and China, respectively.

The Indian government has taken steps to revise the definition of FDI flows in the country. A committee set up by the Reserve Bank of India submitted a report in October 2002 that recommended the Indian definition be put on a par with global practice. In June 2003 the government of India announced that, as the result of its adoption of international norms, FDI inflow figures nearly doubled from US$2,342 million to US$4,029 million in 2000–1 and from US$3,906 million to US$6,131 million in 2001–2 .[2]

Even if the measurement problems are taken into account, FDI inflows in India are low compared to inflows in other economies in the region. Studies of determinants of FDI inflows conducted in the framework of an extended model of location of foreign production (Kumar 2000a, 2002) have found that a country's ability to attract FDI is affected by structural factors such as market size (income levels and population), extent of urbanization, quality of infrastructure, geographical and cultural proximity with major sources of capital, and policy factors (namely tax rates, investment incentives, performance requirements). Although India's large population base is an advantage in terms of these factors, her low income levels, low levels of urbanization, and relatively poor quality of infrastructure are disadvantages. Furthermore, the relative geographical and cultural proximity of China and other East Asian countries with major sources of capital such as Japan and the Republic of Korea (also the United States) may have put India at a disadvantage compared to them.

2. Government of India Press Note, June 30, 2003, DIPP, Ministry of Commerce and Industry.

Unlike China and some other countries, India has not employed fiscal incentives such as tax concessions to attract FDI. India is also at least twelve years behind China in terms of launching reforms. Finally, the ability of China to attract FDI inflows is largely the result of special economic zones that gave foreign enterprises better and specialized infrastructure and flexibility in domestic regulations such as labor laws.

The Sectoral Composition of FDI Inflows and Other Differences

India's post-reform experience suggests that a substantial proportion of FDI has gone to services, infrastructure, and consumer-goods manufacturing industries with low technology intensity—a contrast to the high concentration in technology-intensive manufacturing industries in the pre-reform period. In China and other Southeast Asian countries, the bulk of FDI is concentrated in manufacturing. In the pre-reform period, FDI was consciously channeled into technology-intensive manufacturing through a selective policy. In the post-reform period, however, the opening up of new industries, such as services and infrastructure, to FDI has led to increased investments in them, thus bringing down the share received by manufacturing. Within the manufacturing sector, now that FDI is no longer directed to certain branches, consumer-goods industries with little exposure to FDI in the past have risen in importance. China and other Southeast Asian countries, while following in general a liberal policy toward FDI, have directed FDI to manufacturing with export obligations and other incentives for such pioneer industry programs. Hence, FDI accounts for a relatively high share of manufactured exports in these countries. Although a liberal policy toward FDI may be advisable, broad direction needs to be given to make FDI contribute more to the industrialization and export building capability of the country.

References

Agarwal, A. 2002. "Liberalisation, Multinational Enterprises and Export Performance: Evidence from Indian Manufacturing." *Journal of Development Studies* 38(2): 119–37.

Agosin, M. R., and Ricardo Mayer. 2000. "Foreign Investment in Developing Countries: Does It Crowd in Domestic Investment?" UNCTAD Discussion Paper No. 146. Geneva: United Nations Conference on Trade and Development.

Arthreye, Suma, and Sandeep Kapur. 1999. "Foreign-Controlled Manufacturing Firms in India: Long-Term Trends." *Economic and Political Weekly*, November 27, M-149-51.

Battat, Joseph, Isiah Frank, and Xiaofang Shen. 1996. "Suppliers to Multinationals: Linkage Programmes to Strengthen Local Capability in Developing Countries." Washington, D.C.: Foreign Investment Advisory Service (FIAS), International Finance Corporation.

Chandra, Nirmal K. 1991. "Growth of Foreign Capital and Its Importance in Indian Manufacturing." *Economic and Political Weekly* 26 (March): 679–90.

Correa, Carlos M., and Nagesh Kumar. 2003. *Protecting Foreign Investment: Implications of a WTO Regime and Policy Options.* London and New York: Zed Press in association with RIS (Research and Information System for Developing Countries).

Fikkert, Brian. 1994. "An Open or Closed Technology Policy? The Effects of Technology Licensing, Foreign Direct Investment, and Technology Spillovers on R&D in Indian Industrial Sector Firms." PhD diss., Yale University, New Haven, Conn.

Financial Express. 2002a. "RBI To Correct Massive FDI Underestimation, To Adopt IMF Definition." November 15.

———. 2002b. "Under-estimated FDI Flows: Government Sets up Panel." June 17.

Fry, Maxwell J. 1992. "Foreign Direct Investment in a Macroeconomic Framework: Finance, Efficiency, Incentives and Distortions." Policy Research Working Paper WPS1411. Washington, D.C.: The World Bank.

The Hindu. 2003. December 16 issue quoting *New York Times* source.

International Finance Corporation. 2002. *World Business Environment Survey: Economic Prospects for Developing Countries.* Washington, D.C. March.

Jenkins, R. 1990. "Comparing Foreign Subsidiaries and Local Firms in LDCs: Theoretical Issues and Empirical Evidence." *The Journal of Development Studies* 26: 205–28

Kumar, Nagesh. 1990a. *Multinational Enterprises in India: Industrial Distribution, Characteristics and Performance.* London and New York: Routledge.

———. 1990b. "Mobility Barriers and Profitability of Multinational and Local Enterprises in Indian Manufacturing." *The Journal of Industrial Economics* 38: 449–61.

———. 1991. "Mode of Rivalry and Comparative Behaviour of Multinational and Local Enterprises: The Case of Indian Manufacturing." *Journal of Development Economics* 35: 381–92.

———. 1998a. "Multinational Enterprises, Regional Economic Integration, and Export-Platform Production in the Host Countries: An Empirical Analysis for the U.S. and Japanese Corporations." *Weltwirtschaftliches Archiv* 134 (3): 450–83.

———. 1998b. "Liberalization and Changing Patterns of Foreign Direct Investments: Has India's Relative Attractiveness as a Host of FDI Improved?" *Economic and Political Weekly*, vol. 33, no. 22, May 30.

———. 1998c. "Emerging Outward Foreign Direct Investments from Asian Developing Countries: Prospects and Implications." In *Globalization, Foreign Direct*

Investment and Technology Transfers: Impacts on and Prospects for Developing Countries, edited by Nagesh Kumar et al., 177–94. London and New York: Routledge.

———. 1999. "Trends, Patterns, and Determinants of Overseas R&D Activity of Multinational Enterprises: Evidence from U.S. and Japanese MNEs." *Development Engineering* (Tokyo) 5: 21–36.

———. 2000a. "Explaining the Geography and Depth of International Production: The Case of U.S. and Japanese Multinational Enterprises." *Weltwirtschaftliches Archiv* 136(3): 442–76.

———. 2000b. "Mergers and Acquisitions by MNEs: Patterns and Implications." *Economic and Political Weekly*, August 5, 2851–8.

———. ed. 2000c. *Indian Economy under Reforms: An Assessment of Economic and Social Impact*. New Delhi: Bookwell.

———. 2001a. "Indian Software Industry Development: International and National Perspective." *Economic and Political Weekly*, vol. 36, no. 45, November 10, 4278–90.

———. 2001b. "Determinants of Location of Overseas R&D Activity of Multinational Enterprises: The Case of U.S. and Japanese Corporations." *Research Policy* 30: 159–74.

———. 2002. *Globalization and the Quality of Foreign Direct Investment*. Delhi: Oxford University Press.

———. 2003a. "Performance Requirements as Tools of Development Policy: Lessons from Experiences of Developed and Developing Countries." RIS Discussion Paper No 52. New Delhi: Research and Information System for Developing Countries. Available at www.ris.org.in.

———. 2003b. "Investment on the WTO Agenda: A Developing Country Perspective and the Way Forward for the Cancun Ministerial Conference." *Economic and Political Weekly* 38 (July 26): 3177–8.

Kumar, Nagesh, and Aradhna Agarwal. 2000. "Liberalization, Outward Orientation and In-house R&D Activity of Multinational and Local Firms: A Quantitative Exploration for Indian Manufacturing." RIS Discussion Paper No. 7/2002. New Delhi: Research and Information System for Developing Countries.

Kumar, Nagesh, and Jaya Prakash Pradhan. 2002. "Foreign Direct Investment, Externalities and Economic Growth in Developing Countries: Some Empirical Explorations and Implications for WTO Negotiations on Investment." RIS Discussion Paper No. 27/2002. New Delhi: Research and Information System for Developing Countries.

———. 2003. "Export Competitiveness in Knowledge-based Industries: A Firm-Level Analysis of Indian Manufacturing." RIS Discussion Paper No. 43/2003. New Delhi: Research and Information System for Developing Countries.

Kumar, Nagesh, and N. S. Siddharthan. 1994. "Technology, Firm Size and Export Behaviour in Developing Countries: The Case of Indian Enterprises." *Journal of Development Studies* 31(2): 289–309.

Kumar, Nagesh, and Neelam Singh. 2002. "The Use and Effectiveness of Performance Requirements: The Case of India." New Delhi: Research and Information System for Developing Countries.

Lipsey, R. E. 2002. "Home and Host Country Effects of FDI." Paper for ISIT Conference on Challenges to Globalization, Lindingö, May 24–25.

Lipsey, R. E., and Merle Yahr Weiss. 1981. "Foreign Production and Exports in Manufacturing Industries." *The Review of Economics and Statistics* 63 (4): 488–94.

———. 1984. "Foreign Production and Exports of Individual Firms." *The Review of Economics and Statistics* 66 (2): 304–8.

Lipsey, R. E., E. Ramstetter, and M. Blomström. 2000. "Outward FDI and Home Country Exports: Japan, the United States, and Sweden." SSE/EFI Working Paper in Economics and Finance, No. 369. Stockholm: Stockholm School of Economics.

Liu, L., and E. M. Graham. 1998. "The Relationship between Trade and Foreign Direct Investment: Empirical Results for Taiwan and South Korea." IIE Working Paper 98-7. Washington, D.C.: Institute for International Economics.

Mehta, Rajesh. 2003. *Indian Industrial Tariffs: Toward WTO Development Round Negotiations.* New Delhi: Research and Information System for Developing Countries.

Ministry of Commerce and Industry. 2000. Press Note No. 7, July 14. New Delhi.

Ministry of Finance. 2004. *Economic Survey 2003–2004.* New Delhi.

Moran, Theodore H. 1998. *Foreign Direct Investment and Development.* Washington, D.C.: Institute for International Economics.

———. 2001. *Parental Supervision: The New Paradigm for Foreign Direct Investment and Development.* Washington, D.C.

Pfaffermayr, M. 1994. "Foreign Direct Investment and Exports: A Time Series Approach." *Applied Economics* 26: 337–51.

———. 1996. "Foreign Outward Direct Investment and Exports in Austrian Manufacturing: Substitutes or Complements?" *Weltwirtschaftliches Archiv* 132 (3): 501–21

Pfeffermann, G. 2002. "Business Environment and Surveys, Paradoxes: China vs. India." Presentation made at 2002 PSD Forum Session, *Investment Climate Assessment Methodology: The Investment Climate in India and China— Which is Better?* http://rru.worldbank.org/psdforum/forum2002/documents/Pfeffermann.ppt.

Rosen, D. 1999. *Behind the Open Door: Foreign Enterprise Establishment in China.* Washington, D.C.: Institute for International Economics.

Sharma, Kishor. 2000. "Export Growth in India: Has FDI Played a Role?" Discussion Paper No. 816. New Haven, Conn.: Economic Growth Center, Yale University.

Srivastava, Sadhana. 2003. 'What Is the True Level of FDI Flows to India?" *Economic and Political Weekly*, vol. 38, no. 7 (February): 608–10.

UNCTAD (United Nations Conference on Trade and Development). 1999. *World Investment Report 1999*. New York: United Nations.

———. 2001. *World Investment Report 2001*. New York: United Nations.

———. 2002. *World Investment Report 2002*. New York: United Nations.

———. 2003. *Use and Effectiveness of Performance Requirements: Select Case Studies*. New York: United Nations.

———. 2004. *World Investment Report 2004*. New York: United Nations.

World Bank. 2002. *World Development Indicators*. Washington, D.C.

WTO (World Trade Organization). 2002. *Trade Policy Review: India*. Geneva. Available at www.wto.org.

Index

Note: References to figures, tables and boxes are indicated as *40f*, *89t* and *263b*.

www.ingramcontent.com/pod-product-compliance
Lightning Source LLC
Chambersburg PA
CBHW060126280326
41932CB00012B/1435